ISBN 978-1-5280-7378-3
PIBN 10579782

FB &c Ltd, Dalton House, 60 Windsor Avenue, London, SW19 2RR.
Company number 08720141. Registered in England and Wales.

For support please visit www.forgottenbooks.com

PERSONALITY

DAVID C. McCLELLAND

WESLEYAN UNIVERSITY

A HOLT-DRYDEN BOOK

HENRY HOLT AND COMPANY, INC., NEW YORK

25544–0111

Manufactured in the United States of America

Contents

CONTENTS

Tables

TABLES

Figures

Preface

What I have set out to do in this book is simple enough. I have wanted to produce a theoretically oriented text in the psychology of personality. The need for such a text clearly exists today. We have, on the one hand, a number of excellent introductory texts on personality, mental hygiene, personal adjustment, and the like and on the other, a number of more advanced technical books about personality written from some special viewpoint such as psychoanalysis or the Rorschach Technique. This book is aimed at a level somewhere between these two approaches, a level which will require the knowledge of basic introductory material and make use of specialized contributions within the clinical field. The treatment throughout is theoretical rather than practical and applied. The justification for this, if justification is needed, is that theory must always precede application. Today the social pressure for the application of psychological knowledge to problems of personal adjustment is enormous, yet as Angyal so rightly says, psychiatry, and one might add clinical psychology, is "the application of a science of personality which does not as yet exist." This book is intended as a contribution to the theory of personality. As such it may be useful in some way to clinical psychology, but that is not its primary purpose.

While the purpose of the book is simple enough, its execution is not. To do the job well requires a knowledge of practically all of present-day psychology, since all that psychologists know is needed to conceptualize adequately the single personality. This presents some difficulties. In the first place, how can I or any one person know that much? In the second, what about the prospective student? What must he know before he tackles such a complex subject?

The first difficulty poses some real problems. Consider for a moment what a psychologist ought to know before he ventures to speak with any authority about personality. To begin with, he must be thoroughly grounded in the basic principles of psychology, in learning theory, for instance, where he should be able to deduce a theorem from Hull's postulates, draw one of Tolman's "balloons" properly, master the facts on conditioning and learning, and so forth. He should know the tremendous literature on psychological paper-and-pencil tests from the Bernreuter Personality Inventory to the Minnesota Multiphasic Test. Ultimately this should lead him into the intricacies of factor analysis so that he can understand the contributions of men like Cattell and Guilford. After he has spent a year or so on this he ought to take up anthropology, and travel, mentally at least, through the South Seas with Margaret Mead and Malinowski, to Alor with DuBois, to the Southwest with Kluckhohn and Leighton. After studying culture and personality in books, he should of course spend a year or two in the field, after which he will be ready for psychoanalysis. For who can understand the Old Masters like Freud without three to seven years of "didactic" therapy? Perhaps by choosing one's analyst carefully, some of the views of the neo-Freudians like Horney, Fromm, and Alexander can be learned in the process. To save a little time, our hypothetical well-educated student of personality could take a summer off to attend a Rorschach Institute so that he can make a stab at understanding the some eight hundred studies of personality made with this instrument. But even this is only a beginning. What about the Thematic Apperception Test and its intricate interpretations? How about some of the ancient techniques, like hypnosis, or some more modern ones like nondirective interviewing? Surely he should know these. And if he is to be really educated he should have read the "great books" and should be familiar with the history of culture of Western civilization. How else will he be able to understand the depth and complexities, the richness and variety of human personality?

The list seems a little long, and certainly I do not qualify as an expert in any of the fields mentioned. I have never been psychoanalyzed, never been to a Rorschach Institute, cannot properly interpret a Thematic Apperception Test, space "mhms" correctly in a nondirective interview, deduce a theorem from Hull's postulates, or ask a Navaho informant about his sex life. But perhaps all this is what qualifies me to write this book.

The psychology of personality has unfortunately tended in recent years to become split up into a number of specialized fields presided over by high priests who are jealous of their special skills and who contribute little to efforts at integration of their knowledge into a general science of personality. People nowadays have a horror of the word eclecticism, but eclectic is precisely what this book intends to be. In the very elementary state of our knowledge of personality it has seemed unwise to me to exclude from consideration any source of information about the subject, just as it has seemed unwise to fall into the trap of assuming that this particular source of information is the key which will open all the mysteries of personality. The specialized pleading of any particular school or approach to the subject will be disregarded, and its contribution evaluated so far as possible in terms of the new information it provides about personality.

The dilemma of the unprepared student is more easily solved than that of the unprepared author. This is intended to be an advanced text and probably should not be used with students who have not had considerable prior work in psychology. In trying it out I have found that students should have taken as prerequisites a good course in learning, one in abnormal or dynamic psychology, and one in statistics. Desirable, although by no means necessary, are courses in social anthropology and in experimental psychology. In attempting to keep the text from becoming too theoretical, abstract, and advanced, I have adopted two devices which have proven of help to my students. One is to ask a number of questions at the end of each chapter which are intended to challenge the student's imagination, and to help him to read the chapter critically. They are questions which often admit of no easy answers and should therefore give the student a sense of participation in the quest for knowledge about personality which is one of the most valuable things he can get from studying the subject. The other device is to test any abstract formulations arrived at against the concrete behavior of a single human being.

It is my impression that theories of personality are rather easily constructed. The mind of man being as ingenious as it is, we can readily invent symbol systems and pile one set of elaborate theories on another without really making much progress. What does lead to progress in science is the development of specific methods of measuring our theories and abstractions. So the emphasis throughout this book is always on measurement. Many famous theories of personality will not be fully represented for the simple reason that they have not lent themselves readily to measurement. Specifically there are few experimental articles in the journals dealing with them.

To make this emphasis even more explicit, I have chosen a single individual, Karl, whose behavior will be studied each time a new theoretical construct is introduced. After all, the proof of the pudding is in the eating. Every personality theorist should always ask himself, how will this new construct, how will this new distinction contribute to my understanding of this particular person whose behavior is here before me? It is for this reason also that I have made a practice of having each student analyze his own case as we have proceeded from one theoretical construct and method of measurement to another. Ideally, of course, the student should collect for himself, on his case, all the different types of behavior that we have had available on Karl, but often this is impractical. I have found that a good autobiography, so long as it contains many concrete factual episodes and not too much conceptualization by the author, will serve as a fairly adequate substitute for many of the measures used, although it normally gives more information about schemata and motives than about traits. The case materials on Karl were originally collected by a student, John Perkins, to whom I am much indebted for permitting me to use them. Other students have worked successfully from published autobiographies like *Black Boy*, by Richard Wright, or *Seven Storey Mountain*, by Thomas Merton, from case documents like Harold Holzer (cf. Elkin, 1943) or *Sun Chief* (Simmons, 1942), or from life histories specially written by fellow students or friends.

Working with concrete lives like this, as they proceed through the theoretical discussions in this book, should prevent students or anyone else from gaining the impression that I am trying to present "a system" or "a theory" of personality. No one knows enough at present to build a theory. Rather what is needed and what I have tried to do is to find a number of constructs in terms of which we can collect data about personality, perhaps with the ultimate hope of building a theory. Anyone who thinks through the questions at the ends of the chapters, or who faces the problem of attempting to treat the bewildering variety of Karl's or anyone else's behavior in terms of the theoretical constructs used cannot fail to be impressed by how much there is to learn. But this is as it should be. The science of personality is only at its beginning and the student should know this above all other things.

One practical problem has arisen in presenting the material on Karl. To understand him adequately, the reader should have available all the documents on which the conceptualization of him is based. This has proved impractical for two reasons: first, inclusion of all the data on him in all their detail would seriously interfere with continuity of exposition, and second, one of the major didactic methods of the book is to form a conceptualization of Karl based

on part of the data which is to be used by the student to predict how Karl would react to a variety of situations to which his reactions are recorded in the rest of the data. The method loses its value if the student knows the answers to the prediction questions or can find them out by looking in the back of the book. Because of these difficulties a compromise has been made. Most of the data on which the conceptualization is based are presented at various places throughout the book. These facts and everything else known about Karl are published separately in a manual for the instructor, along with the prediction questionnaires and their answer keys. Thus the teacher can withhold information on Karl as long as he wants to, give the prediction questionnaire (Part I) as often as he wants to, reproduce sections of the case material (e. g., Part II of the autobiography for Chapter 15), or modify any of the interpretations of test data given in the text, since he will have a complete and separate case file on Karl. While this arrangement is made primarily for teaching purposes, it should still be possible for the general reader to move uninterruptedly through the text without reference to the manual, except for reading the second part of Karl's autobiography before turning to the last section of Chapter 15.

In a very real sense this book is a community enterprise: nearly every idea in it has been discussed a number of times with different people over the past several years. Like a squirrel who has collected a bag of nuts, I cannot properly trace the origin of many of my ideas, although I am certain, in many cases, that they came from conversations with others. I can only acknowledge, then, in a general way, my deep indebtedness to a number of people, many of whom have contributed more than they know to the warp and woof of this book. First of all, I should like to acknowledge a deep indebtedness to John Alexander McGeoch, who first introduced me to the mysteries of psychology and to whose inspiration I owe the conviction that a science of psychology and personality is possible. Since this book draws heavily on learning theory, culture and personality theory, and psychoanalysis, I should like to acknowledge also intellectual debts in each of these fields; in learning to Arthur W. Melton, who convinced me of the importance of methodology and to Clark L. Hull who taught me something about the nature of theory; in culture and personality to Abram Kardiner, Clyde Kluckhohn, and Ralph Linton; and in psychoanalysis to Sigmund Freud and Henry A. Murray.

If these men are responsible for my basic orientations in the field

himself, how will this new construct, how will this new distinction contribute to my understanding of this particular person whose behavior is here before me? It is for this reason also that I have made a practice of having each student analyze his own case as we have proceeded from one theoretical construct and method of measurement to another. Ideally, of course, the student should collect for himself, on his case, all the different types of behavior that we have had available on Karl, but often this is impractical. I have found that a good autobiography, so long as it contains many concrete factual episodes and not too much conceptualization by the author, will serve as a fairly adequate substitute for many of the measures used, although it normally gives more information about schemata and motives than about traits. The case materials on Karl were originally collected by a student, John Perkins, to whom I am much indebted for permitting me to use them. Other students have worked successfully from published autobiographies like *Black Boy,* by Richard Wright, or *Seven Storey Mountain,* by Thomas Merton, from case documents like Harold Holzer (cf. Elkin, 1943) or *Sun Chief* (Simmons, 1942), or from life histories specially written by fellow students or friends.

Working with concrete lives like this, as they proceed through the theoretical discussions in this book, should prevent students or anyone else from gaining the impression that I am trying to present "a system" or "a theory" of personality. No one knows enough at present to build a theory. Rather what is needed and what I have tried to do is to find a number of constructs in terms of which we can collect data about personality, perhaps with the ultimate hope of building a theory. Anyone who thinks through the questions at the ends of the chapters, or who faces the problem of attempting to treat the bewildering variety of Karl's or anyone else's behavior in terms of the theoretical constructs used cannot fail to be impressed by how much there is to learn. But this is as it should be. The science of personality is only at its beginning and the student should know this above all other things.

One practical problem has arisen in presenting the material on Karl. To understand him adequately, the reader should have available all the documents on which the conceptualization of him is based. This has proved impractical for two reasons: first, inclusion of all the data on him in all their detail would seriously interfere with continuity of exposition, and second, one of the major didactic methods of the book is to form a conceptualization of Karl based on part of the data which is to be used by the student to predict how Karl would react to a variety of situations to which his reactions are recorded in the rest of the data. The method loses its value if the student knows the answers to the prediction questions or can find them out by looking in the back of the book. Because of these difficulties a compromise has been made. Most of the data on which the conceptualization is based are presented at various places throughout the book. These facts and everything else known about Karl are published separately in a manual for the instructor, along with the prediction questionnaires and their answer keys. Thus the teacher can withhold information on Karl as long as he wants to, give the prediction questionnaire (Part I) as often as he wants to, reproduce sections of the case material (e. g., Part II of the autobiography for Chapter 15), or modify any of the interpretations of test data given in the text, since he will have a complete and separate case file on Karl. While this arrangement is made primarily for teaching purposes, it should still be possible for the general reader to move uninterruptedly through the text without reference to the manual, except for reading the second part of Karl's autobiography before turning to the last section of Chapter 15.

In a very real sense this book is a community enterprise: nearly every idea in it has been discussed a number of times with different people over the past several years. Like a squirrel who has collected a bag of nuts, I cannot properly trace the origin of many of my ideas, although I am certain, in many cases, that they came from conversations with others. I can only acknowledge, then, in a general way, my deep indebtedness to a number of people, many of whom have contributed more than they know to the warp and woof of this book. First of all, I should like to acknowledge a deep indebtedness to John Alexander McGeoch, who first introduced me to the mysteries of psychology and to whose inspiration I owe the conviction that a science of psychology and personality is possible. Since this book draws heavily on learning theory, culture and personality theory, and psychoanalysis, I should like to acknowledge also intellectual debts in each of these fields; in learning to Arthur W. Melton, who convinced me of the importance of methodology and to Clark L. Hull who taught me something about the nature of theory; in culture and personality to Abram Kardiner, Clyde Kluckhohn, and Ralph Linton; and in psychoanalysis to Sigmund Freud and Henry A. Murray.

If these men are responsible for my basic orientations in the field of personality, there are a host of others to whom I am personally indebted for the elaboration in discussion of these orientations. I owe much to my colleagues at Wesleyan, to Alvin M. Liberman, Gordon T. Gwinn, David P. McAllester, John W. Whitfield, Juan Roura and particularly to Robert H. Knapp whose breadth of information and imagination saved me often from sterility and despair. I also owe a very special debt to Dr. Benjamin Simon and to Dr. Jules Holzberg, both then of the Connecticut State Hospital at Middletown, who often gave generously of their time and advice when I was attempting to gain a better understanding of the psychiatric and clinical approaches to personality. This book could never have been completed, certainly in its present form, without the generous support provided by the Research Committee of Wesleyan University and by the Department and Laboratory of Social Relations at Harvard University which made it possible for me to spend a year away from my normal teaching duties. During this year at Harvard I have received much in the way of stimulation and moral support from Jerome S. Bruner, Edward C. Tolman, John W. M. Whiting, Robert R. Sears, Florence Kluckhohn, Gordon Allport, and many others. I am particularly grateful for instruction received in seminars run by Talcott Parsons, by Henry A. Murray, and by David Aberle.

But most of all I am indebted to my students who have forced me again and again to revise or clarify the ideas which have gone into this book. Knowing how much these ideas have changed since my first seminar in personality at Bryn Mawr in 1944-45, I feel sure they will continue to evolve—which is as it should be. To all my students then—at Bryn Mawr, at Wesleyan, and at Harvard—who made me write this book, who made me change it, and who will go on writing it, I hope, I dedicate this book.

Middletown, Conn. D. C. M.
March, 1951

Part One

METHODOLOGY: HOW PERSONALITY IS STUDIED

I

The Scientific Approach to Personality: The History of a Belief

Acquiring a scientific attitude toward human personality is not easy. There are all sorts of emotional and theoretical problems involved, all sorts of implicit assumptions that tend to color thinking and distort judgment unless they are made explicit to begin with. After all, to take a detached, scientific attitude toward a human being is to do a somewhat peculiar, "unnatural" thing. It involves treating another human being as if he were a thing—a tree or a stone—to be analyzed and conceptualized, rather than loved, hated, judged sinful or successful, appreciated or derogated. It involves the assumption that human nature *can* be understood in the same way that a tree or a stone can be understood. This daring assumption is by no means shared by everyone. In fact there are important reasons why people should emotionally resist such an idea. It will therefore be useful to try to discover how it has come about historically that many today assume that they can understand human nature by the scientific method. Tracing the historical development of an idea like this is intrinsically interesting, but for us it will have still another purpose. It will show what difficulties arise in connection with adopting such an attitude so that we may allow for them before starting on our quest for the scientific understanding of human personality.

Origins of Interest in Understanding Personality. People are undoubtedly deeply interested in human personality today. On every side the cry is the same: Man has developed his technical skills, his knowledge and control over nature, to the point where he is about to destroy himself; what we must do is develop our knowledge of human nature to the point where we can understand and control it and perhaps prevent man from ultimate destruction. President Conant of Harvard put the matter as follows in stressing the importance of psychology, anthropology and sociology to the American Association for the Advancement of Science in 1947:

All concerned with medical science, however objective and neutral they may claim to be, are urged forward with a desire to improve the public health and a firm conviction that they will do so. Likewise, the scientist concerned with human relations and the structure of society must have conviction as to the practical objectives of the practitioners in his field and a belief in the possibility of accomplishing at least some of the objectives they have in mind.

These types of work seem full of promise. The point of view of the younger men in these fields indicates that the time is now at hand when rapid advances will be forthcoming, and from these advances flow practical consequences of great value to this nation. (Quoted in the *American Psychologist*, 3, p. 67.)

It is not only the educational leaders who feel this way. Libraries report that circulation of books on psychology and personality is higher than it has ever been. Colleges report that enrollment in psychology courses increased sharply after World War II. Current best-seller lists are headed by such titles as *The Mature Mind* by Overstreet, *Peace of Mind* by Liebman, or *Peace of Soul* by Sheen, all books which attempt to tell man how he should adjust to an increasingly threatening world. Society is turning to the sciences of human relations, to psychology, and particularly to the psychology of personality. Why?

Alexander (1942) has suggested an answer. On the basis of his experience as a psychoanalyst he argues that people become concerned with their own inner workings in times of pain and trouble, when things are not going right in the outside world. He attributes our present concern with psychology to the disasters which threaten to overwhelm us from without—from world wars and the great advances in techniques of mass destruction of human life. Allport puts it this way: "Whenever one is unable to achieve, or continue in, a condition of friendly relations with the environment, he must perforce pay attention to his own shortcomings, and thereby become acutely aware of the incompatibility between himself and the physical and social world outside, and of his isolation. In pleasure, when everything is going well, his separation is not felt; but pain is always referred to the self." (1937, p. 164.) This is just as true of nations as it is of individuals, argues Alexander. When an empire begins to crumble, when a state is unsuccessful in war or turns from prosperity to depression, its citizens often turn to self-examination, to try to find out what the trouble is. Alexander illustrates his point from history, citing, for instance, the changes in the intellectual climate of Athens during the long and costly wars with Sparta. During the Golden Age of Pericles Athens had been prosperous and proud, a great center of learning and culture. Philosophers like Thales and Democritus at this time were chiefly interested in understanding the physical world. Then came the long and costly Peloponnesian War. Athenian philosophers like Socrates and Plato in this time of great strife and material reverses turned their attention from the external world to self-examination, from problems of cosmology and physics to problems of ethics and psychology. In the words of Socrates' motto, taken supposedly from the Delphic oracle, the great object of thought was to "know thyself." "Socrates turned away from speculations about the outside world, and devoted himself to an attempt to apply the scientific method to conduct as thoroughly as it was applied every day to technical processes of manufacture. He repudiated as a useless labor all attempts to know the world without. Its changes are in the hands of the gods, who have hidden knowledge of them from men. Conduct, on the other hand, is our affair." (Lindsay, 1935, p. xxii.) Socrates differed from many of the other skeptics of his time in believing that man *could* know himself. He had faith in man's ability to arrive at ultimate truth, at least so far as human conduct was concerned. Self-knowledge was the path to self-control which in turn was the path to the salvation of the state in a collapsing material world. This faith was a kind of heroic last stand in the face of destruction from without. It is poetically reflected in Aeschylus' great drama *Prometheus* in which the hero ultimately wins out by a supreme act of self-assertion, by holding fast to his secret knowledge despite all the tortures to which fate and the gods subject him. But the faith was not destined to last. Already in Sophocles' great drama *Oedipus Rex* there are intimations of evil forces at work within man which will bring his downfall. Still later in Greek history we come across a play like Euripides' *Medea* in which the hatred and jealousy of a woman reflect fully the uncontrollable forces at work in the human personality. Here there is none of Socrates' optimism about knowledge and control of human nature; instead there is increasing fear of unknowable evil forces within man as well as without.

External disaster therefore may lead to interest in personality but it does not necessarily produce the faith that one can understand and control it. The Hebrews stand as a sharp contrast to the Greeks in this respect. They, too, after a brief period of glory under David, were a dispossessed, unsuccessful nation buffeted about on a geographical bridge between three great empires. They, too, turned inward in their attempt to discover why things were going so badly.

The inward search is most vividly described in the book of Job. Job sits at his campfire with his three counsellors in great material distress and suffering and wants to know why—why should all this have happened to him? What has he done wrong? Hasn't he obeyed God's laws? How can he regulate his life so as to avoid disaster? After much soul searching, he receives an answer which is quite different from the one that Socrates found at Delphi. The voice in the whirlwind appears and tells Job that he is wrong even to ask such questions. To try to know God's will is itself sinful, a sign that man has set himself up against God in wanting to know so much. Job must realize and accept his inability to know such things, his powerlessness: "Canst thou draw Leviathan with a fishhook?" "What is man that thou art mindful of him?" These are the attitudes toward man found in early Hebrew thought, and they are very different from those expressed by Plato and Socrates, who had such great faith in man's power to know himself and find his own salvation. In early Old Testament thought there is a profound pessimism, a conviction that even the wish to know is itself bad, as it presumes too much. The story of Adam and Eve has the same moral: Knowledge belongs to God; the impulse to know is dangerous and sinful, a symptom of man's disobedience and self-will.

Western civilization inherited from these two great traditions two quite different beliefs about whether human nature could or should be known or not. Both the Hebrews and the Greeks had been stimulated by material distress into thinking about man's nature, but they had come to different conclusions. The Hebrews felt that there were dark inscrutable forces within human nature just as there were in the outside world and that even the wish to understand them was in itself bad, in fact a symptom of those evil forces themselves at work. The Greeks, on the other hand, at least in the time of Plato and Socrates, felt that man by reasoning could arrive at understanding and control of himself. They did not wholly overlook the irrational elements in human nature. In fact Book IX of Plato's *Republic* contains a remarkable account of the action of the "unnecessary pleasures and desires."

> Of the unnecessary pleasures and desires, some seem to me to be unlawful. They are probably innate in everyone, but if disciplined by law and by the better desires, and with the assistance of reason, they may in some men be entirely eradicated, or at least left few and weak, while in other men they are stronger and more numerous.
>
> And what are those desires? he asked.

> Those that are active during sleep, I answered. When the rest of soul, the reasoning, gentle, and ruling part of it is asleep, the bestial and savage part, when it has had its full of food or wine, begins to leap about, pushes sleep aside, and tries to go and gratify its instincts. You know how in such a state it will dare anything as though it were freed and released from all shame or discernment. It does not shrink from attempting incestual intercourse, in its dream, with a mother, or with any man or god or beast. It is ready for any deed of blood, and there is no unhallowed food it will not eat. In a word, it falls short of no extreme of folly or shamelessness. (Lindsay's translation, 1935, p. 269.)

This passage is unusual in two respects: It describes with startling accuracy the dream material which centuries later was to provide the basis for the Freudian revolution in psychology and it reflects Plato's deep conviction that the unlawful, instinctual side of human nature could be subjected to rational control, a conviction that was also shared by Freud.

The History of a Belief. With such an inheritance from opposing Greek and Hebrew traditions it can hardly be wondered that beliefs about the feasibility of a scientific approach to personality swung from one extreme to another at different periods in the history of Western civilization. In times of material crisis, psychology, as usual, came to the fore, but sometimes with hope and sometimes with despair. The gradual breakup of the Roman Empire found men like Marcus Aurelius greatly concerned with inner peace and arguing that no matter what happened in the outside world, one could always remain untouched by evil and tragedy in the inmost citadel of his mind. Later Augustine was also concerned over the source of evil and finally located it in man himself, in his willful attempt to disobey God by trying to understand things by himself. Augustine brought something new into the picture by managing to combine both the Greek and Hebrew traditions in a curious way. Like the Hebrews he felt that man by himself was helpless, but if he surrendered completely to God and attempted to do God's will, he might then accomplish all things. Thus a kind of compromise was arrived at over the feasibility of understanding human nature, a compromise which permitted and even required such knowledge but according to a set of established doctrinal rules. Thus the great medieval scholastic synthesis was made possible. One of its major tenets was that although man might not know himself, since even to attempt to do so was a sign of disobedience and sin, he might with God's help work out a system of self-control and obedience which led to salvation. Thus the great scholastics like Thomas Aquinas spent their energies in a somewhat contradictory enterprise: the attempt to work out by reason what reason ultimately could not understand. What made the enterprise possible was the faith that God was revealing himself to man in his efforts, but any little evidence that man might be wanting to know these things on his own accord, out of his own desires, had to be rigorously suppressed as a sign of disobedience. Augustine relates how he had to check himself when he found he was idly watching a spider spin her web and wondering how she did it. Even such a tiny impulse of curiosity (and hence self-will) had to be suppressed.

Such an attitude had important consequences as to the theory of human nature which did develop. In the first place, the universe became *anthropocentric*. All geography, the entire physical world, even the stars above, were arranged in accordance with a moral law which applied not only to human conduct but to the universe without as well. In Dante's *Divine Comedy*, which epitomizes this trend, though perhaps with some poetic license, the earth is conceived as specially designed with a deep pit to handle different types of human sinners, and the planetary orbits in the heavens as created to receive different kinds of saints. In short, the universe was conceived as built according to the demands of the psychological model of the times. Psychology, in the religious sense, ruled supreme over all the branches of knowledge. In the second place, as present-day psychologists might have told the scholastics, a psychological theory which demanded such rigorous control and suppression of antisocial, instinctual desires ultimately led to the projection of these impulses into the outside universe, and men in the Middle Ages became obsessed by the greatest fear of witchcraft in the history of Western civilization. The attempt at rational mastery and control of "evil" impulses according to the demands of Christian law only forced men to disown those impulses and ultimately to attribute them to devils, witches, and sorcerers. The projection was made easy by the belief that the universe was organized entirely around man. At this point man was perhaps farthest from really understanding himself and from believing that he ever could understand himself, although at the conscious level scholastic psychology of the time intended just such an understanding.

The Renaissance broke up this pattern of beliefs. Technical inventions (gunpowder, printing), voyages of discovery to the New World, religious revolt, the revival of Greek learning, all combined to produce major upheavals in every sphere of life, but psychologically their impact was the same: Man began to regain faith in himself and in his own powers. Rabelais expresses this new faith and vigor perhaps more vividly than any other figure of his time. His hero Pantagruel is a lusty infant from birth, demonstrating his great powers in all matters, from sex to athletics or the Greek classics. He typifies man's renewed faith in himself, a faith which was soon to justify itself in man's great and largely successful scientific conquest of the physical universe. Whitehead (1925) calls the period 1550-1660 the "Century of Genius," a century which saw published the great discoveries of Kepler, Galileo, Descartes, Pascal, Newton, etc. Once again the pattern of ancient Greece seemed to be repeating itself. Man's great material success in making new inventions and conquering new continents had turned scientific interest to the physical universe and this time with signal success. There were attempts to extend the new methods of analysis to human nature; Cabanis and LaMettrie felt that man could be pretty well understood as a machine which operated according to the same principles as other machines about which so much was being learned. Locke and his spiritual descendants in the British associationist school felt that since man was essentially a "blank tablet" at birth, society had the power to make of him what it would by the kind of education it gave him.

Thus the Greek faith in man's ability to know and control himself—the faith of Socrates and Plato—had revived even stronger than ever. Perhaps the most fascinating example of its application in practice is the story of how James Mill attempted to make of his son, John Stuart Mill, a kind of paragon of reason. As a young boy he was forced to read, understand, and discuss critically books which ordinarily would be read in college. He began to learn Greek at three. Before he was eight his father

> . . . used, as opportunity offered, to give me explanations and ideas respecting civilization, government, morality, mental civilization, which he required me afterwards to restate to him in my own words. . . . I was continually incurring his displeasure by my inability to solve difficult problems for which he did not see that I had not the necessary previous knowledge. (Mill, 1873, pp. 8, 12.)

No father would have dared attempt such an enterprise who did not firmly believe that he understood human personality and could therefore make of it whatever he wished. The story of John Stuart

Mill's life as he tells it in his autobiography is the more interesting because his father's faith in his methods proved not to be wholly justified. As the son eventually realizes, his father had left out something very important: there was no understanding or education of his emotional life and eventually he fell into a fit of prolonged depression. How he recovered from this depression is interesting. He describes it thus:

> I did not think I could possibly bear it beyond a year. When, however, not more than half that duration of time had elapsed, a small ray of light broke in upon my gloom. I was reading accidentally, Marmontel's "Memories," and came to the passage which relates his father's death, the distressed position of the family, and the sudden inspiration by which he then a mere boy, felt and made them feel that he would be everything to them—would supply the place of all that they had lost. A vivid conception of the scene and its feelings came over me, and I was moved to tears. From this moment my burden grew lighter. . . . I was no longer hopeless . . . thus the cloud gradually drew off, and I again enjoyed life. (Mill, 1873, pp. 140-141.)

Nowadays a clinical psychologist could hardly fail to see the disguised hostility which he is abreacting here toward his father, a hostility which he certainly must have felt according to frustration-aggression principles after being forced to cram his head with ideas all day long for years on end, almost from the moment of birth. To a modern psychologist the catharsis and relief he feels at the thought of his father's death is obvious. Yet to Mill himself this episode obviously had no meaning. To him it remains the mysterious occasion on which he overcame his "melancholy." The faith of the British Associationists and others like them who felt that man could be understood by reason, was unlimited but their psychological knowledge did not wholly justify it.

There were, as usual, throughout all this period in history those who had looked at the other side of the coin and who had argued that man, far from being a rational animal, was in reality an emotional, lustful, power-mad creature. Some of them, like Machiavelli, thought that man should simply accept the fact that power was his main concern in life and make his arrangements accordingly, thus reviving an idea which had been advanced by Thrasymachus and refuted by Socrates in Plato's *Republic* some two thousand years earlier. As usual there were many who shared this view: Nietzsche, Marx, Pareto, even Hitler and Stalin, who according to Alexander (1942) have tended to operate in our time as if they did not really believe in man's capacity for self-knowledge and self-control. To Marx, for instance, the profit motive was essentially instinctual. There was nothing to understand and control. Rather it had simply to be accepted and political and social arrangements made to curb it. For this group of men the unreasoning, instinctual, primitive urges of mankind had the center of the stage, and they shaped their philosophies accordingly.

The Freudian Revolution. On to this scene stepped Freud, with a new idea, an idea which was to alter once again the belief that man had in the feasibility of scientific knowledge of human personality. In Alexander's terms, "Freud took the first step toward converting the ideal of the Greeks and of Locke, the rule of reason, into a scientific reality." (1942, p. 112.) Even though it is obviously unfair to attribute all of this change in attitude to one man, especially when there were many other psychologists who contributed equally to the change in attitude, nevertheless we can dramatize the change most easily by using Freud as an example because he dealt head-on with the issue that had been causing conflict over so many centuries. His idea was simply this: Man, in order to insure the triumph of reason, must extend its domain to those very unconscious, irrational elements which had so long shaken man's belief in the power of reason. In his own words, "Psychoanalysis is the instrument destined for the progressive conquest of the Id." (*The Ego and The Id,* p. 5.) He spent his long life in a reconnaissance in the "underworld" of the aggressive, sexual, antisocial impulses, the existence of which had so long baffled man in his efforts for self-control. Out of his explorations Freud fashioned the rational instrument, psychoanalysis, which he felt was to give man mastery over these impulses.

Interestingly enough, Freud combined in his own thinking the two great contradictory beliefs about human nature that we have traced throughout the history of Western civilization. On the one hand, he had the passionate faith of the Greeks in the power of reason and man's ability to understand himself. On the other, he had the fascination with and sensitivity to the aggressive, antisocial urges, the importance of which was stressed by those whom we have characterized as being in the Hebrew tradition and as being ultimately pessimistic about man. The important fact is that for him these two views were not contradictory: he attempted at least to extend the rule of reason to what had been repressed and not studied because it was so obviously unreasonable. How did he get that way?

It will be worth our while to look into his life a little in our search for the origins of the belief that the scientific study of all of personality is possible. While it is out of the question to attempt any serious personality study of Freud, we can nevertheless note certain major trends in his thinking which suggest what the ingredients of a student of personality are. His cultural environment contained important elements of both the Greek and Hebrew traditions. Coming from a Jewish family in central Europe, he became sensitized early in life to what it was like to be socially isolated and despised as a member of an "undesirable" minority group. In his life then we find repeated the painful conditions in the outside world which, as we have suggested, so often creates an interest in the processes of human nature. Like Job, he might have had reason to ask why he deserved such treatment. More than this, as a Jew, he was thoroughly familiar with the long Jewish tradition of interest in suffering and in the irrational, repressed elements of human nature. Unlike Job he rejected the view that the ultimate design of life was inscrutable to man and must be accepted as God's will. He refused to put his trust in God and to believe that he could not "draw Leviathan with a fishhook." Sachs (1944) in typical psychoanalytical fashion argues that Freud's antiauthoritarian attitude derived from his rebellion against his father, who apparently felt that his son was never going to "amount to much." Whatever the reason, Freud identified himself thoroughly with the rising tide of faith in science which characterized the late nineteenth century. Many of the leaders in this scientific movement had inherited the confidence of men like James Mill in the power of reason, and the great accomplishments of men like Darwin and Spencer seemed to justify their faith. Freud himself started out as a biologist and would, according to Sachs, have been a great research worker in this field, had his interest not turned to psychology. Out of these two great influences on his life, one essentially Jewish and the other Greek, came Freud's synthesis: Man, even in his most irrational, fantastic moods, can be understood by the methods of reason and scientific analysis. Significantly Freud began his work with the meanderings of dreams and free associations which had seemed to all but the soothsayers to be either the merest chance happenings or the signs of the Devil at work. To Freud nothing was to be left to chance, let alone to the Devil. He was to spread man's wildest fancies on the table and subject them to scientific dissection and analysis. The purpose of his analysis was the same as it had always been—mastery and control of human nature. "Psychoanalysis is the instrument for the progressive conquest of the Id."

There is one other aspect of Freud's personality which is of interest in this connection. He kept his distance from people. More precisely, there is throughout much of his writing clear evidence of pessimism about human nature which verges at times on anger and hostility toward people. He often felt that he was being persecuted, that people were against him (which was often the case), and the record of the early days of psychoanalysis is full of quarrels, jealousies, and petty hatreds, over which Freud presided in a now detached, now openly hostile, but never a loving, manner. Even to those who knew him best and remained loyal to him always, like Sachs, he appeared aloof, cold, and distant, the father figure to be admired and respected, but hardly one for whom respect would be mingled with warmth and love. Freud's angry attempts to unmask man's religious self-deceptions are well known. One need only run through the titles of some of his books to be reminded of them: *The Future of an Illusion, Civilization and Its Discontents,* etc. Through all the disagreeable, ordinarily hidden aspects of human nature he seemed to pick his way carefully, like a man who does his duty because he must. Like Leontius in Plato's *Republic* he appears to be forcing himself to look at "dead bodies" because it will be good for him and for the world. Unmasking man would be a nasty job for anyone, and it may have been possible for Freud only because he was able to express his anger at man by exposing the "seamy" side of human nature.

Yet detachment in science is an absolute necessity, however it may be achieved. We have mentioned this side of Freud's personality to illustrate this point. Curiously enough, Roe (1949) in her study of eminent research scientists in biology and physics has discovered that they too have often achieved scientific detachment as a result of personal and social maladjustment. She finds, for instance, that the typical scientist of world renown was isolated in early life. He did not play with other children, was often awkward and embarrassed in social relationships, had difficulty falling in love and often appeared to retreat to the "ivory tower" in order to avoid the embarrassment of emotional contact with others. This seems to be a case where personal maladjustment serves a useful social end, since, as Parsons points out (1949), "affective neutrality" or detachment is one of the prerequisites of a professional scientist. Science in fact has raised objectivity and detachment to the level of a credal dogma to which each of its devotees must subscribe. Only recently, when advancement in the physical sciences seems so threatening, has there been a movement to escape this isolation and to take a moral attitude toward the consequences of scientific discovery.

Psychology, like the other sciences, has made a strong effort after affective neutrality. But the task is harder, since the subject matter of the science is so very close to the affective life. Detachment may have been easy in Mill's time, or even in Titchener's, when psychology dealt with associations or sensations that seemed far removed from the joys and sorrows of everyday living. But what about a psychology that attempts to deal with the innermost core of man's secrets—with his hopes, his fears, his hates, and joys and sorrows? How can we achieve the necessary objectivity with such material, which is the very center of the psychology of personality?

Dislike, anger, and pessimism will accomplish this end after a fashion as they probably did for Freud. We can keep our distance and remain "detached" if we do not like people. But unfortunately this attitude may also distort the picture, and give the darker side of man's nature an undue emphasis. We need affective neutrality, not affective hostility, even though the latter may correct some of the faults of too close a relationship with people. A second approach to the problem is to avoid the issue altogether by skipping lightly over the central areas of personality, usually on the grounds that one does not have the tools to deal with them yet. Historically this is the position taken by psychology in the United States. The chief reaction of most "solid," scientific psychologists in America to Freud in the twenties was distaste, if not disgust. Pavlov and his conditioned reflexes were considered much more important. Much of the distaste for Freud grew out of the lack of scientific sophistication of many of his followers, from their facile and dogmatic overgeneralizations from inadequate data, and to this extent it was wholly justified. But some of it seems to go beyond this point to a rejection of the very material with which psychoanalysts were attempting to deal, however imperfectly. One is reminded of the Queen's remark to her husband in Hamlet: "Methinks he doth protest too much, my lord." Psychology's earlier rejection of psychoanalysis had much that was defensive about it. Neutrality must not be purchased at the price of avoiding the very issues which might challenge it. American psychologists are beginning to realize that they can no longer afford to expend all their energies on depersonalized experiments with segmental aspects of personality or in attempts to show that psychoanalysis is unscientific, irrelevant, and slightly "disgusting" (cf. Sherif and Cantril, 1947).

A third path to detachment is the aesthetic, appreciative attitude toward people, which Allport has recommended (1937) as being the best attitude for a good judge of people to assume. Many clinical psychologists in particular have found it adaptive. Perhaps the greatest example is Hans Sachs, Freud's pupil, whose poetic approach to psychoanalysis (cf. 1948) is a delightful contrast to Freud's dogged, hard pessimism. Sachs was one who could see all, know all, even the darkest regions of man's nature, and yet love and appreciate what he saw. This gives a certain balance to the picture. It is perhaps the best approach for poetry, for literature, for art, and perhaps even for psychotherapy. But it is not the way of science. It may give a kind of objectivity, but it does not lead to system, or to rigor, as any reader of Hans Sachs will testify. He was not the scientist that Freud was nor did he claim to be. The artist often feels that we "murder to dissect" and that we must dissect to be scientists. We do not want to murder, even unconsciously, when we are being scientific.

What then is the solution to this dilemma? Probably there is none, but the ancient one recommended by Socrates and Freud, namely, to make the problem known. Having seen the emotional problems associated with the scientific study of personality clearly, we can, like one of Rogers' nondirective clients, beware of false or inadequate solutions like Freud's, and perhaps recognize that the "neutral" attitude of science toward people is one we need assume only for certain purposes. After all, the scientific mode of apprehending reality is only one possible mode. A person may put it on or take it off according to the demands of the occasion. A chemist can enjoy a steak; he can also analyze it into its organic compounds if he wants to. He need not do both at once. A physiologist can enjoy a cocktail without mentally tracing the deleterious influence of alcohol on the various functions of his body. A physicist can enjoy a sunset without giving a thought to the principles of optics and refraction. A psychologist can love his wife without perceiving that she is "really" a mother figure for him. So in the following pages when we take a scientific, analytic attitude toward personality we will not do so with the imperialistic notion that this is the only attitude which counts. It is merely *one* attitude, one which is useful for purposes which we will assume to be ours at the moment throughout the rest of the book.

Recognizing this should not only help us gain an objective attitude toward the scientific approach to personality; it should also help us avoid some of the excessive faith that men have at times had in psychology and social science. In material crises, as we have seen, the demand for knowledge of human nature is so great that people tend to expect too much of science, as if it could solve *all* the problems that face men. Many of these problems can be solved only in terms of other modes of apprehending reality, in terms of aesthetic or religious modes, for instance. The scientific approach is merely one among several. There should be no surprise and no disappointment if it cannot answer questions which should not have been put to it in the first place. Science may give us a fuller understanding of human personality and this in turn may ultimately give us greater control over behavior, but decisions as to how this knowledge is to be used must often be made in terms of nonempirical assumptions. Only confusion results when science assumes all for herself. We have seen how faith in the scientific approach to personality has developed throughout the history of Western civilization. The extent to which that faith is justified can be tested in the following chapters, but it should be judged in terms of the limited goals which science has. Let us not expect too much of science.

NOTES AND QUERIES

1. This chapter contains a number of generalizations for which adequate proof does not exist at the present time, although they are commonly accepted among experts. Think about how evidence might be collected which would prove or disprove them. Take, for example, the assertion that when men get into material difficulties in the outside world, they become concerned with their own mental processes. Design an experiment which would test this hypothesis among a group of individuals. If you get into difficulties, consult Sears (1942).

2. Suppose you found that this hypothesis was confirmed at the individual level, would this justify you in assuming that it held true for societies also? How would you go about testing the hypothesis as far as societies are concerned? Would comparisons among different cultures help? How?

3. Although it is commonly believed that the notion that "man is the measure of all things" is typical at least of a certain period in Greek intellectual history, it is also true that the Greeks often emphasized the power of fate or necessity as being essentially outside man's control. Would it be possible to correlate the incidence of one or

the other of these ideas with the decline of Athenian material prosperity? What are some of the factors other than material progress which should contribute to belief in man's strength or helplessness? What about geography or climate? How could they support one belief or the other? Design a cross-cultural test for any hypothesis you advance. Beliefs about man's relation to nature will be discussed again in Chapter 8.

4. In what way is the belief in uncontrollable forces in human nature strengthened by attempts at rational self-control? Why aren't attempts at self-control always self-defeating?

5. Granted that there is as much anxiety over and fear of sexual and antisocial impulses in some circles today as there was in the Middle Ages, why is belief in witchcraft less likely to occur today? For discussions of witchcraft in the Middle Ages see Zilboorg (1941) for a historical account; Mann's *Dr. Faustus* (1948) for an imaginative reconstruction; and Seabrook (1940) for a discussion of contemporary beliefs in witchcraft. Show how witchcraft is related to Freud's notion of "omnipotence of thought" (cf. *Totem and Taboo,* 1918).

6. We have suggested that the qualities of sensitivity and detachment are necessary for a good personality psychologist. What exactly is meant by detachment? Why is it necessary? Why should there be resistances against assuming such an attitude? What would be the consequences of maintaining such an attitude consistently in all one's relationships to people? Are there other qualities which are necessary for the scientific student of personality?

7. Why was Freud's attempt to unmask man dangerous? What is the technical name for the defense mechanism we have argued he adopted to cope with this danger?

8. What are the aims of clinical psychology? How do they differ from those of scientific personality study? Can a scientist show "warmth" as a clinician should? What value assumptions does the operating clinical psychologist make? Can they be proved or disproved?

9. What are some of the assumptions that the scientific approach to personality makes? Could the "null hypothesis" that man is no different from a tree or a stone and can be understood by an extension of the same techniques ever be disproved? Is it in the realm of proof or disproof?

10. What value for science do certain nonempirical assumptions have? Consider an example from social psychology: What would be

the disadvantages (if any) for science of making the belief that Negroes, or some other minority group, should not be discriminated against contingent on the *empirical* finding that their intelligence was the same on the average as for other groups? One simple way of testing whether or not a belief is based on empirical or nonempirical grounds is to try to think of conditions which would *disprove* it. If you can think of no way of disproving a belief or of finding evidence that would lead you to abandon it, then the belief may be said to be held on nonempirical grounds. Science usually tries to reduce such beliefs to a minimum, but a certain number may actually facilitate the collection of evidence. Show how this would work for minority groups. Show how the assumption that every individual is worthy of respect as an article of faith (based on nonempirical grounds) might facilitate the collection of evidence on a particular individual as compared with the belief that an individual is worthy of respect only if the evidence warrants it. The essential difference between the two beliefs is that the former is presumably not changed by whatever facts are collected about the person, either positive or negative, whereas the latter is. Are there other ways of keeping evidence and judgment about people separate than by making certain nonempirical, nonscientific assumptions to start with? Show how the considerations discussed here might make the scientific study of Hitler's or Goering's personality exceedingly difficult (cf. Kelley, 1947). This question will be discussed again in Chapter 3.

2

Obtaining the Facts

Faith has grown in the applicability of the scientific method to the study of personality. But is that faith justified? A real answer to such a question requires consideration in concrete detail of the way in which scientific method can be used to study personality. It may help by way of contrast to begin with an *unscientific* approach to personality; that is, with a first impression such as anyone might form on observing another person. Having started with a completely natural and scientifically unsophisticated portrait of an individual, we can then see how various methodological improvements might be introduced to make the portrait into a scientifically satisfactory one.

Students in a personality class were asked to write a first impression of another person they had observed briefly. Two of them happened to observe the same person and wrote reports as follows:

First Student's Impression of Mr. P.

Recently while attending a basketball game in Hartford with several friends, I had an opportunity to make a snap judgment of an individual's personality and a chance to check this judgment through an extended conversation with the subject. The subject sat in front of us and my first impression was gained from gazing at his back and profile, and overhearing several remarks that he made concerning the contest and related affairs. Mr. P. impressed me as being about forty-eight years old, huskily built, without the flabbiness that usually typifies men of his age, well dressed in the latest vogue. In his dress he appeared to be trying to give both the impression of conservatism and the flashiness of youth. This same contradiction appeared in his manner in other ways. Most of the time he sat back with the reserved, detached air of a casual observer; but often he seemed to feel that he must show his youth and vitality by entering verbally and physically into the spirit of the game.

Mr. P. was undoubtedly exceptionally well acquainted with the game and its terminology, also with the players and the schools which they represented—more so than would be expected from a casual spectator. He gave the impression, often seemingly intentionally, that he was in some way attached to the game, the schools, or the players. (It later turned out that he's a coach at one of the public high schools.)

Judging from the tone of his voice and tenor of remarks, Mr. P. appeared to be definitely dominating, extroverted, confident, and self-centered. These are only snap judgments which accounts for the conflict between a couple of the traits. As is so often true, I was attracted by the man because I disliked him from the minute he voiced his first opinion. For this reason my whole impression was undoubtedly tainted, but on talking with the subject and with other people who knew him well, I found that most of the above judgments were correct.

Second Student's Impression of Mr. P.

Mr. P. is a middle-aged, pyknic type of individual, who seems to have found his station in life and seems content with it. His outward appearance indicated a middle-class man who lives comfortably but moderately. He is friendly, talkative, and gregarious, as evidenced by his continuous conversation with a group of us students at a basketball game. With the exception of his eyebrows and his laugh, he reminded me of a certain person on the X— faculty. Telling anecdotes, being one of the boys, enjoying and desiring the center of attraction would probably be some prominent characteristics of his. Beneath his easy-going, jocular "smoke" there is probably a simmering temper which readily steams if sufficiently stimulated. He is not one to be contradicted or provoked extensively. His curiosity about the X— coaching staff and about who the real football coach is, fell in with my general picture of him when I learned that he was a coach himself. Further impressions about his liking for boys, or sportsmanship, and athletics are merely mentioned in the light of this secondary information. The over-all recollection of him was favorable.

As we look at these two judgments of the same person, based on observations made at the same time, we are struck by both the similarities and the differences in the opinions of the judges. On one student Mr. P. made a favorable impression. On the other he did not. On more obvious traits, such as his talkativeness and his knowledge of the game, both judges agreed, although it is worth noting that whereas one of them referred to him as gregarious, the other called what was probably the same behavior "extroversion." When one puts such diverse judgments and impressions as these side by side, it does appear that the task before the psychology of personality is a difficult one indeed. How are these differing pictures to be reconciled? What is the man's true personality? How are we to go about finding out what his true personality is?

Even in such uncontrolled observations as these, however, the elements for beginning a systematic study of personality are present. In the first place both judges made some actual observations of behavior. They noted his blue suit, his jocular, easygoing manner, his talkativeness, the fact that he knew a lot about the game; they noticed his physique, his tone of voice, the number of times that he spoke with the people around him. These are the actual facts on which an impression of personality is built. Secondly, both judges used some sort of general concepts to describe the behavior they had noticed. These concepts included such terms as *middle-class, a coach, extroverted.* One judge said that he had a "simmering" temper. In this case the judge borrowed a term from another kind of experience (with boiling water) to describe a particular aspect of Mr. P.'s behavior. Finally both judges had an over-all picture of the person. They *integrated* their observations into an over-all impression which they either liked or disliked.

Thus we can see that even the most naïve impression of a person involves three elements: observation, conceptualization, and integration. We can begin understanding the scientific approach to personality by studying the improvements which science has introduced in each of these three parts of the process of constructing an adequate personality portrait. Refinements in the methods of making observations will be discussed in this chapter, and improvements in conceptualization and integration will be discussed in the succeeding two chapters.

Observation

Science generally has progressed when man has invented new techniques for making his observations precise. Originally man had to look at the stars with his naked eye. His knowledge of astronomy has increased almost in exact proportion to the sensitivity of the instruments that he has been able to invent to aid his naked eye. Psychology is no exception in this respect. Making an observation such as the students reported above is no easy task for it involves attending to a number of different things at once. As Murray (1938) has pointed out, there are severe limitations set by nature on perceptual ability. A man can only take in so much at a glance and he can only look from one place to another just so fast. While the observer is listening to what Mr. P. says, he may not notice that Mr. P. is scratching himself with his left hand, shoving his knee into the back of the spectator below, and avidly following every play of the game. There are also the limitations arising from the observer's set. He sees to some extent what he expects to see, what he is looking for. Finally he must translate what he sees into some kind of judgment and, if left to his own devices, he will doubtless pick some method of expressing his judgment which is unlike that which would be used by any other judge. One of the most striking things about the two impressions of Mr. P.

is that the very difference in the terminology the observers used would make it quite difficult to obtain a reconciliation of their views. Efforts to improve observation have been directed both toward refining and agreeing on terms in which the judgments will be made and toward improving the techniques of actually perceiving the behavior of the subjects studied.

Improving the Way in Which Judgments Are Made. Historically the earliest attempts to improve observation centered around refining the judging process. The goal was to get observer agreement on what had actually taken place, a goal which arose from the conviction that it would certainly be impossible to develop a science of personality unless observers could agree on the "stubborn irreducible" facts to start with. With attention focused so early on this goal, much has been learned about how judgments may be improved, the ordinary criterion for improvement being whether the judgments are *reliable*. Reliability in this context refers to whether judges agree on what the facts are. It is ordinarily measured quantitatively by correlating ratings made under identical conditions by two or more judges or by correlating successive ratings by the same judge. Symonds (1931) and more recently Krech and Crutchfield (Chapter 7, 1948) have covered very thoroughly most of the advances in this field. We need only touch on some of the main points very briefly as follows:

1. *Agreement on the terms to be used.* The very first and most elementary problem in judgment is to decide what categories or what dimensions of behavior are going to be observed. These categories or dimensions must then be defined as carefully as possible so that all people using them will understand them in the same way. One of the simplest forms in which such a set of categories can occur is the *check list.* In the check list several behavior categories are defined, such as "talking," "laughing," "walking," or "standing still," and the judge simply checks whether or not the behavioral item in question occurs during a given time period. Although such categories as those just mentioned are usually reliably judged (with observer agreement correlations of .90 or better), they may have limited psychological significance. Consequently experimenters have repeatedly tried to get judges to make decisions about more complex characteristics such as leadership, adaptability, friendliness, honesty, and integrity. Repeated experimentation has shown that as one moves from simple overt behavior to more complex personality variables,

such as integrity, the reliability of the judgments decreases (Symonds, 1931). Judges find it more and more difficult to agree as the variable becomes more complex.

In recent years, rather good observer agreement has been obtained for fairly complex judgments provided the behavior in question can be observed over and over again as in a written record like the Thematic Apperception Test. Here the judge may have to decide whether the person is displaying a complex characteristic such as *need for Affiliation* or *Aggression*. Yet McClelland, Clark, Roby, and Atkinson (1949) and Tomkins (1947) report observer agreement correlations up to .96 for judgments of this sort, even though they require the judge to categorize the *meaning* of the behavior in the protocols rather than just the words or acts themselves. The advantage of working with a written record lies in the fact that the judge may review the behavior as often as he wants before he makes a decision, which is not the case when he is checking behavior as it occurs or when he is asked to rate a person's "friendliness" on the basis of his recollection of an indefinite number of prior incidents. It is not therefore so surprising that judgments of increasingly complex characteristics can be reliably made as the behavior on which they are based is available for repeated observation.

2. *Quantification: scaling and ranking.* After it has been decided what categories are to be used, a common next step has been to ask the judge to scale his judgment in some quantitative way. The check list simply asks the judge to record presence or absence of an item, whereas a rating scale may be given the judge so that he can indicate the degree to which the subject shows the characteristic in question. Observer agreement in rating has been found to be a function of such variables as the number of steps in the scale and the carefulness with which each step is defined. As an illustration of a typical rating scale let us consider the following item dealing with the extent to which a person displays "leadership."

Does he get others to do as he wishes?

Probably unable to lead his fellows	Lets others take lead	Sometimes leads in minor affairs	Sometimes leads in important affairs	Displays marked ability to lead his fellows; makes things go

(After Symonds, 1931, p. 70.)

Note that the steps define approximate increases in the frequency with which the subject takes the lead in various situations. Note also that the judge may make five major discriminations or as many finer ones as he wishes, since this is a graphic rating scale. In general it has been found that five to seven discriminations or steps on the scale yield the highest observer reliability (Symonds, 1931). Often many discriminations are permitted the judge but the experimenter then categorizes the judgments in relatively few classes to obtain this higher reliability. One of the problems with rating scales of this sort is that judges tend to use different portions of the scale, which makes judgments not comparable. This difficulty can be met to some extent by converting each judge's ratings into standard scores in terms of the mean and distribution of his own judgments. Usually some attempt to inform judges about distributing their decisions will also help normalize the distribution of their judgments. Graphic aids and special instructions have been devised for this purpose. Most experts in this field caution experimenters against forcing the judges to make quantitative decisions of this sort when they do not feel able to do so. Extreme ratings and ones of which the judges are confident are apt to be most reliable. In some cases therefore a rating scale, though easily devised, is no improvement over a simple check list.

Individuals may also be *ranked* with respect to a particular characteristic, since judges often find it easier to compare individuals than to estimate how much of a characteristic each one has. Ranking may be very carefully done by the method of paired comparisons in which each person is compared with every other one. It too has its problems, however. On the practical side, if there are too many people to rank, the task may become too difficult for the judges. On the theoretical side it is sometimes hard to know how to treat the data obtained, as for instance when inconsistent "circles" arise (A > B, B > C, C > A). Recent developments in the statistics of ranking (Kendall, 1948) promise to increase the usefulness of this technique.

3. *The number of judgments.* As Symonds states (1931, p. 5), "Reliable evidence must be multiplied evidence." Under most conditions the greater the number of times a given judgment can be made, the more confidence can be placed in the reliability of the judgment. Even the clinician working with a projective technique recognizes the importance of this when he shows more than one inkblot to his subject. The single occurrence of a form response to a single inkblot is not considered a dependable index of the tendency of the subject to use form responses in his approach to unstructured material. Of course

there are times when only one judgment is possible (a close play at first base) or when increasing the number of judgments will destroy the validity of the judgment itself. For example, if the judgments are spread over too long a time, the resulting average may obscure a genuine trend.

4. *The number of judges.* Increasing the number of judges increases the stability of their decisions. Symonds (1931, p. 96) presents a table showing how many independent judgments are needed to achieve a high reliability coefficient. To get a coefficient of .90 the number of judgments varies from four for a rating on scholarship to eighteen for a rating on impulsiveness. The virtue of having more than one judge has impressed some psychologists so much that they have concluded that the opinion of a large number of judges is the most *valid* judgment of a trait that can be obtained. Hull (1928), for example, averaged the ratings of a whole fraternity on each of the members of the fraternity. While this will give a very reliable judgment, in the sense that the average rating on a given group of subjects by twenty judges will be very close to that given by twenty other judges, it is, of course, no guarantee that the judgment is accurate. The judgment of any one fraternity member may actually be more valid or correct than the combined group judgment, no matter how reliable it is.

5. *Rating errors.* Much attention has been given to correcting for systematic errors which may creep into judgments. The "halo" error results from a judge allowing a general impression to influence his rating on specific traits. The "generosity" error results from the tendency of judges to overestimate the good qualities of subjects they like. Such errors may often be corrected by converting a judge's ratings to standard scores around his own average judgment, by special instructions to the judge, by reversing the ends of a rating scale so that they run from high to low and then from low to high. or by other such techniques.

Improving the Conditions of Observation. Looking back at the work of our two student judges, we note that they not only gave their reports in an unsystematic manner, but they also observed under very uncontrolled conditions. Each one probably observed Mr. P. at different times during the evening and under various distracting influences from watching the game and talking with friends. Scientists working in this field soon realize that no matter how carefully they define the categories of judgment or how many judges they use to observe an event, if the conditions of observation are not controlled, agreement is impossible to obtain. For example, Ray (1947) has shown a film of a simple hold-up scene to a class of students. Even though the students are warned as to the general nature of the scene, and though the scene itself is only one minute in duration, he found that the students made many errors in answers to the specific questions asked afterward as to what took place. Many of these errors of observation were made even though the subjects were asked to say whether they would swear to the judgment or not in a court of law. To take an extreme example, in answer to the question as to whether the woman in the picture was tall, short, or medium in height, more people gave incorrect judgments than correct judgments. This and many other similar experiments demonstrate the great importance of improving the conditions under which the judge is asked to report what he sees. Considerable progress has been made in this direction. The results of it may be summarized as brief "advices" to those planning observation.

1. *Train the judges in observing the material in question.* There seems little doubt that the more experience an observer has with the behavior on which he is going to be asked for a judgment, the better and more accurate his judgments will be. Many writers have stressed this (cf. Symonds, 1931). One needs only to sit by a coach at a basketball game to be convinced of the importance of this fact. The coach sees literally hundreds of things: movements, plays, fouls, etc., which are "invisible" to the average spectator. The psychological process involved seems to be the redintegration of complex events from small cues based on past experience. An analogy is the difference between the way a child looks at a book when he is reading it and the way an adult looks at the same book. The beginner at reading has to see nearly every word, as eye-movement records will demonstrate, whereas the experienced reader can jump from one portion of the page to the next and redintegrate or anticipate the intervening portions of the material. The skilled judge works in the same way. He has learned what comes next and can short-cut parts of the observing process.

2. *Simplify what is to be observed.* Great advances have been made in this field through the development of a technique which has come to be called *time sampling.* Typical of some of the better uses of this technique is research by Thomas, Loomis, and Arrington (1933) on children's behavior in a nursery-school situation, by Olson (1929) on nervous movements, and by Sears (1942) on the motility of

adolescent boys left alone in a room after failure. This work is of such very great methodological importance that it is worth while considering a representative example of such a study in some detail.

A report by Merrill on mother-child interaction (1946) is an excellent case in point. She was interested in observing accurately the stimulus properties of a mother's behavior toward her child. This general problem is of very great theoretical importance in the field of personality because of the contemporary emphasis on the importance of child-rearing techniques in forming basic personality structure. Merrill, working under Sears' direction, was faced with the problem of choosing categories of mother behavior which would be definable, recognizable, and relevant to the theoretical problem. She decided that she would attempt to define variables which related to the contact between mother and child, to the specificity of control by the mother, and to facilitation or inhibition of the child's behavior. She developed some thirty-two behavior categories, of which the following are typical:

a. Mother is carrying on independent activity at the adult level—any act divorced from the experimental setup, or the child, such as reading magazines, looking out the window, busying self with contents of pocketbook.

d. Mother specifically directs child's actions by command or statement. . . . Example: "Put that block on top of the other ones . . . then make a door right there."

i. Mother interferes by structurizing, interfering, cautioning, stopping, etc. Example: "Don't drink that water—the cup is not clean." Or "Oh dear, now you've gotten your suit wet and there's quite a draft in this room."

(Merrill, 1946, pp. 40-41.)

After memorizing the list of categories, the observer sat behind a one-way vision screen and watched the child playing in the presence of his mother. The observer's task was to write down a symbol for one of the behavior categories every five seconds for thirty minutes. A light signal marked the end of every five-second period. Thus it was possible not only to discover whether or not the behavior had occurred but actually to measure its duration or relative importance by counting the number of checks for a given category out of the 360 possible checks for a half-hour session. With these data it was then possible to measure the agreement between two observers working simultaneously, or to measure the consistency of a mother's behavior from one session to the next. Merrill found that her observer agreement correlations ranged from .86 to .92 for different categories. The mothers were also fairly consistent in the amount of a particular kind of behavior they showed on different occasions. The correlations for relative amount of a certain type of response shown on two occasions varied from .33 to .92 (median around .65) depending on the response.

Since Merrill now knew that the observations she was making were reliable and consistent under normal conditions, she was able to introduce an experimental variable to see what effect it had on maternal behavior. The variation she introduced in this particular case was to motivate the mothers to have their children do well by telling them that she felt their children could play better than they had in the previous session. She found a significant increase in the amount of directing and interfering behavior on the part of the mothers. The great methodological importance of this experimental finding is that Merrill was *not* just relying on over-all impressions or ratings on the part of observers as to whether the mother interfered more on the second occasion. She was not simply multiplying judges to get perhaps stable but inaccurate judgments. Instead, she had actual quantitative records which showed that the mother's behavior had changed in the direction indicated and by such and such an amount.

The value of this approach can scarcely be overemphasized. It should be applied with increasing frequency to observations of this sort, even in field studies done by anthropologists and others. The reason for this can be made clearer by an example. Let us take an item in the Outline of Cultural Materials (formerly the Cross-Cultural Survey) kept at Yale University which deals with severity of cleanliness training in various cultures (item 863). One anthropologist interviews a number of informants in a given culture or makes certain observations which are the basis for a description of "methods of teaching children to wash, bathe, and groom themselves; inculcation of standards of cleanliness, neatness," etc. Another anthropologist gets material on the same issues (which is one great methodological improvement of the Outline) in another culture. But *comparison* of their reports is still difficult without more standardization of the conditions of observation. If both of them could make the same observations and if they could make them under time-sampling conditions, such as those just described, it would be much easier to decide which culture in fact has more severe cleanliness training.

3. *Remove the observer from the immediate situation.* One of the common difficulties in observing is that the observer is often taking

part in the experience which he is trying to record. This may radically change the behavior of the person being watched or it may make the observation inaccurate because of the necessity of responding to the situation as well as recording it. Observation of this sort is much like trying to turn up the gas to get a better look at the dark, to use William James' neat illustration.

The problem can be met in a variety of ways. The recording can be done by another nonparticipating observer or by an instrument; or it can be done by providing a one-way vision screen through which an observer can record the behavior without interfering at all with it; or the role of the participant observer can be fairly clearly defined so that even though he is present, his effect to some extent can be allowed for ahead of time. An example of the last approach is Dollard's description of his role as a field worker in his book *Caste and Class in a Southern Town* (1937). In his introduction Dollard states very carefully who he is and what his presence in a southern town as an interviewer on racial problems would mean to the person being interviewed. In other words, the observer can attempt to define his own stimulus value to the people being observed before he begins his work. This should serve to increase the accuracy of his observations or, what is more important, of the interpretation which he or others put on his observations.

4. *Record the data for future content analysis.* No matter how carefully the experimenter defines his categories, it still will be difficult for an observer to get very accurate judgments of some complex scenes, particularly as they occur in the field. It was one of the advantages of Merrill's study that the mother and child were somewhat circumscribed in what they could do since she placed them in a rather small playroom with a limited number of play objects and asked them to stay there for a given period of time. These conditions cannot always be fulfilled. Consequently, great efforts have been made to record an event accurately while it is taking place and then to make observational judgments later. The advantages of recording are that the observer can make his judgments under optimal viewing or perceiving conditions, that he can make them as many times as he wants to, if the record is such that he can look at it again and again, and that as many different observers as necessary can view the event. Methods for recording behavior have improved greatly in the past ten years. They may be grouped under the following headings.

(A) WRITTEN PERSONAL DOCUMENTS. G. W. Allport has summarized ably the uses to which personal documents can be put in psychological science (1942). They have always been of great interest, but not until recently have psychologists recognized their methodological value. By and large they have been considered by laboratory psychologists as good clinical tools but of little use to quantitative science. Recent advances have shown this is not necessarily the case. It is possible to define a set of behavior or content categories, much like those chosen by Merrill (1946), which can be applied to written behavior contained in personal documents. McClelland, Atkinson, Clark, and Roby (1949) have applied just such a set of categories to Thematic Apperception Test stories and have found that observers can agree in assigning certain written statements to these categories with a coefficient of correlation varying from .91 to .96. Dollard and Mowrer (1947) report similarly high agreement correlations for categorization of written material in a case worker's record. This approach is so relatively recent that perhaps a concrete example is desirable. Theoretically any written record is a piece of "frozen behavior" and can be subjected to content analysis. Actually, different ways of obtaining the record have suggested different methods of categorization, but for the sake of simplicity and easy comparison, we will apply several different methods to the same record. Suppose we take a typical Thematic Apperception Test story written down as it is told:

1. This boy's father was a famous concert violinist before he was born.
2. Unfortunately,
3. he lost his life in a tragic accident.
4. He was drowned.
5. His wife was pregnant
6. and had this chap.
7. Might add that his father was at the peak of fame.
8. Died on the night before the concert.
9. Of course he left his fiddle
10. which was old and valuable to his son.
11. He always had hopes that he would teach his son
12. and his son would play the fiddle better than his father.
13. At the age of one year his mother died
14. and the boy was left with an aunt and uncle
15. who were not too favorably inclined toward fiddlers.
16. Nevertheless they gave him his chance
17. and started him on violin lessons.
18. He didn't show unusual talent,

19. but a fair amount.
20. Now as he sits here,
21. he has just been told about his parents and their wishes.
22. He realizes he isn't overtalented,
23. but he is considering whether he will like it enough for his mother's sake.
24. As he grows older, he will put the fiddle aside
25. and go to something else.
26. He's debating other possibilities.

This story has been broken up into numbered thought units or acts to make cross references easier in the subsequent analyses. Now let us consider some representative methods of classifying and studying such a behavior sample.

i. Discomfort-relief quotient (DRQ). One of the simplest methods of analysis is to obtain a "tension index" by counting the number of thought units which indicate pleasure, relief, or happiness and those which indicate displeasure, tension, unhappiness, discomfort, etc. (Dollard and Mowrer, 1947). The units which indicate neither are simply scored O and omitted from the index, which is computed by dividing the number of discomfort units by the number of discomfort-plus relief units. In the present story, statements 2, 3, 4, 5 might be classified as discomfort, statements 6 and 12 as neither, and statements 1 and 7 as relief. A rough count of this sort yields nine D units out of fourteen units which can be classified one way or the other, yielding a tension index of .63 (63 per cent Discomfort units) which is fairly high. An index based on so few units would probably not be stable, but Dollard and Mowrer have demonstrated that stable indexes can be obtained with larger samples of written behavior and can be used to determine the "drive" or tension level of an individual as it is reflected in successive interviews recorded by a social case worker. Kauffman and Raimy (1949) have shown that the DRQ is also a good index of progress in a nondirective interviewing situation and correlates highly with the PNAvQ, which is another method of classifying content material based primarily on the number of positive, negative, and ambivalent self-references. High observer agreement for computing these indexes is reported in both bases. Dollard and Mowrer feel that ultimately the DRQ can be used to measure the strength of a person's motives (taken perhaps as a whole) since they adopt a tensional definition of motivation.

ii. Interaction process analysis. Bales (1950) has developed a method of classifying behavior in small groups which has been applied by Mills (1950) to written documents with some modifying assumptions. Greatly simplified, the system involves classifying acts (or thought units) as having positive or negative valence in the "social-emotional area" or as giving or receiving information in the "task area." This makes it possible to compute a "positive-negative quotient" which is very much like the DRQ, although individual units may be classified differently. Thus, for instance, unit 2 ("Unfortunately") is classified as a positive emotional act (shows sympathy on the part of the writer), though for the DRQ it was classified as indicative of tension. Despite these differences a quotient of 70 per cent negative emotional reactions is obtained by this method, which is close to the 63 per cent tension index obtained by the DRQ method. It is also possible to compute a "task *vs.* emotional" orientation quotient. Thus in the present instance the subject makes ten statements out of twenty-four, or 42 per cent, which can be classified as emotional whereas the remainder are task-oriented (information-giving). Finally, this method also permits an analysis of the subject's role perceptions since the person giving and the person receiving an act (the "who-to-whom" dimension) can be identified. Thus in unit 23 the son is scored as showing solidarity with the mother. All the son-mother acts can be summated and a picture obtained of how the subject perceives the son-mother role relationship (whether mutually antagonistic or solidary, nonreciprocal love, etc.). Observer agreement coefficients for such classifications are high.

iii. Semantic analysis. Although the problem will be touched on more fully later, it should be mentioned here for the sake of completeness that verbal material may also be broken down into grammatical categories (nouns, verbs, adjectives, adverbs, etc., or clauses, tenses, and the like). Sanford (1942a) has reviewed the extensive work that has been done in this field. The indexes which have usually been considered important are such things as the type-token and verb-adjective ratios. In the former the number of *different* words (types) is divided by the total number of words (tokens) in a given sample. For example, in the first one hundred words in our story the subject uses twenty-four nouns of which seventeen or 71 per cent are *different* words. The size of this ratio is apparently a function of intelligence, at least when it is plotted over successive samples of words. In all subjects the ratio tends to get smaller in successive word samples as the active vocabulary is used up, but the rate of decline is slower with more intelligent people (Zatzkis, 1949). Similarly the verb-adjective ratio in this instance is 23/18 or 1.27 indicating for this subject a much smaller ratio than is usually obtained. This is normally taken to mean that he is relatively more interested in passive description, in qualitative distinctions, in the external world, than in action and the internal world. Such counts as these are easy to make with great reliability but they are hard to interpret.

iv. Value analysis. R. K. White (1947) has attempted to classify content according to what value is referred to in a thought unit or statement. A somewhat simplified scheme has been worked out by Riecken and McClelland (1950) in which many of the values have the same names as Murray (1938) has given to needs or motives. For example, the description in unit 1 ("famous concert violinist") is clearly made with an Achievement value as a frame of reference. The same is true of units 7, 10, 14, 16, 20. Similarly the judgment in unit 2 ("Unfortunately") involves an Affiliation value. And so on. All judgments or evaluative descriptions can be classified in terms of the value they imply.

v. Need-sequence analysis. McClelland, Clark, Roby, and Atkinson (1949) have published a description of a method for scoring the changes which occur in brief imaginative stories under the influence of various induced need states. The scoring follows the problem-solving sequence which involves the following elements: (1) Need; (2) Instrumental Activity; (3) Obstacles; and (4) Goal satisfactions or dissatisfactions, either actual or anticipated. For example, our sample story may be scored for achievement motivation since there is a good deal of achievement imagery in it. Unit 1 is achievement gratification (G+). Units 11 and 12 are anticipated achievement gratification (Ga+). Units 16 and 17 involve *nurturant press* or help given the boy in his efforts after achievement, etc. This method is useful in telling how intense a person's achievement motives are, since, generally speaking, the more such characteristics he shows, the greater the intensity of his achievement motivation. It is also useful in showing exactly how the person perceives his achievement problems. Thus, as in this story, there may be practically no instrumental activity aimed at achievement. Most of the material deals with achievement satisfactions or dissatisfactions. Such a person may have difficulty in getting down to next steps in carrying out his achievement ambitions, etc. The interpretation may become difficult, but the method is a sufficiently precise one for collecting dependable facts about perceptions of motivational problems.

vi. Symbolic analysis. Probably the most controversial method of analyzing content derives from Freud's original attempts to find the "latent" meaning behind the "manifest" content. In our sample story, for instance, the "old and valuable fiddle" becomes the son's penis which he inherits from his father (units 9 and 10). The notion of "playing the fiddle better" (unit 12) disguises the notion of sexual intercourse which suggests in turn the mother, a suggestion which is so anxiety-arousing that the mother must die in the story to be out of harm's way (unit 13). At this point the son is taken with remorse and wonders if he shouldn't give up "fiddling" (e.g., sexuality) altogether (units 23-26). Is this the "true" or latent meaning of this story? No one knows. The average clinician, if he were psychoanalytically oriented, would doubtless start with this as a hypothesis anyway. We cannot worry at this point about the validity of such an interpretation. We can only assert that this type of symbolic interpretation has become so standardized among clinicians with a psychoanalytic orientation that it would probably be easy to demonstrate a fairly high observer-agreement for this method of analysis, although instances in the literature of such agreement correlations are few and far between.

vii. Other methods of content analysis. This by no means exhausts the possibilities. Baldwin (1942) has counted the frequency with which ideas are associated in a series of letters. Murray (1938) has developed elaborate scoring schemes for classifying the material in imaginal productions. Content or sequence analysis on the Rorschach Test has become common practice. Thematic Apperception Test scoring schemes which enable one to make quantitative estimates have also been developed by several others (cf. Bell, 1948). This should be sufficient to suggest the extreme range of techniques which are now becoming available for analyzing spontaneous behavior when it is "frozen" in a written document. All of these methods permit high observer-reliability which is the *sine qua non* for scientific usefulness. They have been sampled briefly here because they seem peculiarly appropriate to personality study and because it has only recently been realized that with proper observer training they can be made to yield facts (classes of behavior) which are just as dependable as responses in a reaction-time experiment. Of course the interpretation of the facts is not clear in many cases, but this is not a problem peculiar to this class of facts alone. It exists for all classes of facts.

Such developments as these throw some doubt on the supposed division between a clinical psychology based on experience and a scientific psychology of personality based on "behavior." Sears (1943) has described the division thus: "The kind of personality science that is more widely used in such work is *behavioral* rather than *experiential,* and since the behavioral way of thinking about personality is of even more recent origin than psychoanalysis, there seems good reason for concluding that a behavioral science of personality has been found more useful in the past and may be expected to be so in the future." (p. 141.) The gap between these two approaches to personality can be closed if the same or similar concepts are applied to the data obtained from the two approaches. For example, the dream is one of the chief sources of information used by the psychoanalyst. But the dream may be recorded or written down, at which point it becomes a piece of behavior and can be classified into various units which may be manipulated statistically or theoretically like any other units of behavior. Experience as recorded in words is far more various than the kind of overt movements categorized by Merrill (1946) or Sears (1942). It should therefore provide a much better basis in some instances than grosser movement responses for approaching the complexities of personality. But the point is, that the method applied to it can be precisely the same as that applied by Merrill, Sears, and others, to overt movements. This is the great methodological change which has made personal documents of renewed interest and importance.

(B) Phonographic recording. The value of phonographic recording has long been recognized and has been used for some time, particularly by anthropologists in bringing back data from field trips. But it is only relatively recently that the improvement in recording techniques has been such as to permit detailed recording of great amounts of spoken material. Great methodological advances were made in the early 1940's at Ohio State University under the leadership of Carl Rogers, who was interested in the recording of counseling interviews. This work has been summarized best to date by Curran (1945). It reveals, among other things, that the notes taken by a counselor on an interview in the usual way cover at the most only about one-third of the items actually occurring in the interview situation as determined from verbatim recordings. Covner, Porter, Curran, and others found that when a check list was devised which a judge could use in scoring the typescript from phonographically recorded interviews, the agreement among the judges as to the classification of items was very high, ranging from .85 to .95. They found that they could use observer agreement to decide which items to include, discard, or redefine so that they could be classified more reliably. Furthermore, as in Merrill's work cited above, they found it possible to count the number of times a given category of response occurred and thus to get a quantitative measure of the importance of that response in the interview situation. This enabled them to study very carefully the changes in the responses given by the client in the interviewing situation and to train a counselor to observe the appropriateness with which he had responded. Entirely apart from the value of this research for its specific purpose, the chief point to notice here is that, like Merrill's study, it provides a great methodological advance over the older method of simply taking notes on an interview. It opens up, as written personal documents do, the whole area of verbal behavior to exact theoretical analysis.

(C) Motion picture recording. Research workers have long recognized the value of recording through motion pictures the complex behavior of people as it occurs. The experimental group which has made most use of the technique to date has been the one at the Child Guidance Clinic at Yale University under the leadership of Dr. Arnold Gesell. They have demonstrated the value of motion pictures for identifying certain patterns of motor behavior, although they have not been much concerned with the quantitative measurement of changes in behavior as a result of experimentally introduced variables. However, there is no reason why the data obtained by motion pictures could not be used for this purpose, just as phonographically recorded data have been. Stone (1950), for instance, has made detailed analyses of acts of aggression in a football game from motion pictures taken for the coaching staff.

Sound motion pictures combine a record of what the observer would both see and hear but have been little used because of the expense involved. This technique has been used to fullest advantage probably only once or twice, notably in connection with the making of the documentary film *Let There Be Light* during World War II at Mason General Hospital under the psychiatric supervision of Dr. Benjamin Simon and the direction of John Huston. This film was made for the Army with all the advantages of the latest Hollywood equipment. Thousands of feet of film were shot of such important events as the behavior of a patient actually undergoing narcosynthesis. Since the film was obtained under natural conditions, as the events actually occurred, it obviously provides a record which is unparalleled in value in the recording of complex personality changes for future and repeated study. Although the full record has not yet been made available by the War Department for scientific study, it illustrates what could be done in this field if the money were available.

Although some of the matters which we have been discussing would seem to be of purely technical importance, they have a significance for the experimental study of personality which is far greater than would appear on the surface. Many people, including psychologists, have felt that the study of complex personality processes would be forever denied to the experimental psychologist. G. W. Allport is merely expressing the opinion of many others when he states: "One cannot approach experimentally such experiences as embarrassment, remorse, falling in love, or religious ecstasy." (1937, p. 21.) Although there will of course be some argument as to what exactly is meant by experimentation, it is certainly obvious by now that it would be possible through advances in recording techniques to get a complete record of just such experiences as he lists, which could then be studied systematically and in detail according to the methods of analysis described above. Thus, for example, religious ecstasies could be recorded in a sound motion picture and analyzed quantitatively for the various types of behavior shown afterward. If this were done enough times under enough different conditions, it might be possible to make some observations as to what the conditions are which produce different varieties of religious experience. Furthermore, much of the literature of confession and mystical experience could be analyzed in this way from personal documents. The fact that one cannot produce some of these phenomena in the laboratory does not mean that they cannot be observed and studied scientifically as they are found in nature. The biologist would be quite seriously limited if he had to confine his study of living organisms to those he could produce in the laboratory. Yet no one declares him less of a scientist because he cannot. What the psychologist working in the field of personality has needed is the improvement of techniques for studying the complex processes of human nature as they occur naturally. And much progress along these lines has been made in the past few decades.

Experimentation

It is also possible to approach problems of observation in a different way. This involves controlling rigorously the behavior the subject is allowed to make or limiting the responses the observer pays attention to. This approach usually falls more nearly under the heading of experimentation proper. In this case the experimenter has some degree of control over the stimulus situation or over the response which the subject makes. The model here is the standard laboratory experiment, such as the one on reaction time. The subject is limited to the response of pressing a key and his response time is plotted as a function of, for example, the intensity of a light stimulus which can be carefully controlled by the experimenter. The situation is represented diagramatically in Table 2.1 in which *S* stands for environmental stimulus conditions, *R* for the organism's response, *Rec* for the record kept by the observer, and ☐ for the control which the observer has over that aspect of the situation. Three types of scientific observation are illustrated: experimentation in

TABLE 2.1

Illustration of Different Kinds of Control Exercised by the Experimenter over Elements in an Observation

1. Experimentation	[S]	[R]	[Rec]
2. Naive observation	S	R	Rec
3. Projective technique	[S] (dashed box)	R	[Rec]

which everything is controlled, even the response which is permitted; naïve observation in which anything can happen and the observer makes any kind of comments he wishes (e.g., the traveler's letters home); and the projective techniques in which there is a fair degree of control on the stimulus side (represented by a ⬚) as in an inkblot, very little control over what the subject says, and very precise recording and analysis of what he says. All sorts of other permutations of control are possible. The student should make them for himself and try to find the traditional label applied to each.

Is there any really controlled experimentation in the field of personality (line 1, Table 2.1)? What are the values of experimentation as compared, for example, with content analysis (which might classify under line 3, Table 2.1)? To answer these and related questions it is necessary to consider systematically the way in which experimental controls can be introduced into the study of behavior. Far too often it has been assumed, in dealing with this problem, that the exact control of the reaction-time type of experiment is the only "respectable" approach, and the conclusion usually has been quickly drawn by clinical psychologists that the experimental approach to personality is of very little value. But, as we shall see, there is actually a continuum of control which can be introduced either on the stimulus side or on the response side in scientific observation.

Control of the Situation. In its simplest form experimentation is usually thought of as involving the introduction of a known variation in stimulus conditions and the observation of its effects on some response. This suggests, on the stimulus side, that the experimenter has a control over the condition which he is introducing. It further implies that since he can control it he understands the nature of the change he is making. It is not essential, of course, that control and understanding go together. Usually they do. For example, in a simple laboratory experiment such as the one described above, the experimenter can control light intensity, and in order to do so he must understand the nature of what he is varying, at least to some extent. However, it is possible to introduce something to a subject whose nature cannot be very precisely defined. A case in point is a Rorschach inkblot in the standard Rorschach Test in which the nature of all the blots is always controlled, although as Rust (1948) has pointed out, it would be very difficult to define precisely the nature of any given inkblot in terms of its stimulus dimensions. The understanding of the situational variation introduced seems to be a more basic necessity than its control, but historically control has often been considered equivalent to understanding. The chief attempts to date which have been made to control the stimulus variable to which a person is subjected may be summarized briefly under several headings.

1. *Symbolic control.* Early workers in the field of personality found it very difficult to produce experimentally or to discover in any other way many of the most important personality characteristics. They

met this problem by producing vital situations symbolically, specifically in the form of verbal representations of situations in questionnaires. For example, it was difficult actually to frustrate people and observe their responses, but experimenters could very easily ask subjects a question such as the following:

> What do you do when you are frustrated?
> (a) Blame yourself
> (b) Blame whatever frustrated you
> (c) Nothing, etc.

Of course this question could be asked in a variety of ways. For example,

> Describe how you reacted to the frustration situation described on the left.

or

> Check the reactions which you showed when frustrated in the ways described on the left.

No matter how the question is phrased, the experimenter is attempting to introduce a situational variable symbolically through a verbal description and is asking the subject to react to this symbolic representation.

The apparent advantage of the procedure is that a great deal of work can be done very quickly. The number of questions which a person can answer in a relatively short period of time is very great indeed. Furthermore, it is very easy to score the subject's answers. Consequently, early work in personality dealt largely with the results of such questionnaire studies. However, psychologists began to wonder about the real value of this procedure. The basic doubt arose over the presumed connection between the question and what it was supposed to represent. Many wondered whether reaction to a question about frustration was the same thing as reaction to the frustration itself. Very few attempts were made to check this rather obvious assumption, but the conviction grew anyway that what questionnaires got at was a response to verbal stereotypes, rather than to the "real" psychological situations that the verbal stereotypes were supposed to represent. The reaction to such stereotypes is, of course, an important part of psychology, but the fundamental research on the other variables involved has to be done at a different level.

2. *Natural control.* It was also obvious from the beginning of personality research that certain conditions could not be reproduced

in the laboratory at all. For example, it is highly unlikely that psychologists will ever have a chance to try out the various methods of child rearing that they might wish to experiment with to test various hypotheses. However, many variations in child rearing occur naturally in different cultures and it is only necessary to go and find them. Thus, while it would be impossible to introduce water as a disciplinary agent in young children, it is perfectly feasible to go to the Crow Indian tribe, where they have poured water down children's noses to discipline them, to observe the effect this has had on personality (cf. McAllester, 1941). Child-rearing techniques are clear instances of natural variation in which one does not have control over the variable in question but can measure its effects, if it is carefully defined. Baldwin, Kalhorn, and Breese (1945), Merrill (1946), and Whiting and Child (1950) have succeeded in defining objectively some of the important dimensions of parent behavior so that they may be rated or checked as they occur in nature. This, in effect, makes a controlled experiment possible, although nature is responsible for the differences in parent behavior being studied. With this technique it would be possible, for example, to *find* two sets of parents who vary only with respect to the amount of acceptance they show for their children and to determine the effects of this difference on the children's behavior and personality.

Such naturally occurring differences are not, of course, restricted to child-rearing techniques. For a long time it has been the habit of psychologists to compare groups of people that are naturally different. It has been standard procedure to develop questionnaires and tests by comparing the responses of people who differ as to sex, age, occupation, or socioeconomic status. One example of this is the Strong Vocational Interest Test, scoring keys for which were developed by comparing the responses of a given occupational group, e.g., artists, with the responses of men in general to the test. While this approach has much practical utility for the purpose of vocational guidance, it does not qualify as a good experimental procedure because the stimulus conditions of being a member of the artist class are not very well understood. That is, if one could find some meaningful psychological dimensions on which artists as an occupational group differed from other people, then the responses of artists could be meaningfully related to the dimensions so defined. The differences in the behavior of artists could then be associated with something more than an occupational name and the case would be parallel to the differences in child rearing mentioned above. But so far this more theoretical approach has not been adopted with such data although there is no reason why it could not be.

3. *Experimental control.* To follow up the example of the effects of parent behavior, we could now turn to an experiment like Merrill's, described above. In this instance she not only took maternal behavior as she found it but she experimentally modified it by her instructions to the mother dealing with the supposed inferiority of the child's previous play behavior. If she had gone on and measured the effects of the change in the mother's behavior on the child, this would then qualify as an example of an experimentally induced variable supposedly influencing personality. In recent years psychologists have succeeded more and more in finding ways for introducing experimentally variables which are significant for personality study. It will be necessary only to mention a few of these for illustrative purposes.

A great deal of work has been done in the field of induced *frustration.* Psychologists have become very skillful in annoying human beings. For example, Dembo (1931), working under Lewin in one of the earliest studies in this field, measured the effects of frustration and anger on general behavior in a problem situation. Sears measured the effect of failure on performance in a learning situation (1937) and also on general motility (1942). McClelland and Apicella (1945) measured the effects of failure-frustration on verbal comments of the subjects. These are just samples of a very large group of experiments in which frustration has been successfully introduced.

A parallel series of experiments on satisfaction or gratification has yet to be done, although Maslow (1948) has pointed to the need for such a series. There have been studies of the effect of success on behavior (Jucknat, 1937) but in general we know less about this than about the effects of failure. There has also been a number of studies dealing with what is usually called *ego-involvement* (cf. Allport, 1943) in which the basic operation seems to be the instruction to the subject that the task he is performing is a measure of his general intellectual ability or some other such quality of presumed importance to him. McClelland and associates (1949) have worked extensively in this field on the assumption that such instructions involve the arousal of achievement motivation. The effects of experimentally aroused motivation of this sort would appear to be a very promising addition to the number of personality variables which the experimenter can control. It is still true that we cannot arouse in the laboratory such complex feelings as falling in love or religious ecstasy, as G. W. Allport has suggested, but we are making progress along these lines. And in the meantime we can always find many of these things as they occur in nature.

4. *Partial control.* Some of the most successful work in the field of personality has involved the introduction of situations which are not very precisely defined for the subject. That is, the stimulus situation is purposely left vague and nondirective in the hope that the responses of the subject will consequently be less a function of the situation and more a function of his own personal characteristics. Examples of this sort of approach are the play behavior of children to relatively unstructured situations, the Rorschach Test, the Thematic Apperception Test, and other such tests of imagination (cf. White, 1944). In these instances the importance of the external variable is deliberately decreased and the kind of inference drawn from the results is somewhat different, as will be indicated below. Here the experimenter controls the situation by reducing the number of hints, as it were, in the environment, as to what the subject *should* do.

Control of the Response. In any of the above situations the subject's response may be relatively free and spontaneous or rigidly limited to a particular one chosen by the experimenter. Historically the psychologist simplified his observational problems typically by directing his attention to only one aspect of the behavior of the subject. For example, in the classical conditioning situation the dog actually makes many other responses besides salivating but the experimenter usually pays no attention to them. Let us consider systematically the kinds of responses to which the experimenter has paid attention in the field of personality study.

1. *Choice responses.* The easiest and most controlled thing to do is to permit the subject to choose one of a number of responses given to him by the experimenter. The prototype of this approach is found in the questionnaire where the subject is asked to respond *yes, no,* or *doubtful,* or *Like, Dislike,* or *Indifferent.* The practical advantages of this approach are tremendous and efforts are still being made to reduce all experiments to situations in which the subject can choose one or more responses. The appeal of this approach to practical Americans is suggested by the enormous development of machine methods of scoring multiple-choice tests.

The disadvantages of this approach have only recently begun to be apparent. Some have appeared on practical grounds, and some on theoretical grounds. On the practical side it has been found difficult, if not impossible, to develop a valid multiple-choice form of such important imaginative tests as the Rorschach (cf. Bell, 1948, p. 150). On the theoretical side much progress has been made toward understanding some of the nonpersonality variables which determine choice behavior. For example, it has been pointed out that the human conception of probability is quite different from the mathematical conception, as it is based on the assumption of a finite rather than an infinite universe. Practically this means that a person will guess in a different way from what would be expected by mathematical chance. He will tend to avoid a long series of similar answers (*Yeses* or *Noes*) as any teacher who has made up True-False examinations knows, and to avoid regular patterns of choice such as simple alternation (Whitfield, 1949a). This means that on a real questionnaire he will be influenced by such patterns of random behavior as well as by the meaning of the questions to which he is supposed to be responding. Of course, as more is known about the ways in which human probability differs from mathematical probability, it will be possible to control for this effect to some extent.

Yet there is an even more serious objection. This revolves around the fact that the subject, when he is given a choice, apparently has time to consider what an answer would mean. For example, he might have time to think whether or not he would be judged neurotic or successful or what not if he answered *yes* to the question: "Do you daydream frequently?" Such considerations as these are usually not relevant to the variable which the experimenter is trying to measure, and this may explain why such tests as the Bernreuter Personality Inventory may yield results which have been found to be misleading in individual cases. Apparently the method of *production* rather than recognition and choice is not as open to the same criticism because the subject, if he has to produce a response in a given period of time, finds it more difficult to evaluate the significance of that response at the same time. This may explain some of the advantages of projective tests, in which the response is not so rigorously limited, over comparable multiple-choice tests (Getzels, 1950).

2. *Efficient responses.* Some of the earliest and most successful work in psychology was done with various motor and mental tests, and with the speed with which subjects could learn to perform well on them. So it was quite natural to measure the effects of various personality variables on these tests of performance. The results, by and large, have been disappointing. For example, some of the early

work dealt with the effects of fatigue or frustration on tests of coordination or learning. It has been repeatedly found that these variables have little or no effect on efficiency. Experimenters have been convinced that fatigue does affect a person but they have not been able to measure it with such tests. For instance, one of the most extensive efforts to measure the effects of prolonged fatigue has been made at Tufts College under Carmichael, Kennedy, and Mead (cf. 1949). They found that subjects who continued long and arduous physical and mental work for two or three days without sleep still showed very little or no falling-off in performance on very complex and involved mental tasks. Yet it was obvious to the experimenters that the subjects were in very bad shape. They could hardly force themselves to perform the tasks, but once they did, efficiency turned out to be impaired hardly at all. Obviously efficiency measures were not sensitive indicators of the profound changes which had taken place in the subjects. This is just the culmination of a long series of similar experiments. Psychologists are gradually becoming convinced that, although performance measures can be very accurately made, they are not going to reflect very sensitively under normal conditions experimentally-introduced personality variables, since the organism apparently is able to compensate in such a variety of ways that it can always manage to produce nearly the same performance output.

3. *Experimentally limited responses.* The experimenter may limit what the subject can do (judge, move, etc.) by the nature of the experimental task and yet not be interested in how *well* the subject performs, as in the case just discussed. Here the emphasis is not on the amount of work accomplished per unit time or the amount of time per unit work, as in the case of efficiency, but on the actual behavior of the subject in response to the task. To make the contrast as sharp as possible, we can turn to some work by Langer (in Murray, 1938) in a learning setup where the interest is normally in measures of efficiency. He used the standard learning measures (namely, number of errors, total time taken, and number of repetitions needed) but he combined them into an over-all learning index. This, in turn, gave him a measure of what he called motor impulsion. In other words, he assumed "that the comparative number of errors made in relation to the other factors [in the learning index] would be an indication of the tendency to act without thinking." (p. 515.) Such a measure as this is not an efficiency measure at all, strictly speaking, but a measure of the relative contribution of a

given factor (here, errors) in the total performance picture. Thus, for example, it might be found that a given experimental condition, such as fatigue, might not change the over-all output but it might change the relative importance of errors in the learning index.

There are many other behavioral measures which have been found useful in personality measurement outside of those that arise in learning experiments. Measures of *expectation,* particularly as represented in the level of aspiration technique, have been found to be related to a significant number of personality variables, even under rigorously controlled conditions. Bruner and Goodman (1947) and others (Postman, Bruner, and McGinnies, 1948) have shown that such *perceptual responses* as are involved in size judgments or recognition thresholds for briefly presented words are sensitive to personality differences. Finally, certain *memory* effects, such as the relative proportion of uncompleted to completed tasks remembered, have also been found to reflect personality differences sensitively (Atkinson, 1950b). In short, in the last few decades the number of such experimentally controlled behavioral responses which have been found to be useful in personality measurement has increased markedly, and we may expect more progress along these lines in the future.

4. *Spontaneous responses.* This includes all the remaining types of responses in which very little control is exercised by the experimenter over what the subject does. Usually there is some kind of limit, such as that placed by having the subject in a specific place or by having him limit his responses to verbal ones. The difference between this type of experiment and the three previous ones lies basically in the fact that the experimenter decides what responses he is going to score quantitatively *after* the subject has produced them and not before. There is no *a priori* judgment as to what is an important response and what is not, what response the subject will be allowed to make and what one he will not be allowed to make. It would be a mistake to assume, however, that the results could not be just as exact and quantitative as in the other methods, as the earlier section in this chapter on methods of content analysis has shown.

Angell (Gottschalk, Kluckhohn, and Angell, 1945) has clarified the issue of prejudgment very nicely in his discussion of Stouffer's work on attitudes toward prohibition. Stouffer first asked his subjects to fill out a standard attitude scale relating to prohibition and then to write full personal accounts of "their experiences and feelings since childhood toward prohibition laws and toward the drinking of liquor."

Several judges read the personal accounts and rated the subjects as to their attitude toward prohibition and toward drinking. Stouffer found that the ratings by the judges correlated very highly with the subjects' expressed attitudes on the standardized scale. Since the attitude-scale approach was obviously much simpler and more economical, and yet arrived at the same results as were obtained by the involved personal-document procedure, the former would seem to have the obvious advantage. But the point Angell makes is that the attitude scale has an advantage only with respect to the particular issue which it measures. If this is the only issue in which the experimenter is interested, all is well and good, but it should be noted that he has decided ahead of time that attitude toward prohibition measured in a particular way is the only thing in which he is interested.

An alternative approach, as Angell suggests, is "to gather good documentary or observational data and then to experiment with various key hypotheses until he finds one that seems to bring the data into some kind of order." In other words, the data determine the order, and not the order the data. The order is introduced *after* the data have been collected instead of before. There are cases, of course, when it is appropriate, because of a theoretical orientation or previous research, to introduce a limitation of response ahead of time. The point being made here is that the freer procedure has been far too often neglected by psychologists in the field of personality who have really no adequate basis for imposing a limitation on the response of the subject beforehand.

Our survey of methodological improvements has not been complete. We have obviously tried merely to sample areas in which significant changes have occurred in the past decade. Nor has our survey come to any definite conclusion as to which particular method is best for studying personality. Obviously there are many possible combinations of limitation of the situation and limitation of the subject's response. The one certain fact on which all psychologists would agree is that control on the observational or recording side is absolutely essential. Our aim has really been to give the student some idea of the variety of ways in which scientifically sound observational methods may be introduced into personality study.

A look at contemporary points of view in the field of personality will justify such an aim. As Murray has pointed out so well, there has tended to grow up a split between the laboratory and clinic in the field of personality. In the laboratory we find what Murray calls "peripheralists," who, "chiefly interested in what is measurable, . . .

are forced to limit themselves to relatively unimportant fragments of the personality or to the testing of specific skills. The aim is to get figures that may be worked statistically." (1938, p. 9.) In the clinic we find, on the other hand, "centralists" who are interested in man's "ambitions, frustrations, apprehensions, rages, joys, and miseries. . . . These have no stomach for experiments conducted in an artificial laboratory atmosphere." It is to be hoped that one of the things learned from this chapter is that such a division is not at all necessary and has arisen, in fact, from a misunderstanding of the nature of scientific method, or rather from the tacit assumption on both sides that scientific method is limited to the kind of experiment in which one has a rigid control of the environmental stimulus and of the subject's response as well as of the record of the experiment itself. If such a narrow interpretation of scientific method had been accepted by biologists and astronomers, they would have been seriously hampered in their experimental work. We may confidently expect that, as some of the improvements in the scientific method for studying personality briefly outlined here get more and more widely used, the gap between the laboratory and the clinic, between the peripheralists and the centralists, will close.

NOTES AND QUERIES

1. Make a time-sampling study of the behavior of some person you are observing. Nervous movements are relatively easy to observe, and a good observation post is the library reading-room. First make a rough impressionistic report of your observation of the person with respect to the behavior under consideration, e.g., nervous movements. Then make up a rating scale with several items on it and rate the person on the various items on the scale after a five-minute period of observation. Finally, make up a check list in which you list a series of categories at the left which you are going to observe and then draw lines at the right representing five- or ten-second intervals. Then, following Merrill's procedure, you can check one of the behavior categories every five or ten seconds, keeping track of time with a wrist watch. Make your observations for at least two five-minute periods, separated by at least three minutes. Then correlate the results you obtained in the two periods to see whether the behavior in question is consistent or whether your observations are reliable. Does such a correlation coefficient violate any of the assumptions necessary for computing it? Then compare your check-list results with your rating-scale results and with your first impression.

What does the check list add to your knowledge of the person? Discuss your results.

2. In Table 2.1 three of the various combinations of control of the stimulus, response, and recording aspects of scientific observation were listed. What other combinations are in common use? What are the advantages and disadvantages of each? Try to think of a concrete experiment in each case which would illustrate the combination in question.

3. How could the conditions for observing maternal behavior under field conditions be improved so as to get better observations, using the criteria laid down in this chapter? Consider the advantages and disadvantages of introducing a standardized situation in which the behavior of mothers could be compared. Make out a check list for maternal behavior which you think could be observed in a field situation.

4. In his *Use of Personal Documents in Psychological Science* Allport writes: "The writers conclude that it is possible, though not economical, to treat life history materials quantitatively in practice. Questionnaires yield essentially the same results and are ordinarily more convenient to use. Hall had reached the same conclusion at the turn of the century." (1942, p. 25.) Evaluate this conclusion. Why, if it is so, have personality psychologists turned increasingly often in recent years to content analyses of various sorts?

5. Design a study which would attack scientifically the experience of falling in love. What methods of observation and measurement would you use? What would be the main methodological difficulties you would meet and how would you overcome them?

6. Classify each unit in the sample Thematic Apperception Test story given in the text according to several different methods of content analysis described. Consult the original sources wherever necessary to get adequate definitions of the scoring categories.

3

Interpreting the Facts

Once it has been settled how we are to observe another person, there is still the problem of how we are going to interpret what we perceive. As Allport puts it so well, in observing another person we may sit back and enjoy him, perhaps identifying with him or sympathizing with his predicaments or "free-associating from one incident to similar incidents" in our own lives (1942, p. 164), or we may make very exact objective descriptions of what he does. But neither of these is enough. As psychologists, we have the task of making "theoretical sense" out of his life. This is the job of the scientific psychologist, just as it is the job of the physicist to make theoretical sense out of his observation of the physical world.

The difficulties of making theoretical sense or choosing the right concepts to interpret what we observe is nicely illustrated by a story told by Gottschalk (1945, p. 52) about two British soldiers serving in the campaign against Field Marshal Rommel in North Africa. "Tired and thirsty after some hard fighting on the desert, [they] return to their barracks and find half a bottle of water. 'God be praised!' says one, 'it's half full.' 'Devil be damned!' says the other, 'it's half empty.'" As Gottschalk goes on to say, "It is obvious that both were accurately describing a situation with regard to which each was a reliable eyewitness." But which interpretation of the event is the correct one? No amount of precision in observation will help solve this problem. It will not improve matters any to know that there are two and one-half inches of water in the bottle or to know the exact number of cubic centimeters it contains. We must interpret our observations, however accurate they may be. Our two student judges in Chapter 2, in describing the coach at the basketball game, did, in fact, employ a large number of concepts to describe the man. They used such terms as "talkative," "a coach," "a simmering temper," etc.

Which of these is a good concept? Which ones shall we, as scientists, choose? Can we ever get psychologists to agree on what concepts they should use? If we can't get them to agree, is there any hope of ever producing a unified picture of a given personality? Certainly, as we look around among psychologists, we find no agreement as to what conceptual frame of reference should be adopted. As Allport puts it (1942, p. 167), "if he (the psychologist) is a Marxist, he sees significance in the class membership of the subject; if he is a Kretschmerian, he bears heavily upon the implications of constitutional types; if he is a Freudian, it is the toilet training or the Oedipus situation that captures his attention. More subtle, but just as effective, are other favorite theories: conditioning, frustration-aggression, cultural-determinism, compensation, functional autonomy." Difficulties such as these press for answers before we try to conceptualize personality.

Perhaps we may begin our solution to some of these problems by asking what the purpose of a concept is. Roughly, a concept may be defined as a shorthand representation of a variety of facts. Its purpose is to simplify thinking by subsuming a number of events under one general heading. As the writers in general semantics have made clear, a concept is usually a higher-order generalization or abstraction covering a number of specific and detailed events. For example, any word or concept is a simplification of the thing for which it stands. The word *cow* does not refer to any particular cow with brown spots, no horns, and eating grass in a particular pasture at a particular moment in time. But the word *cow* is a fairly satisfactory shorthand description of *any* particular cow. It is sufficient to call up a reasonably good image of the chief features of any given cow. A concept in the field of personality has exactly the same function. If we say that a man is a coach, for example, this carries with it a number of implications as to his habits, attitudes, skills, appearance, and so forth. These implications may not be entirely accurate in detail—in fact, they almost certainly will not be—but the use of the term *coach* certainly has great shorthand value in describing the man in question.

With this general background as to the nature and function of concepts, perhaps we can now turn our attention to the sources of concepts which have come into common use in the field of personality.

Observation As a Source of Concepts. Many of the concepts in common use in personality study derive directly from the way in which the person is observed. Two examples will serve to illustrate how this comes about. First, let us return to Merrill's study of maternal behavior (1946). It will be remembered that since she was using a direct observational technique she adopted such behavior categories as "mother directs, interferes, or carries on independent activity at the adult level." These were the aspects of behavior which she could observe reliably. At the same time they suggested to her the kinds of concepts that she could use in interpretation. If the mother showed a lot of the directive type of behavior, Merrill characterized her as "compulsive." Or if she sometimes directed and sometimes did not, Merrill used such terms as "uncertainty" and "inconsistency." The following is a typical example of the kind of interpretation Merrill gives which is obviously based on the behavioral categories that she observed: "This particular mother-child relationship was composed of a rejecting child and a mother whose basic insecurity in her dealings with the child resulted in vacillating handling of him." (1946, p. 48.) It is easy to see how this statement grew out of the kind of behavior she observed, just as it is easy to see that from that behavior she could have made *no* statements, for example, about the mother's anticipations of her child's successes or failures.

A second and even better example is to be found in the interpretation of the scoring categories in the Rorschach Test. The number of stimulus dimensions of an inkblot which can determine a subject's response is limited. Thus the subject may respond to different locations, to the form of the blot, to the color, to supposed movement, or to shading. It is a perfectly straightforward objective task for a judge to determine to what extent a given response involves movement, color, or form. It is quite another thing to interpret in psychological terms what a movement response means. The concepts used by Rorschach testers have apparently been directly suggested in many cases by scoring categories derived directly from the nature of the subject's task. Let us take a particular case, the good form (F+) response, and follow it through from a simple objective-scoring category to its ultimate interpretation as the Rorschach worker understands it.

Beck (1944, p. 20) starts out with the statement that a good form response (F+) "is an index of accurate perception." This, then, in turn suggests "respect for reality" or still later, "critical effort," until finally he concludes that F+ is an index of ego strength. "The stronger the ego, the more F+ associations." We are not raising questions here about the possible validity of this interpretation of the form response. We are simply pointing out the *process* whereby the response observed may directly suggest, often by analogy, the interpretative concepts finally used.

To take just one further example, this time from Klopfer and

Kelley, we find the statement that *m* on the Rorschach (impersonal forces, whirlwinds, etc.) means "the subject experiences his promptings from within as hostile and uncontrollable forces working upon him, rather than as sources of energy at his disposal." (1942, p. 279.) Again the psychological meaning is suggested by the scoring category. We are therefore not surprised to discover that the Rorschach tester makes very little use of such concepts as the *Oedipus complex* or the *anal character*. His data are not such as to permit him to use these concepts. To a very considerable extent, the disagreement among theoretical psychologists in the field of personality arises from the fact that *they are dealing with different data to start with and cannot use each other's concepts.*

Similarities As a Source of Concepts. Other concepts arise from perceived similarities among the observed responses or between a response and some other, usually more familiar, experience of the observer. For example, the observer may be reminded by what he sees of some other common, often sensory, experience he has had, which he then uses to interpret what he sees. Thus we find such terms as a "simmering temper" or "mercurial temperament." In such cases knowledge of the characteristics of the experience with which the response or trait is compared gives a better understanding of the nature of the trait. We can think of a temper which may blow off or blow up at any moment, just as a simmering teakettle might, or we may think of a changeable temperament which is as fickle and changeable as a drop of mercury. Somewhat similar analogies are involved in some of the Rorschach categories. For example, to see movement in a static blot is interpreted to mean a kind of inner psychic movement, e.g., a "prompting from within." Allport and Odbert in their study of trait names (cf. Allport, 1937, p. 309) list a sampling of other terms which might classify here, for example: *aflutter, ashen, animal spirits.*

As Allport and Odbert further point out, these analogies do not necessarily involve other sensory experiences but may involve a comparison with a well-known historical character. Such terms as Machiavellian, Pickwickian, or Rabelaisian have come into fairly common use. At a simpler level we may simply say that John reminds us of Mr. X. In making such statements we are helping to interpret or understand John's behavior by comparing it with the presumably better-known or more distinctive behavior of Mr. X.

A somewhat more sophisticated technique is to search for similarities among a person's responses. This is essentially the method of trait psychology, which groups together under one heading or trait-name a variety of responses which have something in common. Thus we may say that a person is expansive, a term which covers expansiveness in gait, gesture, talking, mode of giving a dinner party, etc. Cattell has argued that this is the fundamental way in which we should arrive at concepts. He proposes specifically that we do not use the scientist's judgment of what goes together but use instead the actual empirical co-variation of behavior elements or responses. He states (1946a, p. 71) that "the unity of a set of parts is established by their moving—i.e., appearing, changing, disappearing—together, by their exercising an effect together, and by an influence on one being an influence on all." This he calls co-variation or going-togetherness, the usual concrete measure of which is the correlation coefficient. In other words, he is proposing that we adopt concepts that are derived from what empirically functions together in the behavior field and not from any theoretical preconceptions. This involves factor analysis and is in effect a statistical method of arriving at a definition of similarity. Others like Allport would argue that similarities can be discovered in a more theoretical way, through the understanding of the scientist.

Social Groups As a Source of Concepts. Many of the concepts in common use in the psychology of personality derive from names given to the groups or classes to which a person belongs. The value of such concepts lies in the fact that certain more or less well-defined traits, interests, habits, and attitudes belong to members of that class. Some of the classes are simply biological in nature. For example, when we say, "He's a man," that carries with it the tacit assumption that he shares, along with other men, certain interests, sexual and otherwise, certain physical characteristics, and certain kinds of knowledge and skill. If we go further and say, "He's a man of forty-five," that carries even wider connotations with it as to his interests, abilities, and probable functions in society.

Such concepts have great shorthand value and are consequently very often used not only by scientists but by the man in the street. It is not sheer human cussedness or just accident that people so often use such descriptive terms as "Nazi," "Jew," "dour Scot," or "warm." Being able to place a man in one of these groups of people carries with it the suggestion of a great many traits without the necessity of enumerating each individual one (cf. Asch, 1946). The fact that a person may not have many of the implied traits has often been emphasized by psychologists, but it has not so often been pointed out that these terms have great shorthand value.

Terms such as these are also used to refer to the cultural groups to which the person belongs. Most common are role and status terms referring to family or association groups. Thus we may say, "He's a father, a coach, and a Mason." Each of these terms helps describe what behavior we may expect of him if we know the behavior which is typical of members of each of these groups. Such terms may also apply to a group of traits a person has because of his particular relationship with some class of physical objects. Thus we may refer to a person as a bicyclist or a farmer and derive from the reference some impression of the activities he will engage in as a result of his relation to certain particular environmental objects. These terms have been called "environmental mold" unities or concepts by Cattell (1946a, p. 64).

Cause and Effect As a Source of Concepts. Other concepts arise from the presumed common origin or common end of a variety of behavior elements. Many of these concepts derive from Freudian developmental psychology. Thus we may speak of a man as representing the "anal character." In doing so we imply that he should show three such dissimilar traits as obstinacy, stinginess, and orderliness because he was presumably fixated at the anal level in his libidinal development. That is, these traits occur together in a personality because they presumably have a common origin. The concept "anal character" refers to that origin and carries with it the implication that the person will have the traits in question. Such concepts as these, many of them derived from abnormal psychology, psychoanalysis, and psychiatry, have become common in describing personality. We use the *origin* or *presumed explanation* of the person's behavior to describe and interpret it. Thus, for example, we may say that a man has an inferiority complex or an Oedipus complex.

There is a whole group of related terms which refer to the *goal* of a variety of responses. These are largely motivational concepts. Thus we may speak of the need for achievement, the need for love, the need for security. When we say that Jones has a high need for achievement, this may serve to summarize a lot of his behavior, which may include: studying hard for examinations, working long hours, being sensitive to the criticism of others, and a whole variety of other responses which would in no way appear similar, at least on the surface. The basis for grouping the responses under a common heading is not their similarity, but their judged relationship to a common end.

Value As a Source of Concepts. Finally there is a whole series of concepts which interpret the behavior of a person in terms of some norms or standards. Allport and Odbert found in their analysis of trait names that this was by far the most common type of concept that they ran across. Yet they feel that so far as possible such terms should not be used in the scientific study of personality. "The psychology of personality must be kept free from confusion with the problems of evaluation (character)." (Allport, 1937, p. 308.) That is, they feel that such terms as *honest, unselfish,* and *law-abiding* have no place in the scientific study of personality. Most psychologists would agree with them. Somehow evaluative characterological sketches must be kept distinct from scientific personality studies. But wherein lies the difference? When is it all right to use a term like *honest,* and when not? Exactly what makes the use of the term *honest* improper anyway? Such important questions demand careful scrutiny, if we are really to understand the nature of conceptual schemes in personality study.

The Conceptualization Process. To unravel some of these complicated issues, let us start as simply as possible and see how and at what point concepts are introduced into the process of understanding another person. Fortunately our quest begins with an object that has a simple operational definition: a person is something that can be pointed to. We can formulate a fancier definition if we want to, e.g., a person is a living, human organism. But this is not absolutely necessary. Since we can point to a person, everyone knows what we mean when we say that the psychology of personality has a person as its legitimate subject. We can go further and say that the person becomes a legitimate object for scientific study only when the person is known to someone else. That is, the person, like any object of scientific knowledge, must "be perceived by other human beings, either directly or through recording or measuring instruments of some kind." (Mowrer and Kluckhohn, 1944, p. 77.) Following these authors further we may analyze the different ways in which a person becomes known to someone else, here the inquiring scientist. Table 3.1 outlines the various ways in which a person's behavior may affect the world around him.

TABLE 3.1

A Schematic Diagram Showing How a Scientific Conceptual Scheme Is Derived from a Person's Responses.

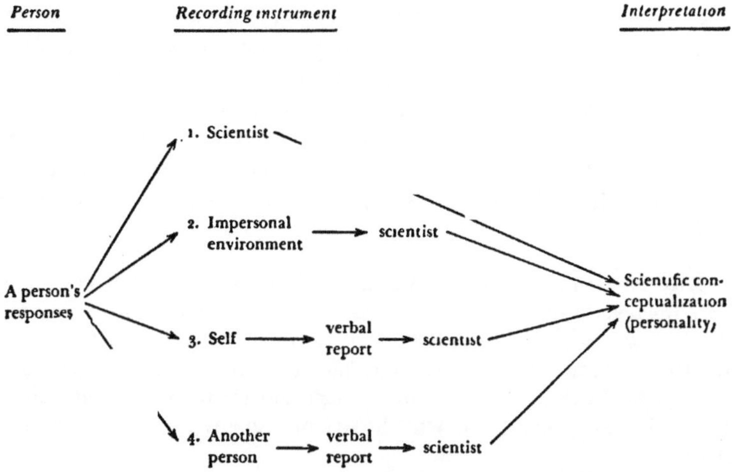

Person | *Recording instrument* | *Interpretation*

1. Scientist
2. Impersonal environment → scientist
A person's responses
3. Self → verbal report → scientist
4. Another person → verbal report → scientist
Scientific conceptualization (personality)

(After Mowrer and Kluckhohn, 1944.)

It shows how the behavior of a person becomes known to the scientist and can consequently be used by him to form a conceptual scheme. We may label this conceptual scheme the person's *personality,* recognizing that it always involves an interpretation of the person's responses. But to understand some of the confusions which have arisen as discussed above, we shall need to consider systematically the various ways in which the scientist arrives at his knowledge.

First of all, the scientist may record directly, according to the techniques covered in Chapter 2, the motor or verbal behavior of the person. This is the method the scientist is using when he adopts a check list to record movements in a time-sampling technique or when he studies the written response of a subject in a Thematic Apperception Test. At least in the beginning this observation has as little interpretation in it as possible. The scientist must have accurate raw data from which to build a conceptualization.

A second, somewhat more indirect approach involves the scientist's observation of the effects of a man on his impersonal environment. This might involve studying carvings on an ancient Egyptian bas-relief and trying to infer from them what kind of a worker the artist was. As anthropologists have pointed out, man leaves about him many art objects, belongings, and other more or less permanent artifacts, which psychologists could use to interpret personality, just as they use observation of actual behavior. Psychologists have not adopted this approach to personality very often. In fact, the best example of its possible usefulness is provided by Sherlock Holmes, who could make "amazing" deductions from a cigar ash or from the way in which the sole of a shoe is worn. An illustration of how this approach could be used in reality is provided by the "belongings test" used in the assessment of men by the Office of Strategic Services (O.S.S.) during World War II. The instructions for the test were as follows:

> This room was occupied several months ago by a man who was a guest here for several days. On his departure he left a number of his things, a number of belongings behind him in the room, planning at the time to return. We have collected these and laid them out so that they are all in plain sight. Your task is to examine them and try to size up the man, to learn all you can about him, what he was like, in any respect. (O.S.S., 1948, p. 92.)

Such data as these could be far more useful to the student of personality than they have been to date.

The third effect of the person is still more indirect and is open to a variety of changes before it gets to the scientist. This is the effect of the person on himself. It includes on the one hand direct observations, such as "I feel unhappy" and on the other, his interpretation of such feelings. That is, direct observations are often colored by the subject's own ideas as to what they mean. For example, he may say, "I feel unhappy because I have an inferiority complex." The statement about an inferiority complex is an attempt at interpretation which the student of his personality may utilize in *his* conceptualization, but it certainly should not be accepted at its face value. Anything which the person says about himself, whether it be simple reporting of subjective facts or complex interpretations of those facts, is grist for the scientist's mill, so long as the scientist is careful not to accept the person's conceptualization as his own. If a person says, "I am abnormal," the psychiatrist is definitely interested in that statement even though he may not regard the person as abnormal at all by his standards.

The last effect of a person may be on another person who then transmits his observations to the scientist. Obviously this effect is very much like the first one, where the scientist is the direct observer, but a distinction has to be made because the scientist's information has often gone through a transforming process when he gets it from an intervening reporter. The fact is that the ordinary observer of another person usually mixes a great deal of interpretation into his report to the scientist. The material as the scientist gets it is definitely secondhand and has been selected, high-lighted, and interpreted in a way which makes it very difficult for the scientist to get at the actual responses on which the observations were based. In fact, such reports may tell the scientist more about the person making the report than about the person being observed.

It is precisely in this way that a legend may grow up which in time may appear to constitute a man's personality. Take the case of Jesus. Scholars are apt nowadays to distinguish between the Jesus of the Church and the Jesus of history, each of whom has a somewhat different "personality." The original impressions of what Jesus said and did were recorded from memory by a few people. These memories were undoubtedly selective, and involved a good deal of implicit conceptualization. They were then in turn subject to interpretation by church writers, who began to react to each other's interpretations and conceptualizations till the very complex picture of His personality developed which is characteristic of present-day theology. The situation is comparable to Bartlett's reproduction experiments (1932) in which a story is told to one person, who passes it on to another, who passes it on to another, until finally the story may have little connection with the original. The changes it undergoes are of very great importance for the study of social psychology and perhaps of the personalities of the men through whose minds it has passed, but the final version is of little value for the study of the personality of the person about whom the story originated. What we are discussing here might be called *reputation,* which is defined as the conception of a man held by his associates or by men in general. But reputation must be distinguished from a scientific conceptualization of personality.

Inductive and Deductive Conceptual Schemes (Personality vs. Character). This brings us back to where we started, since reputation is very similar to what we mean by character. The difference is that now we can see how the opinions of others may be mistaken for a man's personality and yet how they may be utilized by the scientist in his over-all scheme. It remains to show how the opinion of others differs from the opinion of the scientist. It differs in two main respects. First, it is usually not as systematically based on observation and experimentation. Secondly, it often proceeds *deductively* from a frame of reference rather than *inductively* from behavioral fact. To take an extreme case, a minister may be interested in knowing whether Charlie is a sinner. He arrives at his definition of sinning deductively from theological assumptions. Then he attempts to fit Charlie into this conceptual category. From the scientist's view the "sinning" concept may not be applicable to Charlie's behavior, one way or another, but this does not matter to the minister, who is not interested in accounting for Charlie's behavior as simply as possible but in seeing how he fits into an evaluative scheme. He is interested in Charlie's character more than in his personality.

The point is that the *purpose* of a scientific portrait and a religious portrait differ. One proceeds primarily inductively, the other deductively. The purpose of a scientific conceptualization of a person is to account for his responses as completely and as economically as possible. This is the aim of any scientific concept or law. The scientist wants to make sense out of his data, he wants to develop generalizations which will account for the variety of things which he has observed. And he wants to use the minimum number of generalizations which will do the job adequately. This is exactly the task of the scientist working with a person's behavior. He wants to adopt the minimum number of concepts which will account for *all* of the behavior of a given person.

This immediately suggests what makes a concept valid or valuable for scientific use. A concept is valid in personality study to the extent that it has implications which can be defined (i.e., measured) and which have actually been tested and confirmed. Suppose, for example, on the basis of the fact that Mr. Q. returns a purse which a lady has dropped on the street, we decide to label the man honest. Is the concept *honest* valuable scientifically? The answer to this question lies in another question. Does the concept *honest* carry with it a number of implications as to other parts of his behavior? By what other operations are we as scientists going to define the word *honest*? We might decide, for example, that honesty also meant telling the truth, not looking up answers in the back of the book, or returning the right change in a business transaction (cf. Hartshorne and May, 1928). If everyone in the scientific world agreed on what the other operations were that measured honesty in this way, we could then go out and see whether in fact Mr. Q. is honest in general. That is, we could then decide whether the term *honest* was a useful concept to describe his behavior. If he showed very inconsistent behavior in the situations mentioned, we might very well have to search for another concept which would summarize his behavior better. Or we might want to redefine the meaning of the word *honest* to cover his behavior. The basic point here is that for scientific purposes a term must have an agreed-upon set of operations before its usefulness can be tested in a particular case. If the operations cannot be defined because the term is too vague, or if they are defined and are not confirmed, then we can say that the term is no good as a scientific concept, the purpose of which is to summarize behavior economically. The most general statement we can make is that a concept is valid if it has a set of operations which can be precisely defined and which have been tested and confirmed in the individual case.

Now obviously there are other purposes for which concepts may be used and this is where much of the confusion has arisen. The terms *honesty* or *sinfulness,* for example, have quite different uses for a minister, who will doubtless continue to employ them *regardless* of whether or not the scientist finds them economical in describing personality. In analogous fashion a teacher may be asked by a prospective employer whether a certain student is honest or not. It will not satisfy the employer if the teacher answers that he cannot apply the term *honesty* to this student's behavior! The teacher is being asked to make a value judgment, not a judgment as to whether the term is scientifically useful or not. One and the same term can be used for scientific purposes or for quite different purposes. To make this absolutely clear, let us modify Table 3.1 as shown on page 62.

Table 3.2 has been drawn up in such a way as to show how a teacher might arrive at a *recommendation,* using the same methods of getting information as would be available to the scientist, but starting with an evaluative framework and working back to the person's responses rather than the other way around. For instance, the teacher might observe (Method 1) that Charlie's examinations showed considerable irregularity, that he answered some questions well and some poorly, that sometimes his papers were on time and sometimes late. The teacher might also notice (Method 2) that he sometimes left his books lying around and often lost them. When confronted with some of these things Charlie would nevertheless say (Method 3), "I am deeply interested in this course and I don't know why my performance is so irregular." The teacher might then go to the

TABLE 3.2

A Schematic Diagram Showing How an Evaluative Conceptual Scheme is Applied to a Person's Responses.

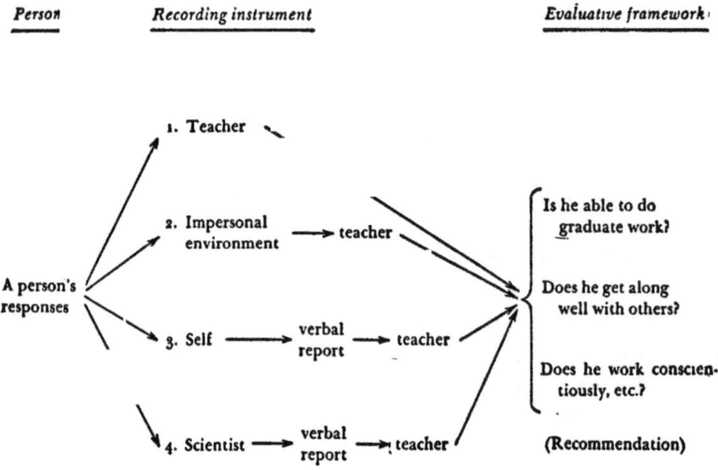

clinical psychologist for a scientific conceptualization of the man's personality (Method 4). This the clinical psychologist might give him in some such terms as the following: "Charlie is suffering from ambivalence about achievement. He has identified himself strongly with his father whom he likes and admires very much, but his father has been a failure. As a result the boy is confused in his achievement ambitions." Taking all these observations together (Methods 1, 2, 3, 4), the teacher sits down and tries to write a recommendation for the student in terms of the questions he must answer, which might run somewhat as follows:

Charlie F---- is a student whose work is best characterized as being of very uneven quality. At times he shows a real grasp of the subject matter and approaches brilliance; at other times he doesn't seem to try at all. He is careless in his work habits and not completely dependable. Though I would like to see him have a chance at graduate work, I am not very optimistic about his eventual success. If he could settle down and straighten out some of his goals in life, I think he might make a very able student. But he has not done this as yet. Personally I find him very likable.

The thing to notice about such a recommendation is that it uses some of the very same concepts that might be used by a scientist trying to give a picture of the boy's personality. But the concepts are used for a different purpose. They are used to give an over-all evaluation of the boy as a student so that the graduate school can decide whether to admit him or not. It is true that the teacher uses concepts that summarize the boy's behavior fairly adequately, but he also chooses his concepts primarily with an eye to their usefulness for the purpose of recommendation. It is this other purpose which distinguishes the portrait of a person drawn by the nonscientist. Such a recommendation may be called a *character* sketch as distinct from a *personality* sketch. The term *character* may be used to refer to an evaluation of a person in terms of some standards, whereas the term *personality* should be restricted to the scientific conceptualization under consideration here.

An analogy may be drawn with the portrait which an artist makes of a still life. He rearranges his imperfect sensory impressions into something which makes artistic sense to him. He is creating, contributing much to what he sees in terms of his artistic values concerning line, color, and form. He has a purpose which goes beyond accounting as simply as possible for what he sees, just as the teacher has a purpose which requires him to arrange what he observes into the categories of judgment required in a recommendation. Similarly the novelist, in describing a character, will select and emphasize the qualities which fit his artistic plans. The scientist, on the other hand, has as his job the adequate accounting for all a person's activities and experiences as economically as possible. His concepts are limited to those which are useful to this particular purpose. Such a limitation may make the scientist at times seem uninspired and pedestrian. Allport quotes Stefan Zweig as saying, "In psychology the field of personality is worked by lesser men, mere flies, who have the safe anchorage of a frame of science in which to place their petty platitudes or minor heresies." (1937, p. 60.) But as Allport also says (1937, p. 63), "If psychology today is discovering only what literature 'has always said' it is nevertheless giving precision and general application to the ancient truths. Less enjoyable, it is more disciplined; less subtle, it is more verifiable; less artful, it is more exact."

Two Contrasting Personality Portraits. The importance of the issue we have been discussing will become obvious if we compare two conceptualizations of the same individual written and published by two different teams of psychologists who had access to substantially the same information. One report is by White, Tomkins, and Alper (1945) on a Harvard student they named Helmler, and the other by Murray and Morgan (1945) on the same man, whom they named Hawk. According to the White team Helmler was a very successful college man who had made a realistic synthesis. "At the age of twenty he has achieved a working synthesis which includes the demands of his culture, the pressure of his own needs, and the conditions imposed by external reality. . . . Our investigation shows that he has known considerable anxiety, that he has been placed in situations of great conflict, and that his adaptation has been won and re-won in the face of successive obstacles." They report him as giving the "impression of maturity . . . partly from his habitual poise and deliberate, well-considered speech." On the campus he is a leader participating "in nearly every kind of college activity. . . . He . . . has made an excellent academic record consisting mainly of A's and B's; this is the more to his credit because he is earning most of his way through college by rather time-consuming office work." (1945, p. 229.) All in all they see him as a person who has great ego strength and who has achieved a "remarkable realism," although at considerable cost since his "self-forwarding career" entails the "sacrifice of friendliness and warmth" which he wants (1945, p. 247).

Murray and Morgan view the same man quite differently. They find him primarily egocentric and unable to adjust to World War II. "We do not believe that his primary motivation in avoiding battle is crude physical fear as such, fear of injury and pain, but rather dread lest a bullet put an end to a magnificent career, the certainty of which rests upon an undeniable presentiment of his own potentialities. He is overcome by pity of a vision cut short by violence. But the vision is not the offspring of world loyalty; it is the outgrowth of a primitive desire for power and glory." (1945, p. 107.) "In the present crisis, there was not a trace of leadership ability in Hawk's behavior. Disillusioned, confused, and unable to bring his own mind into line, he could be of no help to others." (1945, p. 109.) Similarly they find him hostile to religion because it tends to "narrow the mind." ". . . his capacity for dedication and selflessness is deficient. He has no thought of finding his life by losing it. Personal power is what he wants, conscious governance of himself and others —this above all." (1945, p. 165.) On attitudes toward sex he fares hardly better. He is in favor of romance but so far has not been able to develop much romance himself. "The truth is that Hawk is so narcissistically preoccupied with his own personal ambition that he is incapable at present of giving himself wholeheartedly to anything but this." (1945, p. 274.) Only toward his parents are his attitudes positive. ". . . his affection and devotion are undeviating." Perhaps, as they suggest, "Having nothing to fear from his parents he can love them without qualification." (1945, p. 238.)

What a contrast this is to the picture of a "realistic synthesis"! It hardly seems possible that the same person is being described by these two teams of psychologists. Yet he is. What explains the difference? How can he appear "mature" and "realistic" to one group and "confused" and "narcissistically preoccupied" to another? The fact is that the judges were holding him up to different standards. His life had a different meaning depending on which set of norms they referred it to. Murray and Morgan were obviously considering him from the viewpoint of the extent to which he measured up to society's requirements, particularly in time of war. They found him wanting. He did not have the "selflessness" that country, church, or love would require of him. Their conceptual categories were determined in part by the requirements of the evaluative framework to which they referred him. The White group, on the other hand, had adopted an individualistic rather than a social evaluative framework. They asked themselves whether he would succeed, not whether his country would find him an excellent citizen and soldier, or his wife a selfless lover. They judged he was realistic from the value framework of individual success. In this respect they were probably just as correct as Murray and Morgan were to find him egocentric rather than sociocentric. Each group was holding him to a different standard. Each was writing a different kind of recommendation, as it were. But which is the correct one? Neither, according to the view adopted here. A conceptual scheme should be oriented toward accounting for the behavioral facts and not toward any judgmental framework, hard though that may be when value judgments so permeate our relationships with people. This in no way lessens the importance of evaluations. There is no reason why someone should not ask how good a soldier or how good a businessman Hawk will be and no reason why teams of psychologists should not attempt to answer such questions. When they do so, however, they should recognize that they have left the field of personality, of pure science, and have entered the field of character, of applied science. Both are important fields of study but in the interest of clarity they should be kept separate and distinct.

A Systematic Evaluative Framework. Two German scholars, Dilthey (1894) and Spranger (1928), have argued strongly for a scientific, systematic approach to character evaluation. They feel that the approach recommended here, namely, that of working inductively from a person's behavior, has led psychologists to be exclusively interested in causation and development. It is easy to see how this might result. If the scientist is response-oriented, his major problem becomes that of determining the relationship between two or more responses, or of explaining *why* response A is associated with response B, etc. Dilthey argued that psychology should concern itself not only with explanation or with cause, but also with meaning (1894). By *meaning* he had in mind the connection of an act with some larger whole or frame of reference that had value or importance. He differentiated, consequently, explanatory psychology from a descriptive or comparative psychology. He even invented a new term to describe the method used in descriptive psychology. In German the term is *verstehen,* which may be translated *understanding.* This has been taken by Allport (1937) to mean any *intuitive* approach to psychology, although it is doubtful if Dilthey and his pupil, Spranger, meant to imply that the "understanding" approach was any less analytical, comparative, or rigorous than the explanatory approach to psychology. The major contrast they meant to draw was between the *aims* of the two kinds of psychology, not between the *methods* of study.

This difference of aims can best be illustrated by a concrete example. Suppose a person goes to New York. Dilthey and Spranger argue that there are two kinds of questions which may be asked about this act. First is the question, "Why does he go?" An answer to this question might involve a study of his motives, his inner states, or the argument he had with his father the day before. This is the approach the Freudians would presumably use. But we may also ask the question, "So what?" What is the meaning of his act, what is its significance? Answers to these questions might involve considering the economic or social significance of the act. He might be going to New York to earn a living, to meet a friend, or to go to the opera. In other words, his act has economic or perhaps social or aesthetic significance or value.

What difference does this make in the conceptualization of a given personality? The answer to this is best found in the studies of personality made by men belonging to this school. Thus Dilthey wrote a life of Goethe (1910) which was concerned chiefly with Goethe's significance as a writer and not with Goethe's inner feelings or motives or his relationship to his mother. In other words, Dilthey wanted to judge Goethe from the viewpoint of various standards, values, or frames of reference. As a culture historian he wanted to place Goethe in his socio-cultural context.

Spranger (1928) went a step further and argued that there are six frames of reference (*Lebensformen*) in terms of which a personality should be systematically considered. It is from the viewpoint of these six abstract standards or values that a particular life takes on *meaning,* just as an act takes on meaning when it is judged in terms of its economic or social significance or consequences. This normative framework should not be confused with a moral framework for praising or condemning a person. It is simply an abstract system of reference points in terms of which a particular life history may be written or evaluated. These reference points (aesthetic, social, political, economic, theoretical, religious) derive from social structure analysis rather than from developmental stages of the organism as in the Freudian scheme. The difference can be high-lighted by contrasting the two different lives which might be written of someone like Saint Theresa, one of which would deal with its aesthetic and religious significance, the other with the emotional causes of her behavior, with, perhaps, her powerful, sublimated sexual urges.[1]

What are we to make of this proposal? What it seems to involve is an attempt to treat the "social stimulus value" of a person systematically, to consider the place of a person's life within a number of different normative frameworks. Spranger would include the evaluations of the novelist, the priest, or the teacher, but in a more objective systematic manner. We might call this approach *criticism.* Careful and objective criticism of a man's life in terms of standardized frames of reference or values is clearly a task which needs to be done. Someone must concern himself with the meaning of a man's life. To seek an analogy in the realm of physical science, we may also say that someone must concern himself with the "meaning" of water—its economic utility, its artistic qualities, its destructive power, etc. Yet the chemist normally contents himself with the structure of water and leaves its "social stimulus value" to someone else. We might say that the psychologist should do likewise, with one important difference to be noted below. Normally the process of evaluat-

[1] I am deeply indebted to Professor Juan Roura for his patient explanation of the views of Dilthey and Spranger. See also his book, *El Mundo Historico Social,* 1948.

ing a person is left to those who excel in the particular standards in terms of which he is being judged; e.g., the priest, the artist, or the teacher. We have no name for Dilthey and Spranger's normative science of evaluating these evaluations, unless it be characterology, criticism, or philosophy. At any rate, the task of the psychology of personality is more circumscribed; to repeat, it is merely to get the most adequate and economical conceptualization possible of a single person's responses.

There is one aspect of criticism which is a legitimate subject for social psychological study. That is the *process* of arriving at the critical value judgment. The social psychologist is definitely interested in the way evaluations of other people grow up. In their extreme form such judgments may take the form of a legend, such as the legend about George Washington, Abraham Lincoln, or some nonexistent historical figure. Particularly useful for the study of cultural attitudes have been the purely mythical figures, the culture heroes, gods, or demigods. For example, Brown has shown (1947) how Hermes, the thief in ancient Greek mythology, really came to have a personality which was a projection of the desires of the rising Greek middle class. These mythical "personalities" are very useful to the social psychologist and the anthropologist because they reflect fundamental social attitudes, but they are not part of the psychology of personality proper.

The Usefulness of All Sorts of Concepts. Nevertheless we may well want to borrow concepts from the field of social psychology or even from the field of criticism and adapt them to our own scientific purposes. For example, we shall find it very useful in this book to borrow the social role concept as an aid in describing and summarizing a man's personality. This is necessary because most of a man's acts are social in nature and are determined by his interiorization of social norms. It is here that the parallel with water is not exact. The chemist does not find the social stimulus value of water of any use in his scientific understanding of water. But this is not true of the psychologist. To know the social stimulus value of a man, to know that he is a coach, provides us with a concept which not only gives his function in his society but which also may be used to summarize or explain his behavior, since the attitudes and activities expected of a coach are fairly well defined in our society. Nevertheless, we shall find it necessary to distinguish between the term *coach,* as used in the first sense when it is a unit of social structure analysis, and in the second sense when it summarizes Mr. P.'s behavior. The interiorization of the behavorial norms that go with being a coach is never perfect; so we shall need a somewhat different term to refer to this interiorized norm ("role perception"), but it will depend for its meaning very much on the social meaning of the term *coach*.

Likewise we shall borrow concepts for scientific purposes from the other sources listed earlier. We shall use the concept of trait, which is based on similarities of behavior, and the concept of motive, which is based on cause-and-effect relationships. We shall also be influenced by methodological considerations, since, if a concept has a set of operations which cannot be compared with any other set of operations used by scientists, it is of limited general usefulness. For example, the term "promptings from within" has an operational definition. Roughly it is the M response on the Rorschach Test. But if the concept can be related to no other operations, it will die a natural death. Finally we shall be influenced in our choice of concepts by the relation of the concepts to other concepts which have been developed. All along we have been talking as if a concept existed in isolation. Actually, of course, it not only has a relationship to the operations which define it but it has a supraordinate or coordinate relationship to other concepts in the general theory of personality being developed. This aspect of our theoretical problem will be treated more fully in the next chapter.

Definition of Personality. We have finally completed our definition of personality. Starting with a simple operational definition of a person as something one can point to, we have concluded with a definition of personality as the most adequate conceptualization of a person's behavior in all its detail that the scientist can give at a moment in time. This definition of personality requires some further elaboration. First, it is obvious that a person is not his personality any more than a particular color *blue* corresponds to a wave length of a certain frequency with all its connotations in theoretical physics. *Personality is a theoretical interpretation derived from all a person's behavior.* This should reassure those who prefer direct apprehension of another to the scientific method of understanding. It goes without saying that even the psychologist will go on loving his wife in preference to building up a scientific conceptualization of her. We certainly have not meant to judge the theoretical approach to the person as superior to the artistic, the critical, or the intuitive. We have simply tried to distinguish it as sharply as possible from these other approaches.

Second, a person's personality in this sense may change as he changes or as the scientist's insights improve. In fact, since personality is a theoretical construct, it is very apt to change as the scientist's other theoretical convictions are modified or improved. Nowhere is this more obvious than in current definitions of personality given by other workers in the field. Thus Guthrie defines personality as "those habits and habit systems of social importance that are stable and resistant to change" (1944, p. 58). Here it is clear that the author has defined personality in terms of his theoretical orientation toward associative learning as the basis of all behavior. A somewhat more comprehensive definition is given by Allport, who defines personality as "the dynamic organization within the individual of those psychophysical systems that determine his unique adjustments to his environment." (1937, p. 48.) The elements in this definition, if taken separately, reflect all or nearly all of the major theoretical viewpoints in psychology today. The final phrase "unique adjustments to his environment" clearly reflects the contemporary Darwinian emphasis on functionalism, or adaptation for survival. The phrase "dynamic organization," on the other hand, neatly combines two schools, the Freudian emphasis on striving and the Gestalt emphasis on patterning. The word "psychophysical" emphasizes the biological basis of personality or the relation between mind and body, etc.

This is, of course, as it should be. An interpretation will always reflect the theoretical viewpoints of the time. But it should be clear that each formulation of personality, like any scientific formulation, is only approximate—a more or less happy hypothesis—which is subject to change as insights improve. There is no absolute and final truth, at least so far as a conception of a given person is concerned. Truth will always be only approximate.

The definition of personality we have given also requires some further specification of what is meant by an adequate conceptualization. We may begin by saying that an adequate conceptualization is one which leads to the maximum understanding of the person. But unfortunately the word *understanding* has so many subjective meanings, we must specify even further than this. Following the Social Science Research Council as reported by Allport (1942, pp. 170-171), we can set up various criteria for determining the adequacy of the conceptualization in producing understanding of the person.

1. Completeness. The primary consideration would appear to be that the conceptualization conforms with as many facts about the person as possible. It must account for *all* his behavior.

2. Economy. The formulation must not only be complete, it must be made with as few principles and concepts as possible. Obviously a conceptualization which is as varied and detailed as the raw data on which it is based has very little scientific usefulness. It is one of the primary principles of science to get along with as few abstractions as will still give complete understanding.

3. Consistency. The interpretation must be internally consistent. "Parts of an interpretation can be made to confront one another. Logical contradictions raise a suspicion of invalidity." (Allport, 1942, p. 171.) In other words, the elementary rules of logical thinking must be applied to the interpretation. It has often been said rather unkindly of some psychoanalysts that they always start out with two opposite principles and are thus able to explain anything which a person does by using either one or the other.

4. Predictive power. Prediction has a special place in science because it would seem to be the final test of understanding. If our interpretation is correct we ought to be able to predict what the person will do in a specified situation. Unfortunately the difficulty lies as often in specification of a situation as it does in the adequacy of a conceptualization. As the authors of *Assessment of Men* have so aptly put it, "It is easy to predict precisely the outcome of the meeting of one known chemical with another known chemical in an immaculate test tube. But where is the chemist who can predict what will happen to a known chemical if it meets an unknown chemical in an unknown vessel? . . . How, then, can a psychologist foretell with any degree of accuracy the outcomes of future meetings of one barely known personality with hundreds of other undesignated personalities in distant, undesignated cities, villages, fields, and jungles that are seething with one knows not what potential harms and benefits? Fortune—call the old hag or beauty what you will—can never be eliminated from the universe of human interactions. And this being forever true, prophetic infallibility is beyond the reach of social scientists." (1948, p. 8.) Nevertheless, for the situations which *can be specified* by the psychologist—and there are an increasing number of these at least so far as laboratory experiments are concerned—predictions should be made and tested. There is no more convincing proof of the adequacy of a theoretical formulation. It is this con-

sideration which has led Cattell to define personality as "that which predicts behavior given the situation" (1946a, p. 566).

5. Relation to other theoretical concepts. Science is a community enterprise. It would be conceivable for a psychologist to develop a conceptualization of a given person which was completely adequate and fulfilled the other criteria listed above, but which had no relationship to any conceptualization which might be developed for any other person. That is, he might arrive at an absolutely unique formulation. As such it would have distinctly limited utility. The scientist in the field of personality must be guided to some extent by concepts which not only are in use in other disciplines but are in use by other scientists working in the same field. And especially he must be guided by the applicability of the concepts he uses to more than one person.

We shall try to apply these criteria to a case which will be fully developed in this book so that the discussion does not remain on too abstract a level. By this time it should be obvious that the task of the scientist in the field of personality is not easy. Nevertheless it will become easier as it is sharply distinguished from the tasks of others who have legitimate interests in the human individual. It is only by carefully defining our purpose that we can keep from getting hopelessly involved in arguments over what personality really is and how it should be described.

NOTES AND QUERIES

1. One of the best published examples of the conceptualization of a normal personality based on a great variety of careful observations is that given in the book *Assessment of Men,* written by the staff of the O.S.S. training school during World War II. Read the formulation of the sergeant's personality reproduced in full below, pick out half-a-dozen concepts used, and classify them as to their source according to the scheme in the text. Are there any evaluative terms used? Why would they be used?

This competent, energetic, self-confident Sergeant is very well qualified for his assignment by his ability, personality, and background. He is a determined, clear-thinking person who has well-defined values and goals which he pursues with unswerving persistence, fully utilizing his capacity for hard work. In spite of his pronounced tendency toward self-reliance and independence which, combined with his rejection of indiscriminate gregariousness, often leads to bluntness in social relations, he is essentially a person of good will, is frank, sympathetic, sincere, and a good mixer. While his brusqueness and independence may alienate people upon first contact, over a longer period of time the student is likely to win and hold both the respect and the affection of his colleagues. These traits, together with his readiness to take responsibilities for others, to solve problems, and to make decisions, qualify the candidate for a position of leadership higher than one that would be compatible with his rank.

Son of a successful attorney-at-law, the candidate grew up in Oregon and Wisconsin and from an early age developed a great love for outdoor life, becoming proficient in mountain climbing, skiing, riding, and swimming. He was always a good student in school, sociable and active in a variety of extracurricular pursuits. Very close to both parents, and admiring his father's character and achievements, he decided to follow him in the legal profession, and obtained his degree from the University of Missouri in 1941. Expecting to be drafted, he postponed going into practice, and took a job with the U.S. Department of Justice. He enjoyed this work greatly, and in the course of it has acquired some experience in questioning Chinese and Japanese. Inducted into the Army in 1943, he went through basic training and a radio school and has worked as a radio instructor for the last two years. In spite of slow promotion, he has adjusted well to this situation, has enjoyed teaching, for which he obtained the highest ratings, and has utilized his free time for extensive reading in the field of law and social science. He wants an overseas assignment because he feels that he should do more for the war effort and feels capable of handling a strenuous and responsible mission. Although the candidate's strong desire to do well makes him nervous and tense in test situations, or in beginning a new type of work, increasing familiarity with the situation quickly dissolves these tensions; the student is well integrated emotionally and has no disturbing conflicts or fears; while he does not seek danger he is willing to take any risks that the assignment might involve.

This candidate was very highly motivated for all of the situations at S. He entered into the assignments enthusiastically and exerted himself to the utmost in order to achieve a successful solution of his group's problems. Possessing a good measure of forcefulness and self-assertiveness, he was usually the first to make any bid for leadership. Only the lack of sufficient ingenuity in field problems prevented him from carrying out this role with distinction. He is adaptable and flexible—attributes which should stand him in good stead in acquiring the leadership techniques and fundamental knowledge necessary to handle his projected assignment effectively.

He has a strong desire to plan and carry out tasks on the basis of his own ideas. As a result, he tends to be somewhat abrupt with others who have different ideas and he is very likely to overlook their point of view in favor of his own. However, he has sufficient insight into himself so that this characteristic rarely becomes so dominant as to interfere markedly with his social relations. Furthermore, his good will, warmth, and sympathetic understanding of others become more obvious as time goes on. He should therefore wear well with any group with which he is associated over a long period of time.

In situations which he regarded as critical tests of his abilities, his tensions expressed themselves in profuse sweating and quivering limbs. He was aware of his uneasiness and discomfiture but controlled himself so well that he never became upset and never permitted his emotionality to interfere with the work at hand.

He is highly recommended for his proposed assignment overseas.

(Reprinted with permission from the *Assessment of men*. Copyright 1948, Rinehart and Co.)

2. In contrast to this picture we have a portrait such as the following, written by a literary characterologist and quoted in Allport. Contrast this portrait with the one given below. What are the similarities and what are the differences? In what sense is the former more scientific?

Giton has a fresh complexion, a full face and bulging cheeks, a fixed and assured gaze, broad shoulders, a projecting stomach, a firm and deliberate tread. He speaks with confidence; he makes those who converse with him repeat what they have said and he only moderately enjoys what is said. He unfolds an ample handkerchief and blows his nose noisily; he spits to a great distance and sneezes very loudly. He sleeps by day, he sleeps by night; he snores in company. At table and in walking he occupies more room than anyone else. He takes the center and walks with his equals; he stops and they stop; he walks on and they walk on; all regulate themselves by him; he is not interrupted, he is listened to as long as he likes to talk; his opinion is accepted, the rumors he spreads are believed. If he sits down you will see him settle into an armchair, cross his legs, frown, pull his hat over his eyes and see no one, or lift it up again and show his brow from pride and audacity. He is cheerful, a hearty laugher, impatient, presumptuous, quick to anger, irreligious, politic, mysterious about current affairs; he believes he has talents and wit. He is rich. (Allport, 1937, p. 59.)

3. Identify the major theoretical viewpoints in the following definitions of personality. How do they differ from the definition suggested earlier in this chapter?

Personality is "the system of habits which . . . is largely made up of non-adaptive ways of adjusting to conflict situations." (Stagner, 1937, p. 9.)

Personality is "the organized aggregate of psychological processes and states pertaining to the individual. This definition includes the common element in most of the definitions now current. At the same time it excludes many orders of phenomena which have been included in one or another of these definitions. Thus it rules out the overt behavior resulting from the operation of these processes and states, although it is only from such behavior that their nature and even existence can be deduced. It also excludes from consideration the effects of this behavior upon the individual's environment, even that part of it which consists of other individuals. Lastly, it excludes from the personality concept the physical structure of the individual and his physiological processes." (Linton, 1945, p. 84.)

"This expression [integrate in action] is here used to include (1) the meaning or *function,* which an individual's actions have for him, (2) the *conflicts* which exist between his various habit systems, (3) the environment or *field* to which he is accustomed, and (4) the more or less unique way in which he is held together, or *integrated.* These four criteria derived from the four basic assumptions of dynamic theory, thus provide a comprehensive scheme for defining 'personality' in general and for identifying any 'personality' in particular." (Mowrer and Kluckhohn, 1944, p. 77.)

4. G. W. Allport (1937, p. 62) quotes "a famous professor of literature" as describing a character as follows: "The nose, almost invariably the index of mental power, was perfect in fullness, straightness, and strength." Allport says further, "No psychologist could write such a passage without being torn limb from limb by his professional colleagues!" What personality concepts are introduced here and on what basis? What precisely is wrong with them?

5. Try out the belongings test following the instructions reproduced in the text. Go into someone's room (when he is out!) and try to draw as many inferences about his personality as you can from observing his "artifacts." Does the nature of your data set any limits on the concepts you can use? Why has the effect of a person on his impersonal environment seldom been used as a way of finding out more about him?

6. Allport in arguing against the "social stimulus value" theory of personality makes the following statement: "A solitary dweller on a desert island, unknown to any other mortal, has a full-fledged (and intensely interesting) personality." (1937, p. 41.) In what sense is this correct? In what sense incorrect?

7. Mowrer and Kluckhohn (1944, p. 77) state that "when an individual dies, 'personality' in the first sense comes to an end, but in the second sense it may continue or even grow for centuries." According to our treatment of the subject, in what sense may a personality die or continue to grow? Which of the effects of a person disappears at death?

8. There is a sense in which the Spranger scheme marks off regions in a man's sociocultural environment (*Kulturgebiete*) in terms

of which he should be systematically described, in order to give a cross-sectional view of his personality as opposed to a developmental one. Does this interpretation make Spranger's approach scientific in the sense in which the term is used here? Would it satisfy Spranger? Or is there a difference between such statements as "he plays the violin" and "he plays the violin beautifully," a difference so fundamental that we must assign the first statement to his "personality" and the second to his "character" or reputation? Can we get around this dilemma by saying that if a man knows or thinks he knows that he plays the violin beautifully, this item can become part of a scientific portrait of him? Why is it that non-evaluative descriptions of people seem so lifeless, so "meaningless"?

4

Relating the Facts to One Another

Referring back to the elements in the offhand description of another person with which we began our study of personality, we can see that we have covered the improvements made by science in observation and in conceptualization. This leaves the most difficult part of all, namely, the integration of the concepts derived from our observations into an over-all personality picture. We must not only formulate concepts to represent segments of behavior, we must also relate these concepts to each other in some meaningful way. This takes us inevitably into the field of psychological theory. Unfortunately psychological theory is not in a very satisfactory condition and to try to state in any definitive way how it operates in the field of personality is out of the question. Nevertheless, there are certain outstanding problems in connection with the application of standard inferential or analytical thinking to the individual life that we shall have to face at the very beginning. Our chief concern in this chapter will be to state those problems as precisely as possible and to try to indicate the directions in which solutions to them may lie. At this stage in psychological theory we are doing well if we can formulate the problems correctly and indicate a mode of attack. Final solutions will have to be left to future generations.

Kinds of Psychological Laws. Following the lead of Bergmann and Spence (1944), we may begin with the two kinds of empirical relationships or laws found in psychology. The first of these relates a response variable (R) to an experimentally manipulated stimulus variable (S). This may be written symbolically in the following form:

1. $$R = f(S)$$

This formula illustrates the traditional type of empirical relationship or law studied in experimental psychology beginning with the earliest work in Wundt's laboratory. A response (e.g., reaction time) is plotted as a function of some stimulus (light intensity, length of the fore period, set, etc.). This is the prototype of nearly all laboratory experiments in psychology, even in the field of personality. For example, we may measure the influence of success- and failure-stimulation on level of aspiration. Or we may count the number of food objects imagined as a function of number of hours of food deprivation. Such relationships have typically been stated in the "If A, then B" form—if the human being is deprived of food for increasing lengths of time, he will imagine he sees an increasing number of food-related objects (McClelland and Atkinson, 1948) under certain conditions. Or the number of food objects a man will see increases according to a function which may be mathematically described. All of Hull's laws in his *Principles of Behavior Theory* are of this nature. That is, a response of the organism is ultimately tied (via intervening constructs, to be sure) to some change in the environment. For convenience we may refer to this type of law as an "S—R law."

Another type of empirical relationship in psychology takes the following form:

2. $$R_1 = f(R_2)$$

Here one response of the organism is related to another response of the organism. To take but one of the examples given above, we may now relate the number of food objects imagined to the subject's rating of his degree of hunger. Here his imagination (R_1) is related to his judgment of his hunger (R_2). As Bergmann and Spence put it, "As a matter of fact, any correlation between the scores on two different tests is of this type and so is much of the knowledge in the field of personality (correlation of traits)." (1944, p. 20.) We may well ask why most of the laws in personality take this form. The answer lies in the fact that very often in personality we are not interested in changes in the person's responses as a function of some momentary stimulus condition. Rather we are interested in stable personality characteristics which are the result of long-time summations of stimulus conditions. That is, Charlie's behavior is not determined wholly by changes in his immediate external environment, but by his past history as well, by the cumulative effects of his past experience with this and similar situations.

To follow our example still further, Charlie may have a history with regard to hunger experiences, and we may be more interested in that than we are in the effect of temporary food deprivation. In fact, to get at this past-history variable, we very often hold external conditions constant and note what we call *individual differences* in the number of food objects imagined in our situation. "Individual differences" in this sense very often means *unrelated to the differences in the external experimental conditions,* or, the variation in behavior left over after that due to the experimental conditions has been analyzed out or subtracted. These individual differences may of course be related to differences in prior experiences that each subject has had. For example, Charlie may have grown up in an area of plenty, where there was all the food he could eat, whereas Joe may have grown up under conditions in which food was only periodically present in sufficient quantities. These two people may be expected to react quite differently to hours of deprivation as adults. To get at this past-history variable, we should hold hours of deprivation constant and obtain some food-related response of the subject, such as self-ratings or number of food objects imagined. Figure 4.1 has been drawn to illustrate this approach and its relation to a typical S–R function. The solid line shows the simple S–R type of relationship in which mean self-ratings of hunger are plotted against hours of food deprivation. The bar graph shows how individual subjects rate themselves on hunger when food deprivation has been held constant at one hour. Since there are wide variations in these self-ratings when we hold the experimental variable (hours of food deprivation) constant, we must conclude that unknown (as yet) factors in the past histories of the individuals are determining their self-ratings on hunger.

FIGURE 4.1

A Comparison of an S–R Type of Law with the Individual Differences Approach to Personality

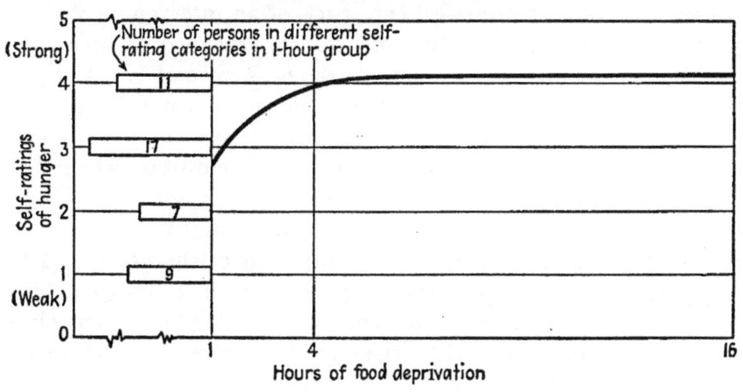

Since we often cannot determine or are not interested in determining what the past-history stimulus conditions were, we are unable to formulate a law of the S–R type. Instead, we must relate one response to another. We may then attempt to see if we can "explain" the differences on rated hunger for the one-hour group by relating the ratings to some other measure (whether they liked the food they had just eaten, their projected need for security, score on an adjustment inventory, etc.).

The R–R type of law has two important consequences for theoretical thinking. In the first place, it does not permit the traditional independent-dependent breakdown in plotting the relationship between two variables. In particular we can no longer think in terms of S (the stimulus condition) *causing* R (the subject's response). As all the elementary texts in psychology point out, a correlation cannot be interpreted in terms of causation. We may find that cigarette smoking is correlated with low grades in high school, but we should be incorrect to conclude that therefore cigarette smoking causes low grades. Technically it would be just as correct to say that low grades cause cigarette smoking. In fact, with this type of law we have to stop thinking about causal relationships altogether. This may actually be an advantage as far as theory construction is concerned, although Bergmann and Spence seem to feel (1944, p. 21) that the R–R type of law is actually inferior.

The reason for this possible advantage is to be found in the second consequence of the R–R type of law. This is that we are forced to think much more carefully about what it is that relates the two responses. We are forced to invent a middle term which "explains" the correlation between the two responses. This middle term—call it a concept, or a hypothetical construct, or an intervening variable, or what you will—is the essence of psychological theory. Technically a middle term is just as necessary in the S–R type of law, but practically the experimenter is not forced to think as carefully about it. The reason for this is that the middle term between an S and an R is often just a class name for the type of conditions which have been found to produce the response. A classic example can be found in the field of memory. A relationship which holds fairly widely for retention is that forgetting (R) is a function of the activity (S) interpolated between original learning and relearning. The theoretical construct or middle term involved in this law is "interpolated activity" but actually it is so close to the variety of experimental stimulus conditions which it describes that many people do not recognize that it is a middle term. That it is such a term is illustrated by the fact that it can be used to mediate deductions about new kinds of interpolations which can be tested experimentally.

The R—R relationship is usually much more difficult to handle than this. For example, suppose one finds a correlation between a certain type of score on a Thematic Apperception Test and the number of words obtained in the middle section of a twelve-minute anagrams test (cf. Clark and McClelland, 1950). What middle term are we going to invent to explain this relationship? We cannot stop with the empirical correlation because as such it is relatively meaningless. But in our search for meaning we are forced to think much more carefully about what kinds of constructs we can legitimately introduce to explain the relationship empirically obtained between two such responses.

A Concrete Example: n Achievement. Since this is a very difficult problem to understand at the theoretical level, let us take a concrete example and follow it through from a simple empirical S—R relationship to a more complex theoretical interpretation of the relationship. We can thus see in actual practice what the advantages and disadvantages are of the various types of middle terms and of how they are used in psychological theory. We will take an actual example from the experimental literature and will use throughout an adaptation of Spence's (1948) scheme for representing different types of laws. The experiment in question is from a series by McClelland and associates (1949) on the effect of ego-involving instructions on the characteristics of written imaginative stories. These stories are comparable to those obtained on the Thematic Apperception Test (abbreviated TAT). McClelland *et al.* discovered that if the subjects were ego-involved by certain instructions and then caused to fail, the stories they wrote after this experience would differ significantly in a number of ways from the stories written by a comparable group of subjects without such prior experience. This is a simple S—R relationship which may be represented as follows:

3. $R_1 = f(S_1)$ TAT score = f ("ego-involving" instructions)

The right-hand portion of Equation 3 states that the TAT score, derived by summing the story characterictics which changed under the new conditions, is a function of those new conditions (ego-involving instructions, induced failure). This is a simple empirical law and presumably some other experimenters, if they wanted to, could obtain, by reproducing the experimental situation, the same changes in stories written by comparable subjects. A next step with such a law might be to refine the nature of the relationship. That is, one could systematically vary the type of ego-involving experience and record the changes in the stories. Or one could try to vary the intensity of the ego-involving experience and then try to plot the size of the shift in the TAT score. This might lead to a more precise statement as to the nature of the law—i.e., as to whether it is linear, positively or negatively accelerated, etc. But the interpretation of the relationship is another and a much more complicated matter. Probably the most that could be said from the empirical law itself is that a subject who has a high TAT score under normal conditions is behaving as if he had just had an ego-involving experience like the one experimentally induced. But McClelland *et al.* (1949) were interested in going further than this. They invented a construct which would help interpret the empirical relationship, as follows:

4. $C = f(S_{t=0})$ Temporary n Achievement = f ("ego-involving" instructions)

In the left-hand portion of the equation, the letter C stands for concept or construct, and is used instead of the letter I (for intervening variable) in Spence (1948) for reasons to be given below. What this equation means is that a construct has been invented which is said to be a function of stimulus conditions at the time ($t = 0$ stands for time at the present). The right-hand portion of the functional equation shows that the construct chosen was what might be called temporary need for achievement (or following Murray (1938), n Achievement). This is strictly a guessed-at or invented relationship. To put it in everyday language, what it says is that the ego-involving instructions have aroused in the subject a state which the authors choose to label temporary n Achievement. But even this does not go very far toward adding meaning to the empirical relationship. As we have seen above, in personality we are much more often interested in the stable characteristics of a person than we are in his temporary states. So another relationship of the following form is guessed at:

5. $C = f(S_{t-n})$ n Achievement = f (Σ past "ego-involving" situations)

Here the formula suggests that the construct is a function of similar ego-involving experiences in the past (t–n). In other words,

Equation 5 assumes the person carries around with him a characteristic amount of n Achievement as a result of his past learning in connection with similar experiences of ego-involvement, failure, success, etc. To put it in another way, a person, as a result of learning, develops n Achievement in proportion to the number and nature of ego-involving experiences like the one experimentally induced. Now it is obviously impossible in any given person at any given moment to specify what those past experiences have been. The general truth of such a relationship can be checked to some extent by a study of individual cases as they develop, perhaps in different cultures, and also by our general knowledge of learning principles, but nevertheless for the most part this, too, must remain a purely hypothetical relationship. If we grant that it is, we can take one further step, as follows:

6. $R_1 = f(C)$ TAT score = f (n Achievement)

We have now arrived at a relationship which is of considerably greater theoretical value than the purely empirical one with which we started. Equation 6 states that we can use the TAT score derived as indicated above as a measure of a person's characteristic level of n Achievement. Such a statement sounds much better than the one with which we started in Equation 3, but wherein does its extra value lie? This is the crux of the theoretical problem.

Actually, as MacCorquodale and Meehl have pointed out (1948), such a term as n Achievement, which was invented to interpret the data, may have two quite different meanings. We may use it first as an intervening variable which has no more meaning than the operations which gave rise to it. That is, n Achievement is simply a TAT score derived in this particular way, no more and no less. If we want to relate some other response to n Achievement, we simply relate it to the TAT score, which is what defines n Achievement.

Perhaps some other examples will serve to illustrate this possible use of a construct more fully. The term *intelligence* is often used in much this sense by some people. When someone says, "Intelligence is what the intelligence tests measure," the term *intelligence* is being used as an intervening variable. What this statement means is that *intelligence* has *no meaning* other than that given by intelligence-test scores. Or, to put it in another way, the common-sense meanings attached to the word *intelligence* are ruled out. To take one other example, a Rorschach worker might say that creativity is M (the movement response) on the Rorschach Test. That is, M is the defining operation for the term *creativity* when used technically. The virtue of such intervening variables is that they may serve to summarize a variety of situations and abstract them under one single heading. But it should be pointed out that the label X, Y, or Z, or some obscure Greek word, might just as well be applied to such an abstraction when the concept is limited in this way wholly to the operations which define it.

Actually, of course, when psychologists use such terms there is almost always "surplus meaning" attached to them. MacCorquodale and Meehl properly insist (1948) that when a term is used in this way it be called something else. They suggest the term *hypothetical construct.* The concept *creativity,* for example, clearly implies or suggests other operations than seeing movements in static inkblots. This is illustrated by Rust's study (1948), in which he attempted to discover if creativity as measured by "ratings of color and pencil drawings by art supervisors" (1948, p. 397) was correlated with the M response on the Rorschach. Obviously he was led to do this research by the surplus meaning inherent in the term *creativity.* Since he found no relationship, the Rorschach testers have the choice of choosing another term to describe M on the Rorschach or of arguing that they were using the term in its strict operational sense and did not mean to imply the kind of creativity which Rust tested. This particular argument over the M response does not concern us here except as it indicates that the meaning of such terms as *creativity* should be clearly stated wherever possible by the people who use them. Historically the most rapid advance in theory would seem to occur when someone hits on a lucky hypothetical construct which has a number of implications which can be tested. MacCorquodale and Meehl illustrate how this happened in physics: "Thus beginning with the hypothesis that gases are made up of small particles which obey the laws of mechanics, plus certain approximate assumptions about the relation of their sizes to their distances, their perfect elasticity, and their lack of mutual attraction, one can apply mathematical rules and eventually, by direct substitution and equation, lead without arbitrariness to the empirical equation $PV = K$." (1948, p. 97.) Once again, the ultimate value of this physical model or hypothetical construction is not our concern here. But we can see how an assumption about the existence of small particles and their various properties led to some useful (at least, for the moment) explanations of empirical relationships actually found in experiments.

How would this same procedure work with the hypothetical construct n Achievement just developed? Quite obviously this term was chosen rather than *abracadabra,* for instance, because it has surplus meaning. What are some of these implied meanings of n Achievement? For purposes of exposition we can state two implied assumptions about the nature of n Achievement which will then be used to deduce, in a very incomplete way, certain additional empirical relationships.

A. n Achievement is a learned result of experiences of success and failure.

1. Younger children should show less consistent TAT shifts in response to ego-involving instructions than older ones.
2. Different patterns of parent behavior especially in regard to independence training should produce discernible differences in TAT n Achievement scores in adulthood.

B. n Achievement is a central excitory state which is more easily aroused by some cues than others.

3. n Achievement should lower recognition thresholds to achievement-related words. This follows from a knowledge of the nature of central excitatory states (cf. Morgan, 1943) and suggests that there should be a relationship between TAT n Achievement score and recognition thresholds for achievement-related words. Such a relationship has been found to exist (McClelland and Liberman, 1949).
4. n Achievement should produce changes in imagination or performance which are similar to those produced by other, similarly aroused central excitatory states. Because learning has been similar, we may infer that other central excitatory states corresponding to different motives, like hunger and insecurity, may produce some of the same effects on imagination as n Achievement does (cf. McClelland, Clark, Roby, and Atkinson, 1949).

Such consequences of the use of the construct n Achievement and its surplus meanings should be taken as merely illustrative of the way in which theory can develop. Obviously no attempt has been made to deduce the theorems rigorously from the premises. The whole development of theory in the early stages is so tentative that it is a waste of time, at least in the beginning, to become more rigorous than the state of knowledge warrants. The theorizing must be kept flexible enough to make such changes as new experiments require. But, on the other hand, it must not be kept so flexible that *any* experimental result can be explained simply by adding an *ad hoc* property to the concept. Criticism of many psychoanalytic interpretations is directed precisely at this point. No one should object to the surplus meanings implicit in such concepts as super-ego or libido, but one can object to the ease with which these surplus meanings are added or subtracted to fit any troublesome fact. This does not lead to increasing precision in the determination of psychological laws. For example, the surplus meaning involved in the term *libido* has often been of a hydraulic character; that is, the libido may be spoken of as being dammed up, diverted, finding subterranean channels for expression, etc. There can be no objection to stating these properties of the libido explicitly if the theorist sticks to them rigorously and discards or refines them as the data require.

One of the most difficult problems in psychological theory arises from the illegitimate personal meanings which attach themselves so easily to its constructs. For example, someone might easily add the following meaning to n Achievement:

C. n Achievement level is what a skilled clinical psychologist judges it to be after prolonged study.

The difficulty with such a proposition is that it is not open to any kind of testing until the operations on which the clinician bases his judgments are known. Often the clinician may object to specifying any particular operations since they may do violence to his overall impression, but so long as he does not, the construct *n Achievement* has no utility in psychological theory, no matter how useful it may continue to be in clinical practice. Subjective or phenomenological meanings like this attach themselves readily to psychological concepts. They do have some value in calling up some of the initial areas for study (cf. MacLeod, 1947) but usually it is very difficult to make them stay put, that is, to state their properties in such a way as to be able to draw consistent deductions from them. In the present instance, the deduction which might be drawn from assumption C is that clinical ratings of n Achievement should be directly related to the TAT measure of n Achievement. This is unfortunately not true (Clark and McClelland, 1950). It then becomes difficult to know what to do next if the basis for the clinical judgment is not known. Fortunately in this case some other data in the Clark and McClelland study suggest what behavior the judges were using in making their ratings and so theory could continue to develop. Nevertheless many psychologists, clinical and nonclinical, will continue to feel that some people who rank high on the TAT measure of n Achievement are not "really" high on n Achievement. What lies behind that word "really" are some implicit operations for measuring n Achievement which must be made explicit before progress can be made. Often when they are made explicit it appears that they belong to some other construct which is interacting with n Achievement.

Concepts Leading Readily to the Formulation of General Laws. In Chapter 3 we discussed which concepts were adequate and which ones were not, and the criteria by which we could decide whether or not a concept was valuable. Have we added anything to this discussion? Our attention has turned from the adequacy of a concept within a given field of data to what might be called its theoretical integrating power. Then we spoke of such criteria as completeness, economy, and consistency. Now we are talking about the ease with which primary principles or postulates can be added to a concept which has been judged adequate according to the former criteria. It is these primary principles or postulates like A and B in our n Achievement example which are used to mediate deductions about empirical relations between responses. To return to our example from physics, the particle concept may fulfill all the criteria of completeness, economy, etc., but it becomes useful theoretically when we can add to it the guessed-at assumption that it obeys the laws of mechanics. So we must choose our concepts not only with regard to the adequacy with which they represent specific data but also with regard to the ease with which they suggest postulates or principles which can be used to mediate further deduction.

The question naturally arises as to where we are going to get these wonderful constructs and the principles that go with them. Psychology, like any other science, will probably have to wait for its Galileo, Newton, Einstein, or Gibbs, but in the meantime there are a few clues which should be of help in selecting constructs.

1. First of all, a construct should be chosen which functions according to the principles of learning. The history of psychology to date has certainly indicated that concepts which have had the properties of innate dispositions, drives, instincts, or what not have little theoretical fertility. The reason appears to be that a "hereditary given" does not suggest additional principles, but stalls thinking instead with a kind of "first cause" which cannot be looked into further. On the other hand, we now know a great deal about the

way in which a person learns, and to say that a construct like n Achievement has been acquired according to the principles of learning is in fact to suggest a great many properties which may be applicable to n Achievement.

2. In the second place, a construct should not have properties which are inconsistent with the known characteristics of neural mechanisms. Neurophysiology may not always tell us what the "surplus meanings" of our variables should be but it *can* eliminate certain properties as impossible, and it may suggest some useful additional ones. Psychologists have argued much about the usefulness of neurology to their science, but the fact remains that any hypothetical state attributed to the organism must operate within the limitations of the nervous system. Looking back at our example of n Achievement, we can readily see that the first principle stated was based on learning and the second on neurophysiology. One of the difficulties with a concept like *libido* is precisely that it did not operate according to the principles of learning (except in such reformulations as have been given it recently by Fromm, Horney, and others) nor did it operate according to known principles of neurophysiology.

3. A theoretical construct should not only fit into the two basic fields of psychological knowledge, it should also, wherever possible, take into consideration the findings of phenomenology, abnormal psychology, and cultural anthropology. Psychologists have argued much about the value of introspective, phenomenological data. In recent years they have tended to discard them except for some recent protests such as that by MacLeod (1947). Despite this, it is reasonably certain that no psychology of personality will be complete that does not adequately theorize about the nature of personal experience. And as we have seen in Chapter 2, it is quite possible to study this personal experience objectively through personal documents, Thematic Apperception Test records, etc. Furthermore, so many facts have been collected by psychiatrists and psychoanalysts working in the field of abnormal psychology that it would seem prodigal for personality theory not to make use of their many findings. Finally, recent advances in cultural anthropology and sociology have clearly delineated many of the interrelationships between man and his social institutions. After all, nearly all social facts are also personal facts. Roles, customs, the nature of social obligations and relationships must exist in the minds of the men making up the society. It would therefore seem essential that any complete theory

of personality take account of such social facts and findings. To return once again to our example, it is certain that n Achievement will be a more useful theoretical construct when postulates can be added to it which relate it to the phenomenology of striving, to abnormal instances of overriding ambition, such as Alexander describes (1942), and to cultural norms as to what constitutes achievement. The fact that such postulates cannot be formulated very well at this stage is an illustration of the inadequacy of our knowledge in these areas.

Application of General Laws to the Individual Case. One of the knottiest problems in the psychology of personality is the relationship between general laws such as we have been discussing, laws which are established for groups of individuals, and their application to the individual person. Allport (1942) has dramatized this difficulty by pointing out that there would seem to be two kinds of laws: laws dealing with regularities in the behavior of groups of people which he calls "nomothetic" after Windelband, and laws dealing with regularities within the individual case which he refers to as "idiographic."

Most laws in psychology would seem to be nomothetic. For example, we discover that under certain conditions a majority of the subjects remember incompleted tasks better than completed tasks. Or we discover that subjects who score high on TAT n Achievement also tend to score high on the middle section of an anagrams test. But there are always some subjects, sometimes a substantial minority, who do not show the expected relationship. What are we to make of George, who remembers more completed than incompleted tasks? Of what use is the general principle in explaining his behavior? Allport puts it this way (1937, p. 4): "The piling of law upon law does not in the slightest degree account for the pattern of individuality which each human being enfolds. The *person* who is a unique and never-repeated phenomenon evades the traditional scientific approach at every step. In fact, the more science advances, the less do its discoveries resemble the individual life with its patent continuities, mobility, and reciprocal penetration of functions."

Although Allport despairs of using such nomothetic laws for the study of the individual personality, he does suggest that laws are possible within a given person. These idiographic laws are not based on frequency of occurrence in a population and may or may not be related to such nomothetic laws. Let us look at this important theo-

which describes more closely. Is there any connection between these two kinds of laws? Are nomothetic laws of any use whatsoever in analyzing the individual case?

Allport strongly stresses this point. "What [illegible] the nomothetic [illegible] is the very real possibility that no two lives are alike in their motivational processes" (1962, p. 57). What he appears to suggest by this statement and elsewhere is that the very concept which we use to describe one person may not be applicable or useful in describing another person. He argues that it is a mistake to assume there are "a few motives common to all men." Specifically this might mean that whereas n Achievement is a useful concept for describing the responses of groups of people, and while it might be useful in describing one person, it may not be applicable at all to another person. For the other person we would have to develop some new construct. If this viewpoint is pushed to the extreme we get into a very perilous situation for a science of personality. If we must always use entirely different constructs to conceptualize different people, then we would soon be lost in a maze of particularity and no science of personality would really be possible.

This is not to deny the possibility that a psychologist could spend his entire career studying one individual person. He could develop a theoretical system which would account adequately for that person's behavior in all its respects, a theoretical system which would meet all the criteria which we have set up for a good one. Such an effort would be interesting, it might be scientific, but it would be of little value, because it is a private enterprise and would appear to be useful to the extent that it can develop theoretical systems which are applicable to more than one individual.

Yet we are still faced with the difficulty about general laws applying to the individual case. Fortunately there is another approach to the problem. We need not conclude that we must have two different kinds of laws. We may need only to make an idiographic application of a nomothetic law or laws. A physicist does not argue that the law of gravity is of no utility in understanding the individual case because a single feather dropped from the leaning Tower of Pisa does not fall as it ought to according to this law. Instead he accepts the general nomothetic law and makes special measurements to apply it to the individual feather. Analogously the specifications of a particular bridge, say the Golden Gate bridge, are "a unique and never-repeated phenomenon," but they are all applications of the same general nomothetic laws of physics.

[illegible]

Reasons Why Every Person Does Not Behave in Accordance with a General Psychological Law.

1. [illegible]

[illegible]

retical problem more closely. Is there any connection between these two kinds of laws? Are nomothetic laws of any use whatsoever in studying the individual case?

Allport certainly doubts it at times. *"What for the nomothetist is hard to contemplate is the very real possibility that no two lives are alike in their motivational processes."* (1942, p. 57.) What he appears to suggest in this quotation and elsewhere is that the very concept which we use to describe one person may not be applicable or useful in describing another person. He argues that it is a mistake to assume there are "a few motives common to all men." Specifically this might mean that whereas n Achievement is a useful concept for handling the responses of groups of people, and while it might be useful in describing one person, it may not be applicable at all to another person. For the other person we should have to develop some new construct. If this viewpoint is pushed to the extreme we get into a very perilous situation for a science of personality. If we must indeed use entirely different constructs to conceptualize different people, then we would soon be lost in a maze of particularity and no science of personality would really be possible.

This is not to deny the possibility that a psychologist could spend his entire career studying one individual person. He could develop a theoretical system which would account adequately for that person's behavior in all its respects, a theoretical system which would meet all the criteria which we have set up for a good one. Such an effort would be interesting, it might be scientific, but it would be of little value. Science is a public enterprise and would appear to be useful to the extent that it can develop theoretical systems which are applicable to more than one individual.

Yet we are still faced with the difficulty about general laws applying to the individual case. Fortunately there is another approach to the problem. We need not conclude that we must have two different kinds of laws. We may need only to make an idiographic application of a nomothetic law or laws. A physicist does not argue that the law of gravity is of no utility in understanding the individual case because a single feather dropped from the leaning Tower of Pisa does not fall as it ought to according to this law. Instead, he accepts the general nomothetic law and makes special measurements to apply it to the individual feather. Analogously the specifications of a particular bridge, say the Golden Gate Bridge, are "a unique and never-repeated phenomenon" but they are all applications of the same general nomothetic laws of physics.

But such analogies as these may be misleading. Let us take, instead, a concrete instance of a general law and try to apply it to an individual case, and see what happens. We may take the R–R law mentioned above, namely, that subjects with high TAT n Achievement scores tend to score high in the middle portion of an anagrams test, a relationship which we have explained by reference to a hypothetical construct n Achievement with certain properties. Now this relationship is actually statistically represented by a correlation of the order of +.40. This is significant and could not have occurred by chance, but it quite obviously means that there will be many individuals who do not obey this "law." We may well ask, why not? And if not, what good is the law? At least, what good is it as far as this particular person is concerned who does not obey it?

Reasons Why Every Person Does Not Behave in Conformity with a General Psychological Law.

1. The first and most important reason is that *we may not have tested the law in question,* at least so far as George is concerned. That is, we may not be measuring, in George's case, the responses to which the law refers. In any psychological law there are implicit assumptions as to the conditions under which it will hold true. One of the most important of these assumptions, for example, is that the subject be naive, at least with respect to the relationship under consideration here. It may be that George has read a book on psychology and knows what the TAT is supposed to be measuring. Or he has somehow misunderstood the instructions on the anagrams test and is trying to make only four-letter words. Obviously either of these situations represents *a radical departure from the conditions under which the law is supposed to hold.*

In fact, it is possible to get group laws *only* on the assumption that the impact of the conditions of the experiment or test are approximately the same for the whole group of subjects. When we ego-involve some students by certain instructions and find certain changes in their TAT stories, we shall always find some individuals who do not show these changes. One logical possibility always is that we have not succeeded in producing the ego-involved situation for those subjects. But the assumption is still legitimate that, had those subjects been ego-involved, they would have shown the same TAT story characteristics as the other subjects did. This is exactly analogous to saying that the feather would have acted according to the law of gravity if it had been in a vacuum, which is the condition under which the law holds. In other words, it is still proper to assume that the relationship would hold in *every* individual case if it were possible to reproduce in every case the conditions under which the law is supposed to hold. We might have to go to some extraordinary means to ego-involve a given individual in order to test the law, especially if he were informed of the tricks of psychologists, but we should not prematurely conclude that the law does not apply to his case without making such an *individualized* attempt to test the law's applicability.

The real gap between nomothetic and idiographic laws has often arisen from the fact that psychologists have not taken the trouble to make an individual determination of a general law. If one is interested in the individual person, or the individual bridge, he must make individual determinations of the general laws of personality or physics. It is quite true that the individual *combination* of measurements of different variables may be absolutely unique for a particular person, but it is not necessary to conclude that therefore we actually need different variables or different concepts to explain or account theoretically for different lives. The psychologist interested in establishing general principles or nomothetic laws in personality cannot take the time usually to determine the meaning of every individual test situation for every person taking the test, but this is exactly what the student of any *one* person must do if he is to make use of general laws in the individual case. Concretely a clinical psychologist, knowing the nomothetic relationship established between n Achievement and the tendency to perform well in the middle of the task, and knowing that this person has misunderstood the anagrams test, can nevertheless easily think up another test to which the general principle should apply. The general theory may have been developed from groups of people *for reasons of economy,* but its ultimate application is always to the individual case.

2. In the second place a law may not hold for a given individual response because *there is more than one law determining the response in question.* For example, aggression is not only a function of the strength of the instigation frustrated but also of the fear of punishment (cf. Dollard *et al.,* 1939). Thus, if a group of people were frustrated at a given strength of instigation and only 70 per cent of them showed aggression, we would not conclude that the relationship between strength of instigation and frequency of aggression does not hold for some people. We would correctly conclude that in order to explain the occurrence or nonoccurrence of aggres-

sion in an individual case, we should need to know *both* the strength of the instigation frustrated *and* the fear of punishment. The 30 per cent who did not obey the law were those presumably in whom the fear of punishment was sufficiently high to inhibit aggression. At least this is a hypothesis to be tested. Correspondingly, even though the conditions under which the TAT and anagrams scores were obtained were faultless, it might still be true that a person with a high TAT n Achievement score might not show a high mid-anagrams score if there are, other factors determining score on anagrams, such as ability, for instance. Far too much despair over the inapplicability of general laws to individual cases has arisen in psychology because the laws in question are *single-variable* laws, whereas it is reasonably certain that any particular response in any given person is actually a function of a number of variables in several different laws.

3. There is still another reason why a general law may not hold in an individual case: *the general law may really be incorrectly stated.* For example, for a long time there was a general empirical law in medicine which stated that there was a correlation between night air and malaria. It was discovered that people who closed their windows at night did not get malaria as often as people who left them open. This law did not hold perfectly in individual cases. In fact Mr. Smith might be quite justified in concluding that it was no law at all if he woke up with malaria one morning after having kept his windows closed tight every night for the preceding year. The reason for the inapplicability of the law in this case is obvious. Night air is associated with mosquitoes to some extent, and so the general empirical law had a certain approximate validity, but it was not until the law was correctly stated by identifying the mosquito that it could be said to have anywhere near perfect application to the individual case. Thus we may find that n Achievement is not the best explanation of the correlation between TAT n Achievement scores and anagrams scores, and when we do find the real connection we may be able to make a much better prediction of an individual's score on the two tests.

In short, we find that the situation is not nearly so bad as it might appear at first glance. There are many ways in which general laws may be applied to individual people. Underneath all this lies the scientist's faith that he can arrive at a general conceptual theoretical system which will enable him to account for the behavior of one individual person. He recognizes that the combination of determinations for each individual may be unique, but he reserves the right to use a common theoretical framework for all.

Derivation of General Laws From Individual Cases. The relationship between the general and the particular is not a one-way street. It is just as likely that a general law may be suggested by a relationship discovered in an individual case, as it is the other way around. In fact, one could make a very good case, as Allport does (1942), for the study of individual cases as a source of suggestions for general laws. This technique has been followed to a very great advantage by Freud and his psychoanalytic followers. Nearly always Freud's important theoretical concepts were suggested by the study of one individual. For example, he apparently arrived at his concepts of resistance and repression from the attempt to cure Dora (Breuer and Freud, 1895), and his theory of the Oedipus complex from his study of Little Hans (1909). The value of such an approach is perhaps illustrated by the fact that although nomothetic psychologists worked intensively at one time with questionnaire studies of likes and dislikes among large groups of people (cf. Pressey, 1921), they did not arrive at any general theory of the nature of ambivalence. Yet Freud and his followers very early arrived at the conclusion that love and hate of the same object produced feelings of guilt. In fact, it is rather hard to imagine how this general principle could have been arrived at from a nomothetic study of a large number of people's responses, but on the other hand it is easy to see how it could be arrived at from the study of one or two individuals.

To take one further example, students of personality have often tried to discover whether there are any differences in the traits of first- as compared with second-born children. The usual conclusion is that birth order has no significant relationship to personality characteristics. Yet the followers of Adler, studying individual cases, came to the conclusion that second-born children tended to develop traits that were consistently different from those of the first-born child. Such a conclusion might have been arrived at by correlating various trait scores of first- and second-born children using the nomothetic approach, but the point is that this, in fact, was not done, and the hypothesis was arrived at more quickly by the study of individual cases.

We are not here concerned with the validity of such hypothetical relationships. In fact, one of the great weaknesses of the psychoanalytic approach has been to generalize far too widely on the basis of a relationship found within a single individual. As Sears points out (1943), the Oedipus complex in its pure form probably exists only in a minority of male children in Western civilization, to say nothing of male children in other cultures. Yet it was common practice for Freud and his followers to assume it was universal. The point is that hypotheses arrived at from the study of individual cases are not necessarily more valid than those arrived at through studies of groups of people, but they may be suggested more readily that way and then be tested for their generality. It would be possible, but not very feasible, to test the hypothesis at the nomothetic level that love and hate toward the same person lead to feelings of guilt. Thus one might secretly arrange with the mothers of twenty college boys to write their sons on the same day that Dad had run off with another woman. If this were done, one might reasonably suppose that if these boys were given a Thematic Apperception Test the assumed correlation between love, hate, and guilt might be discovered. But the fact is, the group approach to the general principle would be cumbersome, to say the least, and a much quicker and probably more valid approach would be through the study of individuals who had reason to love and hate the same person.

A Note on Determinism. So far we have gone boldly ahead with the assumption that we could account for a person's behavior by erecting a theoretical superstructure along the lines suggested in this chapter. Someone is sure to wonder whether this means that the scientist studying personality believes that he can account for everything. Does he seriously believe that he can ever, even if he knows everything, explain a person in his entirety? Is there to be no mystery left? After all, doesn't a person seem to have free will, and if he can arbitrarily choose what he is to do next, what chance has the scientist, with all his theoretical superstructure, to account for this "spontaneous" behavior? Such questions as these arise very insistently for the scientist who is interested in studying the individual person.

There are really two separate issues involved in such questions as these. First, is man free or is he determined? Such a question of course has all sorts of moral and philosophical implications, but what precisely does it mean in terms of the theoretical framework we have just developed? As we look back over the chapter, we may well ask where the concept of cause has entered into our theorizing. When we postulated n Achievement to account for an empirical correlation between two responses, did we mean to imply that n Achievement caused those two responses? When phrased in this way, it becomes evident that the question is somewhat irrelevant. In fact, it is the view of some contemporary philosophers (Whitehead, 1925) that the whole notion of causality is traceable to what has come to be regarded as a misconception of nineteenth-century physics. Freud would probably trace it to a kind of primitive animism, to a desire to attribute power or force to our hypothetical constructs (cf. Totem and Taboo, 1918). Somehow the whole concept of causality seems quite irrelevant when applied to a construct like n Achievement which was invented for theoretical purposes. We can say that n Achievement accounts for the observed phenomenon or correlation, but it seems incorrect to say that n Achievement causes the correlation, at least in any "forceful" sense. Part of this misconception undoubtedly arises from the fact that early empirical laws in psychology were S—R laws, in which it seems possible to refer to the relationship as a causal one in the true nineteenth-century manner. If the experimenter does something to the person, the person reacts in a specifiable way. It is as if the *control* of the experimenter over the subject's response gives a special meaning to the word *cause*. As our analysis has shown, however, even this type of law, just like the R—R law, contains an implicit hypothetical construct which has certain properties or operates according to certain principles or postulates. A theoretical system made up of hypothetical constructs seems to leave out the notion of causality altogether, at least in the sense in which the term is commonly used in discussions of this sort. A system like ours will enable someone to predict with increasing success what a person will do on the basis of other things he has done, but it seems incorrect to say that the system therefore *caused* him to behave that way. There are philosophers who argue that increasing precision of predictions is the only valid meaning that causation has, but they are not usually the ones who worry about whether behavior is determined or not. Consequently we can only say with respect to the free will *vs.* determinism controversy that the issue is based partly on a misconception of the nature of causation in theory construction. The reason for this "misconception" is, however, deeply rooted in the conception of the self (cf. Chapter 14).

The second and related issue is whether or not we can predict a man's behavior with any degree of certainty from our theoretical formulation of his personality. We can assert that if our theoretical system is finally perfect, we should be able to *account* for everything that the person does, but does this mean that we can always *predict* what he will do? As far as predicting for everyday life is concerned, the answer must of course be a qualified *no.* We cannot predict what a person will do for an unspecified situation, any more than a chemist can predict what a known chemical will do when it meets with an unknown chemical under unknown conditions (next Thursday at 3 P.M.). However, to the extent that we can ascertain ahead of time what the situation will be to which a chemical or a person is responding, our predictions should become progressively more accurate. As we have already noted, a law cannot be expected to hold in the individual case unless the conditions which the law presupposes obtain. *If we know those conditions,* we should be able to predict accurately. Thus we can predict with almost 100 per cent certainty that Mr. P. will shave tomorrow morning. This is because we know with reasonable certainty the conditions which will obtain for him tomorrow morning. Of course if he knows we have made the prediction, he is very likely not to shave to prove his "free will," but this constitutes a change in the expected conditions.

Similarly, it is relatively easy to make predictions about controlled laboratory situations. From our knowledge of George we may predict with very reasonable certainty that he will show a better memory for completed than for incompleted tasks in the standard situation used for testing the Zeigarnik effect (1927). In fact, it is one of the best tests of the adequacy of our theoretical conception of a man's personality to predict in a controlled situation like this what he will do. What this adds up to is that since many situations can be specified with reasonable accuracy in advance, we can make a lot of rather good predictions about an individual's behavior, but to the extent that we cannot anticipate the future, there will always be an element of uncertainty in the prediction of an individual's behavior. This is a practical limitation, rather than a theoretical one. If a psychologist were to be given, along with his supposed knowledge of George, the gift of complete foresight as to exactly what will happen to George at a given moment in the future, he should be able to predict what George would do. But since this gift of foresight will probably not be granted, at least until the Duke experimenters learn a whole lot more about "precognition," prediction for everyday life is bound to have a considerable element of uncertainty in it.

The fact remains, however, that the scientist working in the field of personality feels that he should be able to account, with his theoretical system, for everything that the person has done. Once the event has occurred and the subject has responded to it, the theoretical picture should account for it. Such complete theoretical pictures as this do not, of course, exist at the present time. But they are the goal of the scientist working in the field of personality.

The Personality As a Whole. The goal of the psychology of personality is a completely adequate theoretical picture of the single person. We will therefore need general laws like the laws of physics, but general laws that are tested for validity by their application to the individual case just as the laws of physics are. Theoretically there seems to be no qualitative difference between applying a general law to a particular phenomenon in any of the sciences. But, while this might hold true for applying *one single law* to an individual, can we ever hope to apply enough laws to him to get an over-all picture of his personality which is of any value whatsoever? Granted that we shall never by this method give a picture with the kind of "life" and "value" discussed in Chapter 3, we should consider the possibility seriously advanced by some psychologists that such an analytic procedure is of no value at all, not even for prediction purposes.

Allport, as usual, has high-lighted the problem by providing us with a dramatic contrast between analytical and intuitive approaches to personality. Representative of the analytical approach is what he calls "differential psychology." In this approach the person is represented by a series of scores which show his standing on a number of tests relative to a group of individuals who have taken the tests. Such a procedure is quite common in educational and vocational guidance. Sometimes the scores may be connected by a line giving an over-all profile or psychograph. Anyone who has tried to get a theoretical picture of a person from such a psychograph can well agree with Allport that the task is difficult, if not impossible. Allport sums this approach up as follows (1937, p. 9): "Differential psychology has not at all treated the individual as a special *combination* of capacities, accomplishments and tendencies. It has done nothing more than to imply that a person is a simple sum-total of his departures from the average." In contrast to this extreme, there are the more intuitive approaches based on direct perception, empathy, or understanding of the total personality.

The Advantages of Intuition. It is not difficult to show that less analytical approaches are, superficially at least, more successful. One of Allport's students, Polansky (1941), wrote up the same case history in six different modes, including the differential psychology mode and a "structural" mode. He found that the judges much preferred the structural mode and were able to use it more successfully in predicting subsequent behavior of the individual in question. J. G. Miller (1942) tells an interesting anecdote which high-lights the advantages of intuition over analysis. A young lawyer was advised always to make his decisions in terms of his own best judgment and not analytically in terms of his knowledge of the principles of law. He followed this advice and became very successful as a judge, handing down decisions which were famous all over the legal world. Eventually he became so impressed with his success that he thought he ought to try to give the reasons for some of his decisions for the benefit of future generations of jurists. However, when he did, in fact, write out the bases for his decisions, their absurdity was obvious to everyone and he only appeared ridiculous in the eyes of the whole legal profession. Similarly the theoretical psychologist, with his tools of analysis and inference, must often appear ridiculous in the eyes of really good clinical judges of personality who are not forced to give the reasons for their judgments.

At times psychologists have pitted the opinion of a good intuitive judge against the best prediction that could be made on the basis of theoretical knowledge. For example, it is common practice for colleges and universities to develop multiple regression equations based on aptitude scores and high-school grades which will predict the success of an applicant as far as grades in college are concerned. These equations are developed at the cost of a tremendous amount of clerical and statistical labor, but usually the correlation between predicted grades and actual grades does not run over +.60. At Wesleyan University it was common practice for the Director of Admissions to make an estimate at entrance of what each freshman's average would be. Naturally he based his prediction on his knowledge of high-school grades, aptitude-test scores, and many individual personal factors. It turned out in this instance that the judge's predictions correlated about +.80 with the actual grades of the freshman class. Here the human judge was considerably superior to a multiple regression equation based on analytical knowledge used at the same college. Sarbin (1944) has reported instances in which the reverse is true. But this is to be expected because judges differ widely in their capacities for making intuitive predictions. From the practical viewpoint one conclusion might be that it is considerably cheaper to select a good judge than to go to all the trouble of working out a multiple regression equation which in the end may not do as good a job.

Such a conclusion is scarcely satisfactory from a theoretical viewpoint. Are we forced to conclude from all this that the systematic analysis of personality that we have proposed throughout this chapter is in fact inferior to the simple, direct intuitive approach? If so, scientists in this field could be accused of playing an esoteric game of analysis, of possible amusement to themselves, but of little value as far as advancement of knowledge is concerned. Certainly the question demands serious consideration.

What Units of Analysis Shall We Use? To begin with, we need to look more closely at the method of analysis. Analysis requires a breakdown of some totality into smaller units. Ever since Descartes' time, scientists have attempted to follow his advice of choosing the simplest units possible. In describing his analytic method, he states that two of his goals were "to divide each of the difficulties under examination into as many parts as possible, and as might be necessary for its adequate solution . . . to conduct my thoughts in such order that, by commencing with objects the simplest and easiest to know, I might ascend by little and little, and, as it were, step by step, to the knowledge of the more complex" (1637, p. 19). Much of the confusion and argument in psychology has been over how many parts the subject matter should be divided into and over what the simplest units of division are. Descartes merely says that he wants to divide his problem into *as many parts as might be necessary for an adequate solution.* The criticism of the intuitionists would seem to be that the analytic psychologists have, in fact, divided personality into so many parts that an adequate synthesis is no longer possible. The argument is really not over whether or not units of analysis should be used but over what those units of analysis should be.

Allport draws an excellent analogy from the psychology of perception. He points out (1937, p. 544) that prior to the development of Gestalt psychology it was common practice in the structuralist school of Titchener to view perception as the simple summation of discrete sensations. The Gestalt psychologists called attention to the primacy of form and organization, and argued that these could not be derived from simpler components any more than the property of wetness could be derived from a knowledge of the hydrogen and oxygen components of water. The battle cry of this school has been "the whole is more than the sum of the parts."

Allport applies this same approach to personality. ". . . just as geometrical designs are perceived as one unit rather than as an assemblage of discrete lines, so too there is a compulsive tendency for the mind to form pattern judgments concerning people. We cannot help view a personality as one single—if many-sided—structure." (1937, p. 544.) We can agree with Allport that certain analytical units in the psychology of personality may be poor ones to work with, just as everyone would appear to agree nowadays that the old-fashioned sensation elements of the structuralist school are of little value in understanding perception. We can agree further that the units in terms of which a personality is described according to differential psychology seem to have little theoretical value. In fact, test scores as such do not constitute a theoretical approach at all, at least in the sense in which the term *theory* is used in this chapter. In terms of our symbolic equations used earlier a test score may be represented as follows:

7. $$R = f(S_{t-n})$$

This equation has no hypothetical constructs in it. It is a pure empirical relation between an unknown set of antecedent conditions (S_{t-n}) and a response. In this respect it is inferior even to the simple S—R type of law in which the antecedent condition can be specified. Only as one adds hypothetical constructs to this empirical relationship does one begin to build a theory.

This suggests a solution to the controversy which has raged over the choice of units in the analysis of personality. The real argument would seem to be over whether the units of analysis, or hypothetical constructs, as we have called them, have been adequate. The "intuitionists" would seem to have a legitimate basis for criticism on this score, just as the Gestalt psychologists had a legitimate basis for objecting to earlier theories of perception. But it should be noted that even the Gestalt psychologists had to talk about perception in terms of some units. They chose new descriptive terms such as the laws of *good Gestalt*—closure, good continuation, similarity, etc. These were the hypothetical constructs they developed to deal with perceptual facts. The Gestalt psychologists certainly did not argue that perception was an untouchable whole in which a scientist could not distinguish different features. If so, they could scarcely have been scientists at all and could certainly not have theorized about perception, but could only have perceived. They were simply following the Cartesian principle of dividing their problem into the parts which *they* considered necessary for an adequate solution.

We can agree with Allport that "the original sensitivity to form is certainly an *a priori* possession of each individual" (1937, p. 547), but we want to know more. We want to know *what* form, in particular what aspects of form intuitive judges use in synthesizing personality. As Angyal states (1941, p. 13): "The division of the whole into smaller units can be made, therefore, in such a way that the line of division coincides with the structural articulation of the whole itself." The problem is clearly not one of avoiding all hypothetical constructs, but one of finding the right ones. Such a phrase as *structural articulation* is not much help to us in finding these constructs, but it does suggest that the discovery of such parts of a whole is possible. It may very well be that we should be guided in our choice of constructs to some extent by analogous ones developed to handle the somewhat similar problem of perception. But the main point is that the contrast between the analytic and intuitive approaches is not one of a sharp qualitative difference. Rather the real argument dissolves itself into a problem on which both sides can make a contribution.

The Analytic Units Used by a Good Intuitive Judge. Imbedded in this whole controversy is a concrete empirical suggestion for finding units of description or hypothetical constructs which may be valuable in a developing theory of personality. We have seen that judges differ markedly in their skill in judging personality. Why not study the methods that a good judge uses? It may be that he has happened to light upon the most fruitful concepts in terms of which personality can be formulated. Of course, if he tries to analyze the basis of his judgments, as Miller's jurist did, he may not be able to give the right reasons for his success. Nevertheless the psychologist, comparing his imaginative processes with those of a poor judge, may be able to draw inferences as to what the real basis for his excellence is. F. H. Allport and Frederiksen (1941) have outlined a practicable way of approaching this problem. They asked eighteen predictors to write out the response that they thought each of five acquaintances would give to a written dilemma. Then the acquaintances, in turn, were asked to write out their responses to the dilemma. It was then possible to compare the predictions with the actual responses. They found that there were wide variations in the number of successful predictions made by different judges and they were able to compare the approach of the best judges with that of the poorest judges. They suggest that the good judges were aware of goal-directed or "teleonomic" trends in the person they were judging. If this finding is confirmed one might conclude that a hypothetical construct of great value in personality theory might very well be some kind of a dynamic or motivational construct (teleonomic trend). On the other hand, if they had found that poor judges made their predictions primarily in terms of traits or qualities of the person, rather than on the basis of what the individual was "trying to do," there might be some basis for arguing that the concept of traits was not as useful in conceptualizing personality for predictive purposes. Their study is only suggestive and is cited here for its methodological value primarily.

Knowledge and Guesswork. So far we have outlined how a theory of personality consists of *empirical relations* discovered in groups of people or in one individual—empirical relations which are based on *accurate observations* accurately recorded, and which lead to the development of *hypothetical constructs* to explain the relations with the aid of some *basic postulates* or primary principles. Knowledge arrived at in this way can only be arrived at slowly and tediously. Certainly we have no reason to think that the psychology of personality has proceeded very far along this road as of today. In the meantime, what are we to do? Psychologists are required to give theoretical interpretations of personality all the time. The educational or vocational counselor, the clinical psychologist, the psychiatrist, and many others are required to make tentative formulations of personality without the kind of knowledge we have been recommending. As Angyal has so aptly put it, "Psychiatry is the application of a basic science which does not as yet exist." (1941, p. 5.)

There is, then, a sense in which intuition will be necessary for a long time to come. We shall have to guess where we do not know. Understanding a personality today involves a little knowledge, considerable inference, and a whole lot more intuition, or guessing. A distinction should be made of course between *sheer guessing* and *educated guessing*. In the present state of knowledge, much attention should be given to training good judges who can go successfully beyond their knowledge. One can use an approach like the one Allport and Frederiksen used, which requires judges to check their predictions against actual behavior. Or one can use an approach like the one Rogers is using in training nondirective counselors, in which the student counselor can hear and judge the wisdom of his actual responses in a phonographic recording. In fact, the need for good clinical judges will always exist, no matter how much knowledge the scientist may acquire about personality. There will always be room for the skillful practitioner, the person who can take scientific knowledge and apply it imaginatively to the individual case. Just as no physicist without practical experience would dream of trying to build a bridge, so we can expect that the theoretical student of personality will not necessarily be a good judge of personality or a good clinical psychologist. Theory must precede good practice, but it can never take the place of practice.

Psychological science has not actually progressed very far beyond the first impressions given by the two students in Chapter 2. Nevertheless it has been the aim of these three chapters to show the direction in which improvements have been or could be made. Knowledge of what to do next is a great advance, even though it has not yet been applied. In the remainder of this book we will attempt to apply some of these methodological principles to the actual content of the psychology of personality as it exists today. Much of our knowledge, and most of our constructs, fall far short of the criteria set up above, but the purpose of these chapters will have been satisfied, if the student can now see the way in which we can usefully add to the present content of our knowledge of personality.

NOTES AND QUERIES

1. In a summary of his findings Eysenck (1947, p. 245) makes the following statement. "The terms used in the table (suggestibility, persistence, intelligence, rigidity) are not used in a popular sense; they are operationally defined, and have reference to exact, quantitative variables. It is only in this precise sense that they ought to be understood; there is no intention to enlarge our findings beyond this limitation." When we look up the precise operational meaning of the term *persistence* as an example, we find (1947, p. 159) that it represents the length of time that a subject can hold his leg up about one inch from the seat of a chair while sitting on another chair. If Eysenck has no intention of enlarging his findings beyond the limitations of this particular test, why does he use the term *persistence* to refer to the test results? Why shouldn't he use some term like *leg control* instead?

2. Take a concept like persistence, make some assumptions about it, and suggest some testable deductions which follow from the assumptions. Can you make an assumption which relates persistence to n Achievement?

3. Consider the following statement: "The more Charlie tries to succeed, the more anticipations of failure arise and interfere with his performance." Is this an empirical law? Is it the S–R type or the R–R type of relationship? Is it nomothetic or idiographic? How would you go about measuring the variables contained in it?

4. Evaluate in the light of the principles discussed in this chapter the following statement made by Lundberg (1926, p. 61):

> (1) The case method is not in itself a scientific method at all, but merely the first step in scientific method; (2) Individual cases become of scientific significance only when classified and summarized in such form as to reveal uniformities, types, and patterns of behavior; (3) The statistical method is the best, if not the only, scientific method of classifying and summarizing large numbers of cases.

As Allport states (1942, p. 55), Lundberg elaborates this later by saying that individual cases "are, for all larger scientific purposes, quite useless, unless they can be combined and generalized into types and patterns of behavior." Do you agree? Could Lundberg's argument hold for the individual *response* and not for the individual *case*? (Cf. Sarbin, 1944; F. H. Allport, 1937; Cattell, 1946a.)

5. Evaluate in the light of principles discussed in this chapter the following statement made by Allport (1942, p. 59). In particular what is meant by the phrase "entirely peculiar"?

> No nomothetist can tell what his wife would like for a Christmas present by applying the general laws of psychology. He can make this prediction correctly only by knowing his wife's particular patterns of interest and affection. If the reply is made that such knowledge is itself generalization from the wife's past behavior, well and good, but be it noted *it is the single life that is generalized;* in other words, it is purely idiographic knowledge that is employed. A wife's delight will obey certain *laws* in her nature, but the laws may be entirely peculiar to herself.

6. Do you see any connection between our discussion in Chapter 3 of others who have a legitimate interest in people and our treatment of the problem of free will and determinism?

7. Make seven predictions about the behavior of a friend in the next twenty-four hours and report how many of them come true. Discuss.

8. Is there any particular object of scientific knowledge which is *not* a "unique and never-recurring phenomenon"? Consider a particular tree, a particular rock, a particular badger, a particular atom, all at a particular moment in time. What are the important differences between these particular objects of scientific knowledge and the particular, unique individual person?

9. Reproduced in the section immediately following is a fragment of an autobiography written by a college student whom we will call Karl. Read it through carefully and try to get an over-all intuitive picture of what he is like. Then go on to the next section and try to fill out the "Prediction Questionnaire" which deals with a test and a section of his autobiography not included in the fragment of his case history. This should give you some idea of how adequate an intuitive formulation is for predictive purposes. It will also provide a baseline against which we can calculate any improvements in conceptualization of Karl resulting from the many subsequent analyses of his personality that we will make throughout the book. When we have completed our analysis of him in Chapter 15, you can fill out the prediction questionnaire again and see whether you are better able to predict his behavior than you are now.

Autobiography of Karl

(Covering period up to college entrance)

Born: April 7, 1922 Present age: 24 Religion: Protestant Evangelical United Brethren

Grandparents

Grandmother, Grandfather } (Swiss) Grandmother, Grandfather } (German)

Aunt Uncle Uncle Mother (2nd-generation Swiss) Father Uncle Uncle Uncle Aunt (2nd-generation German)

Siblings:

Brother, age 27, married, one child
Brother, age 22
Sister died at age of 6 months

Note. The following autobiography was written while in college for a fellow student by the subject himself by following an outline provided him. The parenthetical notes were added where they seemed appropriate. They were obtained from direct questioning of the subject following an outline taken from Richards' *Modern Clinical Psychology* (1946). Dates, names, and other such data have been changed throughout to prevent revelation of Karl's true identity.

My parents are ordinary hard-working people. Neither went to high school. My grandparents came over from Germany, on my father's side; and from Switzerland on my mother's side. My father is a skilled mechanic, pipefitter, and has always made a living for his family even during the depression. My father worked at everything, brewery, butcher, in a box factory, refrigerating engineer, and is in fair financial condition. My mother is an industrious, but worrisome woman, always concerned about details. (During the depression mother took in washing.) My father is very thorough in all that he does, but is excitable and constantly worried by everyone's troubles. He is rather suspicious of the motives of others and berates the country, world, and officials of all sorts. Money matters seem to give him a great deal of concern. Neither of my parents are in good health. My mother suffers from deafness, (My mother has been deaf for the past five or six years. We obtained a hearing aid for her, but she refuses to wear it.) arthritis, and sinusitis, while my father has had a back injury which has induced arthritis. My father's chief diversion is gardening. He dislikes his present job to the point where he would like to quit and raise chickens or farm. At any rate, he seems to be quite dissatisfied with life. Neither parent goes to church. My mother reads the Bible and argues it, but my dad says very little though he claims Christianity as his faith. Nevertheless both parents are kind, rather generous, and have done quite a bit of community work in the past.

The general atmosphere of the home is comparative harmony, although details are argued about and a lot of worrying is done for nothing. (I have lived all my life with my parents and been cared for by them.) My parents love all their children; that love is reciprocal. My older brother seemed to be my father's favorite. He bears his name. My younger brother seems to be my mother's favorite. We were never given allowances and had to work after school and on Saturdays around the house. When we were younger, my parents always took time to read us the funnies and play games with us. We were not neglected, neither were we objects of over-solicitation.

My favorite parent, although my affection for both is nearly equal, was at first my mother. But after high school, my father seemed to come to the fore in my affections.

My attachment to the family was always a close one, although now I am indifferent. I always resented the fact when small that I never had the spending money other boys and girls had, but I realize that in so doing I learned the value of a dollar.

I do not resemble either parent in temperament particularly, although I have the tendency to worry about details.

Our discipline at home was fairly strict. The rod was not spared but also not used too frequently. (Punishment was by a yardstick whipping.)

We grew up to acquire a name in town as being "well-raised, well-mannered boys." The punishments received had no detrimental effect, either mentally or otherwise. They seemed to do us good.

I have two brothers, one older and one younger. There are about two and a half years between our ages. My older brother is calm, cool, and collected . . . now married, one child. He can turn his hand to anything and make a success of it. Very accomplished in music, electricity, flying, woodworking, to list a few of his achievements. My younger brother is a quiet, easygoing gent who minds his own business and is mainly concerned with having a good time. Nevertheless, he saves his money and is preparing for the future. Both are at college studying aeronautical engineering and both served in the Navy Air Corps during the war.

I feel inferior to my older brother, but superior to my younger, mainly due to my limited abilities in other fields. (I get along all right with my brothers. We fought when we were kids. Recalls having told brother to drink ink at age of four or five, and that mother was angry with him. The war tightened the bonds. We lend each other money.)

Our family circle, taken as a whole, is very loose. All grandparents are dead and I haven't seen some of my cousins and uncles for years although they live only three miles away. Two uncles, one aunt on mother's side; three uncles, one aunt on father's side.

I was born and raised in the country. Our home was comfortable, but not elaborate. The town I live in has a population of 600 people. We always had plenty to eat and good wholesome fare.

* * *

I was born on April 7, 1922. It was a natural birth. I was breast-fed. I don't recall the weaning time. I remember when I was three years old sitting before our cookstove to keep warm one bitter winter. My mother would open the oven door so that we could warm our feet.

I depended very much on my parents and felt secure with them. In fact, I was a rather timid soul and felt inclined to cry easily. Hence, my parents were a great source of refuge to me.

My development was normal. I can't recall when I walked and talked but I believe it was at the average time. (Sphincter and bowel control, normal. Enuresis, normal.) I had chicken pox at five, scarlet fever at seven, and measles at different times. (No temper tantrums recalled. Flu in high school. Measles on the 4th of July, so that my brother shot off the fireworks as I couldn't.)

A girl took care of both my brother and me when I was about three or four years old. I liked her. She used to make fudge for us and read to us.

I never had any habits such as nail biting, bed wetting, etc., but did have a temper which flared up occasionally. I always ate my food and still do. We had to eat what was on our plate and were taught never to waste any food.

I played "cops and robbers," "cowboys and Indians," and the normal games of youth. Always had friends to play with. In fact the others vied with each other for my friendship, as I was easygoing and friendly to all. Two fellows, however, had it in for me, picked on me constantly because I was rather timid, until one day my temper flared up and I beat them both up, separately. This gave me some confidence which I needed badly.

We always had rabbits, guinea pigs, dogs, and cats for pets, and I always liked caring for them.

My favorite heroes were the French Foreign Legion and knights of old. Roland was my favorite knight. I used to imagine myself as living in those days and being the hero that the knights were.

I was always cooperative and obedient, a good student, but influenced by others which sometimes led me into trouble. I was always sensitive and my feelings were and still are easily hurt.

Went to school, grammar school, at five, graduated at thirteen years of age. Very good marks, head of the class, of eighteen. I always liked geography and history. Got the best marks in those courses. Liked math. least of all, although I received good marks in it. I had many friendships, (Got along all right with the teachers.) and was regarded favorably by other boys and girls. I was always bashful around girls and was kidded a lot about it. I was very gregarious. In the younger days, third and fourth grades, I was occasionally picked on, but after a couple of fist fights, which I was goaded into, I was left alone.

In high school my marks were excellent. I was at the head of the class, in many activities, Pres. of the class for four years, on the football team, All-state guard, editor of the school paper. I worked well with all groups. My high school days were very happy and gratifying ones. I was very ambitious, wished to become a chemical engineer. I always did my work conscientiously and thoroughly and never wasted a minute. I always went to Sunday school, kept myself pure, and led a fairly model life. I graduated when seventeen years of age. I was very confident working in groups when I knew the people, received cooperation, and was usually chairman or a "wheel." I was very anxious to get ahead in the world and was ever zealous toward going to college. (During freshman year, I was pinched for stealing corn during daylight on a Halloween day. I was scared. There was a whole crowd of us. Parents sore. Stole watermelons, but didn't get caught. Everyone does it down there.)

For amusement I played sports, went to the movie shows, etc., but not as much as the average. I was sometimes more content to sit at home and read. I did a great deal of reading during my youth.

Hobbies: collected stamps and souvenirs. Sports. Photography at present. Liked to read when a kid. Didn't have the patience to build model airplanes. Played a little music on the guitar and harmonica. Took piano lessons (5) and quit or the teacher never came back. I was lazy about practicing.

I had no particular heroes. I always liked the cowboy heroes of the Westerns, Tarzan, and others in the Saturday serials. I looked up to my football coach to an extent but not too greatly.

Additional excerpts referred to in subsequent interpretations:

1. I have dreamed intensely of living a life with an ideal mate. Nothing is so satisfying as to cast oneself into a dream world, wherein you and the woman you love are together high on a windy hill, looking out upon the world. Just to hold the woman of your choice in your arms and lavish your love upon her seems to be the source of greatest delight. I particularly care for a girl typed as rugged individualism; one who is athletic as well as retaining her intrinsic femininity.

I believe one hundred percent in marriage as a noble institution. I believe that a couple can only make the most of their lives, living in harmony and satisfaction of a happy union. However, I believe in marriages where the participants are of tender years; 25 to 30 years, in my estimation is the ideal time for a man to take the step and for a woman, a couple of years younger.

* * *

2. I would like to see the world remodelled on the Christian ethical standard, the Sermon on the Mount, with the law of love pervading the hearts of men. I believe this is the answer to our social economic, political and all problems of society. I should like to take my place in such a world as a citizen of it, not necessarily as a leader, because in such a society, leaders can be dispensed with. It is an ideal society. Perfection perhaps, but it is the essence of the Kingdom of God principles. My general estimate of the social world is that it consists of a lot of selfish grasping individuals, perhaps so because of the competitive spirit or law of survival which seems to pervade our society. Nevertheless, I believe that given a chance, man will regard his fellow man with equity and be generously disposed toward him.

* * *

3. I have heard voices every once in a while starting about 5 or 6 years ago. They reoccur occasionally. I don't recall what they say. They are different people who talk ordinary talk, usually when alone. No thoughts of anyone planning to do away with me. No enemies recalled.

KARL
Prediction Questionnaire (Part I)

When he entered college, Karl took the Strong Vocational Interest Test so that we have his reactions to a good many specific questions. Circle Like (L), Indifferent (I), or Dislike (D) as you think he did. A second part of the questionnaire asks you to predict certain general aspects of his behavior and performance in college. Your answers will be compared with his actual behavior.

A. Excerpts from the Strong Vocational Interest Blank (Strong item numbers are given in the second column from the left beginning 191. etc.)

1.	191	Handling horses	L	I	D
2.	192	Giving "first aid" assistance	L	I	D
3.	193	Raising flowers and vegetables	L	I	D
4.	194	Decorating a room with flowers	L	I	D
5.	195	Arguments	L	I	D
6.	196	Interviewing men for a job	L	I	D
7.	197	Interviewing prospects in selling	L	I	D
8.	198	Interviewing clients	L	I	D
9.	199	Making a speech	L	I	D
10.	200	Organizing a play	L	I	D
11.	211	Pursuing bandits in sheriff's posse	L	I	D
12.	212	Doing research work	L	I	D
13.	213	Acting as yell leader	L	I	D
14.	214	Writing personal letters	L	I	D
15.	215	Writing reports	L	I	D
16.	216	Entertaining others	L	I	D
17.	217	Bargaining ("swapping")	L	I	D
18.	218	Looking at shop windows	L	I	D
19.	219	Buying merchandise for a store	L	I	D
20.	220	Displaying merchandise in a store	L	I	D
21.	221	Expressing judgments publicly regardless of criticism	L	I	D
22.	222	Being pitted against another as in a political or athletic race	L	I	D
23.	223	Methodical work	L	I	D
24.	224	Regular hours of work	L	I	D
25.	225	Continually changing activities	L	I	D
26.	226	Developing business systems	L	I	D
27.	227	Saving money	L	I	D
28.	228	Contributing to charities	L	I	D
29.	229	Raising money for a charity	L	I	D
30.	230	Living in the city	L	I	D
31.	231	Climbing along edge of precipice	L	I	D
32.	232	Looking at a collection of rare laces	L	I	D
33.	233	Looking at a collection of antique furniture	L	I	D

Comparison of interest between two items. Indicate his choice of the following pairs by checking (√) in the first space if he preferred the item to the left, in the second space if he liked both equally well, and in the third space if he preferred the item to the right. Assume other things are equal except the two items to be compared.

34.	321	Streetcar motorman		Streetcar conductor
35.	322	Policeman	.. .. ..	Fireman (fights fire)
36.	323	Chauffeur	.. .. ..	Chef
37.	324	Head waiter	.. .. ..	Lighthouse tender
38.	325	House-to-house canvassing	.. .. ..	Retail selling
39.	326	House-to-house canvassing	.. .. ..	Gardening
40.	327	Repair auto	.. .. ..	Drive auto
41.	328	Develop plans	.. .. ..	Execute plans
42.	329	Do a job yourself	.. .. ..	Delegate job to another
43.	330	Persuade others	.. .. ..	Order others
44.	331	Deal with things	.. .. ..	Deal with people
45.	332	Plan for immediate future		Plan for five years ahead
46.	333	Activity which produces tangible returns	.. .. ..	Activity which is enjoyed for its own sake
47.	334	Taking a chance	.. .. ..	Playing safe
48.	335	Definite salary	.. .. ..	Commission on what is done

Reprinted from E. K. Strong, Jr. *Vocational Interest Blank for Men (Revised)* with the permission of the author and the publishers, Stanford University Press.

B. Predictions about college adjustment.

Karl took Ethics, German, Mathematics, English, and Chemistry during Freshman year.

49. Karl's average grade for the year was:
(Check Honors, Average, or Below average)

A— B+ B B— C+ C C— D+

..(Honors) ..(Average) ..(Below average)

T F 50. He got an A in his Freshman year.
T F 51. He got an E in his Freshman year (flunked a course).
T F 52. He did his best work in Mathematics.
T F 53. He was elected an officer of the Freshman class.
T F 54. He played football in his Freshman year.

Roughly 75 per cent of the students receive a bid to a fraternity at the men's college which Karl attended.

T F 55. Karl joined a fraternity.
T F 56. Karl joined one of the "high prestige" fraternities.
T F 57. He tried out for the editorial staff of the college paper during his Freshman year.

58. Check how many friends you think he made.
..Few
..Average number
..Many

59. Check how deep and lasting these friendships were.
..Deep and lasting
..Average depth and duration
..Superficial and short-lived

The following items refer to his Sophomore year. He elected German, Mathematics, Physics, Spanish, and Chemistry.

60. Karl's average grade for his Sophomore year was:
(Check Honors, Average, or Below average)
A– B+ B B– C+ C C– D+
..(Honors) ..(Average) ..(Below average)

T F 61. He got an A in his Sophomore year.
T F 62. He got an E in his Sophomore year (flunked a course).
T F 63. He was elected an officer in the Sophomore class.

64. Check the amount of drinking you think he indulged in.
..Very little or none
..Average amount
..A lot

65. Check the amount of student roughhousing or fighting he was involved in.
..Very little or none
..Average amount
..A lot

66. Check the amount of heterosexual activity he was involved in.
..Very little or none
..Average amount
..A lot

67. Check the amount of time you think he spent in "bull sessions" sitting around and talking with other students.
..Less than average
..Average
..More than average

T F 68. He changed his vocational ambition during this period.
T F 69. He gave up playing football to study harder.
T F 70. He took on a lot of outside work.

Part Two

TRAIT AS A PERSONALITY VARIABLE

5

Expressive Traits

Trait psychology represents one of the earliest attempts to introduce some kind of order into the multiplicity of human responses. Its approach is simple. It consists of looking for consistencies in behavior. "The scientific evidence for the existence of a trait always comes from demonstration by some acceptable method of consistency in behavior (the consistency being not a matter of stereotyped habits, but of equivalent responses)." (Allport, 1937.) This approach to personality has been greatly favored by psychologists, probably because a trait can readily be conceived as a set of learned responses or a habit, a conception which fits it into a large framework of learning facts and theories. We shall not at this time inquire further into trait theory, but instead shall turn our attention to the kinds of data which have been handled most readily in terms of traits. Having first obtained some general notion of the empirical findings in this field, we shall be in a better position to discuss the theory of traits and to evaluate its contribution to the psychology of personality.

Physique Traits

One of the problems which has fascinated observers of human nature almost from the beginning of history is whether or not there is any relationship between physique and personality. This problem fits into our discussion here because physique is often conceived of as a determinant of consistent behavior and therefore of traits. From the time of Hippocrates, physicians, poets, and philosophers have noted an apparent correlation between physique and temperament. This view is still rather widely accepted in our culture today. We can say with Shakespeare, "Yon Cassius has a lean and hungry look," or think of Santa Claus as "fat and jolly." It is inevitable that such a widely held view should have been subjected to careful scientific study. As a matter of fact, the study has not been as careful or as scientific as it ought to have been, and many psychologists, by and large, have not been impressed with the correlations found between physique and personality variables. It is not our purpose to review this literature here because it has been very ably done in a number of other places (cf. Paterson, 1930, Sheldon, 1944, Eysenck, 1948). Instead, we shall single out for closer scrutiny one of the most careful and extensive studies done in this field, published in two volumes, entitled *The Varieties of Human Physique* by Sheldon, Stevens, and Tucker (1940), and *The Varieties of Temperament* by Sheldon and Stevens (1942).

Physique Typing. Sheldon and his associates differed from earlier workers in the field by attempting to get some quantitative measurements of different physique types. Nearly everyone who has studied human physique extensively has come to the conclusion that there are three major types of physique—the heavy-broad, the tall-narrow, and those in-between. Eysenck (1948, p. 75) has brought together in one table reproduced below some of the names given these three basic body types. The table also suggests how extensive the work in the field has been.

TABLE 5.1

Types of Physique

Author	*Leptomorph*	*Mesomorph*	*Eurymorph*
Hippocrates	Habit. Phthicus	—	Habit. Apoplecticus
Rostan (1828)	Respiratory-Cerebral	Muscular	Digestive
Carus (1853)	Asthenic	Athletic	Phlegmatic
Mills (1917)	Asthenic	Sthenic	Hypersthenic
Brugsch (1918)	Narrow-chested	Normal	Wide-chested
Bean (1923)	Hyperontomorph	—	Mesontomorph
Stockard (1923)	Linear	—	Lateral
Davenport (1923)	Slender	Medium	Fleshy
Aschner (1924)	Slender	Normal	Broad
Pende (1924)	Hypovegetative	—	Hypervegetative
Bauer (1924)	Asthenic	—	Arthritic
Kretschmer (1925)	Asthenic	Athletic	Pyknic
Huter (1928)	Empfindungstypus	Krafttypus	Ernährungstypus
Viola (1933)	Microsplanchnic	Normosplanchnic	Megalosplanchnic
Sheldon (1940)	Ectomorph	Mesomorph	Endomorph

Reprinted with permission from H. J. Eysenck, *Dimensions of Personality.* Copyright 1947 by Routledge and Kegan Paul.

Sheldon, as the table shows, is no exception in arriving at the same three basic components, but he does differ in the way he arrived at them. He developed a technique for photographing the naked male figure from three different angles under standard conditions which permitted him to study simultaneously a great number of human physiques. On the basis of his observation of some four thousand photographs of male college students he was able to select three morphological extremes. The first of these, endomorphy, "means relative predominance of soft roundness throughout the various regions of the body . . . the digestive viscera are massive and tend relatively to dominate the bodily economy." The second, mesomorphy, "means relative predominance of muscle, bone, and connective tissue. The mesomorphic physique is normally heavy, hard, and rectangular in outline." The third, ectomorphy, "means relative predominance of linearity and fragility. In proportion to his mass, the ectomorph has the greatest surface area and hence relatively the greatest sensory exposure to the outside world. Relative to his mass he also has the largest brain and central nervous system." (1940, p. 5.)

Having identified the extremes in this way, Sheldon and others next assumed that each of them was a component of every human physique. They therefore assigned ratings from one to seven for each of the three components for any given physique. Thus, for example, a physique rating of 171 represents a person who is very low in endomorphy, very high in mesomorphy, and very low in ectomorphy, whereas a 444 is a person who is average in all three components. To provide a quantitative basis for his ratings in the three components, Sheldon worked out an anthropometric technique which involved a number of measurements for seven different regions of the body, which could be made on his standardized photographs. These measurements are taken according to a carefully specified procedure and cover such things as facial breadth, trunk thickness and breadth at several different points, etc. The figures from different regions of the body are then combined into one over-all index of physique (IP), which is also referred to as a person's somatotype.

A Case: Karl. Throughout this book we shall refer again and again to our case, Karl, who, except for his fictitious name and some other changes to prevent identification, is a real person. Our procedure will be to report data on Karl which illustrates the approach to personality under discussion. In this way we shall hope to discover on the concrete level what contribution this approach can make to our understanding of an individual person. We can begin with his physique. It is described as follows by three observers:

A fraternity friend: "He is blond, slightly bald, with a sturdy build."

A teacher: "He is blond, big and muscular (square) and looks as if he'll round out with the years."

A psychiatrist: "The subject is a plethoric, ebullient, pyknic young man of obvious Teutonic origin."

There seems little doubt from these observations that Karl belongs in the heavy-boned [illegible] of physiques, although the different [illegible] to describe him. Sheldon would [illegible] more than this. Unfortunately, as we do [illegible] photographs necessary for a careful somatotype, it will be necessary to use some short cuts suggested by Sheldon, Stevens, and Tucker (1940). As an approximation we may start with his height, which is [illegible], and his weight, which varies somewhere between 180 and 185 pounds. From this we derive a height-over-the-cube-root-of-weight ratio from a table given by Sheldon (1940, p. 267). In another table he gives the somatotype most frequently associated with various indices derived in this way. We find that Karl's index is 12.3, which is associated with two somatotypes, 362 and 542. The first indicates a dominance of the second or muscular component, whereas the second indicates a dominance of the first or endomorphic component. Since Karl was a wrestler on the 165-pound class in college and was captain of his football team in high school, and since the observer describes him as muscular, we can conclude that it is much more likely that he belongs to the 362 somatotype. Of course this is only an approximation and, as Sheldon points out, it is possible that somatotypes associated with the height-weight indices may be the exception. But in this case it seems fairly accurate, especially when compared with Sheldon's description of the 362 [illegible]

[illegible] powerful physique [illegible] clearly [illegible] and muscular without being weaker. The [illegible] characteristics of [illegible] the [illegible] an increase of the first order of endomorphy. [illegible]

[illegible] that is thick and [illegible] whites [illegible] These [illegible] heavy, solid, [illegible]

This description [illegible] physique as it would be [illegible] as Sheldon; it also provides us with [illegible] good sample of the physique descriptions contained in Sheldon's [illegible]ok. Naturally questions have arisen as to the validity and particul[illegible] the permanence of a somatotype. What happens if a person [illegible] weight? Quite certainly Karl will gain weight; in fact, his face h[illegible]lready filled out, as a glance at his Freshman picture taken so[illegible]en years ago readily shows. This in turn will change the ratio [illegible]x and the associated somatotypes. Although Sheldon feels that [illegible] easiest time to make a valid somatotype is in the young adult[illegible]e, he also is strongly of the opinion that nothing, not even th[illegible]st drastic changes in metabolism, will change the basic somat[illegible]. "A 444 is not changed by nutritional disturbances to a [illegible] anything else. He only becomes a fat or a lean 444, or [illegible]n extremely fat or an emaciated and wasted 444. . . . It can[illegible]id that the case has yet to occur in which a nutritional dist[illegible] has caused a physique either to become unrecognizable or t[illegible] another somatotype strongly enough to cause any justifiabl[illegible]n." (1940, p. 221.) Recently serious doubt has been thrown on t[illegible]pinion of Sheldon's by some work of Lasker and others [illegible]udied according to Sheldon's technique the somatotypes of a nu[illegible] of men who underwent prolonged starvation at the Labo[illegible] Physiological Hygiene at the University of Minnesota. This [illegible] clearly showed that emaciation changed nearly every me[illegible]t on which the somatotype was based and produced a mark[illegible]ft in all individuals toward ectomorphy. For the time bein[illegible]ver, we will assume that the somatotype derived in this wa[illegible]od way of representing the human physique under normal n[illegible]nal conditions.

Temperament Typing. The ne[illegible]p was to derive an index of temperament which would [illegible]e associated with differences in physique. Sheldon and Ste[illegible]) went about this problem [illegible] in an empirical fashion. [illegible]cted some 650 trait descrip[illegible] which they refined through u[illegible]ion and use to some 50 traits. [illegible] then proceeded to r[illegible]me thirty-three male college [illegible] a long series of a[illegible]nterviews extending over an [illegible]. They then interco[illegible]d the trait ratings and tried [illegible]sters of traits wh[illegible]ated highly with each other [illegible] with traits in oth[illegible]sters. They found that if they [illegible]cluster correlations [illegible] least +.60 and inter-cluster [illegible] at least [illegible]30, they were able to identify three clusters [illegible] then proceeded to add traits to these three primary

There seems little doubt from these observations that Karl belongs to the heavy-broad classification of physiques, although the different observers used different terms to describe him. Sheldon would require a more precise classification than this. Unfortunately, as we do not have the standard photographs necessary for a careful somatotype, it will be necessary to use some short cuts suggested by Sheldon, Stevens, and Tucker (1940). As an approximation we may start with his height, which is 5′ 8″, and his weight, which varies somewhere between 160 and 165 pounds. From this we derive a height-over-the-cube-root-of-weight index from a table given by Sheldon (1940, p. 287). In another table he gives the somatotype most frequently associated with various indexes derived in this way. We find that Karl's index is 12.4, which is associated with two somatotypes, 361 and 542. The first indicates a dominance of the second or muscular component, whereas the second indicates a dominance of the first or endomorphic component. Since Karl was a wrestler in the 165-pound class at college and was captain of his football team in high school, and since the observers describe him as muscular, we can conclude that it is much more likely that he belongs to the 361 somatotype. Of course this is only an approximation and, as Sheldon points out, it is possible that somatotypes associated with the nearby ratio indexes may be the true ones. But in this case it seems fairly accurate, especially when compared with Sheldon's description of the 361, which runs as follows (1940, p. 209):

> The 361 is a massive and extremely powerful physique . . . closely similar to the 261, but . . . heavier and rounder without being weaker. The head is large, and some of the cubical characteristics of extreme mesomorphism have been lost in the rounding and filling out which accompanies an increment of the full degree of endomorphy. But the face is still strongly mesomorphic, with a massive bony skeleton and great muscular strength clearly predominant. The mouth is strong, straight, and firm. The jaw is square and wide. It is a face which appears as though a well-delivered blow would glance off without doing any particular damage. The trunk is long, the shoulders are broad, the thoracic girdle is powerful and erect, and the chest is deep and mobile. . . . The 361 is strongly inclined to professional athletics, but once out of his teens, he has a hard time keeping down his weight. These great muscles which are diffused with an endomorphic 3, seem as thirsty for fat as a sponge for water, and the 361 passes over to a heavy, stolid, barrel-bodied middle age.

This description not only gives us a fairly accurate picture of Karl's physique as it would be described by his friends if they were as fluent as Sheldon; it also provides us with a good sample of the physique descriptions contained in Sheldon's book. Naturally questions have arisen as to the validity and particularly the permanence of a somatotype. What happens if a person gains weight? Quite certainly Karl will gain weight; in fact, his face has already filled out, as a glance at his Freshman picture taken some ten years ago readily shows. This in turn will change the ratio index and the associated somatotypes. Although Sheldon feels that the easiest time to make a valid somatotype is in the young adult male, he also is strongly of the opinion that nothing, not even the most drastic changes in metabolism, will change the basic somatotype. "A 444 is not changed by nutritional disturbances to a 443, or to anything else. He only becomes a fat or a lean 444, or perhaps an extremely fat or an emaciated and wasted 444. . . . It can be said that the case has yet to occur in which a nutritional disturbance has caused a physique either to become unrecognizable or to simulate another somatotype strongly enough to cause any justifiable confusion." (1940, p. 221.) Recently serious doubt has been thrown on this opinion of Sheldon's by some work of Lasker and others (1947) who studied according to Sheldon's technique the somatotypes of a number of men who underwent prolonged starvation at the Laboratory of Physiological Hygiene at the University of Minnesota. This research clearly showed that emaciation changed nearly every measurement on which the somatotype was based and produced a marked shift in all individuals toward ectomorphy. For the time being, however, we will assume that the somatotype derived in this way is a good way of representing the human physique under normal nutritional conditions.

Temperament Typing. The next step was to derive an index of temperament which would presumably be associated with differences in physique. Sheldon and Stevens (1942) went about this problem also in an empirical fashion. They collected some 650 trait descriptions which they refined through inspection and use to some 50 traits, on which they then proceeded to rate some thirty-three male college students, after a long series of analytic interviews extending over an academic year. They then intercorrelated the trait ratings and tried to discover clusters of traits which correlated highly with each other and negatively with traits in other clusters. They found that if they required intra-cluster correlations of at least +.60 and inter-cluster correlations of at least —.30, they were able to identify three clusters of traits. They then proceeded to add traits to these three primary clusters until they had 20 representing each. From an inspection of these clusters they decided to name them viscerotonia, somatotonia, and cerebrotonia. "Viscerotonia, the first component, is so named because the complex of traits to which it refers is closely associated with a functional (and anatomical, we now know) predominance of the digestive viscera. . . . Somatotonia, the second component, is so named because the complex of traits to which it refers is associated with functional and anatomical predominance of the somatic structures—the moving parts of the bodily frame . . . the voluntary muscles. The somatotonic individual . . . desires more than anything to do something with his muscles, to move about assertively, to conquer, to experience physical adventure in combat. The third component (cerebrotonia) was not so easy to name. . . . the prepotent activity seems to be that of conscious attention which involves an inhibition or 'crushing' of other activities of the body." (1942, p. 22). A more complete understanding of each of the three components may be gathered from Table 5.2, reproduced from their book, showing the short form of the temperament rating scale which contains the 10 out of 20 traits under each component which are most easily rated on the basis of short acquaintance with a subject.

TABLE 5.2

Shortened Scale for Temperament

Select One for Each

(1 = extreme antithesis, 7 = extreme manifestation of trait)

	Viscerotonia		*Somatotonia*		*Cerebrotonia*
(4)	Movement	(6)	1. Assertiveness of Posture and Movement	(4)	1. Restraint in Posture and Movement, Tightness
	2. Love of Physical Comfort	(6)	2. Love of Physical Adventure		
	3. Slow Reaction	(7)	3. The Energetic Characteristic		3. Overly fast Reactions
		(6)	Exercise	(3)	Privacy
					5. Mental Overintensity, Hyperattentionality, Apprehensiveness

TABLE III (Continued)

	Viscerotonia		Somatotonia		Cerebrotonia
		[illegible]	6. Love of Risk and Chance	[illegible]	6. Secretiveness of Feeling, Emotional Restraint
[illegible]	7. Love of Polite Ceremony	[illegible]	7. Bold Directness of Manner	[illegible]	7. Self-conscious Motility of the Eyes and Face
[illegible]	8. Love of Social [illegible]	[illegible]	8. Physical Courage for Combat	[illegible]	8. Fear of Social [illegible]
		[illegible]	9. Competitive Aggressiveness	[illegible]	9. Inhibited Social Address
[illegible]	[illegible] Evenness of Emotional Flow				
[illegible]	[illegible] Tolerance	[illegible]	[illegible] The Unrestrained Voice	[illegible]	[illegible] Vocal Restraint and General Restraint of Noise
[illegible]	[illegible] Complacency				
[illegible]	[illegible] The "Untempered" Characteristic	[illegible]	[illegible] Overmaturity of Appearance	[illegible]	[illegible] Youthful Intentness of Manner and Appearance
[illegible]	[illegible] Smooth, Easy Communication of Feeling, Extraversion of Viscerotonia				
[illegible]	Mean		Mean	[illegible]	Mean

Reprinted with permission from W. H. Sheldon and S. S. Stevens, The Varieties of Temperament. Copyright 1942 by Harper and Brothers.

[illegible]

According to Sheldon the scale for temperament should be used only by a person [illegible] [illegible] psychology and who has [illegible] [illegible] [illegible] [illegible] [illegible]. [illegible] [illegible] [illegible] [illegible] [illegible] [illegible] [illegible] the variables of the scale. [illegible] [illegible] [illegible] [illegible] [illegible] these variables we may choose one or [illegible]. [illegible] [illegible] and [illegible] Sheldon's descriptions [illegible] [illegible]. [illegible] [illegible] is described as "[illegible] [illegible] [illegible] [illegible] [illegible] clusters until they had 20 representing each. From an inspection of these clusters they decided to name them viscerotonia, somatotonia, and cerebrotonia. "Viscerotonia, the first component, is so named because the complex of traits to which it refers is closely associated with a functional (and anatomical, we now know) predominance of the digestive viscera. . . . Somatotonia, the second component, is so named because the complex of traits to which it refers is associated with functional and anatomical predominance of the somatic structures—the moving parts of the bodily frame . . . the voluntary muscles. The somatotonic individual . . . desires more than anything to do something with his muscles, to move about assertively, to conquer, to experience physical adventure in combat. The third component [cerebrotonia] was not so easy to name, . . . the prepotent activity seems to be that of conscious attention which involved an inhibition or 'crushing' of other activities of the body." (1942, p. 20.) A more complete understanding of each of the three components may be gathered from Table 5.2, reproduced from their book, showing the short form of the temperament rating scale which contains the 10 (out of 20) traits under each component which are most easily rated on the basis of short acquaintance with a subject.

TABLE 5.2

Shortened Scale for Temperament
Filled Out for Karl

(1 is extreme antithesis, 7 extreme manifestation of trait)

	Viscerotonia		*Somatotonia*		*Cerebrotonia*
(4)	1. Relaxation in Posture and Movement	(6)	1. Assertiveness of Posture and Movement	(4)	1. Restraint in Posture and Movement, Tightness
(4)	2. Love of Physical Comfort	(6)	2. Love of Physical Adventure		
(2)	3. Slow Reaction	(7)	3. The Energetic Characteristic	(4)	3. Overly fast Reactions
		(6)	4. Need and Enjoyment of Exercise	(5)	4. Love of Privacy
				(4)	5. Mental Overintensity, Hyperattentionality, Apprehensiveness

TABLE 5.2 (*Continued*)

Viscerotonia	*Somatotonia*	*Cerebrotonia*
	(5) 6. Love of Risk and Chance	(3) 6. Secretiveness of Feeling, Emotional Restraint
(3) 7. Love of Polite Ceremony	(6) 7. Bold Directness of Manner	(1) 7. Self-conscious Motility, of the Eyes and Face
(6) 8. Love of Society Sociophilia	(7) 8. Physical Courage for Combat	(1) 8. Fear of Society Sociophobia
	(7) 9. Competitive Aggressiveness	(2) 9. Inhibited Social Address
(2) 12. Evenness of Emotional Flow		
(5) 13. Tolerance	(6) 13. The Unrestrained Voice	(3) 13. Vocal Restraint, and General Restraint of Noise
(4) 14. Complacency		
(4) 16. The Untempered * Characteristic	(5) 16. Overmaturity of Appearance	(2) 16. Youthful Intentness of Manner and Appearance
(4) 17. Smooth, Easy Communication of Feeling, Extraversion of Viscerotonia		
(3.8) Mean	(6.1) Mean	(2.9) Mean

(Reprinted with permission from W. H. Sheldon and S. S. Stevens, *The Varieties of Temperament.* Copyright 1942 by Harper and Brothers.)

* Meaning "flabby," etc.

According to Sheldon this scale for temperament should be used only by a person who is well versed in constitutional psychology and who has interviewed and studied his subjects for at least a year. Training is necessary, as in the case of all rating scales, to familiarize the judge with the variables to be rated. To get a better idea of the nature of these variables we may choose one in particular, V-8, S-8, and C-8, and study Sheldon's descriptions more in detail. V-8, *sociophilia,* is described as "love of company. Appetite for people . . .

conviviality, and emotional delight upon being surrounded and supported by others. There is a deep, persistent craving to have people about, a rich satisfaction in being one among many, and a strong sense of loneliness and weakness when cut off from the fulfillment of this craving. The viscerotonic individual warms up and expands in company." (1942, p. 37.) In direct opposition to this we find C-8, *sociophobia,* which is associated with cerebrotonia. It means "dislike of being socially involved. Antithesis to conviviality. The individual avoids and deeply distrusts social gatherings. He is strained, distressed and uncomfortable in the face of any social relationship, especially those of a temporary or superficial nature." (1942, p. 78.) S-8, *physical courage for combat,* is described as "Courage for actual or potential combat. An essential and unquestionable physical fearlessness. Confident dependence upon the sturdiness, skill, and muscular strength of the body. The individual depends upon his soma as the viscerotonic depends upon social good-will, and as the cerebrotonic depends upon the exercise of exteroceptive acuity and wariness." (1942, p. 55.) This illustrates concretely how a given trait may have two polar opposites, although the antithesis to S-8 is conceived to be cowardice, which involves an element of both V-8 and C-8.

After becoming thoroughly familiar with the trait variables and with the subjects after a year's close study, one can rate them on each of the sixty traits, using a 7-point scale. The average rating on each of the three scales represents the rating on that component of temperament and the resulting three numbers give the index of temperament (IT) corresponding to the index of physique (IP) developed as described above.

The procedure followed here is the standard one for developing rating scales of this sort. Like all such scales, it raises two questions:

1. Are the individual traits under a given component really independent measures of that component? There is a paradox involved here. Obviously in setting up this temperament scale, the authors wanted to produce a complex of traits which related highly with one another, so that they would be measuring a unitary over-all trait function. However, in choosing traits which correlated highly with each other, what they may have been doing is selecting traits which were so similar that for all practical purposes the judges *could not discriminate among them* in assigning ratings. A look at the trait descriptions given above, or at any two traits in a given scale in Table 5.2, suggests how this overlapping may occur. Take, for ex-

ample, the first two traits under viscerotonia, "relaxation in posture and movement" and "love of physical comfort." Both the trait names and the trait descriptions given suggest that it would be a very difficult thing for a judge to discriminate between these two variables. Would it really be possible to rate someone high in love of physical comfort who did not also show relaxation in posture and movement? The fact that this did not occur, as is shown by the high positive correlation between the ratings on these two traits, does not necessarily indicate that the traits are associated in the personalities investigated. It *may* simply mean that the judge could not make two independent judgments. In other words, this procedure at times comes dangerously close to asking a judge to rate the same variable twice. This criticism is not peculiar to the particular temperament rating scale developed here, although it seems particularly applicable. Also it is not necessarily a disadvantage to ask a judge to make repeated estimates on the same variable. This may be the most reliable method of getting a valid judgment. The only danger arises when someone interprets the results as meaning the traits under consideration are really different and are correlated in the person being judged, whereas they may be simply *indiscriminable in the judge's mind.*

2. The second question arises over the reliability of the trait ratings made for this scale. Sheldon reports that they are fairly high. In eighty-three cases which he re-rated after re-interviewing them, the correlation between his first and second temperament typings was +.96. Since he might have been influenced by knowledge of his earlier ratings, he also reports a correlation with an independent observer which varied from +.81 for the first component to +.89 for the second, and +.87 for the third. This indicates satisfactory reliability of judgment made by people well trained in the technique. He also reports that people who are not very well trained do not give judgments which agree with those of a trained observer like himself (1942, p. 417).

Karl's Temperament. In Table 5.2 we have placed in front of each of the ten traits under each component the rating assigned to Karl by a fraternity brother who had known him well over a two-year period, and who was also familiar with Sheldon's trait descriptions. Once again we must be content with an approximation because the student judge was obviously not highly trained nor did he have the requisite analytical knowledge of the person, although he had made a careful study of Karl for a personality term paper. Also he used the short form of the temperament rating scale which Sheldon reports correlates with the long form somewhere between +.61 and +.73 (1942, p. 419). Recognizing all its limitations, we arrive at an index of temperament for Karl of 463, which represents the rounded mean rating on the ten traits for each of the three scales.

Physique and Temperament. Of course the primary motivation behind all of this analysis of physique and temperament has been to attempt to show the relationship between the two. As Sheldon and Stevens so aptly put it, the fascinating question is, "Can we predict a man's likes and dislikes by measuring his body?" (1942, p. 1.) A partial answer to this question is to be found in the correlations obtained between the physique and temperament components of the two indexes. They found that "the correlations between morphology and temperament are +.79 for the first component, +.82 for the second component, and +.83 for the third." (1942, p. 401.) This indicates a very high degree of relationship between the ratings of the physique component and the ratings of the temperament component. Similarly the temperament components are negatively related to each other because of the way the scales were devised and consequently are also negatively related to the other physique components. Sheldon's table comparing the physique and temperament indexes for a group of two hundred cases shows that the two are highly congruent although seldom exactly the same.

In Karl's case we note that the correspondence is fairly close. His IP was estimated at 361, his IT at 463. The first thing we note is that our judge has supplied us with an "impossible" temperament type. The components usually add up to 10 or 11, but never to more than 12. We can lay this to lack of experience with the distribution of trait elements and conclude that Karl is probably a 362 (which keeps the rank order of the three components) with a strong suggestion of what Sheldon calls "overloading." By this he means that when a person begins to get high ratings on all three components there is apt to be sharp conflict of interests and attitudes. In discussing a case of 363 temperament, for instance, he describes him as follows: "This youth has shown academic as well as general ability in numerous little false starts that he has made. But always an acute somatotonic restlessness seems to get the better of him, and then he is soon off on a new tangent. . . . In spite of having twice left college in the midst of semesters he made a respectably passing record. At present he is studying chemistry, but unsuccessfully and unhappily. He wants to be more active. . . . This case probably represents a remarkably persistent effort to harness incompatible impulses. . . ." (1942, p. 337.)

Unfortunately none of the 361 physiques reported by Sheldon had IT's like Karl's but, from Sheldon's general description and case studies of dominant somatotonia, we can get some idea of what Karl should be like. "The second component is the 'motional' element in life . . . the craving for vigorous action . . . the resolution to subdue the environment to one's own will." (1942, p. 258.) After describing a number of more or less physical characteristics of the somatotonic personality, such as eating too much, sleeping deeply, and feeling good in the morning, Sheldon goes on to say that he is liable to religious conversions, noisy, lacking in introspective insight, fond of alcohol and stimulated by it, and susceptible to routine (1942, pp. 259-265). With these additional notes as well as the rating scale, we now have a portrait of Karl based on his physique which we can check against other information as we come to it.

The Meaning of Correlations Between Physique and Temperament Traits. The interpretation of such relationships between physique and temperament is, however, fraught with difficulties. In the first place there is the problem of *bias,* as the authors of the book well recognize. That is, the people making the temperament ratings were also well aware of the physical type of the person they were rating. To what extent would they therefore be influenced in their ratings by a knowledge of physique? "It is impossible altogether to exclude this danger in the assignment of temperamental rating, for the investigator cannot make the ratings without seeing the subject, and if the investigator is well trained in constitutional methods of analysis he cannot look at a subject without somatotyping him, approximately at least." (1942, p. 392.) Although Sheldon is aware of what he calls the "halo error," he feels that his knowledge of what to expect from a given somatotype may actually make it easier for him to discriminate deviations from this expectation. Essentially his defense is that the investigator would not *consciously* introduce a correlation where there was none. In this we can believe him. However, before psychologists will be willing to draw any conclusions about physique causing temperament traits, it will be necessary to disentangle the two variables in the judge's mind. They have had too much experience with honest investigators whose unconscious expectations have tricked them. The procedure suggested by Sheldon of making the temperament ratings without seeing the subject on the basis of full case-history information would appear to recommend itself for this purpose.

But this immediately suggests another difficulty, or at least another way of conceiving the association between physique and temperament. How, in fact, could the ratings be made without seeing the subject? Most of the trait definitions include terms which refer to the subject's body. For example, S-8, *physical courage for combat,* is described as "confident dependence upon the sturdiness, skill, and muscular strength of the body" (1942, p. 55); or C-1, *restraint in posture and movement, tightness,* means "the body as a whole is carried stiffly" (1942, p. 69); or we have variables such as *youthful intentness of manner and appearance, fast or slow reaction,* etc. Would it be possible to rate such variables without seeing a person? Some of them, yes; but many of them, no. In other words, even in making the rating of a given trait, the judge must take into consideration the physique variables so that *the ratings are contaminated by body characteristics from the very beginning.* It is no wonder, then, that we find a high correlation between physique and temperament ratings. Such contaminations are extremely common in studies in which such characteristics as voice, gestures, gait, handwriting, etc., are matched against personality sketches. Frequently the sketches contain adjectives which characterize the expressive feature in question. For example, it is not so surprising that a judge will match a statement like "He is quick and restless" with a handwriting specimen which is obviously a hasty scrawl. What this proves is not so much that expressive features can be used to diagnose personality but that judges often use adjectives describing expressive features in writing personality sketches.

This suggests a re-evaluation of Sheldon's work in somewhat different terms. He was interested in discovering whether certain physiques were associated with certain temperamental differences. We have suggested that the association he discovered was put there to begin with. But this is not necessarily a disadvantage unless the association is misinterpreted as a cause-and-effect relationship. Instead we may simply conclude that it is useful to summarize certain behavioral characteristics by organizing them around physical characteristics. What we are saying is that it is useful to define certain traits largely in physical terms. For example, V-1, S-1, and C-1, referring respectively to relaxation, assertiveness, or restraint in posture and move ment, would seem to define a useful dimension for characterizing the behavior of different people. That is, we have brought together under one heading a number of gestures, postures, attitudes of the body, eye movements, etc., and called them "restraint in posture and movement." We have found a consistency in behavior and thus satisfied Allport's definition of a trait. To this consistency we give a trait name which has an obvious physique reference. Thus it would seem to be useful to refer to Karl as assertive in posture and movement, since it certainly helps to describe one aspect of his personality.

However, it is probable that Sheldon and his associates had a much grander design in mind than this. They wanted to provide a basis for the conceptualization of the whole personality sphere. They appear to argue that the sixty traits on the temperament scale are a fair representation of the different aspects of personality as a whole. Other psychologists would of course disagree with this. They would ask, where is the trait of suggestibility? Where is the concept of motivation? Where is n Achievement or n Security? Where is intropunitiveness? Or creativity? The authors of *The Varieties of Temperament* might well answer that some of these variables are in fact covered by their temperament scale or at least referred to tangentially. They might argue that sociophilia meant a need for social approval, sociophobia a deep-seated n Security, or that a somatotonic might be expected to have high n Achievement. But this does not really answer the question at issue. The point is that it may not be useful or convenient to force all the many aspects of a personality into physique-related variables. Some aspects of personality fit readily into this scheme and some do not. Some may be much more easily conceptualized in other terms.

In conclusion, we should not feel that such a scheme as they have developed is of no use for describing personality. On the contrary, it would seem quite useful for the limited purpose of summarizing behavior which is clearly related to physique. On the other hand we must not assume too much for it. One of the weaknesses of psychologists has been that whenever they develop a new measuring instrument they tend to try to generalize it to cover the whole of personality. We shall meet this tendency again and again in subsequent discussions of other approaches to personality. The term somatotonia is at once too broad and too narrow. It is too broad in including areas of personality which may be better conceptualized in other terms, and it is too narrow in assuming that wide areas of personality can best be described in physique-related terms.

In what sense does physique *cause* temperament? In much the same sense that a bicycle "causes" the trait of bicycle riding. In both cases a behavioral trait or group of traits is associated with some physical object in the environment, in one case the body. and in the other the bicycle. We name the group of traits in terms of the physical object which helps define them. Thus it is not surprising to learn that with his relatively massive physique Karl has been a successful football player and wrestler, just as it is not surprising to discover that a person interacts with a bicycle in a certain way, by pushing the pedals, holding on to the handlebars, etc. We could refer to the latter as bicycle traits. Physique undoubtedly influences sensitivity, reaction time, and movement; and also to a considerable extent determines the reaction of society to the person. Thus big, fat, heavy bodies move slowly and are of little use for fencing. On the other hand, bodies like Karl's are useful in football playing. It is therefore no surprise to learn, knowing as we do the pressure put on high-school boys to play football, that Karl has, in fact, become a football player. The determinants of such complex traits as "courage for combat" or football playing are therefore very complex. They involve social as well as physical factors. We need to know much more how these physical and social influences interact according to the principles of learning to produce some of the complex temperament traits we have discussed here. For the moment then we can come to two tentative conclusions. (1) Physique and temperament are related to the extent that the temperament traits are loaded with physique or movement terminology. (2) To the extent that the temperament traits include behavior not directly associated with physique and movement, other variables enter into their determination and have to be taken into account in "explaining" the traits. As soon as this is done it no longer becomes convenient, and in fact it may be misleading, to associate these traits too closely with a single determinant—namely, physique.

At any rate, we now know something about Karl which is important in the general picture of his personality and which we could not have obtained in any other way. What we know might have been a little more precise if Sheldon and associates had stuck to posture and movement variables and not tried to drag in so much else, but even with this limitation, they have made an important contribution to our knowledge in this field.

Movement Traits

Psychologists have been interested for a long time in a person's expressive movements in the "conviction that all the mobile features of the body are avenues for the expression of personality." (Allport and Vernon, 1933, p. 173.) Consequently psychologists have searched for consistencies, or congruences, among such features as posture, pose, movements with the hands or legs, gait, handwriting, etc. Unfortunately in the early stages of research in this field a tendency grew up for workers to divide into two completely opposed camps, one of which argued that expressive movement was the royal road to understanding personality, the other of which, led by Hull and Montgomery (1919) and others, claimed that the "facts . . . should go a long way toward counteracting the view that there is a functional unity between mind and body." (Paterson, 1930, p. 158.) The former group unfortunately did much of its research without the benefit of modern scientific methods, including statistics, and the latter was often handicapped by a too rigid interpretation of those same methods. It is only recently that a middle group of scientists has begun to develop that has investigated the problem with both an adequate theoretical orientation and a careful application of scientific methods.

Movement, as we have seen, is closely related to physique. In fact some of the early work in the field was directed at showing that men with different physiques showed different expressive movements. We have noted above that perhaps the most valid, physique-related traits are those which refer to expressive postures and movements. Thus, for example, the trait described by Sheldon under C-1, "restraint in posture and movement, tightness," has been noted by Enke (1930) in his study of psychomotor types associated with various Kretschmerian physique types. Enke's leptosome, who corresponds to Sheldon's ectomorph, tends to express himself in "movement that is hesitant, cautious, critical, tense, stereotyped. . . . It does not matter, for example, whether the typical leptosome is writing with a pen, carrying a glass of water, or reacting to music; he is found to be uniformly tense and cautious." (Allport and Vernon, 1933, p. 9.) Enke's study, as Allport and Vernon point out, was done with the usual care of the German analytic school but without the benefit of modern statistical analysis. Nevertheless his finding is congruent with that of Sheldon's. Furthermore, a much more recent study, done by Pascal, performed with adequate experimental techniques, would also support the conviction that there is some relationship between physique and expressive movement. He found (1943a, p. 243) that men high in mesomorphy who would be assertive in posture and movement according to Sheldon tended to write with greater average pressure and wider pressure range than men low in mesomorphy and than women.

But what are some of the established expressive movement traits? One of the most extensive investigations in this field was performed by Allport and Vernon, and summarized in their book entitled *Studies in Expressive Movement* (1933). They limited themselves in the first instance to an attempt to discover whether there were any individual consistencies in overt movements, putting aside for the moment the question of whether these consistencies were representative of a wider personality configuration. Table 5.3 adapted from Bell (1948) illustrates some of the tests and measures they used.

TABLE 5.3

Experiments in Expressive Movement Conducted by Allport and Vernon (1933)

Experiment	*Measures Obtained*
Counting Aloud	Speed
Walking, out of doors; walking, indoors	Speed; length of strides
Strolling, indoors	Speed; length of strides
Estimation of angles with rotating arm	Overestimation of angles
Estimation of handshake	Strength of normal grip
Circles drawn on paper, with right hand	Speed; average area; proportion of unoccupied space
Squares drawn on paper, with left hand	Speed; average area; proportion of unoccupied space
Length of self-rating checks on rating sheet	Length
Writing sentence and signature on pressure board	Speed; area; point and grip pressure
Writing *eee's* in sand with pointer attached to feet	Area

Reproduced with permission from J. Bell, *Projective Techniques,* p. 277. Copyright 1948 Longmans, Green, and Co.

They ended with some thirty-five such measures drawn from every type of movement in different parts of the body which they could imagine. The first question they attempted to answer was whether or not subjects were consistent from one time to the next in the way they moved in a given test situation. They found that the average of their uncorrected repeat reliability coefficients was +.684 which justified their conclusion that "single habits of gesture as we have measured them, are stable characteristics of the individuals in our experimental group." (1933, p. 98.) This finding, which was based upon twenty-five subjects, has been sufficiently confirmed by other investigators, some of whom have been critical of Allport and Vernon's other results (cf. Bell, 1948), for it to be accepted as a fact.

A more interesting question is whether different movements from different parts of the body, performing different functions, correlate highly. To answer this question they intercorrelated all their measures and found that although there were about twice as many significant correlations as one would expect by chance, the average intercorrelation was quite small. Consequently they were led to the conclusion that there was no general over-all movement factor. However, an analysis of the correlation table led them to conclude that there were three group factors, the first of which appeared to be an *areal* or *expansive* factor. Table 5.4 reproduced from their book (1933) shows the measures which led them to arrive at this general factor.

TABLE 5.4

Average Intercorrelation of Several "Areal" Measures with the Sum of the Other Eight Measures

Measure	r
Area of Total Writing	+.69
Total Extent of Figures	+.67
Area of Blackboard Figures	+.64
Slowness of Drawing	+.52
Area of Foot Squares	+.48
Overestimation of Angles	+.45
Ratings on Movement during Idleness	+.39
Length of Self-Rating Checks	+.38
Length of Walking Strides	+.37

The average intercorrelation of the variables taken two at a time is +.333 for this factor, which is just about at the 5 per cent level of significance. They named this general trait *expansiveness* in terms of the size or area factor which seemed to be involved in all of its measures. They also found a factor which they called the "centrifugal group factor" (1933, p. 112) which saturated such measures as the overestimation of distance from the body with the hands or with the legs, and a third group factor, called "emphasis," which was associated with voice intensity, ratings on movement during speech, writing pressure, etc. (1933, p. 114). The average intercorrelation of the components of these last two factors is somewhat less and in fact Eisenberg (1940) has questioned whether there really is very good evidence for such group factors. However, common sense, as well as other experimental evidence (cf. Bell, 1948), would seem to support at least the first and third of these group factors as trait names descriptive of two dimensions of expressive movement. That is, it makes sense to speak of the areal characteristics of expression (that is, its general expansiveness), and also the intensity characteristics of expression (that is, its emphasis or insistence).

Psychodiagnostics. Most of the argument in this field has not been over what descriptive trait terms should be adopted to describe expressive movements. Instead, most of the claims and counterclaims have dealt with the validity of measures of expressive movement for diagnosing more complex personality characteristics. This is precisely the same problem which we met in connection with physique, where Sheldon and others raised the question as to whether measurements of the body would enable us to predict what a person's likes and dislikes would be. Here the question is whether measurements of the body's movements will enable us to tell something about a person's likes and dislikes. The argument has waxed particularly hot over what can be determined about personality from handwriting, although Wolff (1947) has made extensive claims for the diagnostic significance of *all* expressive movements. At the one extreme are the elaborate psychodiagnostic systems of Klages and Saudek described in full in Bell (1948) which attempt to derive a complete personality picture from handwriting. At the other extreme is to be found the widely quoted study by Hull and Montgomery (1919) in which they found that the average correlation between ratings on a series of personality traits and various handwriting measures was —.016. It is not our purpose to review this controversy here because such an attempt would go far beyond the scope of this book. Careful review of the status of graphology can be found in Allport and Vernon (1933) and Bell (1948). Instead we shall take a single study by Pascal which appears to be a significant contribution to methodology in the field, since it was carried out in accordance with careful experimental procedures.

Pascal (1943b) began with twenty-two male undergraduate Harvard students who had been extensively analyzed in the Harvard Psychological Clinic as part of a larger study under Murray's direction (1938). These students had been rated on thirty-six carefully defined personality variables after very extensive clinical and experimental analysis. Pascal made thirty-nine handwriting measurements from specimens supplied by these subjects, who were asked to write with their favorite fountain pen as naturally as possible "an account of their experiences since leaving college." Measurements were read to .2 of a millimeter, and explicit directions are given in his article for making the measurements used. Table 5.5 summarizes five of the nine relationships between handwriting variables and personality characteristics which were significant at or beyond the 1 per cent level of confidence. In each case enough of the definition of the handwriting measurement and the personality characteristic is given so that some idea of the nature of the relationship can be obtained.

TABLE 5.5

Sample Handwriting and Personality Relationships Found by Pascal (1943b) to Be Significant at the .01 Level

1. Upper projection (mean vertical height of the letters *b, h, k, l,* taken consecutively about one third down the page) is positively correlated with playful attitude (meaning "to relax, amuse oneself, seek diversion and entertainment . . . avoid serious tension").
2. Mid-zone ratio (width of the letters *m, n, u,* divided by the height of the same or similar letters) is positively correlated with projectivity ("the disposition to project unconsciously one's wish-engendered or anxiety-evoked beliefs").
3. Distance between words is positively correlated with playful attitude.
4. Distance between point of the letter *i* and its dot divided by the width of *m, n, u,* is positively correlated with infavoidance (meaning "to avoid failure, shame, humiliation, ridicule").
5. Upper projection (the height of the letters *b, h, k, l*) minus lower projection (the length of the letters *g, j, q, y,* and *z,* excluding capitals) is negatively correlated with abasement, and positively with dominance and defendance.

Pascal is rightly unwilling to draw any very extensive conclusions from such findings as these, especially since he is dealing with such a very small and selected group of subjects and with such a large number of correlations that a few of them could be expected to be significant by chance. The fact remains that his study is one of the few carefully controlled ones in which significant relationships have been found. It differs from earlier attempts to disprove relationships in this field chiefly in the carefulness with which the personality measurements were made.

But supposing, for the sake of argument, that his findings are generally applicable, what sense can we make of them? Of the relationships listed in Table 5.5 we note first of all that 1 and 3 would appear to be related to the dimension defined by Allport and Vernon as the expansive or areal factor. Distance between words and a tendency to use high upper projections both indicate the using up of greater space. Similarly the fifth relationship appears related to the factor of emphasis; that is, if pressed we could make a case for the tendency to push upward against gravity as indicating an over-all assertive or dominant attitude (cf. Wolff, 1947), provided the general areal factor is subtracted out as it is in the formula. Finally it should be noted that the relationships under 2 and 4 both deal with ratios of vertical to horizontal distances. If we reverse the ratio in 4 so that both represent width over height, we come out with a striking confirmation of the general fact that handwriting which is wide relative to its height is associated with *low* shame avoidance and *high* projectivity. To put this in another way, a person who does not hide his anxieties but projects them, tends to express himself in horizontal, rather than vertical, movements.

To show how widely applicable such a finding may be, we note that Mira, in his Myokinetic diagnosis, reports results which would tend to confirm this result. He uses a technique in which the subject is asked to draw vertical and horizontal lines with either his right or his left hand, beginning at the left or at the right or the top or bottom. He reports that depressed patients tend to draw lines which are about twice as long in the horizontal direction as normal people, whereas the same depressed patients tend to draw vertical lines which are shorter than for normal people. His figures, which can be found in a table reprinted in Bell (1948, pp. 334-336), do not agree exactly with Pascal's and furthermore the suggestion that they correspond with Pascal's involves the assumption that depressed patients have a lot of the same sort of anxieties as led to high ratings on projectivity and low ratings on infavoidance for Pascal's subjects. Nevertheless the correspondence is striking and is pointed out simply because it illustrates the need for the integration of various diverse research findings in this general field. It seems sufficiently clear that handwriting traits, like physique traits, are not going to provide the key which unlocks all the mysteries of personality, but on the other hand it is time psychologists stopped trying to prove this obvious point and got to work to attempt to show how this important aspect of personality can be usefully measured, described, and integrated into the total over-all picture.

Karl's Handwriting. Let us return to our individual case and see what his handwriting looks like. It is reproduced in Figure 5.1 along with some handwriting samples from another person. Two of the samples are Karl's and two were written by another male college student. Can you pick the two samples written by the same person? Can you decide which pair belongs to Karl?

FIGURE 5.1

Four Handwriting Samples, Two of Which are Karl's.

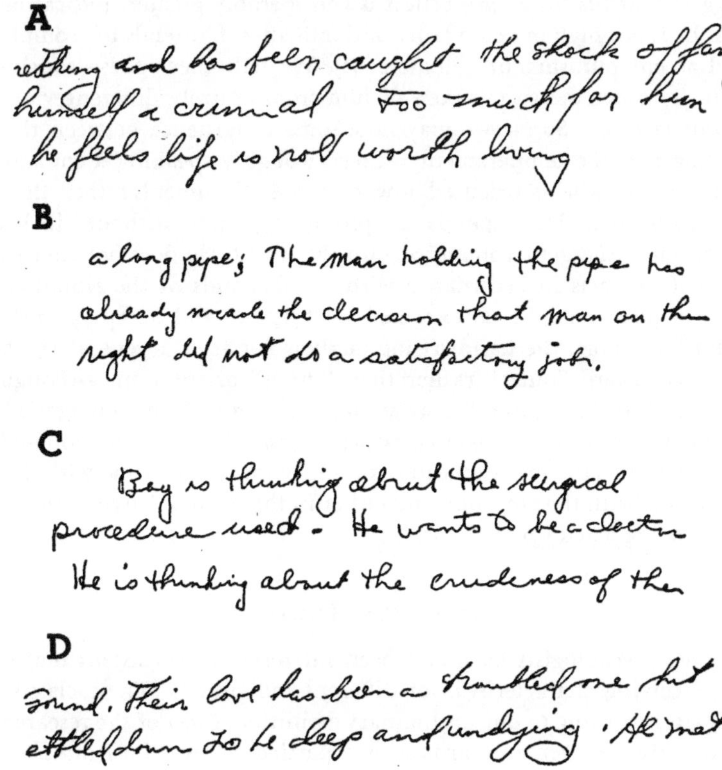

A

rething and has felt caught the shock of fan
himself a criminal too much for him
he feels life is not worth living

B

a long pipe; The man holding the pipe has
already made the decision that man on the
right did not do a satisfactory job.

C

Boy is thinking about the surgical
procedure used. He wants to be a doctor
He is thinking about the crudeness of the

D

Sound. Their love has been a troubled one but
ettled down to be deep and undying. He met

These are the two traditional questions asked by experimenters who have used the matching technique to measure the consistency of expression and the agreement of expression with over-all personality characteristics. Of course you have no over-all picture of Karl as yet but at least you have some impressions of him from the physique and temperament data.

Handwriting samples A and D were written by Karl. Can we draw any conclusions about his personality by looking at the relationships found by Pascal? Unfortunately Pascal did not provide norms since he worked with ranks instead of actual scores, but we can make a few inferences by way of illustration. Thus we might argue that his upper projection and distance between words is above average and conclude that therefore he has a tendency to be more playful than the average person. It is extremely difficult to draw any conclusions about width relative to height in his case without norms, but a comparison of upper projection with lower projection would strongly suggest that his lower projection is considerably greater, indicating that he is not high in defendance or dominance, but tends to "comply and accept punishment" (abasement). We will check these conclusions by other measures taken of him from entirely different viewpoints later on. So far we may note some congruence between this finding and the temperament ratings. Roughly speaking a somatotonic is one who is oriented toward the environment rather than toward himself. He responds to "promptings from without" in his "motional" energetic commerce with the world. He does not consult himself but acts in accordance with the demands of the situation. Such a person might be expected to "comply and accept punishment." In short, the handwriting analysis confirms a general trend in Karl toward "outer" rather than "inner" orientation, although at first blush "compliant" may seem far removed from "energetic." In fact we are forced to assume rather awkwardly that these opposed traits are surface manifestations of the same underlying wish for commerce with the environment, either in the form of "acting upon" it or "being acted upon" by it.

Perceptual Traits

Some psychologists have also been interested in consistent modes of perceiving characteristics of different individuals. These classify as traits according to our preliminary definition. Most of the research in this area has centered around one particular test—the Rorschach

Test—although there have been some efforts to work with other materials, such as cloud pictures, reproduction of visual, Gestalt patterns, mumbled speech, etc. (cf. Bell, 1948). The basic idea has been to classify the ways in which the subject perceives the world about him. In an inkblot test like the Rorschach he is given a series of ten blots (some in color) and is asked what he sees, what he can make of them. The way in which he goes about responding to this unstructured material is then carefully analyzed by the psychologist in the hope that it will provide significant clues to his mental approach to the world in general. For example, the argument might run that if the subject consistently sees details in the blots, he will tend to pay attention to details in all life's activities. The parallel between this approach and that of expressive movements is fairly obvious. In the one case the psychologist is interested in the consistency of motor responses; here he is interested in the consistency of perceptual responses. In both cases he ends with a trait description which serves to summarize the way in which the person reacts in that modality, and which also supposedly has general diagnostic significance.

Consistent modes of visual perception have been the subject of prolonged and very extensive research in the Rorschach Test, and the results of this research have proved so useful for clinical psychology that this test has without exception become the most widely used psychological instrument in the study of personality. For this very reason the literature on the subject is enormous. Bell (1948), for example, in a recent survey of the Rorschach literature lists 798 references. They reflect not only the wide use of the test, but the care with which the details of administration and scoring have been worked out. In fact the test has become so specialized that it is difficult to work with it without considerable training which special Rorschach Institutes have been set up to give. Detailed case studies appear in the literature along with numerous research findings, particularly in the field of clinical diagnosis of various types of personality disorder.

We cannot therefore begin to go into this test as a working clinical tool. All we can hope to do is to gain a knowledge sufficient to learn something of its contribution to the total personality picture and something of its theoretical meaning in our conceptualization of personality in general. Perhaps the simplest approach is to begin with a concrete case, our subject Karl, and see how he responded to the standard inkblots when the test was administered to him by a clinical psychologist well-trained in the Rorschach technique. Shown in Figure 5.2 are blots VI and VII with the responses which he gave to each. At the right of each response appear the scoring symbols used by the clinical psychologist in his analysis of the record.

FIGURE 5.2

Karl's Responses to Two Sample Rorschach Blots

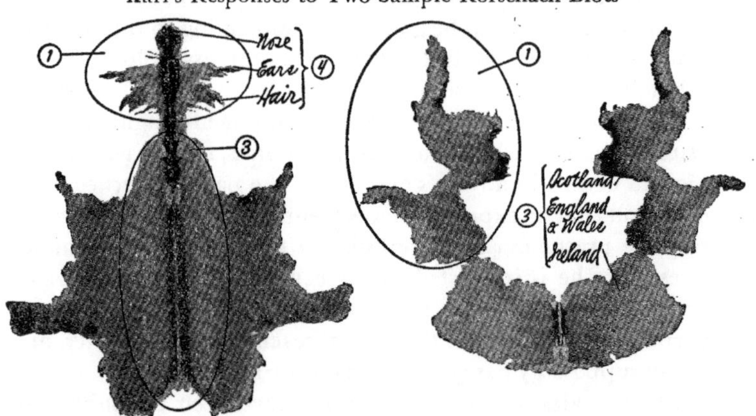

(Reproduced by courtesy of Hans Huber Medical Publisher, Berne. From Rorschach, *Psychodiagnostics*. Sole agents for the U.S.A.: Grune & Stratton, Inc., N.Y. 16.)

Card VI

	Response	Scoring
1.	Radio tower on top—antenna	D F– Sci
2.	Bottom = massive—another skin spread out	W F A P
3.	Female genital organs	D FK Sex
4.	Fox's head with cow's nose	D F– Ad

Card VII

	Response	Scoring
1.	Frolicking fauns in wood dancing around trees—Disney characters—Siamese fauns	D M H P
2.	Might be centaur—heavy body	W F A
3.	British Isles—map	W F– map

Card VIII

	Response	Scoring
1.	Cut open human being—inside abdomen red = blood	W CF At

The first response to Card VIII, which contains a good deal of color, has been included to illustrate some of the other types of possible responses. Table 5.6 lists some of the commonest scoring symbols, the frequency with which they appeared in Karl's record, the scoring definitions (cf. Bell, 1948), and the approximate psychological meaning for each.

TABLE 5.6

The Meaning of Some Common Rorschach Scoring Categories and the Frequency with Which They Appear in Karl's Record

Blot Characteristic	*Sample Scoring Symbols*	*Frequency in K's. Record*	*Scoring Definitions*	*Approximate* Psychological Meaning*
	R	42	Total number of responses	
1. Location	W	12	Whole blot used	Intellectual
	D	26	A normal detail	Approach
	Dd	4	A rare detail	
	S	8	White space used	Negativism
	DW	0	Detail made into whole	Confabulation
2. Form	F	26	Form response	Control
	F+	17	Good or poor form	
	F–	9	responses	
3. Movement	M	3	Movement response	Creativity
4. Color	C	9	Pure color response	Emotion
	CF	6	Color dominates form	
	FC	4	Form dominates color	
5. Shading	FK	2	Vista responses, third dimension	Anxiety
6. Content	A	17	Animal	Determined by
	H	3	Human	associational
	At	7	Anatomical	sequences and
	Art	5	Art	inferences of judge
	P	7	Popular response	Conformity with social thinking

* An item has meaning only in terms of the total context of other responses. Various ratios of responses such as the relation of W to M are given particular meanings.

The material in this table is merely illustrative. Actually there is considerable variation in the use of such symbols among the different Rorschach workers. Bell (1948) lists some thirteen pages of different scoring symbols and the slightly different interpretations given by different Rorschach experts. After a record has been scored in this manner, the next step is usually to sum up the different scoring categories for the total record and to prepare an over-all picture, sometimes in the form of a psychogram, which the Rorschacher can use as the basis for his personality diagnosis. The diagnosis involves, as has already been suggested in Chapter 3, the use of personality concepts which are based on the perceptual categories actually used in the scoring. It is important to make a distinction at this point. The process of applying the correct scoring symbol to a subject's response is an objective one which can be learned fairly easily to the point of high inter-scorer reliability after the usual training. As in the case of expressive movements, such modes of perceiving as seeing wholes (W) or movements (M) seem to be unobjectionable *as purely descriptive categories for an aspect of behavior.* But the second process, that of drawing inferences from the scoring categories to wider areas of personality, is not only more difficult, involving a thorough knowledge of personality, but also rests on a series of rather involved theoretical assumptions.

The intermingling of perceptual categories and personality constructs can only be illustrated by a concrete example. Let us follow the process of analyzing Karl's record one step further. Here is the first section of the clinical psychologist's interpretation of his record:

Rorschach Record of Karl
Analysis by Dr. Jules D. Holzberg

The subject produced an adequate Rorschach record quantitatively (42 R). There does not appear to be any disturbance in the manner in which he intellectually approaches a problem. Although he tends to be a practical person and deals with the commonplace (63% D), he is nevertheless capable of some abstractual thinking and generalization (28% W) while not ignoring the less significant in his environment (9% Dd). He does not engage in alogical thinking (no DW). Although there is no undue stereotypy in thinking, he does not however permit much flexibility in ideation (50% A) although potentially capable of high average intellectual functioning and possibly higher (42 R, 12 W, content).

We may pause here to notice what has happened. The psychologist has taken the fact that 63 per cent of his location responses are to details and generalized to the statement that therefore he tends to deal with the commonplace and is a practical person. On the other hand, his whole responses suggest abstractual thinking, and the fact that 50 per cent of his content responses are animal responses suggests ideational inflexibility because he does not depart much from the animal figures "normally" suggested to people taking the test. This illustrates how the analyst's picture of Karl's ideational or intellectual processes, of his *intellectual* approach to the world, is based on his *perceptual* modes of responding.

Let us take a further section of the clinical interpretation, to see how this works out for other areas of personality:

At present, his achievement strivings are beyond his functioning capacity (12 W: 3 M). Although his level of aspiration is not abnormally high, he is nevertheless incapable of achieving this level because of his emotional problems. One is dealing here with a problem of emotions rather than ideation.

In this excerpt perceptual characteristics are interpreted first in motivational terms ("achievement strivings") and then in emotional terms.

Basic to his personality problems is marked negativism and contrariness (8 S), and a push to mold his environment to his own needs.

Note here how the use of the background white space rather than the normal figural black part of the card is taken to mean that the subject is contrary-minded; that is, he tends to mold his environment rather than to accept the figural responses strongly suggested by the blot. The analyst again generalizes from a "perceptual contrariness" to a general contrariness (negativism). It is worth noting that this "push to mold his environment" is almost exactly the description used by Sheldon for somatotonics when he speaks of their "resolution to subdue the environment to one's own will." Such parallels as these are what give clinical psychologists faith in the Rorschach and theoretical psychologists faith in the consistency of personality as displayed by different measures.

He is therefore a narcissist and his emotional reactions would tend to confirm this (6 CF). Emotionally, he is very labile (9 C) and easily aroused by emotionally-charged situations (50% R Cards VIII-X).

The significance of this last comment is that 50 per cent of his forty-two responses occurred in connection with Cards VIII-X, which are blots containing a great variety of color of different hues and shadings. Color is roughly equivalent to emotion to the Rorschacher, just as form is equivalent to control.

When so aroused, he may react with narcissistic and explosive displays of emotional behavior (6 CF) and it is clear he is incapable of coping with his feelings. Although there is an attempt to express mature, warm emotions in interpersonal relationships (6 FC), he is unable to sustain this and eventually his emotional reactions become inappropriate and poorly controlled (2 FC–). Any sensitivity for the problems of others is lacking (no c), again a reflection of his narcissism. He appears to accept humans in his attempt to establish rapport (3 H out of 42 R).

A portion of his unstable emotionality is absorbed through phantasy (3 M), but much of his phantasy is itself infantile and regressive (2 FM) and may therefore not be sufficiently capable of absorbing his affects.

Basically, he is an extratensive personality (3 M: 9 C) who seeks satisfactions in and works out his problems on the environment.

The ratio of M to C is one of the most important relationships in the Rorschach Test. To Rorschach it meant the person's "experience balance"; that is, the extent to which he was extratensive or introversive. Generally speaking, a person who shows more movement responses would seem to be more creative, that is, adding more of his own attitudes to the response, than a person who is determined in his responses by striking features of the environment. On the common-sense level one can see that color, especially in a series of black blots, is an impressive experience which would appear to suggest a response, whereas motion is something which the subject has to introduce on his own into the static blot. The person who responds primarily in terms of color, like Karl, is regarded as extratensive, that is, as directed toward his environment rather than toward himself. He responds to "promptings from without" (C) more than to "promptings from within" (M). Once more we find confirmation of a characteristic found both in the temperament ratings and in the handwriting analysis.

However, his unstable emotionality and his hostility (8 S) may interfere with adequate relationships with others. This will produce conflict and therefore anxiety (2 FK). In view of the possibility that the direction of his strivings is not functioning satisfactorily, he may resolve anxiety by turning in upon himself with the possibility of depressive mood reactions (7 At, 1 FC′) which appear to have their roots in infantile fears of overwhelming parent figures, particularly the mother ("massive representation" appearing with the depressive percept and with the percept "female genital organs"). Even here, however, this possibility of internalized aggression is limited, since he is likely to resort to hostile reactions ("cut open human being"). He is constantly experiencing struggle with his environment (people "tugging against each other").

Here and in the last paragraph the analyst makes use of the actual content of the subject's responses rather than their perceptual characteristics alone. This part of a Rorschach interpretation really does not belong under the heading of "expressive traits" at all, but it is included here so that the unity of the over-all Rorschach approach will not be violated.

One defense he attempts in coping with unstable affects is repression and intellectualization (65% F, 5 Art). That this mechanism does not serve to allay anxiety is clearly demonstrated by the unstable emotional reactivity and the low level of accuracy at which he perceives and interprets his environment (65% F+). This latter factor further indicates that the ego and the ability to moderate between id strivings and the demands of social reality is poorly integrated and weak. Ego strength particularly weakens under the guilt and anxiety for hostile wishes and feelings.

Sexual preoccupations play a major role in his phantasies ("shapely angels," etc.). With the exception of one instance ("female genital organs") all reference to sexual material is sublimated. However, invariably sexually-tinged percepts give rise to debilitating anxiety and cause ego-disruption (F–). A vicious cycle is demonstrated in that hostility gives rise to anxiety, which further reinforces and intensifies hostile reactions. His only defense is intellectualizing and repression (F) but these are incapable of coping with the emotions that run rampant. It is here that it becomes apparent that interest in art, present in this record, is one manifestation of the use of intellectualization as a defense against anxiety and the fact that some of his art percepts have sexual symbolic significance would suggest that this interest of the subject also serves as sublimation for his sexual preoccupations.

Note that in this section of the interpretation attention has shifted somewhat from Karl's traits to some attempt at analyzing the reasons for some of these traits. In other words, the content of the Rorschach responses often suggests the reason for some of the responses obtained. It is here that the full subtlety of the Rorschach analyst must be brought into play. Note how, in this case, some rather minor clues are worked up into a plausible hypothesis (fear of the mother, sexual anxiety) which would appear to explain Karl's perceptual behavior and therefore possibly his general behavior. For example, in Figure 5.2 we note the deterioration in form resulting from sexually tinged responses. Response 3 ("female genital organs") to Plate VI is followed by an F– response, whereas the centaur reference in response to Plate VII is also followed by an F– response. It is as if the sexual associations aroused have disconcerted the subject and aroused enough anxiety so that his next response is not as good. This disrupting effect of anxiety is well known in the experimental literature (cf. Sears, 1937), and the conclusion that this particular sequence means anxiety is therefore not pure conjecture.

The clinical interpretation ends with an over-all summary of Karl's strengths and weaknesses.

In summary, this Rorschach record reveals an emotionally unstable personality who is struggling with unacceptable affects. Basically narcissistic and hostile, he is unable to establish and maintain warm human contacts in spite of his extratensive personality structure. With a relatively low level of tolerance for anxiety, ego strength is weak and under sufficient stress may be unable to serve its moderating role. Mechanisms of defense lie in intellectualization and repression, both of which are presently failing to protect him from his anxiety. The essential core of his phantasy is sexual and infantile fear of overpowering parent figures is suggested. Of positive strength in this personality picture is the absence of deviant thinking, some absorptive phantasy, a desire for human contact, and a fair level of intellect.

This concrete example has given us a good idea of the two major functions of the Rorschach Test. In the first place it gives a picture of the perceptual mode of approach of the subject. Whether or not the picture obtained from a single Rorschach Test is a reliable index of the way in which the subject perceives his world is unfortunately still a somewhat debatable question. Attempts have been made to measure the reliability of this instrument, but an over-all evaluation is still lacking. The reason for this is that no one has yet developed an exactly equivalent form of the test so that the results on one occasion can be correlated with the results on another. Even this method of testing reliability would not be without criticism, since taking one of the tests would doubtless influence responses on the next. The usual methods of measuring reliability have been applied, however, to the responses obtained to the standard ten blots. That is, retests over varying intervals of time have been shown by Fosberg (1941) to yield highly comparable psychograms. Hertz (1934) has reported odd-even correlations for individual types of responses varying from +.70 to +.90 and averaging +.829. Finally, attempts to discover whether two Rorschach analysts scoring the same record come out with the same result have been hampered to some extent by the fact that there are minor differences in scoring technique which make comparisons difficult. However, the data show, by and large, that there is a very high degree of agreement between two independent analyses of the same record (cf. Bell, 1948).

The second function of the Rorschach Test is what makes it so important clinically. It is not only supposed to give a picture of consistent perceptual traits; it is supposed to suggest the person's mode of approach in general to all of life's problems. Not only this, it often gives hints as to some of the person's basic conflicts. Here the technique verges on the kind of psychodiagnosis for which handwriting and physique have also been used. Essentially we are dealing here with the problem of whether or not the perceptual traits and content responses found on the Rorschach are representative of broader personality trends. Here again research has proved difficult for the simple reason that in many cases we have no more adequate measures of these general personality trends than the Rorschach itself gives. This is particularly true when the characteristics in question are defined in such a way that they can be measured *only* by the Rorschach. For example, M on the Rorschach is supposed to mean inner creativity. If we attempt to check the "validity" of this notion, we find some other measures which define creativity as well or better than M on the Rorschach, such as artistic creativity (Rust, 1948) or scientific creativity (Roe, 1949), and test the extent to which the Rorschach agrees with these measures. If it does not agree, as in Rust's and Roe's analyses, then the Rorschacher can always argue that this is not the kind of creativity he had in mind. He can state the definition of creativity in such a way that only the Rorschach can measure it; the same is true of extrotensiveness which is similar to but different from extroversion and could not therefore be checked against measures of extroversion. The difficulty with this approach is that it prevents contact between different ways of measuring personality and limits the predictive power of the Rorschach ultimately to perceptual behavior.

Where there are independent estimates of personality trends or conflicts, particularly in psychiatric diagnoses, the record of the test has been good. That is, Rorschach workers have been able to arrive at an interpretation based solely on their test results which agrees very closely with prolonged case studies (cf. Bell, 1948). In one instance Benjamin and Ebaugh (1938) found that in thirty-nine out of forty-six cases the diagnosis arrived at by the Rorschach agreed entirely with that arrived at by psychiatrists, and in the remaining seven cases the difference was not great. Glueck and Glueck (1950) report that Rorschach analysts were able to separate delinquent from matched nondelinquent boys on the basis of Rorschach records alone in well over 90 per cent of the cases. A rather striking and somewhat unusual confirmation of the test's validity has come from a study by DuBois and Oberholzer on the Alorese (1944). Here Oberholzer, working independently from Rorschach records alone, arrived at a picture of the basic personality structure of the Alorese which was highly congruent in most important respects with the one arrived at by an anthropologist (DuBois) and a psychiatrist (Kardiner) working with anthropological data.

The ability to match Rorschach interpretations with psychiatric interpretations shows the clinical usefulness of the test, but unfortunately it does not give us much insight as to what is involved theoretically. Nevertheless it should lead us to conclude that the Rorschach is an extremely promising approach to personality which theoretically oriented scientists should make use of in trying to refine their concepts for handling personality structure. For example, what clearly needs to be done is to follow the procedure outlined in Chapter 4. We need to take a given Rorschach concept like *negativism* or *hostility* which is based on the perceptual use of white space and analyze carefully its surplus meanings. Obviously the word *negativism* is used precisely because it does have surplus meanings for other areas of personality. No one is particularly interested in perceptual negativism *per se*. But so far no one has attempted to define *precisely* what the surplus meaning of negativism is and how its manifestations in other areas of personality could be tested. Does it mean, for example, that a person with high S should also choose *atypical responses* in a personality questionnaire, or on the Strong Vocational Interest Test? Before we make such deductions as these we should probably have to make some assumptions (postulates) about the nature of negativism and then try to understand how it would manifest itself, not only in perception but in other types of behavior as well. It is only when this kind of painstaking analysis is completed that we shall have added a concept to the field of personality study which is more than merely suggestive. Most of the Rorschach concepts, unfortunately, are just suggestive at this stage of the game, which makes them very useful for clinical work, but not so useful for a rigorous theoretical system. On the other hand, it does not mean, as some students of personality have assumed, that the Rorschach concepts are of no use. On the contrary, they are some of the best and most suggestive that we have, and what we need to do is to attempt to apply them more rigorously to other types of personality data.

STYLE

Psychologists have also interested themselves in the extent to which individuals show a consistent style in the many different ways in which they express themselves. Wolff has conducted a series of extensive and ingenious researches on this subject (1943). He has worked with such expressive aspects of personality as photographs of silhouetted profiles and hands, mirrored handwriting, phonographic records of voices, style in telling a story, movies of gait, etc. Generally he reports that judges can match samples from such widely different areas of the same person better than would be expected by chance. He argues, as does Allport, that style is the overall consistent way in which a person expresses himself. Allport regards style as the external aspect of a marked internal *consistency* or organization of personality. When psychologists show that they can successfully match different expressive aspects of personality they are merely confirming the widely-held critical and commonsense view that a man's style of life can be recognized in whatever he does. It is on this assumption that literary, musical, and artistic criticism is based. "From style alone we may recognize compositions by Chopin, paintings by Van Gogh, and pastry by Aunt Sally." (Allport, 1937, p. 490.)

Table 5.7 abbreviated from Allport (1937, p. 479) shows some of the typical results from matching different aspects of personality. It will be noted from this table that even such diverse aspects as handwriting and phonographic recording of voices can be matched with better than chance accuracy, as is shown by the contingency coefficients (C's) which are several times their probable errors (P.E.'s).

TABLE 5.7

Results of Matching Different Aspects of Personality

	C and P. E.
Four photographs of bodies (with heads removed) matched with five photographs of heads; (the latter were taken at a different time, when different clothes were worn). (Vernon)	0.42 ± .046
Pairs of drawings of a house and a man by 490 children (10-13 years), arranged in 70 sets. Each set of seven matched with a time limit of 30 seconds by educated adults. (Vernon)	0.59 ± .062
Handwritings matched with phonograph records of the voices of the writers. (Wolff)	0.39 ± .042
Photographs of hands matched with silhouettes of profiles. (Wolff)	0.14 ± .052
Handwriting specimens matched with portraits of the writers. (Arnheim)	0.25 ± .055
Eight themes written by 70 students matched with one or more other themes by the same authors. Two judges matched groups of five authors at a time. The result is the average of 112 experiments. (Allport, Walker, and Lathers)	0.60 ± 1.42

Reproduced with permission from G. W. Allport, *Personality*, p. 479. Copyright 1937 by Henry Holt and Co.

A slight variant of this approach is to have judges match personality descriptions derived from a study of different expressive aspects of personality. Reproduced in Table 5.8 are brief samples from interpretive reports on a single girl, Sally, based respectively on the Rorschach, on graphology, and on an art technique, as reported in a study by Munroe (1945).

TABLE 5.8

Test Reports on Sally

Rorschach (1940)	*Graphology (1941)*	*Art Technique (1942)*
This student seems to be a well-adjusted pedant. She is intelligent . . . and ambitious. She is methodical, accurate, acute. She works hard, gleans masses of facts which she can use with a certain aptness. What she lacks is any sort of broad sweep, any emotional warmth and creative impulse. For all her systematic methods of working, she seems to be basically pretty scattered. There is no *inner* organization and focus.	She is by no means brilliant, but she has a good average intelligence. She is a diligent and conscientious worker who is good in routine performances. Her mechanism of learning is based more on absorption and identification than on assimilation. She possesses little phantasy and imagination, and has a rather sober and plain approach to given material.	A highly constricted person . . . Is intelligent and reliable . . . Suppression of emotion . . . hampered in being creative.

(From Munroe, 1945.)

This table illustrates both the strengths and the weaknesses of the matching technique. The reader can judge for himself the degree of congruence in these reports. On the one hand it is easy to see how, on the basis of such descriptions as these, a judge might be able to put together three descriptions that belong to Sally as opposed to three other descriptions belonging to some other girl. On the other hand the question arises as to what value such a correct matching has. The situation recalls one of Dr. Samuel Johnson's famous remarks: "Sir, a woman preaching is like a dog walking on his hind legs. It is not done well; but you are surprised to find it done at all." Psychologists have felt the need of proving by matching experiments that there *is* consistency in personality, but having done so and marveled at the result, they have not been able to think of much more to do about it. The matching technique is excellent for showing that a phenomenon exists, but not for showing what the phenomenon is. Certainly the descriptions of Sally written by the three different analysts are so different that it would be difficult to state precisely on what basis a correct match might be made. Many writers have argued that the basis for the matching is not external characteristics but an interpretation of those characteristics based on an over-all conceptualization of a personality. If this is so, then what we need to do is to go beyond matching experiments into more careful conceptualizations which are standardized enough to permit a more precise understanding of the consistencies noted.

Speech and Personality. One attempt to break style down into simpler components has been to concentrate on linguistic style which can be analyzed quantitatively. Language has been considered one of the most representative aspects of a man's style. To quote Ben Jonson, "Language most showeth a man; speak that I may see thee." Fortunately speech may be broken down into units and ratios of units which can be handled quantitatively with ease. Under the leadership of men like Busemann and Krachel in Germany, and Korzybski, Wendell Johnson, and Sanford in America, some very accurate and painstaking analyses of word usage have been made. The typical approach is to take a word sample of given length—say a thousand words—and to count the number of grammatical forms of different sorts in it, e.g., nouns, pronouns, adjectives, adverbs, verbs, prepositions, and articles. A distinction is made between the number of different words used (types) and the total number of words used (tokens). Chotlos (1944) and others have shown that such speech characteristics as the over-all type-token ratio are highly consistent from one word sample to another of the same person if each of the samples consists of a thousand words or more. The correlations run over +.90 for samples of this size. Starting with this discovery of intra-individual consistency, Sanford (1942b) has analyzed for two subjects such speech characteristics as the type-token ratio, hesitating sounds, sentence lengths, verb tense, concrete-abstract nouns, grammatical types of adjectives, verb-adjective ratios, subject-object ratios, pointing words, etc. He calculated in all some 7,488 separate scores. Nevertheless on the basis of these minute speech segments he was able to build up a synthetic picture of the styles of these two individuals. For example, he was able to define a trait of "cautiousness of response" as follows:

a. Many noun clauses
b. Many cause clauses
c. Many concession clauses
d. Frequent concept of cause
e. Many static copula clauses ("It seems that")
f. Low certainty-uncertainty ratio ("is," "seems")
g. Many modal auxiliaries ("could," "would," "might")
h. Many quotation marks in Autobiography

(1942b, p. 189.)

Having built up a number of traits in this manner, he was able to summarize one of the person's styles as follows:

> Thus Merritt's speech is *complex, perseverative, thorough, uncoordinated, cautious, static, highly definitive,* and *stimulus-bound.* If we go one step further toward synthesis and generalization, we might conceive of his whole style as *defensive,* and *deferent.* Most of his verbal behavior seems to reflect a *desire to avoid blame or disapproval.* He is cautious and indirect, rarely making a simple or bald statement. Once he makes a judgment he explains it and presents all aspects of it, leaving little to the auditor's imagination and little for the auditor to question. . . . (Sanford, 1942b, p. 190.)

This speech characterization has been presented in some detail because it represents the extent to which a psychologist can place on a quantitative basis characteristics of literary style which critics have usually arrived at intuitively. After having read Sanford's analysis, we can scarcely doubt that his characterization is excellent so far as Merritt's speech is concerned. But here, as in all previous cases of studies of expressive behavior, psychologists have wanted to use speech characteristics as diagnostic of other personality traits. When Sanford concludes that Merritt is cautious, this does not necessarily mean that he is cautious in all that he does. It does mean that his speech may be characterized as cautious, but inevitably we want to add the surplus meaning that he is cautious in other fields of activity as well.

Thus psychologists, as well as others, have not been slow to draw very far-reaching conclusions from a study of speech habits. Led by Korzybski (1941), a whole semantic movement has grown up which claims to be able to diagnose very complicated personality processes from speech characteristics (cf. Sanford, 1942a). Korzybski, in fact, has developed a whole theory of psychoneurosis based on poor speech habits. "The hypothesis, stated broadly, maintains that the individual who applies rigid Aristotelian class-words to a world which is not rigid and not Aristotelian will sooner or later run afoul of the inevitable misfit between his words and the world." (Sanford, 1942a, p. 824.) Here there is assumed a correlation between personal adjustment and speech habits, although as Sanford also points out, it is not clear whether a paranoid personality will produce poor speech habits, or the poor speech habits a paranoid personality. Others have attempted to correlate such indexes as the type-token ratio with intelligence test scores and generally have found a significant relationship (Chotlos, 1944). Once again it would be impossible to summarize all the work which has been done in this field. Perhaps the best over-all summary has been made by Sanford (1942a), who concludes as follows: "All along the line there are data, reasonable arguments, insights, and hunches, adding up to the conviction that by his words a man may be known. We can accept it as a fact that speech and personality are related. But before we can get to the bottom of this relationship there are many bridges to cross." (p. 840.)

Karl's Speech. To illustrate how speech analyses are made, we can turn to a sample of Karl's written language and analyze it according to some of the standard techniques used by psychologists working in this field. Here is a sample of what Karl wrote in an elementary psychology class one day in response to the topic: "What I would like ideally to get out of a course in Psychology." It is reproduced with his spelling and punctuation, and with one word ("it") added to make the sense clear.

I had several reasons in mind when I signed up for the psych course. Believing in the true liberal arts tradition it seemed necessary to me to round out my more or less heterogeneous study program with a couple of semesters of psych. To me the individual represents such a predominant segment in society and the state, that [it] is imperative that we know as much as possible, in the words of a popular book title, "What Makes Sammy Run." Everyone is interested, it seems in what makes himself and his fellow associates tick. I do believe that the puzzling and sometimes baffling behavior of ourselves and our acquaintances, can be greatly clarified and elucidated through a study of psych. Psych, and its attendant knowledge can be of tremendous practical value in our understanding and appreciation of our fellow man. We must live in society, hence it seems necessary that we know as much as possible concerning the behaviour, attributes and character of those we contact. In other words to use a vernacular expression, we must be able "to figure out" people in order to lead a *more* successful life. Along with this trend of thought, I might add that psychology would seem to supply many of the missing links in the problems of philosophy and other sciences. Especially in this day and age in which rapid technological advances force us to decision, must we muster all our intellectual resources to face the ever increasing problems of life and its functions. We need a well-rounded store of knowledge, especially about ourselves and human behaviour in order to live a richer, fuller and happier life. I believe the problems of religion can have a great deal of light shed upon them through an intelligent study of psychology. This is one of my chief reasons for taking psych. We are all interested in religion more or less and key to the whole business seems to rest in human behavior.

I think that one can more readily understand and appreciate his capabilities, talents and potentialities if he is fully aware of them. An introspection into ones character and personality, a consideration of these facts through self-analysis, such as a serious study of psych provides, can give to the individual a new concept of purpose and value and enable him to lead a more useful life for himself and for society.

I believe . . . .

Zatzkis (1949) took the sample of four hundred words reproduced above from the total theme and broke them down into the usual grammatical categories, not only for Karl but for nineteen other similar subjects. Some of his results are reproduced in Table 5.9, which has been prepared for illustrative purposes. It shows Karl's word counts for some of the most important parts of speech and gives the type-token ratios (TTR) in each case which are supposed to be related to intelligence. The absolute size of the TTR is obviously a function of the number of words in the sample. The over-all TTR is small, because it includes many repeated articles and pronouns.

TABLE 5.9

Frequencies of Various Grammatical Categories in the First 400 Words of Karl's Theme and Rank Order Comparisons of Those Frequencies with the Results from Nineteen Other Subjects

	Tokens	*Rank*	*Types*	*TTR*	*Rank*
Nouns	88	2.5	60	.68	12.5
Verbs	64	19	39	.61	2
Adjectives	54	5	43	.80	9
Adverbs	24	19	13	.54	19
$\frac{\text{Verb}}{\text{Adjective}}$ ratio	1.18	17			
Total type-token ratio (TTR)				.39	8

Of importance here are the persistent tendencies to use one type of speech rather than another. For example, one characteristic which has figured in speech analyses is the relative number of verbs and adjectives. Boder (1940), Busemann (1925), and others have argued that many verb responses indicate, like the M response on the Rorschach, a tendency toward introversion, with little adaptation to reality, whereas many qualitative responses, like the color responses on the Rorschach, indicate extroversion with closer adaptation to reality. As Sanford says, "It might be expected that the individual who injects action into an inkblot will make a similar injection into the scenes and situations which he verbally depicts." (1942a, p. 828.) Karl is relatively very low in the use of verbs and adverbs, whereas he is quite high in qualitative expressions, such as nouns and adjectives, indicating a static approach to life. Does this fit with the results obtained on the Rorschach? Referring back to an earlier section, we find that he used only three M (movement) responses as compared with nine C (color) responses, which confirms the predicted tendency. In both cases we find that Karl shows a static, qualitative rather than an active, moving approach to his material. For the fourth time we find confirmation of his orientation toward the world (description) rather than toward himself (injection of action). He is an active person behaviorally but is responding to promptings from without, acting in and on the environment which is more important to him than his own inner states which would lead him to add to his perception of the world. Thus we are beginning to distill out of our analysis of this individual case a hypothetical construct which might be labeled something like "suggestibility" or "environment orientation" and which has already four different sets of operations. We might go further and predict on the basis of the surplus meanings suggested by the construct that Karl would be very much disoriented in Witkin's tilted room (1949), since he should be influenced more by visual cues (promptings from without) than by proprioceptive ones (promptings from within), although such an extension of the meanings of our construct might turn out to be unwarranted. It is only by the gradual building up and refining of such constructs that we can begin to extend the meaning of an expressive trait found in one area of behavior to other areas of behavior. Unfortunately we are only in a position to illustrate such relationships at the present time.

A Theoretical Note. This chapter has sampled some representative approaches to expressive traits without attempting to do complete justice to any one of them. Throughout all of the discussion two questions have insistently arisen: (1) What is an expressive trait? And (2) when is it a valid indicator of some other personality characteristic? The answer to the first question cannot be given in full until the chapter on trait theory, but we can give a tentative answer now. An expressive trait is the characteristic way in which a person learns to adapt to certain recurrent problems. Consider the problem of walking, for example. Every person has to walk. Yet there are a variety of possible ways in which a child can learn to walk. He can walk quickly, leaning forward, or slowly and deliberately, or rapidly with small steps. Which of these particular responses he happens upon is determined by a large number of factors which in any individual case would be hard to analyze. They would certainly include physical variables, social conventions, and probably some deeper underlying motivations. It is instructive to observe how these adaptive responses are learned in a completely new situation. A person can be given a new task, such as waving a baton or using a cane for the first time, and the observer will notice that after some preliminary trial and error his responses often settle down to a consistent pattern. It is this pattern which forms the basis of our conclusion that he has developed an expressive trait. What we mean by a trait in this instance is a recurrent similar response pattern to a given situation. The economy of adopting a regular habitual motor response to recurrent problems is obvious from the adaptive viewpoint. It fits in with all we know about the principles of learning.

The second question as to when we can use an expressive trait like this as an index of another and usually more important personality characteristic is much more difficult to answer. Yet, as we have repeatedly seen, this is what has chiefly interested psychologists. To get from one class of responses to another in this way requires some kind of common language, some common set of symbols or hypothetical constructs, which have operations in different areas of behavior (perception, movement, speech, etc.). And it is just here that psychologists dealing with different kinds of expressive behavior are weakest. Each has a language of his own. Each tries, as Wolff points out (1947), to interpret the hieroglyphs of different forms of expression, but there is no Rosetta stone to translate one set of constructs into another. Thus the Rorschacher or the semanticist cannot speak to the graphologist, or the graphologist to the somatyper.

For example, when Wolff speaks of expressiveness in punching a balloon (1947, p. 203), what is the relationship of this expressiveness to the movement response on the Rorschach, expansiveness in handwriting, or the energetic characteristic rated by Sheldon and others? When Wolff states: "Narrow movements connected with low pressure seem to indicate discouragement" (1947, p. 211), what is the relation between the discouragement measured in this way to the vista response on the Rorschach or the relatively high number of verbs used by anxiety hysterics?

The problem here is not what some psychologists have frequently assumed that it is. Many of them have argued that such statements as Wolff's are simply invalid. By validity they mean whether or not the response in question "measures what it is supposed to measure," but who knows what it is supposed to measure? What is the basic defining operation for discouragement? The notion of validity *assumes that there is one way of measuring (defining) a construct which is better than (or "truer" than) any other measure.* All other measures can then be tested for validity against this standard measure. Such a notion has a great deal of use in applied psychology where such "true" measures exist (as when, for example, a psychologist is trying to predict on the basis of a test score whether a person will pass or fail a criterion). But in personality theory there is often no basis for arguing that any *one* measure is any better than any other. Consequently the notion of validity is not very useful and ought not to be invoked as often as it is in the field. In its place we may use the criteria of inductive rigor and deductive fertility. That is, a concept is useful theoretically (1) to the extent that the person using it makes explicit its operational meanings and (2) to the extent that those operations cut across and are confirmed in different areas of behavior. So our question should be: What are the different ways of measuring "discouragement" or any such similar construct? Can we test them? Is there agreement or a rational relationship among these different measures of discouragement? If not, hadn't we better consider giving up "discouragement" in favor of a construct that will have different behavioral measures which do relate to one another in a rational way? We should make a sharp distinction at this point between *unverified* and *unverifiable* constructs. In the former instance we have a hypothetical construct that has implications which can be explicitly stated but which have not as yet been checked. In the latter we may have a term whose meaning is so vague that no rigorous deductions can be made from it which can be checked. Most of the thinking in psychodiagnostics is not so *unverifiable* as many psychologists would have us believe. On the other hand, most of it is *unverified.* What we would appear to need to do is to take such statements as Wolff's or the statements that the Rorschach workers make and subject them to the theoretical analysis which has been repeatedly suggested in the preceding discussion. We need to make surplus meanings explicit so that they can be explicitly checked. When we find that an implication is not confirmed, we need not throw out the concept but may instead refine the surplus meanings that we have intuitively given it.

The probable reason for failure to develop a science of personality in this direction is that most of the psychologists working in the field have been practical men who have had a clinical function to perform. That is, they have been concerned with making as shrewd guesses as they possibly could from the data they have used, for purposes of curing somebody or making a recommendation about school or vocational placement. When the emphasis is taken off such immediate practical objectives, we can expect eventually to develop a science of personality in which the constructs have a theoretical, as well as a purely practical significance. It is only when such a science develops that there will be a common language for all to understand and use.

NOTES AND QUERIES

1. In a very interesting discussion of whether or not the constitutional approach is fatalistic at the end of their book, *The Varieties of Temperament,* Sheldon and Stevens make the following statement: "It may be in one sense fatalistic to suppose that Christopher (an extreme ectomorph) cannot become a heavyweight champion, or that Boris (an extreme mesomorph) will never read cuneiform. Yet to try to fit Christopher and Boris to an indiscriminate behavioral or mental mold would seem a cruel misanthrophy. This would be to pretend psychological alchemy." (1942, pp. 437-438.) Make a careful analysis of this statement in the light of the discussion in the text on cause and effect. Is there any critical difference between the statements made about Christopher and Boris?

2. There are several ways in which knowing a person's physique will help predict his behavior. What are they? Is there any difference theoretically between predicting behavior from a knowledge of physique and predicting behavior from a knowledge of socioeconomic status? For instance, we might predict that because a person is poor, he will have a trait of shooting craps. In what sense does being poor "cause" crap shooting? This anticipates a little the discussion of the theoretical nature of a trait in Chapter 7, but this is a

natural context for trying to figure out the relation between *situations* and consistent behavior.

3. Rate someone on Sheldon's temperament scale. Then assign him tentative ratings on each of the three physique components. Check these ratings, if possible, through the tables giving the height-divided-by-cube-root-of-weight index in *The Varieties of Human Physique* (1940, pp. 287 and 267). Do you find much agreement between your physique and temperament indexes? To what extent did physique influence or enter into your original temperament ratings?

4. Make a list of factors which influence handwriting other than what we have been calling personal expressive traits. In other words, what besides personal dispositions may influence handwriting?

5. Ludwig Klages stands in the same relationship to handwriting analysis as Rorschach does to perception analysis. He makes a distinction between "bond" and "release" which is quite similar to the distinction Rorschach makes between "promptings from without" (bond) and "promptings from within" (release). "If inner impulses are stronger than requirements of external world, there will be indications of release; if conscious will for adaptation to external resistance prevails there will be greater indications of bond." (Bell, 1948, p. 302.) Bell lists the handwriting characteristics of each in part as follows:

Release	*Bond*
largeness	smallness
lack of pressure	pressure
width	narrowness
slant to right	vertical writing
upper lengths longer than under-lengths	under lengths longer than upper lengths
ascending lines	descending lines
irregularity	regularity
increasing left margins	decreasing left margins

From these measures can you relate the constructs of bond and release to the constructs used by Pascal in Table 5.5, who employed some of the same measures? For instance, how is *bond* related to *submissiveness* or *release* to *playfulness*? Analyze the handwriting specimens reproduced in Figure 5.1 for these characteristics. Try to decide whether Karl shows more bond or release and then see if your finding confirms the inferences drawn about his orientation toward the environment.

6. Why do you suppose that Klages' work is practically unknown and unused by psychologists in America as compared with Rorschach's work, which is widely known and used? Is there any inherent advantage for diagnostic purposes that perceptual modes of responding have over motor modes of responding?

7. Below are listed four samples of oral speech which were phonographically recorded and typed up. The subjects were telling stories in response to pictures for the Thematic Apperception Test. Try to match the two stories in each case which were spoken by the same person, and choose the pair spoken by Karl. Then analyze as well as you can the basis on which you made your match. Would quantitative analyses of the speech characteristics help make your match? Are there any elements in the verbal style which could apparently not be covered by such quantitative analyses?

A. This boy's father was a famous concert violinist before he was born. Unfortunately, he lost his life in a tragic accident. He was drowned. His wife was pregnant and had this chap. Might add that his father was at the peak of fame. Died on the night before the concert. Of course he left his fiddle, which was old and valuable, to his son. He always had hopes that he would teach his son and his son would play the fiddle better than his father. At the age of one year his mother died and the boy was left with an aunt and uncle who were not too favorably inclined toward fiddlers.

B. Looks like a mother and her son. Apparently something has happened—I'm going to use my imagination and say something particular happened. Well, I'd say he just came in and told his mother some bad news—I don't know what it is yet. But he's certainly taken her by surprise—she doesn't know what to say or what to think about it. Neither does he—I guess he had a hard time explaining what happened, by the look on his face.

C. Oh boy! Look at the background. What is it, a poster in the background? (Make it whatever you want.) Oh, I see. This chap has recently come home from overseas where he was with combat troops. While he was over there——He's a plenty wild character. He played havoc with the native women. He was favorably disposed toward them. He's quite a lustful fellow . . . a gigolo . . . Romeo . . . he likes to get around . . . .

D. This is a young fellow who thought he could get away with some petty crime and he has just been apprehended by a couple of policemen. You can see by the expression on his face he was not a bad boy at heart, etc., he just took this to make a meal on his own—how foolish it was and it wasn't the idea that crime doesn't pay so much as he didn't realize the sense of values, etc. He knows now and he was convinced all along that it was wrong—but it just took this one act to—the police got ahold of him—caught him with the goods so to speak—that brought him to . . . .

8. Figure out type-token ratios for two samples of your own verbal behavior on two different but comparable occasions. How closely do they agree? Take a third sample from a noncomparable situation (e.g., examinations *vs.* themes or letters). Does the nature of the situation change your speech habits much? Why?

9. Take any Rorschach concept and illustrate how you would go about making it into a theoretically useful one. Define its surplus meanings in such a way that they could be tested in other ways than through perception.

10. Summarize the trait characteristics that run through all of Karl's expressive behavior beginning with his posture and movement, his handwriting, his modes of perceiving, and his written speech. Are there any characteristics common to all these modes of expression? Write a brief summary of your knowledge of him to date, covering the *expressive* aspect of his personality and omitting any references to other aspects which appeared in the Rorschach analysis and elsewhere.

11. Try to demonstrate how the adjectives used in a personality sketch may influence the success of matching. Write sketches of three people you know very well, obtain a handwriting sample from each, and find a number of judges who are willing to match the handwriting with the sketches. Now prepare each sketch in two slightly different alternative forms so that one form contains adjectives which obviously refer to energy or movement characteristics (such as quick, alert, sluggish, etc.) and one form does not. Make sure that both forms describe the person equally well, however. Then ask one set of judges to match Form A with the handwriting samples, and another set Form B. Discuss the meaning of your results.

6

Performance Traits

A vast fund of information about personality which we have not as yet tapped is to be found in educational tests and measurements covering achievement, specialized abilities, and general intelligence. Looked at from the viewpoint of trait psychology, these tests may reveal how people respond consistently to a variety of different work situations with respect to such behavior characterizations as the amount of different types of material mastered in a given period of time, the ability to maintain a steady output, the ability to adapt quickly to a new situation, etc. Some people do consistently well—that is, cover a lot of ground—in certain types of tests, but not in other types of tests. Some people consistently start slowly but catch on quickly. Some people can never finish their work on time and others are always punctual. What we seem to be dealing with here are a number of traits which cluster around working, or performing, standardized laboratory tests. Let us coin the term *performance trait* to cover a variety of different consistent modes of responding to problem situations. Certain ways in which people perform cannot readily be reproduced in laboratory test situations. For such cases measures of the traits involved have had to be obtained by ratings or check lists based on the techniques of controlled observation discussed in Chapter 2. For this reason we will deal first with performance traits derived from standardized tests and second with performance traits based on ratings of behavior under field conditions.

Serious theoretical problems arise when we try to integrate the results of educational measurement into personality theory. The raw material with which we work is no longer behavior but the outcome of behavior. The question no longer is, does this person consistently approach a perceptual situation wholistically (W on the Rorschach), but, how many problems can this person solve in which W is presumably needed for solution? Trait information is derived from the second type of question by a more devious route which involves (1) inferences about the relative strength of the trait in question from comparison with the number of similar problems solved by other people under similar circumstances and (2) inferences about what behavior is required for the solution of a particular problem or class of problems. This last procedure may be particularly hazardous, since, as clinicians are fond of pointing out, a particular problem may be solved in a variety of different ways. Two persons may get exactly the same score on a block-design test but one may proceed cautiously and systematically, the other spasmodically, relying on quick perceptual reorganizations.

A further problem arises because the testing movement has been oriented mainly toward *evaluating performance* rather than toward characterizing adequately the behavior of individuals. Such an orientation is an instance of the evaluative approach discussed in Chapter 3 as typical of the theorists who are interested in *character* rather than personality. We were critical of Murray and Morgan (1945) for judging Hawk in terms of whether or not he would make a good soldier, on the grounds that while this was an important question, it was not the business of personality theory proper. Similarly statements of how intelligent a person is are evaluations in terms of a judgmental framework. In fact Stoddard (1943) has defined intelligence to include such standards as "adaptiveness to a goal, social value, the emergence of originals" and "resistance to emotional forces" along with the more conventional standards of difficulty and abstractness of problems performed, etc. In so doing he makes clearer than ever that intelligence judgments involve various value standards that are relevant to estimating social effectiveness but not to describing personality according to the scientific standards we laid down in Chapter 3.

But this does not mean that we cannot use for our purposes the data which Murray and Morgan or the intelligence testers collect to make their evaluations. It is just that the task will prove more difficult than if the data had been collected for our purposes to begin with. Concretely we will be interested in the percentile standing of Karl on a particular test for the insight it will give us on how he behaves in a certain standardized work situation. From this we should be able to predict what his behavior will be under similar work situations, but we will not be interested in asking whether he is "up to scratch" or meets certain standards of brightness or intelligence in those situations. The distinction is tricky and hard to keep clear because exactly the same datum (test score) can be used to draw inferences about Karl or, as is much more common, to make a judgment as to how smart he is, how well he will do in college, etc.

Tests

Any consideration of efficiency or of methods of working leads inevitably into the field of intelligence and intelligence testing. We may have to pause a moment to justify the inclusion of intelligence in a book on personality. Strange as it may seem, it has become customary to consider intelligence and personality as separate. As Cattell says (1946a, p. 396): "In some psychological writings it has become almost customary to omit abilities when studying personality." Yet certainly as the term *personality* has been used and defined in this book, intellectual functioning is just as legitimate a part of it as is any other kind of behavior. Furthermore, as any clinical psychologist knows, intelligence and personality cannot in fact be separated when the individual person is the object of study. Some of the reasons for this split between intelligence and personality will become apparent in the discussion which follows. Probably the most important reason is the evaluative orientation already mentioned, combined with the lack of any determined effort to integrate the theory of intelligence into a more general theory of personality.

Intelligence Measurement. Probably the most widely publicized achievement of psychology has been the ability to test intelligence. Even though it is not as true now as it once was, many people still think of a psychologist as someone who "gives tests"—even, as some of the most cynical among them might add, if he cannot interpret them. This, strangely enough, is the nub of the problem. The psychologist has never been sure exactly what his tests measure. He has been well aware of this fact and has often publicly admitted it. In doing so he may in quiet desperation simply say that intelligence or musical ability or what not is simply what an intelligence or musical-ability test measures, which is scarcely satisfying to the layman, or to the theoretical psychologist either, for that matter. Or he may make a bold attempt to define intelligence broadly as "the global capacity of the individual to act purposefully, to think rationally, and to deal effectively with his environment" (Wechsler, 1944, p. 3) and then go on to claim that his test measures whatever such a statement implies.

But the fact remains that our theoretical understanding of intelligence is not satisfactory. It has lagged far behind our technical competence in developing scales for discriminating the more from the less intelligent. Psychologists have worked long and hard in standardizing their tests, putting out instructions for their use, training test examiners, and refining their data statistically to make sure the tests discriminate equally well over all sections of the scale. But no comparable advances have been made in understanding what the tests measure. We have advanced a very long way since Binet's time in our knowledge of what items are good to use in intelligence scales, at what different age levels, and in other such items of practical importance, but we have not advanced nearly as far in understanding the theoretical nature of that part of personality which has come to be called intelligence. Psychologists agree that certain tests are not tests of intelligence (e.g., high jumping) and that test problems should somehow involve the higher mental functions. But, although the area of higher mental functions is pretty well agreed upon, to judge by the kind of tests that are used, still it is hard to define precisely what intellectual functions are involved in the tests. To illustrate this point, let us take a look at one of the most popular adult intelligence tests, the Wechsler-Bellevue Intelligence Scale.

The Wechsler-Bellevue has ten sub-tests and one alternate vocabulary test. Table 6.1 names the tests and gives a brief description of the mental functions supposed to be measured by the tests according to Wechsler, at least so far as he could tell from a rough analysis of what is required to do well on them.

TABLE 6.1

Approximate Mental Functions Measured by Wechsler-Bellevue Sub-Tests According to Wechsler (1944, pp. 77-101)

Test Name	*Task*	*Mental Function*
1. Information	Answering wide variety of questions; e.g., "Who is President of the U.S.?"	Range of information
2. Comprehension	Answering "What would you do if" questions	Common sense
3. Arithmetical reasoning	Solving arithmetic problems	"Mental alertness"
4. Memory span for digits	The number of digits which can be retained after one presentation repeated forwards or backwards	Rote memory and attention

TABLE 6.1 (*Continued*)

Test Name	*Task*	*Mental Function*
5. Similarities test	For example, "In what way are an orange and a banana the same?"	Logical or abstractive character of the S's thinking
6. Picture completion	Name missing part in a picture on a card	Ability to "differentiate essential from unessential details"
7. Picture arrangement	Arrange pictures to make a sensible story	Ability to comprehend and size up a whole situation
8. Object assembly	Put pieces together, to make a form (e.g., hand)	Whole-part modes of approach
9. Block design	Make a design with colored blocks like the one on a card	Synthetic-analytic ability
10. Digit symbol	Placing digits under symbols according to a key	Speed of learning
11. Vocabulary	For example, "What does *apple* mean?"	Learning ability; range of information

The "Mental Functions" listed in this table are "hypothetical constructs" with surplus meanings in the sense in which the term was defined in Chapter 4. Since they refer to the outcome of behavior (success or failure on a variety of tasks), they are usually called "abilities" rather than traits. Traits, as we have used the term, refer more to the consistent modes of behavior that produce success and failure. They seem better adapted to personality theory than ability constructs, since the purpose of such a theory is to predict behavior rather than the results of behavior. Nevertheless the two kinds of constructs overlap. "Speed of learning," for instance, is an ability construct which predicts that if a person scores high on the digit symbol substitution test he ought to do well in other types of learning situations. The outcome of his behavior in one test situation is used to predict the outcome of his behavior in other similar test situations. But as soon as the generality of this ability construct is checked, it will appear that predictions are good for some types of test situations and not for others. A person with high "speed of learning" on digit symbol substitution will probably also get a high score on a language-learning test, but not on a mechanical assembly learning test. These differences lead the theorist to suppose that what lies behind the speed of learning outcomes are a variety of behavioral traits that make success probable in one situation and not in another. The theorist may then go on to describe two hypothetical trait constructs: symbol orientation and spatial orientation. One person may think characteristically in terms of symbols which makes him quick in learning a digit symbol task; another may think in terms of visual images which will make him adept at learning a mechanical assembly task. Factor analysis, as we shall see later, may provide a more systematic means of going from ability constructs to trait constructs in this way.

An obvious feature of Table 6.1 as it stands is the miscellaneous nature of the mental functions or hypothetical constructs listed on the right-hand side. They have been drawn as accurately as possible from Wechsler's own descriptions of his tests and what they presumably measure. Although he recognizes the importance of defining what his tests measure, he does not specifically state anywhere how each of these particular mental functions is related to the task in question. Nevertheless the table is helpful, if not systematic, in suggesting what some of the major intellectual traits are: abstractive thinking, analytic-synthetic approach, attentiveness, differentiation of cues, etc. It does not cover the whole field of intellectual traits because the intelligence tester will eliminate those tests which do not discriminate among his criterial groups. No matter how useful a test might be considered for describing some aspect of a person's behavior in performance situations, it will be discarded if it does not discriminate the more from the less intelligent. For instance, if it were found that a certain test evoked an analytic mode of approach in most people, it would not appear in intelligence tests because it would not help spread people along an intelligence dimension. Yet it might be an excellent situation for checking how consistently analytic a person was in his approach to problems. Because of their emphasis on discriminating power, intelligence tests probably do not sample the entire range of performance traits.

Another rich source of information about possible intellectual traits is to be found in the case reports written by clinical psychologists who have been more interested in behavior than in the outcome of behavior. A good example is *Case Lanuti* by Hanfmann, Rickers-Ovsiankina, and Goldstein (1944). Not a single test score is reported in this study although the patient was given many tests. The reason is that the authors were interested in his behavior on the tests and not in how well he did on them. They were interested in characterizing his performance traits, as we are. For instance they write: "The only adequate mode of behavior for Lanuti is that of concrete immediate action." (1944, p. 23.) He could not recognize a key unless he used it in a door, a pencil until he wrote with it, etc. "Any task that requires detachment from the momentary situation, thinking in categories, spontaneity, initiation of action at will, shifting voluntarily, is outside the scope of the patient." (1944, p. 70.) They were able to arrive at this characterization of the patient's behavior after observing his response to many different test situations. The point is that his test performance was used to characterize him rather than to evaluate him. Wechsler makes similar comments from time to time: "The Object Assembly, like the Block Design Test, seems to get at some sort of creative ability, especially if the performance is done rapidly." "Successful reproduction of the Object Assembly items depends upon the subjects' familiarity with figures and their ability to deal with the part-whole relationship." "It sometimes reveals the ability to work for an unknown goal." (1944, p. 98.)

Such individualistic analyses are lost sight of and may be impossible in large-scale group testing, the purpose of which is evaluation. Often a particular test is processed by machine scoring and yields only a collection of standard scores which are not of very much assistance in trying to characterize an individual's behavior. Neither the problems with which the person was faced nor the particular kinds of successes or failures he made are evident to the observer: all he has is the outcome of a complex, unanalyzed behavioral process. It is small wonder that those who have been mainly interested in characterizing the individual—the psychoanalysts, for example—have found little use for standardized test scores in their case studies.

Karl's Test Results. To illustrate concretely what we have been discussing in a general way, let us see what we can learn about Karl from his test results. He obtained the following scores on the College Entrance Examination Board tests.

Test Name	*Standard Score*
Verbal	535
Social Studies	619
Language	461
Mathematics	598
Science	677

Since the mean of each of these tests has been set at 500 with a standard deviation of 100 we can tell from this table how well he did in comparison with others and we can compare his score on one test directly with that on another. For example, we note that he did quite well on the social studies test—above the 85th percentile, in fact—and that he was below average on the language test. In general these scores tell us that he is a pretty good bet for college and should be able to get fairly high marks. They might even suggest to us that he should avoid languages and should concentrate in social studies or sciences. But beyond this we are not given very much to go on to figure out how he operates intellectually. We do not know what types of items he attempted and which ones he failed. We did not watch him at work. There is a great deal of information about his behavior that we would like to have.

To illustrate how some of this information may be recaptured by a more careful interpretation of tests, let us turn to the scores he obtained on the Iowa Silent Reading Test, which provides a variety of scores on a number of ingenious sub-tests. Table 6.2 tells the story.

TABLE 6.2

Karl's Iowa Silent Reading Test Scores

Test Name	*Raw Score*	*Standard Score*		*Percentile Standing in Freshman Class*
1. Rate-comprehension			95	57
Rate	36	88		
Comprehension	27	101		
2. Directed reading	10		89	50
3. Poetry comprehension	8		80	8
4. Word meaning	47		99	58
5. Sentence meaning	39		99	80
6. Paragraph comprehension			100	71
Central idea	10	94		
Development	22	105		
7. Location of information			77	15
Use of index	8	80		
Selection of key words	8	74		
Median score			95	63

Karl's over-all median score is in the 63rd percentile of a group of comparable entering Freshmen but there are some rather wide differences in his ability to perform on different parts of the test

He is above average on most of the test but falls down sharply on "Location of Information" and "Poetry Comprehension," while he is very good at Sentence Meaning. Studying the nature of these subtests may give us some further clues as to his methods of thinking. In the Poetry Comprehension Test, the task is to read through a rather complex allegorical poem entitled "Wisdom" and then to answer pointed questions about the meaning of the poem. The specific task is for the subject to find the number of the clause in the poem which contains the answer to a question like "What feeling inspired the poet to write?" Even though the subject may understand the poem quite well, he may have difficulty locating the exact phrase with its corresponding number that answers the question. Much the same sort of task is involved in the other test on which he did poorly, the one which requires the location of information through the use of an index. A sample question is, "Does the index tell where to find information about the industrial uses of cork?" The subject must then decide under what topic to look in the index in order to answer *yes* or *no* to this question. As in the case of poetry comprehension, the process involved here of breaking a whole meaning down into a salient feature is very difficult for Karl, although he is obviously excellent—in fact, much better than the average—at comprehending whole sentences and paragraphs.

But with sentence and paragraph comprehension the task is different. What he has to do is to answer *yes* or *no* as fast as he can to a series of questions like, "Is an undesirable reputation often based on a record of misbehavior?" This task does not appear to require the same detailed analysis and searching that the other two do. In short, we appear to have isolated two of Karl's consistent intellectual traits. On the one hand he seems very good at grasping general meanings, and on the other he seems consistently poor at breaking those general meanings down into details. He is global rather than analytic in his thinking. Somewhat similar traits were discovered in his Rorschach analysis, where it was reported that he gave a fairly large number of whole responses (W) indicating the same tendency toward "abstractual" thinking as we have noted here. The evidence of the Rorschach on whether he can break down whole responses (e.g., general ideas) into salient details is not clear-cut although his distribution of 12W, 26D, and 4Dd indicates a disproportionate emphasis on whole responses (W!) which in Beck's words is "the sign of an overall thinker." (1944, p. 14.) There is also no evidence for the orderly sequence of W, D and Dd which one would expect from the "dehumanized professor" who ought to be very good with indexes.

Factor Analysis. Our analysis so far has illustrated how information about performance traits may be suggested by or teased out of various test results, but the problem remains of systematically developing a comprehensive set of traits for describing this aspect of personality. Case analyses like Lanuti's or Karl's are a step in the right direction, but they do not solve the theoretical problem of deciding what intellectual traits we need in our systematic description of personality. Factor analysts have been interested in this problem. They have tried to get behind the actual test scores to the "factors" within the person which account for the scores. Their method has been to work with correlation coefficients, which means that they have attempted to base their theoretical interpretations on co-variations of test scores. As Cattell puts it: "The unity of a set of parts is established by their moving—i.e., appearing, changing, disappearing—together, by their exercising an effect together, and by an influence on one being an influence on all." (1946a, p. 71.) This is both a definition of a factor arrived at by factor analysis and of a psychological trait. So Cattell and others have argued that factor analysis is the royal road to discovering the fundamental psychological traits not only in the intellectual sphere but in all other spheres of personality as well. Thurstone (1938) would call these factors abilities rather than traits, but his purpose is the same as Cattell's. It is to discover the fundamental theoretical units in terms of which the variety of test behavior may be explained or described.

Factor analysis is a very large and complicated subject, but we will approach it, as we have equally difficult matters, through a concrete example. The example has been chosen for its simplicity rather than for its contribution to knowledge in this field. It is a study by R. A. Clark on the problem of "closure" in mental organization (1947). Clark was simply interested in determining whether there was any single factor, trait, or ability which produced high intercorrelations among a variety of tests purporting to measure "closure" as the term is generally understood in Gestalt psychology. Put in another way, his problem was to find perceptual, motor, and cognitive tests which could be scored for the subject's tendency to draw disparate elements together into an over-all coherent structure. Having assembled such tasks, he could then correlate the "closure" scores on all of them to see if the trait in question was sufficiently general to characterize different kinds of behavior. In selecting his tests he followed Guilford's advice (1940) of trying to pick ones which could be solved only by the behavioral approach under study. If the tasks are complex, the resulting factorial structure is likely to be complex too, and the interpretation in terms of any particular one or two traits becomes exceedingly difficult.

The best way to understand this approach is to describe the tests used, paying particular attention to the kind of behavior needed for their solution.

Clark chose some twenty tests in all, sixteen of which were used in his final factor analysis and nine of which are described here.

1. Street Gestalt. This test was adapted from one invented by Street and used by Thurstone (1938), and consists of a number of pictures, large sections of which are missing. The figures are printed in India ink on white cardboard and were presented tachistoscopically for three seconds on a screen. The subject's task was to try to identify the figure, which was of some common object, such as a violin, a rabbit, a stove, or a clock. The subject's score was the number of correct identifications or "closures" in the time allotted for each picture.

2. Mutilated words. The material in this test is very similar to that in the first. It consists of a number of words printed in India ink on white cards, parts of which have been erased, and the subject's task is to identify the words. Both this test and the Street Gestalt require the subject to synthesize discrete perceptual elements.

3. Reversible figures. The material for this test consisted of four figures, which could be seen in two entirely different ways. One was the well-known picture which could be seen either as an attractive young woman or as an ugly old hag. The score was the number of seconds it took the subject to see the second figure after he had seen the first. The task is more complicated than the first two but involves the same elements. Now the subject must synthesize into a figure elements which are, however, not just discrete but part of another figure.

4. Mirror tracing. This was the standard laboratory test in which the subject has to trace a star seen in a mirror. It was included in this test battery following a suggestion made by Peters (1946) that it measured flexibility which, as in test 3, should indicate the ability of the subject to combine cues in a new synthesis.

5. Motor flexibility. This test is better known under the name of motor perseveration. It consisted of six sub-tests adopted from R. B.

Cattell, who has done extensive research and theorizing in this field (1946b). Each test requires the subject to perform an ordinary task as many times as possible within sixty seconds and then to perform the same task in an unaccustomed or reversed manner as many times as possible in sixty seconds. The six specific tasks were (1) to write the word *ready* forward and then backward, (2) to write the sentence "John has gone to the store for meat" normally and then alternating lower-case letters and printed block capitals, (3) writing the same sentence normally or writing it with each letter doubled, (4) reading a passage normally, followed by reading it with both words and lines backward, (5) writing one's own name normally, followed by writing it backward beginning at the right-hand end, (6) writing the number 653 normally, followed by writing it with backward strokes. In each case the number of times that the subject was able to perform the unusual task in sixty seconds was divided by the number of times the subject was able to do the same task normally in sixty seconds. This gave a flexibility rather than a perseveration score since the higher the ratio, the better the subject was able to perform the unaccustomed task, or make a new synthesis.

6. Anagrams. This is a test adapted from Thurstone (1938) in which the subject has to make as many words as possible in four minutes from the key word *generation*.

7. Scrambled words I. Here the task was to rearrange a jumbled series of letters to make a word with a special kind of meaning, e.g., to rearrange the letters *itgre* to spell the name of an animal.

8. Scrambled words II. The task here was to rearrange the letters of a word to make a new word with a special meaning, e.g., to rearrange the word *melon* to spell the name of a fruit. Tests 6, 7, and 8 all seemed to involve a kind of conceptual as opposed to perceptual synthesis or closure.

9. Memory figures. The subjects were presented with five simple geometric figures, each of which was presented for six seconds. Each of the figures contained some slight defect (for example, a circle with a gap in the top of it) and the subjects were instructed to observe the figures as carefully as possible in order to be able to recall them later in the session. After about forty-five minutes the subjects were shown six slides in each of which was included the original figure along with eight others very similar in size, shape, etc. The subjects' task was to select the figure which they considered to be the original one and the answer they gave was scored for its approximation to good-Gestalt, as the term is understood in Gestalt psychology. For

example, subjects who chose figures in which the gap was smaller were scored for closure or good-Gestalt. Here memory closure is being measured as contrasted with perceptual closure in tests 1 and 2.

Most of these tests have been used often before by other investigators, either in this form or in a slightly modified one. Incidentally, many of them could be considered tests of intelligence in the broadest sense (cf. Thurstone, 1938). Clark then gave these tests, along with the seven others in the battery, to thirty subjects and intercorrelated their scores on the sixteen tests. The intercorrelations for the nine tests just described are shown in Table 6.3.

TABLE 6.3

Tetrachoric Correlation Coefficients among Various "Closure" Tests
($N=30$, $r_t=.48$ at 1% level of significance)

	Str. Gest.	*Mut. Wds.*	*Rev. Fig.*	*Mir. Trac.*	*Mot. Flex.*	*Ana.*	*Scr. Wds.I*	*Scr. Wds.II*
1. Street Gestalt	—	+.82	+.75	+.48	+.68			
2. Mutilated words		—	+.38	+.66	+.74	Cluster I		
3. Reversible figures			—	+.47	+.28			
4. Mirror tracing				—	+.65		Cluster II	
5. Motor flexibility					—	+.52	+.72	+.25
6. Anagrams	+.06	+.06	−.09	+.48	Cluster I	—	+.94	+.89
7. Scrambled words I (nonsense)	+.20	+.03	+.46	+.21	vs.		—	+.90
8. Scrambled words II (sense)	+.30	+.10	+.31	+.06	Cluster II			
9. Memory figures	−.40	−.02	.00	−.10	−.04	+.17	−.10	−.30

Since these correlations are tetrachorics and based on very few subjects, they are to be taken as suggestive. The correlations do not give a very good estimate of the extent of a relationship, but do indicate whether it is significant or not. A tetrachoric correlation of around .48 is significant at the 1 per cent level with this number of subjects. The correlation table has been arranged in such a way as to show the fact that there are two distinct clusters of high intercorrelations, one including tests 1-5 and another including tests 5-8. It will be noted that in the first cluster there are eight out of ten correlations significant at or beyond the 1 per cent level, whereas in the second cluster there are five out of six correlations significant at the 1 per cent level. Furthermore, as the lower left-hand cluster of correlations in the table shows, the two clusters do not intercorrelate significantly. Out of the twelve intercluster correlations there is only one which approaches the 1 per cent level of significance. Note also that Motor Flexibility is contained in both clusters and that Memory Figures is contained in neither. These results suggest immediately that closure is not an over-all unitary trait or ability. At least tests purporting to measure closure in perception do not correlate highly with tests involving verbal closure. Instead there seem to be two closure factors and the two motor tests, especially Motor Flexibility, involve both factors. One suggests perceptual synthesis, the other cognitive synthesis.

The whole correlation matrix, including all 16 variables, was subjected to a factor analysis following Thurstone's centroid method. As anyone would readily guess who is familiar with this procedure, the factor analysis provided a very good simple structure, leading to a two-factor solution centering in the two clusters already noted, but with an important exception which can be observed in the factor saturations given below:

Factor I

Street Gestalt	.90
Mutilated words	.82
Reversible figures	.74
Mirror tracing	.60
(Motor flexibility	.25)

Factor II

Anagrams	.97
Scrambled words I	.91
Motor flexibility	.80
Scrambled words II	.67

Notice what happens to Motor Flexibility. Although it was contained in the *cluster* which included Street Gestalt, Mutilated Words, etc., it turns out to have a very low saturation on the *factor* which includes these same tests. On the other hand it turns up with a very high saturation on Factor II, corresponding to the second cluster. The explanation for this lies in the fact that the Motor Flexibility tests must have behaved like the tests in Factor II with regard to the seven other variables in the matrix and unlike the tests in Factor I with regard to those same seven variables. This shows how factor analysis can often add information to that which results from a simple cluster analysis. Of course not many correlation tables can be so readily broken down into clusters as this particular one, which was chosen as an example largely because its structure is so simple. Note also that the Memory for Figures Test, which is a good closure test, as far as the principles of Gestalt psychology are concerned, still does not fit in with the other tests. Apparently the tendency toward closure in perception and in memory are not the same thing. The person who synthesizes perceptual cues does not necessarily synthesize memory traces in the same way, at least so far as these fallible measuring instruments are concerned. Probably other factors enter into the memory process.

But the central theoretical problem is to try to analyze the nature of the two factors which have been obtained by this elaborate statistical analysis. It is here that the factor analyst's ingenuity is taxed to the utmost. Often many of them seem at a loss by the time they arrive at their factors and they end up with names which are about as miscellaneous as the names which Wechsler used to describe his various tests. Factor I in this instance is easily identified with a factor called "speed of perception" found by Thurstone (1944), which saturated highly the first two tests listed here (as well as "speed of dark-adaptation" and "span of visual peripheral vision") but did not saturate "Reversible Figures" or "Mirror Tracing" because these tests were not included in Thurstone's battery. Unfortunately "speed of perception" is not too informative a trait or ability title. What does quick dark-adaptation have in common with mirror tracing? Or span of peripheral vision with the ability to fuse discrete visual cues into a Gestalt? Perhaps all these tests involve the subject in perceptually unfamiliar situations and the scores on all of them reflect his ability to get information or organized percepts from strange cues. Unfortunately, as the list of tests which saturate the factor increases, it becomes harder and harder to infer what psychological process or processes are involved in getting a high score on all of them.

The difficulty is even greater with Factor II. It too appears at first glance to be similar to one of Thurstone's factors which he labels W for "word fluency" in his book *Primary Mental Abilities* (1938). His factor saturates anagrams and what he calls "disarranged words" very highly, also spelling and grammar tests (1938, p. 84). The joker is that Clark's Factor II includes the motor flexibility test. This test (much more commonly known as *motor perseveration*) has plagued psychologists for a long time. In an attempt to resolve the "riddle of perseveration," as he calls it, Cattell cites (1946b) some thirty different studies of perseveration of one kind or another. Certainly the presence of this test in Factor II is puzzling and means that we cannot label the factor "word fluency," since words are not involved in motor perseveration in any very obvious way.

At this point there are two attitudes that one can take toward the naming problem. One can regard a factor as an intervening variable (cf. Chapter 4), in which case a name is chosen for the factor which has as its operational meaning the tests which go to make up the factor. In this case we might turn to some Greek word and perhaps refer to Factor II as the catoptric or "mirror-image" factor or something of the sort. If anyone asks what this factor means, the only appropriate answer is to tell him to look at the tests, because they are what the factor means operationally. This is the answer sometimes preferred by Thurstone and by those who have difficulty in finding a theoretical definition of intelligence.

The other approach involves the use of hypothetical constructs, based on an attempt at further analysis of the mental processes required for solving the problems in the tests themselves. In the present case, for instance, we might argue that all the tasks in Factor II may be solved by hard, conscientious effort, suppression of distractions, and systematic building up of small units. In contrast, the tests in Factor I require perceptual reorganization which does not necessarily result from hard, conscientious effort. The next step would be to create a hypothetical construct for each factor—"persistence" (Factor II) and "flexibility of perceptual organization" (Factor I) for instance —and to explore more fully the surplus meanings of each by constructing purified tests that maximize the necessity of these traits for solution (cf. Lovell, 1944). In this way a number of performance trait variables might be isolated from factor analyses.

The Weakness of Present-Day Factor Analysis. Factor analysts are seldom able to proceed in as simple and straightforward a way as this. Instead they usually start off with so many tests of complex structure that it is nearly impossible to identify any simple trait constructs of the sort just proposed. To illustrate the difficulties, let us take a look at some of the evidence in Clark's study which has so far been suppressed. In the first place, factors in Cattell's compendium of factor analytic studies (1946a) which, like Clark's Factor II, saturate highly such tests as anagrams, generally saturate motor flexibility not at all or negatively! Yet these two tests were associated in Clark's results. This raises the question of whether the factorial composition of a given test is invariant or dependent on the other tests in the battery (cf. Thurstone, 1947), a question of considerable theoretical importance which is too complex to treat here. In the second place, Clark threw some other test scores into his correlation matrix which have so far not been mentioned. In addition to the nine tests described, he used the Allport-Vernon Study of Values Test because he was interested in determining whether closure had any personality correlates. It turned out that Factor I (flexibility of perceptual organization) saturated .49 on the Economic scale and —.52 on the Social scale of this test. Furthermore, the Religious scale saturated —.72 on Factor II (persistence). What are we to do about naming our hypothetical constructs now? Can we somehow reformulate perceptual flexibility as a descriptive title so that it includes an interest in and liking for economic values and a dislike for social values? Must we conclude that people with high religious values are low in persistence? Obviously not. What appears to have happened now is that relationships are being found which may have some deeper motivational connection. The picture is obscured rather than clarified by the addition of such measures from a totally different area of personality. If we include a wide miscellany of tests in a battery, we shall get out miscellaneous factors—factors which saturate such a variety of tests that we cannot make much real theoretical sense out of them. If we put in purified tests, and understand thoroughly the nature of performance on them, we are likely to get out factors whose meaning we can also understand.

The real difficulty has been that some factor theorists assume that "blind" factor analysis is the royal road to psychological theory. Its advantage seems to them to be that, starting with a miscellaneous assortment of tests, the real nature of which is unknown, one can by intercorrelating them arrive at the fundamental dimensions of the mind. And furthermore, they sometimes assume that order is "out there" in nature and all the factor analyst does is discover it by a purely empirical method without any theoretical preconceptions. Thurstone has demonstrated that by intercorrelating miscellaneous measures of physical objects one can arrive by factor analysis at the three theoretically important dimensions of space (length, width and height). This would appear to justify the use of a "blindly empirical" approach to theory. But why didn't he discover the space-time dimensions of modern physics? Obviously here as elsewhere what was obtained from the factor analysis was largely determined by the implicit theoretical preconceptions that were involved in the *choice of measurements* made in setting up the correlation matrix in the first place. Sometimes factor analysis is useful in making explicit a theorist's unconscious assumptions.

A study reported by Eysenck (1947) illustrates the point. He factor analyzed the answers to an item sheet filled out by psychiatrists for about seven hundred patients "suffering from the mainly reactive types of mental illness." (1947, p. 33.) Some of the items on the sheet called for objective data about the patient's family or work history, and some called for a judgment on the part of the examining psychiatrist. For instance, the psychiatrist checked whether in his judgment the patient was: *badly organized, dependent, anxious, irritable, narrow in his interests, of little energy,* etc. When these ratings were included in a factor analysis along with some fairly objective criteria like: *boarded out of the army, dyspepsia, tremor, unemployed,* etc., Eysenck discovered a factor which he labeled *neuroticism* because it saturated highly on: "badly organized personality, dependent, abnormal before illness, boarded out [of the army], narrow interests, little energy, abnormality in parents, schizoid, dyspepsia . . ." (1947, p. 36). But psychiatrists, if they are well-trained in their profession, undoubtedly have general conceptions of what they mean by "neuroticism," "hysteria," "dysthymia," and "hypochondriasis" (other factors found by Eysenck). These general conceptions will cause their ratings on individual items to be associated, which in turn will produce factors corresponding to their preconceived notions. To put the matter simply, the factor analysis discovered that psychiatrists have learned as part of their training that certain symptoms belong together in syndromes—that unemployed are apt to have badly organized personalities, that badly organized personalities have little energy and are apt to be unemployed, etc. This is interesting. It may show that psychiatrists group symptoms together in ways different from what they had supposed they did. It may be used to change their conceptions of disease patterns. But the point is that the theoretical dimensions of personality supposedly "discovered" by the "blindly" empirical factor analysis were in part already consciously or unconsciously in the minds of the psychiatrists filling out the item sheet on which the statistical analysis was based. Knapp (Goodrich and Knapp, 1950) has actually capitalized on this fact and factor analyzed a series of his own judgments of successful teachers' personalities to get a sounder basis for discovering what his general impressions were.

Greene has summarized the relation of factor analysis to psychological theory as follows: "When the tests are constructed so that the same scores may represent very different sorts of ability, then no clear explanation of factors can be made. When tests are constructed to allow only one method for success, however, then factor analyses will yield results that can be clearly recognized by psychologists." (1941, p. 341.) In other words, Greene is arguing that theory must enter to some extent into the choice of measurements and that factor analysis is essentially a methodological tool like any statistic and must serve theory rather than create it. Clark fortunately had fairly definite hypotheses as to what it took to succeed on his tests and consequently he came out with two factors which are more meaningful (exclusive of the Allport-Vernon test results) than many of the factors reported in the literature.

Does this mean that we can make no use of the results of factor analysis to date? Fortunately things are far from that bad. In spite of the limitations of factor analysis, Cattell (1946a) has attempted with considerable success to match factors obtained in a wide variety of different investigations. Just in the area of the kind of test we have been discussing, he lists (1946a, pp. 399-407) approximately 180 factors! By some ingenious cross-matching he manages to reduce these into five basic types of factors dealing with (1) *ability* (general, mechanical, spatial, etc.); (2) *persistence* (will-character, plodding application, inhibition); (3) *variability* (oscillation or fluctuation); (4) *speed* (fluency or tempo); and (5) *perseveration* (disposition rigidity or flexibility). Perhaps the meaning of all these is sufficiently clear except for the last, which refers to the motor flexibility tests described above, in which the subject has to make a "creative effort" to perform a task in some unaccustomed manner. As noted above, effort and suppression of distractions seem to distinguish the behavior involved here from the "flexibility of perceptual organization" factor found in Clark's study.

Summary of Test Performance Traits. Keeping in mind Cattell's findings and those of the testing movement, let us try to list the basic performance traits of personality. Since all tests are problems which have to be solved, we can begin our inquiry by noting the different ways in which a person can go about working on or solving a problem. Figure 6.1 has been prepared to help isolate performance traits from a schematic analysis of the different ways in which people can behave in problem situations.

FIGURE 6.1

Schematic Diagram to Illustrate Different Types of Performance

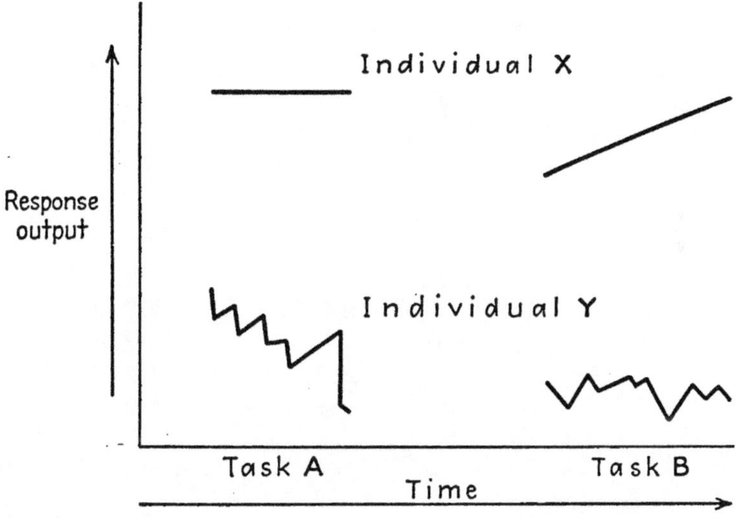

1. **Mode of Approach.** On Task A in Figure 6.1 individual X shows a higher response output than individual Y. The meaning of this difference in trait terms is determined, as we have seen, from an analysis of the requirements of the task. If, for instance, the task requires a wholistic approach, we conclude that individual X approaches problems wholistically. It was in just this fashion that we concluded that Karl was an over-all thinker who had difficulty with tasks that required a breakdown of global units into smaller ones. What are the major modes of approach that have been isolated by this method? Any final answer to such a question is impossible at this stage of our knowledge, but the following traits are strongly suggested by the evidence to date.

a. **Whole-Part Approach.** One of the simplest ways to characterize problem-solving behavior is in terms of whether the person thinks or tries to think in terms of the whole pattern or whether he works with small parts of it. The simplest illustration of this trait is the

l if purified over their presen
f what the hierarchy is for an
example, Hanfmann and Kas

e in the performance of ind
6.1 is the fact that X is able t
What is apparently involve
ions, boredom, discomfort, c
presented in Clark's Factor I
on had to work hard and pe
do well on the tasks involve
this trait at length and sugges
nces as the average strength
will endure a painful shock
a person will spend on a ta

ure 6.1 shows much greater u
ndividual X. Some people wo
re, others show wide variatio
ne index of variability (e.g., t
. Some people are consisten
and. Cattell (1946a, p. 418) l
the existence of such a trait

vidual X has difficulty in p
reas individual Y does not.
e cannot shift readily from o
tasks in Clark's Factor I seem
mode of sol ion to anoth
others have sed this tr
appears to b olar oppos
is mustered e for the
ce in a wid of tasks.

er outp sponses
n indi . While
ns t his do
sts that

W response on the Rorschach which appeared more frequently than normal in Karl's record. We also found evidence of this trait in Karl in the way he approached different sections of the Iowa Silent Reading Test. Other evidence for it could be found in noting the way a person attempted to solve such Wechsler-Bellevue tests as Picture Completion, Block Design, and Similarities. None of these tests is pure, however. Now that we have a hunch such a trait is important, the next step is to define it more carefully and attempt to design tests which can be solved *only* by a whole or a part approach. Then we could get purer measures of the strength of the trait for a given person, its generality, etc.

b. **Dominant Symbol Type.** Evidence that people characteristically use certain types of imagery or symbols in thinking is widespread. Witkin (1949), for instance, has demonstrated that some people use proprioceptive cues and others visual cues in spatial orientation. The traditional classification of abilities as visual or spatial, numerical, mechanical, and verbal may simply represent a way to break down the characteristic images or symbols used by a person in solving a set of problems. A person who, for instance, consistently reacts to a problem situation by a stream of visual-spatial images will probably be able to solve easily the problems that require such symbols. Likewise a person who thinks predominantly in verbal terms may do well on a vocabulary test but will have difficulty in some of Thurstone's tests involving arrangement of blocks in three-dimensional space. What we are proposing here is a slightly different interpretation of the results of the testing movement rather than anything completely new. In short, we are arguing that the many so-called "abilities" may represent *habitual modes or styles of thinking* in problem situations, modes which are similar theoretically to the modes of expression in speech, gesture, etc., as discussed in the last chapter. It is even conceivable that, in brain-injured patients like Lanuti, behavior may seem to become excessively concrete because the injury has made impossible the use of higher order symbolic approaches and forced the use of tactile-kinaesthetic imagery, which is not as adequate for solving certain types of abstract problems. This suggests further that all modes of symbolic approach are possible for any person, just as all types of expressive movement are possible. Some simply become preferred over others through learning for a particular person. That is, as a result of long practice and probably reinforcement, the various symbolic approaches become organized into a habit hierarchy. Performance or thinking tests should, if purified over their present complex form, permit the discovery of what the hierarchy is for any individual (cf. the Vigotzky Test for example, Hanfmann and Kasanin, 1937).

2. **Persistence.** A further difference in the performance of individuals X and Y on Task A in Figure 6.1 is the fact that X is able to maintain his output while Y is not. What is apparently involved here is a capacity to resist distractions, boredom, discomfort, or fatigue. The trait seems fairly well represented in Clark's Factor II since we concluded there that a person had to work hard and persistently, in the face of distractions, to do well on the tasks involved. Cattell (1946a, p. 415) has discussed this trait at length and suggests that it may even cover such performances as the average strength of maintained grip, the time a subject will endure a painful shock or hold his breath, or the length of time a person will spend on a task before giving up.

3. **Variability.** Individual Y in Figure 6.1 shows much greater ups and downs in his output curve than individual X. Some people work steadily, with little fluctuation in score; others show wide variations. The usual measure of this trait is some index of variability (e.g., the standard deviation) of sub-test scores. Some people are consistently variable, paradoxical as that may sound. Cattell (1946a, p. 418) has discussed at length the evidence for the existence of such a trait of oscillation.

4. **Flexibility.** In Figure 6.1 individual X has difficulty in performing Task B after Task A whereas individual Y does not. In short, he shows negative transfer. He cannot shift readily from one task to another. A good many of the tasks in Clark's Factor I seemed to require a difficult shift from one mode of solution to another. Frenkel-Brunswik (1949) and many others have discussed this trait under the title of "rigidity," which appears to be the polar opposite of flexibility. Cattell (1946a) also has mustered evidence for the existence of such a trait from performance in a wide variety of tasks.

5. **Fluency.** Individual X shows greater output of responses per unit time on both Task A and Task B than individual Y. While his poorer performance on B may give indications as to what his dominant mode of approach is, his over-all high output suggests that he is *fluent* in producing whatever responses are required on the tasks.

Cattell (1946a, p. 421) reports that this trait is represented by such measures as associative fluency (number of responses to an inkblot or to a stimulus word), verbal fluency (anagrams test), or perceptual fluency. The last measure may also indicate flexibility, since a person who shows a high number of perceptual reorganizations of the field is probably also a person with high flexibility, particularly if he produces them when one type of organization is dominant in the situation (as in the reversible figures test). In its most general sense this trait might be called *energy* in the sense of sheer output of responses without regard to their appropriateness.

This list is far from exhaustive. It attempts merely to summarize the possible performance traits from two points of view: (1) a systematic analysis in Figure 6.1 of the ways in which performance *can* vary, and (2) a list of the traits which have repeatedly been found in previous testing, the evidence for each of which is best summarized in Cattell (1946a).

Karl's Performance Traits. Let us try to apply this list of traits to Karl and see what information we have on this area of his personality. His performance on a typical task will be helpful in this analysis. Table 6.4 shows the number of words he was able to make out of the key word *generation* in successive two-minute intervals of an anagrams test.

TABLE 6.4

Karl's Anagrams Scores

Minutes	*Number of words obtained*	*Rank out of 30 students*
1–2	25	1
3–4	9	13.5
5–6	11	2.5
7–8	14	1
9–10	10	2.5
11–12	4	21.5
Total score	73	1

The efficiency of his performance on various parts of the test as shown by his rank position in comparison with a group of thirty students gives us some information about his performance traits, at least for this task. We may summarize our conclusions about him in Table 6.5 based on these and previously reported data.

TABLE 6.5

Karl's Performance Traits

Trait Name	*Measures*
1. a) Over-all non-analytic thinker	Rorschach Test
	% and quality of W
	sequence of W and D
	Iowa Silent Reading Test
b) Dominant imagery	(no evidence)
2. Moderate persistence (?)	Final anagrams score
3. High variability	Anagrams sub-test scores
4. High flexibility	Initial anagrams score
5. Fairly high fluency	Rorschach response total
	Anagrams response total

The evidence for most of these traits is rather skimpy, with the possible exception of the first one. The final anagrams score is not a good measure of *persistence* because it is dependent in part on how many words the person has extracted by the time he gets to this point in the test. Karl is certainly *variable* as far as this test goes, although again we really need unavailable evidence as to how variable he is in comparison with others. His *flexibility* is merely suggested by his good initial adjustment to anagrams. It is confirmed indirectly, however, by the variability of the anagrams scores, since this is the kind of test in which one can succeed either by systematic rearrangement of the letters, which should yield a steady output, or by quick perceptual shifts which yield the kind of variable output characteristic of Karl's record. It is especially unfortunate that Karl was not given a series of ability tests which would have made inferences about his mode of symbolic approach possible. The College Entrance Tests are nowhere near as 'pure' as Thurstone's Primary Mental Abilities Tests and only suggest that neither the verbal nor numerical approach has clear predominance in his thinking. Thus in conclusion we can only say that the picture of Karl's performance traits is extremely sketchy and serves only to indicate in a general way how an analysis of this sort could properly be made.

Other Tests. We have not covered in this discussion a good many other tests which yield results normally included under trait psychology. An outstanding example of such an omission is the whole series of personality questionnaires, whose scores are usually interpreted in terms of traits. For example, the *Bernreuter Personality Inventory* purports to measure some six different traits, including neuroticism, self-sufficiency, and dominance. It is just one of dozens of such inventories. The reason the results from these tests are not discussed here is that they are difficult to analyze in terms of any meaningful theoretical units. Sometimes they reveal ideas or attitudes (cf. Chapter 8), sometimes self-conceptions (cf. Chapter 14). But often they involve a miscellany of correlated responses out of which it is nearly impossible to make any theoretical sense. In Allport's words, "As the statistics grow better and better, the intelligibility grows less and less. . . . (From one highly sophisticated empirical scale comes this extreme instance: Children who give the response word 'green' to a stimulus word 'grass' receive a score of +6 for 'loyalty to the gang'—an example of empiricism gone wild.)" (1937, p. 329.) Empirical correlations may be useful for practical purposes: the length of the big toe may predict Mental Age, the association "green" may predict who will be a good gang member, open windows at night may predict who will get malaria, number of digits forward may predict who will pass in school. But in all these cases some kind of intervening variables or hypothetical constructs must be discovered before the empirical correlations contribute anything to theory. And some of the relations are so complex or contaminated that the invention of adequate theoretical variables to explain them seems out of the question. (Cf. Maller, 1944.)

Ratings of Performance Traits

Psychologists have recognized from the very beginning that there are a number of traits which people display which cannot readily be observed in standardized test situations. When faced with this problem they have resorted to ratings. The great advantage of ratings is that the judge can arrive at a score after having observed the subject under a much wider variety of conditions than can be reproduced in a laboratory test of any sort. But to the extent that ratings can cover such a wide variety of behavior, they also have the theoretical disadvantage that the number of variables which can be rated is practically infinite, limited only by the imagination of the judge. Rating scales can be made up almost at will, and in fact they have been. Cattell again (1946a, p. 295) has made a heroic attempt to reduce the over-all number of trait variables which have been rated to a minimum number through factor analysis. He started with thirty-five "established" trait clusters based on a survey of the literature. In each cluster there were at least two or three sub-traits, so that actually he used about one hundred trait descriptions, stated in terms of polar opposites. The following are typical of the names given his trait clusters:

Self-assertive	–v–	Self-submissive
Willful, egotistic, predatory	–v–	Mild, self-effacing, tolerant
Surly, hard	–v–	Good natured, easygoing
Insecure, infantile, hostile	–v–	Mature, kind, tactful
Cheerful, enthusiastic, witty	–v–	Unhappy, frustrated, dour
Adventurous, lusty	–v–	Generally inhibited, timid
Imaginative, introspective, constructive	–v–	Set, smug, thrifty
Sociable, hearty	–v–	Seclusive, shy

(After Cattell, 1946a, pp. 295-299.)

Cattell reduces these by cross-matching to twelve traits, but since the names for these twelve get their meaning from the traits under them, there is little point to listing their titles here. A better demonstration of the possible utility of this approach is provided in a study by Fiske (1949), who made use of Cattell's findings. Fiske wanted to get a series of traits which would be useful in evaluating graduate students in a clinical psychology program. He chose the traits presented in Table 6.6 from Cattell's list. As you read through them try to fill them out for Karl.

TABLE 6.6

Rating Scale Definitions
(After Fiske, 1949 and Cattell, 1946a.)

(For ratings on this scale, 1 is extreme on left side, 8 on right side)

Note: These attributes refer to behavior which can be directly observed on the surface. In using this scale, disregard any inferences about underlying dynamics.

1 2 3 4 5 6 7 8

1. Readiness to cooperate Generally tends to say yes when invited to cooperate. Ready to meet people more than half way. Finds ways of cooperating despite difficulties.	–v–	Obstructiveness Inclined to raise objections to a project. "Cannot be done." Not inclined to join in. Inclined to be "difficult."

1 2 3 4 5 6 7 8

2. Predictable Consistent in day-to-day attitudes and behavior	–v–	Unpredictable Frequent shifts in attitudes and behavior. Shows changing, unpredictable moods and impulses.

TABLE 6.6 (*Continued*)

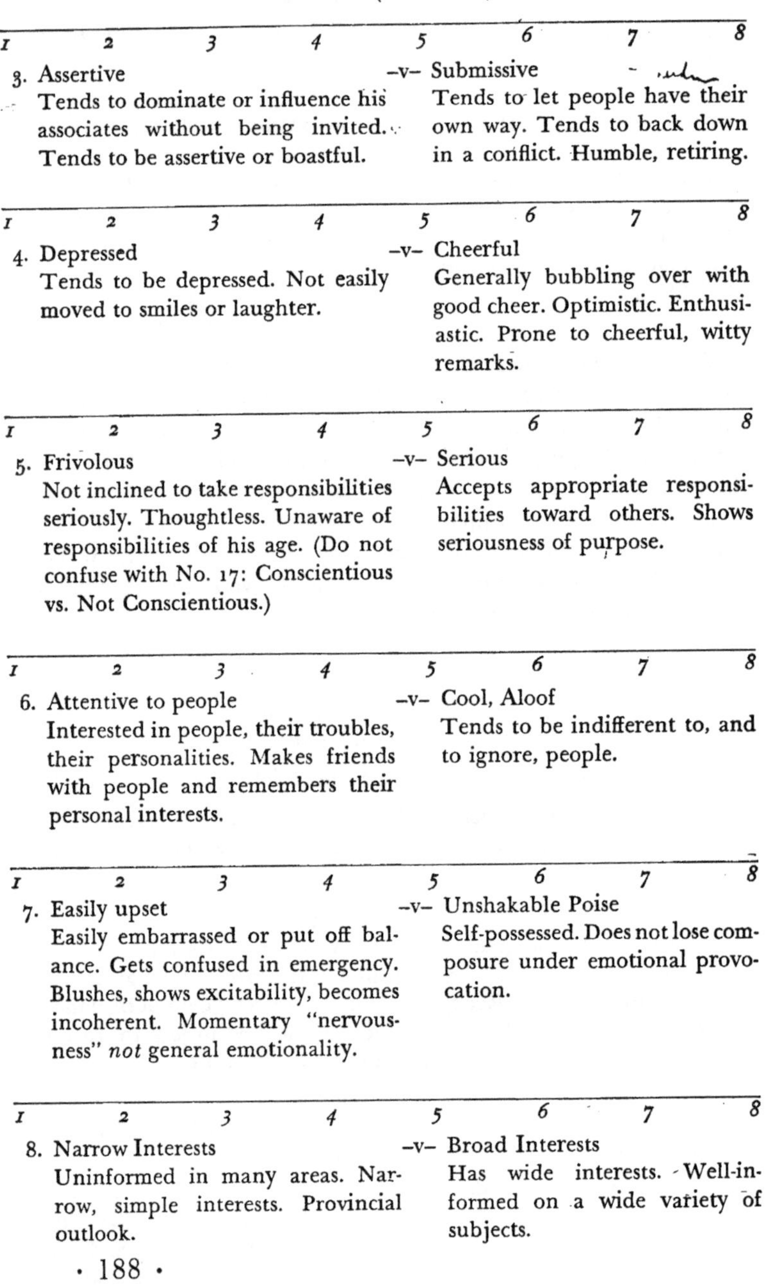

1 2 3 4	5 6 7 8
3. Assertive –v–	Submissive
Tends to dominate or influence his associates without being invited. Tends to be assertive or boastful.	Tends to let people have their own way. Tends to back down in a conflict. Humble, retiring.
1 2 3 4	5 6 7 8
4. Depressed –v–	Cheerful
Tends to be depressed. Not easily moved to smiles or laughter.	Generally bubbling over with good cheer. Optimistic. Enthusiastic. Prone to cheerful, witty remarks.
1 2 3 4	5 6 7 8
5. Frivolous –v–	Serious
Not inclined to take responsibilities seriously. Thoughtless. Unaware of responsibilities of his age. (Do not confuse with No. 17: Conscientious vs. Not Conscientious.)	Accepts appropriate responsibilities toward others. Shows seriousness of purpose.
1 2 3 4	5 6 7 8
6. Attentive to people –v–	Cool, Aloof
Interested in people, their troubles, their personalities. Makes friends with people and remembers their personal interests.	Tends to be indifferent to, and to ignore, people.
1 2 3 4	5 6 7 8
7. Easily upset –v–	Unshakable Poise
Easily embarrassed or put off balance. Gets confused in emergency. Blushes, shows excitability, becomes incoherent. Momentary "nervousness" *not* general emotionality.	Self-possessed. Does not lose composure under emotional provocation.
1 2 3 4	5 6 7 8
8. Narrow Interests –v–	Broad Interests
Uninformed in many areas. Narrow, simple interests. Provincial outlook.	Has wide interests. Well-informed on a wide variety of subjects.

TABLE 6.6 (*Continued*)

1	2	*3*	*4*	*5*	*6*	*7*	*8*

9. Suspicious	–v–	Trustful
Believes rather too quickly that he is being unfairly treated. Imagines on insufficient grounds that people strongly dislike him. Interprets things as having reference to himself when none is intended. Feels persecuted.		Accessible. Free from suspicion, but not to the extent of gullibility.

1	2	*3*	*4*	*5*	*6*	*7*	*8*

10. Good-natured, Easy-going	–v–	Self-centered, Selfish
Generous with his property, time or energy. Gives people "the benefit of the doubt," when their motives are in question.		Gets irritable or resentful if property or rights are trespassed on. Inclined to be "close" and egotistical.

1	2	*3*	*4*	*5*	*6*	*7*	*8*

11. Silent, Introspective	–v–	Talkative
Says very little; gives the impression of being introspective and occupied with thoughts.		Talks a lot, to everybody. Takes the initiative in conversations. When addressed, responds quickly.

1	2	*3*	*4*	*5*	*6*	*7*	*8*

12. Cautious	–v–	Adventurous
Avoids the strange and new. Looks at all aspects of a situation overcautiously. Keeps clear of difficulties. Avoids new things. Does the safe thing.		Ready to enter into new experiences and situations. Ready to face emergencies.

1	2	*3*	*4*	*5*	*6*	*7*	*8*

13. Socially poised	–v–	Clumsy, Awkward in Social Situations
Polite, poised and tactful in social situations. Deals with people gracefully and skillfully. Refined speech, manner, etc. Familiar with good etiquette.		Tactless in social situations. Crude in speech and manners. Omits proper formalities. Does not meet people gracefully. (Note: applies to relationships with one or more people.)

TABLE 6.6 (*Continued*)

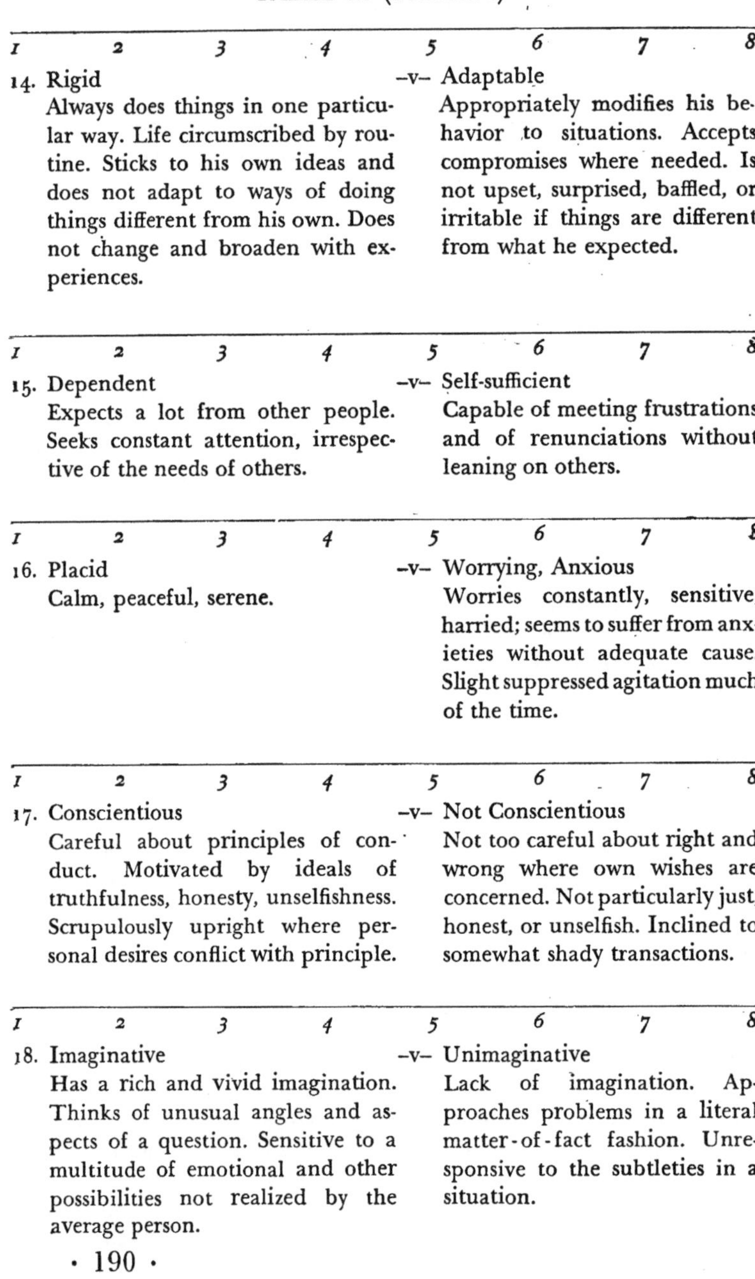

1 2 3 4 5 6 7 8

14. Rigid Always does things in one particular way. Life circumscribed by routine. Sticks to his own ideas and does not adapt to ways of doing things different from his own. Does not change and broaden with experiences.	–v–	Adaptable Appropriately modifies his behavior to situations. Accepts compromises where needed. Is not upset, surprised, baffled, or irritable if things are different from what he expected.

1 2 3 4 5 6 7 8

15. Dependent Expects a lot from other people. Seeks constant attention, irrespective of the needs of others.	–v–	Self-sufficient Capable of meeting frustrations and of renunciations without leaning on others.

1 2 3 4 5 6 7 8

16. Placid Calm, peaceful, serene.	–v–	Worrying, Anxious Worries constantly, sensitive, harried; seems to suffer from anxieties without adequate cause. Slight suppressed agitation much of the time.

1 2 3 4 5 6 7 8

17. Conscientious Careful about principles of conduct. Motivated by ideals of truthfulness, honesty, unselfishness. Scrupulously upright where personal desires conflict with principle.	–v–	Not Conscientious Not too careful about right and wrong where own wishes are concerned. Not particularly just, honest, or unselfish. Inclined to somewhat shady transactions.

1 2 3 4 5 6 7 8

18. Imaginative Has a rich and vivid imagination. Thinks of unusual angles and aspects of a question. Sensitive to a multitude of emotional and other possibilities not realized by the average person.	–v–	Unimaginative Lack of imagination. Approaches problems in a literal matter-of-fact fashion. Unresponsive to the subtleties in a situation.

TABLE 6.6 (*Continued*)

1 2 3 4		*5 6 7 8*
19. Marked Overt Interest in Opposite Sex. Dates a good deal and/or talks a lot about opposite sex. Extremely aware of women as women. (Disregard *inferred* needs or drives.)	–v–	Slight Overt Interest in Opposite Sex. Talks very little about women. Does not use opportunities for contacts with women.
20. Frank, Expressive. Comes out readily with his real feelings on various questions. Expresses his feelings, sad or gay, easily and constantly.	–v–	Secretive, Reserved. Keeps his thoughts and feelings to himself.
21. Dependent-Minded. Intellectually dependent on others. Generally accepts the opinion of the group or of authority without much thought. Unsure of own opinion.	–v–	Independent-Minded. Thinks things out for himself and adopts a clear and definite independent position. Examines every question persistently and individualistically. Makes up his own mind about it.
22. Limited Overt Emotional Expression. Is apathetic and sluggish.	–v–	Marked Overt Emotional Expression. Shows hyperkinetic, agitated behavioral responses; is overly excitable and overdemonstrative.

(Reproduced by permission from D. W. Fiske (1949). Copyright by the American Psychological Association.)

In Fiske's study a group of graduate students in clinical psychology were rated according to this scale by members of the teaching staff, by fellow graduate-students and by themselves. He then intercorrelated the ratings obtained in each of these ways and subjected the resulting three correlation matrices to Thurstone's centroid method of factor analysis. He came out with several factors in each matrix which could be matched with factors obtained in the other two matrices. In other words, he found that the traits tended to cluster in the same way no matter who did the rating. In several cases particular traits were added to the factor pattern by different sets of observers, but the observers agreed pretty generally about the core traits defining a factor. Fiske isolated five general traits in all, each of which deserves some individual discussion.

1. Social adaptability.

Cheerful	–v–	Depressed
Talkative	–v–	Silent, Introspective
Adventurous	–v–	Cautious
Adaptable	–v–	Rigid
Placid	–v–	Worrying, Anxious

As Fiske says, "These traits suggest a pattern of behavior with high social value. A person possessing these traits is good company. . . . Others like to be with him. . . . He is spontaneous, responsive, and *Socially Adaptable*." (1949, p. 335.) If our preceding analysis has been correct, Karl should rate high on at least the first four out of these five variables. He is certainly "spontaneous and responsive," though this will make him "good company" only in terms of the standards for good company set up by the particular group which is evaluating him. Actually here, as in many of the trait ratings, Fiske has not made the clear distinction that we require between personality description and character evaluation.

2. Emotional control.

Unshakable	–v–	Easily upset
Self-sufficient	–v–	Dependent
Placid	–v–	Worrying
Limited	–v–	Marked Overt Emotional Expression

Fiske describes this factor as follows: "From this inspection we can designate this recurrent factor as Emotional Control or emotional self-possession, keeping clearly in mind that this is probably mature guidance of emotional expression, not an inhibitory, constricted pattern. Further explorations may well identify it more definitely as emotional maturity." (1949, p. 335.) Once again it would seem preferable to leave any judgments as to the "wisdom" of emotional control out of a trait description. If we think of the word "control" in the sense of whether or not a person displays his emotions, we can reserve judgments as to whether this trait means "constriction" or "maturity" for occasions on which such judgments are called for. Karl probably rates fairly low on this trait. Certainly by his own account, which should yield the same results, according to Fiske's findings, he worries a good deal and has many emotional ups and downs.

3. Conformity.

Readiness to cooperate	–v–	Obstructiveness
Serious	–v–	Frivolous
Trustful	–v–	Suspicious
Good-natured, Easygoing	–v–	Self-centered, Selfish
Conscientious	–v–	Not Conscientious

"These characteristics describe the person who does the 'right thing,' who obeys the social mores. He is the 'good child in our society,' grown older. Probably the clinicians see a strong superego in him, while he sees himself as well-behaved, dependable, and *conforming*." (Fiske, 1949, p. 337.) Again this trait appears to fit Karl's behavior, so far as we know it, very closely. He is a "good man" in the sense that he does what is expected of him; he follows the social norms of good behavior closely. This trait seems almost impossible to untangle from the normative frame of reference in terms of which the behavior is classified.

4. The Inquiring Intellect.

Broad interests	–v–	Narrow Interests
Independent Minded	–v–	Dependent Minded
Imaginative	–v–	Unimaginative.

It is harder to define this trait since so few ratings were common to all three factor analyses. According to Fiske, "It seems . . . appropriate to emphasize the aspect of intellectual curiosity, for here are the attributes of the active exploring mind." (1949, p. 337.) In saying this he is attempting to find a common source for these surface traits and manages to isolate a common core which would probably be called a Need for Cognizance or Understanding by Murray (1938). We might avoid such interpretations and call this trait simply "intellectual activity," meaning the extent to which a person is active in intellectual pursuits. From what we know of Karl it is difficult to form any firm opinion as to how he stands with respect to this trait, though he is probably not conspicuously high in it.

5. Confident Self-Expression.

Assertive	–v–	Submissive
Talkative	–v–	Silent, Introspective
Marked Interest	–v–	Slight Overt Interest in Women
Frank, Expressive	–v–	Secretive, Reserved

There was agreement on this trait complex in Fiske's study only for teammate and self-ratings. Since no staff rating factor matched this one very closely, there is more uncertainty about it than the others. It is especially interesting that the teammates added some unfavorable characteristics to this core—namely Self-Centered and Marked Overt Emotional Expression—which suggests that to them the trait was a kind of "Spontaneous Egotism" according to Fiske (1949). The self-ratings, however, added Attentive to People and Socially Poised, which suggested that to them this trait appeared to be a kind of "Social Initiative." Part of the difficulty with defining this factor arises from the fact that several of the terms like "Self-Centered" have such strong value connotations that agreement between self and others would be unlikely. Whatever this factor really is, Karl appears to be fairly high in it, since he is the kind of person who expresses himself fairly freely. Whether this free expression is judged as "Egotistic" by his friends or as "Social Initiative" by himself is a little beside the point, and brings in value judgments that are irrelevant to the task of describing his personality.

Fiske's work is one of the best examples as to how a practical problem in rating others may contribute to our knowledge of a particular individual. Since the rating, as in this case, is nearly always done with some value standards in mind, the variables chosen will not be as pure as they should be for descriptive purposes, but we can nevertheless learn a good deal about the person from them if we strip off the value terminology wherever possible. In doing this we are following the same line of attack as we did in discarding judgments of how intelligent a person was and paying attention to what the test score told us about the way the person behaved. From this rating scale we have systematized a number of our miscellaneous impressions about Karl and concluded that in social situations he is *spontaneous, responsive,* and *expressive;* in emotional situations he is *variable;* and in ethical situations he is *conforming.*

Ratings Based on Controlled Observation. Ratings such as those just described are based on behavior in a wide variety of situations. The basic assumptions are that the opportunities to observe any particular person will be a representative sample of the situations in which the behavior in question may occur. Presumably a person will be able to observe himself in the widest range of situations calling for cheerfulness, his teammates the next widest, and the staff the narrowest. The fact that Fiske found agreement suggests that the sampling by each of the three sets of judges had something in common. Obviously if the staff, for instance, had seen each student on only one occasion—let us say just prior to a Qualifying Examination—the ratings on Cheerfulness would probably not have agreed in any way with those made by the Self or by Teammates.

The lack of control of the conditions under which observations and ratings are made has bothered psychologists and attempts have been made to expose individuals to a standard set of "real life" situations so that the bases for judgment will be more comparable. The outstanding example of this approach is the assessment of men carried out by the Office of Strategic Services (O.S.S.) during World War II under Murray's leadership (cf. *Assessment of men,* 1948). Murray and his associates approached the problem by controlling the experiences to which candidates were exposed during a limited time period and having numerous judges around to observe how they reacted. To accomplish this end the O.S.S. selection staff took over a large country club to which candidates for the service were sent for an intensive period of testing. For three days the men were completely at the mercy of the psychologists, who made use not only of standard laboratory tests, but also of actual lifelike situations which were standardized but realistic in that they called for the total activity of the person in a natural setting.

A typical situational test was the construction problem. Here the candidate was assigned the job of directing two associates or helpers to build a frame structure out of wooden poles and sockets (1948, p. 102). The functioning of the two assistants is perhaps best described in the words of the O.S.S. staff:

> These two members of the junior staff traditionally assumed the pseudonyms of Kippy and Buster. Whoever played the part of Kippy acted in a passive, sluggish manner. He did nothing at all unless specifically ordered to, but stood around, often getting in the way, either idling with his hands in his pockets, or concerned with some insignificant project of his own, such as the minute examination of the small-scale model. Buster, on the other hand, played a different role. He was aggressive, forward in offering impractical suggestions, ready to express dissatisfaction, and quick to criticize what he suspected were the candidate's weakest points.

The two assistants were not permitted by their secret instructions to disobey orders, and they were supposed to carry out whatever directions were given them explicitly. Within the bounds of this ruling, though, it was their function to present the candidate with as many obstructions and annoyances as possible in ten minutes. As it turned out, they succeeded in frustrating the candidates so thoroughly that the construction was never, in the history of S, completed in the allotted time. (O.S.S., 1948, p. 103.)

The behavior of the candidate under these frustrating conditions was noted carefully by staff observers and formed part of the basis for their ratings on emotional stability, leadership, and energy and initiative. The advantage of this approach is that it permits the judge to observe the reactions of the person under standardized but lifelike conditions. It represents therefore a decided improvement over ratings based on uncontrolled observations made on a series of individuals as they encounter entirely different situations in the normal course of living. The O.S.S. training staff developed a variety of situational tests like this one, on the basis of which they made their ratings.

The variables which they finally chose for rating were: (1) motivation including energy, (2) effective intelligence, (3) emotional stability, (4) social relations, (5) leadership, (6) physical ability, (7) observing and reporting, and two other variables more specifically related to the job for which the candidates were applying. The choice of these seven traits was dictated to some extent of course by the specific task for which the candidates were being evaluated. Nevertheless they are comparable in many ways to the variables used by Fiske (1949) to evaluate clinical students, which suggests that the consensus as to what traits should be rated is greater at the practical than at the theoretical level.

Intellectual Traits in Life Situations. In order to get an idea of how situational tests modify the rating process, let us take one of their traits and study more closely how they defined and judged it. "Effective intelligence" is perhaps best for this purpose, since we have already discussed intellectual traits rather extensively in connection with the testing movement. They chose the term *effective intelligence* so as to make it clear they meant *more* than paper-and-pencil test results, and then decided on theoretical grounds to divide it into afferent and efferent functions. On the afferent side they felt that intelligence involved collection of data (perception, memory, note-taking, watching, listening, etc.) and diagnosis of the situation (interpretation, inference, anticipation of possible contingencies, etc.). (1948, p. 267.) On the efferent side it included conception of plan (selection of the most strategic goal, scheduling of projects, communicating plans to others) and execution of action (managing, administering or leadership activities and "striving with perseverance until the goal is attained"). (1948, p. 267.) They detached many of the afferent functions and rated them under the separate variable of observing and reporting, ratings on which, however, saturated nearly as highly on a final intelligence factor as the effective intelligence rating itself. The important point in all this is that they tried to analyze *what behavior* they were going to rate and in so doing got some trait measures which could subsequently be held up to *various* standards of evaluation, depending on what traits were demanded in a particular situation.

For measuring effective intelligence on the efferent side they used the Construction problem already mentioned, a Brook problem (transferring some material across a deep ravine with the help of others), a personal Interview, Discussion, and Debate. In observing individuals performing in these natural situations they found it very difficult to decide what was intelligent behavior and what was not. In discussing the Brook test they state:

> One member of the group would be the first to notice the worn stump of a branch on a tree across the water (suggesting the possibility of throwing over it the noose of a rope), another candidate would propose a practical overall plan for the division of function. . . . Should a significant observation be rated as high as an outline of strategy? Should a verbal "know-how" be rated higher than an unarticulated "can-do"? And then how much should be subtracted from a man's score because of his having made this or that impractical or stupid suggestion? (1948, p. 274.)

This difficulty illustrates nicely the point we have been trying to make throughout this chapter: namely, what will be judged as intelligent depends on the standards you adopt and on what the situation calls for. Therefore it is better to describe behavior as economically as possible *without reference to any particular standard.* Behavior should first be described and then evaluated for whatever purpose is relevant.

In spite of the confusion of standards, the O.S.S. staff was able to resolve their rating problems in the same way, since two judges observing the same people under the same situations produced ratings which correlated highly with each other. For the Brook Test, for example, the agreement correlation ratio was +.71 for Effective Intelligence, whereas it went as high as +.86 for the Discussion situation. In other words, they were able to judge reliably the effective intelligence shown by an individual in a given situational test. Furthermore, there was a fair degree of agreement between the ratings in one situation and those in another, indicating considerable generality for this trait. For example, the rating in a situation in which the person was assigned a leadership role correlated +.59 with his rating when he was assigned a subordinate role. Or again, the ability to select important information from four purported enemy documents (SIX–2 Test) correlated +.29 with rated effective intelligence in a Debating situation. Of course some of the intercorrelations were insignificant, but the median intercorrelation among twelve ratings of effective intelligence based on different situations was +.29, which was beyond the 1 per cent level of significance. Furthermore, an inspection of their table of intercorrelations led them to conclude that there were at least four types of effective intelligence:

> 1) Physical-Social (Outdoor-Practical) Ability as measured by the Brook and the two Assigned Leadership tests. . . . The median intercorrelation of these three tests was .41. . . . 2) Verbal-Social (Speaking) Ability, as measured by Discussion, Debate, Judgment of Others, and Vocabulary. . . . The median intercorrelation of these four tests was .52. . . . 3) Verbal-Abstract (Writing) Ability, as measured by the Otis Vocabulary and SIX–2. The median intercorrelation of the three tests is .43. . . . 4) Non-Verbal Abstract Ability, as measured by Mechanical Comprehension, Non-Verbal, and Otis. . . . (1948, p. 279.)

This breakdown of intellectual traits may be compared with the one arrived at from our analysis of the results of paper-and-pencil tests at the end of the preceding section of this chapter. The trait names used here are based partly on an attempt to name the situations (Social, Practical, Writing, etc.) in which they were important, and partly on an attempt to classify the imagery types involved (Verbal, Mechanical, etc.) in working successfully in these situations. It would be simpler theoretically to stick to the latter approach, at least so far as trait psychology is concerned. What is needed here, as in the case of paper-and-pencil testing, is a more thorough knowledge of what traits are needed or used in successful performance in situational tests. This will require that the observers pay more attention to the actual *behavior* of the subjects in the situations (and here the O.S.S. breakdown of effective intelligence into a variety of functions should be a useful guide) rather than to the effects of the behavior (work accomplished, success, failure, etc.).

NOTES AND QUERIES

1. Make a list of the dominant symbolic approaches ("imagery types") that on logical or empirical grounds you feel would qualify as intellectual traits to be measured for a person. Consult Thurstone's *Primary Mental Abilities* (1938) and other factor analytic studies (cf. Cattell for review of the literature, 1946a). Compare your final list with the list arrived at by the O.S.S. Staff from a totally different approach to the problem. Is there any hope of reconciling the two lists? Try to define at least one of your traits very carefully. State its surplus meanings in the form of hypotheses as to what kinds of tests and situations a person should do well in.

2. What is the relationship between the five basic traits discovered by Fiske and the seven rated by the O.S.S. Assessment Staff? Is there enough similarity for you to attempt a resolution of the lists into a common, more accurately defined list?

3. How does the decision to treat intelligence as showing itself through a number of "intellectual traits" relate to the problem of whether intelligence is "inherited" or "acquired"? Traits are learned responses, as we shall see in the next chapter. Granting this, can you see how intelligence tests might discriminate unfairly against lower socioeconomic groups as Davis and Havighurst (1948) claim that they do? What conditions would favor the acquisition of certain symbolic approaches over others?

4. Davis and Havighurst (1948) argue that the "academiclike problems" in standard tests of intelligence do not permit the pupils in the lowest socioeconomic group "to show, in the final test, any of the activities at which they are superior or equal." They then propose that tests should be devised that will permit "fair" estimates of intelligence. Is this possible? Is there any *one* standard for judging the merit of one symbolic approach over another? Will Stoddard's criteria of complexity and difficulty work? Redefine the notion of validity in the light of this discussion, referring back to our definition of it in connection with expressive traits, if necessary.

5. Can you foresee a rational resolution of the number of traits in the personality sphere or do you think the best approach is empirical, i.e., to collect, as Cattell has, all the traits that have ever

been rated and then try to reduce them by intercorrelation and matching? In what sense are most trait ratings or tests "impure" from the rational viewpoint? How would one go about measuring traits that had been isolated on rational or theoretical grounds? The pursuitmeter which is a common laboratory performance task was developed out of the desire of some psychologists to figure out the different ways in which a phonograph motor could be used in a psychological laboratory. Does this suggest why it has been difficult to isolate performance traits?

6. Would you expect any of the "closure" tests to be related to Rorschach traits?

7. What handwriting traits might be related to the rigidity-flexibility trait—e.g., the "resistance to willed change of old established habits . . . manifested . . . most clearly in motor performances?" (Cattell, 1946a, p. 437.)

8. It is at least a tenable hypothesis that schizophrenics become "concrete" or incapable of "abstract" thinking because they, like Lanuti, have given up the types of symbolic thinking which enable a person to solve abstract problems. Why should visual imagery, for instance, be "given up"? In what sense is it "given up" (presumably the person's visual acuity is just as good as ever)? Could anxiety over a certain type of experience change the hierarchy of symbolic approaches? Would it be possible to inhibit altogether a particular approach through anxiety? Which modes of approach would be most likely to be affected by anxiety? Can you see any connection between hysterical "blindness" and loss of capacity for abstract thinking?

7

Trait Theory

That man whom you saw so adventurous yesterday, do not think it strange to find him such a coward the day after: either anger or necessity, or company or wine, or the sound of a trumpet had put his heart in his belly. This was not a courage shaped by reason; these circumstances have made it firm; it is no wonder if he has now been made different by other contrary circumstances.

All contradictions may be found in me by some twist and in some fashion. Bashful, insolent; chaste, lascivious; talkative, taciturn; tough, delicate; clever, stupid; surly, affable; lying, truthful; learned, ignorant; and liberal and miserly and prodigal.

—MONTAIGNE

The theory of personality traits has developed from the kind of data we have been reviewing in the past two chapters. The observation that people tend to react in similar ways on similar occasions has necessitated the invention of a construct which would account for such consistencies. Having reviewed some of the consistencies as they have been found under more or less controlled conditions, we are in a better position to study and evaluate the theory of traits which has been developed to explain these consistencies. There have been two serious attempts to study the nature of traits and to base a psychology of personality on them. One such attempt was made by G. W. Allport (1937) and one by R. B. Cattell (1946). Both of these men agree that the trait construct should be used to explain the consistencies in personality. In Allport's words: "Traits are not directly observable; they are inferred (as any kind of determining tendency is inferred). Without such an inference the stability and consistency of personal behavior could not possibly be explained." (1937, p. 340.) To Cattell *trait* is the name given to a pattern of covarying behavior elements. He finds the concept essential in explaining the unities we observe in personality. "A trait, whether unique or common, is a collection of reactions or responses bound by some kind of unity which permits the responses to be gathered under one term and treated in the same fashion for most purposes." (1946, p. 61.) Furthermore, for him covariation is the indicator of unity. "A unity can be detected from the fact that the constituent behavior elements in a trait *covary*." (1946, p. 72.) In other words, for both theorists it is the similarity, consistency, or covariation of behavior elements which leads them to the trait concept.

But just exactly what is a trait? In choosing empirical examples of traits we have been guided by the criterion of behavioral consistency, but we need a more precise definition than this. It leaves many theoretical questions as yet unanswered. For example, how do we know a trait exists? How general are traits? Do they cover single habits or groups of habits? Or are they broad determinants of personality? Is the trait concept sufficient to account for all of a person's behavior? Or are other concepts necessary? As an approach to some of these problems we may begin with the formal definition of a trait given by Allport. "We are left with a concept of trait as *a generalized and focalized neuropsychic system (peculiar to the individual), with the capacity to render many stimuli functionally equivalent, and to initiate and guide consistent (equivalent) forms of adaptive and expressive behavior.*" (1937, p. 295.) Although this definition is very general and inclusive, it readily breaks down into two parts. What Allport appears to be saying is that a trait, on the one hand, renders stimuli equivalent and, on the other, initiates equivalent responses. These two functions of a trait can be illustrated by the simple diagram in Figure 7.1.

FIGURE 7.1

Schematic Representation of Allport's Definition of a Trait

	S_1		R_1	
Situations	S_2	trait	R_2	*Responses*
	S_3	(*hypothetical construct*)	R_3	
	·		·	
	·		·	
	·		·	
	·		·	
	S_n		R_n	

This figure shows how a trait for Allport is a kind of intervening hypothetical state which serves to unite or knit together what might otherwise be dissimilar stimuli and responses. He apparently feels that a trait is both an inference the observer finds necessary to explain equivalences (on the S or R side) and a living reality or force which acts within the individual to produce the equivalences.

To make this definition more understandable, we need a concrete example. We could choose any one of the traits discussed in the preceding two chapters. Suppose we take the finding, based on the M:C ratio on the Rorschach, that Karl is extratensive, that is, that he tends to respond to "promptings from without" rather than from "within." What this means operationally in terms of the Rorschach test is that when asked to give perceptual responses to static inkblots, he does not tend to inject much movement into them. We observed a somewhat similar tendency in his written speech behavior: he used relatively few verbs as compared with adjectives. Now we can see how Allport's trait definition works. We could say that Karl has a trait which we shall call, for convenience, *extratensiveness,* which has rendered two situations equivalent: that is, we can postulate the existence of something within Karl which has served to make the situation of trying to find words to write a theme similar to a situation in which he was trying to find words to describe an inkblot. Furthermore, this "something" within Karl served to produce equivalent responses: few movement responses in the one case, and few verbs and adverbs in the other.

But such an example serves only to raise more questions. In particular it raises the question as to how we decide when situations and responses can be considered equivalent. On closer analysis the definition appears somewhat circular. In this particular instance we probably decided the situations were equivalent because Karl gave equivalent (similar) responses to them. But how do we know the responses are similar? Must we answer that they are similar because they are given to equivalent situations? To escape this circularity we need some rational, independent basis for defining similarity or equivalence.

If we accept this viewpoint, the problem then becomes one of finding bases on which situations and/or responses can be grouped together as similar. The problem is not a new one. We met it before in Chapter 3, when we were trying to locate the sources from which concepts have been drawn to describe personality economically. Our task is here, as it was there, to find some basis on which different responses can be grouped together and treated as a unity. Cattell (1946a) lists some six different methods which have traditionally been used for grouping responses together and calling them traits, but we shall limit ourselves to three general methods which include and cut across his six.

Social Norm Traits. As we pointed out in Chapter 3, personality has been repeatedly conceptualized for purposes of evaluation in terms of some theoretical, religious, or aesthetic system. In the process of fitting the person into one or another of these value systems, certain concepts have been used to describe the person, often because they fit into the system rather than because they fit the person's behavior particularly well. We may take punctuality as an example. Dudycha (1936) studied when college students arrived for a variety of campus events: eight-o'clock classes, college commons, appointments, extracurricular activities, vesper services, and entertainments. He found that for each type of event there was a normal distribution of times of arrival with the peak frequency of arrival being a few minutes before the start of the event. What he was interested in was whether or not people were consistently late or early in different situations. He found significant, although not high, positive correlations among times of arrival for different events.

Our concern here is not so much with his findings as it is with the question of why he chose *punctuality* as a trait to measure. The answer lies partly in the fact that "being-on-time for things" is an accepted social norm in our society (although it is not in some others). We *expect* some consistency in "arrival" behavior because society decrees that this kind of behavior should be consistent. That is, society defines, at least to some extent, what being-on-time means and what situations it applies to.

Perhaps an even better example of a "social norm" trait is honesty, which was extensively investigated by Hartshorne and May in the Character Education Inquiry (1928). They devised a number of tests to measure three basic types of dishonesty—namely, cheating, stealing, and lying. They gave school children opportunities to cheat under a variety of conditions. It will aid our theoretical analysis of traits to take a closer look at some of the tests they used to measure dishonesty.

> 1. The duplicating technique. One of the common forms of classroom cheating is for the pupil to make an illegitimate use of answers in the back of the book. To measure this they gave the children a test, collected the papers, recorded the answers, and then returned the papers for the children to grade themselves with the use of an answer sheet. The difference between the answers recorded the first time and those after self-scoring was the measure of the deception which the child had practiced in grading his own paper.
>
> 2. The improbable achievement technique. Here, as the title suggests, the child was given a chance to say whether or not he

had done something successfully which it was actually impossible to do in the time allotted. For example, they used a puzzle peg test, in which the task is to remove all the pegs from the board by jumping and removing adjacent ones. If any child reported that he had correctly solved the problem in the time allotted, it was concluded he must have cheated by pulling the pegs out because no one tested under normal conditions could perform the task in this amount of time.

3. The double testing technique. The method here was to have the children take two equivalent forms of a test, such as arithmetic, once with an answer key available and once when it was not available. The difference in score on the two occasions, if it is above that to be normally expected from practice, is regarded as a measure of deception.

4. Cheating in athletic contests. The children were introduced to an athletic contest in which they competed against each other on such tests as measuring the strength of one's handgrip, chinning oneself, or making a standing broad jump. The method for measuring deception was to instruct the child in the test by giving him three practice trials, the best of which was mentally noted by the examiner. The child was then told to make his actual competitive trials by himself while the examiner explained the test to the next child. If the child reported a score which was better than that noted by the examiner in practice, it was concluded that he had cheated, since on physical tests of this sort it is nearly impossible, because of fatigue effects, to get a better score on later than on earlier trials.

This sample of the tests used should be enough to give an idea of how they went about measuring dishonesty. They measured *lying* by asking the children whether or not they had cheated on any of the tests. Since they knew whether or not the children had cheated, it was possible to determine whether the children lied in answering this question. One of their primary theoretical interests was to discover whether children consistently cheated on the various tests. They also wanted to know whether the children who cheated also lied and stole. In general they found low positive correlations among their various tests of deception (1928, p. 212). This was interpreted by them as meaning, not that there was a general trait of honesty of the sort Allport has proposed, but that the various tests had elements in common which produced the correlations. "If they have nothing in common, the correlations will be zero." (1928, p. 215.) In other words, the transfer of learned responses of honesty from one situation to another on the basis of similarity accounted for what consistency they found, and they felt it unnecessary to attribute to a child a trait of honesty as a "psychological entity with any real existence." (1928, p. 379.) But their results have also been interpreted by others as meaning precisely the opposite, namely, that there is some general tendency for children to be honest (Allport, 1937). Perhaps the best summary of the situation is given in Figure 7.2.

FIGURE 7.2

Percentages of children who took advantage of varying numbers of opportunities to cheat.

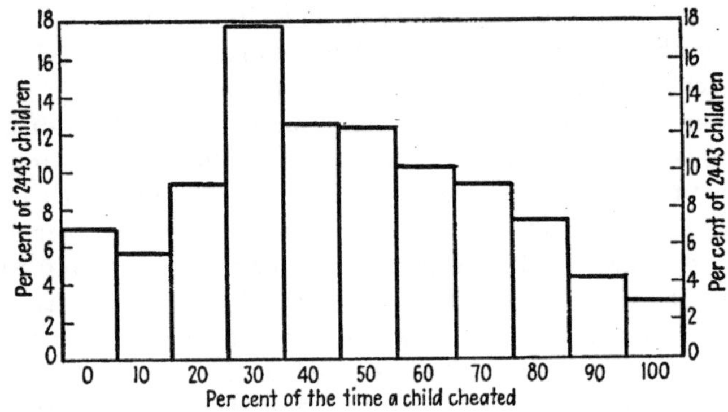

(Reproduced with permission from H. Hartshorne and M. A. May, *Studies in Deceit.* Vol. 1, p. 386. Copyright 1928 by The Macmillan Co.)

This figure shows the largest single group of children cheated three times in ten opportunities, while only 7 per cent never cheated (that is, were consistently honest). On the other hand, only 3.2 per cent cheated at every opportunity. "The other 90% cheated all the way from once to nine times in every ten opportunities." (1928, Vol. II., p. 221.) Once again the actual results do not concern us so much as the basis on which Hartshorne and May decided to investigate a trait called honesty. Quite obviously they chose to study honesty because society says there is or should be such a trait. There is a social norm or code of honesty, just as there is one of punctuality. Honesty is a virtue which is supposed to include certain kinds of behavior. Hartshorne and May had little difficulty in finding test situations which would yield responses which society would readily label honest or dishonest.

But although honesty is a virtue which has clearly understood behavioral referents, it is not necessarily a good trait term to use for describing a given individual's behavior. After all, widely diverse forms of behavior have been included by Hartshorne and May under the general heading of dishonesty. What response elements do looking up answers in the back of the book and surreptitiously pulling pegs out of a board have in common? In what sense are adding inches to a broad jump and changing an answer to an arithmetic problem equivalent responses? They are equivalent because morality (society) says they are. They both involve passing something off as something else and all such responses society has decreed should be grouped together and labeled dishonest. Although, as we have seen, it will continue to be necessary to describe a person's behavior in terms of such value systems as these, it does not follow that honesty is a very useful concept for describing and summarizing the consistencies in a given person's behavior, particularly in view of the data in Figure 7.2. Allport summarizes this argument very neatly, as follows: "The error of probing for consistency in the wrong place (and failing to find it, pronouncing in favor of specificity) has been likened by G. B. Watson to the absurdity of asking whether a person using the public library has a trait causing him to take out only books with red or with blue covers. Of course he hasn't. If only the bindings were studied, no consistency should be expected. But if the *subject-matter* of the chosen books was investigated, well organized traits of interest would appear." (1937, p. 256.)

Individual vs. Common Traits. This discussion raises a serious theoretical problem which must be faced sooner or later. Repeatedly we have mentioned the possibility that terms like honesty, which society uses to evaluate the behavior of people in general, may not be very useful for describing the consistencies of any given individual's behavior. By a simple extension of the argument we might land in the predicament of discovering that any trait term whatsoever that the scientist might decide to use could not be perfectly applicable to more than one person. Might not the attempt to use any trait term to describe the behavior of a number of people actually force into one mold behavior elements which may belong together for one person but *not for any other*? Allport has raised this question most insistently, and has argued vigorously that we should recognize that there are individual traits and common traits. Common traits may be considered as distributed in the general population, but individual traits apply to only one person (1937, p. 341). Common traits refer to inter-individual consistencies (e.g., this person is the most aggressive in his group in all situations); individual traits refer to intra-individual consistencies (e.g., this person is consistently aggressive in all that he does). Furthermore, the trait names usable for groups of individuals are only approximately accurate in describing intra-individual consistencies. Does this mean that we must develop two entirely different sets of trait concepts? We seem to be caught here between the too particular and the too general. Fortunately there is a little empirical evidence which would suggest that the dichotomy between individual and common traits is not so sharp as Allport at times appears to suggest.

The problem has been attacked experimentally by Baldwin (1946), and theoretically by Cattell (1946a, pp. 96 ff.). Baldwin made use of behavior ratings on a number of nursery-school children for a series of twenty consecutive days. With these data he could do one of two things. First he could intercorrelate the average ratings over the twenty-day period on such variables as affectionateness and aggressiveness. These inter-individual correlations would show, for example, whether high ratings of aggressiveness would be associated with high ratings on affectionateness and perhaps with low ratings on cooperativeness. A table of these intercorrelations for the thirty variables rated could be obtained and a factor analysis performed to discover which behavior ratings belonged together under one general trait heading as far as the group of children is concerned. This procedure was followed with Baldwin's data and led to the definition of a common nursery school trait of *desirability* which saturated highly on such behavior elements as aggressiveness, competitiveness, gregariousness, leadership, originality, and planfulness.

Secondly, Baldwin could and did make quite a different use of the same data. He intercorrelated the ratings on the thirty variables *for a given individual* for the twenty different days. What such correlations show is whether two trait elements (or behavior ratings) for a given child varied together regardless of where those same ratings stood with respect to the group as a whole. He has prepared a figure, reproduced as Figure 7.3, which illustrates how this could happen.

In Figure 7.3 trait behavior elements A and B are highly correlated from day to day for the particular individual under study. That is, when the rating on Variable A goes up, the rating on Variable B also goes up. In other words, they *covary*. However, the *mean* rating on Variable A for all twenty days is *above* the general population mean, while the mean rating on Variable B is *below* the general population mean. Thus as far as the group is concerned, this individual would contribute to a *negative* correlation between these

FIGURE 7.3

Covariation of Two Behavior Elements Displayed by *One* Child on Successive Days

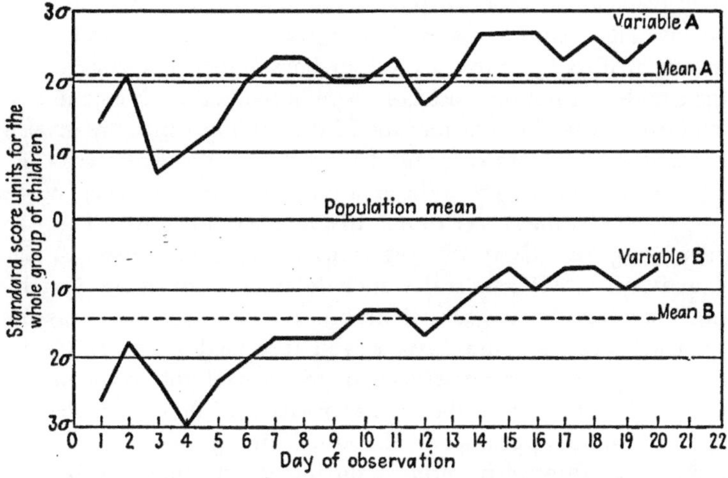

(Reproduced with permission from Baldwin (1946, p. 155). Copyright by the Duke University Press.)

trait elements. That is, he is high as far as the group is concerned on one, and low on the other, which would lead to a negative correlation between the two trait elements if other individuals have mean ratings that stand in the same relationship. This figure then illustrates how it is possible for two elements to be correlated positively from day to day within the individual and yet contribute to a negative correlation as far as the group as a whole is concerned. If this happened very often, one could easily see how the traits arrived at for groups of individuals (common traits) might be quite different from those derived from the study of individual cases (individual traits).

When Baldwin (1946) had intercorrelated the behavior ratings on twenty different days in this manner for four nursery-school boys, he then performed factor analyses in the usual way for the table of intercorrelations for each of the boys. In order to eliminate temporal change as a factor and to help locate the first axis in rotation, he introduced time as a thirty-first variable which he intercorrelated with all the other thirty behavior ratings. Locating his first axis through the time variable, he was able to arrive at factor solutions for each boy, which yielded the results on Factor I shown in Table 7.1 reproduced from his article.

For three of the boys (Arnold, John, and Ned) there seems to be fairly high agreement as to saturations on individual items in the set of behavior ratings. To put this in another way, he found that the day-to-day pattern of variations in the ratings tended to be fairly similar, at least for three of the four boys. There is also agreement between the saturations based on these individual analyses and those obtained on the group factor labeled *desirability* which are given in the righthand column of Table 7.1. In Baldwin's own words, "The variables on which there is the greatest agreement are (1) aggressiveness, (2) cheerfulness, (3) competitiveness, (4) fancifulness, (5) frequency of gross activity, (6) gregariousness, (7) planfulness, (8) vigor of activity. . . . These scales include almost all those variables which had high loadings on 'desirability' in the group analysis. The factor was labeled 'desirability' because it seemed to express the general concept held by nursery-school teachers of the 'good nursery-school child.' In view of the high correlation of these variables with time, it would appear that the usual nursery-school child goes through an adjustment process during which time his behavior tends toward the 'desirable.' " (1946, pp. 157-159.)

Baldwin further points out that although Arnold, John, and Ned adjust to nursery school in a similar way, there are differences which can be noted by an inspection of the table. For example, Arnold's and John's adjustments are characterized by affectionateness, whereas Ned's is not. Ralph, on the other hand, is quite different from the other three boys and also from the group. This, as Baldwin points out, is because Ralph started out in nursery school as an outcast, who looked unhappy and felt social ostracism very much. As time went on, he became less inhibited and more able to express his emotions aloud, until finally he became accepted in the group and was delighted with his newfound status. Consequently his behavior ratings would obviously not vary in the same way as would those of

TABLE 7.1

Factor Saturations on Different Behavioral Elements for Individual Boys and for the Group of Children as a Whole

(After Baldwin, 1946.)

Loadings on Factor I—Temporal Change

Variable	*Factor—Temporal change*				*Cross-sectional Factor I*
	Arnold	John	Ralph	Ned	(Desirability)
Affectionateness	.90	.90	.80	—.32	...
Aggressiveness	.76	.79	.16	.88	.64
Cheerfulness	.59	.71	—.55	.63	.35
Competitiveness	.88	.87	.04	.99	.80
Conformity	—.14	.37	.71	—.08	...
Cruelty	.56	.88	.79	.80	.23
Curiosity	.94	.65	—.24	.95	.23
Emotional control	.49	.48	.64	.01	...
Emotional excitability	.88	.60	.54	.79	...
Fancifulness	.64	.79	—.03	.88	.62
Frequency of gross activity	.90	.81	—.55	.65	.68
Friendliness	.20	.62	.79	.13	.71
Gregariousness	.82	.81	—.66	.62	.70
Intensity of emotional response	.64	.47	.86	—.04	...
Jealousy	.82	.19	—.10	.59	...
Kindness	.81	.28	.00	.83	.52
Leadership	.90	.51	.34	—.58	.88
Obedience	.53	.01	.84	.22	...
Originality	.63	.88	—.40	.96	.72
Patience	.12	.04	.50	—.22	...
Physical apprehensiveness	.86	.71	.22	—.85	.27
Planfulness	.96	.81	.76	.92	.71
Quarrelsomeness	.48	.63	.78	.74	.25
Resistance	.79	.54	.64	—.33	...
Sense of humor	.42	.77	.54	.19	.44
Sensitiveness	.21	.76	.28	.49	.54
Social apprehensiveness	.74	.90	—.40	—.86	.35
Suggestibility	.70	.87	.87	.59	...
Tenacity	.98	.87	.37	.50	.40
Vigor of activity	.50	.59	—.73	.66	.66
Time	1.00	1.00	1.00	1.00	

(Reproduced by permission from Baldwin (1946, p. 158). Copyright by the

the normal child in the course of adjustment to nursery school. Adjustment meant something quite different to him from what it did to the others.

This problem illustrates the extent to which one can expect to find agreement between common and individual traits. As far as three of the boys were concerned, the common trait of desirability or nursery-school adjustment meant substantially the same thing with respect to the behavior denoted. And as far as they were concerned, the trait could nearly as well be arrived at by a study of inter-individual as intra-individual correlations. But as far as Ralph was concerned, the "adjustment" trait was not defined by changes in the same behavioral items. Since he was different to begin with, the behavior which characterized his increasing adjustment or "desirability" was quite different.

This study illustrates rather neatly both the promise and the limitations of a psychology of personality based on groups of individuals. In Baldwin's own words, we can conclude from it "that the group analysis gave reasonably accurate interpretations of the behavior of three of the four individuals, but that the fourth individual was not described adequately in terms of the group factors. Even in cases where group factors were approximately accurate, some aspects of the individual's personality were not revealed." (1946, pp. 167-168.)

We can further conclude that there will be important differences in the extent to which common traits will correspond with individual traits. In some cases the agreement may be so slight as to force us to abandon the use of the common trait and perhaps of the trait concept itself. In other cases the similarity between common traits and individual traits would appear, at least on rational grounds, to be so close that we shall feel justified in continuing to use the trait concept, even though it refers to common elements in the behavior of a number of people. For example, in talking about consistencies of expressive movement, it would seem safe to predict that the trait of expansiveness would not only be common to a group of people but would also adequately describe many intra-individual consistencies.

But how do we know when we are justified in assuming that common and individual traits correspond reasonably well? What is the difference in value between nursery-school adjustment and expansiveness as trait concepts? We shall consider this question more fully later in the chapter, but we can conclude now that trait concepts based on social norms (such as nursery-school desirability, honesty, or punctuality) are not apt to be as useful for describing intra-individual consistencies as are some other traits based on other consistencies in behavior. Social norms like honesty, punctuality, desirability, and neuroticism represent groupings of responses which *covary more in social expectation than in individual behavior.* They are therefore especially likely to crop up in rating studies where the observer's expectancies will create "halo" effects (covariation in the judge's mind, not in the subject's behavior). But for this very reason they will tend not to be very useful in cross-cultural studies where the judge's expectancies may lead him to look for consistencies in behavior in the wrong places.

Common traits based on such norms will correspond somewhat to individual traits, since the interiorization of social norms influences behavior, but we shall find it more convenient to speak of the child's *conception of honesty* as a social norm rather than to consider honesty as a trait describing consistency in his behavior. We must find some other basis for grouping responses together than the arbitrary one of social custom and usage if we are to avoid the problem of coming out with traits which apply accurately to only a very few highly socialized individuals in the group.

Goal-Directed Traits. Responses may also be considered equivalent because they serve the same end. The result is what Cattell calls "a dynamic trait unity. . . . In traits of this kind the behavior manifestations are united by being all directed to a single goal." (1946a, p. 62.) The goal usually gives the trait its name. Thus we may speak of the traits of being sociable, keeping clean, being polite, or being generous. A great variety of responses may serve any one of these ends. In order to keep clean a person may brush his teeth, comb his hair, have his shirts laundered every other day, take a bath twice a week, etc. Taken individually these different responses may seem to have little similarity, but they are grouped together because they appear to serve the same goal.

A consideration of this type of unity of behavior has led Allport to distinguish between driving and directing traits or dynamic and expressive traits. He would refer to expansiveness in movement as an expressive trait, whereas cleanliness or sociability would be considered dynamic or driving traits. The distinction becomes clear in his discussion of the origin of the trait of sociability. He traces the hypothetical development of such a trait beginning with the young child's discovery that his wants are satisfied in the presence of his mother.

consistent habits. To handle such inconsistent behavior he feels the concept of need or motive is absolutely necessary.

This argument is not entirely fair to Allport. As we have seen from his treatment of the development of the trait of sociability, he includes the need concept under the heading of dynamic traits. In fact, he specifically argues (1937, p. 2[illegible]) that means and ends cannot be separated. That is, a specific motive like n Achievement cannot be separated in the individual life from the actions which serve the achievement goal. Thus he prefers a more all inclusive term, such as dynamic trait, which covers both the goal and the actions which lead

At this point the issue becomes close to being a terminological dispute. Certainly we need two concepts—one which will account for the consistencies and recurrences and one which will account for the inconsistencies and sudden, dramatic changes in behavior. For this purpose we may choose the terms *stylistic* and *dynamic* traits, as Allport does, or we may, following Murray, choose the terms trait and motive. We shall follow Murray on the grounds that the two kinds of behavior under consideration are sufficiently different to require different hypothetical constructs. Unlike Allport and unlike Cattell, we find it awkward to use the trait concept to cover behavior oriented around social norms or around individual goals. Consequently we shall eliminate these two meanings of the trait concept and leave it to refer in a more restricted sense to recurrences in behavior, much as Murray defines them above. The other meanings given the term by Allport and Cattell will be taken up in later sections of the book in connection with our other variables.

Traits As a Recurrent Response Pattern. When we have eliminated in this way trait entities based on social norms and on goals, we are left with traits which are somehow based on similarities or recurrences in response patterns. Here we need to return to the empirical data which led to the use of the trait concept in the first place. In Chapters 5 and 6 we noted a number of consistencies and similarities in moving, perceiving, thinking, remembering, talking, etc. It is for such consistencies that we need the concept of trait. We need terms which will cover the fact that a person consistently, in a variety of situations, produces a lot of words per unit time, or the fact that a person introduces a lot of empathic movement into static situations, or the fact that a person generally performs well in a new situation. These are the kinds of observations on which the trait

This in time leads the child to seek the presence, not only of his mother, but of other people. "A trait (not an instinct) of gregariousness develops. The child grows eager for social intercourse; he enjoys being with people. When isolated from them for some time, he misses them and becomes restless. The older he grows the more ways he finds of expressing this gregarious interest. He seeks to ally himself with groups of people at the lodge, at the theater; at church; he makes friends and keeps in touch with them, often entertains them, and corresponds with them. These separate activities are not habits. They are varied (but equivalent) aspects of a trait of sociability. . . . Under guidance of this trait new and effective expressions may be found to satisfy the craving for social intercourse. Habits no longer dominate the trait; rather it is the trait that forces the formation of new habits, congenial and serviceable to the trait." (1937, p. 292.)

This quotation illustrates rather neatly what Allport had in mind when he devised his formal definition of a trait as something which rendered stimuli equivalent and guided equivalent responses. It also suggests that part of what he had in mind was what many other theorists would call a *motive*. When he speaks of the "craving for social intercourse" or of the person "seeking to ally himself with groups of people" it is apparent that he intends to broaden the concept of trait to include what many psychologists refer to as motivation. If we return to our original definition of a trait as a concept which was devised primarily to account for the consistency in behavior and the stability in personality, it appears that Allport has stretched the term *trait* a little too far. He is now using it to account for inconsistencies in behavior, new responses which seem primarily determined by the person's wishes or goals, rather than by his past adjustment in similar situations.

Murray argues (1938) that the concept of trait is very useful for describing consistencies of behavior or recurrent patterns of behavior. He claims that "one cannot properly speak of a trait until one has observed a number of similar or equivalent bits of behavior." (1938, p. 712.) That is, we arrive at the concept of trait "by observing the frequent repetition of similar or equivalent trends." (1938, p. 713.) Murray then goes on to state that he feels trait psychology is overly concerned with recurrences in behavior and does not adequately account for sudden inconsistencies, creative impulses, irrational thoughts, dreams, and neurotic behavior. He points out that to the trait psychologist a baby has no personality because it has no consistent habits. To handle such inconsistent behavior he feels the concept of need or motive is absolutely necessary.

This argument is not entirely fair to Allport. As we have seen from his treatment of the development of the trait of sociability, he includes the need concept under the heading of dynamic traits. In fact, he specifically argues (1937, p. 241) that means and ends cannot be separated. That is, a specific motive like n Achievement cannot be separated in the individual life from the actions which serve the achievement goal. Thus he prefers an over-all inclusive term, such as dynamic trait, which covers both the goal and the actions which lead to the goal.

At this point the issue becomes close to being a terminological dispute. Certainly we need two concepts—one which will account for the consistencies and recurrences, and one which will account for the inconsistencies and sudden, irrational changes in behavior. For this purpose we may choose the terms *stylistic* and *dynamic* traits, as Allport does; or we may, following Murray, choose the terms *trait* and *motive*. We shall follow Murray on the grounds that the two kinds of behavior under consideration are sufficiently different to require different hypothetical constructs. Unlike Allport and unlike Cattell, we find it awkward to use the trait concept to cover behavior oriented around social norms or around individual goals. Consequently we shall eliminate these two meanings of the trait concept and leave it to refer in a more restricted sense to recurrences in behavior, much as Murray defines them above. The other meanings given the term by Allport and Cattell will be taken up in later sections of the book in connection with our other variables.

Trait As a Recurrent Response Pattern. When we have eliminated in this way trait unities based on social norms and on goals, we are left with traits which are somehow based on similarities or recurrences in response patterns. Here we need to return to the empirical data which led to the use of the trait concept in the first place. In Chapters 5 and 6 we noted a number of consistencies and similarities in moving, perceiving, thinking, remembering, talking, etc. It is for such consistencies that we need the concept of trait. We need terms which will cover the fact that a person consistently, in a variety of situations, produces a lot of words per unit time, or the fact that a person introduces a lot of empathic movement into static situations, or the fact that a person generally performs well in a new situation. These are the kinds of observations on which the trait concept is based. Can we formulate a definition which will cover these facts?

The following definition appears to sum up most of our discussion to date: *A trait is the learned tendency of an individual to react as he has reacted more or less successfully in the past in similar situations when similarly motivated.* To put this in a slightly different way, we can say that when a man is faced with what he perceives to be the same situation with the same variety and intensity of motivation, he tends to utilize the type of response which satisfied the demands of the situation and the motivation in the past. Since *exactly* the same situation scarcely ever recurs, nearly every repeated occasion involves transfer or generalization of the exact response reinforced previously. Hence we must think of traits as *patterns* or *types* of responses classified together (and covarying) on the basis of some similar element. In short, a trait is a hypothetical construct serving to place a number of different response elements under the same heading on the basis of similarities among them. Let us proceed by means of a concrete example to analyze in detail what the implications of this general definition of a trait are. We can start with the often-mentioned trait of expansiveness in movement and gesture. In terms of our general definition we can say that when a person is faced by the repeated situation of having to move, he may learn to move expansively. What are the implications of this simple statement?

Trait As a Learned Response. In the first place it is perfectly clear that we have defined a trait, as a learned response or habit would be defined by a learning psychologist like Hull (1943) or McGeoch (1942). This means concretely that a trait is a group of responses which are acquired according to the laws of learning, and retained according to the laws of memory or forgetting. One of the major advantages of our particular definition is that it permits the application to traits of the considerable body of knowledge about the principles governing learning and retention. For example, our definition implies that a trait is acquired according to the law of effect. In terms of our example expansive movements must somehow have satisfied the motivation involved in situations requiring movement: Expansive movements must have been reinforced. Since we are dealing with a hypothetical example, we can only guess as to what motivation could be involved in such a case. But such guesses are not difficult to make. For instance, for a person of relatively massive physique, like Karl, it might be quite fatiguing to make small precise movements. In other words, expansiveness might develop in order to satisfy the motive of fatigue- or pain-avoidance. It is in just such ways as this that we can imagine physique entering into the determination of a trait response. A less likely hypothesis might be that expansiveness was greeted by parental approval on the grounds that it suggested the child was likely to become a successful actor. Such approval for expansive gestures and movements might reinforce them sufficiently so that they would recur again in similar movement-requiring situations. A third hypothesis might be that expansiveness was instrumental to a need for dominance or for being noticed.

The application of the law of effect to the acquisition of traits is only one example of the advantage of considering a trait as being subject to the laws of learning. A trait might also be studied in the light of other reasons for the learning of a response, such as frequency of reinforcement, punishment, generalization, the effect of extinctions interspersed among rewards, etc. A problem which has traditionally been of more interest to personality theorists has been why traits seem to persist so long. The answer to this question involves the application of our knowledge about the reasons for the forgetting of a response once learned. Allport (1937) has been so impressed by the persistence of traits that he has argued that the ordinary laws of forgetting do not appear to apply to them. Instead he has argued that traits become *functionally autonomous.* He feels that while it may be correct to say that the trait of expansiveness originally developed to satisfy some such motive as social approval, it is incorrect to argue from this that the trait continues in adulthood because it is still satisfying the same motive. On the contrary, what started out as a mode of satisfying motives appears to become independent of its origin and to develop a driving power of its own. It was this observation which led Allport to conclude that a trait like expansiveness, which might have started out as an expressive, stylistic trait, would often end up as a dynamic or driving trait. The mechanism becomes a drive (cf. Woodworth, 1918). In Allport's own words: "Workmanship is a good example of functional autonomy. A good workman feels compelled to do cleancut jobs even though his security, or the praise of others, no longer depend upon high standards. In fact, in a day of jerry-building, his workman-like standards may be to his economic disadvantage. Even so he cannot do a slipshod job. Workmanship is not an instinct, but so firm is the hold it may acquire on a man that it is little wonder Veblen mistook it for one." (1937, p. 196.)

Is it really true that we shall have to suspend the laws of forgetting in order to account for the persistence of such traits as expansiveness or carefulness in workmanship? The issue as Allport presents it is complex because he has not restricted the meaning of the term *trait* as we have here. Consequently when he chooses an example like the one quoted above, he may be referring to what we would call a motive. That is, the workman may have a *need for order* which is quite different from the trait of neatness in the restricted sense of a similar response to similar situations under similar motivation. If we restrict ourselves to this second meaning of the term *trait,* the problem of functional autonomy is not so difficult. It becomes one of discovering whether the conditions which are known to produce forgetting have actually occurred. To return to our example, what are the conditions which would lead to the dropping out of the response of expansiveness once it has been reinforced to a certain level of habit strength?

Reasons for Disappearance of a Trait. In the first place, we could not expect the trait simply to die out with the passage of time. Although there is still some unexplained evidence to the contrary (cf. McGeoch, 1942), the prevailing opinion among learning psychologists is that responses are not forgotten through disuse. Instead, forgetting seems to be largely a function of retroactive inhibition or the learning of a new response which replaces the old one, usually through differential reinforcement. Part of Allport's argument for functional autonomy seems to rest on the assumption that a response, once it is no longer used, will tend to die a natural death. Since a number of the trait responses he observes do not die the death he expects them to die, he is forced to the conclusion that there is something in them which keeps them going. A simpler conclusion would be that the conditions necessary for forgetting or unlearning have not occurred, and consequently the response continues.

What are the conditions which would lead one to expect cessation of a trait response like expansiveness? McClelland (1942) has gone into the question in some detail but his discussion may be summarized rather briefly here. In the first place, a response may drop out because the situation which gives rise to it does not recur. This is what McGeoch refers to as the *change of context* basis for forgetting. In retention theory it is illustrated by the inability to recall a person's name in a new context. In our example it would be illustrated by the disappearance of the trait of expansiveness if the person were suddenly stricken by paralysis and never had to move again. There must be some recurrence of a situation to observe consistent responses to it. Of course there are all degrees of similarity of recurring situations. A person who is normally reclusive in gesture may lose this trait if he has to perform on a platform in front of people where the situation is so different from the normal ones in which he moves that it does not evoke the usual responses. Still, for most expressive traits, the situations are seldom different enough so as to fail to evoke the well-learned normal responses. Thus we find that the first cause of forgetting—at least as far as a trait like expansiveness is concerned—would hardly ever operate, and we could not therefore expect the trait to drop out for this reason.

In the second place, a temporary extinction of a response may be brought about by *withdrawal of reward.* Extinction, as it has been observed in the laboratory, is a very special kind of forgetting and is so temporary that it could hardly be considered a serious reason for the disappearance of a trait like expansiveness. The person has to move for various reasons, and if expansive movements satisfy his desires to get from one place to another, that particular style of movement is going to be reinforced. The only apparent way of extinguishing the style of movement would be not to reinforce movement at all, and it would be difficult to imagine such a circumstance.

In the third place, the disappearance of a response may be caused by the learning of a new response under conditions of *differential reinforcement.* This is the interference theory of forgetting and it states in effect that a new learned response replaces the old one. In order for a new response to be learned, it must be reinforced, and the old one usually must be punished or not reinforced. Once again it is difficult to see how this situation could arise with a trait like expansiveness. Undoubtedly one could get rid of the trait of expansiveness by bringing the subject into the laboratory and shocking every expansive movement and approving every restricted one. It would take considerable practice for the subject to learn to make smaller constricted movements in handwriting and gesture, but with proper training it probably could be done. But the point is that it would seldom happen in real life. Apparently this cause of forgetting also would occur so seldom that we could not normally expect a trait to die out for this reason either.

We have exhausted the usual reasons given for forgetting and found that they would in fact seldom occur as far as a trait like expansiveness is concerned. We may therefore expect that once acquired it would persist as Allport observes it does persist, and we need not assume that the laws of forgetting have been suspended and replaced by a new principle of "functional autonomy." Nevertheless it may be objected that we have chosen our example judiciously and that the conditions for forgetting might more easily arise for some of the other traits previously discussed. It is difficult to meet such an objection entirely, but a glance at the traits discussed in Chapters 5 and 6 would certainly suggest that they do not differ very much from expansiveness in this respect. Ways of doing things—ways of perceiving, of moving, of talking, of working, of thinking—once acquired, are not easily lost for the simple reason that the conditions which cause the forgetting of a response do not often occur for such responses. The apparent reason for this is that many of the situations occur very frequently and represent problems that the subject must solve repeatedly. A person must walk, talk, perceive, think, *somehow,* and once he has discovered a way of doing these various things, it tends to be repeated because it continues to solve these problems and the conditions for causing it to disappear do not occur. The biological economy of such traits is obvious. If we had continually to relearn or rediscover ways of adapting to such common everyday problems, life would be a much more complicated affair than it is. Traits are the stable adjustive mechanisms by which we adapt to recurrent problems in our environment. As William James so aptly put it, traits or habits are the great "flywheel of society."

Similar Responses. Another part of our trait definition states that we must note whether a person is reacting now as he has reacted in the past. This raises the old problem of similarity of responses. How do we know that he is reacting the way he did before? What constitutes a similar response? We shall have to define similarity more narrowly than Allport did if we are to avoid the difficulty of calling any two responses equivalent regardless of what they have in common. We may be tempted to define similarity on the basis of identical elements in the responses, as the transfer theorists were in the habit of doing some years back. But as Allport points out (1937), this really begs the question, since no one has been able to define what an "element" or what an "identity" is. He quotes Thorndike to the effect "that a person's ability to estimate the length of 100 mm. lines is essentially independent of his ability to estimate the length of 50 mm. lines. Since in experimental investigations it is found that training in one of these abilities does not appreciably affect the other ability, they are regarded as containing no appreciable elements in common. One wonders whether the abilities involved in estimating lines of 100 mm. and 75 mm. are still separate; and how about the abilities to estimate lines of 100 mm. and 99.999 mm.?" (1937, p. 269.) Allport further argues that we cannot rely on identities of the muscular contractions involved in the responses since "writing with a crayon held in the right hand, left hand, toes, or teeth shows transfer effects, but the muscles involved in these cases are entirely different." (1937, p. 272.) Since Allport felt that the identical element theory of response similarity was untenable, first because it led to an infinite variety of elements, and second because it provided no basis for defining identities, he concluded that the much broader theory of equivalence of responses was necessary. He therefore postulated the existence of traits as focal dispositions which rendered responses "equivalent" even though they might be as varied as listening to a symphony, reading a sonnet, looking at a sunset, or playing golf.

Fortunately we are not forced to this extreme—an extreme which, as we have seen, has meant that the trait concept has been broadened beyond its real usefulness to include behavior which might more easily be conceptualized in other terms. On a common-sense basis at least, there certainly seem to be *ways* of thinking, perceiving, moving, and working which appear highly similar. In determining what responses to group together as similar, we can be guided in the first instance by theoretical convenience. That is, we may set up hypotheses as to response similarity, based on rational analyses of the ways in which an organism can function. For instance, to choose an example from Chapter 6, we may decide on theoretical or *a priori* grounds that one of the ways in which an organism can function in a work situation is to show wide fluctuations in output. Consequently we set up the hypothesis that there may be a trait called *variability* or *oscillation,* which will show itself in fluctuations in performance of all sorts. The next step is to try to discover whether such a trait exists by correlating variability scores in different types of performances. On the basis of such a correlational analysis we may find that there is such a trait unity, but that it is restricted to a certain group of tests. Or of course we may find that there is no consistency in the variability which subjects show even on the same test. In either case this will necessitate a change in our hypothesis that there is such a trait as variability or a revision in the surplus meanings attached to our trait construct. In other words, Cattell's method of *covariation* may be utilized to discover whether or not a postulated trait consistency exists. To his approach should be added the requirement that a rational analysis of the dimensions of behavior be made prior to factor analysis. If such a theoretical analysis is made, it tends to insure the discovery of factors which will be meaningful and not as miscellaneous as some that have been discovered to date. In other words, we are arguing here as we did in Chapter 6, that factor analysis is a useful tool for testing whether or not traits exist and for refining our conceptions of the responses they include. Furthermore, it is a more sensitive tool for this type of analysis than is the transfer of training approach discussed by Allport (1937). On methodological grounds it seems safer to conclude that Responses A and B can be grouped together as similar if they covary than to assume they belong together if the learning of A facilitates the learning of B. Covariation is a more direct approach to defining empirical similarity than is transfer of training.

It is pertinent to ask on what basis we set up a hypothesis that two responses are similar or are going to covary. A complete answer to this question would require an analysis of the whole set of theoretical constructs used to cover personality, but a partial answer may be found in the other elements of our trait definition which are yet to be discussed.

Similar Situations. Our formal trait definition also refers to "similar situations." Once again we are faced with the problem of defining similarity. How do we know when a situation has occurred again? How much deviation from the original situation are we going to allow before we call the second situation different from the first? We cannot answer these questions by falling back on Allport's notion of equivalence for the same reason that it was not satisfactory in defining equivalence of responses. We also cannot fall back on covariation, as we did in the case of defining similar responses, since we cannot correlate elements in the situation. Nor are we helped much by reference to identical elements, since we are again faced with the problem of defining what is meant by an element and by an identity.

The solution once more must lie in theoretical convenience. We shall have to begin by stating on rational or phenomenological grounds that certain types of situations are similar. If we discover that the situations are not similar in the sense that they do not appear to mediate consistent responses, then we have to revise our definition of what situations belong together.

In practice the problem is not so difficult as this may sound. What defines the similarity of situations in the laboratory or clinic is the task set under which the subject is performing. The similarity in task set is in turn established by the similarity of the instructions and working conditions accompanying the task. For example, when a psychologist presents the subject with an inkblot and asks him, "What might this be?" the subject is faced with a situation which may be substantially duplicated any number of times. In such cases we say that the test administration procedure is *standardized*. Standardized situations are similar situations.

However, a standardized situation need not be an *identical* one. For example, asking the subject to write *eee's* with a pointer between his toes, in his teeth, or in his right hand is a standardized task situation, and even though the responses called for are different, it seems fair to test them for covariation as similar responses to a similar task set. It would be possible to cite a great number of such examples. Let us take one more. A fairly standardized test instruction to a subject is to say: "Your score on the last trial was X; what are you going to try for on the next trial?" This is what is commonly referred to as the level-of-aspiration technique, which, with some variations in the way the second question is asked, has become standardized and is applicable to a wide variety of test situations. Since what the subject is asked to do is the same, we may regard the situation as similar and look for consistency in the responses of the subject to the various test situations in which such an instruction is used. As a matter of fact, there is considerable evidence that level-of-aspiration responses tend to be fairly consistent in different situations and therefore constitute a trait, as defined here (Lewin, Dembo, Festinger, Sears, 1944). Once more this seems comparable to looking for consistencies in performance tests which have been classed as similar because they require the same kind of behavior for solution.

The definition which we have so far given of similarities of situations in terms of standardized problems which the subject must solve is only approximate. We may hold the situation constant or let it vary within a prescribed range, yet the subject's conception of the situation may be quite different from what we expected it to be. It is possible to perform experiments and give tests because the subjects, by and large, conceive of the testing or experimental situations as we expect them to conceive them. However, we occasionally find that the subjects have given themselves self-instructions that are quite different from what we intended. There is a sense, then, in which similarity must ultimately be defined in terms of what Koffka (1935) has called the subject's "behavioral" environment; that is, his internal environment, as opposed to the external environment. To use Koffka's example, a man may be walking across a frozen snow-covered lake and react to it as if it were solid ground, although we, as independent observers, know that it is really a frozen lake. Nevertheless, as far as the subject is concerned in his behavioral environment, it is solid ground. Similarly in the Rorschach Test situation if the subject responds to the question, "What can this be?" by defining the situation as one in which he must be very careful lest he be sent to a mental hospital, the situation is not similar to that under which others take the test, or under which the same subject might take it again, under different circumstances. Unfortunately for theory, some of these individual differences in interpretation of testing situations go undetected and we may falsely conclude that there is no trait consistency when our correct conclusion should be that we have not kept the situation similar as far as the subjects are concerned.

Common and Uncommon Traits. This discussion contains a clue to the answer of the problem of common versus individual traits. We discover common traits in common situations which have the same meaning to a great number of people. Everyone has to move. Nearly everyone has to perceive, to talk, to solve problems in one way or another. These situations are so common that they are nearly universal for every living human being. Presumably there are a limited number of ways of reacting to these universal situations to which everyone must adjust. Furthermore, these situations are not only *universal;* they are *recurrent.* A person has to move again and again; he has to perceive repeatedly; he has to solve problem after problem. The situations are common not only with respect to the fact that they occur in everyone's life, but with respect to the fact that they recur again and again in every person's life. It is no wonder, then, that we discover common ways of solving such similar problems.

One may make a case from this line of reasoning for limiting traits to biologically recurrent situations. For instance, everyone has a physique, a body. And nearly every person must learn to move it about. Furthermore, he must move it again and again in similar situations (standing up, sitting down, eating, etc.). It is easy to see how trait concepts would cover this type of behavior very conveniently. On the other hand, there are certain common, recurrent social problems which many—if not all—people have to solve in one way or another. For instance, everyone, except a few hermits, has to adjust constantly to the problem of reacting to meeting another person. Presumably the number of ways in which a person can respond to this recurrent social situation is limited. One might then look for consistencies in behavior in such face-to-face contacts, as we did in Chapter 6 in discussing the trait of sociability in connection with a rating scale of social behavior. The difficulty with this type of analysis is that the social interpretation of such situations is of such great importance. One behaves differently to one's mother-in-law, one's son, or one's wife. It therefore becomes more crucial to know the subject's interpretation of the face-to-face relationship than to look for consistencies in his behavior based on an apparent similarity of the situations. Social traits, as they might be called, depend to a very large extent on social and cultural norms and are therefore more subject to different interpretations than are biologically-oriented traits. This is not to deny that social traits exist, but they will certainly be less universal and determined less by past reactions in similar situations than by the subject's conception of what the situation calls for. In other words, social traits involve heavily the social schemata and attitudes to be discussed later. Biological traits also involve to some extent social norms, e.g., as to how a person should walk, talk, or behave with a "football" physique. But the social determinant is much less important and to the extent that it is so, the past experience of the person in similar situations becomes decisive, and the resulting consistency in behavior fulfills more nearly our definition of a trait.

Situations need not be universal in order to give rise to comparable behavior. A group of people who live in a very high altitude may develop modes of adjustment which an anthropologist studying that group would want to identify as traits (e.g., carefulness in movement), even though the trait terms he used would not be applicable to a group of people living at normal altitudes. A recurrent problem which must be adjusted to may be universal, as in the case of moving one's body, or it may be limited to a group, as in the case of adjusting to a high altitude. Or finally, it may be limited to the life of a single individual. For instance, a person may have a physical anomaly which is unique, such as a club foot, to which he must learn to respond. Furthermore, the chances are that he will learn to respond to it in a unique but consistent fashion. That is, the club foot may be a common element in a variety of situations, to all of which he responds in a consistent way, by withdrawal or quiescence, for example. In the individual life, situations may come to be similar through constant association or learning. Someone may come to regard as similar two situations which would be different for most people, or two situations which we may think present similar problems for most people may be interpreted differently by a given individual. When dealing with individual traits, we must take individual perceptions or self-instructions into account rather than assuming that the group instructions have exactly the same meaning for everyone in the group. To illustrate this point, we may return to Baldwin's study of the reaction of children to various nursery-school situations. As far as most of the nursery-school children were concerned, it was safe to assume that the adjustment situation with which they were faced was substantially the same, and their responses to it could be compared and studied for consistency from day to day. On the other hand, for one of the children, Ralph, the adjustment situation obviously had a personal meaning and was therefore not similar to the ones which the other children faced. Nevertheless Ralph's daily adjustment problems were similar to each other and it is perfectly possible to look for consistency within his responses to those recurrent and (for him) similar situations.

What this adds up to is that there is room for both common and uncommon or individual traits. The area of common traits is probably much larger than Allport assumed because there are a relatively large number of situations to which all or nearly all people must adjust and in a limited number of ways. Most, but not necessarily all, of these problems are oriented around the biological equipment of human organisms, and involve such common situations as perceiving, walking, talking, and working. On the other hand, there are recurrent similar situations which are unique to the individual life. And as Allport rightly insists, these must be studied especially by the clinical psychologist. In both cases, however, the problem of identifying a trait is the same. Covariant behavior is sought in the one case in recurrent problems within the life of one individual, and in the other case, in recurrent problems common to a large group of individuals.

Similar Motivation. The last part of our trait definition states that we should look for traits in situations in which the motivation has remained substantially the same. Why do we insist upon similarity of motivation? The reason is simple. What our trait definition says in effect is that what a person has learned in the past will influence what he does in the present *provided* the meaning of the situation and his motivation stay the same. As in many physical laws the effect of one variable, such as temperature or pressure, can be measured only when the other variables are held constant. As we have seen in the preceding section, we cannot expect consistency of responses in situations which are not similar, either in the experimenter's or in the subject's eyes. Similarly we cannot expect consistent behavior, even in similar situations, if the motivation of the subject has changed markedly.

A simple example will suffice to illustrate this point. In tests of expansiveness of movement, the normal motivation of the subject is to get where he's going (in a free response situation), to do what the experimenter asks him to do, or to cooperate as best he can with the instructions. But suppose his motivation changes to one of trying to confuse the experimenter's results, or suppose he decides to hit the experimenter on the head. In either case his reactions (e.g., expansive movements) will scarcely be consistent with those he makes under "normal" motivational conditions. Any number of studies show that test results are markedly modified by what the subject is trying to do. If he is trying to cheat, to make a favorable impression or to fake a particular kind of score (cf. Strong, 1943), his responses will not be consistent with what they would be under conditions of normal motivation.

On the other hand, it has been clearly shown that situations which normally differ can be made equivalent for a group of subjects by introducing a common motive in both of them. For example, introduction of achievement motivation through the technique of ego-involvement has been shown to make behavior consistent which was inconsistent prior to the introduction of the motive. Specifically, confidence ratings on how well a person felt he had done on a number of tests were uncorrelated under conditions of normal motivation, but as soon as the subjects were ego-involved, an appreciable positive intercorrelation among the confidence ratings was introduced (Klein and Schoenfeld, 1941). Or motivation may serve to make different stimulus situations equivalent. McClelland and Atkinson (1948) showed, for example, that hunger produced many more food-related responses to ambiguous stimuli than had appeared under conditions of food-satiation. In other words, ambiguous stimuli which had formerly been interpreted differently now tended under the influence of hunger to evoke similar perceptions of food objects. In short, motivation is another variable which influences the consistency of responses, and it must be held constant if the effect of past learning in similar situations is to be measured. And it is this carry-over from the past, this consistency, that we are interested in when we measure traits.

Motivation should be similar, not only with respect to kind, but also intensity. As our later discussion of needs will show, increasing the intensity of a motive may also markedly change the subject's response. Perhaps Rosenzweig's demonstration of the influence of increased achievement motivation on the Zeigarnik effect is the simplest illustration of this point. He found (1943) that under task orientation or low n Achievement his subjects tended to recall more incompleted than completed tasks, whereas under ego-involvement or strong n Achievement the tendency was reversed (cf. also Atkinson, 1950b). Consequently anyone looking for a consistency in the tendency to remember completed or uncompleted tasks would have to keep achievement motivation at a constant intensity.

Trait Consistency and Generality. Two of the traditional problems in trait psychology are illuminated by the preceding discussion. One deals with how consistent traits are, that is, with the tendency of the same situation on different occasions to evoke similar responses, and the other deals with how general traits are, that is, with the tendency of similar situations to evoke similar responses. As far as consistency is concerned the answer would appear to be that one can expect it to the extent that the responses have been strengthened by past reinforcement and that the other conditions of our formal trait definition are met. Changes in motivation and in the understanding of the situation are bound to introduce inconsistencies in the subject's responses. To a certain extent the same answer applies to the question of how general a trait is. However, somewhere the trait theorist has to make a decision as to how general a given trait should be; that is, as to how many situations it will try to cover. If it is too broad, it will be inconsistent; but on the other hand, if it is too specific, it will become less useful as a means of summarizing the person's behavior. The only ultimate answer to this question is an empirical one. We must set up hypotheses as to what situations should be included under a given trait concept and then attempt to discover whether these hypotheses are, in fact, fruitful. But when we test for their fruitfulness (that is, for whether they lead to consistent responses) we must be careful to make certain that the other specifications of the trait definition are observed. That is, the motivation of the subjects must be kept within the normal range and the meaning of the situation to the subject must be as constant as possible.

Both consistency and generality are functions of past learning. To go to the extreme, one could not expect perfect consistency or perfect generality after one repetition of a similar response in a similar situation. One repetition or several is not enough to produce learning. It follows that traits should become more consistent and more general, the more often the person has reacted to a given situation in a way which is reinforced. This suggests that traits will be more consistent and probably more general in older people. One of the criticisms that has been made of Hartshorne and May's study of honesty (cf. Allport, 1937) is that they worked with children who were too young for any consistent modes of responding to have developed.

To sum up, we find that trait generality and trait consistency, as well as other trait characteristics, are a function of the three variables in our definition of a trait, to wit: (1) *learning* (2) *in similar situations* (3) *under similar motivation.* To put it in another way, we have defined a trait as a covariation or consistency in responses which is a function of past learning in similar situations under similar motivation. Such a definition is much narrower than that given by either Allport or Cattell, and implies the existence of two other personality variables to which we must soon turn our attention.

Summary of Karl's Traits. Our theoretical discussion of the nature of traits may be all very well, but can we apply it to our individual case, Karl? In the preceding chapters we have covered a good deal of ground and assigned him in the process a good many traits varying in complexity all the way from "assertive in posture and movement" to "abasive" or "emotionally labile." Is there any way in which we can boil these various characterizations down into a single trait list of finite length? The apparently overwhelming complexity of the task illustrates the great weakness of personality study today. Everyone uses his own instrument for measuring the dimensions of personality and discovers aspects that are essentially untranslatable into those discovered by any other person. To cut this problem down to size, let us review the prescriptions we have made throughout our discussion as to how we might simplify trait theory:

(1) Restrict the term trait to consistencies in behavior in similar situations under similar motivation; (2) Define a trait carefully with surplus meanings that reach across different response elements; (3) Detach evaluations from descriptions of the traits themselves; (4) Distinguish carefully between behavior and inferences about it drawn from the outcomes of behavior; (5) Give up the isolation implicit in attempting to characterize the whole trait sphere with any one single instrument. Now let us see if we can apply this pious advice to the concrete problem of trying to list Karl's traits.

Table 7.2 represents an attempt to find a classification of common traits that will apply not only to Karl but to any other person as well. It is based in part on a "rational" analysis of common situations to which all people must adjust in one way or another and in part on a study of the traits discovered by existing instruments as covered in the past three chapters.

Obviously a bare list of traits like this can have little meaning apart from the operations involved in measuring each one. Consequently reference is made after each trait to the studies which have made use of it as discussed somewhere in the preceding three chapters. Thus for instance the first trait—"Energetic–v–Weak"—is found, at least in part, in Allport and Vernon's *Studies in Expressive Movement* (1933), in Sheldon's characterization of the somatotonic (1942), and in Fiske's (1949) Social Adaptability Factor (cf. especially "Adventurous –v– Cautious"). The reader should trace back in a similar manner the sources of all fifteen of the traits if they are to be anything more than a collection of names. The traits with an asterisk after them we have found to characterize Karl. On some of the others, either the dimension does not apply to him, or we don't have information, or he falls somewhere in the middle of the two extremes. But with all the reservations about the adequacy of our data in mind, we may summarize this aspect of his personality as follows:

> Karl is energetic and expansive in movement; wholistic and fluent, but oriented outwards in perception; variable and distractable in performance; labile and expressive emotionally; gregarious and adaptable socially; and conscientious with respect to following approved social norms.

Is such a trait portrait satisfactory? Wherein are its weaknesses and strengths? (1) In the first place it should be obvious that it is only a first step toward a scientifically sound trait description because we have not *adequately* specified the operations for measuring each of

TABLE 7.2

A Classification of Common Traits

Common Stimulus Situations	*Associated Behavior*	*Common Trait Dimensions (Sources indicated)*
Chapter 5		
A. Position of the body and its parts	Moving	Movement characteristics (1) Energetic* –v– Weak (AV,S,R) (Emphasis characteristic) (2) Expansive* –v– Restrained (AV,K) (Areal characteristic)
B. Problems to be solved	Perceiving Thinking (Speaking)	Symbolic approach characteristics (3) Wholistic* –v– Analytic (T,Ro) (4) Visual, verbal, numerical or other symbol style (T) (5) Fluent* –v– Inhibited (T,Ro,R) (Imaginative –v– Unimaginative) (6) Inner –v– Outer Orientation* (Ro,Sp,K)
Chapter 6		
C. Work to be performed	Performing	Performance characteristics (7) Variable* –v– Even (T) (8) Flexible –v– Rigid, Perseverative (T) (9) Persistent –v– Distractable* (T)
D. Pleasure and pain	Emoting	Emotional characteristics (10) Labile* –v– Even (R,Ro) (11) Expressive*, Open –v– Inhibited (S,R) (12) Cheerful –v– Depressed (R)
E. Other people	Interacting	Social interaction characteristics (13) Gregarious, Responsive* –v– Autonomous (R,S) (14) Assertive –v– Submissive, Adaptable* (R)
F. Social Norms	Conforming	Conformity characteristics (15) Conscientious* –v– Not Conscientious (R,T)

Key to symbols:
- * trait probably characterizing Karl
- AV Allport-Vernon, Expressive movements (1933)
- S Sheldon, et al. Temperament (posture and movement) traits
- K Klages, handwriting characteristics
- Ro Rorschach, perceiving characteristics
- Sp Speech characteristics
- T Test results (Cattell 1946a, etc.)
- R Rating results (Cattell 1946a, Fiske 1949, O.S.S. 1948, etc.)

these traits. Consequently we can at this point make no meaningful estimates of the degree of strength of any of these traits, though our trait dimensions *assume a continuum* from one extreme to the other. Nevertheless we have taken a *first* step in indicating in Table 7.2 what class of operations is involved for each trait description. The second step of returning to obtain *purified* measures of each of these traits is now perfectly feasible either for Karl or any other subject. The lack of purity of our measures as they stand is nicely illustrated by the fact that Karl's school friend rates him in Table 5.2 as assertive, bold, adventurous, etc., whereas we have judged him to be primarily adaptable rather than assertive in his social relations (Trait 14). The difficulty arises over the confusion of the "Energetic" characteristic which Karl possesses to a high degree with social assertiveness which is not the same thing.

(2) What is the trait "Conscientious" doing in the list, when we have so carefully eschewed all evaluative trait descriptions? The answer is in part based on simple convenience: *some* measure of conformity (integrity, honesty, etc.) is nearly always required in a personality description. It is also in part based on the fact that "Conscientious" when used in the sense intended here is not really an evaluative term. What it connotes is simply whether or not the person is "good" in the sense of following social norms consistently or not. In some people (cf., for example, the small percentage of Hartshorne and May's cases who were *always* honest), conformity becomes an outstanding characteristic. For them such a trait dimension is a useful way of classifying behavior. For many others it may not be particularly applicable.

(3) Is there anything sacred about this list of fifteen traits? Can they be reduced? A glance at Table 7.2 suggests that there may be several instances of overlap. Is it really possible to distinguish usefully between a person whose performance is *variable* and one whose performance is *distractable*? And are both of these manifestations of emotional *lability*? In each case there is considerable evidence that the traits are independent, but subsequent research may show that they are related in such a way as to reduce them to a single new trait or to redefine each of them. In particular we do not know whether traits that appear similar but which refer to different situations (variability in emotions and in performance) should be grouped under a single heading, although what evidence there is suggests that they should not be, particularly since the range of motives involved

in each is not likely to be the same, as is required in our trait definition.

Can this list be expanded? What has become of the thousands of trait names listed by Allport and Odbert (1936) or used by the many other workers in the field? Can we really get along with so few? There is, of course, no adequate answer to such questions. Anyone who has ever made up a rating scale or invented a test like the Rorschach is bound to exclaim that this list is no good for *his* purposes, that it plainly does not do justice to the richness and variety of personality. And he will be right. *No* scientific scheme will ever do justice to the richness of personality, but since the purposes of a scientific conceptualization are economy and adequacy for understanding and prediction (cf. Chapter 3), we shall have to be contented with *some* kind of a finite set of traits. Many of those who grant this will still be unhappy with the list we have chosen. They should modify it then or make up a better list of their own, following the rules for building scientific concepts. This particular set of traits is obviously only a first approximation to be modified and refined by subsequent research. It also does not claim to describe *all* of personality. We have decided for reasons of convenience to use the trait variable *to describe the surface or stylistic manifestations of personality only*. Many of the objections to this list may disappear when it becomes clearer how we are to conceptualize other areas of personality. We are dealing here with a person's *style* of life, with general characterizations of his *mode of approach*. Later we will attempt to relate his style to his ideas, his conceptions of himself, and his underlying motives.

(4) Will any one of our instruments provide us with measures of all fifteen traits? How about rating scales? Perhaps the first impulse of someone who has read this far and who is willing to go along with this approach would be to construct a rating scale with these fifteen trait titles on it to be checked by some astute judge. How simple! But how inadequate! As we pointed out in Chapter 6, ratings are perhaps the most inadequate measures of all because they are based on observations of behavior in an unknown sample of situations of unknown characteristics. Perhaps a series of standardized situations for behavior observation and rating could be constructed along the lines followed in the O.S.S. assessments, but this would be to move in the direction of the painstaking operational definitions of our trait terms which are absolutely essential.

How about the Rorschach? While most of the instruments discussed, from temperament typing to handwriting, have laid claim to being the "Open Sesame" of trait analysis, probably the Rorschach would have the most serious backing for this post by the largest number of psychologists. A glance at Table 7.2 will show why. There is scarcely a trait in the list which a good Rorschacher could not make inferences about from his test results. The amount of emotional lability, for instance, which we propose to measure through observing the person's mood changes, he feels he can estimate from the number of color responses, the proportion of responses to the colored plates VIII-X, the number of white-space responses, etc. In a similar fashion he might estimate fluency from the number of responses, flexibility from the percentage of animal responses, etc. It would certainly be convenient and extremely economical if we could get even approximate estimates of a wide variety of traits from a single testing situation involving a perceptual or any other mode of approach. There is sufficient common-sense confirmation of the usefulness of the Rorschach for this purpose to encourage Rorschachers to make careful studies of the extent to which their measures will predict trait strength as measured by other, more direct measures. But they should clearly realize what the problem is and not redefine the trait so that it applies only to perceptual behavior, if what they are trying to do is estimate *from perception* what behavior in other types of situations will characteristically be like.

NOTES AND QUERIES

1. Answer Montaigne's statement quoted at the beginning of the chapter. Can it be used as an argument against trait consistency?

2. What is the relation between a trait as defined in this chapter and an attitude? A trait and a habit? A trait and a symptom?

3. Evaluate in the light of the discussion in this chapter the following argument for functional autonomy from Allport. What kind of a trait is "interest in a subject"?

"A person likes to do what he can do well. Over and over again it has been demonstrated that the skill learned for some external reason, turns into an interest, and is self-propelling, even though the original reason for pursuing it has been lost. A student who at first undertakes a field of study in college because it is prescribed, because it pleases his parents, or because it comes at a convenient hour, often ends by finding himself absorbed, perhaps for life, in the subject itself. . . . The original motives are entirely lost. What was a means to an end had become an end in itself." (1937, p. 201.)

4. Ask someone what one of your own outstanding traits is and try to analyze how it got learned and under what conditions it appears. How *general* is it? How *common* is it? Why may it be easier to find one of your traits by asking someone else than by asking yourself?

5. List three factors which would promote trait generality drawing from your knowledge of the factors which promote *positive transfer* and *response generalization,* as well as on our formal trait definition. Could a teacher make use of them in developing a "trait" of honesty?

6. Define honesty and then try to fit it into our formal trait definition. Can you explain why, in terms of our definition, Hartshorne and May did not find much of a unitary trait of honesty?

7. List all the traits ascribed to Karl in Chapters 5 and 6 (between 30 and 40) and try to figure out how each fits under the 15 traits in the final list. What is the best approach to traits that don't appear to fit?

8. Show how each of the 15 traits in Table 7.2 could lead to *positive* or *negative* evaluations depending on the standard used. Under what conditions is "Energy" valuable and not valuable? etc.

9. What difficulties would arise if an attempt were made to use social norm traits like "honesty" or "readiness to cooperate" in cross cultural studies? Is there any trait in Table 7.2 which could not be used cross culturally?

10. Suppose a person is "cooperative" largely because he is afraid. Should we classify his cooperativeness, supposing it to be a consistent response pattern for him, along with the trait of cooperativeness found in a number of other people for whom fear was not part of the motivating situation when their cooperation was measured? Should there be two traits of cooperativeness, one based on one class of motives and another on another class of motives? How can the range of motives be established within which we will attempt to measure a given person's cooperativeness? Obviously there are certain situations in which no one will be cooperative and certain others in which everyone will be. What we need is some "middle range" of situations. Can you define it for this trait?

Part Three

SCHEMA AS A PERSONALITY VARIABLE

8

Ideas and Values

So far we have been dealing with the person's style of living, his manner of approach to life. But somehow trait psychology seems to give us only the outward view. We do not know what is going on inside the person, what he is thinking, feeling, or wanting. We do not know what his conceptions of the world are; we only know how he reacts consistently in some common recurring situations. Psychologists have long been hampered in their efforts to get at what might be called the inner cognitive structure of man. For one thing, the task has seemed incredibly difficult. We were somewhat dismayed when we attempted to discover a limited number of traits in terms of which we could describe a single person like Karl. But suppose we undertake the task of assaying the contents of Karl's mind. Would it not take a lifetime to discover everything that he knows, remembers or conceives?

Krech and Crutchfield (1948) have been impressed both by the need for this type of study and by its difficulty. "To arrive at anything approaching a complete account of what 'Negro' or 'Communism' or 'free enterprise' means to the individual by simply observing his behavior or by asking him to respond to 20 scale items would be manifestly impossible. What is needed is the most intensive, searching, and prolonged investigation of cognitive contents, and there is no short cut to this goal. The contents of an individual's beliefs and attitudes about a single object, Adolf Hitler, for example, might be so detailed and complex as to require many hours to describe." (1948, p. 248.) As they go on to point out, the expenditure of time and energy necessary for a task of this sort would be tremendous. Furthermore, methods for analysis and synthesis of cognitive content have not yet been developed. Nevertheless they feel that possibly "the next major advance in the field of belief and attitude research will come along these lines." (1948, p. 249.)

Plan of the Next Three Chapters. However, if we approach the problem systematically, we may be able to whittle it down to size. Let us consider it for a moment from the viewpoint of a newborn infant who is turned loose in a welter of stimulation, out of which he must make sense in order to survive. Can we usefully distinguish different aspects of this stimulation around which his developing ideas will cluster? To begin with we may note, as Kluckhohn and Mowrer have (1944), that this matrix of stimulation is part physical or geographical in nature, part biological, part social, and part cultural. That is, one important source of stimulation for the child is the physical environment in which he lives. If he is born in Africa he will be exposed to certain climatological conditions, certain sights and sounds, certain fauna and flora that will be quite different from those experienced by a child born and brought up in New York City. Likewise a person born with a strong right arm or into a narrow family group will have a different range of experiences from that of a person who is born weak or into an extended kinship system. Finally, even though the range of stimulation given from without in the objective environment is nearly the same for two individuals, different cultures and different family units within a given culture will tend to emphasize different aspects of this range, so that the modal stimulation within any given dimension may still be different for a particular child.

Having distinguished in this way the major sources of stimulation or, as they have sometimes been called, the major determinants of behavior, we may next infer that the individual who receives this stimulation must have the capacity to organize, integrate, or schematize it, if he is to be able to find his way successfully through the "blooming, buzzing confusion" of incoming impulses. This organizing process is not completely mysterious. As psychologists we know a good deal about it, particularly as it works at simpler levels, just as we know enough about how consistent responses are acquired to enable us to understand something about the nature of traits. Fortunately not all of the organizing has to be done by each new infant starting completely from scratch. Instead, each culture provides a good many ready-made solutions to the problems of organization which are of tremendous value, adaptively speaking, to each person as he learns his way about the world of stimulation.

Table 8.1 may help to show how far we have come in our analysis and where we go from here.

This schematic diagram shows how we have simplified our initial problem. Instead of a task of seemingly overwhelming complexity we are now faced with three more specific problems, each of which can be attacked with some hope of moderate success. First of all we can attempt to identify the important sources of stimulation, par-

TABLE 8.1

Schematic Diagram Showing the Relations between Cultural Patterns and Personal Schemata As They Will Be Discussed in the Next Three Chapters

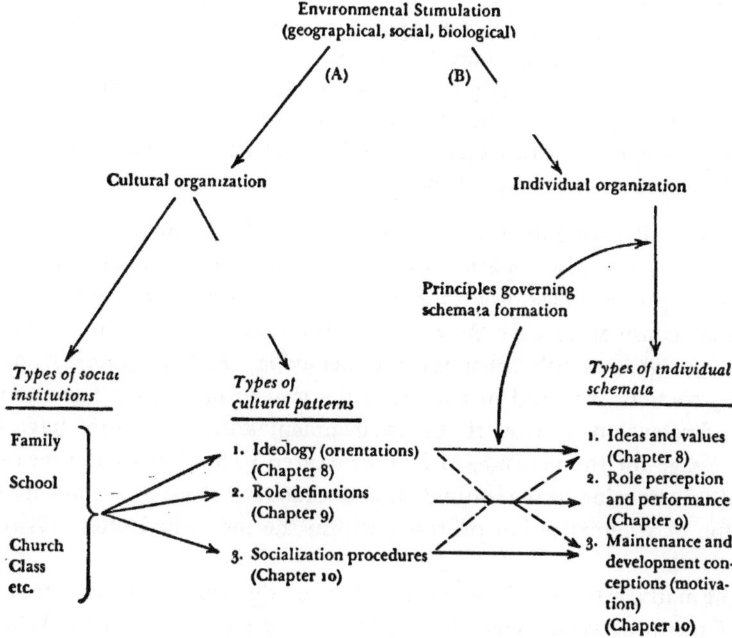

ticularly as they are patterned by the culture in which the person lives. What are the sources, limits, and ranges of environmental stimulation starting at the top of Table 8.1? At the individual level this is not so formidable a task as it may at first seem. Thus when Karl says, "My parents are ordinary hard-working people . . . I was born in a small town in New Jersey," this alone tells us a good deal about the ranges of stimulation to which he was subjected as a child. From the geography or ecology of rural New Jersey, we can estimate with a fair degree of certainty what things he has experienced regularly and what things he has experienced seldom, if ever. Thus it is certain that his experience of space is quite unlike that of a nomadic Arab living on the Sahara Desert, that he has probably never seen a camel except in a zoo and that his experience with palm trees is minimal. We know further that he will probably have been exposed to certain types of agricultural techniques, modes of transportation, a particular kind of kinship system, etc. It is here that sociologists and the cultural anthropologists are of great assistance to the psychologist working with the individual person because through their analysis of social structure and culture, they can make explicit predictions as to the kind of modal experiences or cultural patterns that a given person will be exposed to. Note in Table 8.1 that the individual's schemata may be organized either directly by himself via route B or indirectly via the much more common route A and its cultural patterns. Thus an analysis of cultural patterns may often be a short cut to discovering the individual schemata located in the lower right-hand corner of the table.

Secondly, we must turn our attention to the schematization process. How are culture patterns assimilated and what happens to them in the process of assimilation? In order to answer these questions we must consider in part the *means* of transmission to the individual (language, parent's attitudes and behavior, reading, public-school instruction, etc.) and in part the rules governing schema formation and retention. It is as if the environment and the culture have a message for the person which is structured somewhat by the means of transmission to the individual and somewhat more by the assimilation or schematization processes within the individual after it is received.

Finally, we must face the problem of describing the end result of this process—namely, the individual's system of schemata. What are the individual's beliefs, frames of reference, major orientations, role perceptions, ideas, and values? Unfortunately there is a terminological problem involved here, since psychologists have not agreed on what to call the "cognitive maps" (after Tolman, 1948a) the person builds up of his world. Perhaps the term *attitude* has been most often used by psychologists, although for our purposes it has two serious limitations: it implies conscious awareness, and it has the connotation of being for or against something or of a tendency *toward* an object. Since what we are talking about is not always conscious and does not necessarily imply either an object or the "for or against" dimension, we will prefer some more general term like conception, schema (plural schemata), or cognitive map.

The next problem is to classify the schemata to be discussed. From the cultural viewpoint we may conveniently distinguish three major types of influence which the culture has on its members—namely, its ideology or belief system, its role definitions, and its socialization procedures. Each of these has been given a counterpart in the individual's schemata structure under a slightly different name in Table 8.1 and arrows have been drawn to indicate that, while a particular schema type may derive chiefly from its corresponding cultural pattern type, it may draw in part from all three. The first type of cultural influence deals with the most general problems of orientation, with such matters as location in space and time, answers to questions as to what life means (religious systems), how men work, how they can enjoy themselves, or how they should be governed. This is the cultural ideology, which is partly drawn directly from the environment and partly from cultural emphases on aspects of it. It is of such fundamental importance in structuring all the other kinds of influences to which the person is subjected that it will be discussed first in this chapter. Secondly, the culture gives the individual guidance for behaving in many rather specific social situations. These behavioral or attitudinal norms have traditionally been subsumed under the *role* concept and will be discussed in the next chapter. Finally in Chapter 10 we will turn to the important orientations the culture gives the individual through its institutionalized child-rearing practices. From the individual's viewpoint socialization comes first in order of learning, roles second, and ideology third. We have inverted the order to correspond to the assumed relative order of importance of the three areas of cultural influence. Furthermore, as Table 8.1 suggests, socialization leads naturally into the next section of the book on motivation, since "maintenance and development conceptions" comes very close to defining motivation.

Principles Governing Schemata Formation. Before we turn to the specific task of this chapter, we will need to take time out to explore how cultural and environmental stimulation gets organized into a person's ideas. Having once analyzed the principles of schemata formation carefully, we can assume that they operate in other areas of culture as well and we need not refer to them over and over again. Just what has psychology to tell us about how external stimulation gets organized into ideas, schemata or cognitive maps inside the person? Let us begin with some very simple cases and work up to more complex ones.

1. Field Organizational Factors. Perceptual schemata are organized according to such Gestalt principles as figure-ground, good continuation, closure, similarity, proximity, and the like (cf. Koffka, 1935). The exact application of these principles to ideational material has not been worked out, although Wertheimer (1945), Allport and Postman (1947), and others have attempted it. Whenever they have been most successful in finding Gestalt processes at work in thinking or memory which are analogous to those found at the perceptual level, it often appears that the cognitive processes are loaded with visual imagery, which *ought* to function according to Gestalt laws. This may mean that such laws are not of much help in determining what happens to incoming stimulation of a nonvisual (e.g., verbal) nature. The difficulty with much ideational material (of a nonvisual nature) lies in trying to specify what constitutes similarity, proximity, etc., so that one can predict what organization the stimulus material suggests to start with.

2. Successive Stimulation. One of the simplest bases for schema formation in the field of memory is successive stimulation within a single sensory dimension or narrow range of dimensions. Sir Henry Head (1926) was one of the first to attack this problem carefully in his consideration of the coordination of posture and movement. Head felt that the afferent impulses must be organized on their entry into the brain into more or less enduring dispositions or schemata, in relation to which subsequent appropriate responses could be made. He thought of these schemata as "a model of ourselves which constantly changes" or "that combined standard against which all subsequent changes in posture are registered before they enter consciousness." This "body image," as it has been called, is formed unconsciously, although it may become conscious, out of serial sensory stimulation, which must get organized into some kind of a pattern. He conceived this organized postural schema both as a record of past sensory imput and as a determinant of future responses, as Oldfield and Zangwill point out (1942).

A simple empirical demonstration of the production of such a schema was given as early as 1909 and 1910 by Hollingworth (1909), who was working with what he called the "central tendency" effect in judgment. For example, in one series of judgments he had the subjects move their pencils through grooves varying in length from 10 to 70 mm. They then had to draw a line on a piece of paper equal in extent to the movement they had just made. He found that when the subjects tried to reproduce lines at the short end of the scale, that is, around 10 mm., they tended to make their lines too long and if they tried to reproduce lines at the long end of the scale they made them too short. They reproduced most accurately a line near the middle of the series, that is, around 35 mm. in length. In short, there appeared to be a norm or central tendency somewhere near the center of the range of lines to be drawn which summed up previous sensory experiences (of line drawing) and influenced subsequent judgments. When he shifted in another experiment to a different range and asked the subjects to reproduce lines varying in length from 30 mm. to 150 mm., he found that the subjects reproduced most accurately lines around 70 mm. in length rather than around 35 mm. as in the previous series. Furthermore, the 70 mm. line which had been underestimated in reproduction in the earlier series was now being reproduced accurately as it came closer to the central tendency of the new range of line lengths.

A great deal of subsequent experimental work has been done in this area which has been integrated by Helson (1948) into a single theoretical formulation which provides a mathematical formula for calculating the central tendency, or "adaptation level," as he calls it, from such variables as the frequency, intensity, and range of previous stimulation and its figure-ground characteristics. The particular mathematical formula he has derived appears to be sufficiently general to apply to a number of different sense modalities. It may prove of even greater importance if it can be applied to such higher order functions as the formation of a single individual's opinion as a function of the range, intensity, etc., of similar opinions expressed by other individuals in a group discussion. Certain preliminary findings by the Research Center in Group Dynamics at the University of Michigan suggest that the same principles may apply in such a situation. However, the chief importance of these experimental and theoretical formulations here is in demonstrating more exactly how schemata develop out of successive stimulations.

3. **The Fate of a Single Impression.** Another rather simple case of schema formation is that of an impression which occurs only once and then interacts with the total trace system or apperceptive mass of the person. Here the process is a little more difficult to analyze meaningfully because the other sensations or the pre-existing schemata which interact with the single impression are usually unknown. Nevertheless the phenomenon has been rather extensively studied,

beginning with some early work by Bartlett (1932) on remembering and coming up to a more recent work by Allport and Postman (1947) on the psychology of rumor. As an example of Bartlett's work we may take the following story which a subject reads to himself twice for the initial impression.

The War of the Ghosts

One night two young men from Egulac went down to the river to hunt seals, and while they were there it became foggy and calm. Then they heard war-cries, and they thought; "Maybe this is a war-party." They escaped to the shore, and hid behind a log. Now canoes came up, and they heard the noise of paddles, and saw one canoe coming up to them. There were five men in the canoe, and they said:

"What do you think? We wish to take you along. We are going up the river to make war on the people."

One of the young men said: "I have no arrows."

"Arrows are in the canoe," they said.

"I will not go along. I might be killed. My relatives do not know where I have gone. But you," he said turning to the other, "may go with them."

So one of the young men went, but the other returned home.

And the warriors went on up the river to a town on the other side of Kalomo. The people came down to the water, and they began to fight, and many were killed. But presently the young man heard one of the warriors say: "Quick let us go home: that Indian has been hit." Now he thought: "Oh, they are ghosts." He did not feel sick, but they said he had been shot.

So the canoes went back to Egulac, and the young man went ashore to his house, and made a fire. And he told everybody and said: "Behold I accompanied the ghosts, and we went to fight. Many of our fellows were killed, and many of those who attacked us were killed. They said I was hit, and I did not feel sick."

He told it all, and then he became quiet. When the sun rose he fell down. Something black came out of his mouth. His face became contorted. The people jumped up and cried.

He was dead.

(Reproduced with permission from F. C. Bartlett, *Remembering*. Copyright 1932 by the Cambridge University Press.)

Subjects were asked to reproduce the story they had read, at various time intervals after the first impression. The following is a reproduction of the story by one subject nearly three years after he had first read it:

Some warriors went to wage war against a ghost. They fought all day and one of their number was wounded.

They returned home in the evening bearing their sick comrade. As the day drew to a close he became rapidly worse, and the villagers came round him. At sunset he sighed; something black came out of his mouth. He was dead. (Bartlett, 1932, p. 75.)

Bartlett observed the transformation of the content of this story from a form much more closely approximating the original to this final end-product by obtaining repeated reproductions every month or so after the original impression. On the basis of his analysis of these changes and of the final product, he concluded that remembering is predominantly schematic; that is, it seldom involves very accurate reproductions but instead leads to "omission of detail, simplification of events and structure, and transformation of items into more familiar detail" (1932, p. 93.) He further feels that there is a good deal of reconstruction and rationalization in memory. For example, the subject stated in connection with the reproduction above "there was something about a canoe but I can't fit it in. I suppose it was his soul that came out of his mouth when he died." (1932, p. 75.) In other words Bartlett contended that remembering was an organized constructive process dependent upon attitudes toward the material, and he therefore adopted the term *schema* to refer to the serial "thread" which runs through repeated reproductions. Actually what interests us most here is the way in which his research illustrates how complex experiences, such as the initial impression of a story, get changed and reformulated into some sort of generalized conception, because we can assume that it is in much the same way that *all* of the individual's conceptions of his world develop, becoming simplified and reorganized with the passage of time.

4. Cultural Patterns. The schemata we have so far been discussing have developed out of controlled or uncontrolled experiences that the subject has had in an experimental situation. They are the product of personal and often unique experiences coming in a particular order with unique variety and intensity. But as Table 8.1 shows, many schemata are cultural products, that is, the products of prior organization by other people, and all the individual does is to take them over more or less ready-made. If he had to produce all the organization of his "blooming buzzing" experience himself, his task would be far more difficult than it actually is. Society fortunately does most of his work for him ahead of time. That is, many of the common problems which individuals in a given society must meet have already been tentatively solved by individuals in that society who have met the problems before. These problem solutions we call culture patterns or perceptual and behavioral norms. For example, Karl may develop out of his own personal and unique experiences a conception of how a father behaves (Route B in Table 8.1). On the other hand he is undoubtedly exposed to ready-made conceptions of the father role which his culture has already devised for him (Route A in Table 8.1). These social schemata are of tremendous importance in shaping his individual conceptions of the world.

Sherif (1936) has provided us with an excellent demonstration of how group conceptions or norms get built up and determine individual schemata. He made use of the well-known autokinetic phenomenon—namely, the tendency for a pin point of light in a dark room to be perceived as moving. When subjects are asked to judge how far and in what direction the point of light moves, they gradually establish a frame of reference with regard to the extent of the movement. That is, they build up a generalized conception or schema of how far the light is moving. When two or three individuals make their judgments together there is considerable disagreement at first in their perception of how far the light moves, but gradually their judgments converge and a group norm or frame of reference is established. This group standard continues to determine the judgment of the subject even if he returns to the situation alone. Likewise, a person who has set up an individual standard will be influenced in his judgment if he is placed in the group situation. Finally Sherif (1936) showed that a person's frame of reference could be experimentally modified by pairing him with a "stooge" who was instructed to make judgments of the extent of movement in a prearranged manner.

Although we are dealing here with a very ambiguous situation in which the subject has very little to go on, it has commonly been supposed that many social situations are likewise ambiguous and the person is guided in his perception largely by the judgments and perceptions of his social group. For example, Simmons tells the story in his book *Sun Chief* (1942) of how he and Don, a Hopi Indian whom he was studying intensively, went to visit a rock near the village. To Simmons the rock was just another rock in the desert, possibly interesting on geological grounds but no more. However, he described vividly how Don would not go near the rock because he interpreted it as the dwelling place of the much-feared and powerful Spider

Woman. In other words, Don's perception of a simple physical stimulus was markedly determined by the cultural interpretation of the meaning of that stimulus just as Simmons' perception of it was likewise colored by his cultural background. Bartlett (1932) found that his memory schemata were markedly subject to alteration due to cultural attitudes. In fact, one could argue that there is a social as well as a personal determinant in nearly all schemata.

5. **The Shaping Influence of Symbol Systems.** There is considerable evidence that symbolic representations, particularly verbal ones, have a very important effect on the shaping of impressions as they enter the mind. At the simplest level, there are experimental demonstrations of nonverbal stereotypes. Numerous Gestalt experiments have shown that complex objects tend to be reproduced in a more simple form or to get assimilated to a "better figure" or at least to a better known form, as in the following example from Bartlett.

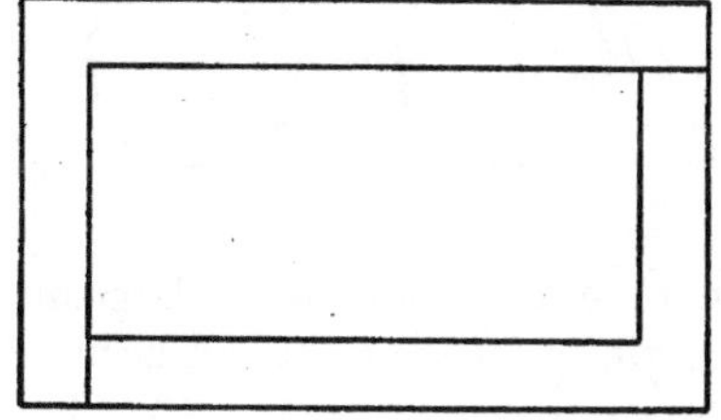

When this figure was reproduced sometime later it came out like this:

Apparently the standardized image of a picture frame influenced the initial impression markedly. In similar fashion Thouless (1931) found that ellipses were often judged by subjects to be circles turned on an axis out of the frontal parallel plane. The standard image of a circle as "squarely" in front of the face determined judgment.

Bruner, Postman, and Rodrigues (1950) in an ingenious experiment have shown that a color patch is perceived as more orange, as demonstrated by a color-wheel match, when it has the shape of an orange than when it does not. In other words a person has a certain stereotyped schema of an orange which includes a certain shape and a certain color. The adaptive utility of such standardized or stereotyped conceptions of picture frames, circles in the frontal parallel plane, or oranges is obvious. Without them perception and thought would be much more complicated since organization would have to start from scratch each time.

The phenomenon is even more impressive when a schema is shaped by a *verbal symbol.* A simple illustration from an experiment from Carmichael, Hogan, and Walter (1932) will demonstrate how this works. They exposed the following figure to two groups of subjects, naming it "eyeglasses" for one group and "a dumbbell" for the other:

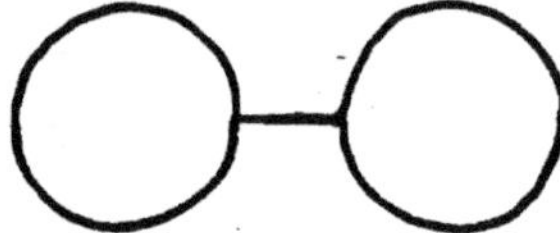

When it had to be reproduced along with a large number of other such line drawings, the group for which it had been labeled "dumbbell" tended to reproduce it as follows:

Dumbbell

And the group for which it had been labeled "eyeglasses" tended to reproduce it in this way:

Eye glasses

The role of *language* in organizing our incoming impressions can scarcely be overemphasized. Whorf (1940) has put it this way: "We dissect nature along lines laid down by our native languages. The categories and types that we isolate from the world of phenomena we do not find there because they stare every observer in the face; on the contrary, the world is presented in the kaleidoscopic flux of impressions which have to be organized by our minds—and this means largely by the linguistic systems in our minds. We cut nature up, organize it into concepts, and describe significances as we do, largely because we are parties to an agreement to organize it in this way—an agreement that holds throughout our speech community and is codified in the patterns of our language." (Newcomb and Hartley, 1947, p. 214.) Kluckhohn and Leighton have made a similar point in discussing the Navaho language. They state that it is "an excessively literal language, little given to abstractions and to the fluidity of meaning that is so characteristic of English." (1947, p. 199.) For example, for the Navaho it would be impossible to say simply "he went to town." Instead the Navaho would have to specify *how* he went to town, whether by wagon, airplane, boat, on horseback, at a trot, a run, or a gallop. A Navaho with inflections of the same verb form can say "I kick him," "I gave him a kick on repeated occasions," "I gave him repeated kicks on the same occasion," and "I gave him repeated kicks on repeated occasions." (1947, p. 207.) The English language on the other hand would have to make such fine distinctions with many words, as these translations indicate, or by the context in which the word occurred. The excessive abstractness or "fluidity of meaning" of the English language is perhaps best illustrated by Lorge's semantic count of common words (1949) which shows, for example, that the simple word "run" has some eight hundred different meanings. All of this demonstrates how a great deal of the "blooming, buzzing confusion" of entering impressions is organized into schemata for the person in terms of the particular language symbol system which he learns to use.

The use of language in forming a person's schemata may be illustrated at a somewhat more concrete level. The French psychologist Piaget has reported extensively on the questions a child asks in trying to get his picture of the world organized. In one case he recorded 1125 spontaneous questions asked by a boy named Del between the ages of six and seven. He wanted to know, for instance, "Is it (this pool) very deep?" or "Are the clouds much, much higher than our roof?" "How long is it till Christmas?" "Mr. J. has eaten a lot, hasn't he?" "Where is New York?" "Why do you teach me to count?" "Why are you not sure?" "Why do you do that to the poor little table?" (1926, p. 209.) The way in which these questions are framed and the kinds of answers Del got will go a long way toward shaping his conceptions of the world of nature. Many of the questions deal with attributive differences ("how big?" "how deep?"), others with classifications (who?" "what?"), or with explanations ("why?"). The developing ideas of causality as indicated by different types of "whys" are analyzed particularly by Piaget (1930), and yet we are told by Lee that among the Trobriand islanders with a different language system the concept of teleology or cause is almost totally absent (cf. Newcomb and Hartley, 1947, p. 219). What Piaget did not study and what would be of great importance in the present context is the kind of answers that Del got to his questions, for these would be of great importance in shaping his future empirical ideas.

Language begins to be more influential than ever when the person begins to read, because here common cultural explanations are given to the child in the most compact, symbolic form. Sometimes they are given in the form of a concrete set of symbols like the Boy Scout oath, and sometimes they structure the child's expectations more subtly and implicitly. Child, Potter, and Levine (1946) have provided us with an excellent example of how these cultural norms may be transmitted indirectly to people through their reading. They classified the contents of children's textbooks used in third and fourth grade according to the Murray need-press (1938) categories. As a typical example of their findings they report that stories dealing with affiliation, cognizance, and nurturance were very frequent, whereas stories dealing with infavoidance and rejection were quite infrequent. This and other findings suggested to the authors that "a major defect of the readers from this point of view is what might be called their unrealistic optimism." The stories seldom dealt with children trying to adjust to failure but on the other hand nearly always dealt with rewarded behavior. "Yet from the point of view of contribution to the solutions of problems of everyday life, failures ought to receive a larger proportion of attention, for it is they that pose problems." (1946, p. 45.)

Table 8.2 selects some more of their findings which are of general interest. Note that seeking information (cognizance) and friendship (affiliation) are rarely punished, while acting independently (autonomy) and trying to avoid blame (infavoidance) are pictured as often punished.

TABLE 8.2

Percentage of Reward, Punishment, and No Consequence for Each Category of Behavior (in all of the 3,409 Thema Which Were Analyzed)

Category of behavior	*Per cent of Thema in which behavior is rewarded*	*Per cent of Thema in which behavior is punished*	*Per cent of Thema in which behavior results in no consequence*
Cognizance	86	9	5
Succorance	84	10	6
Affiliation	82	8	9
Dominance	74	16	8
Acquisition	64	31	3
Autonomy	48	40	12
Aggression	35	52	11
Infavoidance	8	74	18

(After Child, Potter, and Levine, 1946, p. 43.)

It is only as we begin to understand such modal cultural propositions that we can fully understand the personality of any member of that culture. The table does not show that any given individual will have a need for cognizance or affiliation, but it does indicate that children in our culture will be made aware of the general respect for cognizance, affiliation, and the like. As any clinical psychologist knows, these implicit cultural assumptions enter very largely into the solution that a person works out to his problems. For example, a person may repress his aggression because of the strong cultural pressure against displaying aggression which is reflected in the figures in this table.

Summary of the Schematizing Process. This survey of psychological knowledge about the schematizing process has necessarily had to be brief and highly selective. Important topics such as the influence of motivation on schemata, the variables influencing schema strength (cf. Bruner, 1950), or the role of schemata in forming anticipatory sets in thinking (cf. Woodworth, 1938) have not been touched on at all. Nevertheless the survey will have served its function in this context if it has made the process itself less mysterious. Psychologists do not know nearly enough about how stimulation from without, e.g., cultural ideology, is incorporated and made over into individual ideology, but they do know something, and that something is enough to provide the basis for further experimentation in the same field.

Let us summarize what some of the main principles are which derive from this knowledge: (1) Experience tends to get organized into something which is simpler than the original. This "something" may be called a schema, a hypothesis, or conception. (2) These schemata have been found to be of great importance at all levels of experience—sensation, perception, memory, and thinking. (3) They are built up gradually and often without the subject's awareness. That is, the subject may not be able to verbalize the frame of reference in terms of which he is operating. They are constantly being modified by new experiences. (4) The way in which they are built up is not clearly understood, although Bartlett's work would suggest that they are determined in part by the serial order in which the experiences occur and in part by outstanding details. Helson's formula (1948) provides a method for predicting how certain "level" schemata (standards) are built up in the simpler psychological dimensions. (5) Schemata are built up out of personal experiences but an important part of these personal experiences are social schemata, or organizations of experience which have already been worked out by the culture in which the person lives and which are communicated to him by members of that culture. (6) One of the most important social determinants of schemata is language, as it shapes the way the person perceives the physical and social world. (7) There have been two main methods of measuring schemata: by inferring their existence from the judgments the subject makes, and by analyzing introspective phenomenological reports. (8) Whether or not these schemata are formed according to the principles of learning is not as yet definitely known. It has been customary to think of experiences piling in on top of each other and forming a general apperceptive mass in a way which did not require application of the laws of learning. Gestalt psychologists in particular have argued that organization of the sort we have been discussing is a capacity of the organism just as learning is. However, as Bateson (cf. Newcomb and Hartley, 1947, pp. 121-128) and Harlow (1949) have pointed out, it is possible to develop learning sets from solving a number of similar problems. Subjects appear to "learn how to learn." These experiments may eventually throw some light on how schemata are learned or formulated. For the moment we shall simply have to take them as they come.

Methods of Classifying Cultural Content. Returning now to the problem of cultural ideology, we will find it convenient to break down this complex subject into general topics for the purpose of discussion in connection with our individual case, Karl. There are several methods of analysis we might adopt. At one extreme there is the fairly specific classification of cultural patterns to be found in a library catalogue or a more systematic account like the *Outline of Cultural Materials* (1950) in the Human Relations Area Files (formerly the Cross-Cultural Survey). In the latter, which is probably the best system that exists for classifying materials of this sort, there are seventy-nine major headings covering such items as religious beliefs, family, travel and transportation, recreation, ideas and customs regulating different aspects of the life cycle, etc. Each of these in turn is broken down into many smaller units. Obviously, if we were to apply such a system to the culture into which Karl was born, we would be faced by a problem of bewildering complexity, even if the data existed, which, in this particular case, they do not. At the other extreme are attempts to simplify the major orientations or ideas of a culture under relatively few general headings. Table 8.3 is a reproduction with slight modifications of a valuable scheme of this sort constructed by Florence Kluckhohn (1950).

TABLE 8.3

Scheme for Representing Profiles of Cultural Orientation (After F. Kluckhohn, 1950.)

What are the innate predispositions of men?	Evil	Neither good nor bad (or mixed)	Good
What is man's relation to nature? (Includes man's own physical nature)	Man subjugated to nature	Man in nature	Man *vs.* nature, rational mastery over nature
What is the significant time dimension?	Past	Present	Future
What type of personality is to be most valued?	Being	Being in becoming	Doing
What is the dominant modality of the relationship of man to other men?	Lineal	Collateral	Individualistic

The use of this table can perhaps best be illustrated by the emphases the author feels would be provided in the culture of which Karl is a member. "The profile for what Dr. Jurgen Ruesch has called American 'core culture' can be drawn by an accenting of the following orientations: *individualistic* relational orientation; the *achieving* orientation, wherein judgment of a person's value is primarily on the basis of his accomplishments, his productivity; the *man-against-nature* or rational-mastery orientation; the *future-time* orientation; and the definition of human nature as *evil but perfectable*." She points out that of course there are substitute profiles of emphasis in a given culture, particularly in as complex a society as that of the contemporary United States, but contends that this provides a useful set of dimensions on which to erect such profiles so as to compare different cultures, or sub-cultures. Its applicability to the study of an individual case would arise from the attempt to discover the extent to which these orientations were in fact a part of Karl's cultural environment and the extent to which he accepted them as part of his ideology. Since she further argues that the position taken on these dimensions will determine to a large extent ideas held on much more specific matters, it is obvious that such a scheme has a great deal of potential value as far as simplifying the analysis of cultural ideology is concerned. Although we will make use of it therefore in analyzing Karl, we will find it necessary to introduce other aspects of cultural ideology, since it is a little too simple for our purposes.

A quite different attempt to simplify and classify the effects of the environment has been made by Murray (1938). He decided to classify what happens to a person (what he calls *press*) not in terms of its cultural content, but in terms of its effect or potential effect on the subject. As illustrative of the way his system works, we may take the following statement which he quotes as coming from the autobiography of one of his subjects: "I remember one windy day walking to school, that I was afraid of the wind as I started to cross [the street] and that I clung to a lamppost until someone came and took me by the hand."

In the analysis of an incident like this, Murray is primarily concerned with the influence of environmental events on the subject. He states, "By 'effect' here we *do not mean the response that is aroused in the subject* (a mode of classification that has been abandoned): we mean what is done to the subject before he responds (ex: belittlement by an insult) or what might be done to him if he did not respond (ex: a physical injury from a falling stone). . . ." (1938, p. 117.) "The *press* of an object is what it can do *to the subject or for the subject*—the power that it has to affect the well-being of the subject in one way or another." (1938, p. 121.) Thus in the above example the fact that someone comes and takes the subject by the hand Murray would classify as *press nurturance* or p Nurturance. Some typical examples of press and their definitions follow:

p Affiliation, a friendly, sociable companion

p Nurturance, a protective ally

p Dominance, restraint, an imprisoning or prohibiting object (1938, p. 121).

It is clear from these examples that Murray is attempting to classify the behavior of the *environment* (press) in exactly the same manner as he would classify the behavior of a *person* in connection with his system of need analysis. This approach has some advantages for certain purposes, but as compared with a more direct study of cultural patterns and ideology, it seems unnecessarily thin and overly concerned with one aspect of the pattern, namely the *directionality* of the interaction between the person and his environment. It will not prove of much value to us in studying the content of Karl's ideas and values, although it will prove of some use in helping to classify the kinds of behavior that he will expect from others.

This brief survey of some representative attempts to classify the impact of the sociocultural matrix on the individual suggests that in the present state of knowledge it may be most practicable to adopt an approach that is less extreme than any of those presented, but which will make use of the viewpoints to be found in each. A sort of middle ground is provided by the traditional, old-fashioned analysis of experience by culture historians into relatively few *Kulturgebiete* or cultural areas. Spranger (1928), a pupil of the culture historian, Dilthey, has provided us with a breakdown into six general areas which at least have the advantage of some previous usage in personality psychology because they were the basis for the construction of the well-known Allport-Vernon Study of Values Test. The way in which culture is divided up into six areas and associated activities itemized for each by Allport and Vernon is perhaps best illustrated in composite form as in Table 8.4.

Actually as this table suggests there is some lack of corresponden between the three columns. Sp ager's contribution was the sta nent that people who concent d in a given area of activity lemarcated by the cultural hist n were people who were predo nantly motivated by a partic value. Thus when Allport a 'ernon made up their test, the ad to assume that a person w ngaged in reading and other olarly pursuits in preference ther activities was apt to be a son who was interested in tru or its own sake. This is not n rily true, of course. Many of t ctivities listed in the right han olumn might be undertaken f ny one of the values listed by nger. A person who scored hi n the Religious scale in the might in actuality be a pers whose chief value was pow r, who sought power through re ious activities, and who prefer them for that reason on the te Nevertheless the test and Sp r's classification will provide racticable introduction to lem of defining a limited nu er of areas of experience which l cover approximately the wh of the sociocultural impact of nvironment on the person. A lthough we cannot assume th value Spranger mentions is n sarily implied by preference tivities in a given area, we c rgue that scores on the six sc the Allport-Vernon test will g s some idea of the areas y which a given person empl sizes or de-emphasizes for reasons. To this extent at lea he test provides a key to th 's orientations by demonstrati what areas of cultura f importance or weight to hi And what is importan ht" is one meaning of the wo alue, even though y the meaning which Spran ntended With this introd can now turn our attention he immediate pract summarizing the influence he culture on Karl under different headings.

Theoretical-Empirical Ideas can begin with what is perha he most important area e for our own culture, name he area of empirical know ience. As Parsons puts it (195 'Science as a part of cultur defined as a systematically ganized and verified body of r 'beliefs' about, or 'knowled of the empirical world. It is the 'cognitive orientation' men which is socially structured the sense of being held in co mon by considerable numbers of eople within the same soci and which, as part of the cult tradition, is socially 'inherit

TABLE 8.4

Content Analysis of the Allport-Vernon Study of Values Test

Culture area	*Value involved* (Spranger)	*Associated activities, attitudes, etc.* (Items selected from Allport-Vernon Test)
Theoretical	Truth for its own sake	God is unnecessary because of science Interest in a stranger's knowledge as shown in his books Spending Sunday by reading serious books
Economic	Utility	Teaching economics Reading Real Estate and Stock Market sections of Sunday *Times* Encouraging children to take vocational training
Aesthetic	Beauty, harmony	Great artists are justified in being selfish Bible should be regarded more from viewpoint of beautiful mythology Spending Sunday going to an orchestral concert
Social	Love, interpersonal relations	Self-analysis leads to insincerity Great general progress through freeing slaves and the "enhancement of value placed on individual life" Good government should aim mainly at aid for the poor, sick, and old
Political	Power	Wars won't be abolished because man is inherently aggressive It is just to have a small proportion of rich people since they got there mainly through "push and ability" Spend Sunday trying to win at golf, or racing
Religious	Unity of all experience	Man is not inherently aggressive The Bible is spiritual revelation Spend Sunday hearing a really good sermon

(Reproduced with permission from G. W. Allport and P. E. Vernon, *A Study of Values*. Copyright 1931 by Houghton Mifflin Co.)

Actually as this table suggests there is some lack of correspondence between the three columns. Spranger's contribution was the statement that people who concentrated in a given area of activity as demarcated by the cultural historian were people who were predominantly motivated by a particular value. Thus when Allport and Vernon made up their test, they had to assume that a person who engaged in reading and other scholarly pursuits in preference to other activities was apt to be a person who was interested in truth for its own sake. This is not necessarily true, of course. Many of the activities listed in the right-hand column might be undertaken for any one of the values listed by Spranger. A person who scored high on the Religious scale in the test might in actuality be a person whose chief value was power, but who sought power through religious activities, and who preferred them for that reason on the test. Nevertheless the test and Spranger's classification will provide a practicable introduction to our problem of defining a limited number of areas of experience which will cover approximately the whole of the sociocultural impact of the environment on the person. And although we cannot assume that the value Spranger mentions is necessarily implied by preference for activities in a given area, we can argue that scores on the six scales of the Allport-Vernon test will give us some idea of the areas of activity which a given person emphasizes or de-emphasizes, for whatever reasons. To this extent at least, the test provides a key to the person's orientations by demonstrating what areas of cultural ideology are of importance or weight to him. And what is important or "has weight" is one meaning of the word *value,* even though it is not exactly the meaning which Spranger intended. With this introduction we can now turn our attention to the immediate practical problem of summarizing the influence of the culture on Karl under these six different headings.

Theoretical-Empirical Ideas. We can begin with what is perhaps the most important area of knowledge for our own culture, namely, the area of empirical knowledge or science. As Parsons puts it (1950), "Science as a part of culture may be defined as a systematically organized and verified body of 'ideas' or 'beliefs' about, or 'knowledge' of the empirical world. It is part of the 'cognitive orientation' of men which is socially structured in the sense of being held in common by considerable numbers of people within the same society, and which, as part of the cultural tradition, is socially 'inherited' from previous generations or diffused from other societies, additions continually being made to this received base." The distinguishing characteristic of this kind of knowledge is its "empirical verifiability." That is, we may include under this heading anything from a simple sensation of blue all the way to Einstein's Theory of Relativity because in each case operations exist for checking the sensation or the idea that the person has. These "checking" or "pointing" operations distinguish this kind of knowledge from that classified under other headings (Aesthetic, Religious, etc.). Thus we may distinguish for practical purposes the scientific knowledge that the psychologist obtains about personality from the poetic or appreciative knowledge that the novelist or dramatist has of personality (cf. Chapter 3), or the scientific knowledge that the physicist has of the physical principles which produce the beautiful colors of a sunset and his appreciative knowledge of that same sunset. Obviously any particular set of sensations can be viewed *in relation to* a number of different frames of reference. The point we are making here is that some cultural knowledge is regularly viewed from the standpoint of its empirical verifiability. Thus a chemist may get an aesthetic thrill out of his equations, or be impressed by the economic or technological utility of them, but chemistry as a branch of *knowledge* is normally considered to fall within the empirical-theoretical area of culture. We cannot hope to summarize the full extent of Karl's empirical knowledge from Abacuses to Zebras, although Roberts (1950) has attempted to do something like this with individuals in preliterate societies where symbolic control of knowledge through reading is less highly developed than in our own culture. But we can assert from our knowledge of Karl's education and achievement test scores that he has sampled rather widely from the existing areas of empirical knowledge and that in the process he has formulated certain basic ideas or orientations which serve to organize or give meaning to his various items of information. These ideas may perhaps best be characterized in terms of "size," "growth," and "relative importance" orientations as in Table 8.5.

In this table are listed on the left-hand side the basic orientations which are supposed to characterize this area of American culture according to sociologists (Cf. Kluckhohn and Kluckhohn, 1947; Sirjamaki, 1947; Naegele, 1949; etc.) On the right-hand side are listed Karl's ideas which are derived in part from cultural orientations and in part from his own idiosyncratic experiences. Each of these ideas is labeled according to the portion of his records from which it was inferred. Sometimes he is fully conscious that he has such an idea: there

TABLE 8.5

Some Typical American Cultural Orientations Toward Empirical Phenomena and Their Associated Representations in Karl's Schemata

American Cultural Orientations (Cf. Kluckhohn and Kluckhohn, 1947.)	*Karl's schemata with source indicated*
A. Size	
1. The more information one has the better.	(1) A well-rounded education is valuable since it opens up all areas of knowledge to the person. (A) (B)
2. Larger things are more important, valuable, etc. (Cf. Bruner and Goodman, 1947.)	(2) Bigness (including my size), is valuable.
B. Growth (progress)	
3. Time discriminations are important especially with future reference.	(3) The future is very important. (C)
4. Knowledge is growing all the time.	(4) The growth of knowledge presents problems to men. (A)
5. Nature can be conquered, manipulated for man's benefit.	(5) Nature can be conquered if we understand human nature. (A)
6. Human nature can be understood and conquered too, though the task is less far advanced.	(6) Knowledge is not so important in itself but as a means to the higher value of happiness. (A) (E)
C. Relative importance of knowledge to other values.	(7) Empirical explanations are to be preferred to non-empirical, religious ones wherever possible. (D)

Sources

(A) Essay on "What I would ideally like to get out of a course in Psychology." (Cf. Chapter 5.)
(B) Autobiography.
(C) Number of future tenses in essay; high TAT n Achievement Score.
(D) Religion questionnaire.
(E) Allport-Vernon Study of Values Test.

is an actual statement by him of the idea in question. In other cases the idea is an inference by the observer. A case in point is his *future orientation*. F. Kluckhohn (1950) has argued that Americans, particularly of lower-middle-class background like Karl, are oriented toward the future (cf. also Israeli, 1932), but that does not mean, of course, that Karl necessarily is. Furthermore, he does not say in so many words that he is "chiefly concerned about the future," but we can infer that he is from the high frequency of future tenses in his essay, as compared with others writing under similar conditions (rank 4th out of 14), and also from the high frequency of "forward-looking" achievement characteristics in a Thematic Apperception Test, again as compared with others taking the same test (cf. Chapter 13). In this case an idea, orientation, or schema is *inferred* from the data. Inference may even be necessary when there is a direct conscious expression of an idea, since it may not be the reflection of a truly representative idea for the person but of a desire to please, conform, or defend himself.

At the present time there are no methods available for making a systematic ideological census of this sort. We can therefore only proceed using the hints given us either by sociological analyses of American culture or by Karl's comments in his autobiography and elsewhere, in the hope that methodological improvements will someday be made on both sides. There are indications of such improvements already. In the first place, many more sociologists and anthropologists are paying attention to the problem of defining dominant cultural ideas or values. In the second, clinical psychologists have for years found it indispensable to discover a patient's major ideas, at least roughly, and have collected a good deal of data which can be used as a basis for more systematic analyses. At the crudest level this involves such simple orientation questions as, "How long have you been here in the hospital," "Where are you?" "What time is it?" or "In which direction is your home?" At a more complex level it involves information questions (as in the Wechsler-Bellevue test) and concept formation tests like the Vigotzky (cf. Hanfmann and Kasanin, 1937) in which an attempt is made to find out how well a person can categorize his experience perceptually and to some extent ideationally. There is no reason why the Vigotzky test approach could not be extended to discover how a normal person classifies more complex experiences than blocks of different shapes, colors, and sizes. In the third place, experimental psychology has made advances in studying individual differences in perceptual modes which may in time aid in defining a person's major ideological orientations. For instance, Witkin (1949) has developed a way of telling whether a person's orientation in space is made primarily in terms of visual or proprioceptive cues. Some day in a similar manner experimentalists may be able to show us how to determine whether the idea "Knowledge is growing" is a major orientation in a given person's life. What is needed is a method for determining central tendencies among ideas comparable to the ones we have for determining central tendencies in judgmental scales.

In the meantime we shall have to be content with the kind of common-sense approach represented by Table 8.5. Some further comment on each of the ideas in the table is in order, particularly to show the evidence on which each is based. In this and subsequent discussions we will refer to a given idea by number so as to be able to integrate them all into an ideological system for Karl at the end of the chapter. (1) The value of knowledge and education in America is well attested by many facts. Perhaps it is sufficient to quote only one statistic from F. Kluckhohn on this point: "The check of a sample of older brothers of the high school age boys (the sample included the brothers of all boys in one school grade in each of three towns) shows that 62 percent have achieved a higher educational level than their fathers and only 7 percent have had less education." (1950.) Karl clearly participates in the trend toward upward mobility through education. Neither of his parents went to high school but he and both his brothers have gone beyond high school to receive professional training. In his essay on his interest in psychology he states "We need a well-rounded store of knowledge" and "It seemed necessary to me to round out my more or less heterogeneous study program . . ." To him a "well-rounded education" is clearly a value.

(2) Size and bigness are part of the American "technological growth" complex according to sociologists. Cities are getting larger, buildings are getting taller, more people are being educated, fewer people are dying of disease, the average soldier in World War II was heavier and taller than in World War I. All this is implicit in the thinking of most Americans whether they like it or not. We may assume that Karl shares this orientation, although there is little direct evidence for it except in connection with a corollary notion about the value of his own size. He is a big person, as our somatotype analysis has shown, and his "bigness" has inevitably made an important difference in his adjustment so far. He can beat up people

who pick a fight with him, play a high prestige role in the "youth culture" by being prominent on the football team, etc. These are all experiences which should contribute importantly to a "size" schema, even though it is doubtless an implicit one which could be confirmed only by more direct methods.

(3) Future orientation in America goes with the "size and growth" complex (F. Kluckhohn, 1950). It derives in part historically from the expectation of immigrants that their children would surpass them and leave behind their foreign ways (cf. Gorer, 1948). Concern about future time has trickled down from this general orientation until it permeates every part of modern urban living. Murray describes it thus: "Personalities construct schedules which permit the execution of as many conations as possible, one after another. . . . Time will be set aside for the carrying forward of one or more serial programs. . . . Under the conditions which generally prevail today, especially in highly integrated, urban communities, a man lives by a clock-determined schedule. The stimulus for eating is not emptiness in the pit of his stomach but the factory whistle or the hands of his watch indicating that the pre-arranged moment has arrived." (Kluckhohn and Murray, 1948, pp. 18-19.) The importance of this time orientation is illustrated by the contrasting example of a student who failed as a subject in an experiment on judging short time intervals. He was unable to make time discriminations or reproduce time intervals accurately that were reproduced with little error by the typical American college student. It later turned out that he had been brought up on a small island in the Mediterranean where the style of life required very little in the way of time judgments. There were no trains to catch, no stop watches for high-school athletic events, no places to speed in an automobile, etc. Consequently he had simply not learned as yet to think in terms of time or to make as accurate time discriminations as the average American does.

Again Karl appears to be typical. As a third-generation lower-middle-class American he should have been most exposed to the stress on future success, on scheduling life's activities in terms of tomorrow. What evidence there is strongly suggests he has such a future orientation, as the number of future tenses in his essay and his high TAT n Achievement score both attest.

(4) and (5) The faith in man's ability to conquer nature through the advancement of knowledge is supported by technological advance on every side. More and more people are coming to share Karl's view, as we have seen in Chapter I, that only by understanding *human*

nature through science will we be able to reap the benefits of our conquest over nature. In his words:

> Along with this trend of thought, I might add that Psychology would seem to supply many of the missing links in the problems of philosophy and the other sciences. Especially in this day and age in which rapid technological advances force us to decision, must we muster all our intellectual resources to face the ever increasing problems of life and its functions.

(6) and (7) It would be difficult to conclude how important some of these orientations are in American life relative to some other orientations to be discussed below. But for the individual the problem is not so difficult. Karl's comments and three of his tests tell us where he stands on this issue:

> We need a well-rounded store of knowledge, especially about ourselves and human behavior in order to live a richer, fuller and happier life.

In short, truth and knowledge are for him instrumental values. He goes on to say that psychology may be the key to religion which "we are all interested in . . . more or less." Although he does not accept any theological opinions (such as belief in God as a "Heavenly Father") which appear to go against empirical facts (see p. 276), he does think of those empirical facts merely as *means* to the more important values of happiness and adjustment to the universe (Religion). This view is fully confirmed by his score on the Theoretical Scale of the Allport-Vernon Values Test which places him in the 20th percentile for college students and which ranks this value for him in a tie for fourth and fifth place out of six value scales. His Theoretical interest is surpassed both by his interest in Religion and in Social affairs on this test in direct confirmation of the above quotations from his writings. Finally his scores on the Strong Vocational Interest Test for various occupations confirm the relatively low position of "knowledge for its own sake" in Karl's ideological hierarchy. Out of the thirty-three occupations on which standard scores were available for Karl there were three (Mathematician, Engineer, Chemist) which could be classified as occupations in which theoretical-empirical ideas could be considered as of being of central importance to the men engaged in them. On these three Karl's average standard score was only 22.7 (a C+ rating) which corresponds to around the 21st percentile rank in all his occupations. (See notes at the end of the chapter for details.)

These test scores illustrate several methodological points. (1) A single fact can and probably should be approached in several different ways. Here an inference about the relative importance to Karl of knowledge for its own sake is confirmed in three ways (Essay, Allport-Vernon Test, Strong Interest Test). (2) Psychological tests are most useful in determining the *relative importance* of an idea once it is defined. Unfortunately what is needed in this area is a technique for determining *what ideas* are important to a person. But once this problem is solved, the related question of *how important* the idea is can be determined by existing measurement techniques. Note, however, that the tests do not show *why* knowledge is less important to Karl, though this is readily apparent in his essay in which knowledge appears as instrumental to other ends. (3) Relative importance can be measured within an individual as well as among individuals. That is, we have compared Karl's standing on various groups of occupations in comparison with his standing on all occupations and have been able to find meaning in the intra-individual comparison just as we also have in comparing his standing with others.

Economic Ideas. Under this heading we include ideological emphases in the culture concerning working and earning a living. Parsons (1950) has made a strong case for the fact that America perhaps even more than most European countries has been dominated by what might be called "utilitarian economic theory." This theory holds that "the individual is and should be basically on his own."

> He "knows what he wants" and sets out to get it. In the process he encounters others and he and they tend to come to terms with each other to mutual advantage. Each perceives that indirect ways of getting what they want through producing something that they can "sell" to others are more productive than trying to do everything for themselves. Money as a medium of exchange facilitates this process. Since most of what is wanted can be bought for money the immediate goal of productive effort tends to focus on money income. The pursuit by each of his self interest in a system of market exchange relationships, through the self-regulating action of competition, tends to maximize production and conduce to the welfare of all. (Parsons, 1950, p. 31.)

This ideological framework has seemed peculiarly fitted to the expanding economy and the opening frontier which has characterized the United States in the past one hundred years. Let us look for elements of this economic ideology in Karl's autobiography and other records.

First of all we note that both his father and his mother worked during the depression when their means of livelihood, like that of so many other American families, seemed to be severely threatened. He states that his mother is "industrious" and that his father is "very thorough in all that he does." The boys in the family were taught the values of thrift and hard work early in life.

> I always resented the fact when small that I never had the spending money that other boys and girls had, but I realized that even in so doing I learned the value of the dollar.
>
> I was born and raised in the country. Our home was comfortable but not elaborate. . . . We always had plenty to eat and good, wholesome fare. . . .. I always ate my food and still do. We had to eat what was on our plates and were taught never to waste food.

From the cultural economic ideology and from these excerpts we may summarize two of Karl's economic views as follows:

(8) The individual is on his own and must make a living by his own efforts.

(9) The primary goal of work is money.

As support for this last statement, we note further that he says in connection with his father that "money matters seem to give him a great deal of concern." There is also evidence that Karl came in frequent contact with another of the economic ideas prevalent in his culture, namely the prevalence of competition with others in the pursuit of one's own economic welfare. He states about his father that "he is rather suspicious of the motives of others" and in outlining his own philosophy, "I would like to see the world remodeled on the Christian ethical standard, the Sermon on the Mount, with the law of love pervading the hearts of men. I believe this is the answer to our social, economic, political and all problems of society. . . . My general estimate of the social world is that it consists of a lot of selfish, grasping individuals, perhaps so because of the competitive spirit and law of survival which seem to pervade our society." This makes clear that he accepts the view that economic life involves a competitive struggle for survival, but rejects the utilitarian notion that this will be conducive to the welfare of all. These ideas may be expressed as follows:

(10) Competition is an inherent part of economic life.

(11) Competition promotes selfishness and is not conducive to the welfare of all.

Throughout all this we note the typical middle-class emphases on effort and hard work, thrift, property and money (Kluckhohn and Kluckhohn, 1947), all of which carry implications as to the discipline and self-control necessary to obtain them. How important are these economic orientations to Karl? Once again we can turn to the Allport-Vernon and Strong Vocational Interest Tests for an answer. On the former, economic ideas receive relatively more emphasis than the theoretical-empirical ones, but his raw score of 27 is still only in the 40th percentile among college students and ranks only third out of his six value scores. As far as the Strong test is concerned, the many "practical" or utilitarian occupations (e.g., the office occupations and the skilled trades such as printer, carpenter, farmer, etc.) all tend to show very low interest ratings, the mean standard score being 25.7, which is in the 30th percentile of all his occupational scores, again somewhat higher than for the "theoretical" occupations but still quite low. It is of some interest to note that his overt vocational ambition on entering college was to become a chemical engineer. In this it seems likely that his father's occupation (skilled mechanic) and interests played some part, as well as the general American expectation of upward mobility, since the occupation is of the same general sort as his father's but at a higher level, requiring more education. That this ambition represents the influence of environmental press more than inner conviction is definitely indicated by the results of the Strong Vocational Test, which show that his actual interests in fields allied to this one are quite low as compared to his interests in other occupations, particularly those dealing with people in a service relationship, as we shall see later.

Aesthetic Ideas. In this area are included all the sentient or sensuous aspects of life which may reach their highest and most institutionalized forms in art, music, and poetry. There is almost no evidence in Karl's autobiography of interest on his parents' part in this area of experience, or of any direct or important experience on his part with such activities. It is therefore not surprising to discover that he scores in the 10th percentile on the Aesthetic value scale for the Allport-Vernon test and has a mean standard score on the four occupations relating to this area (artist, musician, architect, author-journalist) of only 20.3, which is in the 14th percentile of all his occupations. From this we derive:

(12) Formal artistic experience is of relatively little importance in life.

In this respect Karl is again rather typical of his culture, which emphasizes the *doing* or *achieving* rather than the *being* or *becoming* virtues (cf. F. Kluckhohn, 1950). Work leaves little time for sensuous enjoyment. Nevertheless, at the noninstitutionalized level, there is a good deal of concern and uneasiness about personal happiness. The two themes that seem to run through this material are these:

(13) Achievement does not bring happiness.
(14) Life is rather painful, full of suffering and worry.

Thus in describing his parents he states that his father is "excitable and constantly worried by everyone's troubles. . . . My mother suffers from deafness, arthritis, and sinusitis while my father had a back injury which has induced arthritis. My father's chief diversion is gardening. He dislikes his present job to the point where he would like to quit and raise chickens for a farm. At any rate he seems to be quite dissatisfied with life." In another section he states that "A lot of worrying is done for nothing." In his own case, organized attempts at recreation or enjoyment seem to include chiefly caring for a series of pets, playing sports, and reading a good deal. Underlying all is the fundamental implicit feeling that something is lacking in life, that one ought to enjoy life more. Along with this feeling of lack there are few positive notions as to how it can be fulfilled, other than through the establishment of the "law of love in the hearts of men," which serves as a final goal rather than as a next step.

Political Ideas. What are the main cultural orientations toward problems of power, authority, government, and war? Sociologists and anthropologists in general seem agreed that to contemporary Americans authority as such is considered bad. In Parsons' words (1950): "Everything went so well, it was maintained, because men had become sensible enough to liberate themselves from interfering restraints, of which there were two main types: Political authority with its 'monopolistic' controls, and irrational 'custom.'" Gorer notes in the same connection that most of the immigrants who came to America "escaped at the same time from discriminatory laws, rigidly hierarchical social structures, compulsory military service and authoritarian limitations of the opportunities open to the enterprising and of the goals to which they could aspire. But the rejection of home and country could not be piecemeal; the supports had to be abandoned with the restraints; individually the immigrants had to try and transform themselves into Americans." (1948, p. 25.) In many instances the father became symbolic of the old rejected ways and hence it was impossible for him to maintain, according to Gorer, a position of much authority in a family in which the children knew more about the desired American ways than he did. Thus "the land of the free" meant freedom from authoritarian political and social systems in which the father is the dominant symbolic figure. Ideally of course this should lead to a society of equals in which no man is better than any other and in which there are no classes. There is evidence of this ideological dislike of authority and class distinctions in several different places in Karl's record. For instance, we have seen that his father "is rather suspicious of the motives of others and berates the country, world, and officials of all sorts." In speaking of the world remodeled on the Christian ethical standard Karl states further, "I should like to take my place in such a world as a citizen of it, not necessarily as a leader, because in such a society, leaders can be dispensed with." Finally we find that Karl makes every effort to put his belief in the "brotherhood of man" into practice since in filling out the Bogardus Social Distance Scale (cf. Newcomb and Hartley, 1947) he showed no racial or religious discrimination, stating that he would be willing to admit members of other races and faiths into the closest personal relationships. Karl seems to have interiorized the following two elements of the American creed:

(15) All men are equal.
(16) Power and authority are essentially suspect and undesirable.

Yet he is not without ambivalence on this point, nor, in fact, is his culture. For one thing it is perfectly obvious that not all men are equal in the economic privileges they have or in the power and authority they enjoy. As Parsons (1950) puts it, "the growth of organization invalidates even for the man on the street the simple paradigm of individuals producing things and trading with each other to mutual advantage. Above all the elements of authority and discipline, as well as differentation of wealth and privilege, become conspicuous. On this count it is only a minority who enjoy the full advantages of the system." To put it in another way, if Karl is to follow out his own economic ideal of getting ahead he must "climb the ladder of privilege" which already exists (although it shouldn't) and may sooner or later find himself in a position of leadership or authority it is undesirable for anyone to hold. This ambivalence is nicely expressed in the contrasting scores he gets on the Allport-Vernon Values Test, which place him in the 20th percentile (rank 4.5 out of 6 values) on interest in political affairs (or in power) and on the Strong Interest Test, on which he rates rather high in vocations involving managerial responsibility. His mean standard score on such occupations as Policeman, City School Superintendent, Production Manager, and President of a Manufacturing Concern is 38.5, which places this group of "power-oriented" vocations in the 77th percentile of all his occupations. How can we reconcile an apparently explicit distaste for authority relationships with an implicit interest in the kind of occupations which involve such relationships? His father's attitude is revealing in this connection. On the one hand his father is suspicious of the interference of others and dislikes the government, yet, on the other hand, in his own home he is apparently something of an autocrat requiring his children to obey him almost in the European pattern of the patriarchal father. Thus the father dislikes authority in others, but sanctions its use by his own behavior. The same conflict appears in Karl. At the more conscious level he is opposed to authority, but implicitly he apparently identifies to some extent with his father and believes discipline is a good thing. "We grew up to acquire a name in town as being 'well-raised, well-mannered boys.' The punishments received had no detrimental effect, either mentally or otherwise. They seemed to do us good." We can therefore say that the following proposition is accepted implicitly by Karl:

(17) Authority is also good and desirable.

The conflict between propositions 16 and 17 is fairly obvious to Karl and he has made several attempts to rationalize it. Thus in one place he makes a distinction between the real and the ideal, apparently holding that in order to meet the selfish competitiveness of others, some kind of counteractive striving for prestige and power is essential, although it could be done away with in a society run according to the law of love. A more subtle adjustment between these two values is suggested by the following remarks referring to his high-school experiences. "I was very confident working in groups when I knew the people, received cooperation and was usually chairman or a 'wheel.'" Here the view seems to be that leadership is permissible if it is the "will of the people." In American life generally, it is considered undesirable for any person to want too much to hold an important position. Instead he is supposed to be "drafted." Karl apparently holds somewhat similar views, although in his case it is quite clear that this is not a ruse designed to deceive anyone. Instead, he seems genuinely to mean it when he says that leadership for him is possible only when he is secure in the approval and cooperation of others. We might summarize this view as:

(18) Power should only be exercised if subordinates wish it and ask for it.

It is therefore not surprising to discover that in a rating of the relative seriousness of various vices (see notes at the end of the chapter), Karl places such items as disrespect and rebelliousness as least important on the scale. Rebellion against authority is all right, particularly if it is arbitrary authority rather than the "will of the people."

Social Ideas. Broadly speaking, this topic includes the structure and patterning of all sorts of social relations in a given culture and the ideas which the culture holds with regard to these relations. As we have already seen, the culture into which Karl was born was primarily an individualistic one which plays down or minimizes solidary relations of all sorts. The philosophy of economic utilitarianism implies that the "individual acted on his own, not in his capacity as a member of a solidary group." (Parsons, 1950.) This philosophy was aided in America by the necessity of breaking with older authoritarian patterns and by the conditions which existed in a frontier community. As a result of all these processes as well as the Protestant ethic to be discussed below, national, class, religious, and family solidarities all tended to be played down. In Parsons' words, "The psychological and sociological complexities of the spheres of the family, sex roles and the relations of the sexes were also completely bypassed. . . . There has in fact been an opening for another type of individualistic emphasis here, which has played a great part in the mythology of romantic love, in feminism, in the ideological appeal of 'vulgar' Freudianism." In terms of the kinds of analysis made by Florence Kluckhohn as to types of family relationship as presented in Table 8.3, the American system is definitely individualistic in emphasis, as opposed to collateral or lineal. The typical family is the isolated conjugal unit, and the typical individual passes from one (the family of orientation) to another (the family of procreation) in the course of his lifetime. His obligations are limited first to his parents and then to his wife and to some extent to his children, although the latter often cease as soon as the children are of age.

All of these elements appear to be present in Karl's family relations. He says, for instance, "Our family circle taken as a whole is very loose. All grandparents are dead and I haven't seen some of my cousins and uncles for years although they live only three miles away." And further, "My attachment to the family was always a close one, although now I am indifferent." A psychiatrist who later interviewed Karl to round out our picture of him comments: "The general attitude toward the family is cold, lacking in deep attachment levels." In relation to his brothers he states, "I get along all right with my brothers. We fought when we were kids. The war tightened the bonds. We lend each other money." In all of this there is evidence of the individualistic emphasis at least at the family level. Family obligations are loose, warm affectional ties are missing.

Yet as a part of the whole complex, or because of it, Karl greatly idealizes romantic love as the solution to all problems. As he puts it in his autobiography,

> I have dreamed intensely of living a life with an ideal mate. Nothing is so satisfying as to cast oneself into a dream world wherein you and the woman you love are together high on a windy hill, looking out on the world. Just to hold the woman of your choice in your arms and lavish your love upon her seems to me the source of greatest delight. . . . I believe one hundred percent in marriage as a noble institution. I believe that a couple can only make the most of their life, living in harmony and satisfaction of a happy union.

As Parsons suggests, perhaps the reason for the importance of the romantic-love complex in our society is the de-emphasizing of other sources of solidarity—the family, the church, the nation, etc. Karl at any rate fits into such a pattern very clearly. To him romantic love is all important. In one of his TAT stories which seems to be autobiographical in view of the above quotation, he puts it this way;

> He is at a loss at times to describe his feelings. Nobody seems to understand. The one thing that will snap him out of this, where he will seek to free himself from a shackled existence . . . where he will assert himself and conquer his doubts and fears, the thing that will do the most toward putting him on the right road will be for him to marry the girl he loves. Otherwise this chap's life is in vain. He will not be accomplishing anything worth while. He will lead a blighted existence, but were he as I have said before, to love the right girl and marry her, the future would be a bright one indeed.

As we shall see in discussing religion this idea of the importance of love has fused with the Christian conception of the "law of love" to form a central ideological complex in Karl's life. We may summarize it as follows:

(19) I am without strong solidary, affiliative ties.

(20) Love, especially through marriage to a woman I love, is the key to existence.

Confirmation of this trend is to be found in a number of places in Karl's records. In the Allport-Vernon test his score on the Social Value scale is in the 96th percentile, only slightly below the score on the Religious Value scale. In rating his vices he places *intolerance* among the more serious sins, as would be expected from his own lack of intolerance as shown by the Social Distance scale. Furthermore, by all odds the most serious vice to him is *lack of courage*. It is probable that courage as a virtue has a peculiar place in the American individualistic ideological emphasis, since if the individual is "on his own," he must be able to stand by himself on his own feet and ward off all dangers. It is probably no accident that the poem "Invictus" ("I am the master of my fate, I am the captain of my soul") has been so popular in America, even though in the extent to which it emphasizes *self*-reliance it is definitely irreligious in the Christian sense. It would seem almost necessary for a society which de-emphasizes solidarities to stress such virtues as courage and self-reliance. It is probably for this reason, at least in part, that for Karl,

(21) Lack of courage is the most serious vice.

The results of the Strong Test are in line with all of this. Karl scores highest on those occupations which involve service to other people. On such scales as Y.M.C.A. Secretary, Social Science High School Teacher, Personnel Manager, Minister, etc. his mean standard score is 44.5, which is well above his average (91st percentile). Another check shows that of thirteen occupations which can be classified as involving primarily relations with people, Karl scores high (B, B+ or A) on eleven out of the thirteen, whereas of the nineteen occupations dealing with things, he scores high on only two. The difference is significant well beyond the .01 level, even when corrections are made for the lack of independence of the various scores on the different occupations. In all this he appears to be typical of the rising generation of Americans who have attempted to reconcile two conflicting ideas, "love thy neighbor" and "maximize your money returns" (Parsons, 1950), by turning to those business occupations which are service-oriented (e.g., Physician, Personnel

Manager, etc.). In a somewhat oversimplified fashion we may state this as:

(22) One's occupation should involve service to people.

Religious Ideas. Religion deals essentially with what Parsons calls the "non-empirical reality systems." Every culture takes some position on such important, but nonempirically-answerable questions as: What is the nature of man? What is the nature of God or the supernatural? What is the relationship between man and God? The Protestant ethic which is part of Karl's background has been repeatedly analyzed by a number of different writers, notably by Max Weber, the great German sociologist. It would be impossible to do justice to this complex subject in a short space, but we may select three ideological emphases of major importance for brief discussion: (a) God is the all-powerful source of creation and requires respect and obedience. Implicit in this idea are many of the elements of the Old Testament conception of God as a more or less authoritarian patriarchal father. (b) Man is responsible for his own salvation. This dominant idea, though it went through as many transformations as there were Protestant sects, formed the basis for the Protestant revolt at the time of the Reformation. It has two somewhat opposed corollaries. The first is the emphasis on individual responsibility for salvation ("the priesthood of all believers") as opposed to the many supports provided by the "Mother church." The other is the notion that salvation is tied up with inner perfection. Christ as Mediator between God and man became the example of the perfect Man after whom individuals should model themselves as much as possible. Yet in Christ's life and in His teachings there is strong emphasis on the "being and becoming" virtues as opposed to the achieving ones. The Sermon on the Mount stresses such virtues as humility, service, self-sacrifice, meekness, peaceableness, and the "law of love pervading the hearts of men." (c) Man is responsible for the coming of the Kingdom of God. Especially in Saint Paul's time there was a strong emphasis on active effort to bring about the Kingdom of God which he felt was required in his lifetime. This idea has been stressed often in Protestantism and has contributed to the notion that man must conquer nature and especially human nature if he is to bring about the Kingdom of God. There is something of a conflict here between evaluating man for what he *is* in terms of the Christ ideal and in terms of what he *does* to bring about the Kingdom of God on earth.

It is fairly clear that all these ideological elements were present in

Karl's environment and received their peculiar emphasis in his own ideas. He states, "Neither parent goes to church. My mother reads the Bible and argues it, but my dad says very little though he claims Christianity as his faith. Nevertheless, both parents are kind, generous, and have done quite a bit of community work in the past." His mother's reliance on the Bible rather than on the authority of the church is typical of Protestant individualism in its earlier form. From this we can infer the following idea:

(23) The individual must seek salvation (happiness) on his own.

Karl himself was given a rather extensive religion questionnaire which is reproduced in full at the end of the chapter, to show how he answered each item. Table 8.6 summarizes the extent of his agreement with various statements on this questionnaire.

TABLE 8.6

Summary of Karl's Answers to a Religion Questionnaire

Yes	*Agree Sometimes*	*No*
Fellowship with God in prayer	God can forgive sins	God a Heavenly Father
God outside himself	God can perform medical miracles	God as all-powerful
Men are God's "little children"	God can give power to cope with difficulties	God desires human love
Preoccupation with death	God should be adored	Religion requires abstinence
Self-sacrifice is good	We should atone for our sins to God	Personal conversion
God gives benefits	Man is sinful in disobeying God	Personal philosophy primarily religious
Confession to God feels good	Majesty of Presence of God	Bible is literal truth
	Love of the flesh is bad	God the main thing in life
		Man ought not to need the world
		God saves by grace

From the "yes" column it is relatively easy to draw the conclusion that he conceives of God as a source of comfort, security, benefits, and peace of mind. In a sense his conception fulfills the role of a "security system" in Kardiner's sense; Kardiner argues that all projective systems, including religion, serve the function of protecting the person against fear and insecurity (checked by Karl as sources of his religion). On the other hand he does not conceive of God as a Person (Heavenly Father) but as a vast impersonal spiritual principle (not *desiring* love, etc.). This is in line with the propositions about reality he has acquired in his study of science and shows that the need for security is not the only determinant of his religious conceptions.

The second column suggests a doubting acceptance of God's power. It is as if he were saying: "God may be powerful (able to perform miracles, forgive sins, etc.) and an object of awe and adoration." This is consistent with his ambivalent attitude toward authority mentioned earlier. On the other hand, the final column argues that to him God is not the only or central issue in life around which everything else is organized. He rejects the more extreme religious stands (abstinence, fundamentalism, etc.). We might summarize his position as follows:

(24) God *may* be powerful and require respect and obedience.
(25) God is the principle of love working to help men who are dependent on him.

It is relatively clear from this that it is the loving aspect of God which appeals to Karl. At least in the realm of religion there is very little emphasis for him on the striving or achieving dimension. In fact, he wants to bring about a world as we have seen in which competitive striving and achieving will be replaced by the principles of the Sermon on the Mount. Although he is definitely ambivalent about it we can perhaps express his attitude this way:

(26) Man ought to be evaluated for what he *becomes* rather than for what he *does,* but the world legislates otherwise.

The relative importance of religious ideas to Karl is best indicated by the fact that on the Allport-Vernon scale of values he ranks highest of all on the religious scale and, comparatively, in the 98th percentile of all male college students taking the test. The score for Minister on the Strong test is also high but not this high.

The Summing Up: Integration of Karl's Ideology. We have listed, in all, twenty-six ideas which seem to be central in Karl's conception of the world. Can we integrate them in any way? Do they hang together into a consistent pattern? Where are the sources of conflict and tension? Which ideas are of central importance and which are secondary? Unfortunately there is no simple methodological scheme for determining how these ideas order themselves. Figure 8.1 represents one such integration which shows that the ideas are not unrelated to one another and in fact do form a coherent, if conflicting, pattern. The reader should try other integrations of his own. There is some rephrasing of Karl's ideas in the table for purposes of economy, but the numbers in parentheses refer back to the full statements scattered throughout the chapter. In this diagram some of the sources of the ideological structure of the American man are placed on the outside. In the center are the particular ideas which are stressed by Karl and the solutions which he has apparently adopted when those ideas conflict. Arrows have been drawn to attempt to show some of the major connections among the ideas and their sources, although it has obviously been impossible to show *all* such connections. The easiest way to read the diagram is to start at the bottom left-hand corner and go upward, to the right, and then down again. It has been difficult to indicate adequately the central conflict in Karl's ideological structure, which is between individualism on the one hand and the need for solidarities on the other. Many factors, as we have seen, have contributed to the stressing of the importance of the individual: the Protestant ethic, pioneer life, the theory of economic individualism, extreme social mobility in an expanding community, political revolt against older solidarities, etc. In Karl at least, and probably in many others brought up in the American social system, there is a strong need for security and solidarities of one sort or another, a great feeling of "aloneness." These two contradictory needs, one for achievement and one for security, have fused to produce a number of different solutions, all of which are fairly typical of the contemporary scene. First and foremost to Karl is the great value of romantic love. Essentially this is an individualistic type of solidarity, since it involves winning another person's affections and then standing united with the one other person as a small unit against the world. Secondly, there is the solution of continued achievement or striving which may bring security eventually through the accumulation of money or perhaps authority and prestige. Karl apparently has no particular faith in either of these routes. At least in this stage of his life money does not seem adequate for the real support and affection he needs. Possibly it is devalued because it apparently did not bring his father happiness and because it is somewhat at variance with his religious ideology. Authority and prestige are more likely possibilities for him, although here again they conflict with his political ideology of the equality of all men, and he can accept the value of leadership only if it is ac-

FIGURE 8.1

Diagram Showing Karl's Major Ideas (in circles), Their Sources (in boxes) and Interconnections (arrows)

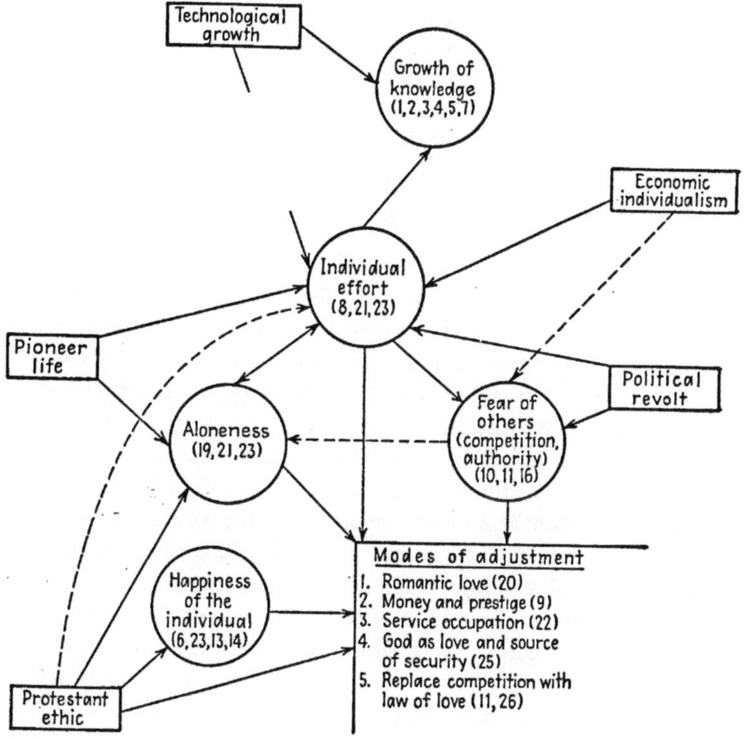

companied with the love of those who are being led. A third approach is a kind of unreal, ideal solution in which the competitive system would be replaced by the law of love, in a kind of realization of the Kingdom of God on earth. Since he realizes that this is an unreal solution, he is ready with a compromise which involves the kind of occupation which requires service to others rather than competition with them. We have then four solutions to the conflict between excessive individualism and the need for solidarity: romantic love, individualistic striving for money or prestige, the unreal Kingdom of God on earth, and individualistic striving for service to others. There is a certain real sense in which this basic conflict and the alternate solutions reflect the "basic ideological structure" of the American man in much the same sense as Kardiner speaks of the "basic personality structure." These themes and conflicts will enter to a greater or lesser extent into the thought patterns of anyone born in Karl's culture, but only an analysis of this sort will give the peculiar emphasis that any individual gives to them. The question as to *why* certain ideas and conflicts are stressed over others in Karl can be answered only after we have analyzed motivational structure and its relation to cognitive structure. For the moment we must be content with our "ideological census" *per se.*

NOTES AND QUERIES

1. What is a value? What is the difference between an individual value and a cultural value? How would you measure each? How is a value related to a sentiment defined by Murray and Morgan as "an acquired psychophysical disposition to respond affectively to a certain entity or to entities of a certain class." (1945, p. 28.) How is a value related to an "important idea?"

2. Trying to find the relations among ideas is not unlike trying to find the relations among individuals in a group from likes and dislikes of the members of the group. In other words, we may proceed to construct an "ideogram" as we would a "sociogram" provided we can make simple judgments as to whether idea A leads to idea B, or B leads to A, or both lead to each other. To do this would require a large square matrix which in Karl's case would have the twenty-six ideas listed across the top and down the side or down the diagonal. In each square the judge would then place a sign indicating his perception of the relationship between the two ideas. The methods developed by Katz (1947) and others could be used to select the important ideological clusters and group them so that a person could perceive them readily. Try this in Karl's case. Whatever else it does, it insures the placing of every idea in conjunction with every other one and so avoids errors of simple oversight in constructing the over-all picture.

3. Why has there not been more discussion of attitude scales in this chapter? What attitude scales could be used that would help round out the picture of Karl's ideology and values?

4. Take F. Kluckhohn's cultural orientation scheme presented in Table 8.3 and attempt to derive each of the twenty-six central ideas attributed to Karl from the five orientations typical of America. Do

you need any additional assumptions? Is there any way to tell which are central and which are derivative orientations?

5. Kluckhohn and Leighton (1946, pp. 223-232) list the premises underlying the Navaho philosophy of life as follows:

1. Life is very, very dangerous.
2. Nature is more powerful than man.
3. The personality is a whole.
4. Respect the integrity of the individual.
5. Everything exists in two parts, the male and the female, which belong together and complete each other.
6. Human nature is neither good nor evil.
7. Like produces like and the part stands for the whole.
8. What is said is to be taken literally.
9. This life is what counts.

Can you summarize in a similar fashion the basic premises of Karl's philosophy of life? How many of them are similar to these? How should the premises in a personal philosophy of life be related to the premises in the philosophy of life of the culture of which the person is a member? How do you arrive at the latter?

6. Is there anything in the notion of "basic ideological structure" for a given cultural group? How would you go about proving or disproving your answer? For example, Kluckhohn and Kluckhohn (1947) list the following characteristics of American ideological structure:

1. Effort and optimism (including moral purpose and rationalism).
2. Romantic individualism (including the cult of the Average Man and the tendency to personalize).
3. Change as a value in itself.
4. Pleasure principle.
5. Externalism.
6. Simple answers.
7. Humor.
8. Generosity.

How many of these are consistent with the American core values in Table 8.3? With the ideological emphases in Karl's record in Figure 8.1? Can you design ways of measuring each of these ideas and seeing whether in fact individuals or groups of individuals think in these terms? How many of them could be tested simply through linguistic usages?

7. The Rorschach analyst has this to say about Karl in one part of his report:

> His only defense is intellectualizing and repression (F) but these are incapable of coping with the emotions that run rampant. It is here that it becomes apparent that interest in art, present in this record, is one manifestation of the use of intellectualization as a defense against anxiety and the fact that some of his art percepts have sexual symbolic significance would suggest that this interest of the subject also serves as sublimation for sexual preoccupations.

How would you reconcile this finding with the apparent lack of interest in art displayed in Karl's autobiography and tests?

8. Discuss the advantages and disadvantages of describing a person in terms of some important determinant of behavior—either biological ("he's a desert rat, plains-dweller," etc.) or cultural ("he's a plains Indian, a Zuni, a minister," etc.).

9. A number of Karl's test results have been given at various places throughout the chapter. This procedure is naturally open to the objection that scores are selected to prove whatever point is at issue. Perhaps there are other scores which disprove the same point. In order to make the detection of such errors possible, the full results are reproduced here. The reader should check through them to see if there are points which have been obviously overlooked or overstressed.

A. The Allport-Vernon Study of Values Test.

	Actual Scores	*Approximate Percentile*
Religious	55	98
Social	46	96
Economic	27	40
Theoretical	23	20
Political	21	20
Aesthetic	19	10

B. Karl's self-ratings on vices.

Rate yourself regarding the following "vices." Scale A indicates your attitude toward the relative seriousness of the vice. Scale B indicates how much you are characterized by the vice. Scale C is an indication of how guilty you felt if you have ever expressed that vice. (6) is high, (1) is low rating.

a. *Disrespect* for those in authority—parents, professors, business superiors.
A–Seriousness 1 2 ③ 4 5 6
B–Involvement 1 2 ③ 4 5 6
C–Guilt 1 ② 3 4 5 6

b. *General dishonesty,* e.g., cheating, petty thievery, misrepresenting, etc.
A–Seriousness 1 2 3 4 ⑤ 6
B–Involvement 1 2 ③ 4 5 6
C–Guilt 1 2 ③ 4 5 6

c. *Lack of courage* in face of danger.
A–Seriousness 1 2 3 4 ⑤ 6
B–Involvement ① 2 3 4 5 6
C–Guilt 1 2 3 ④ 5 6

d. *Rebellion,* e.g., acting against some express rule of authority—home, school, church, etc.
A–Seriousness 1 2 ③ 4 5 6
B–Involvement 1 2 3 ④ 5 6
C–Guilt ① 2 3 4 5 6

e. *Narrow-mindedness* (intolerance, prejudice, etc.)
A–Seriousness 1 2 3 ④ 5 6
B–Involvement 1 ② 3 4 5 6
C–Guilt 1 ② 3 4 5 6

f. *Overindulgence*—eating or drinking too much, laziness, playing around too much.
A–Seriousness 1 2 ③ 4 6
B–Involvement 1 2 3 ④ 6
C–Guilt 1 ② 3 4 5 6

A kind of rough over-all index of the importance of a given virtue can be derived from Karl's answers to this rating scale. It is obtained by adding the seriousness and guilt ratings and subtracting the amount of involvement. In other words, the greater the seriousness and guilt, and the less the involvement, the more important the virtue would appear to be. When this is done we discover that courage is by all odds the most important value to Karl of the ones listed. It is followed by *honesty* and *tolerance* and then at a much lower level by *respect, obedience,* and *moderation.*

C. Karl's Religious Conceptions. An attitude questionnaire, as we have observed, is nearly always used to measure the amount rather than the content of an attitude. But this need not be the case. Content can be obtained from such a scale, though not without difficulty. By way of illustration we have reproduced here a section of Karl's answers to a "Religious Attitude Inventory." This questionnaire was based in part on one used by Allport, Gillespie and Young (1948) and was designed by Rhodes (1948) to give an over-all "religiosity" index and an index of transcendent as opposed to immanent religiosity. The scores he obtained were utilized in the normal manner in establishing relationships in a group of subjects. Here we are interested specifically in *what* one person believes, namely Karl.

In Part I of the inventory Karl checked statements indicating that religion of a conservative Protestant sort had had a marked influence in his upbringing, but that he had reacted against it and had prayed not at all in the last six months. As being influential in making him religious at times he listed the following factors: mother (not father), personal influence of people other than parents (not conformity with tradition), fear or insecurity (not gratitude), studies in school or college (not a mystical experience), and church teachings. Most of the remaining items in Part I and in Part II are reproduced in full below. They are the basis for the content summary of Karl's religious beliefs in Table 8.6.

7. The deity (check the one statement which *most nearly* expresses your belief):

___ 1. There is an infinitely wise, omnipotent Creator of the universe and of natural laws, whose protection and favor may be supplicated through worship and prayer. God is a personal God.

___ 2. There is an infinitely intelligent and friendly Being, working according to natural laws through which he expresses His power and goodness. There is the possibility of communication with this Deity in the sense that prayer may at least affect our moral attitude toward nature and toward our own place in the scheme of things.

_X_ 3. There is a vast, impersonal, spiritual source or principle throughout nature and working in man, incapable of being swayed or communicated with through prayer.

___ 4. The only power is natural law. There is neither a personal creator nor an infinite intelligent Being. Nature is wholly indifferent to man. Natural law may be spoken of as "spiritual force," but this in no way adds to or changes its character.

___ 5. Because of our necessary ignorance in this matter, I neither believe nor disbelieve in a God.

8. The person of Christ (check the position best corresponding to your own view):
   ___ 1. Christ, as the Gospels state, should be regarded as divine—as the human incarnation of God.
   _X_ 2. Christ should be regarded merely as a great prophet or teacher much as the Mohammedans accept Mahomet, or as the Chinese accept Confucius.
   ___ 3. In all probability Christ never lived at all, but is a purely mythical figure.
9. Immortality (check the position that best corresponds to your own view):
   _X_ 1. I believe in personal immortality, i.e., the continued existence of the soul as an individual and separate entity.
   ___ 2. I believe in reincarnation—the continued existence of the soul in another body.
   ___ 3. I believe that a person's immortality resides merely in his influence upon his children and upon social institutions.
   ___ 4. I disbelieve in immortality in any sense.
   ___ 5. Other

Part II

The following cross check questions are more specific than the foregoing. They may be answered quickly. Do not be disturbed if your answers are inconsistent with each other or with those checked in Part I.

If at times you agree with the statement and at other times do not, place your check under "agree sometimes."

	Yes	*Agree sometimes*	*No*	*No opinion*
1. Do you believe that God can help you				
a. by restraining people who could harm you (for instance, on the battlefield?)	*			X
b. by forgiving your sins?		X		
c. by performing medical miracles?		X		
d. by having fellowship with you through prayer?	X			
e. by giving you power to cope with life's difficulties?		X		
2. Do you think of God				
a. as a Heavenly Father?			X	
b. as a Being outside yourself?	X			
c. as all-powerful?			X	

* Filled in and then erased.

	Yes	*Agree some-times*	*No*	*No opin-ion*
d. as desiring human love or adoration?			X	
e. as an Object of praise and adoration?		X		
f. as a Being to whom we must atone for our wrongdoings?		X		
3. Do you believe mankind is basically sinful in that he continually disobeys God?		X		
4. Do you agree with the conception that Christians are "little children" in the eyes of God?	X			
5. Within the last six months have you been preoccupied with the idea of death?	X			
6. Do you feel it necessary to abstain from certain "pleasures" (sex, liquor, overeating, etc.) for religious reasons?			X	
7. Do you feel that self-sacrifice raises the quality of the spiritual life?	X			
8. Have you ever had an experience wherein you felt "overwhelmed by God's presence,' e.g., a religious conversion?			X	
9. Is your "philosophy of life" primarily concerned with religion?			X	
10. Can you accept the Bible as literal truth?			X	
11. Indicate your agreement with the following sayings abstracted from the writings of famous religious persons:				
a. "Seek a convenient time to think on the benefits of God."	X			
b. "Life's most majestic experience is to have felt the Presence of God."		X		
c. "Verily we deceive ourselves by inordinate love of our flesh."		X		
d. "All other things in the world, save only to love God and serve Him, are vanity."			X	
e. "A man ought to strengthen himself so that he needeth not to seek any consolation from the world outside."			X	
f. "God saves man by Grace."			X	
12. A person feels better after confessing his sins to God (or God's representative).	X			

D. Karl's Strong Vocational Interest Test (scores grouped according to Spranger's value types and also showing factorial grouping).

		Standard Score	*Rating*	
1. Theoretical				
Group II *	Mathematician	12	C	
	Engineer	23	C+	
	Chemist	33	B−	Mean=22.7 (21 percentile)
2. Economic				
Group VIII	Accountant	29	C+	
	Office man	34	B−	
	Purchasing agent	21	C	
	Banker	27	C+	
Group IV	Farmer	32	B−	
	Carpenter	10	C	
	Printer	27	C+	Mean=25.7 (30 percentile)
3. Aesthetic				
Group I	Artist	16	C	
	Architect	11	C	
Group VI	Musician	25	C+	
Group X	Author-journalist	29	C+	Mean=20.3 (14 percentile)
4. Political				
Group III	Production manager	40	B+	
Group IV	Policeman	41	B+	
Group V	City School Sup't	40	B+	
	Personnel manager	46	A	
Group XI	Pres. Mfg. Concern	25	C+	Mean=38.5 (77 percentile)
5. Social				
Group V	YMCA phys. director	54	A	
	Personnel manager	46	A	
	YMCA Secretary	42	B+	
	Soc. Sci. H. S. Teacher	42	B+	
	City School Sup't	40	B+	
	Minister	36	B	
Group I	Physician	38	B	Mean=44.5 (91 percentile)
6. Religious				
Group V	Minister	36	B	Score=36 (69 percentile)

…SONALITY VARIABLE

	Standard Score	Rating	
[illegible]	28	C+	
[illegible]	25	C+	
[illegible]	51	B−	
[illegible] salesman	52	B−	
[illegible] salesman	[illegible]	B	
[illegible]	26	C+	Mean = 31.9
[illegible]			(54 percentile)
[illegible]	54	B−	
[illegible] teacher	[illegible]	B+	Overall mean = 31.0
			SD = 10.1

[illegible] show which occupations belong together according [illegible]

9

Roles and Role Moals

DEFINITION ROLE

The scene opens in a fraternity ho e in an Eastern men's college. One of the "brothers" is standing o e table in the front hall surrounded by a cheering crowd. He ra his hand for silence. "Men," he says in hard-boiled, commandin nes, "we'll find him all right. I'll take on the job." "Atta boy, S ' somebody shouts from the owd. They all cheer him on and try to look impressed. "Who saw m last?" demands Sam, sternly. ere is a confused babble of nts. Sam again raises his hand silence. "Joe, you take over. their stories and call the I utenant to tell him what you Ted, you look in the dorm ies. I'm going to look for him al's." "Oh, will you ever fid him, Sam?" quavers some- uld I be dictating this r rt to you, Effie, if it weren't t all right?" shouts Sam he leaps from the table and s of laughter heads for S the local tavern. Sam Spade, ammett's radio detective, ff on his latest caper.

esting part about this episode, and the part which is so his fraternity brothers that the hero of the story hesitant and self-critic hat, far from being the hard- pade, he appears reticen nd indecisive in everything he r, as soon as he assum he role of Sam Spade, which often at the delighted sistence of his "brothers," he l and gives at least a reonably good performance as nt, hard-boiled privat etective. Is this *role* which or drop a real part of personality? If it is, how are nd it and include it ur systematic analysis of per- e?

ection it appears at assuming the role of Sam extrem example of what all of us do frequently ves. We may not often be called upon to assume te detective, but we do have to display such pat- s are appropriate t being a man or a woman, a or salesman. Mo of us in such situations have t of behavior r attitudes are expected and

Miscellaneous		Standard Score	Rating	
Group I	Dentist	28	C+	
	Psychologist	25	C+	
Group IX	Sales manager	31	B−	
	Real estate salesman	32	B−	
	Life insurance salesman	37	B	
Group X	Advertising man	26	C+	Mean=31.9
	Lawyer			(54 percentile)
Group IV	Forest service man	34	B−	
	Math. phys. science teacher	42	B+	Overall mean=31.0
				SD=10.1

Note: (*)—The group numbers show which occupations belong together according to a factorial analysis.

9

Roles and Role Models

Definition of Role

The scene opens in a fraternity house in an Eastern men's college. One of the "brothers" is standing on the table in the front hall surrounded by a cheering crowd. He raises his hand for silence. "Men," he says in hard-boiled, commanding tones, "we'll find him all right. I'll take on the job." "Atta boy, Sam," somebody shouts from the crowd. They all cheer him on and try to look impressed. "Who saw him last?" demands Sam, sternly. There is a confused babble of shouts. Sam again raises his hand for silence. "Joe, you take over. Listen to their stories and call the Lieutenant to tell him what you find out. Ted, you look in the dormitories. I'm going to look for him down at Sal's." "Oh, will you ever find him, Sam?" quavers someone. "Would I be dictating this report to you, Effie, if it weren't coming out all right?" shouts Sam as he leaps from the table and amid bursts of laughter heads for Sal's, the local tavern. Sam Spade, Dashiell Hammett's radio detective, is off on his latest caper.

The interesting part about this episode, and the part which is so amusing to his fraternity brothers is that the hero of the story is normally so hesitant and self-critical, that, far from being the hard-boiled Sam Spade, he appears reticent and indecisive in everything he does. However, as soon as he assumes the role of Sam Spade, which he does fairly often at the delighted insistence of his "brothers," he is transformed and gives at least a reasonably good performance as a self-confident, hard-boiled private detective. Is this *role* which he can put on or drop a real part of his personality? If it is, how are we to understand it and include it in our systematic analysis of personality structure?

On closer inspection it appears that assuming the role of Sam Spade is only an extreme example of what all of us do frequently throughout our lives. We may not often be called upon to assume the role of a private detective, but we do have to display such patterns of behavior as are appropriate to being a man or a woman, a guest, a Methodist, or a salesman. Most of us in such situations have a general idea of what sort of behavior or attitudes are expected and furthermore we can exhibit that behavior more or less correctly. The ability of people to transform themselves at least partly in accordance with the demands of a situation has long been observed by students of human nature and has an honorable place among the concepts used by social scientists. William James, for instance, spoke of our having as many "social selves" as there are social situations in which we find ourselves. Sociologists like Weber and Veblen have emphasized the importance of the requirements of an occupation in shaping the cast of a man's mind. In consequence such terms as "the bureaucratic personality," the "military mind," or the typical "schoolmarm" have come into common usage. Playwrights made use of such stereotypes long before the social scientists began their study of them. In the Latin plays of Plautus and Terence, for instance, there are typical stock characters such as the *Miles* or "braggart soldier" whose behavior could be correctly predicted by the members of a Roman audience as soon as they recognized him.

Psychologists as well as sociologists have been interested in the concept of role. J. F. Brown (1936) for example speaks of "membership character" and its importance for determining attitudes and beliefs. For instance, as a member of the Methodist church a man would or should have certain beliefs about the nature of God. But it has remained for an anthropologist, Ralph Linton, to give what is perhaps the clearest current formulation of the social role concept. He distinguishes first of all between *status* and *role.* By status he simply means the position of a person in the social structure without regard to how "high" the position is. A person's status then may include his position in a family group, an age group, an occupational group, a religious group, etc. Associated with each of these statuses are certain expected patterns of behavior or social norms. A configuration of these patterns may be referred to as a "status personality." "The study of such Status Personalities, as I have chosen to call them, can scarcely fail to produce results which will be significant for the understanding of many personality phenomena. Common status provides one of the simplest and at the same time the most significant frames of reference within which groups of individuals can be observed and compared. Persons who share a common status within a society are all subject to the same sort of formal social pressure and are expected to learn and adhere to similar culturally patterned forms of overt behavior." (Linton, 1949, p. 166.)

Where does the status personality concept fit into our over-all picture of the relation between personality and culture? From Table 8.1 (p. 241) it would appear that status presents the individual with a class of problems to which he must adjust more or less according to the specific solutions laid down by his culture. In Chapter 8 we discussed the orientations or ideas provided for the individual by the culture with respect to the class of problems dealing with what might be called "life's basic issues." Now we turn to the class of problems associated with the different social positions in which a person finds himself at birth (e.g., sex category) or at different times during his life (e.g., age and occupational categories). Generally speaking, the solutions to such problems laid down by the culture are more specific than the general orientations dealt with in the last chapter. They are therefore more difficult to treat in any over-all summary fashion. In this respect our problem seems somewhat like the one we faced in attempting to deal with the multiplicity of personality traits. There seem to be just as many social roles as there are personality traits that a person can display. This suggests that the solution to the problem of multiplicity of roles may be the same as it was to the multiplicity of traits: we will have to find the common problems, associated with common social positions, for which certain common behaviorial solutions are socially approved.

Trait and Role. Let us pursue the analogy between trait and role a little further in the hope that it will help us understand the role concept better. Suppose we take the hypothetical case of a young woman who is about to become a schoolteacher. In the course of her development we may assume that she has adjusted to such ordinary everyday recurrent problems as walking, talking, and interacting with other people, in characteristic or consistent ways which we have labeled traits. Let us further suppose that she is quiet, unassuming, dependent or submissive in social relationships, restrained and controlled in gesture and movement, since these are traits which would perhaps be favored by her physical constitution and by her culture as appropriate for a person with feminine status. Now when she walks into the classroom, her task presents her with a whole new set of problems. Specifically she must (1) be seen, (2) be heard, and (3) maintain discipline. She may quickly find that her old modes of responding, her old traits, are no longer successful. If she talks in her usual voice, the children do not hear her. If she makes her usual restrained gestures, they will not see what she is pointing at. And if she maintains her old dependent relationship to others, the children will soon be running her. In this confusing new situation, what does she do? Certain courses of action (new responses) are suggested to her directly by the situation: She begins to talk louder. Other new responses come from her observation of other teachers who have already solved these problems or from her memories of how her own teachers behaved. From these sources she learns to some extent what she cannot do. She knows, for instance, that she cannot use a bull whip on that boy in the back row, although she might like to. She also learns what she can do to maintain discipline. In time, reacting to the pressures of the situation and the guidance provided her by others, she becomes the "typical" schoolteacher: she speaks louder, gestures more expansively, and develops techniques for dominating the classroom situation and controlling the children more or less well (cf. Waller, 1932). Either that or she quits her job or is fired. Out of the classroom in other social positions she may continue to display her former habits, reserving her schoolteacher "status personality" for the classroom, but in the end there will probably be some transfer to other situations as well and she may display some typical schoolteacher characteristics: "a certain inflexibility, a stiff and formal manner, a flat didactic tone of voice, dignity, lack of spontaneity, and on the whole a lack of creativeness, and a strong desire for security." (Komarovsky and Sargent, 1949, p. 146.)

The point to notice particularly about this adjustment process is that it is common to all the women who go through it. The problems presented by the classroom situation (being heard, being seen, etc.) are practically the same everywhere, and so are the social limitations on the ways in which they can be solved. Is it any wonder then that schoolteachers the country over develop certain characteristics in common? When this happens—that is, when the situation "dictates," as it were, the common characteristics which several people display we call the resulting trait pattern a *social role*. Of course there are many individual variations, particularly in the extent to which the "classroom personality" generalizes to situations outside it, but certainly there is a common enough pattern of traits which would justify us in referring to them as a role.

The Reciprocal Nature of Roles. From the individual's viewpoint the role pattern is important in two ways. On the one hand it is a pattern of behavior which he displays or attempts to display in a given social situation and on the other it forms a basis for his expectations as to how *other* people will behave in such a situation.

In either case roles tend to have great economic utility for the organism since role traits come in "packages." That is, a person can put himself in the place of a schoolteacher or Sam Spade and produce a variety of expected behaviors reasonably well. What is perhaps more important: the cluster of associated role traits provides a kind of social shorthand which enables a person to react more or less properly to other people. Thus in seeing a woman walk toward him on the street, an individual may think, "Oh, she's a schoolteacher," and on the basis of this cue expect that she will behave in certain ways in greeting him, and that he in turn will behave in certain ways toward her. The operation of this process is perhaps best illustrated by an experiment reported by Kelley (1949), as follows:

> A person unknown to the subjects was introduced in each class as temporarily replacing their instructor. Half of the class was given biographical information including the information that the stimulus person is "rather cold." The remaining subjects were independently given identical information except that it included the statement that the stimulus person is "very warm." The stimulus person led each class in a twenty minute discussion, a record being kept of the frequency of students' participation. Afterward, first impression ratings of the stimulus person were obtained from all

> The subjects given the "warm" expectation rated the stimulus person as more considerate than others, less formal, more sociable, more popular, more humorous, more human, and better matured. They also participated in the discussion significantly more than the subjects given the "cold" ex-

This experiment, patterned after earlier work by Asch (1946), illustrates nicely how a single label, in this case "warm" or "cold" rather than "schoolteacher," can determine the traits perceived in a person and can influence the frequency of interaction with him.

Summary of Role Characteristics. From this preliminary illustrative discussion we may now draw a more formal definition of role: *A role is a cluster of traits (or pattern of behavior) which serves as the culturally normal or modal solution to recurrent, usually social problems peculiar to a particular status or position in society.* Certain elements in this definition need further explanation.

By *cluster of traits* we mean (a) the tendency of the status or its name to evoke a certain limited number of responses with fairly high frequency, or (b) the lesser tendency of any one of the traits in a cluster to evoke the other traits with a fairly high frequency.

dren will soon be running her. In this confusing new situation, what does she do? Certain courses of action (new responses) are suggested to her directly by the situation: She begins to talk louder. Other new responses come from her observation of other teachers who have already solved these problems or from her memories of how her own teachers behaved. From these sources she learns to some extent what she cannot do. She knows, for instance, that she cannot use a bull whip on that boy in the back row, although she might like to. She also learns what she can do to maintain discipline. In time, reacting to the pressures of the situation and the guidance provided her by others, she becomes the "typical" schoolteacher: she speaks louder, gestures more expansively, and develops techniques for dominating the classroom situation and controlling the children more or less well (cf. Waller, 1932). Either that or she quits her job or is fired. Out of the classroom in other social positions she may continue to display her former habits, reserving her schoolteacher "status personality" for the classroom, but in the end there will probably be some transfer to other situations as well and she may display some typical schoolteacher characteristics: "a certain inflexibility, a stiff and formal manner, a flat didactic tone of voice, dignity, lack of spontaneity, and on the whole a lack of creativeness, and a strong desire for security." (Komarovsky and Sargent, 1949, p. 146.)

The point to notice particularly about this adjustment process is that it is common to all the women who go through it. The problems presented by the classroom situation (being heard, being seen, etc.) are practically the same everywhere, and so are the social limitations on the ways in which they can be solved. Is it any wonder then that schoolteachers the country over develop certain characteristics in common? When this happens—that is, when the situation "dictates," as it were, the common characteristics which several people display we call the resulting trait pattern a *social role*. Of course there are many individual variations, particularly in the extent to which the "classroom personality" generalizes to situations outside it, but certainly there is a common enough pattern of traits which would justify us in referring to them as a role.

The Reciprocal Nature of Roles. From the individual's viewpoint the role pattern is important in two ways. On the one hand it is a pattern of behavior which he displays or attempts to display in a given social situation and on the other it forms a basis for his expectations as to how *other* people will behave in such a situation.

In either case roles tend to have great economic utility for the organism since role traits come in "packages." That is, a person can put himself in the place of a schoolteacher or Sam Spade and produce a variety of expected behaviors reasonably well. What is perhaps more important: the cluster of associated role traits provides a kind of social shorthand which enables a person to react more or less properly to other people. Thus in seeing a woman walk toward him on the street, an individual may think, "Oh, she's a schoolteacher," and on the basis of this cue expect that she will behave in certain ways in greeting him, and that he in turn will behave in certain ways toward her. The operation of this process is perhaps best illustrated by an experiment reported by Kelley (1949), as follows:

> A person unknown to the subjects was introduced in each class as temporarily replacing their instructor. Half of the class was given biographical information including the information that the stimulus person is "rather cold." The remaining subjects were independently given identical information except that it included the statement that the stimulus person is "very warm." The stimulus person led each class in a twenty minute discussion, a record being kept of the frequency of students' participation. Afterward, first impression ratings of the stimulus person were obtained from all subjects.
>
> The subjects given the "warm" expectation rated the stimulus person as more considerate than others, less formal, more sociable, more popular, more humorous, more human, and better matured. They also participated in the discussion significantly more than the subjects given the "cold" expectation.

This experiment, patterned after earlier work by Asch (1946), illustrates nicely how a single label, in this case "warm" or "cold" rather than "schoolteacher," can determine the traits perceived in a person and can influence the frequency of interaction with him.

Summary of Role Characteristics. From this preliminary illustrative discussion we may now draw a more formal definition of role: *A role is a cluster of traits (or pattern of behavior) which serves as the culturally normal or modal solution to recurrent, usually social problems peculiar to a particular status or position in society.* Certain elements in this definition need further explanation.

1. By *cluster of traits* we mean (a) the tendency of the status or its name to evoke a certain limited number of responses with fairly high frequency, or (b) the lesser tendency of any one of the traits in the cluster to evoke the other traits with a fairly high frequency.

SCHEMA AS A PERSONALITY VARIABLE

The "cluster" phenomenon is characteristic of all schemata as we have seen in Chapter 8. In Kelley's (1949) and Asch's (1946) experiments the key element in the trait complex, namely "warm," was enough to evoke other responses such as sociable, popular, etc., more frequently than other traits. The phenomenon does not seem to be a case of pure verbal stereotypy but rather to be a genuine perceptual phenomenon. In an ingenious experiment Bruner, Postman, and Rodrigues (1950) have demonstrated that more red is needed in a color wheel to match the color of a lobster claw than is needed to match the exactly equivalent color of another object of about the same size but of a different shape. In other words the lobster claw appears genuinely "redder" to the observer. The shape and the color are part of a perceptual "cluster" just as the characterizations "warm" and "sociable" are in Kelley's experiments. Psychologists have long studied this phenomenon in connection with race prejudice. Katz and Braly (cf. Newcomb and Hartley, 1947), for instance, asked Princeton undergraduates "to select the traits from a prepared list of 84 adjectives to characterize ten racial and national groups." This provides a more direct test of the cluster phenomenon in the social field since the problem is to discover whether certain traits are consistently associated with national or racial status. For certain groups they found a fairly high degree of stereotypy, e.g., for Negroes and Germans. The following list shows the percentage of one hundred Princeton students assigning each of various traits to these groups.

Negroes	
superstitious	84%
lazy	75%
happy-go-lucky	38%
ignorant	38%
musical	26%
ostentatious	26%
Germans	
scientifically-minded	78%
industrious	65%
stolid	44%
intelligent	32%
methodical	31%
extremely nationalistic	24%

For certain groups the stereotypy was by no means so obvious, for instance the Chinese:

Chinese	
superstitious	35%
sly	30%
conservative	30%
tradition loving	27%
loyal to family ties	23%
industrious	19%

(After Katz and Braly, in Newcomb and Hartley, 1947, p. 207.)

Data such as these have usually been reported as examples of how faulty and incorrect people are in forming such stereotypes, since obviously many members of these various groups do not have the characteristics in question. While this certainly is true, more emphasis needs to be placed on the fact that it is just such clustering that makes adaptation to the social matrix possible. The fact that such schemata may be incorrect should not blind us to the fact that in many instances they are accurate enough for the purposes at hand and provide an indispensable guide for conduct in various social situations.

As an example of the importance of status-associated behavioral norms we may cite the case of Doris Fleischman (Bernays), who has given an amusing account of the results of her feminist attempt to do away with the "Mrs." title in her own life. She wanted to continue to be known as Miss Fleischman after her marriage, and found the hazards to be great. Since people were unsure of her status, they were unsure of how to react to her. "At a party I am assailed by 'Oh, do you know him? Oh, you're his wife? What? You're his partner? What?—you're Miss? You're Mrs.? The hell with it. Let me get you some tea.'" (1949, p. 165.) She tells of difficulties in getting a passport, in registering at hotels in the same room with her husband, in disillusioning unattached males who wanted to take her out, in explaining to schoolteachers that her children did not come from a broken home. All these difficulties arose from the fact that the behavior appropriate both from and toward a woman with single status differs considerably in our society from what it would be for a woman with married status. Nothing could illustrate more vividly the social utility of having role norms to guide people through the sociocultural matrix. To sum the matter up in Linton's words, "thus in dealings between complete strangers, simple recognition of the social position of the two individuals involved makes it possible for each to predict how the other will respond to most situations." (Linton, 1945, p. 130.)

2. It is the *modal* as well as the stereotyped character of most social roles that makes them useful in social adjustments. In other words, if a particular stereotype or cluster of traits were known only to a few people, its social usefulness would be restricted to those people. It is not just the fact that certain acts are associated with single female status—availability for dates, not sleeping in a hotel room with a man, not having children, etc. It is the fact that since single women typically behave in these ways everyone will know what to expect and can respond "appropriately," at least as the culture defines appropriateness. This process goes on so easily under most circumstances that we become aware of the utility of such role conventions only when they are inappropriate as in the case of race prejudice or in a case like Miss Fleischman's in which a person who occupies one status tries to act as if he occupies another.

3. The role solutions to status problems are part of an individual's knowledge and therefore part of his personality. This may seem like an obvious statement, but it is worth making in view of a somewhat different position adopted by Linton who states "that any one individual of such a group manifests this response proves nothing about his personality except that he has normal learning ability. His personality dispositions will be revealed not by his culturally patterned responses but by his deviations from the culture pattern . . . until the psychologist knows what the norms of behavior imposed by a particular society are and can discount them as indicators of personality he will be unable to penetrate behind the façade of social conformity and cultural uniformity to reach the authentic individual." (Linton, 1945, p. 26.) Our view is that the psychologist must know what the norms of behavior imposed by a particular society are, not to discount them, but to use them to gain a more adequate theoretical formulation of the person's behavior in *all* its aspects. The façade of social conformity *is* part of the authentic personality in the sense in which we have defined personality in Chapter 3. In short, we will need to know what a person's conceptions of social norms or social roles are in order to predict or account for many of his responses.

4. The fact that we have classified a person's role conceptions as part of his knowledge or the schemata he has of his social environment suggests that from this knowledge *alone* we will be able to predict his role behavior or role performance. This is not the case. How any person behaves as a father or as a schoolteacher or as an unmarried woman is *partly* a function of his knowledge of the be-

havior expected in this position, but it is also a function of his motivational state, his desire to perform the role, and also of his past adjustments or learned responses to similar status situations. Role *knowledge* and role *performance* are two different matters. We will discuss the latter more fully later on.

5. As we have defined the role concept, it is clear that one of the central tasks in understanding a particular role is to analyze the nature of the problems which the person has to face in a given status. We have demonstrated how it is possible to analyze such problems in our illustration of the schoolteacher and the adjustment problems presented her by the classroom situation. This is essentially the task of sociology, which has already made considerable progress in defining the requirements of particular statuses. For example, Parsons argues (1949) that "affective neutrality" is one of the requirements of the medical profession. That is, a doctor cannot be permitted by society to get emotionally entangled with his patients if he is to continue to perform his professional role adequately. From the personality psychologist's viewpoint the task in this case is one of observing how a particular individual doctor discovers and defines problems of affective neutrality and how he learns the appropriate modal solutions to this problem as they are practiced and approved by other doctors and sanctioned by society. It is at this point that students of social structure and students of the individual adjustment to the problems that social structure presents must work very closely together.

Types of Roles

Having considered in a general way what roles are, we must now turn to the concrete problem of attempting to discuss what some of the important roles are and illustrate each of them with the conceptions of them which our subject, Karl, has developed. Fortunately Linton (1945) has provided us with a convenient classification of the major statuses and their associated roles, as follows: age, sex, family position, occupation, and association group membership. That is, different role behavior is expected of people of different ages (age-grading), of people of different sex (sex-typing), from fathers, sons, sisters, brothers, aunts, cousins (family statuses), from lawyers or from unskilled workmen (occupational statuses), and finally from Rotarians, Methodists, Dixiecrats, or Boy Scouts (association group statuses). A given individual may occupy several of these statuses at the same time or in succession, spread out over the course of his life.

SCHEMA AS A PERSONALITY VARIABLE

Linton has given an excellent account of the way a particular person's behavior will vary according to the different statuses he occupies in the course of a hypothetical day. It is so vivid that it is worth reproducing in full here:

> Let us suppose that a man spends the day working as a clerk in a store. While he is behind the counter, his active status is that of a clerk, established by his position in our society's system of specialized occupations. The role associated with this status provides him with patterns for his relations with customers. These patterns will be well known both to him and to the customers and will enable them to transact business with a minimum of delay or misunderstanding. When he retires to the rest room for a smoke and meets other employees there, his clerk status becomes latent and he assumes another active status based upon his position in the association group composed of the store's employees as a whole. In this status his relation with other employees will be governed by a different set of culture patterns from those employed in his relations with customers. Moreover, since he probably knows most of the other employees, his exercise of this culture pattern will be modified by his personal likes and dislikes of certain individuals and by considerations of their and his own relative positions in the prestige series of the store association's members. When closing time comes, he lays aside both his clerk and store association statuses and, while on the way home, operates simply in terms of his status with respect to the society's age-sex system. Thus if he is a young man he will at least feel that he ought to get up and give his seat to a lady, while if he is an old one he will be quite comfortable about keeping it. As soon as he arrives at his house, a new set of statuses will be activated. These statuses derive from the kinship ties which relate him to various members of the family group. In pursuance of the roles associated with these family statuses he will try to be cordial to his mother-in-law, affectionate to his wife and a stern disciplinarian to Junior, whose report card marks a new low. If it happens to be a lodge night, all his familial statuses will become latent at about eight o'clock. As soon as he enters the lodge room and puts on his uniform as Grand Imperial Lizard, in the Ancient Order of Dinosaurs he assumes a new status, one which has been latent since the last lodge meeting, and performs in terms of its role until it is time for him to take off his uniform and go home. (Reproduced with permission from R. Linton, *The Cultural Background of Personality,* copyright 1945, by Appleton-Century.)

Turning now to Karl we will consider two people as they simultaneously occupy different status positions—namely, Karl himself as an adolescent boy, and Karl's father. We have chosen to analyze his father for two reasons. In the first place, his father's behavior in his various statuses will provide Karl with expectations as to how fathers in general will behave and perhaps even general expectations as to how adult males in superior positions will behave. Secondly, his father's behavior will presumably provide an important source of information on how he himself should behave when he assumes some of the statuses later on that are now active for his father—e.g., when he becomes a father, an adult male, a member of an occupation, etc. The role behaviors which Karl himself displays as an adolescent male will provide a contrast and at the same time may suggest the ease or difficulty with which he will adjust to new status problems when he goes to college or assumes more adult responsibilities.

Table 9.1 provides a rough summary of the various statuses occupied by Karl's father broken down according to Linton's scheme. Under each is listed a limited number of problems associated with that particular status together with a comment from Karl's autobiography indicating how his father characteristically adjusted to those problems.

TABLE 9.1

Role Adjustments Made by Karl's Father

Status classification	*Associated problems*	*Role adjustments*
I. Family or kin	Problems facing a father	
	1. Family support	"My father has always made a living for his family even during the depression."
	2. Nurturance of children	"My parents always took time to read us the funnies and play games with us . . . [they] love all their children."
	3. Control of children	"Our discipline at home was fairly strict."
II. Age-sex	Problems facing an adult male	
	1. Work habits	"My father is very thorough in all that he does . . ."
	2. Outlook on life	". . . but is excitable and constantly worried by everyone's troubles."
	3. Recreation	"His chief diversion is gardening."

TABLE 9.1 (*Continued*)

Status classification	*Associated problems*	*Role adjustments*
III. Occupation	Problems facing a skilled tradesman	
	1. Job fluctuations	"My father is a skilled mechanic. During the depression he worked at everything."
	2. Job adjustment	". . . dislikes his present job to the point where he would like to quit and raise chickens."
IV. Association	Problems facing a Christian	
	1. Belief	"My father says very little though he claims Christianity as his faith."
	2. Church attendance	"Neither parent goes to church."
	3. Ethical dealings with others	"Nevertheless both parents are kind, rather generous, and have done quite a bit of community work in the past."

There are problems associated with various statuses to which the father is not a guide, and which are therefore not adequately represented in this table. From some of these Karl gets guidance from his mother, and for others from people outside the home. There are also problems for which his father's conduct is a guide that have not been included in the table because there is little or no information about them in Karl's autobiography. For example, his father will provide information on how a husband behaves toward a wife. In particular his father's statuses in various association groups have not been considered, in the expectation that his membership in the church is representative, since there is no information on other groups. In one sense the selection represented in Table 9.1 is meaningful rather than arbitrary since it represents the selections spontaneously made by Karl in his autobiography and therefore represents his father as *beta* press (cf. Murray, 1938), or the way in which Karl thinks of him.

Role Performance and Role Perception. There are two general uses to which Karl can put the information contained in Table 9.1. First of all he can use his father's behavior as a guide to solving his own similar status problems, if and when they arise. Secondly, his father's behavior can serve as the basis for his developing ideas of what to expect from men who occupy his father's positions in life. The perception or schema of the father, particularly in this last more generalized form, has given rise to the concept of the *father image* or *imago* which is of very great importance in psychoanalytic thinking. In view of the constant contact of a child with his parents and of his need for guidance in many problems presented by various common social situations, we can scarcely doubt the formation of some kind of generalized parental images and should therefore analyze carefully how they are acquired and what their influence is. We shall treat the problem in its most general form in this chapter and return to it in Chapter 14 when we discuss how certain aspects of these images are incorporated into the self to become part of the super-ego and the ego-ideal.

Role Models

The Parent As a Guide in Role Performance. Returning to the first function of the father image, we can see that many difficulties will arise if Karl attempts to adopt literally his father's behavior as a pattern for his own life. We might make a very rapid summary of the father schema given in Table 9.1 as follows:

> My father is nurturant and strict with respect to those dependent on him, hard-working, adaptable but unhappy in his adjustment to life, and essentially solitary or nonparticipant in various association groups.

As soon as we begin to think of Karl's applying these role traits to his own problems, it is apparent that most of the statuses involved are *latent* as far as he as an adolescent male is concerned. That is, the problems to which his father is adjusting are problems to which he will also adjust someday, but need not now. This is the first difficulty in applying to his own life the information gained from his father's conduct. With respect to family status, for example, there are simply not other people dependent on him as there are on his father, and therefore what he learns about how to behave toward such people will have to be held over until he becomes a father, or until he gets a chance to practice some of these traits on his younger brother or younger playmates.

In the field of age-sex statuses, there are peculiarly difficult problems of adjustment, since the boy is encouraged to copy his father in some ways and not in others. As Flugel points out, "the little boy is allowed, encouraged, and enjoined to copy his father in many respects, in the ordinary habits of cleanliness and hygiene, in courage and patience in the face of pain or disappointment, in control over emotional expression, in innumerable small skills and habits exhibited in daily life . . ." (1945, p. 61.) On the other hand, he may not imitate parental behavior in many instances, particularly according to the psychoanalyst in the sexual sphere, and also in such other matters of privilege as "smoking, swearing, staying up late, entering places of alcoholic refreshment, etc." (1945, p. 62.) As a result it may often seem to the boy that he should imitate his father with regard to some of the more difficult aspects of life without being able to enjoy some of the privileges or pleasures of adulthood. He may have to learn irksome table-manners to copy his father but not be allowed to speak as freely at the table as his father does. Such conflict may be accentuated by the fact that parents often hold a higher standard of conduct for their children than they do for themselves. Many parents are put in the position of teaching "Do as I say, not as I do," or "You ought to be better than I am." This is particularly important in America, as Kluckhohn and Kluckhohn point out (1947), because children are often seen as the chief means of improving the family's position in society. Thus from the child's viewpoint the parents are often in the position of preaching one standard of behavior and practicing another.

This often is particularly true in the field of aggression training. Many fathers (including Karl's) are put in the position of using aggression to suppress aggression, thereby sanctioning the behavior which they are trying to inhibit. The boy may solve the resulting conflict by being aggressive in some situations and not in others. He may learn to show aggression only in self-defense as Mead has suggested (1942), or he may be aggressive not toward superiors but only toward inferiors as his father was toward him.

In the field of preparation for occupational roles, the difficulties in the way of getting much help from the father's behavior are even greater. In nearly all urban occupations the father works outside the home and the son gets little opportunity to observe what he does or to learn from him how to behave under similar circumstances. All that the son usually does get is a general idea of how hard his father works and of what he thinks of his work, as Karl's comments about his father's occupation suggest. This is in sharp contrast to some societies like the Comanche, whose patterns, as Linton points out, "are diametrically opposed to our own in this respect. Comanche childhood is a careful and continuous preparation for full adult status. As soon as the child can walk, he is dressed in miniature replica of adult costume. He is given tasks which are like those of adults but carefully adjusted to his strength. Every device is employed to make him vigorous, individualistic, aggressive and competitive in order that he may become a successful warrior." (1949, p. 169.) The typical American father's guidance for his son, on the other hand, exists chiefly in recreational areas (e.g., gardening in Karl's case), rather than vocational ones. One of the reasons for this state of affairs is the expectation on the part of many Americans, particularly in the class position of Karl's parents, that their sons will have better occupations than their fathers anyway (F. Kluckhohn, 1950).

Finally, a son may have difficulty in applying his father's role behaviors to his own life because he may regard some of his father's traits as desirable and some as undesirable. Thus it is clear that Karl admires the hard-working thoroughness of his father, but does not like the way he worries so much and hopes *not* to follow him in this respect. Thus he states in one place in his autobiography, "I do not resemble either parent in temperament particularly, although I have the tendency to worry about details." This comment suggests what is probably the fact in many cases, namely, that the father will have some direct effect on the son's behavior ("I tend to worry too"), that the son's attitude will also have an influence ("I do not want to worry like my father does"), and that the end result will be a product of both influences ("I do not resemble my father exactly").

After listing the many difficulties in the way of a son's following his father's role adjustments, we may wonder why it is that the father image is supposed to be of such great importance. Must we assume some instinctive mechanism of imitation? Or does the son unconsciously identify with the father as psychoanalysts suggest and therefore follow his behavior no matter how unadaptive it may be? One thing seems clear at any rate. Such mechanisms as imitation and identification need not be considered as automatic or mysterious as has sometimes been assumed. After all, children come in contact with their parents on thousands of occasions during the period when generalized parental schemata are first being formed. In many instances where children do meet the same problems as their parents are meeting (table manners, general attitude toward life), the child may adopt the parents' adjustments simply because it is easier to solve the problem in this way than it is to find a solution through trial and error. Furthermore, such copying behavior often gets rewarded. On the other hand, in those problem situations which we have just been emphasizing, in which the child cannot *immediately* apply what he observes, there nevertheless develops a generalized picture of how other people in such positions behave. We therefore need to distinguish sharply between *role perception* and *role performance.* Actually much of the clinical material on the importance of parent images has referred to perception rather than performance. To put the contrast very simply, "This is the way I am going to behave when I become a father or an adult male" is a less important function of the father image than "This is the way fathers act."

The Parent As a Guide in Role Perception. Psychoanalysts have really had a percept in mind in their use of the "father image" concept. Specifically they have argued that conceptions of and resulting attitudes toward the father generalize rather widely to other persons or "figures" occupying the same or some of the same status positions as the father does. The dimensions of generalization they assume seem to be chiefly these two: to others of the same sex, and to others in similar positions of authority or higher prestige. For example, the conception of the father is conceived as generalizing to all older men or to men in general. The following comment made concerning the Navaho is perhaps typical of how the father comes to represent all men: "Men are always a little undependable. The father is affectionate to the child, but from the very beginning he comes and goes; the child can never really count on his comfort. Man is fickle —but is never thought to be otherwise." (Kluckhohn and Leighton, 1947, p. 138.)

A somewhat similar analysis in the American family might run as follows according to psychoanalytic principles. The father is a competitor and usually a successful one for the mother's love. This competition is particularly accentuated by the small size of the typical American family group. Therefore men in general come to be regarded as dangerous competitors, particularly in the field of love. Furthermore, to follow the Oedipus triangle a little further, this competition will breed jealousy and hatred for the father, followed by guilt arising from love for the father, and the final father image will therefore be composed of both harsh and forbidding aspects and loving and forgiving ones. This image is then transferred to other men and perhaps ultimately even to God and the Devil, who represent, according to Ernest Jones (1944), a decomposition of the father image into its good and bad aspects.

Claims for generalization along the authority dimension have been as sweeping as this and usually have gone along with assertions about transfer to other male figures. Thus, for example, the father as a stern disciplinarian becomes the prototype of *all* authority, in particular the authority of the state (cf. Fromm, 1941b) and the child develops his expectations, perhaps even his needs, for a certain type of government of an authoritarian character out of his original relationship to his father. Gorer (1948) has followed such an approach to the problem. He finds a certain similarity or consistency between political attitudes and attitudes within the family, a consistency which is indicated by the title of his first chapter: "Europe and the Rejected Father." He states, "The making of an American demanded that the father should be rejected both as a model and as a source of authority. Father never knew best." "And once the mutation was established, it was maintained; no matter how many generations separate an American from his immigrant ancestors, he rejects his father as authority and exemplar, and expects his son to reject him." (1948, p. 31.) He regards this attitude as typical of American attitudes toward all sorts of authority: "Authority is inherently bad and dangerous; the survival and growth of the state make it inevitable that some individuals must be endowed with authority; but this authority must be as circumscribed and as limited as legal ingenuity can devise; and the holders of these positions should be under constant scrutiny, should be watched as potential enemies." (1948, p. 32.) The fundamental importance to psychoanalysts of the father figure concept is further illustrated by the way in which neuroses are supposed to be cured in the analytic situation by the creation of a new father figure in the psychoanalyst of whom new and better schemata can be developed.

The same type of generalization is supposed to occur for mother figures. Thus to psychoanalysts like Kardiner the Virgin Mary becomes a projected image of certain portions of the mother role in Western society (1945), to Kluckhohn and Leighton Changing Woman is the image of a Navaho mother "who is either all bad or all good" (1947, p. 138), and to Gorer the Statue of Liberty represents a "most beautiful and resounding promise of maternal solicitude and welcome." (1948, p. 52.) Gorer goes further and argues that since mothers and female schoolteachers are largely responsible for the right behavior of children, "the American conscience . . . is predominantly feminine. . . . Beauty and right conduct become feminine figures." (1948, p. 56.) Examples such as these can be multiplied many times. They all proceed from the assumption that conceptions and attitudes developed in connection with the parents generalize widely to all areas of life.

Karl's Parent Images. What evidence is there that such generalization actually does occur? Let us turn once again to Karl and try to discover some general principles in the study of the extent to which his parental images have generalized. Table 9.1 has already given us some evidence from his autobiography of his conscious picture of his father. As it happens, a more systematic description of his father is available in a number of ratings of various traits which Karl made, and which are reproduced in Table 9.2, along with similar ratings for his mother.

TABLE 9.2

Karl's Ratings of His Parents

Rate your parents for the following: (1 is low, 6 is high)

	Father						*Mother*					
a. strict	1	2	3	(4)	5	6	1	2	(3)	4	5	6
b. helpful	1	2	3	(4)	5	6	1	2	(3)	4	5	6
c. domineering	1	2	(3)	4	5	6	1	2	(3)	4	5	6
d. friendly	1	2	3	(4)	5	6	1	2	(3)	4	5	6
e. selfish	1	(2)	3	4	5	6	1	2	3	(4)	5	6
f. self-confident	1	2	(3)	4	5	6	(1)	2	3	4	5	6

The interesting thing to note about this table is that the mother is viewed less favorably than the father. She is rated as less strict, but also as less helpful, less friendly, and as more selfish than the father. Neither parent is given very high marks on any of the favorable qualities, and both appear low in self-confidence, as we would expect from the autobiography. The following description of his mother is relevant here;

My mother is an industrious but worrisome woman, always concerned about details. During the depression she took in washing. She suffers from deafness, has been deaf for the past five or six years. We obtained a hearing aid for her, but she refuses to wear it. She also suffers from arthritis and sinusitis. . . .

These then are the conscious parent images with which we may start. What evidence is there from other sources that these pictures have generalized? First of all, with respect to the autobiography itself Karl has little to say about his conception of men in general, although he does say that "the social world . . . consists of a lot of selfish, grasping individuals." The information about women is more explicit. "I have dreamed intensely about living a life with an ideal mate. Nothing is so satisfying as to cast one's self into a dream world, wherein you and the woman you love are together high on a windy hill, looking out upon the world. Just to hold the woman of your choice in your arms and lavish your love upon her seems to be a source of greatest delight."

Father and Mother Figures in Imagination. This idealized picture of woman is found again and again in Karl's Thematic Apperception Test (TAT) stories also. In several of the stories a woman is portrayed as a simple, loving, innocent, and trusting person who is always better than the man who tries to trick her, especially if she stays innocent and trusting. In his last story he says again explicitly, "He will lead a blighted existence, but were he, as I said before, to love the right girl and marry her, the future would be a bright one indeed . . . the key to the lock is the girl he loves." So far this does not seem very consistent with the picture of his mother as a worrisome, not very friendly woman. The female image is inconsistent.

Perhaps the difference lies in the fact that these references are to a future love relationship rather than to a mother-son role relationship as described in his TAT. An analysis of the actions of a mother in Karl's stories toward her son, according to the method described by Bales (1950) and Mills (1950), reveals that she shows five actions indicating solidarity and only two indicating antagonism or a negative relationship. The son shows five positive actions toward mother figures in the stories and seven negative ones. These data, scanty as they are, suggest a relationship of mutual solidarity between mother and son. In six protocols printed by Murray (1949), no other subject perceived the mother-son relationship in this way. Most of them showed either a preponderance of negative reactions from the mother or from the son. This seems to be a fairly accurate reflection of Karl's statement that "My parents love all their children; that love is reciprocal." The same reciprocal-love relationship appears in his TAT stories for the relationship between the male heroes and their loved ones. If the "son-mother" and "son-love object" relationships are pooled, sixteen out of twenty or 80 per cent of the reactions from the mother or lover to the son are positive whereas only 40 per cent of such reactions are positive in the normative group of six subjects. Similarly fifteen out of thirty or 50 per cent of the actions of the son toward either the mother or love object are positive as compared with only 29 per cent for the normative group. In short, as far as the generalized picture obtained in imaginative stories is concerned, Karl pictures a much higher mutual-love relationship than is normal and than we would expect from his picture of his mother in Table 9.2. We might be tempted to argue that the imaginative or perceived picture is *complementary* to the one he had in real life.

What about the men? Generally speaking, in the TAT they are bad actors, commonly deceiving women or failing to live up to their parent's expectations. The inadequacy notion, which is represented in several different stories, may reflect accurately his father's own feeling of inadequacy as described in the autobiography and also in the rating of the father. Furthermore, the father-son relationship whenever it appeared in the TAT indicates predominantly a negative relationship of the son toward the father (seven out of twelve actions between father and son are negative acts from son to father). So far as the normative cases are concerned, this rebellious attitude appears to be the usual way in which the son-father relationship is pictured in the TAT. Perhaps the only other point worth noting is that the father is usually dead in the TAT stories, possibly indicating either the hostility of the son or the unimportance of the father figure in Karl's thinking. All this evidence, inadequate though it is, appears to add up to the conclusion that the generalized father picture obtained from his imaginative stories is fairly congruent with Karl's conception of and attitude toward his own father.

This somewhat limited case analysis suggests that, while a set of generalized expectations about fathers and mothers or parent-child relationships probably do develop, much as the psychoanalysts claim, they almost certainly do not derive *in any simple fashion* from the actual characteristics of the parents or the child's relationship to the parents. In this instance the father or male image appears to come directly from Karl's own experience with his father whereas the mother or female image does not. There are many influences which enter into the formation of such generalized conceptions. Social norms and individual motivations are almost certainly of equal importance to direct personal experience. Thus in the case of Karl's idealized conception of women, he has probably drawn on the romantic love notion prevalent in our culture and also on a strong motivational need for security arising from a felt lack of love and support from his own mother. These other sources of role conceptions will be discussed more fully later.

An important source of confusion has arisen from assuming that transfer goes only in one direction, i.e., from assuming that the father-son relationship, for instance, since it occurs first, is the *cause* of later perceived or imagined characteristics of authority figures. It seems to be almost equally likely that subsequent experiences with authority figures modify the conception of the father. The "father figure" idea may serve as a convenient symbol or schema not only for the psychoanalyst but also for the person being analyzed in representing and integrating his ideas, gathered at many different times in his life, as to what to expect from a person in superior status. In a sense then the term "father figure" is inaccurate since it gives a primacy to the father-son relationship which it probably does not have. Some term like "authority figure" would be more appropriate. This might make it clearer that when someone like Gorer speaks of a "father figure" he means a convenient symbol or schema which derives its characteristics from many sources, of which the actual father is only one, and which is labeled "father," perhaps even by the person with the schema, only because it makes communication easier.

Even this, however, leaves essentially unexplored the problem of how *general* in a person's life the influence of such figures or images really is. Experimentation in this field is greatly needed. As a simple illustration of the kind of study of the generality of such "images" which might be made, Rhodes (1948) attempted to correlate the father conceptions of a group of college students with their conceptions of God, since a correlation of this sort is supposed to exist according to some psychoanalytic theorists (cf. Ernest Jones. 1944). Rhodes found that parallels existed but were exceedingly difficult to establish. On the whole, psychoanalysts might have been checked somewhat in their enthusiastic claims for such wide generalization if they had made use of the principles of transfer and generalization available in learning research. It seems likely that progress in the field will be slow until experiments are designed which take into account these principles.

Age Mates As Role Models: Adolescent Statuses and Roles. As another point of reference in analyzing the variety of social problems a person faces during his lifetime, let us now turn from Karl's parents as role models to the status problems he faces as an adolescent, to the role adjustments to them sanctioned by his age mates, and to an analysis of the extent to which he followed the sanctioned patterns of behavior. Table 9.3 is parallel to Table 9.1 and is designed to show Karl's own role adjustments to the problems facing him in high school.

TABLE 9.3

Role Adjustments Made by Karl As an Adolescent Male

Status classification	*Associated problems*	*Role adjustments*
I. Family or kin	Problems facing a son	
	1. Parents	"We grew up to acquire a name in town as being "well raised, well mannered boys."
	2. Siblings	"I feel inferior to my older brother but superior to my younger. . . . I get along all right with my brothers. We fought when we were kids. The war tightened the bonds."
II. Age-sex	Problems facing a male adolescent	
	1. Like-sex associates	"I played the normal games of youth. Always had friends to play with . . . I was very gregarious."
	2. Opposite-sex associates	"I was always bashful around girls and was kidded a lot about it."
	3. Adults	"I was always cooperative and obedient, got along all right with the teachers."
	4. Recreation	"For amusement I played sports, went to the movie shows, etc., but not as much as the average. I was sometimes more content to sit at home and read."

TABLE 9.3 (*Continued*)

Status classification	*Associated problems*	*Role adjustments*
III. Occupation	Problems of preparing for occupational status	
	1. School work	"I was very anxious to get ahead in the world. My marks were excellent. I was at the head of the class. I always did my work conscientiously and thoroughly and never wasted a minute."
	2. Odd jobs	He worked on a farm and sold magazines.
IV. Association	Problems of voluntary group membership	
	1. Church	"I always went to Sunday School, kept myself pure and led a fairly model life."
	2. Cliques and school organizations	"I worked well with all groups." "In High School, I was in . . . many activities, president of the class for four years, on the football team, All-State guard, editor of the school paper."

Although it is difficult to get an accurate picture of what normal behavior is for Karl's group, there is every indication in this table that Karl was largely a conformist rather than a deviant in his role adjustments. In other words he adjusted easily and successfully to the adolescent "sub-culture." Parsons (1949) has made an attempt to define the major characteristics of normal adjustment to adolescence. He argues that an adolescent male in our culture will be expected to have a good time and be irresponsible since he does not have adult status, that athletics and all-around attractiveness or being a "swell guy" will be conceived as the dominant roads to achievement, and that rebelliousness against authority is also typical. Of these characteristics Karl shows the ones which would define him as a success in the adolescent sub-culture. That is, he has been president of his class, has many friends, and is an outstanding football player. In his own words, "My high school days were very happy and gratifying ones." On the other hand, he does not show the irresponsibility or rebelliousness one would "normally" expect, according to Parsons (1949). In fact, he repeatedly emphasizes his cooperativeness and obedience and mentions only one episode in which he was "pinched for stealing corn in daylight on a Halloween day." But even here he mentions that, "There was a whole crowd of us" and "I was scared." In short, from the adult viewpoint (as represented by the very high recommendation for college given him by his high-school principal) he was a "model boy," even though sociologists might not regard him as typical.

Social Class Roles. Sociologists have seldom been content to follow the molecular type of status analysis so far made in this chapter. Generally speaking they have preferred to deal with higher order role clusters associated with such larger units of social classification as rural-urban, or caste and class. That is, certain problems of social adjustment seem to come in groups or clusters associated with some larger category such as living in the country, being a Negro, or being middle-class as compared with lower-class. One very active group of sociologists in particular has studied the roles associated with different parts of the class system. Thus Davis and Dollard (1940) emphasize the importance of social class training in organizing the child's social world. "The times and places for his recreation, the chores required of him by his family, the rooms and articles in the house which he may use, the wearing of certain clothes at certain times, the amount of studying required of him, the economic controls to which he is subjected by his parents, indeed his very conceptions of right and wrong, all vary according to the social class of the child in question." (Sherif and Cantril, 1947, p. 195.)

Hollingshead (1949) has reported in detail how adolescent behavior may be associated with class position. In a study of high-school-age students in a small middle-western town, he has been able to show that such behavior as attendance at athletic events, high school dances, plays and parties, etc., is a function of position in the social class hierarchy. Students from the upper classes (I and II) attended more frequently than those from the lower classes (IV and V). He also showed that children from families which were perceived as belonging in a certain class (as determined by the ratings of informants) tended to associate with children of families in the same class. They chose their best friends and dates predominantly within the class group. Typical other findings were that regular church attendance was more common in Class III than in any other class and that the percentage of children participating in such diverse organizations as the Boy Scouts or the high school decreased markedly from Class I to Class V. On the basis of such data Hollingshead concludes "that children in the same class, living in the same neighborhood, learn similar definitions of acceptable and unacceptable behavior relative to the family, the job, property, money, school, the government, men, women, sex, recreation." (1949, p. 442.) In short, the family and neighborhood sub-cultures in which a child is brought up "provide him with roles and teach him how to play them." (1949, p. 445.) This is just a sample of many similar studies (cf. Davis and Havighurst, 1947; Centers, 1947; Ericson, 1947) which have shown that attitudes, activities, child-training practices and the like are associated with status in the class hierarchy. From the systematic viewpoint being developed here, class status is a higher order concept integrating under a hierarchical position in the social structure certain common problems from family, occupation, or association group status categories. In a sense one may speak of a class "role" as referring to an integrated pattern of role behaviors, associated with the status problems that go to make up a particular class position.

Acquisition of Roles

Sources of Information About Role Behavior. (1) *Adults.* In our earlier discussion of the influence of parents on the role adjustments their children make, we came to the conclusion that parental influence has tended to be exaggerated by psychoanalysts and that there were probably other important sources of guidance for the growing child. Parents *are* important, particularly in providing information as to what to expect from people occupying a particular set of statuses, but for every child there are other exemplars outside the home. These may be schoolteachers, other relatives, friends of the family, or even movie stars. Karl says, for instance, "I looked up to my football coach to an extent, but not too greatly." (2) *Age mates.* Even more important is the guidance provided by the behavior of age mates, especially for role performances. As we have seen, many adult role behaviors are temporarily inapplicable to an adolescent's status problems and therefore the behavior of other adolescents assumes a much greater importance in aiding his contemporary role adjustments. Hollingshead (1949) describes vividly how the behavior of individuals is kept in line by [illegible] mates. He cites the case of a girl who accepted a date for a [illegible] dance with a Class IV boy and subsequently had other [illegible] with him. This behavior was so disapproved that she was "i[illegible] house" with her clique mates and acceptable boys. She r[illegible] and commented upon it as follows:

> You see I'm in the G.W.G.'s, bu[illegible] around with the G.W.G.'s all the time. I'm kind of in betw[illegible] G.W.G.'s and the other kids. I was out of the G.W.G.'s for a whi[le] because they made me mad. They drew the social line too fine. I dated .. they didn't like. We went to the dance and they just ignored me. I just couldn't stand that. It hurt me, so I pulled out of there; but now I've more or less started to go back with them. (1949, p. 235.)

As a result of many such observ[ations] as these, Hollingshead concludes, "The effective definitio[n th]at he follows appears to be more closely related to the definiti[on] other children place upon the situation, at least what he thin[k]s others think, than it is to definitions his parents, teachers, mi[nist]er, police, and other adults place upon it." (1949, p. 446.) In oth[er] words, "traits exhibited by adolescents tend to be along lines ap[pro]ved by the clique mates, who also tend to be members of the sam[e cl]ass." (1949, p. 446.)

(3) *Reading* is also an important source of guidance for role behavior. For instance, Karl stat[es th]at in grammar school his "heroes were the French Foreign Legi[on] [illegible] favourite knight. I used to ima[g]ine [illegible] and being the hero that [illegible] knights [illegible] he says, "[A]lways liked [illegible] [co]wboy heroes of the Westerns, Tarzan, and oth[er] [illegible] the Satu[rday] [illegible]." The exact influence of this type of rea[ding is n]ot kn[own, alt]hough it should certainly bear on the kind [illegible] he [illegible] will attempt to display and which he [illegible] to ev[illegible] other co[illegible]. An illuminating study of sex ty[illegible] [illegible] in pu[blic sch]ools has been made by Child. [illegible]). Th[illegible] that there were marked dif[ferences] [illegible] and [illegible] stories read by public-school [illegible] characters, for example, are [illegible] [illegible]ing affiliation, nurturance, and [illegible], females are less frequent rela[illegible] activity, aggression, achievement. [illegible] girls and women are thus being [illegible]

tionship, the brave Hansel and the dependent, crying Gretel, occurs fairly frequently in the stories read by children in our own culture. It is hard to imagine how this could fail to have an influence on the conception girls and boys develop of each other and of how they should behave toward one another and in problem situations. Such stories have the social function of myths and folk tales in preliterate cultures in defining role patterns approved by the society. As we concluded in an earlier connection, Karl probably got his idealized conception of women from such sources, rather than from any realistic relationship that he had with any particular woman.

(4) Finally, *explicit social norms* or codes of behavior represent more direct attempts to influence role behavior. The Ten Commandments or the Boy Scout code could be taken as illustrative of these. Since Hartshorne and May demonstrated some years ago (1928) that moral knowledge and moral behavior were uncorrelated, [illegible] been customary to belittle the importance of such explicit [illegible] This is a mistake. Even though there is no one-to-one relationship between a norm for conduct (e.g., honesty), and actual conduct (honest behavior), knowledge of how one ought to act is *one* of the determinants of actual behavior [illegible] of *feelings* about behavior. In recent years some evidence has accumulated to show that these explicit codes affect mostly what a person "thinks others think," and "what others think" is an important determinant of behavior, even though it may not produce behavior in direct conformity with what others think. For example, during World War II Crespi (1945) [illegible] groups of people rate their own attitude toward [illegible] objectors and then estimate what the attitude of [illegible] conscientious objectors was. In every group the "own" attitude was more lenient than the attitude attributed to others. Even though individuals privately had a different attitude from the one they attributed to others, it seems reasonable to conclude that, were they to react to a conscientious objector in the presence of other people whose attitudes were unknown, they would be influenced in what they said and did by their stereotyped conceptions of what the others were thinking. This kind of mechanism is responsible for many of the statements by restaurant owners and hotel men that "I personally have no objection to Negroes, but I would lose my clientele if I let them in." In a similar fashion the presence of an older person will often inhibit free and easy communications between adolescents not because he does disapprove of what they are [illegible]

of individuals is kept in line by clique mates. He cites the case of a girl who accepted a date for a high school dance with a Class IV boy and subsequently had other dates with him. This behavior was so disapproved that she was "in the dog house" with her clique mates and acceptable boys. She realized this and commented upon it as follows:

> You see I'm in the G.W.G.'s, but I don't run around with the G.W.G.'s all the time. I'm kind of in between the G.W.G.'s and the other kids. I was out of the G.W.G.'s for a while because they made me mad. They drew the social line too fine. I dated a boy they didn't like. We went to the dance and they just ignored me. I just couldn't stand that. It hurt me, so I pulled out of there; but now I've more or less started to go back with them. (1949, p. 235.)

As a result of many such observations as these, Hollingshead concludes, "The effective definition that he follows appears to be more closely related to the definitions other children place upon the situation, at least what he thinks others think, than it is to definitions his parents, teachers, minister, police, and other adults place upon it." (1949, p. 446.) In other words, "traits exhibited by adolescents tend to be along lines approved by the clique mates, who also tend to be members of the same class." (1949, p. 446.)

(3) *Reading* is also an important source of guidance for role behavior. For instance, Karl states that in grammar school his "heroes were the French Foreign Legion and knights of old. Roland was my favourite knight. I used to imagine myself as living in those days and being the hero that the knights were." Later on in high school, he says, "I always liked the cowboy heroes of the Westerns, Tarzan, and others in the Saturday serials." The exact influence of this type of reading is not known, although it should certainly bear on the kind of behavior which a child will attempt to display and which he will come to expect of other people. An illuminating study of sex typing in the readers used in public schools has been made by Child, Potter, and Levine (1946). They found that there were marked differences in the way boys and girls in the stories read by public-school children were characterized. "Female characters, for example, are more frequent among those displaying affiliation, nurturance, and harmavoidance. On the other hand, females are less frequent relatively among characters displaying activity, aggression, achievement, construction and recognition. Girls and women are thus being shown as sociable, kind and timid, but inactive, unambitious, and uncreative." (1946, p. 47.) It seems that the Hansel and Gretel rela-

tionship, the brave Hansel and the dependent, crying Gretel, occurs fairly frequently in the stories read by children in our own culture. It is hard to imagine how this could fail to have an influence on the conception girls and boys develop of each other and of how they should behave toward one another, and in problem situations. Such stories have the social function of myths and folk tales in preliterate cultures in defining role patterns approved by the society. As we concluded in an earlier connection, Karl probably got his idealized conception of women from such sources, rather than from any realistic relationship that he had with any particular woman.

(4) Finally, *explicit social norms* or codes of behavior represent more direct attempts to influence role behavior. The Ten Commandments or the Boy Scout code could be taken as illustrative of these. Since Hartshorne and May demonstrated some years ago (1928) that moral knowledge and moral behavior were uncorrelated, it has been customary to belittle the importance of such explicit codes. This is a mistake. Even though there is no one-to-one relationship between a norm for conduct (e.g., honesty), and actual conduct (honest behavior), knowledge of how one ought to act is *one* of the determinants of actual behavior or of *feelings* about behavior. In recent years some evidence has accumulated to show that these explicit codes affect mostly what a person "thinks others think," and "what others think" is an important determinant of behavior, even though it may not produce behavior in direct conformity with what others think. For example, during World War II Crespi (1945) asked various groups of people to rate their own attitude toward conscientious objectors and then to estimate what the attitude of others toward conscientious objectors was. In every group the "own" attitude was more lenient than the attitude attributed to others. Even though individuals privately had a different attitude from the one they attributed to others, it seems reasonable to conclude that, were they to react to a conscientious objector in the presence of other people whose attitudes were unknown, they would be influenced in what they said and did by their stereotyped conceptions of what the others were thinking. This kind of mechanism is responsible for many of the statements by restaurant owners and hotel men that "I personally have no objection to Negroes, but I would lose my clientele if I let them in." In a similar fashion the presence of an older person will often inhibit free and easy communications between adolescents not because he does disapprove of what they are saying but because they think he would. In all these instances an

expectancy about the behavior or attitudes of others influences the adjustments to social situations. And such expectancies are often derived from explicit formalized codes about what behavior is correct or ideal.

Role Adjustment. Repeatedly throughout this chapter we have insisted on a distinction between role perception and role performance. The distinction is necessary because the two are not perfectly correlated. Knowledge of a role and performance of it are two different things. But what are the variables which influence whether or not a person performs a given role? Cottrell (1942) has provided us with an excellent discussion of these factors which we will condense and rearrange somewhat under four new headings.

1. Clarity of Cultural Definition of the Role. Sometimes roles are not very well defined, either by the culture or by the particular member of the culture under consideration. College students were less able to agree on what characteristics to expect from a Chinese than from a German or a Negro. What appears to be involved in a role definition is a series of responses more or less frequently associated with a certain status by a group of people. The responses constitute a kind of habit family hierarchy (cf. Hull, 1943) in which some traits are agreed upon more often by the group than others. An example will probably make this clearer. Suppose we ask a group of male students to answer the Strong Vocational Interest test *as they think women would.* To assume a set like this is relatively easy, as Strong showed (1943) in demonstrating that a group of students could obtain very high scores on the Engineering scale of his test if they pretended they were engineers in filling out the blank. In answering the questionnaire as a woman would, a very large percentage of male students will state that women like to decorate a room with flowers (item 194) and that they dislike operating machinery (item 190). These are sex-typed responses, at least from the male viewpoint, and they have no *necessary* connection with the way women will actually answer these two items. Men *perceive* these responses as belonging in the feminine role. But for another item such as "meeting new situations" there will be little agreement among the men as to what women will like or dislike. In other words, such an item is *not* clearly defined as part of the feminine role. Whether they like it or not most women will also be aware of what the sex-typed responses are. That is, they will know that there are certain things which are expected of them and certain others about which expectations are confused or differ. The point is that adequate role performance will be more likely to occur for those responses on which there is agreement and less likely to occur on those responses on which there is disagreement. In short, a person cannot perform a role unless he knows what it is. Knowing what it is will in turn depend on the agreement among the members of society on what responses define it and on the extent to which an individual has come in contact with the socially agreed-upon definition.

2. Conflicting Role Patterns. Adequate role performance is less likely to occur if there are conflicts as to what the appropriate role is. Such conflict may arise from many different sources. For example, a person may occupy two statuses simultaneously that require different behaviors. Linton (1949) is fond of citing the case of the Scotchman who, having killed a man, went to the dead man's brother to claim his protection as a host. The host then had a severe role conflict. As a brother he had to avenge his kinsman, but as a host he could not do so while the man was his guest. He solved the conflict by leading the murderer out of his territory and then killing him. Such conflicts are very numerous. Karl describes a very common one in one of his TAT stories in which a man is caught between duty to his mother and duty to his wife. In the story a prosecuting attorney is faced with the problem of prosecuting his own brother-in-law. His wife urges him to let her brother go free, while his mother wants him to live up to her ideals and those of his profession. He compromises and lets his brother-in-law off easily but is tortured by qualms of conscience thereafter. As Linton points out, such conflicts are not so frequent as they might be because statuses are occupied successively rather than simultaneously, but when two statuses become active at the same moment, conflicting obligations are apt to lead to serious trouble, and an inability to perform either role adequately. The modes of reaction to such conflicts (blocking, suppression of one response pattern, compromise) are the same as in any instance of competition of responses (cf. Hovland and Sears, 1938).

Other conflicts arise from conflicting sources of information as to how to behave. A boy may have two different exemplars who behave differently in a certain situation. For instance, Karl's father worries a good deal. Tarzan does not. A boy may strive to behave confidently as Tarzan does, but come closer to behaving the way his father does. Another source of conflict, already mentioned, arises from the pressure to copy certain aspects of an exemplar's behavior (e.g., the father) and not others. Thus a boy like Karl may learn to behave like his father as far as acting decisively and responsibly is concerned but he must not carry this trait into the family councils where his father has the sole determining voice. Still other conflicts arise between explicit codes and implicit expectancies. Thus Karl was expected not to steal, but a gang that he went with, at least on one occasion, demanded and obtained this behavior from him. The "do as I say and not as I do" attitude of many parents often results in conflicts of this sort. Finally, different sorts of conceptions of a particular role pattern may arise at different periods in development. A father image, for instance, may be quite different in early childhood from what it is later on and a child's role perception or performance may reflect the confusion in the two images. These are only samples of the types of conflict that can occur. There are obviously many others. The important point is simply that adequate role performance is possible only when the sources of information about role performance do not conflict.

3. Motivational Factors. The relation of a role to the motivational structure of the individual is of very great importance in determining whether or not he performs the role. As Cottrell puts it, "The degree of adjustment to the roles of specified age-sex categories varies directly with the extent to which the role permits the individual to realize the dominant goals set by his sub-cultural group." (1942.) In short, if the role becomes a means to satisfying individual needs it will be performed, whereas if it leads to heightened deprivation or frustration it will tend not to be performed unless it leads on to some other role which "promises the desired gratifications." Some roles may lead to temporary frustrations, of course. An embarrassed novice at psychodrama may be very much disturbed at having to play the role of an irate authoritarian father, but presumably his performance of the role will lead to subsequent satisfactions in the form of approval from the therapist or his friends or from himself for having gone through such an unpleasant ordeal. What is true of a temporary artificial role-playing situation like psychodrama is also true of life situations in which a person's role performances are part of his major adjustments to life. A schoolteacher may not like the traits which she apparently has to acquire

and exhibit in order to do a job successfully, but to the extent that they are reinforced by community sanctions and success at her job they tend to become part of her normal role adjustment to life.

4. **Transition Factors.** A person must perform different roles at different periods in his life. This means that one set of traits or habits must be given up or partially given up for a new set, a transition which usually takes place gradually. All of the factors which learning theorists have shown to produce negative transfer should inhibit the transition from one role to the next. Typical of such factors would be (a) the habit strength of the original role pattern and (b) the difficulty of discrimination between the old and the new patterns. As an example of the former factor there is the case of the college student who has been extremely successful in giving the approved role performance in the "youth culture" by achieving on the football field, being elected to offices, being popular with the coeds, etc., but who, because of the strength of these earlier habits, has difficulty in adjusting to the requirements of adult statuses. The second difficulty arises when the difference between the old and the new roles is subtle. Thus a professor who has been elevated to the presidency of a college may continue for awhile to maintain his old familiar social relations with his friends, until he learns that the requirements of his office do not permit this behavior, partly because other members of the faculty will think that he is playing favorites. He may think that his new situation does not or should not change his role relations with fellow faculty members, and superficially this seems to be so, but in time a gradual role adjustment will take place, and a new type of relationship to his old friends will develop. Karl may have difficulty in transferring from high school to college. He has been so successful in high school that one might expect him to transfer many of his successful role performances to the college situation on the grounds that its requirements are very similar. Yet they are not identical. Chief among the differences is the important fact that he will be away from home, and such a difference will in time promote new adjustments.

Very few careful analyses exist of the way in which role performances are expected to change with changes in status. Simmons (1942), however, has attempted to show how aggression patterns vary with age and prestige status in Hopi society. Figure 9.1 is reproduced from his book as an example of the kind of careful analysis that might be made.

FIGURE 9.1

Hopi Aggression Expressed in Violence

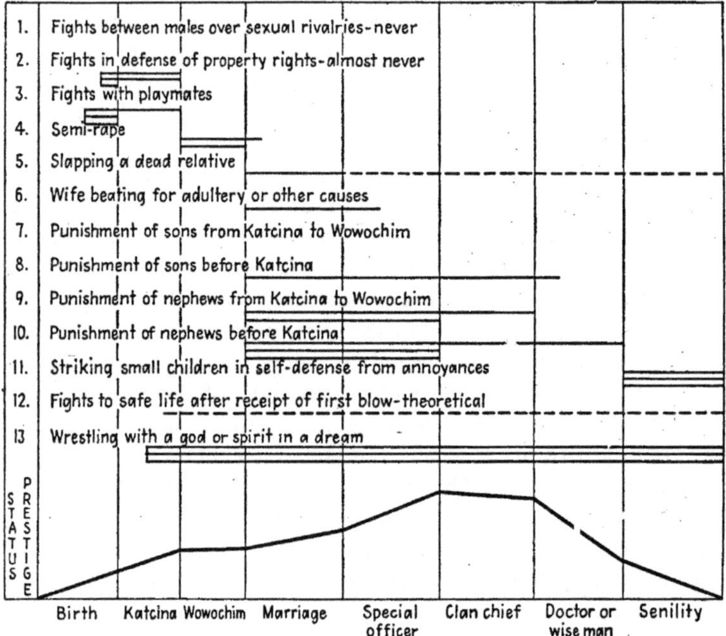

(Reproduced by permission from L. Simmons, *Sun Chief*. Copyright 1942 by Yale University Press.)

This chart lists the types of violence which are prohibited and the positions in life when they are permitted. A dotted line under an item in the list indicates the time of life when that particular type of violence is theoretically permissible and occasionally occurs. For example, in number 12, anyone is theoretically permitted to fight in order to save his life after the first blow has been passed, but such behavior almost never occurs. A single heavy line under an item indicates that this form of violence does occur but is not very common, as illustrated in number 6, "Wife beating for adultery." Two heavy lines under an item indicate that for that period of life the form of violence which is listed is regarded as normal. Three heavy lines under an item indicate that it is more or less expected behavior. (Simmons, 1942, p. 406.)

To rephrase Simmons' findings in terms of age roles it is clear that a young adult married man is expected to punish his nephews before Katcina but never afterwards; he may beat his wife for adultery but never fight with another male over a sexual rivalry, etc. For an older male the permitted aggression drops out, including punishment of nephews, until practically the only kind left is wrestling with a god or spirit in a dream which is expected at all ages from the time the child is old enough to understand the behavior pattern.

The point is that the transition from one of these patterns to another is not an automatic affair. Thus little boys are supposed to give up fighting with playmates after the Katcina ceremony, but the single line demonstrates that they do not always do so. Not all transitions involve giving up a formerly sanctioned role pattern. In some cases the individual has to display behavior formerly disapproved. Thus the Hopi adult is expected to punish his nephews after he gets married and thus to display aggression toward others which up to this time has been inappropriate. Fathers in our own society may have some of the same difficulty in learning to display the appropriate forms of aggression to control their children. Before marriage almost no form of aggression is approved; afterward, punishment of children is often required.

Measuring the Results of Learning About Roles. Since the social role concept has been developed chiefly by sociologists who are interested in role from the viewpoint of its function in the social system rather than in an individual's conceptions of various roles, not too much attention has been given to the problems we have been concerned with in this chapter. From the standpoint of personality theory, we need to know the answers to such questions as the following: What are the important social roles which we ought to include in the conceptualization of a given individual? How are those roles defined? How does our individual *perceive* and *perform* those roles? Adequate answers to these questions will probably depend on better measuring instruments than have so far been widely used.

The typical approach to the definition of a particular social role has been to interview members of a culture about it or to infer what its components should be from the requirements of the social problem situation. Thus in our example, taken from Waller (1932), of the schoolteacher role, information was gathered from both of these sources, both from observations and interviews with teachers, and from inferences as to the kind of behavior they had to show in order to meet the problems arising in a classroom situation. Most role definitions have been the product of shrewd observations and analysis rather than careful measurement. Typical of this "clinical" approach to social role analysis at its best is a recent study of the roles of husbands and wives in a Mexican village (Lewis, 1949). The author points out that the husband ideally is considered the head of the family and master of the household. He is supposed to receive obedience, respect, and service from others and to give in return support and control of a social behavior. The wife in turn is supposed to be industrious and frugal, submissive, faithful and respectful to her husband as well as uncritical, incurious, and not jealous of what he does. The data for such a conclusion were empirical, gathered on the basis of very extensive observation and interviewing, and one will have confidence in the conclusion in the same degree as one would have confidence in the personality analysis made by a clinical psychologist on the basis of thorough empirical but non-quantitative observations. How can such observations be made more quantitative?

1. Role questionnaires. The first improvement in technique involves the use of a questionnaire in which the person is asked what behavior is appropriate for a person occupying a particular status. For example, Stouffer (1949) discovered in this way the role pattern defined for a proctor on a final examination. He asked a group of students who answered his questionnaire to imagine themselves in the following situation:

> Imagine that you are proctoring an examination in a middle-group course. About half-way through the exam you see a fellow student openly cheating. The student is copying the answer from previously prepared notes. When he sees that you have seen the notes as you walk down the aisle and stopped near his seat, he whispers quietly to you, "O.K., I'm caught. That's all there is to it." *You do not know the student.* What would you as proctor do:

A. Take away his notes and exam book, dismiss him, report him for cheating.
B. Take away his notes, let him finish the exam, but report him for cheating.
C. If he can be led to withdraw from the exam on some excuse, do not report him for cheating; otherwise report him.
D. Take away his notes, but let him finish the exam, do not report him for cheating.
E. Act as if nothing had happened and do not report him for cheating.

These are only part of the instructions but they illustrate the form of the questionnaire and Figure 9.2 summarizes some of the main results he obtained with it.

FIGURE 9.2

Percentage Saying that a Specific Action As Proctor Would Be Approved by Authorities and by Fellow Students, Respectively

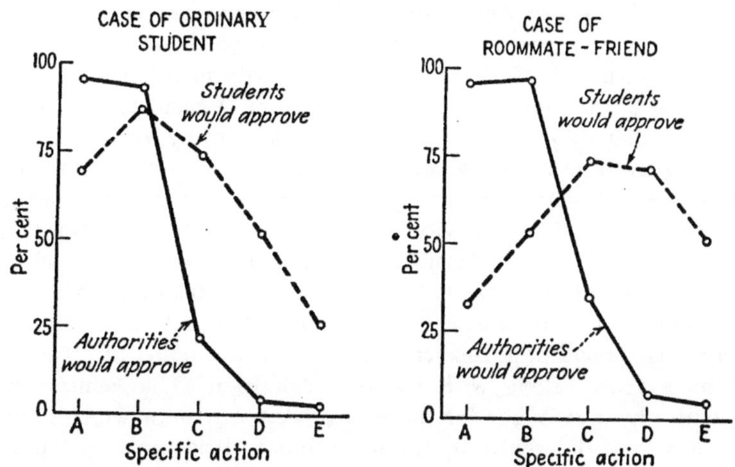

(Reproduced by permission from S. A. Stouffer, An Analysis of Conflicting Social Norms. *Amer. Sociol. Rev.*, 1949, 14, 707-717.)

This figure shows the percentage of students who thought that different specific types of action would be approved by authorities or fellow students both in the case of a student they did not know and of a student who was a roommate-friend. It is clear from the two graphs that the proctor's role was fairly well defined and included the action in any case of not permitting the student to finish the examination and in most cases to report him for cheating. Stouffer goes on to show that what the students actually said they would do (role performance) is a function of what they thought other students would approve of and of their relationship to the imaginary cheater. In terms of our earlier discussion of what leads to role performance, we may note in passing that there are conflicting roles here: one based on the occupational status of being a proctor, another on age-sex status, and still another on an association status (friendship).

A questionnaire such as this is most applicable to fairly specific and well-defined roles in which the relevant actions are known ahead of time and can be phrased in multiple-choice form. In many cases, however, the chief problem may be to determine what actions are judged by a culture to be relevant to a particular status, or are included by the culture in a particular role definition. A modified approach to the questionnaire may be adopted for this purpose. Individuals may be asked to assume that they occupy a certain status or are playing a particular type of role and to answer a questionnaire in terms of this "set." We have already mentioned the "assumed sex" questionnaire in which a group of men, for example, imagine that they are women filling out the Strong Vocational Interest Test. The results of such an analysis show which items are sex-typed and which are not. These responses may then be used to define the classes of behavior which are *perceived* as relevant to being a female (cf. also Fernberger, 1948). Once again it should be pointed out that the results bear no one-to-one relationship to the way women actually answer the test, since their role performance, even their *modal* performance as a group, is a product of other influences acting along with the role definition. The Femininity-Masculinity answer key for the Strong Test will show which items are answered differently by the sexes, but will not provide a pure measure of what is perceived as constituting the female role. In a similar manner individuals may be asked to assume any particular role set and respond to various situations in terms of it. For instance, one experimenter (Orne, 1949) has regressed students under hypnosis to six years of age and asked them to take a Rorschach Test. He found that while there was occasionally fair agreement among students as to what behavior six-year-olds would display on a Rorschach Test (e.g., poor form responses), these agreed-upon responses were not the ones that six-year-old children actually did give to the test. Once again role perception (the college student's view of a child's behavior) differs from role performance (the child's actual behavior). For the moment we are interested in the former.

2. Role apperception tests. An outgrowth of the multiple-choice role questionnaire is the open-ended role questionnaire, in which the role is suggested in the first part of a sentence and the remainder of the sentence is left for the subject to fill out. For example, "Her mother is . . ." or "Her father is. . . ." The spontaneous completions of such sentences as these will give the range of behaviors appropriate to mother or father status, particularly if contrasted with sentences beginning "He is . . ." or "She is . . ." or "She. . . ." A more elaborate approach to the same problem involves the use of the TAT, which contains a number of pictures suggestive of differ-

ent role relations. For instance, card 6BM shows an elderly woman in the background and a young man in the foreground who are usually taken to be mother and son. An analysis of a number of stories told about this picture reveals that in a male college student population the son's behavior toward the mother includes the following: (1) a son should tell his mother his troubles, (2) should feel ashamed in front of her for failure, (3) shouldn't hurt her feelings, (4) must revolt sometimes, (5) should seek reconciliation of his mother with his wife, (6) should support his mother, etc. The mother on her part is pictured as (1) holding her son to high standards, (2) nurturing and supporting him, (3) expecting and urging him to achieve, (4) being interested in his wife, (5) being patient and able to "take almost anything." These acts taken together illustrate the range of behaviors which are *perceived* as belonging to the mother-son role relation in a college student sub-culture. In a large sample of protocols certain of these behaviors will appear more commonly than others, suggesting that there is a habit family hierarchy of role responses associated with a particular status (mother or son). The results in terms of the present TAT pictures will not be adequate since they were not specifically chosen to get at common, social behavior patterns but rather at individual idiosyncrasies or motives. A modification of the test in the direction of more clearly identified status problems should provide better role definitions.

Analogous studies can be made using a projective technique like doll-play. Radke and Trager (1950), for instance, recorded the spontaneous comments and actions of children playing with Negro and White dolls. They found among other things that children tended to associate certain occupations, certain types of clothes, and certain housing arrangements with racial status.

3. Experiments on perceptual norms or schemata. Reference has already been made to various experimental techniques for determining what aspects of a percept "hang together." They range all the way from form-color associations (Bruner, Postman, and Rodrigues, 1950) and age-size associations (Rosenblith and White, 1949), to resistance to seeing incongruities (Bruner and Postman, 1949) and to Kelley's experiment (1949) on changes in the perceptual qualities of a person by the introduction of the characterization of "cold," or "warm." All of these techniques may be adapted to study social role expectancies by using social status as the stimulus material. Thus the degree of association of some perceptual characteristic with a status label (e.g., a stern facial expression with being a traffic policeman)

could be tested by asking a subject to pick a correct match in a set of comparison stimuli, by noticing the length of time it took the subjects to observe a perceptual incongruity (a smiling policeman), or by noting the changes in rating the severity of expression which accompanied labeling a figure "policeman." The problem is new, but the experimental techniques for handling it are well-developed. Future research along these lines should be profitable.

4. Measuring role performance. Interest in exact measurement of role performance has also not progressed very far, but two techniques deserve special mention. The first is role playing, a technique originally exploited by Moreno (1946) for therapeutic purposes. He arranged spontaneous dramas in which his patients were assigned roles which they had to carry out on the spur of the moment. These roles were often assigned in terms of the needs of the patient. Thus a person who had difficulty in expressing aggression or anger of any kind might be given a role in which he had to play the part of a typical outraged Victorian father who has just discovered that his daughter has been seduced. The technique was developed even further in the assessment program of the Office of Strategic Services in World War II when candidates for the service (O.S.S. 1948) were made to assume "cover personalities" during the several days that they were being tested. All the candidates at the assessment center had false identities and attempted during the time they were there to behave in every way consistently with their assumed personality. In this instance the role-playing technique was adopted to test the extent to which a person could play a new role and conceal his true personality, since this was one of the skills related to espionage work. But there is no reason why it could not be used to determine accurately how well a person understands or can perform a particular role, provided such methodological improvements were introduced as making observations of behavior more precise, standardizing status situations, and obtaining behavioral norms for the standardized situations.

A second technique is one developed by Bales (1950) in which individuals are placed in particular role situations and their behavior noted and classified either directly or from a recording. For example, Strodtbeck (1950) has classified and analyzed the behavior of a husband and wife trying to settle a point on which they had previously given different independent judgments. From these data he has determined how many times the husband or wife wins an argument, what types of items each wins on, the techniques used by each to gain control, etc. In short, he can arrive at a behavioral analysis of the husband-wife role relationship. This technique has very great promise for determining a person's role behavior in all sorts of statuses and for comparing this performance with some of the role perceptions as elicited by some of the techniques discussed earlier.

5. Extent of role conformity. While psychologists have not been so interested in the nature or content of a particular role perception or performance, they have collected a good deal of data about the extent to which a person conforms to a role pattern—irrespective of how it is defined. The situation is the same as it was in the last chapter, where we found psychologists not so much interested in *what* a person's ideas or attitudes were but in measuring *how much* of any old attitude he had. The Strong Vocational Interest Test is probably the best example of measurement of how much a person conforms to various social roles. There are four different types of "role" scales which are in common use in connection with this test. The first is the Masculinity-Femininity scale which measures the extent to which an individual gives responses which are typical of either males or females who have taken the test. The second is the Interest Maturity scale which measures the extent to which a person gives responses typical of his age group; the third is the Occupational Level scale which measures the extent to which an individual gives responses typical of different positions on the occupational prestige scale; and the fourth type is represented by the occupational scales themselves, which measure the extent to which a person has interiorized the responses which are typical of a particular occupational status. Let us see how Karl makes out on these various scales to illustrate what kind of role information this test provides us with. Many of his occupational-scale scores have already been discussed. On the Masculinity-Femininity scale he scores in the 26th percentile of a reference population of high school boys, which means that he gives less than the average number of responses characteristic of men as compared with women. On Interest Maturity he is in the 85th percentile, indicating that he gives responses that are more typical of twenty-five-year-olds than fifteen-year-olds. And on the Occupational Level scale he is in roughly the 35th percentile for a comparable reference population, which is again rather low. In fact his score falls below the mean scores of various professional groups taking the test but above the mean scores for skilled and semiskilled workmen. From all these scores we get an idea of the extent to which

Karl displays on this questionnaire the same kind of behavior which is displayed by groups of people classified according to sex, age, and occupational status. But we do not know *what* behavior they display or exactly how Karl deviates from the normative pattern. An analysis of the Strong answer keys might help provide some of this information but it has not as yet been carefully made.

Nevertheless these scores tell us something. The high Interest Maturity score, for instance, confirms the "miniature adult" behavior that Karl states in his autobiography was characteristic of his performance in high school. Likewise the Occupational Level score appears to mirror somewhat his father's occupational status, while the fact that it is somewhat higher than his father's confirms his upward mobility, which we have discovered before and which is also represented by his ambition to go to college and enter into a professional career. The low identification with masculine interests is somewhat surprising in view of his participation in sports and his general success in high school, but it probably reflects his feelings about his own timidity and insecurity and his interest in reading, all of which lead to characteristically feminine responses on the test.

Summary of Karl's Role Adjustments

It will be difficult to give an adequate summary of Karl's roles, partly because roles, like traits, are often fairly specific to particular situations, and partly because much of what we have had to say has been programmatic rather than the outcome of previous research. Actually the role concept has not been applied very often to the study of the individual personality. Nevertheless we have had considerable to say about Karl's role adjustments at different places in this chapter and some attempt should be made to draw them together into an over-all picture.

Turning back to Tables 9.1 and 9.3 we can take his parents and himself as points of reference, as focal points for a number of role definitions. As we have seen, he views his father as essentially authoritarian, hard-working, but unhappy, and somewhat solitary in his recreational and associational habits. His mother also appears as hard-working and unhappy, and also somewhat unfriendly toward him. Karl pictures himself in high school as a very gregarious boy who works very hard and who is obedient and conforming to adult standards of behavior. These overt pictures all contain elements which promise difficulties in future role adjustments. The father's role adjustments, to begin with, contain some elements which he will want to copy and others which he will not. Specifically he has apparently completely interiorized the strong achievement emphasis in his father's behavior. He admires his father's thoroughness, his hard-working qualities, his versatility, and the extent to which he has always supported his family. This admiration for male self-sufficiency also comes out in describing his older brother who, he says, can "turn his hand to anything and make a success of it. Very accomplished in music, electricity, flying, woodworking, to list a few of his achievements." Furthermore, Karl describes his younger brother as more interested in having a good time than in preparing for the future, again reflecting the strong emphasis on male achievement.

The difficulties begin with the fact that like any upwardly mobile son Karl cannot identify completely with his father because he clearly expects to surpass him on the occupational scale. His overt occupational choice at the time he entered college is something of a compromise. He wants to be a chemical engineer, which is an occupation somewhat related to his father's but at a higher level. A more important difficulty than this, however, arises from the fact that his father is so unhappy and worries so much about money matters, the motives of others, etc. Karl does not want to identify with his father in this respect. As a psychiatrist who interviewed Karl puts it, his father himself always felt inferior, which gave rise in Karl to a similar fear of inferiority and unhappiness which in turn probably reinforced his strong counteractive achievement strivings. His father's anxious striving is likely to favor the same adjustment in Karl. Furthermore, his father is more solitary than Karl would like to be. Thus there are several grounds for predicting that Karl will have difficulty in assuming male adult roles, particularly toward work, because his chief role model, his father, is so satisfactory in some respects, and not in others. If he had a strong father image that he could either completely identify with or reject, his adjustment would be easier than it is here where identification extends to some areas and not to others. Nevertheless Karl is fairly aware of these conflicts and should therefore be able to adjust to them eventually. At the present time he only wishes that things had been otherwise, that the world was ruled by the principles of the Sermon on the Mount so that there would be no need to fear failure so much through the competitive selfishness of other individuals.

The interesting thing about the mother picture is that the fantasy picture of women differs so much from it. At the reality level his description of his mother is somewhat cold and divorced from emotionality, as if she had done her duty toward him and no more. In the TAT the mother either deserts or demands something of her son. On two different occasions, separated by about a year, Karl told a story about the "mother-son" picture (TAT 6BM) in which the mother demands something from the son which he cannot perform. In one story the mother is a "very sacrificial woman who has given her entire life to raising her son to manhood." She wants him to prosecute his wife's brother-in-law but he feels he cannot and ends up feeling very guilty for being "unfaithful to his mother's devotion." The other story is reproduced in full below.

> The young man and his mother are having a serious talk. She is shocked and hurt; also disappointed. He feels sorry for her and is trying to justify his decision. The young man has a job in a café. He is a bartender. His mother had hopes that he would become a great teacher or doctor and would go to school. However, he has just returned from the service and wants to earn a living. His mother wants him to go to school. He wishes to keep his job and he wants to give her sufficient reasons for his actions; he is trying to think of something to pacify his mother and perhaps ease his conscience. He will go back to the bar job and be happy at it. His mother will become reconciled to it, and they will understand each other.

The ending of this story contains the other element which is characteristic of Karl's fantasies about women, namely, their strong, loving, nurturant aspect. Thus at the unreality level the female image has split into a demanding aspect associated with the mother and a nurturant aspect usually associated with a lover. In either case the son often sees himself as deceitful and betraying the trust of a woman. This suggests that there will be considerable difficulty in Karl's adjustment to women, particularly in marriage. On the one hand he has the strong fantasy wish for their love and support ("high on a windy hill") and on the other hand he fears they will be demanding and/or deserting him. The extremeness of these two pictures at the unreality level, together with their apparent lack of connection with the conscious mother image, suggests that the conflict arising over the negative aspect of women is not very well understood by Karl, which will probably make his adjustment to women even harder. In fact, we have evidence in his autobiography that he has always had difficulty with girls and was teased for it when he was younger.

Finally, while his adjustment to high school would seem to be so ideal, we should note that he is still playing the role of a "good boy" who responds to situations as they are defined by adults rather than by his age mates. As we have seen, the "normal" adolescent shows more rebelliousness and irresponsibility than Karl has displayed to date, probably because of his strict parental controls. But in the transition from high school to college or from adolescence to adulthood he will be facing status situations, the approved adjustments to which are not defined by superiors but by his age mates or perhaps even by inferiors. What will happen when he gets on his own? He has so far had little practice in making role adjustments that are not clearly defined from above. We may therefore predict that he will have much more difficulty in adjusting to a situation in which behavioral norms are not enforced by superiors than a boy would who has shown more rebelliousness and who therefore has had more practice in finding norms defined as correct by age mates or inferiors.

NOTES AND QUERIES

1. How do you decide whether a given act is part of a role performance or a personality trait?

2. Suppose a person had a role perception which you wanted to change for some reason (e.g., suppose he perceives father figures as authoritarian or Negroes as filling menial occupational roles). How would you go about changing his conception? Would you use techniques that would differ in any way from the ones you would use for (a) extinguishing any response or (b) getting him to give up a personality trait?

3. In attempting to get a picture of how students perceive the behavior expected of a proctor, Stouffer asked them to judge which of the various alternative actions for dealing with someone caught cheating they thought would be approved and disapproved by the authorities. In a sense this involves perception of the probabilities of sanctions being invoked by the authorities, and is a little like asking what behavior someone thinks will be rewarded or punished. In view of this, would it be better to ask what they as a proctor *ought* to do under the circumstances? What is the difference between perceiving what *should* be done and perceiving what would be approved or disapproved?

4. Some authorities distinguish between an ideal role performance

and a typical role performance. Is there any difference in perception between the two—let us say between the way you perceive women should act and the way you think they do act? What accounts for the difference?

5. Frequently we say that a person playing a role is not being his "real self." In what sense is this true, and in what sense untrue?

6. Design a role apperception test which would give you the information you would want about a person's conception of the major role relations in his life.

7. Take an answer key to the Strong Vocational Interest Test, study the items which are scored one way or the other and try to figure out some kind of pattern which integrates and describes the male and female roles in our society. Consult Strong's discussion of the scale in his *Vocational Interests of Men and Women* (1943). Or note the changes that occur in frequency of responses to various items as a function of changes in age status (Strong, 1931) and try to generalize these into changing role patterns associated with different age statuses.

8. Look up the principles in any learning text (cf. McGeoch, 1942) governing positive and negative transfer and apply them (1) to the problem of predicting to what stimulus patterns attitudes toward the father will generalize, and (2) to the problem of predicting what factors will produce maximal interference in the transition from one role pattern to the next.

10

Socialization: The Sources of Schemata and Motives

Students of personality theory have always stressed the tremendous importance of child training in the development of the person's conceptions of his world. The reason for this has been in part theoretical, in part historical, and in part empirical. On theoretical grounds it has seemed logical to suppose that the best place to study the behavior which a culture expects of its members is at the time of their indoctrination in group customs. Historically, Freud and his followers in the psychoanalytic school always emphasized the tremendous importance of the early years in laying down the basic personality structure. Again and again they found that the cause of a neurosis appeared to lie in the first years of childhood. And when Freud and others of his students began to apply their findings based on individual cases to the study of society, they laid great emphasis on parent-child relationships. For example, Freud in his early study *Totem and Taboo* (1918) argued that the relationship of the son to his father and mother (the Oedipus complex) was responsible for the incest tabu, the nature of religion and many other social phenomena. While most psychologists have viewed with suspicion simple analytic formulations of this nature, many of them have accepted the underlying assumption that the early years of life are of fundamental importance in understanding the relationship between culture and personality.

Finally, on empirical grounds a number of relationships have been discovered by anthropologists which would support the contention that early childhood training is of very great importance in determining adult personality structure. A dramatic instance of this sort is that noted by McAllester (1941) who studied the effects of the use of water as a disciplinary agent among the Crow Indians. He reported that it was common practice for Crow parents to pour water down the noses of their babies to quiet them when they cried. He then found in the cultural institutions of the Crow many evidences of the fear of water. Members of the tribe refuse to eat anything that lives in the water or is associated with water in any way.

They also fear water monsters and go near water as little as possible. To throw water at someone is to shame him completely. Isolated relationships of this sort have been repeatedly reported in recent years (cf. Bateson, 1944) but it has remained for Whiting and Child (1950) to demonstrate that they are not just fortuitous. These authors have found significant relationships cross-culturally between certain child-training practices and different theories of disease in a study which will be reported more fully later in the chapter.

While such findings underline the great importance of child training in the study of personality structure, they do not necessarily imply that the child training is simply the cause and personality and culture the result, as some enthusiastic psychoanalysts have seemed to imply. It is just as logical to assume that the society's general conception of the nature of illness makes their attitude toward weaning harsh (for example) as it is to assume that harsh weaning-practices cause adults in a society to conceive of illness as associated with oral activity. Nevertheless the relationship between early child training and later adult conceptions has been demonstrated to exist empirically. Consequently for this and the preceding reasons it is necessary to look closely into the process of child rearing and its influence on people's ideas of the nature of the world and of the way to maintain one's self in it.

Kardiner's Contribution. A very stimulating and controversial approach to the relationship between childhood experiences and personality formation has been made in recent years by the combined efforts of psychoanalysts and anthropologists, led chiefly by Kardiner, who has collaborated with DuBois in an analysis of the Alorese culture (1944) and later with Linton and others (1945). He was trained as a psychoanalyst and attempted to apply his variation of the Freudian system to the study of personality formation in Alor. We may consider his approach in some detail as illustrative of the one adopted by a number of culturally oriented psychoanalysts. He begins by presenting the analysis of a neurotic who came to him for treatment. "A man of thirty complains of having great difficulty with women, of a constant anxiety state in addition to several specific phobias, the chief of which is the fear of making a speech, constant feeling of unworthiness, incapacity to compete, and hence a sense of failure." (Kardiner, 1945, p. 17.) The man further has intense longings for leadership but is actually "obsessed with a feeling of helpless ineffectuality." (1945, p. 18.) Kardiner concludes that the man's difficulties have arisen out of a peculiar relationship which developed in connection with his mother. She had given him good maternal care until he was about twenty months old, when a change in the family fortunes required her to work in her husband's store and thus prevented her from giving her child the attention he had received heretofore. As a result "the tensions of hunger, the wish to be fondled, and so forth, could no more be satisfied in the usual way." (1945, p. 18.) Out of this desertion and some subsequent events the patient developed eventually a mistrust of his mother together with an unconscious longing for her. To him women appear powerful and resourceful while he is weak, "helpless and unable to enforce his will" (1945, p. 19). As a result he feels insignificant and inferior and yet tries to compensate for this by grandiose dreams of achievement and longings for success.

Having analyzed this particular person in this way, Kardiner asks the legitimate question as to whether these findings could be utilized in any way in the study of society. He feels that a society might exist in which the childhood circumstances which produced this particular personality structure were institutionalized. If this were so, "then we would expect that the trend in their personality formation would follow along the lines indicated by the subject we have just discussed." (1945, p. 21.)

He finds that the Alorese culture fulfills, to a considerable extent, the prerequisite condition of poor maternal care. He therefore attempts to use his psychoanalytic knowledge based on the study of his patient to understand personality formation in Alor. Since Alorese women work in the fields to produce nearly all the staple foods consumed, children are cared for after birth by their mothers only for a very short period amounting to usually not more than two weeks. At the end of this time the mother returns to the fields, leaving the child alone from early in the morning until late in the afternoon. Naturally the child gets very hungry and in need of comfort. He may be given premasticated food or picked up and fondled by anyone who happens to be around but does not develop any strong "parental image as a reliever of tensions from hunger or other sources." (Kardiner, 1945, p. 147.) "The intermittent appearance of the mother in the morning and at night cannot relieve the situation. In fact, it must in the long run act as an additional irritant, because the only image of the mother that can emerge as a consequence of her intermittent attention is the emphasis of her tantalizing and frustrating aspects to the disparagement of the kindlier side." (1945, p. 148.)

As a result of this poor maternal care Kardiner feels that the basic personality in Alor "is anxious, suspicious, mistrustful, lacking in confidence, with no interest in the outer world. There is no capacity to idealize parental image or deity. The personality is devoid of enterprise, is filled with repressed hatred and free floating aggression over which constant vigilance must be exercised." (1945, p. 170.) To rephrase these conclusions in the terms used in Chapter 8 we might say that the average Alorese child learns to act in accordance with certain propositions or premises which may be stated as follows:

Premise 1. Life is very painful.
Premise 2. People are not to be trusted, women especially.
Premise 3. Failure of one's efforts is to be expected.
Premise 4. Financial transactions are important because they insure the supply of food.

This last statement is derived from the observation that most of the adult males spend a large proportion of their time in financial transactions, while the women work in the fields. It can readily be seen how the first three of these propositions, at any rate, are directly derived from the struggle which the young infant has with the tensions created by the desertion of the mother. It is also not difficult to see how the interest in finance could develop from the same anxiety over food. Kardiner goes on to show how this fundamental cultural configuration also leads to personality traits such as absence of persistence. That is, he finds in the Alorese a "lack of constructive ability and systematization; no interest in crafts, absence of idealization, poor aesthetic development; easy abandonment of hope and enterprise . . ." (1945, p. 238). He also finds what we will refer to as a need, namely, the strong need for love or nurturance. The personality portrait which he draws is based on a world view or set of ideas derived almost entirely from what happens to the child in the first year or so of his life. In all of this he is typical of, though more explicit than, other psychoanalysts working in this area who stress the importance of early training in determining implicit adult ideas and values. They all start from the assumption that a culture may institutionalize certain child-training practices which they have found lead in individual cases to certain types of adult personality structures.

Whether or not one agrees with Kardiner's final analysis, his method of approach to the problem set some valuable precedents. He not only made extensive use of standard ethnographic material collected on the Alorese culture, but studied detailed autobiographies obtained by DuBois to check his general formulations. In addition he had dream material from individuals and Rorschach protocols which were independently analyzed by Oberholzer (cf. DuBois, 1944). The whole project is an excellent example of the kind of co-operative effort between students of personality theory and students of culture which is likely to produce the most progress, certainly in the aspect of personality which we are now discussing.

The Navaho View of Life. By way of contrast to Kardiner's approach we may turn to the Navaho view of life as it has been presented by Kluckhohn and Leighton (1947). As it happens, it would not be difficult for a psychoanalyst to see in the Navaho basic personality structure an example of the anal complex of traits which has been observed in individuals who have fixated at the anal stage of libidinal development. Freud and particularly Abraham developed the idea of the "anal character" as including predominantly the traits of orderliness, obstinacy, and parsimony (cf. Healy, Bronner, and Bowers, 1930, p. 318). Psychoanalytic theory holds that individuals who for various reasons do not progress beyond anal cathexis to the normal genital stage will display these traits as adults. The anal character has been extensively studied. A classical literary example is Balzac's Père Grandet in *Eugenie Grandet* whose stinginess is so great that it overcomes all other motives.

Table 10.1 shows how one could find traits in the Navaho personality which seem to correspond rather closely to the anal complex.

TABLE 10.1

Evidence for Anal Character Traits Among the Navaho

Anal complex of traits	*Navaho traits*
1. Orderliness	1. Maintain order at all costs
2. Obstinacy	2. Do nothing in the face of danger
3. Parsimony	3. High value on possessions Waste disapproved

(Kluckhohn and Leighton, 1947, p. 220.)

As for the trait of orderliness, Kluckhohn and Leighton repeatedly emphasize the extreme ritualism of the Navaho. "By seeming to bring the areas of actual ignorance, error, and accident under the control of minutely described ritual formulas, the People create a compensatory mechanism. . . . This is achieved by the compulsive force of order and reiteration in ritual words and acts." (1947, p. 224.) This is typical of the ritualistic observances of the anal erotic. As for obstinacy, to the outside observer, at least, the Navaho must seem stubborn and obstinate because of his basic assumption that in situations of danger it is best to do nothing or be impassive. This refusal to act is also typical of the anal erotic. Finally, as Kluckhohn and Leighton point out, possessions are very highly valued by the Navaho. "By Navaho standards one is industrious in order to accumulate possessions—within certain limits—and to care for the possessions he obtains. Uncontrolled gambling or drinking are disapproved primarily because they are wasteful. The 'good man' is one who has 'hard goods' (turquoise and jewelry mainly), 'soft goods' (clothing, etc.), 'flexible goods' (textiles, etc.) and songs, stories and other intangible property, of which ceremonial knowledge is the most important." (1947, p. 220.) This concern with possessions which extends to great carefulness in dress and to metal molding is again typical of the anal character who has a strong cathexis for material objects, plus a horror of waste.

If we look into Navaho child training to attempt to discover, as Kardiner would, whether or not there is any basis for assuming that the culture institutionalizes a form of bowel training which would lead to the development of this basic personality structure, we even find hints that this may be the case. Leighton and Kluckhohn report that while bowel training is not severe or harsh, it is begun *along with weaning* and "after a time, the youngster who continues to wet or soil himself is unmercifully teased by all present." (1947, p. 35.) To the Freudian the withdrawal of oral gratification coupled with the sudden insistence on bowel control would be an excellent method for emphasizing the libidinal aspect of the excretory function. Among the Navaho, feces are not considered disgusting and there is no exaggerated emphasis on cleanliness, but after a time the child learns that Navaho adults take extreme care in disposing of their feces. "When the toddler goes with mother or with older sister to defecate or urinate, he must notice a certain uneasiness which they manifest by their careful concealment of the waste matter. The mother is now revealed not as omnipotent but as herself very uneasy and afraid, though helpful in that she is teaching the child one way of protecting himself." (Leighton and Kluckhohn, 1947, p. 40.) Once again in orthodox psychoanalytic terms this would provide a mechanism which would emphasize the value of excrement to the child. If it were not important, there would be no need to conceal it so carefully to prevent its usage in witchcraft against the person.

But Leighton and Kluckhohn properly do not adopt the simple procedure of attempting to explain the whole of Navaho adult personality in terms of this single child-training experience. Instead, they argue that "the child naturally comes to feel that the important thing in life is to be safe." (1947, p. 40.) Navaho religion was summed up by one informant in the simple statement, "We do not believe; we fear." (1947, p. 139.) Under the circumstances it seems far too simple to attribute all the fear of the Navaho to a single kind of experience with cleanliness training in childhood. Instead they develop the viewpoint that a Navaho is influenced in all that he does by a way of life which is itself a joint product of the physical environment, the history of The People, and the personalities which go to make up the tribe at any given moment in time. The Navaho physical environment, for example, may have contributed largely to the conception implicit in their view of life that nature is more powerful than man. They live a life which is exposed to all sorts of dangers from nature. A typically nomadic people, they live in relatively isolated units in a semiarid land where the dangers of torrential rains, prolonged lack of water, a lonely illness or accident must soon be obvious to everyone. They do not have the same solidary support from others that Indians living in pueblos have. The idea that life is dangerous may have been reinforced by experiences in their cultural history such as their mass imprisonment by the Whites in the 1860's. Under the circumstances The People may have learned to adjust to danger by ritualistic practices which would ensure safety. Viewed in this light the problem of bowel training becomes simply one more kind of possibly dangerous situation which would be handled in the same way as all other dangerous situations. As such, it also serves incidentally to reinforce in all children the general cultural approach to life, since all of them are faced with the problem of elimination control sooner or later. The general conclusion from this line of reasoning is that child-training problems tend to be handled in a way which is consistent with the over-all point of view adopted by a culture but are not the sole determinants of that point of view though they may be used along with other means to reinforce it.

The peculiarly important contribution of psychoanalysis according to this interpretation is that Freud and his followers discovered a mode of adjusting to a difficult, fear-producing learning problem (bowel control) which proved to be rather generally adopted by individuals in such situations. In the case of neurotics who are true "anal characters," bowel training doubtless has been a serious traumatic or fear-producing situation against which they defend themselves by developing character traits (orderliness, etc.) which turn out to be highly comparable to the modes of response that a culture or other individuals might adopt to other, or more generalized, fears. Should anyone doubt the statement that the fears were more general in the Navaho culture, it should be pointed out that there are characteristics of the "anal complex" which The People do *not* show. For instance, they are not especially clean (for lack of water), or overly compliant and obedient, or obstinate because possessive, all of which are traits which can be traced more specifically to toilet-training traumata (cf. Healy, Bronner, and Bowers, 1930, p. 322).

Furthermore, it should also be noted that it is possible (if not as likely) for another person or another culture to learn to adapt to such fears in a different way. Thus in white America the traditional, "normal" response to danger has been to strive hard and to gain security and safety through individual success and achievement. "When in trouble, *do* something." (Kluckhohn and Kluckhohn, 1947.) This idea was present in Karl's autobiography. It is constantly being reinforced by examples in public life in America today. When Congressman Bloom of New York died, for instance, the papers made much of the fact that he was a man who had risen to the peak of worldly success, respectability, and renown despite his origins as a penniless immigrant. The "rags to riches" or Horatio Alger story is a myth with an important moral for our culture: "When in trouble, *do* something; you can achieve security by effort and hard work."

General Conclusions. From these important pilot studies on the relationship between individual and cultural modes of adjustment we may draw a number of preliminary conclusions. (1) The study of an individual's adjustment to or ideas about a particular problem may *suggest* ways in which it has become normal for a group of people to adjust to or conceive of a common similar problem. (2) The hypotheses as to modes of adjustment derived from individual study must be checked in any given culture to find the actual behavioral norms or conceptions current in that society. These cultural patterns are an important part of the equipment with which any individual member of that culture meets his problems of living. (3) The point at which the individual comes in contact with these norms is in childhood predominantly. Every member of a culture must adjust to certain common problems such as weaning, elimination control, walking, and talking. The culture adopts rearing practices which are consistent with its general philosophy of life and it is in part through these rearing practices that the child learns what the way of life is. That is, a culturally patterned child-training technique is both a product of the culture and a method of reinforcing its dominant ideas and modes of adjustment. (4) There are variations within any given culture as to the particular way in which the culturally approved patterns of child rearing are applied. This may determine the extent to which the person adopts the cultural conception of life, but whether he adopts it as his own or not, he always acts in terms of it as a frame of reference. In other words, no individual is a passive creation of his culture; as Simmons points out (1942), he is a *creator* as well as a *carrier* of his culture. But his creations are always made with the culture as a starting point or frame of reference.

Why Should Childhood Experiences be so Important?

Psychoanalysts like Kardiner have not been overly concerned with this question. They have been content for the most part to know that in the case of some individuals early traumata have had important effects on adult adjustments. Can we add anything to this bare fact from our general knowledge of the way schemata develop or are acquired? Are there any theoretical reasons why early childhood experiences should be relatively more important than later ones? When the question is put in this way, it is immediately apparent that there are a number of factors which should operate to make early experiences more important than later ones, factors which derive from theories and experiments about how schemata are acquired.

1. **Primacy.** As long ago as 1897 Jost formulated two hypotheses about associative learning which have subsequently come to be known as Jost's laws: "If two associations are of equal strength but of different age, a new repetition has a greater value for the older one," and "If two associations are of equal strength but of different age, the older diminishes less with time." (McGeoch, 1942, p. 140.) These "laws" have been confirmed by experiments in the laboratory

over relatively short intervals of time, but as McGeoch points out, they do not have much explanatory value because of "our ignorance of the effective variables which differential age brings with it." (1942, p. 142.) If we think of age of associations ontogenetically, it is clear that associations formed in childhood all have the benefit of age according to Jost's laws. We can further argue that the reason why age is an advantage in this case is that they are assimilated less to pre-existing trace systems. Certainly as far as young children are concerned positive and negative transfer from previous experiences must be relatively much less than with older children or adults. The child has fewer previously formed associations, less "apperceptive mass" into which new experiences are assimilated and modified. In fact, early experiences, simply because they occur first, are probably of greater importance in setting up the frames of reference in terms of which subsequent experiences are classified and modified. In experiments like Bartlett's (1932) on serial reproduction of a story or a perceptual figure, there is considerable evidence to indicate that the first impression is more important in determining the "final" conception than are any subsequent impressions, although data on this point are hard to collect (cf. Asch, 1946, Hanawalt, 1937). Numerous experiments on regression in animals (cf. Mowrer, 1940) have indicated that a response learned first becomes prepotent over subsequent learned responses, especially if frustration is introduced. Finally, experiments on the recognition process (Bruner and Postman, 1949) have demonstrated that the hypotheses brought to a situation tend to shape subsequent perception to a marked extent. From such evidence it seems safe to infer that *part* of the relatively greater importance of childhood events lies in the mere fact that they occur first and therefore can shape rather than be shaped by other conceptions and later experiences.

2. **Undeveloped Symbolic Processes.** A child experiences a great many things during the first eighteen to twenty-four months of his life before he has symbol systems developed to the point where they can adequately represent what he has experienced. We have discussed in Chapter 8 how important language is in shaping mental content. What about all those experiences which occur before language or "consciousness" develops? One can either assume that they are of relatively little importance in determining subsequent behavior because they have not been symbolized, or that they go on influencing behavior but in a way which is relatively independent of

the symbol systems developed in connection with later experiences. The latter assumption, which certainly seems more reasonable, is essentially the one the psychoanalysts have made in arguing for the importance of the "unconscious." If we read for "unconscious" some such term as "unverbalized" or "unsymbolized," it is easy to see on theoretical grounds why early experiences might continue to exert a disproportionate influence on subsequent behavior because they are not under symbolic control. Not enough experimental attention has been given to this important theoretical problem, but several experiments demonstrate the greater resistance to extinction of unverbalized learning (cf. Hilgard and Marquis, 1940, pp. 267-268). In short, early experiences may assume such great importance in personality because they are not represented by the kinds of symbols, particularly verbal, which facilitate subsequent discrimination, assimilation, extinction, and control.

3. **Repetition.** Few people have commented on the fact, although it is readily apparent to young parents, that many of the important problems of early childhood occur over and over again, providing almost unexcelled opportunities for fixation and reinforcement. For instance, the average infant is fed from three to six times a day for the first year at least and perhaps for the second year as well. Conservatively we may estimate that the problem of feeding arises around three thousand times in the first two years of an infant's life. The parent for reasons of economy acquires certain methods of handling the feeding problem and the infant in turn learns to expect certain responses from the parent. Is it then so surprising that responses and expectations which have been reinforced thousands of times should be of importance in determining the subsequent conception a child develops of the world? Or take the problem of bowel control. The average infant probably soils himself from six to ten times a day, at least in the beginning. In the first year alone the problem of changing his diapers or cleaning him up must arise somewhere around two thousand times. One does not need to assume any extraordinary learning capacity on the infant's part to infer that many expectations and habitual modes of reaction will be acquired during all these repetitions of a problem situation. D. P. Marquis (1941) has shown that newborn infants can learn a certain feeding schedule in a matter of a few days (25-35 paired repetitions). But the habits we are speaking of here would have many thousands of opportunities for a particular association to be formed and

strengthened. When one considers how often the Alorese child associates his mother with the pangs of frustration and hunger, it seems reasonable to assume that he might develop the kind of anticipation of frustration from women that Kardiner postulates (1945). The fact is that there are few situations as important to the organism, outside early child training, that give such extensive opportunities through sheer repetition for the learning of attitudes, expectations, and modes of adapting to problem situations.

4. **The Conditions for Forgetting.** Although we may accept readily the importance of some of these learned expectations for the child when he is a child, we can still question whether they are of any great importance for later on. Perhaps they are simply unlearned or replaced by subsequent associations. Why assume that what is learned during the first year is of importance in the second year, the third year, or the twenty-third year? This takes us directly into the problem of unlearning or forgetting. What are the conditions for forgetting? In recent years, the general consensus among learning theorists is that forgetting is not due to *disuse*. McGeoch in particular has argued that forgetting is "not a matter of passive decay." "Decrements in retention are a function of three fundamental conditions: (a) interference by intervening activities; (b) altered stimulating conditions; (c) inadequate set at the time of the measurement of retention." (1942, p. 457.)

How would each of these factors operate to produce forgetting of early experiences? As the child grows older he will learn new responses but under somewhat different stimulating conditions. For one thing, he is simply bigger, and the world looks different to him. Consider for a moment how the world must look to a child of one or two. It must be populated largely with feet and legs, with the underneath surfaces of chairs and tables, with large obstacles such as steps to be crawled over. The context changes radically as he grows bigger. In terms of retroactive inhibition theory, this means that his new responses will be attached to new stimulating conditions and older responses will not necessarily be unlearned or forgotten as a result of this new or "interpolated" activity. In fact, careful consideration of the conditions which McGeoch sets down for forgetting would lead us to expect that the rapid growth of the child would favor the acquisition of new learning without corresponding decrements in old learning. In technical terms, such a state of affairs would show up as reproductive interference making it difficult for the child to *recall* earlier learning, because of new learned responses, while some other method of measuring retention such as a savings score in relearning would demonstrate that earlier experiences were still retained. Actual unlearning is apparently most likely to occur when the same situation gives rise to incompatible responses, one of which may then be extinguished by lack of reinforcement. But such an opportunity for unlearning is not so likely to occur in the rapidly growing infant (a) when stimulus situations change quickly and (b) when similarities among situations are not as great as they are when they can be grouped under a common symbol.

Let us take a concrete example to make the point clear. Suppose for the sake of argument that an infant develops on the basis of earlier experiences with his mother an expectation that she will be harsh and punishing. As he grows older he learns a new expectation based perhaps on the fact that she is no longer harsh and frustrating since he is now toilet-trained, which removes the source of most of her irritation. The new expectation, however, is tied to somewhat different stimulus conditions (he has grown up), and there is no reason for supposing on the basis of contemporary theories of forgetting that the earlier expectation is completely wiped out. It may be difficult to recall, except under conditions of free association and fantasy, as the psychoanalysts have demonstrated, but that is no reason to assume that its influence is entirely lost. As savings scores demonstrate, the influence of past learning persists long beyond the point when recall is reduced to zero. Subsequent learning, to be sure, produces *some* unlearning (cf. Melton and Von Lackum, 1941). but the point that needs emphasis here is that conditions do not seem adequate to account for complete forgetting of early childhood associations.

Furthermore, there are other reasons why early experiences are not as readily forgotten as later ones. Much early learning which occurs before the child has developed the symbol systems discussed above, must be exceedingly generalized and vague. Extinction and forgetting occur most readily when the elements in a stimulus-response-reward sequence are easily discriminated by a rat or a human. When, however, such sequences are made to be vague or variable through aperiodic reinforcement (Jenkins and Stanley, 1950), or random variation of "correct" cues, correct responses, or time delay to reinforcement (cf. McClelland and McGown, 1950), extinction or unlearning becomes much more difficult to produce. Yet vari-

strengthened. When one c nsiders how often
ciates his mother with th ngs of frustratio
reasonable to assume that might develop
of frustration from women hat Kardiner r
is that there are few situat ns as import
early child training, that ve such e
sheer repetition for the arning
modes of adapting to problm situa

4. **The Conditions for** rgetting
ily the importance of son of the
child when he is a child, e can st
any great importance for ler on P
or replaced by subsequen associat
learned during the first w ks of in
third year, or the twenty ird year
problem of unlearning o orgetti
forgetting? In recent yea the ge
theorists is that forgettin is not
ticular has argued that f getting
"Decrements in retention a fu
tions: (a) interference by te
lating conditions; (c) inadequate
of retention." (1942, p. 455)

How would each of the fa
early experiences? As the chil
sponses but under som it
one thing, he is simply b
Consider for a moment h
or two. It must be popul
underneath surfaces of
as steps to be crawled
grows bigger. In terms
that his new response
tions and older respo
gotten as a result o
careful consideratio
for forgetting wou
child would favo
sponding decre
state of affairs

n the basis
aat she will
ew expectat
and frustrat
urce of most
ied to somew
, and there is
ary theories of
ly wiped out. It n
of free association
trated, but that is
ly lost. As savings see
g persists long beyond
subsequent learning, to
on and Von Lackum, 19
e is that conditions do
orgetting of early childh

why early experiences
later Much early learning wh
devel ne symbol systems discu
gen and vague. Extinction

bility of the elements in a learning sequence is probably the rule in early childhood. All Johnny learns is that sometimes "something" painful may happen when he has done "something." In the beginning at least such associations may be so general as to be very hard to extinguish. The isolation of "cue" and "response" and "reward" (cf. Miller and Dollard, 1941) is an achievement of later childhood or of an experimenter who is careful to isolate these elements in a regular and systematic fashion for the animal or child performing in the typical learning experiment. As the apperceptive mass gets more differentiated, as discriminations become easier to make in terms of language and other symbolic systems, what is learned becomes increasingly specific and therefore increasingly easy to forget or unlearn by altered motivation, changed stimulus conditions, etc.

In conclusion, then, it is apparent that many considerations based on our knowledge of the learning and forgetting process would lend support to the psychoanalytic position that early childhood is of very great importance in determining "basic personality structure." Since the reasons derive directly from learning theory, careful reasoning and experimentation along the lines suggested above ought to quiet many theoretical psychologists' doubts about a mysterious "unconscious" which obeys laws of its own. Often psychoanalysts have been right for the wrong reasons. Their lack of training in formal learning psychology has not enabled them to give satisfactory explanations as to why unconscious early learning should be so important and the explanations they have resorted to have seemed so anthropomorphic and strange to other psychologists that many psychoanalytic formulations have been dismissed without the serious consideration they deserve (cf. Sherif and Cantril, 1947).

The Important Learning Problems of Childhood

Having found a basis in learning theory for the importance attached by psychoanalysts and cultural anthropologists to childhood experiences we may now turn to a more systematic treatment of the socialization process. Our task can be divided into three parts: (1) What are the important problems which arise in every infant's adjustment to his environment? (2) What parent behaviors are particularly significant in altering the nature of these problems? (3) What is the effect on personality of variations in the nature of these problems and the way they are handled by parents?

Leaving aside the last question until later, we may first attempt a classification of the important learning problems faced in one form or another by every human infant. An adequate basis for such a classification at this stage of our knowledge is difficult to find. On the one hand we may begin with the problems of socialization which psychoanalysts have traditionally emphasized as of great importance —e.g., nursing and weaning, sex and aggression training, cleanliness training, etc. There is much historical precedent for such an approach. It is the one most commonly used in analysis of the socialization process by contemporary research workers in the field like Davis and Dollard (1940), Davis and Havighurst (1947), Leighton and Kluckhohn (1947), Kardiner (1945), and many others. Any classification scheme must include these problems, but it should also be more systematic if possible. That is, a careful consideration of the functional or adaptive problems of a developing child suggests that there are certain areas of learning which are of considerable importance in the child's development, but which for one reason or another have not been treated extensively by psychoanalysts. Our problem here is essentially the same as it was when we attempted in Chapter 8 to distinguish different areas of cultural ideology. We must find some rational scheme which will order the problems known to be of importance and which will suggest others which may be of importance.

Table 10.2 is an attempt at such a classification. The left-hand column lists four major types of problems which the child must face. They cover relatively broad areas of learning, centering respectively around problems of protection, affection, mastery, and control. Under each of these headings is listed some, but by no means all, of the important more specific problems that fall within this area. For example, under *problems of protection,* every child must somehow be fed, nursed, and shielded from pain and danger. The way in which the problems appear to him—the amount and frequency of feeding or protection, the sequence of hunger, pain, and satisfaction, etc.—will presumably be of great importance in determining the child's conception of the world—whether it is friendly or unfriendly, supporting or nonsupporting, etc. There are two main sources of variation in the way such a problem as this is defined—one arising primarily from the requirements of the situation (column 2) and one from the way in which the parent defines the problem and helps the child to solve it (column 3). In the former category fall those episodes, events, or "accidents" that have appeared to modify the nature of the learning problem according to psychoanalysts and others working in child psychology. For instance, the cradleboard provides a kind of protection from danger for the Navaho child which should modify the nature of his expectations about protection and support. Or again, loss of the mother or prolonged ill health are major events which can scarcely fail to redefine what is to be learned in this area. Similarly the sheer presence of lots of other people, especially adults, from whom the child can get support presents a very different type of situation with respect to learning about protection from the situation which would arise for a relatively isolated Navaho child for whom the frequency of interaction with others is considerably less than for a child born in a pueblo. In the third column are listed sample types of parent behavior as rated by Baldwin, Kalhorn, and Breese as the basis for their elaborate cluster analysis of patterns of parent behavior (1945). They are meant to be suggestive of the different ways in which parents can structure for the child the particular problem under consideration. A more detailed discussion of how they were derived, and of other sources of variation in parent behavior, will be given later in the chapter.

TABLE 10.2

Classification of Learning Problems for the Child with a Sampling of Circumstances and Parent Behaviors of Importance in Determining the Nature of the Problems for the Child

Learning problems	*Variations in childhood circumstances* *	*Variations in parent behavior*†
I. Protection and support		Indulgence-Neglect
		4.2 Sheltering-Exposing
a. Nursing and weaning‡	Loss of mother Cradleboard	4.1 Overhelps-Withholds help
b. Pain and danger	Realistic dangers	1.91 Child centered-Child subordinate
c. Aggression from others (teasing, ridicule, deceit)	Health Birth traumata Frequency of interaction with others	7.2 Devotion-Rejection 7.1 Anxious-Nonchalant over child's well-being
II. Expression and regulation of affect		Acceptance-Rejection
a. "Mothering" expectancies (tickling, cuddling, etc.)	Loss of mother Birth order and interval to next child	7.2 Devotion-Rejection 8.4 Rapport-Isolation

TABLE 10.2 (*Continued*)

Learning problems	*Variations in childhood circumstances* *	*Variations in parent behavior* †
b. Object choices (affectional) ‡	Kinship system etc.	8.3 Affectionate-Hostile
c. Mode of expression of affect (smiling, contact tabus, etc.)		5.2 Approval-Disapproval in direction of criticism
III. Mastery		Acceleration ("Democracy")-Indifference
a. Motor skills—walking, hunting, working	Illness Native intelligence Loss of father	3.3 Accelerational attempt
b. Symbolic skills—talking, reading, etc.	Age of parents at birth Cultural ideology (Mythology, schooling, etc.)	6.1 Satisfies-Thwarts curiosity
c. Cognitive maps or reality systems, etc.		3.22 Optional-Mandatory suggestions 3.14 Consistency-Inconsistency in policy (Rational *vs.* Arbitrary policy) 3.15 Child shares in formulation of policy
IV. Self-direction and control		Autocratic-Permissive
a. Sphincter control (cleanliness, toilet training) ‡	Nature and number of socializing agents Loss of father	3.14 Arbitrariness of policy 5.2 Approval-Disapproval in direction of criticism
b. Aggression control ‡	Institutionally approved forms of aggression	
c. Hierarchy of controls		
d. Self *vs.* Social controls (Autonomous *vs.* Heteronomous Morality)	Traumatic fixations	3.22 Optional-Mandatory suggestions (Nurturance/inhibition ratio)

* Cf. Kluckhohn, 1946.
† After Baldwin, Kalhorn, and Breese (1945, 1949).
‡ Of particular importance in psychoanalytic theory.

Problems of Affection. The decision to place certain traditional socialization problems under one heading or another is to some extent arbitrary, as a consideration of the affectional area of learning quickly demonstrates. The manner in which the infant is nursed not only leads to a definition of the problem of support but also to expectations about love from others. That is, the nursing relationship provides the opportunity for learning about protection and support and also about the expression and expectation of love. It also defines at one stage of development the chief source of cues (the mouth) which are associated with primary gratification. Thus, according to the psychoanalysts, affective learning is first associated with the mouth, later with other parts of the body which provide gratification (the anus, the genitals), and finally with people in the immediate or distant environment (self, mother, father, homosexual, heterosexual object choices, etc.). The order of progression of such object choices is supposed to be controlled instinctively according to some Freudians but it is certainly a function of such factors as the major source of gratification at the time (e.g., the mouth during nursing), the availability of persons (self *vs.* others), and social controls, such as incest tabus based on kinship systems. Psychoanalysts have also stressed the difficult learning problems set for the child by competition for love. The child may compete with one parent (e.g., the father) for the love of another (e.g., the mother), and he may compete with another child for the love of the parents, a problem which usually arises in full force shortly after the birth of a sibling. The conflicts resulting from competition for love may become particularly acute because of the narrowness of the typical family group in Western civilization, and they have therefore come in for a good deal of study by psychiatrists (cf. Levy, 1937). They are mentioned here only as representative of the type of problem that can arise in the area of channeling affectional expressions and expectations.

Problems of Mastery. The area of learning which includes problems of mastery has for some reason been rather exclusively the province of traditional American psychology, just as problems of affection have been more or less exclusively the province of psychoanalysis. Gesell and his co-workers (1940, 1943) have analyzed in great detail with the help of motion pictures the developmental sequences of motor coordination. Like Freud, Gesell argues that there are biologically determined orders of emergence of various behaviors. For example, the child first lifts his head in the prone position, then his trunk; later he can sit supported, then sit without support, then perhaps roll from prone to supine and sit up, then stand with support, then stand without support, and finally take a first step. The lines of motor development are, generally speaking, from head to foot and from the trunk to the extremities. This type of analysis is strikingly parallel to Freud's in that it assumes an innate biological force which determines the order of emergence of these skills, just as the libido governs successive object choices. Despite this parallelism there has been almost no contact between the two systems of thinking, the Freudians being essentially uninterested in problems of motor development and Gesell and his co-workers uninterested in sequences of object cathexes. Actually of course it is not necessary to assume a strictly biological determinism in either case. The fact that the child must sit up before he can stand up and stand up before he can walk does not seem to depend so much on biological growth "forces" as on the fact that each successive skill needs the preceding one before it can be successfully performed. There appears to be a true hierarchy of skills in which higher ones require the prior mastery of lower ones. Here, as in the case of object choices, it seems preferable to attribute the sequence found in all children to the kinds of situations in which they are progressively placed by biological and social factors and by past learning rather than to resort to an innate, instinctual driving force.

Factors which influence the rate at which skills are acquired have traditionally been a part of educational psychology. They include variables all the way from presence of the father in the home, to provide instruction and example for some of the higher-order skills, to native intelligence, or the extent to which the parents accelerate the child. Thus it has been demonstrated, for example, that whereas in middle-class America there is an effort to get children to acquire these "ego-executive" skills earlier than in lower-class circles (Davis and Havighurst, 1946), in other cultural groups like the Alorese no effort is made to help children master normal problems like walking, talking, or working at various tasks (DuBois, 1944).

Problems of Control. When we move into the area of control skills it is again obvious that the psychoanalysts have made the major contribution by their emphasis on the importance of cleanliness training and sex and aggression control. Generally speaking, the problems which fall within this area are those centered around the gradual regulation of the child's behavior to fit into the cultural mold. He must learn to tolerate a certain degree of frustration, to channel his acts of aggression, and to inhibit certain forms of antisocial behavior either through the inner controls of conscience or the outer ones of shame or fear of punishment. There must be some

lations in the ... [illegible] rents' behavior undoubtedly [illegible] time these correlations indi- [illegible] a high and satisfac... [illegible] observer reliability. The au- [illegible] ne fifth visit to the home and [illegible] over any clusters or syndromes [illegible] isolate three clusters of parent [illegible] variables showed a high cor- [illegible] correlation with variables in [illegible] three syndromes *Acceptance* [illegible] *y in the home*, then divided [illegible] intensity levels and classified [illegible] amily studies into one of the [illegible] ble 10.3.

[illegible] grees of freedom in a classifi- [illegible] position on one of the three [illegible] a limited number of positions [illegible] e to find seven different com- [illegible] ion of Table 10.3 which ac- [illegible] amilies studied. The way in [illegible] syndromes is determined by [illegible] s illustrated in Table 10.4.

[illegible] s with the Number of Families [illegible] n and Breese, 1945.)

		N	Total N
[illegible]	Acceptant	36	124
[illegible]	Indulgent	46	124

kind of at least partially integrated control system so that when decisions must be made, one alternative or the other may be chosen. Of considerable importance in this area are such variables as who does the socializing and how much control is required of the child. For instance, it has been argued that cross-sex punishment leads to ambivalence toward the opposite sex which may later lead to difficulties in marital adjustments. That is, if the father punishes the daughter she may in time come to have such an unpleasant picture of men that she may have difficulty in marrying one happily. The death of the father may cause special strains for male children since it necessarily leaves discipline to the mother, etc. Some cultures attempt to avoid creating such ambivalence toward people by having outside agents rather than the parents do the punishing (e.g., the Hopi Katcinas).

Parent Behavior Patterns

In all the areas of learning just discussed, parent behavior is of great importance in defining what the child learns. Therefore it is time we considered in more detail the analysis of parent behavior as outlined roughly in the third column of Table 10.2 on the basis of one of the few objective studies ever made in this field. Traditionally the method used in studying parent behavior has been either to infer what it must have been from the free associations of a patient on a psychoanalytic couch or from answers to questions in an interview, or to observe it under relatively uncontrolled conditions on field trips to other cultures. The observations to be discussed here from Baldwin, Kalhorn, and Breese (1945, 1949) were made as a part of the work of the Fels Research Institute's Home Visiting program and show many methodological improvements over previous studies. They will therefore be presented in some detail here, not so much because they provide any final answers, but because they indicate the way in which future research should progress in this field. Baldwin *et al.* obtained repeated ratings by a home visitor of parent behavior on some thirty different behavior variables, ranging from the activity level of the home to the tendency of the parent to make "suggestions, requests, commands, hints and other directive attempts." (1945, p. 7.) The ratings by the home visitor were found to be quite reliable when correlated for two visits separated by six months and even when compared for two visits made three years apart. The median intercorrelation between the two ratings made three years apart was about .62, with many of the correlations in the .70s. Since the parents' behavior undoubtedly changed somewhat over this period of time these correlations indicate a high and satisfactory degree of observer reliability. The authors then chose the ratings made on the fifth visit to the home and intercorrelated them to attempt to discover any clusters or syndromes of parent behavior. They managed to isolate three clusters of parent behavior in each of which the defining variables showed a high correlation with one another and a low correlation with variables in the other two clusters. They labeled the three syndromes *Acceptance of the child, Indulgence,* and *Democracy in the home,* then divided each of these "dimensions" into three intensity levels and classified each of the hundred and twenty-four family studies into one of the three levels. The results are given in Table 10.3.

Furthermore, they found that the degrees of freedom in a classification of this sort were limited. That is, a position on one of the three dimensions tended to be associated with a limited number of positions on the other dimension. They were able to find seven different common patterns listed in the bottom portion of Table 10.3 which accounted for about 75 per cent of the families studied. The way in which a family's position in one of these syndromes is determined by ratings on specific behavioral variables is illustrated in Table 10.4.

TABLE 10.3

Parent Behavior Dimensions and Syndromes with the Number of Families in Each (After Baldwin, Kalhorn, and Breese, 1945.)

A. Dimensions of parent behavior

	N		N		N	Total N
I. Rejectant	31	Casual	57	Acceptant	36	124
II. Nonchalant	26	Mixed (Nonch.-Indulg.)	52	Indulgent	46	124
III. Autocratic	42	Mixed (Aut.-Dem.)	46	Democratic	36	124

B. Common syndromes

1. Rejectant-Nonchalant
2. Rejectant-Active (Autocratic)
3. Casual-Indulgent
4. Casual-Autocratic
5. Acceptant-Indulgent
6. Acceptant-Democratic
7. Acceptant-Democratic-Indulgent

TABLE 10.4

Parent Behavior Profiles for Two Types of Homes

No	Variable		
1 1	Adjustment of Home	Maladjusted	Well-adjusted
1 2	Activeness of Home	Inactive	Active
1 5	Discord in Home	Harmony	Conflict
1 6a	Sociability of Family	Reclusive	Expansive
1 7	Coordination of Household	Chaotic	Coordinated
1.91	Child-centeredness of Home	Child-subordinate	Child-centered
2 11	Duration of Contact with Mother	Brief contact	Extensive contact
2 12	Intensity of Contact with Mother	Inert	Vigorous
3 11	Restrictiveness of Regulations	Freedom	Restriction
3 12	Readiness of Enforcement	Lax	Vigilant
3.13	Severity of Actual Penalties	Mild	Severe
3 14	Justification of Policy	Arbitrary	Rational
3 15	Democracy of Policy	Dictatorial	Democratic
3 16	Clarity of Policy	Vague	Clear
3 17	Effectiveness of Policy	Unsuccessful	Successful
3.18	Disciplinary Friction	Concordant	Contentious
3 21	Quantity of Suggestion	Non-suggesting	Suggesting
3.22	Coerciveness of Suggestion	Suggestion optional	Mandatory
3 3	Accelerational Attempt	Retardatory	Acceleratory
4.1	General Babying	Withholds help	Over-helps
4.2	General Protectiveness	Exposing	Sheltering
5 1	Readiness of Criticism	Uncritical	Critical
5 2	Direction of Criticism	Disapproval	Approval
6 1	Readiness of Explanation	Thwarts curiosity	Satisfies curiosity
7 1	Solicitousness for Welfare	Nonchalant	Anxious
7.2	Acceptance of Child	Rejection	Devotion
8.1	Understanding	Obtuse	Keen
8.2	Emotionality toward Child	Objective	Emotional
8.3	Affectionateness toward Child	Hostile	Affectionate
8.4	Rapport with Child	Isolation	Close rapport

○ ACCEPTANT - INDULGENT

● CASUAL - INDULGENT

(Reproduced by permission from A. L. Baldwin, J. Kalhorn, and F. H. Breese. Patterns of Parent Behavior. *Psychol Monogr.*, 58, No. 3. Copyright 1945 by the American Psychological Association.)

In the profiles illustrated in this table the mean for the whole group of 124 homes on a particular variable is represented by the line down the middle and any mark beyond the first line to the left or right of center is significant at the 5 per cent level and any mark beyond the second line is significant at the 1 per cent level. Thus in this illustration it is clear that the Acceptant-Indulgent pattern is differentiated from the Casual-Indulgent pattern by the greater affectionateness (8.3) and approval (5.2) shown the child, by the presence of a greater number of suggestions (3.21), and by a more successful policy in dealing with the child (3.17). The two syndromes have in common the Over-helping and Over-sheltering tendencies associated with Indulgence (4.1, 4.2) but differ on the Acceptance dimension (7.1 ff.).

These three dimensions of parental behavior are roughly parallel with the first three problems the child must adapt to as listed in Table 10.2. The *Indulgence-Nonchalance* dimension seems clearly to be related to the amount of *protection* provided the child. Protectiveness does not necessarily mean love, however, as the two separate dimensions in Table 10.4 show (4.2, 8.3). Affectionateness and sheltering are not necessarily present in the same families. This is a familiar finding to clinicians who have argued that in some cases protectiveness and general babying are a reaction formation against unconscious rejective tendencies. *Acceptance-Rejection* (or the "warmth" dimension) on the other hand seems most clearly related to problems of affectional learning as listed in Table 10.2. The amount of love and gratification received from various sources will determine, at least to some extent, the nature and strength of the child's object choices, his conception of the world as friendly or unfriendly, etc. Finally, the *Democratic-Autocratic* dimension relates to problems of learning involving *both* Mastery and Control. Either the Democratic or Autocratic home usually requires a considerable degree of mastery from the child and either may be associated with Accelerational attempt. The true opposite of this dimension as far as the mastery skills are concerned would seem to lie in the mixed group of parents who have no consistent or clear policy, either Democratic or Autocratic, with regard to problems of mastery. The dimension of parent behavior related to mastery problems might therefore be rechristened *Acceleration-Indifference.* A somewhat similar lack of congruence arises in connection with control problems since here the relevant dimension appears to be something like *Autocracy-Permissiveness.* Here the word *Autocratic* does not refer so much to mere arbitrariness as to the restrictiveness and coerciveness of socialization requirements. Some families and some societies are relatively lax in the amount of control of aggression or other asocial behaviors required, whereas others demand a great deal of control and at a relatively early age. It is this high "level of aspiration" parents have for their children with respect to control skills that, according to psychoanalytic thinking, makes the adjustive responses or expectations learned in connection with these problems so important later on. Thus early and strict emphasis on control in one area (e.g., bowel training) may generalize to structure the whole universe as demanding compliance, orderliness, etc. (the anal character discussed earlier).

Such an analysis of parent behavior does not cover all the important dimensions of child-rearing practices. However, it does suggest what some of these dimensions are and how they may be grouped in the higher-order syndromes listed in Table 10.3. It also suggests how some of the other variables known to be influential in child rearing can fit into an over-all scheme. Since we cannot begin to treat all these other variables adequately, we will select three for special treatment, about which a considerable amount of information has accumulated.

1. **Parent Behavior Extremes.** Clinical and anthropological data clearly show that extreme deviations from the "norm" on any of the dimensions listed above (Indulgence-Neglect, Affection-Rejection, Acceleration-Indifference, Autocracy-Permissiveness) will accentuate the problems in this area for the child. *Either* overprotection (cf. Levy, 1943) or neglect, for instance, seems to lead to fear of the unknown and insecurity arising from fear of desertion by the parents. Whiting and Child have shown (see Table 10.6 below) that *high or low* nurturance tends to be associated with a belief in spirits as causes of disease, spirits which presumably represent projections of a strong need for dependence on someone. Similar difficulties arise from extremes in the other dimensions. Overaffectionateness may lead to object fixations which are hard to break, whereas lack of affection or rejection has been eloquently treated by a number of clinicians and dubbed "affect hunger" by Levy (1937). The accelerational emphasis on competitive mastery in our own culture, with its attendant dangers of neurotic striving, peptic ulcers and the like, has received particular attention from many psychiatrists (cf. Alexander, 1942), whereas Kardiner warns us (1945) that the lack of concern for ego executive skills in Alor results in "lack of constructive ability." The list could be extended but the point is simply that *any extreme* in parental behavior is likely to stress the importance of the problem for the child, though in somewhat different and as yet unclearly understood ways. With the variables defined in this way, it should be possible to investigate more systematically what their

effects are. Whiting and Child (1950) have come nearest to this in making ratings of initial indulgence and of severity of training for different types of socialization problems.

2. Sequences of Parent Behavior. So far parent behavior has been treated as a static, cross-sectional phenomenon, whereas actually it varies with the age of the child and often in a patterned way. For example, a child may be initially indulged in nursing, getting both high protection and high affection, and then be suddenly and harshly weaned, perhaps because of the birth of a sibling. Such sequences are thought, on the basis of clinical data (cf. Kardiner's case discussed earlier), to be of very considerable importance, possibly because the early experiences lead to expectations of what is to come next which are then severely frustrated. Under these circumstances, on theoretical grounds one would expect a rather slow adjustment to the new circumstances because of the factors favoring the strength of early learning as discussed earlier in the chapter. A rather simple but important illustration of this point is provided by some observations reported by Sears and Wise (1950) on the frequency of weaning disturbance among three groups of babies, one of which was weaned at birth (cup-fed), one of which was weaned between two weeks and three months, and one of which was weaned after three months. The frequency of weaning disturbance was significantly greater "the longer the child has been fed by sucking." The interpretation given is that frequent association of sucking cues with feeding led to the establishment of a habit (expectation) which was much stronger than if such early reinforcement had not occurred (cup-fed group). To put it in another way, once the expectation of oral gratification has been set up through nutritional sucking, unlearning such an expectation is more difficult and frustrating than if it had not been set up in the first place.

The age at which training is begun is likely to determine the relative importance of the problem to the child and possibly to the adult, for reasons given earlier in the chapter. For example, if independence training is begun before the child is really capable of performing adequately or well the skills which are required of him, his thinking is likely to be colored thereafter by an achievement orientation which takes precedence over orientations stressed at later points in the developmental sequence (cf. Friedman, 1950). If achievement training is begun later, after the person has developed his "apperceptive mass" or his various symbol systems, it will assume less of an all-pervasive importance to him because he can differentiate more easily between achievement-related and non-achievement-related situations. Similarly, early food deprivation appears to have more permanent effects on food-related behavior than docs late deprivation (cf. Hunt, 1941). This problem will be discussed more fully in Chapter 12.

3. **Motives Utilized in Socialization.** So far we have touched on such questions as the following: What are the problems a child has to solve in the process of socialization? How does a parent define or emphasize these different problems? What are the patterns of behavior expected from the child as solutions to these problems? In what order must the problems be mastered or at what age must the child start mastering a particular one? This leaves until last perhaps the most important question of all: Why should the child solve the problems at all which are presented to him in the course of socialization? What reasons has he for doing what the culture wants him to do?

It has been traditional to assume that the child does not want to proceed along the road to socialization. Since progress seems to involve sacrifice and renunciation of earlier gratifications, the child is conceived as reluctant and unwilling. Alexander puts it this way: "There is a marked emotional resistance in the child against this process of maturation. Psychiatric observations offer the most convincing evidence for the strong resistance which the ego puts up against accepting the gradually increasing independence which biological maturation brings." (Kluckhohn and Murray, 1949, p. 333.) Whiting and Mowrer (1943) designed a D-maze as an analogue of the socialization process. A rat is first trained in it to go down the short path to the goal (infant gratification) and then a block is put across the throat of the D and the rat must go the long way around (growing up). This view is oversimplified. As Murray so aptly puts it, "All individuals do not go through life 'tied to their mother's apron strings' with backward glances at the joy that has been denied them. Children clearly exhibit a tendency to change, to wander, to explore, to test their powers of mastery, act like 'grown ups,' gain self-reliance and creatively conceive of things that are 'higher' than any things their parents taught them." (1938, p. 725.)

The truth appears to incorporate both of these notions. The child solves the problems presented him by socialization in part *because of his own motives* and in part because of frustrations, rewards, and punishments administered to him from the outside. As Murray points out, the infant's own need for achievement or mastery will lead him to solve increasingly complicated problems, whose solutions give him his own approval more or less irrespective of the approval or disapproval of others, once the motive (n Achievement) has been established. It would be difficult indeed to account for the progress of the child through Gesell's stages of successive mastery of complex motor skills if it were true that the child was reluctant to give up one stage for another and had to be prodded by rewards and punishments from outside. In fact, if this were true, one might suppose that walking might be less universal, that somewhere along the line the rewards and punishments from the outside would have failed in their purpose and some child would never have given up being carried around.

On the other hand, the kind of motivational control used by a parent is certainly of major importance in how the child gets socialized. Specifically the parent can vary the motive which he appeals to in attempting to get the child to do what he wants. Consider the following alternative motivational appeals:

1. "If you do that, I won't love you."
2. "If you do that, you'll be disapproved, rejected, teased."
3. "If you do that, I will punish you (or reward you)."
4. "If you do that, I will suffer (or be pleased)."

These may occur either in the negative or positive form: e.g., "If you do that, I *will* love you." There has been a good deal of clinical speculation, as yet without too much experimental basis, as to the effects of these various forms of control. For example, the first statement is the "conditional love" formula so characteristic of middle class white Americans according to Margaret Mead (1942). She argues that in many American families, love is conditional on achievement or proper behavior. The second formula apparently underlies the *shame* or situational morality complex in which the person avoids doing something in anticipation of the disapproval or ridicule of others. If caught he is shamed, but if he is not caught, or if the possibility of being caught is not great, the control is not effective: hence the term "situational morality" indicating that morality is contingent upon the situation (Kluckhohn and Leighton, 1947). The third formula leads in its most extreme form to paranoid tendencies in which the person is controlled wholly by fear of hostility or punishment from without, either real (e.g., the police) or unreal (e.g., Hell and Damnation). The fourth formula may give rise to guilt if the child has identified sufficiently with the barent, since if he has, he knows that this will cause the parent to be unhappy or in extreme cases to suffer. For this mechanism to work, the parents must have nurtured and loved the child sufficiently for identification to have taken place (cf. Sears and Whiting, 1950). Some evidence for the differential effects of these control mechanisms is to be found in a study by MacKinnon (cf. Murray, 1938) which contrasts psychological discipline (formulas 1 and 4) with physical punishment (formulas 2 and 3). He compared a group of college men who had not violated a prohibition with a group who had. He found that 78 per cent of the fathers of violators had used physical as opposed to psychological discipline whereas only 48 per cent of the fathers of the non-violators had used physical punishment. Furthermore, 75 per cent of the non-violators reported that they often felt guilty, whereas only 29 per cent of the violators admitted often feeling guilty (Murray, 1938, pp. 497-499). In short, psychological discipline was associated with more frequent guilt feelings and with non-violation of prohibitions as compared with physical punishment, which was associated less often with a sense of guilt and more often with violation of prohibitions when no one was supposed to be watching.

Positive and Negative Sanctions. It is not only the *kind* of motive which is used to control the child's behavior: The *way* in which the control is applied is also thought to be of importance. To begin with, a sanction can be either positive or negative. This has led to the concept of the "reward-punishment balance" used especially by Kardiner (cf. DuBois, 1944). That is, the parent can emphasize either the positive gain associated with a certain act ("If you do that I will be happy," etc.) or its negative consequences ("If you do that, I will be unhappy," etc.) Many specialists in socialization have argued in favor of the use of reward, largely on the basis of findings in learning experiments that punishment appears to be less effective in weakening or inhibiting a response than does learning a new response to replace the wrong one. Mowrer and Kluckhohn are particularly eloquent on the importance of continuous satisfaction "during the first few months of extra-uterine life. . . . Responsively answering the child's expressions of need . . . should promote confidence and trust in a predictable world, for each primitive striving is rewarded. It should encourage an alert, outgoing attitude . . . social responsiveness . . . and facilitate the early establishment of positive emotional attachment to parents." (1944, p. 88.) Kardiner, on the other hand, has emphasized that the average Alorese parent is so predominately negative in his approach to child rearing that this must have contributed to the Alorese individual's suspicious, mistrustful view of the world.

At the present stage of knowledge it is too early to make recommendations as to what procedure is "best" or most "natural," but sufficient evidence has accumulated to argue that reward-punishment balance is one of the important dimensions of child-rearing practices. In further support of this view, Whiting and Child have argued (1950) partly on empirical and partly on theoretical grounds that different combinations of nurturance and punishment will lead to different forms of conscience or control over behavior. Thus, for instance, high nurturance with frequent denial of love as a technique of punishment might lead predominantly to the control of behavior by *guilt,* whereas low nurturance and high punishment might lead to control of behavior through externalized fears.

Regularity in Parent Behavior. Application of sanctions can also vary in the consistency with which they are associated with the response to be controlled. At the one extreme, sanctions may occur promptly and appropriately, just after the response to be reinforced or inhibited. At the other extreme, which is more characteristic of life situations outside the laboratory, the occurrence of parental sanctions may be irregular, inconsistent, aperiodic, or delayed. Analogous irregularities in animal experiments would lead us to expect that such conditions will lead to the acquisition of associations which are less "reality-bound," less easily modified by changes in the situation. For instance, if the experimenter responds to the clock rather than to the responses of a pigeon and reinforces the pigeon every two minutes, regardless of what his pecking activities have been, the bird will develop a stronger pecking habit than if the reinforcement schedule had been geared to his *responses* (cf. Jenkins and Stanley, 1950). The parallel seems rather close to the parent who responds to the clock in feeding an infant according to a time schedule rather than in accordance with the infant's hunger pangs or cries for food. Here, too, one might expect that such inconsistent (from the child's viewpoint) behavior might lead to a heightened concern over food and a lack of appropriateness of such concern to the cues which should evoke hunger or be associated with satisfaction. In short, one might expect a "neurotic," not "reality bound," need for food to develop (cf. Mowrer and Kluckhohn, 1944). Such parallels as these are interesting and point the way to further research on children, but it would certainly be premature to draw, on the basis of such analogies, any firm conclusions about the way children *ought* to be brought up.

The Effect of Child-Rearing Practices on Personality

Having demonstrated at the beginning of the chapter some empirical correlations between childhood experiences and personality formation, we then looked more closely into the reasons why these correlations might exist and into the different kinds of socialization procedures which have been considered to be of importance. This leaves the most important question in need of careful analysis. In exactly what way do these socialization problems and procedures influence personality, particularly adult personality? Although psychoanalysts and many cultural anthropologists are persuaded of the very great importance of early childhood, there are still those who feel that the importance has not been demonstrated. Orlansky after a careful review of the literature concludes "that the rigidity of character structuring during the first year or two of life has been exaggerated by many authorities and that the events of childhood and later years are of great importance in reinforcing and changing the character structure tentatively formed during infancy." (1949, p. 38.) In view of this conflict of opinions we will have to approach this subject carefully and cautiously. Just what is the evidence on this point?

To begin with, we must distinguish between clinical and experimental evidence. It is the former which has largely given rise to the belief that early childhood is important. Psychoanalysts and clinical psychologists have reported in hundreds of cases the world over the importance of some childhood trauma in determining the whole future course of a person's development. The skeptic may grant that this is suggestive but certainly far from conclusive. After all, a patient on a psychoanalytic couch may search his memory for a childhood event until he finds one which fits the psychoanalyst's purpose, or he may even invent such a memory. There is no real way to demonstrate that the memory he finds bears a causal relationship to his present symptomatology. The experimentalist would want to introduce the variable in childhood or to observe it at that time, and then to check its effect years later on the same people grown up. Even though he may accept such a relationship in an individual case when the evidence from outside sources is convincing, he may still argue that this is the exception rather than the rule, since the person being analyzed is sick. Normal personalities do not drag their infantile experiences around with them but leave them behind, or grow out of them (cf. Allport, 1937).

Since such an argument as this is not likely to be soon settled, we must turn to the evidence which arises from direct observation of early experiences and their effects later on. Here again there are two approaches. We may either work with natural differences in parent behavior, observing them as they occur, in which case the difficulty is to isolate the effects of any particular difference, or we may introduce a particular variable under experimental conditions, in which case the difficulty is that we must either work with animals and extrapolate to humans or with humans, using relatively unimportant variables over short periods of time. Despite all these difficulties there are important findings that contribute to our knowledge on this point. At the animal level there are now a whole series of experiments which clearly demonstrate that certain experiences will have one effect if they occur early in life and a different effect if they occur later. Hunt (1941) and others have demonstrated that infant feeding frustration will lead to adult hoarding in the white rat, Wolf (1943) that sensory deprivation in infancy leads to inadequate sensory functioning in adulthood if the rat is placed in competition with another rat, and Christie (1950) that early exploration under simulated wild conditions will enable a rat to make better use of his experience with water bottles and food cups in adulthood. All these findings are suggestive but since they are based on animals may be considered inconclusive for our purpose.

At the human level there is first of all the evidence that parents' behavior definitely influences their children's behavior *at the time*. Table 10.5, which is reproduced from Baldwin, Kalhorn, and Breese (1945) presents behavior ratings for children in nursery school when classified according to the type of home from which they came. The ratings are expressed in standard scores and, if in italics, deviate significantly at the 5 per cent level from the mean for the whole group of children. The data provided in this table are only the beginning of the kind of study which ought to be made. They do indicate that at least the Democratic syndrome and the Active or Autocratic-Rejectant syndrome have important effects on children's

TABLE 10.5

Intellectual and Social Development of School-Age Children As a Function of Parent Behavior Patterns

	REJECTANT		CASUAL		ACCEPTANT		
Variable	*Noncha-lant*	*Active (Auto-cratic)*	*Auto-cratic*	*Indul-gent*	*Demo-cratic*	*In-dulgent*	*Democratic-Indulgent*
Nursery school							
N=	19	10	14	17	14	11	9
IQ change	—.9	—.3	1.9	4.4	7.1	.5	8.6
N=	8	7	6	12	11	8	7
Originality	51	*40*	49	49	*57*	*43*	46
Planfulness	53	47	49	49	*58*	51	46
Fancifulness	46	44	49	47	*60*	46	47
Tenacity	51	*42*	49	50	51	45	47
School-age interview ratings							
N=	9	7	7	too	6	6	7
Sociability	50	53	52	few	*60*	46	53
Shyness	51	*41*	50		46	56	*42*
Quarrelsomeness	52	*60*	46		53	46	53
Hostility to father	53	54	50		*40*	48	*43*
Emotional dependence	51	*43*	57		56	42	56

(Reproduced with permission from A. L. Baldwin, J. Kalhorn, and F. H. Breese. Patterns of Parent Behavior. *Psychol. Monogr.*, 58, No. 3. Copyright 1945 by the American Psychological Association.)

behavior. Both types of Democratic home (which we associated with acceleration of mastery skills) show an increase in I.Q. as measured three years apart in the course of normal nursery-school testing of all children. This growth in mental development is apparent also in the ratings on such intellectual variables as Originality, Planfulness, and Fancifulness. It is interesting to note that when Democracy is combined with Indulgence (protectiveness) there is an increase in tested intelligence but not in the traits of Originality and Fancifulness. These results support the argument presented earlier that the Democratic syndrome is related to Acceleration of mastery techniques and skills. In contrast to this the Actively Rejectant parents appear to produce children who are significantly low on Originality and Tenacity, a finding which is entirely in agreement with Kardiner's conclusion that the institutionalized Rejectant pattern among the Alorese produces people who are notably lacking in creativeness and tenacity.

But we still have not demonstrated the effects of all this on *adult* personality. Such data as these, however, strongly suggest that there must be such an effect even though it may be indirect and continuous. Take the matter of I.Q. change alone. Here the effect of the parent behavior variable (Democracy or Accelerational attempts) is so important (I.Q. increase) that further changes as a result of I.Q. changes can be predicted with considerable certainty. Thus children who have achieved more and are more planful, original, and fanciful are almost certain to receive more reward for school work, to remain achievement-oriented, etc. In fact, under such circumstances it seems unreasonable to assume that such a chain of events would stop rather than continue on to influence adult personality in important ways. In many instances in Table 10.5 the ratings affected seem to deal with what might be called "motivational traits" such as planfulness, fancifulness, or tenacity which should continue to influence what the child decides to do, what kinds of knowledge he accumulates, the way he thinks, etc., long beyond the particular period of nursery school under observation at this point. Further support for this point can be gained from the study of Johnny and Jimmie (McGraw, 1935), two identical twin boys, one of whom was given extensive and very early training in complex motor skills like skating and the other of whom was allowed to develop normally. McGraw, who made the study, found that although the "normal" twin caught up to his accelerated brother as far as motor skills were concerned, the two were markedly different in the attitudes toward life which they had developed. The accelerated twin seemed much more confident, for example, in new situations in later life.

This last example is essentially the case-study method again but with an important difference. Here the experimenter knows exactly what has been done to the child and checks up on his development at a later time. A somewhat analogous approach has been used by anthropologists who attempt to correlate a specific child training practice which they have observed with certain adult personality characteristics. The individual case here is a culture rather than a person. The literature abounds in illustrations of this sort. Kardiner's correlation between poor maternal care and adult personality structure among the Alorese (1945) is one example. Bateson's correlation (1944) between teasing in childhood and the avoidance of climaxes in adulthood in Bali is another. Kluckhohn (1947) has likewise wondered about the significance of the cradleboard in forming the character of the Navaho. He feels that the early security which the cradleboard provides should, according to psychoanalytic principles, lead to relatively great security among adult Navaho. Since this is not the case—since the Navaho are actually suspicious and mistrustful—he argues that other later experiences must have entered in to change what should otherwise have come about. Even though his original assumption is probably incorrect (overprotection also leads to insecurity), his conclusion seems reasonable enough. The difficulty with all such arguments is that they do not permit us to isolate the effects of a particular childhood experience. This is always true so long as we deal with a single case (either a single person or a single culture) since there are so many causes (childhood events) and so many effects (personality systems) that it is impossible to connect any *particular* cause with any *particular* effect.

A much more satisfactory methodological approach has been adopted by Whiting and Child in their study (1950) of the association in a large sample of cultures of a particular childhood training experience with a particular theory of disease. By increasing the number of cultures in which the observations were made, they presumably randomized the "other events" occurring in childhood and any resulting relationship they found should be due to the particular variables they were studying. Specifically, they had three judges rate some 76 cultures on which data were available in the Yale Outline of Cultural Materials on initial indulgence, age of the beginning of training, and severity of training for each of five socialization practices: nursing and weaning, toilet training, sex training, independence training, and aggression control. Some of their most important preliminary findings are summarized in Table 10.6.

What this table shows is that certain child-training practices are associated more often than one would expect by chance with certain specific "magical" explanations of sickness. For instance, if the nuclear family is chiefly responsible for socialization of the child, conditions should be favorable for the child to identify with a *particular* parent and to accept as his own the parent's attitudes of approval and disapproval for a particular act (guilt mechanism: cf. Chapter 9). Fur-

TABLE 10.6

Relationships Between Child-Rearing Practices and Theories of Disease in 50-76 Cultures

Cause of the disease	*Associated child-rearing practices*
1. The patient feels himself responsible (Guilt mechanism: "I feel sick because I have done something I shouldn't have.")	Nuclear family controls socialization Frequent use of denial of love as technique of punishment
a. Broken a food tabu	Severe weaning
b. Broken a sex tabu	Severe sex training
c. Broken an aggression tabu	Severe aggression training
2. Sorcerers (Paranoid mechanism: "I feel sick because some person is hostile toward me.")	Severe punishment for heterosexual play
3. Spirits ("I feel sick because the spirits have deserted me, stolen my soul," etc.)	Either high nurturance or neglect in infancy
a. Increased importance of animal spirits	Severe aggression training

Note: All relationships are significant at or beyond the 5% level.

(From Whiting and Child, 1950.)

thermore the finding that the use of "denial of love" as a form of punishment is associated with guilt as the explanation for sickness confirms the theoretical argument, presented earlier in the chapter, that "psychological discipline" should lead to high guilt feelings. Interestingly enough, the nature of the violation about which the person feels guilty seems determined by the emphasis placed on feeding, sex or aggression control in childhood, again confirming our theoretical hypothesis that early stressing of a particular socialization problem will tend to organize the person's conception of the world around that problem. Further evidence for this position has been obtained by Friedman (1950), who has shown that there is a significant correlation between the number of achievement characteristics in the myths of a culture and the amount of emphasis placed on independence training in childhood.

Returning to Table 10.6 we note the explanations of disease involving *sorcerers* or *spirits* as agents are associated in each case with child-rearing variables which should lead to precisely such results according to psychoanalytic theory. Thus Freud has emphasized the connection between homosexuality (which should be correlated with punishment for heterosexual play) and paranoia, and a number of psychoanalysts have stressed the frequency with which desertion or rejection in childhood leads to the creation of "magic helpers" or spirits which, in the present instance, apparently desert or become hostile when the person feels sick. Furthermore, the fact that animal spirits are more frequently important causes of disease when aggression control is severe strongly suggests the Freudian mechanisms of projection and displacement. That is, high punishment for aggression should evoke hostile impulses in the child which should be unacceptable and projected out into the environment again, particularly if the parents are also highly nurturant because high nurturance should lead to guilt over hostility toward the source of nurturance. The fact that the projected hostility is displaced from the parents to animals would then have to be explained either in terms of the inconsistency of attributing hostility to highly nurturant parents or to the fear of attributing hostility to potentially rejecting parents. When the connections are traced out in this way, it is not so difficult to see how certain common childhood experiences may lead to common cultural beliefs—particularly if those beliefs are in the nature of what Kardiner (1945) calls projective or "nonempirical" reality systems. A mutually reinforcing process is set up. All members of the culture are presumably exposed to a modal type of child-rearing which is molded by certain theories about the nature of nonempirical reality (including disease). The child-rearing practice in turn serves to reinforce that particular theory of disease in the members of the culture when they grow up. The belief predisposes the parents to a certain kind of socialization practice, which predisposes the children to accept the belief and to follow the same practice when they become parents, etc.

To sum up, the evidence is most clear-cut for a connection between early childhood experiences and adult projective systems: i.e., general orientations, attitudes, or conceptions, particularly unreal, imaginative, or nonempirical ones. Thus we have come back to where Freud started since it was *just such "unreal" imaginative productions on the psychoanalytic couch* which first led him to believe in the importance of childhood experiences. Our conclusion is not surprising on theoretical grounds either, since "reality" systems should continue to grow, develop, and be modified by subsequent stimulation much more than the projective or nonempirical systems which are more the product of unconscious, or unsymbolized, experiences, which according to our earlier arguments are so characteristic of early childhood. Having reached this conclusion, we may now attempt to apply it, as Freud did, by starting with Karl's imaginative ideas and trying to draw from them some inferences about the nature of his childhood experiences.

Karl's Socialization As Reflected in His Imaginative Productions

The Thematic Apperception Test (TAT) has been widely used by clinicians to get at some of the more unconscious, "unreal" conceptions guiding a person's adjustment to life. Murray and Morgan (1945), who invented it, have found it particularly useful in getting at childhood events or experiences or their schematic precipitates which are not readily available to conscious recall. In this respect they have confirmed Freud's initial finding that relatively spontaneous or "free" associations are of great value in providing information about unconscious aspects of personality. Karl cooperated willingly in taking the TAT and produced the following story in response to the first picture, which shows a boy looking at a violin:

> This boy's father was a famous concert violinist before he was born. Unfortunately he lost his life in a tragic accident. He was drowned. His wife was pregnant and had this chap. I might add that his father was at the peak of his fame. Died on the night before the concert. Of course he left his fiddle, which was old and valuable to his son. He always had hopes that he would teach his son and his son would play the fiddle better than his father. At the age of one year his mother died and the boy was left with an aunt and uncle who were not too favorably inclined toward fiddlers. Nevertheless they gave him his chance and started him on violin lessons. He didn't show unusual talent, but a fair amount. Now as he sits here, he has just been told about his parents and their wishes. He realizes that he isn't overtalented, but he is considering whether he will like it enough for his mother's sake. As he grows older, he will put the fiddle aside and go to something else. He's debating other possibilities.

The usual method of interpreting a story lik
assume that Karl has identified with his hero an
expressed depict his relationship with his own fa
fest level, this would involve the guesses that his
cerned with achievement, that they expected him
his father, and that he didn't feel capable of d
father. At the latent level the violin would prob
penis symbol, in which case the story would be
unconscious wish to take over the father's sexua
which is so dangerous that it leads to the death of
consideration of renunciation of sexuality altogeth

But how can any of these be verified? Such gue
ingenious as it often appears to be, has seldom
ses that can be systematically tested by ordina
cedures. However, there is some material in th
subsequent stories which can lend itself to a fairl
titative analysis. Such an analysis will be attemp
illustration of how one could go about studying su
for the information it gives us about Karl's socializat

Analysis of Deaths in Karl's Record. The mater
centers around the deaths in his stories. This first st
in that both parents are mentioned and quickly kill
that the father dies by drowning and the mother by
cause. Unfortunately, adequate norms for the vario
the Murray TAT do not exist (cf. Rosenzweig and Fl
but in the protocols of six undergraduate subjects prin
ray (1949) there is not a single instance in which a par
the stories told for this particular picture. This in itself
clusive but it does suggest that a further analysis of
throughout the whole record would be profitable.

First of all, the number of deaths in Karl's record is
higher than normal. In Murray's six protocols th
of somewhat less than four deaths for the ten
also in the set of pictures ... Karl. Th
in Karl's record, which is ... mor
ber in any record in the ... up.
that the norms are ade...
frequency of deaths i...
tation is that there ...

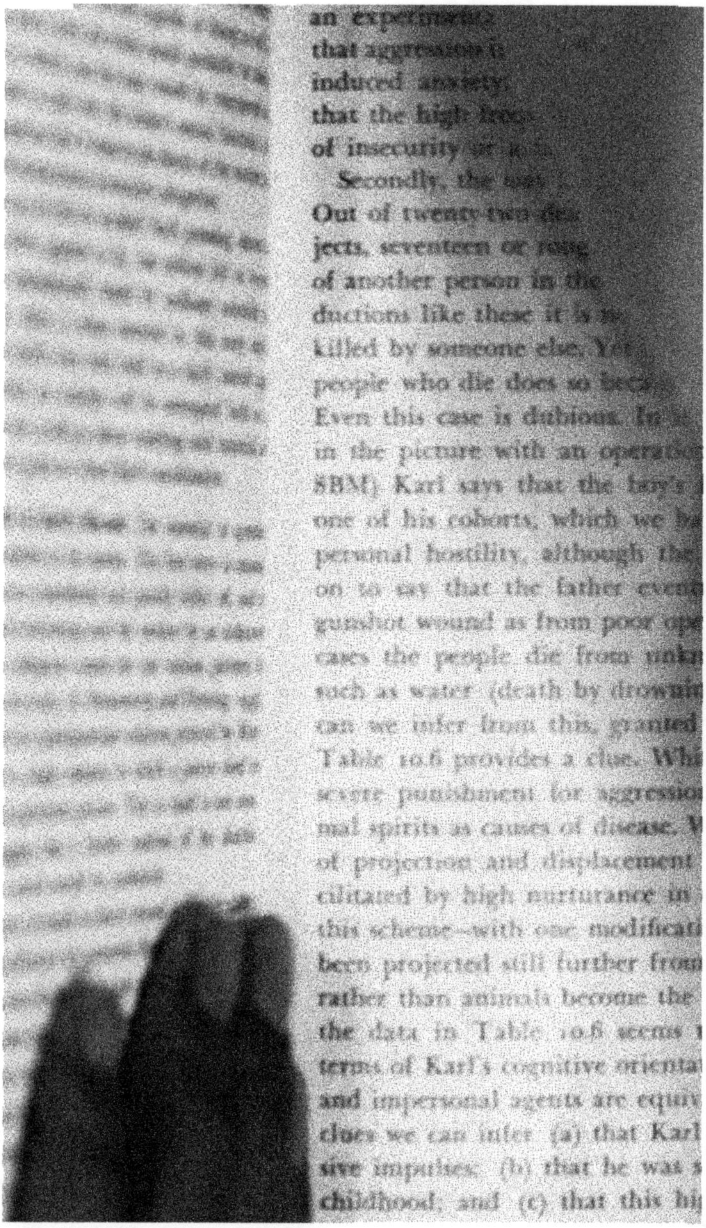

an experimental
that aggression is
induced anxiety;
that the high leve
of insecurity or a
Secondly, the
Out of twenty-two
jects, seventeen or
of another person in the
ductions like these it is
killed by someone else. Yet
people who die does so beca
Even this case is dubious. In
in the picture with an operatio
8BM), Karl says that the boy's
one of his cohorts, which we ha
personal hostility, although the
on to say that the father event
gunshot wound as from poor ope
cases the people die from unkn
such as water (death by drownin
can we infer from this, granted
Table 10.6 provides a clue. Wha
severe punishment for aggressio
mal spirits as causes of disease.
of projection and displacement
cilitated by high nurturance in
this scheme—with one modificati
been projected still further from
rather than animals become the
the data in Table 10.6 seems
terms of Karl's cognitive orienta
and impersonal agents are equiv
clues we can infer (a) that Karl
sive impulses; (b) that he was
childhood; and (c) that this hi

The usual method of interpreting a story like this would be to assume that Karl has identified with his hero and that the attitudes expressed depict his relationship with his own family. At the manifest level, this would involve the guesses that his parents were concerned with achievement, that they expected him to do better than his father, and that he did not feel capable of doing as well as his father. At the latent level the violin would probably be taken as a penis symbol, in which case the story would be interpreted as the unconscious wish to take over the father's sexual position, a wish which is so dangerous that it leads to the death of the mother and a consideration of renunciation of sexuality altogether.

But how can any of this be verified? Such guessing, shrewd and ingenious as it often appears to be, has seldom led to hypotheses that can be systematically tested by ordinary scientific procedures. However, there is some material in this story and in subsequent stories which does lend itself to a fairly careful quantitative analysis. Such an analysis will be attempted both as an illustration of how one could go about analyzing such material and for the information it gives us about Karl's socialization.

Analysis of Deaths in Karl's Record. The material in question centers around the deaths in his stories. This first one is unusual in that both parents are mentioned and quickly killed off, and in that the father dies by drowning and the mother of an unknown cause. Unfortunately, adequate norms for the various pictures in the Murray TAT do not exist (cf. Rosenzweig and Fleming, 1949). In the protocols of six undergraduate subjects quoted by Murray (1943) there is not a single instance in which a parent died in the stories told for this particular picture. This in itself is not conclusive but it does suggest that a further analysis of the deaths throughout the whole record would be profitable.

First of all, the number of deaths in Karl's record is considerably higher than normal. In Murray's six protocols there are an average of somewhat less than four deaths for the ten pictures which were also in the set of pictures given to Karl. There are eleven deaths in Karl's record, which is considerably more than the highest number in any record in the Murray group. Assuming for the moment that the norms are adequate, what can we make of the unusual number of deaths in Karl's stories? The rather obvious interpretation is that there is a lot of aggression in the subject since ag-

organism survive. (Cf. Dollard, *et al.*; 1939.) But what does aggression in a person's stories mean? Maybe Karl just likes to tell gory stories. It is here that most interpretations of imaginative material have broken down, but fortunately we have evidence from an experimental study by McClelland, Birney, and Roby (1950) that aggression in stories like these is increased under experimentally induced anxiety. We may therefore infer as our first hypothesis that the high frequency of aggression in Karl's stories is indicative of insecurity or a fairly high anxiety level.

Secondly, the way in which people die in these stories is curious. Out of twenty-two deaths in the records of our six normative subjects, seventeen or roughly 80 per cent were due to the hostile act of another person in the story. In other words, in imaginative productions like these it is normal for people to die because they are killed by someone else. Yet in Karl's stories only one of the eleven people who dies does so because of the hostility of another person. Even this case is dubious. In telling a story about the young boy in the picture with an operation scene in the background (TAT 8BM) Karl says that the boy's father was "accidentally" shot by one of his [illegible], which we have checked as being indicative of personal hostility, although the hostility is minimal and he goes on to say that the father eventually dies not so much from the gunshot wounds as from poor operating techniques. In all the other cases the people die from unknown causes or impersonal agents such as water (death by drowning), windstorms, disease, etc. What can we infer from this, granted again that it is an unusual fact? Table 10.6 provides a clue. Whiting and Child (1950) report that severe punishment for aggression is associated with belief in animal spirits as causes of disease. We suggested further that this kind of projection and displacement of reactive hostility might be facilitated by low nurturance in childhood. Karl's case seems to fit this scheme—with one modification: in his stories the hostility has been projected still further from the self so that impersonal forces rather than animals become the agents of death. The parallel with the data in Table 10.6 seems rather close if we assume that in terms of Karl's cognitive orientations death is equivalent to disease and impersonal agents are equivalent to animal spirits. From these clues we consider (a) that Karl has acute anxiety over his aggressive impulses, (b) that he was severely punished for aggression in childhood, and (c) that this high punishment was probably asso-

The usual method of interpreting a story like this would be to assume that Karl has identified with his hero and that the attitudes expressed depict his relationship with his own family. At the manifest level, this would involve the guesses that his parents were concerned with achievement, that they expected him to do better than his father, and that he did not feel capable of doing as well as his father. At the latent level the violin would probably be taken as a penis symbol, in which case the story would be interpreted as the unconscious wish to take over the father's sexual function, a wish which is so dangerous that it leads to the death of the mother and a consideration of renunciation of sexuality altogether.

But how can any of this be verified? Such guessing, shrewd and ingenious as it often appears to be, has seldom led to hypotheses that can be systematically tested by ordinary scientific procedures. However, there is some material in this story and in subsequent stories which does lend itself to a fairly careful quantitative analysis. Such an analysis will be attempted both as an illustration of how one could go about studying such material and for the information it gives us about Karl's socialization.

Analysis of Deaths in Karl's Record. The material in question centers around the deaths in his stories. This first story is unusual in that both parents are mentioned and quickly killed off, and in that the father dies by drowning and the mother by an unknown cause. Unfortunately, adequate norms for the various pictures in the Murray TAT do not exist (cf. Rosenzweig and Fleming, 1949), but in the protocols of six undergraduate subjects printed by Murray (1949) there is not a single instance in which a parent died in the stories told for this particular picture. This in itself is not conclusive but it does suggest that a further analysis of the deaths throughout the whole record would be profitable.

First of all, the *number* of deaths in Karl's record is considerably higher than normal. In Murray's six protocols there are an average of somewhat less than four deaths for the ten pictures which were also in the set of pictures given to Karl. There are eleven deaths in Karl's record, which is considerably more than the highest number in any record in the Murray group. Assuming for the moment that the norms are adequate, what can we make of the unusual frequency of deaths in Karl's stories? The rather obvious interpretation is that there is a lot of aggression in the stories since aggression has customarily been defined as "injury to an organism or organism surrogate." (Cf. Dollard, *et al.*; 1939.) But what does aggression in a person's stories mean? Maybe Karl just likes to tell gory stories. It is here that most interpretations of imaginative material have fallen down, but fortunately we have evidence from an experimental study by McClelland, Birney, and Roby (1950) that aggression in stories like these is increased under experimentally induced anxiety. We may therefore infer as our first hypothesis that the high frequency of aggression in Karl's stories is indicative of insecurity or a fairly high anxiety level.

Secondly, the *way* in which people die in these stories is curious. Out of twenty-two deaths in the records of our six normative subjects, seventeen or roughly 80 per cent were due to the hostile act of another person in the story. In other words, in imaginative productions like these it is normal for people to die because they are killed by someone else. Yet in Karl's stories only one of the eleven people who die does so because of the hostility of another person. Even this case is dubious. In telling a story about the young boy in the picture with an operation scene in the background (TAT 8BM) Karl says that the boy's father was "accidentally" shot by one of his cohorts, which we have checked as being indicative of personal hostility, although the hostility is minimal and he goes on to say that the father eventually dies not so much from the gunshot wound as from poor operating techniques. In all the other cases the people die from unknown causes or impersonal agents such as water (death by drowning), windstorms, disease, etc. What can we infer from this, granted again that it is an unusual fact? Table 10.6 provides a clue. Whiting and Child (1950) report that severe punishment for aggression is associated with belief in animal spirits as causes of disease. We suggested further that this kind of projection and displacement of reactive hostility might be facilitated by high nurturance in childhood. Karl's case seems to fit this scheme—with one modification: in his stories the hostility has been projected still further from the self so that impersonal forces rather than animals become the agents of death. The parallel with the data in Table 10.6 seems rather close if we assume that in terms of Karl's cognitive orientations death is equivalent to disease and impersonal agents are equivalent to animal spirits. From these clues we can infer (a) that Karl has acute anxiety over his aggressive impulses; (b) that he was severely punished for aggression in childhood; and (c) that this high punishment was probably associated with high nurturance. A less likely hypothesis might explain these findings in terms of severe punishment for heterosexual play which might have been responsible for the "paranoid" nature of his explanations of death in which the aggression is projected as far from the self as possible.

Thirdly, the *kind of person* who dies in Karl's stories is unusual. It is nearly always (eight out of eleven cases) a nurturant loss, that is, the death of a parent or relative of the hero. In the normative group of subjects only six of the twenty-two cases falls in this category, a proportion that is significantly less than for Karl at beyond the 5 per cent level, even taking into account the fact that the observations are not completely independent. What does this mean? Two hypotheses are immediately suggested. First, the death of the parents usually signifies desertion for the hero: he is an orphan as a result. This suggests again that something is amiss in the Nurturance-Neglect dimension of his child training, particularly in view of the Whiting-Child finding that either extreme leads to belief in spirits (often conceived as spirit *loss* or desertion). Second, Karl may be expressing hostility toward his parents in killing them off so frequently.

It is interesting to note that the Rorschach analyst came to similar conclusions about "infantile fears of overwhelming parent figures" on the basis of quite different imaginative material. Here are the relevant portions of his comments:

> In view of the possibility that the direction of his strivings is not functioning satisfactorily, he may resolve anxiety by turning in upon himself with the possibility of depressive mood reactions (7 At, 1 FC′) which appear to have their roots in infantile fears of overwhelming parent figures, particularly the mother ("massive representation" appearing with the depressive percept and with the percept "female genital organs"). Even here. however, this possibility of internalized aggression is limited, since he is likely to resort to hostile reactions ("cut open human being"). . . . Sexual preoccupations play a major role in his phantasies ("shapely angels," etc.). With the exception of one instance ("female genital organs") all reference to sexual material is sublimated. However, invariably sexually-tinged percepts give rise to debilitating anxiety and cause ego-disruption (F–). A vicious cycle is demonstrated in that hostility gives rise to anxiety, which further reinforces and intensifies hostile reactions. . . .

So far we have worked pretty much within the framework of imaginative material. What outside evidence do we have which confirms or fails to confirm our various hypotheses? Let us combine our inferences somewhat, state them as propositions, and attempt to find evidence on them elsewhere in the case material.

1. Karl has many hostile impulses (probably toward his parents) which he has projected into impersonal forces. In his normal social relationships, Karl gives the impression of being very nonaggressive and mild. After interviewing him concerning his experiences as a subject, a research worker commented, "exceedingly agreeable, friendly, seemed eager to be helpful, cooperative, etc." But this is exactly what we would expect if his aggressive impulses arouse anxiety in him. If he feared his hostile trends sufficiently to project them into impersonal forces, he would in all likelihood show his defense against hostility as a reaction formation in the form of extreme mildness. Furthermore, there is confirming evidence from everyday life that he does project his aggression there as he does in his stories. The psychiatrist interviewing him states that he suffers from claustrophobia and pyrophobia, both of which appear to be instances of fearing hostility projected into impersonal forces (closed places, fire). Perhaps the single most dramatic confirmation of this mechanism lies in the following statement from his autobiography: "I have heard voices every once in a while, starting about five or six years ago. They reoccur occasionally. I don't recall what they say. They are different people who talk ordinary talk, usually when alone. No thoughts of anyone doing away with me. No enemies recalled." What appears to have happened here is that when the hostility is projected less far from the self (people rather than the impersonal environment), it loses a good deal of its hostile character. Either that or we have striking confirmation of Whiting and Child's finding that rejection or overprotection leads to concern with "spirits."

2. Karl fears his aggressive impulses. The evidence as to why this is so is not clear-cut. There are two possibilities, one based on the following dynamic mechanism: Fear of rejection ⟶ anxiety ⟶ hostility ⟶ fear of further loss of love ⟶ repression of aggression. The other derives from the known severe punishment for aggression shown in his household. Both Karl and the psychiatrist agree that his parents were autocratic. Table 10.7 gives their ratings on this variable as well as on the Acceptance-Rejection and Indulgence variables found to be important by Baldwin, Kalhorn, and Breese (cf. Table 10.2).

TABLE 10.7

Behavior Patterns of Karl's Parents as Judged by Himself and a Psychiatrist

1. Acceptance-Rejection (The degree of affection, acceptance and rapport shown for you or the active dislike or hostility expressed in the manner and form of criticism, the intent and intensity of criticism, etc.)

	Acceptance			Rejection		
Karl	1	2	③	4	5	6
Psychiatrist	1	2	3	4	⑤	6

2. Democratic-Autocratic (Were there restrictive regulations you had to follow without question or were things explained to you? Were rules handed down in an authoritarian manner or was family policy decided by everyone concerned? Was policy handed down without justification?)

	Democratic			Autocratic		
Karl	1	2	3	4	⑤	6
Psychiatrist	1	2	3	4	5	⑥

3. Indulgence (The amount of protectiveness, solicitousness shown by the parent toward you. The degree to which the parent is child-centered as against self-centered. The amount of time spent by the parent with you—the amount of "anxious affection," worrying about you and planning your welfare.)

	No Indulgence			Extreme Indulgence		
Karl	1	2	3	4	⑤	6
Psychiatrist	1	②	3	4	5	6

Karl's own comment on his discipline runs as follows:

> Our discipline at home was fairly strict. The rod was not spared but also not used too frequently. (Punishment was by a yardstick whipping.) We grew up to acquire a name in town as being well-raised, well-mannered boys. Punishments received had no detrimental effect, either mentally or otherwise. They seemed to do us good.

This comment provides us with a slightly different hypothesis as to why Karl fears his aggression and projects it so far. The fact that he felt the punishment would be good for him indicates that he had identified with his parents. He felt sufficient guilt for his misdeeds to accept punishment, to feel that he deserved it, and that it made a better man out of him. In short, his aggression is controlled not only because of fear of punishment, or loss of love from the outside, but also because of his internalized guilt feelings arising from identification with his parents.

3. Karl shows insecurity or anxiety probably stemming from rejection or fear of rejection in childhood. Confirmation for this proposition is a little more indirect, but convincing. On the basis of the Whiting-Child study one would expect the peculiar projection of aggression he shows to be associated with rejection or over-indulgence and severe aggression training. The psychiatrist who interviewed Karl rates the parents as very low both on acceptance and indulgence. But Karl himself rates his parents quite high on indulgence and fairly high on acceptance. Who is right? As a matter of fact, we can accept the judgment of either one and come out with pretty much the same interpretation according to the Whiting-Child results. If we assume for the moment that Karl is correct, we could argue that he is rating his parents so high on indulgence because of their extreme anxious concern over his welfare which he refers to over and over again in his autobiography. They not only worried about him, but they worried, according to his report, about everything. This is not the same as warm affection, but there must have been strong enough nurturance for Karl to identify sufficiently with his parents to display guilt over his own behavior and a "rationalization" of their autocratic disciplinary methods. Still their anxious affection was not sufficient to give him a feeling of security and firm loving support. On the other hand, if we assume that the psychiatrist was right to conclude that Karl really did not receive much love and support, we can then explain Karl's more favorable judgment of his parents as an instance of rationalization stemming from the guilt and fear of further desertion arising from his hostility toward them, or we may argue that the psychiatrist knew Karl's parents showed indulgent, anxious affection for him but interpreted this simply as a defense against a fundamentally rejective tendency. Any of these interpretations supports the basic proposition that Karl felt insecure in childhood.

No elaborate inferences are really necessary to prove this point, since he repeatedly refers to his insecurity himself. "I depended very much on my parents and felt secure with them. In fact I was a rather timid soul and felt inclined to cry easily. Hence my parents were a great source of refuge to me." We can scarcely doubt that as a child Karl felt insecure, although it is not perfectly clear as to why he felt insecure. The evidence, however, points to a perceived (not necessarily a real) desertion by the parents. There are a number of possible events or parental attitudes which may lie at the root of this fear of desertion. We can list them as follows:

1. Actual parental lack of affection.
2. Parents' preference for other brothers. His father preferred his older brother, his mother his younger brother.
3. Parents' own insecurity, their constant worry and illness.
4. Death of younger sister when he was between one and two years old. One could easily argue that his jealousy over the birth of a sibling could have given rise to intense guilt and fear of desertion when the hostility apparently resulted in her death according to the "omnipotence of thought" principle (cf. TAT Story 5).
5. Strict parental discipline combined with nurturance may have given rise to hostility toward his parents which could have resulted in guilty fear of desertion by them. This thema may have been reinforced by his fear of alienating people by his realistically dangerous, somatotonic aggression (see Chapter 11).

Whatever the final "explanation" is of Karl's insecurity (and any one of these would probably suffice for the average clinician), the underlying thema which ties all this material together can be reconstructed somewhat as follows:

TABLE 10.8

Reconstruction of a Schematic Thema Based on Karl's Child-Training Experiences

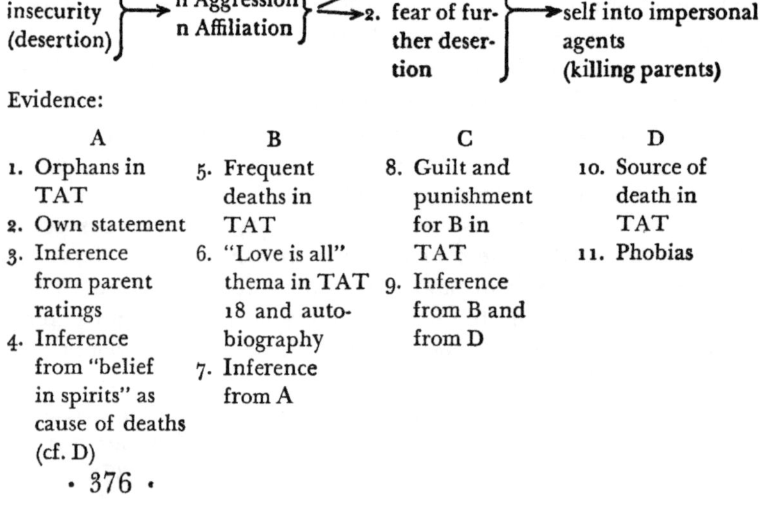

Evidence:

A	B	C	D
1. Orphans in TAT	5. Frequent deaths in TAT	8. Guilt and punishment for B in TAT	10. Source of death in TAT
2. Own statement	6. "Love is all" thema in TAT 18 and autobiography	9. Inference from B and from D	11. Phobias
3. Inference from parent ratings	7. Inference from A		
4. Inference from "belief in spirits" as cause of deaths (cf. D)			

This formula explains how it is that the death of parents in the TAT can at one and the same time be an *explanation* for subsequent aggression (desertion) and also satisfy *hostility* toward the parents as long as the hostility is disguised by projection into impersonal forces. There are a number of different variations on this central theme in the different TAT stories told by Karl. Some stories such as the one told to Card 13 (incest of father with daughter because of wife's desertion) contain nearly all elements in the thema. A further consideration of these variations will be deferred until the next chapter on motivation, since we are primarily concerned here with the effects of socialization.

Just what is the status of the thema that we have outlined? What does it tell us about Karl? What it seems to be is a series of events which are connected in this particular way for Karl. We have discovered the connection partly by the content of the stories he tells, and partly from our knowledge of connections based on experimental studies of fantasy. Finally we must assume that these connections exist primarily at the unconscious, or nonconscious level. We found the connections largely at the unreal level. We have argued that they were produced predominantly in the "unreal" world of childhood. So it would be a serious mistake to assume that this thema is the only or even the major determinant of Karl's behavior. We need the ideological system discovered in Chapter 8 to explain much of his behavior, certainly most of his reality-oriented behavior. What we need this thema and others like it for is to explain the unreal, fanciful, or "unreasonable" behavior that he may display. It is best fitted to account for such things as his phobias, his dreams, and some of his implicit attitudes toward men and women. The difficulty has been that psychoanalysts have often claimed too much for this type of formulation, largely because they were mostly interested in symptomatology or behavior which was not "reality-bound." To establish a balanced viewpoint, at least for normal people like Karl, we must recognize the importance of such formulations as these but still assign them their place as only one of several approaches to understanding personality.

NOTES AND QUERIES

1. What inferences can be drawn from the following statement made by Orlansky (1948)? "The best observations we have to date indicate that the newborn infant knows neither anxiety nor con-

fidence, fear nor happiness, but exists in an affectless and presumably consciousless state." He is arguing against anthropomorphism in infants. Because an infant does not "know" these states of mind, does it follow that he does not experience them? Is the problem partly semantic? What other terms are available to describe different central excitatory states, whether conscious or not?

2. Compare the following two statements made by Freud and Gesell. In what respect are they similar? In what respects, if any, would you modify them? What is responsible for the *stages* in affective and motor development?

The forces which we assume to exist behind the tensions caused by the needs of the id are called *instincts* . . . they are the ultimate cause of all activity. . . . We have been able to form a picture of the way in which the sexual impulse, which is destined to exercise a decisive influence on our life, gradually develops out of successive contributions from a number of component instincts, which represent particular erotogenic zones. . . . We have followed in a striking example the way in which these energies (and primarily the libido) organize themselves into a physiological function which serves the purpose of the preservation of the species. (Freud, 1940.)

Now it may as well be pointed out here that no one taught the baby this progressive series of eye-hand behaviors. He scarcely taught himself. He comes into his increasing growth powers primarily through intrinsic growth forces which change the inmost architecture of his nervous system. . . . Environmental factors support, inflect and modify; they do not generate the progressions of development. The sequences, the progressions come from within the organism. . . . The growth of the child mind is not altogether unlike the growth of a plant. Of itself it brings forth its tokens; it follows inborn sequences. (Gesell and Ilg, 1943.)

3. Aberle, Cohen, Davis, Levy, and Sutton (1950) have drawn up a list of functional prerequisites of a society—e.g., provisions which a society *must* make if it is to avoid extinction or dispersion, apathy of its members, war of all against all, or absorption into another society. In short they argue that at least the following things must get done if a society is to survive.

A. Provision for adequate relationship to the environment.
B. Role differentiation and role assignment (to avoid "everyone . . . doing everything or nothing").
C. Communication.
D. Shared cognitive orientations.
E. A shared, articulated set of goals.

F. The normative regulation of means (*how* the goals under E are to be reached by the people assigned the roles under B).
G. The regulation of affective expression.
H. Socialization.
I. The effective control of disruptive forms of behavior.

How many of these are also functional prerequisites for a personality system? Many of them seem comparable to the types of problems we have listed in Table 10.2 as representative of what the child *must* solve in order to maintain himself as a "going" personality system. Can you draw up a new and better list of problems of adjustment for a personality system on the basis of this analysis of a social system? The mode of attack runs as follows: If a person is to maintain and develop himself, then he must discover more or less adequate solutions to the following problems, etc. This might also be a way of discovering what the basic motives of all individuals are, on the grounds that a person *needs* to perform these functions, e.g., n Security, n Mastery, n Communication (Expression), n Cognizance, etc. (after Murray, 1938). Follow this line of reasoning as far as you can, attempting to discover its advantages and disadvantages.

4. Psychologists and anthropologists who study the socialization process are given to making suggestions about how children should be handled, of which the following is typical, at least at the moment. "In our own children, it is essential that we should provide a firm basic security in the infant, that his bodily needs be satisfied consistently, his developing social needs receive systematic response, and that such social discipline as is required be administered with regularity." (Gillin, in Kluckhohn and Murray, 1948.) What would be the consequences of this form of socialization on the child's maintenance and development conceptions? In terms of what American values (Chapter 8) are they desirable?

5. It is important to note that all of the information about Karl's parents' behavior or childhood experiences comes from himself. Is this a serious drawback? Should we know how his parents *actually* treated him? What improvements in our conceptual scheme would be likely to result if we did know? Rogers has argued that how the person perceives his past in the present is what really matters. Is he correct?

Whereas psychology has, in personality study, been concerned primarily with the measurement of the fixed qualities of the individual, and his past in order to explain his present, the hypothesis here suggested would seem to concern itself much more with the personal world of the present in order to understand the future. . . . (Rogers, 1947, p. 368.)

6. Take any parent behavior extreme (Indulgence, Acceleration, etc.) and try to derive what the consequences should be in terms of an analysis of the way it structures problems for the child to learn, develops expectations, etc. In particular, why should extremes like Overindulgence and Rejection lead to the same result? or should they?

Part Four

MOTIVE AS A PERSONALITY VARIABLE

11

Motivation: Clinical Approach

> It is not a matter for a calm mind to judge us simply by our outward actions; we must sound inside and see what springs set us in motion. But since this is a high and hazardous undertaking, I wish fewer people would meddle with it.
>
> —MONTAIGNE

Psychologists have long been fascinated by the search for the causes of human behavior. There has probably been more speculation on motivation than on any other aspect of personality. Man has always wanted to "sound inside" for the deeper determinants of behavior which lie behind the seeming contradictions of everyday life. This fascination has led to so much speculation that we may feel inclined to agree with Montaigne that it would be better if fewer people meddled with the problem. The only feasible approach in such a welter of confusing theories is to take a firm grip on the facts which necessitate the concept of motivation and see how different sets of facts have led to different motivational theories.

Probably it is the variability of human behavior which has more or less forced scientists to make use of the concept of motivation. Trait psychology developed to explain recurrent responses and consistencies in behavior, in order to explain the *how* of behavior. The *schema* or *attitude* concept developed to handle the problem of *what* the person knew, of what the symbolic contents of his mind were. The motive concept has developed in answer to the question *why*. Why do people behave as they do? Often we feel that we can understand the richness and variety of behavior only in terms of the goals which it serves. Onetime events seem particularly to require the motivation concept. Responses seem so variable that we can find no meaning in them, no repetitive lawfulness to them, unless we go behind the surface phenomena and seek an explanation in terms of underlying motives, purposes, or goals.

A good example of the kind of data which has necessitated the motivational concept is provided in a study by Dembo (1931). She observed continuously for hours at a time the behavior of a person who was trying to solve an insoluble problem. After noting the sudden shifts in the subject's behavior, Dembo comes to this conclusion:

"If one studies a number of records, one comes more and more to the point of view that there exists no lawfulness in the sense that after a certain event *A* a certain event *B* follows. A violent emotional outbreak is one time preceded by weak emotional manifestations, another time by an apparently calm demeanor; as a substitute act there is sometimes a violent effort to get at the solution, and sometimes a turning away from the work; an attack on the experimenter follows sometimes after a pause, other times after a failure, and so forth. A thoroughgoing investigation reinforces the impression of irregularity that contributes to the view of emotional events as being without law. In reality, such a *temporal* presentation of a law 'if *A*, then *B*' is incorrect, and indicates a trend to quasi history. . . . Certainly in our investigation it was especially striking that the first act was interrupted or replaced by other types of acts. Not infrequently a later phase was connected with an earlier phase —but whether it was stronger or weaker or whether it was longer or shorter, or something else, is *not* adequately determined by the structure of the *course of events itself*." (1931, p. 17.) In other words, as a pupil of Lewin, Dembo is arguing that we must go behind the sequence of surface events (phenotypes) to conceptualize them in terms of some underlying motivational or goal structure (genotypes).

Murray has also stated this viewpoint very clearly in contrasting trait psychology with motivational psychology: "According to my prejudice, trait psychology is over-concerned with recurrences, with consistency, with what is clearly manifested (the surface of personality), with what is conscious, ordered and rational. It minimizes the importance of psychological occurrences, irrational impulses and beliefs, infantile experiences, unconscious and inhibited drives as well as environmental (sociological) factors. Hence, it does not seem fitted to cope with such phenomena as: dreams and fantasies, the behavior and thought of children or savages, neurotic symptoms (morbid anxiety, phobias, compulsions, delusions), insanity and creative activity (artistic or religious)." (1938, p. 715.)

Both of these quotations give illustrations of the kind of data which motivational concepts have been adopted to explain. Murray in particular is right in pointing to fantasy material and neurotic symptoms as the source of much dynamic theory. Historically the greatest impetus motivational theory ever received was from the work of Freud and his co-workers, who began with just such data. The full-blown, mature psychoanalytic theories of motivation are far too complex and in many cases far too speculative for us to take the time to summarize them adequately here. But we can return to the kind of empirical observations which first led Freud to formulate his dynamic theory. Freud's book *The Psychopathology of Everyday Life* (1904) gives some of the most detailed descriptions of how he went about his observations and analyses. Its value as a study of associational processes and of the way to draw inferences from them has been largely lost sight of in subsequent controversies over the adequacy or inadequacy of the theories which Freud developed out of his essentially empirical approach. It has become so fashionable either to criticize Freud or to accept him whole-heartedly that it will be worthwhile to return for a moment to the data he initially worked with, to get an idea of how he handled it, and to consider alternative ways of treating it.

Freud's Analysis of a Temporary Memory Loss

As an illustration we may take an instance of memory lapse which Freud analyzes in some detail (1904). One day he and a traveling companion fell into a discussion of the handicaps of being a Jew at that time in Europe. His companion was ambitious and was expressing his disappointment over being held back by racial prejudice. In trying to express his feelings on the subject he tried to recollect a line from Vergil's *Aeneid* in which Dido leaves vengeance to posterity. He managed to recollect the following:

"Exoriar(e) ex nostris ossibus ultor!"
(May an avenger arise from our bones!)

Freud's companion realized that he had left out a word and Freud supplied him with it. It was the word *aliquis,* meaning *some* or *someone.* They then proceeded to try to find out why he had been unable to recall this word in the quotation. After a somewhat extended period of free association in which the word *aliquis* was divided into *a* and *liquis,* the subject finally discovered, through several devious associational routes, that it referred in his mind to a woman's monthly period. He then confessed to Freud that he was very much worried at the moment over whether a woman he had visited in Italy was missing her monthly period and had become pregnant by him. They then concluded that he had forgotten the word *aliquis* because the idea of an avenger arising from his bones was painful to him and because the particular word in the quotation he forgot had particular formal associations with the event he so much feared.

If we study this simple episode carefully, we can find in it nearly all the characteristics of the Freudian position on motivation. In the first place we notice that Freud does not accept the possibility that the forgetting of the word *aliquis* is chance or accidental. *All* behavior is motivated. Secondly, he accepts the fact that the causes or motives behind behavior are often unknown to the person himself, i.e., are unconscious. Thirdly, he goes about uncovering the unconscious motive in an empirical fashion. He does not tell his companion what his motive is (presumably because he does not know what it is) until the person has revealed it through free association. Fourthly, he finds in the free associations of the subject a good many somatic references. The word *aliquis,* for instance, is elaborated into the "liquefication" at the time of a woman's monthly period. Lastly, he finds ultimately that sexual guilt or anxiety is the underlying motive. The word *aliquis* is forgotten because its appearance in consciousness arouses anxiety over a sexual act. In more modern terminology we might say that the act of forgetting the word was instrumental to the goal of anxiety reduction.

As we shall see in a moment, all of these characteristics are fundamental parts of the fully developed Freudian motivational scheme. The important point to notice now is how closely this elaborate theoretical scheme was originally connected with empirical observations. Those who are dissatisfied with the Freudian motivational scheme should ask themselves how else they would account for the events in this little episode. We may study this problem for a moment because it is an interesting one in the light of the subsequent development of Freudian motivational theory.

Freud's picture of this episode leaves two questions only partially answered. First, what is the *precise* nature of the motive which was responsible for forgetting the word? The thing which impressed Freud so much about episodes and free asosciations like these was the great frequency with which a sexual *motif* was uncovered. This led him in time to develop his essentially monistic conception of motivation as consisting of the *libido* or sexual impulses. In his *History of the Psychoanalytic Movement* (1910) Freud tells how he was forced to his conclusion about the universal importance of the sexual motive in all neurosis by repeated observations of this sort and also by the comments of other psychiatrists who apparently had come to much the same conclusion although they were unwilling to admit it. He quotes Charcot as saying, for instance, "C'est toujours la chose génital, toujours—toujours—toujours," although Charcot apparently did not stick to this position publicly (Freud, 1910). But although a sexual matter is clearly involved in the *aliquis* episode the question arises as to whether it is the sexual *motive* which is responsible for the forgetting of the word *aliquis*. Obviously libidinal satisfaction in the ordinary sense of the term is not directly gained by forgetting the word. The psychoanalytic interpretation might run somewhat as follows: No, sexual gratification narrowly conceived is not the motive behind the memory lapse, but the super-ego is involved. But what is the super-ego? Is that another motive? No, but it too involves the libido because while the libido begins by loving (cathecting) the self as one of its objects (primary narcissism), it later cathects the ideal self or ego ideal (secondary narcissism). This means that in order to gratify the portion of the libido which cathects the ideal self, the person must act in such a way as to maintain this idealized image. In order to do this the ego acts defensively and forces out of consciousness the word which would interfere with this conception and so fail to gratify this portion of the libido. Such an explanation is only one of several possibilities, but it serves to illustrate how involved the theoretical structure of the libido concept has become and how far removed in some cases it is from the original data on which its formulation was based. To many people it has seemed simpler to postulate a plurality of motives and values and to explain behavior like the forgetting in this episode in terms of them rather than in terms of an all-embracing libido concept.

The second question not fully answered by Freud's picture of this episode is: What is the precise nature of the motive which leads the subject by free association to provide a solution to the mystery of the "forgotten word"? Once again is it the libido in one of its various forms? Or ought we to postulate the existence of some need such as the need for social approval, the "effort after meaning," or the need for cognizance which serves to motivate the subject to free associate and eventually come up with an answer to the problem? If we accept Freud's dictum that all behavior is motivated, we must find a motive behind the free-association process. Freud does not concern himself with this question, although doubtless it too could be answered in terms of some vicissitude of the libido. Other psychologists, less concerned with seeking causes of neurosis, should be as much interested in finding out the motives which underlie behavior such as this as in discovering what motives are responsible for lapses of memory, symptoms, etc.

Characteristics of the Freudian Motivational Scheme

With this empirical introduction to our topic we may now turn to a more systematic exploration of the characteristics attributed to motivation by Freud and the psychoanalytic school. In doing this we cannot proceed from the internal frame of reference of psychoanalysis but must consider instead its impact on the outside observer. In some ways this approach may be superior to the exposition of psychoanalytic doctrine by a Freudian because, like the person who gives a conceptualization of himself, he might be less aware of some of the basic implicit assumptions in terms of which he operates. Furthermore, if we stick to these basic assumptions, we may be able to avoid some of the intricacies of psychoanalytic doctrine and to emphasize instead the places where psychoanalytic thinking has contributed either positively or negatively to everyone's thinking about motivation.

1. **All Behavior Is Motivated.** Freud was probably the most persistent determinist that psychology has ever known. He didn't want to leave anything to chance. Other psychologists have been willing to accept the fact theoretically that all behavior is determined, but few of them have gone to the lengths that Freud did to demonstrate that even the most casual acts had a *motive*. He made a specialty of analyzing the causes of odd bits of behavior—superstitions, faulty actions, slips of the tongue, jokes, dreams, etc. One of his most striking demonstrations was the attempt to show that he could discover by free association the reason why a particular number was chosen when a person was asked just "to think of a number at random." All such phenomena had been (and are) regarded by other psychologists as having explanations (and being determined in that sense) but not as being goal-directed. Unfortunately Freud confused motivation with determination. To him psychic causation is not accidental, mechanical, or associational, but dynamic and purposeful, though often unconsciously so. *All* behavior was goal-directed. In this sense he was an extreme functionalist. Like other psychologists and biologists of the nineteenth century he had been much influenced by the doctrine of evolution with its attendant notion of adaptation for survival. Unlike them, he pushed the ideas of adaptation and the functional significance of acts to their logical

extreme and concluded that *all* behavior has functional significance and can be explained in terms of some underlying motive or goal related to survival or death. According to the view adopted here, motivation may be involved in all acts but it is only *one* of the constructs needed to account for behavior (traits or habits and schemata being the other two). Under certain conditions, motivation may be of little or no importance in determining a response as compared with these other two factors—a position that Freud would not have accepted, at least not in practice.

Karl's controlled associations. As an illustration of the way in which apparently random responses may sometimes be explained in motivational terms, we can turn to some associations given by Karl to the word *success* in a word-recognition experiment. In this test, words were flashed for .01 second on a screen at a level of illumination which, in the beginning at least, was so low that the subject could not possibly identify the word. The level of illumination was gradually increased and the subject was instructed to guess what the word might be as soon as he had any idea of what it was and to continue guessing until he had correctly identified it. Karl guessed freely in this situation and to the word *success* made the following responses on successive exposures:

either
become
woman
mother
empire
secure
success

Knowing what we do about Karl we can almost reconstruct from these words the connection which security and success have for him. The justification for an attempt to interpret the meaning of this series of associations lies in the fact that the word *success* did start brain processes before it was recognized and in the fact that associational processes connected with security and achievement had already been started by earlier words in the series. With this in mind our interpretation might run as follows: His first response, *either,* suggests the conflict between security and success. He wants to *become* successful but the way seems to be through a *woman,* especially through gaining his *mother's* love, which represents the *empire* of security which makes *success* possible. Apparently the stimulus word *success* sets off a train of associations about security which we can explain as representing his conception of the only way in which the success motive may be gratified. But what, for contrast, is suggested to him by the subliminal stimulus word, *security*?

leaving
avenue
leaving
lexington
review
storage
security

Here we are baffled. And unfortunately this is all too often the case. Apparently unrelated associations of this sort are actually much more common than the striking series of associations Karl gave in the first instance, which seem to have an underlying explanation. It is true that we can fall back on the hypothesis that we could explain the connection between *Lexington* Avenue, *leaving, storage,* and *security* if we knew enough about Karl. But at least for the moment we must confess our ignorance and be content with the conclusion that while *success* suggests *security,* the reverse is not true. *Security* does not suggest *success.* This may be important in Karl's motivational structure. It suggests that success is secondary and dependent on the more primary satisfaction of his security motives.

This example and Freud's investigation of "chance" behavior both serve to illustrate an important corollary derived from Freud's assumption that all behavior is motivated. This corollary is that *a motive is a "convenient construct" which serves to unify, tie together, or give a common meaning to a variety of dissimilar responses.* We cannot explain Karl's associations in terms of the *trait* concept: no one of his responses is "similar" to any other. We cannot explain them very well in terms of the *schema* concept: they do not suggest a coherent conception of anything. But they do suggest a common need for security which is shaping, directing, or "warping" his train of thought. So we explain them in terms of an underlying motive or goal which they are all serving or expressing, each in a somewhat different way. The value of the motive concept lies precisely in the fact that it abstracts out of a number of concrete behavioral phenomena an inference as to their cause. It seeks the reality behind the appearance, the *e pluribus unum,* or in Lewin's terminology, the genotype behind the phenotype.

2. Motives Are Persistent. Freud was repeatedly impressed with the fact that certain motives appeared again and again behind various symptoms in his patients. From this he developed the theoretical position that motivation consists of continuous underlying tensions which will continue to express themselves no matter how they are blocked or disowned by the person. He concludes his detailed analysis of chance and faulty actions with the following statement: "But the common character of the mildest, as well as the severest cases to which the faulty and chance actions contribute, lies *in the ability to refer the phenomena to unwelcome, repressed, psychic material, which, though pushed away from consciousness, is nevertheless not robbed of all capacity to express itself.*" (1904, p. 178.) By this doctrine he opposed the view that motivation is phasic in nature, and dependent upon situational factors. Rather he conceived of it as a continuously driving force which persisted from birth to death despite attempts of the environment to mold and deflect it.

This viewpoint is congruent with the prevailing experimentalist view of a motive as a "persistent stimulus" (cf. Hull, 1943). As we shall see, the biologically oriented psychologists tended to absorb this view of Freud's as consistent with their researches on hunger and other physiological tensions. It has remained for the neo-Freudians and others to emphasize the importance of situational and cultural factors.

3. Motives Are Often Unconscious, Unknown to the Subject. From the earliest days of his publications, Freud's doctrine of the "unconscious" has been frequently attacked and rejected *in toto* by other psychologists, particularly from the experimental schools (cf. Cole, 1939). In retrospect this seems somewhat odd, because actually Freud was more fundamentally a biologist than they were in thinking of motives as physiological tensions of which the subject was only imperfectly aware. As time has gone on, this view of Freud's has also been incorporated into some biologically oriented theories of motivation (cf. Dollard *et al.*, 1939). To these theorists the problem is to explain consciousness, not unconsciousness. It would seem more natural to suppose that motivation like any other biological process would begin by being unconscious (i.e., unverbalized) and would become symbolically represented later on and then somewhat imperfectly. The value of the Freudian approach has been that it has shown how various conscious phenomena could be explained in terms of the assumption of unconscious motives or determinants. While many dislike the conscious, phenomenological terms he uses to describe unconscious determinants, there seems little objection today to the notion that there are such unconscious determinants. We have already shown in the previous chapter how it is possible from Karl's behavior (particularly at the fantasy level) to infer the existence of an intense need for security of which he is only partially aware (cf. also Chapter 14). It was the Freudian school which originally demonstrated the importance and value of making this kind of inference.

4. **Motivation Is Essentially Tensional in Character.** Freud conceived of life as a fairly grim business. More than any other psychologist he showed up the importance of sadistic, aggressive, and hostile trends in human nature. In his own words "the bitter truth behind all this—one so eagerly denied—is that men are not gentle, friendly creatures wishing for love, who simply defend themselves if they are attacked, but that a powerful measure of desire for aggression has to be reckoned as part of their instinctual endowment. The result is that their neighbor is to them not only a possible helper or sexual object, but also a temptation to them to gratify their aggressiveness on him, to exploit his capacity for work without recompense, to use him sexually without his consent, to seize his possessions, to humiliate him, to cause him pain, to torture and to kill him. Homo homine lupus; who has the courage to dispute it in the face of all the evidence in his own life and history?" (Freud, 1930.) Life appeared to Freud so full of aggression and frustration that the major task of man seemed to be to try to find ways to alleviate pain, avoid anxiety, and reduce tension. It is no wonder then that the major gratifications in life often appeared to be those which brought relief from external dangers or internal pressures from the id. From this it was only one step further to the conclusion that motivation was tensional in character and reward or gratification resulted from the reduction of tension.

This view has gained very wide acceptance also among biologically oriented psychologists, as we shall see in the next chapter. It fits in with the assumption that motivation like hunger consists of a persisting stimulus, since the stimulus can be thought of as the tension and a reduction in total stimulation as the tension reduction necessary for gratification.

As we noted in the last chapter, the idea that growing up is a constant struggle for impulse control or tension reduction can be readily translated into a rat experiment in which the animals are forced to renounce easy gratifications for more complex and difficult ones (Whiting and Mowrer, 1943). The comparison is instructive in showing how frustration is an important source of motivation but it does not take sufficiently into account the organism's "positive" or "creative" motives to explore, seek change, test its powers of mastery, etc., as Murray has pointed out (1938).

5. **There Is One Motive, the Libido, Which Will Account For All or Nearly All Striving.** Freud's thinking on the subject of motivation was essentially monistic, or at the most dualistic, as Horney has suggested (1939). Apparently in the beginning he explained all striving in terms of a great fundamental conflict between two major drives, the sex or libido instinct, and the ego or self-preservation instincts. In keeping with the evolutionary doctrines of the nineteenth century to which he had been exposed, he at times apparently thought of this conflict as between the tendency toward cooperation and the tendency toward competition. On the one hand was the self-preservation drive, patterned after hunger, which governed the ego and led man to compete with his fellows for food or other forms of gratification. On the other hand was the sexual drive which, since it required two people for its fullest consummation, forced man to make cooperative arrangements. In this way his motivational scheme incorporated the prevailing evolutionary doctrines of "survival of the fittest" and "cooperation for survival."

Later on, as Horney points out, Freud reduced this dualism to a monism in which the libido remained the primary instinct and the conflict arose between the portions of the libido which remained attached to the self and the portions which were directed toward others. Primary self-love or narcissism became the equivalent of the self-preservative or ego instinct whereas the libido in the post-genital phases normally developed beyond this to attach itself to objects outside the self. In short, the conflict now became one between *earlier* and *later* object choices of the same fundamental motive. Finally he developed a second dualism, this time between the libido or life instinct and the death instinct. This last development was probably influenced by his increasing conviction of the importance of hostile trends on the one hand and possibly by his awareness of developments in physical science which were emphasizing the concept of entropy, or the tendency for the world to run down, as it were, or to go from order toward increasing disorder and chaos. In this dualism the libido became the life instinct which operated to maintain order for a short time in the face of the pressures toward disintegration (entropy or the death instinct). This position is consistent with such modern viewpoints as that taken by the physicist Schrödinger in his book, *What Is Life?* (1945), in which he points out that the curious fact about life is that it maintains order and regularity with many fewer atoms and molecules than would be necessary for similar order in the nonliving universe. To Schrödinger life is characterized by the capacity to resist entropy, which was exactly Freud's position in this last phase of his motivational theory.

The significance of all this theorizing on motivation which engaged Freud's attention throughout his long life is the emphasis he placed on the reduction of all complicated strivings to one or two simple principles. Once again, while many psychologists have disagreed with the specific conclusions that Freud drew about the nature of these one or two principles, they tended to accept his underlying assumption that motivation could be explained in terms of a "few motives, common to all men." Freud's position may be rephrased in terms used by theologians in the Christian church in their discussions of the nature of God. He was essentially a *monist,* but from time to time he tended toward the "heresy of Manicheanism" in that he had to admit the existence of an independent principle of "Evil" (the death instinct) outside "God" (the libido). He was not, however, a "henatheist"—willing to admit that others might find equally valid single motives. His "God" (the libido) was a "jealous God" and he "excommunicated" Jung and Adler when they attempted to replace the libido principle with others. And he was certainly not a "polytheist" believing in the existence of a variety of independent, culturally determined motives.

6. Motivation Is Basically Instinctual in Nature. Freud was first, last, and always a biologist, as Horney again makes clear (1939). He thought of motivation in biological terms. But once again his biological orientation was so radical, so thoroughgoing that other biologists turned against him. From his biological orientation developed some of his most important and also most controversial views on the nature of motivation. We may summarize them as three corollaries derived from the basic instinctual position.

a. The Regular Stages in the Pattern of Libidinal Development. Freud thought of the libido as developing or unfolding in much the same way as any other part of the body would develop and grow. He believed it was part of the equipment of all men just as a leg or an arm is. He also conceived of it as going through various developmental stages just as the foetus does or the leg or the arm. A closer analogy, as we saw in Chapter 10, is with the stages in motor development noted by Gesell and his co-workers as always following in an apparently preordained manner as a result of biological determinants. Just as there are stages of creeping, crawling, sitting up, standing and walking, Freud thought that there were stages in the development of the libido. These stages could be distinguished first by the portion of the body which the libido sensitized or eroticized. The first zone to be so sensitized was the mouth, then the anus, then the genitals, then the body as a whole. Finally the libido turned outward toward other people. Such a theory, stated in these terms, would probably not have met the violent criticism that Freud's theory did when he first advanced it. Part of the reason for the initial objections to the theory was probably that he stated his conclusions about the nature of the libido in words that were so highly psychic in content that they tended to mask the essentially biological nature of the theory. Thus, for instance, instead of speaking of the mouth as being sensitized by some biological drive, the practice was to speak of the mouth as being the object of love or cathexis.

By his doctrine of the developmental stages of the libido, Freud was enabled to enlarge and generalize his initially sexual drive to include all sorts of strivings which were manifestly not sexual in nature, at least as the term sexual is normally understood. Freud's original, empirically founded observation that the sex motive lay behind many otherwise inexplicable surface phenomena was generalized by him into a theoretical system which eventually enabled him and his co-workers to account for all strivings. In order to do this, he had to divest the term sexuality of much of its original meaning. In Horney's words, "Sexuality is not an instinctual drive directed toward the opposite sex, aiming at genital satisfaction; the heterosexual genital drive is only one manifestation of a non-specific sexual energy, the libido." (1939, p. 49.) Freud, through his developmental theory, was able to explain other motives as developing from various stages in the vicissitudes of the libido or as resulting from the fixation or regression to a certain developmental stage. It would be fruitless to try to give in any detail the extremely elaborate developments of the libido theory. Attempts to discover whether some

of the consequences of such a theory can be checked by actual observation have not led to any striking confirmation of it, at least in its original form. Sears has surveyed the experimental literature on this point and come to the following conclusion:

> One conclusion stands out above all others: emotional development, as couched in terms of successive object choices, is far more variable than Freud supposed. This is not to say that none of the classical elements appear. They do; but with too many exceptions to be accepted as typical. The conditions under which object choice is made explain why this is. Object choice is essentially a function of learning and what is learned is a function of the environment in which the learning occurs. Since there is no universal culture pattern for intrafamilial relationships, there can be no universal pattern of learned object choices. (1943, p. 57.)

This represents as briefly as possible the position which many students of Freud's theory have adopted. They are willing to accept many of his observations on the stages of libidinal development, but they interpret them differently. They do not attribute them to biological instincts, but rather to cultural conditions. It is true that children show a great deal of interest in the mouth and in the pleasure which they get out of sucking at the time that Freud says they should. As we noted in Chapter 10, Sears and Wise (1950) have shown that it is the children who receive prolonged gratification through sucking at the bottle or breast who later develop an "erotogenic" interest in the mouth which presumably explains their increased disturbance at weaning. In a similar fashion, one might suppose that the interest children show in bowel control, in feces, or in their genitalia might also be culturally conditioned since the control of these activities is a point of major concern to many cultures. In short, the tendency is to accept the Freudian assumption that one finds the beginnings of motivation in infant gratification, but to reject his theoretical position that the nature and sequence of these gratifications are wholly determined according to some innate instinctual mechanisms.

b. **The Somatic Patterning of All Motivated Behavior.** Another important derivative of Freud's underlying biological position is his conviction that all psychological or higher motives tend to seek gratification in a manner which is patterned after the way in which the underlying biological drive was originally satisfied. Psychoanalysis has a tendency to rely very heavily on somatic analogies, to believe that all behavior is sublimated "body language." For example, Franz Alexander, in discussing the psychological causes of gastric disturbances, states, "In all of our cases we see in the unconscious a deep oral regression to the parasitic situation of the infant"—a statement which evokes a somatic image which he then translates into the "psychic" language of "an extreme and violent craving for love and the need for dependence and help" (in Tomkins, 1944, p. 129). What has happened here is that the psychoanalyst observes that the child during the oral stage is predominantly a helpless, dependent creature whose major mode of existence is through sucking and intaking. He then infers that if a person for some reason becomes fixated at this oral receptive stage, he will show behavior trends as an adult which are *patterned after* those which he showed as an infant when under the influence of the oral drive. Thus he may go further than Alexander does and state that the true "oral" character is one who is interested in ingesting, sucking, or "mouthing" the world. By analogy such a person would be an optimist, certainly as compared with the person whose character is based on the oral aggressive pattern of "spitting out" the world. These somatic analogies are one of the most distinguishing features of psychoanalytic literature. All psychic phenomena tend to be referred back to the body in one way or another. Thus stinginess is related to tightness of the sphincter, anxiety to castration anxiety, envy to penis envy, achievement to urethral competitiveness, an overcoat to a condom, etc. This tendency has become so widespread that the so-called "latent" content of psychological imagery is nearly always the somatic analogue of the image. Anyone who has read psychoanalytic literature at all cannot fail to be impressed by the ease with which a somatic parallel can be found for nearly any image a patient uses.

Criticism of this tendency has been violent and widespread. Boiled down, the criticism resolves itself into two main points. First, body symbolism is far more plastic and variable than has sometimes been assumed. Anna Freud states, for instance, "Symbols are constant and universally valid relations between particular id-contents and specific ideas of words or things." (1937, p. 16.) It cannot be denied that sometimes elaborate manifest content does disguise body imagery. Farber and Fisher have shown that *some* subjects, who were presumably naïve with respect to Freudian theory, were able to give the correct somatic interpretations of various symbols under hypnosis. They report the following instance: "Several female subjects were given this dream: 'A boy was sitting at his desk studying when the waste basket caught on fire. He ran and got a pitcher of water and put the fire out.' Their immediate response was 'Oh, he wet his bed,' or 'He should have gone to the bathroom.'" (From Tomkins, 1944, p. 508.) However, they also found that many subjects under hypnosis were *not* able to give the "correct" interpretations of dreams. The symbolism was by no means universally understood. These experimenters also asked subjects to dream under hypnosis after experimentally inducing certain states. As a result of this work they conclude that "A familiar dream symbol may portray a variety of human experiences. Thus, tooth pulling may represent not only castration and child birth but also socially insulting predicaments; the attack with a hammer may represent not only homosexual assault but also scholastic rivalry." (Tomkins, 1944, p. 516.) In short, the dream work *may* have a somatic reference, but often it has not but refers instead to a psychological experience of a much more complex nature. The basis for such modifications of the Freudian theory is once again that in its orthodox form it does not allow sufficiently for the variety of learning experiences to which a person growing up in the culture may be subjected. Body imagery may express complex motives for some people and not for others. It is probable that this criticism does not apply so cogently to some of Freud's earlier works since he was always careful to have the person involved give by free association his own interpretation of a dream symbol or a chance action. What appears to have happened is that the body symbolism reoccured so frequently that later psychoanalysts tended to universalize the relationships discovered in a way that was not originally envisaged.

The second major criticism of the somatic patterning of all behavior has been made especially strongly by Horney (1939), who argues that the Freudian analysts have confused cause and effect. She feels that the fundamental weakness of their position is that they feel they have explained something when they refer it to its somatic analogue. In her own words, "Thus the difference in point of view may be expressed in this way: a person does not have tight lips because of the tenseness of his sphincter, but both are tight because his character trends tend toward one goal—to hold on to what he has and never give away anything, be it money, love, or any kind of spontaneous feeling. When in dreams an individual of this type symbolizes persons through faeces, the libido theory explanation would be that he despises people because they represent faeces to him, while I should say that representing people in symbols of faeces is an expression of an existing contempt for people." (1939, p. 62.) In other words she rejects the biological *explanation* of adult character trends but feels that the character trends may express themselves in biological terminology. In short, since "body language" is merely one way in which a motive expresses itself, it is a mistake to try to understand the nature of that motive solely in terms of this one mode of expression. Her criticism is certainly valid at least in part. It does appear at times as if psychoanalysts feel they have explained complex psychological phenomena if they can refer them to an analogous somatic pattern. On the other hand, it should be stated that sometimes the somatic analogies appear to have been fruitful in suggesting the ways in which a motive *may* express itself at psychological levels. A moderate viewpoint would appear to be that a biological pattern of response may suggest ways in which a motive may later find expression. If such an analogy is regarded strictly as an analogy, rather than as a cause-and-effect relationship, it is possible that it may prove useful in suggesting observations to be made on the motive in question at more complex behavioral levels. Some of Alexander's work seems to be of this order. At the moment it is still very debatable as to whether these somatic analogies have seriously interfered with progress in the study of motivation or whether they have contributed important suggestions as to the ways in which motives may express themselves.

c. The Importance of Early Childhood in Motivational Development. A further corollary of Freud's general instinctivist position is that the early manifestations of the libido are of greatest importance in character formation. Later motivational developments are derivative and for the most part substitutions for "aim-inhibited strivings." That is, when the libido cannot reach its original aims because of the frustrations of socialization or for other reasons, it is forced to adopt substitute aims. These secondary goals are the basis for the complicated nonsexual strivings of adult life, but they always remain as substitutes for the "real" or primary ends which may be reestablished by traumatic incidents, etc. This suggests strongly that even in adult life the primary biological aims of the libido (oral, anal, and genital object choices) are still very important. It is

for this reason [illegible]
out of adult conflicts in terms of the readjustment of the p
biological aims of which later motives are simply reflections.
practical significance of this viewpoint is that it leads natura
the reinterpretation of all adult motivational goals in terms of
of childhood. We have already seen, for instance, how Alex
found it useful to explain a need for security and support in
of the primary oral drive of infancy.

Later strivings are, if possible, referred to sublimations, d
tions, fixations, or regressions of the primary biological in
which unfolds according to a regular and inevitable patt
growth and development. Nowhere is this clearer than in the
ency to explain adult role motivations in terms of the Oedipus
plex. Freud argued that one of the first and most important
choices of the libido, after various parts of the body, would b
mother. Furthermore, the attachment of the libido to the mo
so strong that the male child especially wants to eliminate all
petitors for the mother's love, particularly the father. The ho
toward the father in turn creates on the one hand fear of retali
and on the other hand guilt for hating an object (the fath
which the libido is also attached. In this situation a number o
tives appear to be present: a primary desire for the mother, a
for aggression against the father, a need for the father's lov
approval, fear of punishment, and a need for the reduction o
anxiety resulting from the conflict of motives which in turn
a forgetting or repression of the whole complex. A thorough an
of how each of these motives arises would be difficult to ma
indeed it has ever been made in any rigorous fashion by p
analysis. But whatever their origin, these motives become th
mary ones in the explanation of behavior which may occur
years after the original Oedipus situation. It is in this way th
contemporary motivation tends to be referred to, and expl
in terms of, much early development of a biological instinc
its various object choices.

In a general way this viewpoint of Freud's has been very
ential. Many clinical psychologists, anthropologists, and perso
psychologists have come to believe that the early years of chil
are of great importance in developing the basic motivational
ture of an individual. On the other hand, this belief has bee
ject to violent attack from men like Lewin, and Allport, or m

cently Orlansky (1949), and even by psychoanalysts who bega within the Freudian framework. Horney, who may be considere typical of so-called neo-Freudians, has objected particularly to wh she calls Freud's "instinctivistic and genetic psychology" (1939, p. 8 She and others in her group have emphasized the importance of cu tural, environmental, or sociological factors in motivational develo ment. In other words, she believes the motives are genuine learne products of experience and do not simply reflect always the ain inhibited striving of a primary biological instinct. In her words, ". prevailingly sociological orientation then takes the place of a pr vailingly anatomical-physiological one" and the "one-sided emph sis on genesis" is relinquished (1939, p. 9). Her view comes close t the position taken in Chapter 10 that there are special reasons wh early childhood experiences are of greater importance in motiv tional development than later ones but that they do not therefo continue to mold, almost single handed, all adult motivational stri ings. From this standpoint motives are the product of *all* learnin experiences to which the initial childhood ones contribute heavil but certainly not exclusively.

Other Views of Motivation

In discussing Freud's contribution to the psychology of moti tion, we have tried to point out what his views have been accepte rejected, or modified by other writers, but many of these oth to make positive contributions of their ow which they regard as substitutes for much of the Freudian fram work. It is difficult to do justice to the great variety of clinical co tributions to the theory of motivation but we can make a very bri survey of some of the major viewpoints. Nearly all theorists wh have worked with clinical data have accepted the first four chara teristics of the Freudian scheme, that is, they have agreed th motivation is one of the fundamental variables of human person ity, that motives are persistent, that they are often unconscious, an that they are tensional in character. By and large, these same peop have also vigorously rejected the sixth characteristic of Freud scheme, namely, the insistence upon the basic somatic, instinct nature of motivation. They can be discussed therefore in terms what attitude they have taken toward point five, that is, in terms whether or not they have accepted a "monistic" view of motivati

for this reason that psychoanalytic therapy emphasizes the working out of adult conflicts in terms of the readjustment of the primary biological aims of which later motives are simply reflections. The practical significance of this viewpoint is that it leads naturally to the reinterpretation of all adult motivational goals in terms of those of childhood. We have already seen, for instance, how Alexander found it useful to explain a need for security and support in terms of the primary oral drives of infancy.

Later strivings are, if possible, referred to sublimations, deflections, fixations, or regressions of the primary biological instinct which unfolds according to a regular and inevitable pattern of growth and development. Nowhere is this clearer than in the tendency to explain adult male motivation in terms of the Oedipus complex. Freud argued that one of the first and most important object choices of the libido, after various parts of the body, would be the mother. Furthermore, the attachment of the libido to the mother is so strong that the male child especially wants to eliminate all competitors for the mother's love, particularly the father. The hostility toward the father in turn arouses on the one hand fear of retaliation, and on the other hand guilt for hating an object (the father) to which the libido is also attached. In this situation a number of motives appear to be present: a primary desire for the mother, a desire for aggression against the father, a need for the father's love and approval, fear of punishment, and a need for the reduction of the anxiety resulting from the conflict of motives which in turn causes a forgetting or repression of the whole complex. A thorough analysis of how each of these motives arises would be difficult to make, if indeed it has ever been made in any rigorous fashion by psychoanalysis. But whatever their origin, these motives become the primary ones in the explanation of behavior which may occur many years after the original Oedipus situation. It is in this way that all contemporary motivation tends to be referred to, and explained in terms of, much earlier development of a biological instinct and its various object choices.

In a general way this viewpoint of Freud's has been very influential. Many clinical psychologists, anthropologists, and personality psychologists have come to believe that the early years of childhood are of great importance in developing the basic motivational structure of an individual. On the other hand, this belief has been subject to violent attack by men like Lewin, and Allport, or more recently Orlansky (1949), and even by psychoanalysts who began within the Freudian framework. Horney, who may be considered typical of so-called neo-Freudians, has objected particularly to what she calls Freud's "instinctivistic and genetic psychology" (1939, p. 8). She and others in her group have emphasized the importance of cultural, environmental, or sociological factors in motivational development. In other words, she believes that motives are genuine learned products of experience and do not simply reflect always the aim-inhibited striving of a primary biological instinct. In her words, "A prevailingly sociological orientation then takes the place of a prevailingly anatomical-physiological one," and the "one-sided emphasis on genesis" is relinquished (1939, p. 9). Her view comes close to the position taken in Chapter 10 that there are special reasons why early childhood experiences are of greater importance in motivational development than later ones, but that they do not therefore continue to mold, almost single-handed, all adult motivational strivings. From this standpoint motives are the product of *all* learning experiences to which the initial childhood ones contribute heavily, but certainly not exclusively.

Other Views of Motivation

In discussing Freud's contribution to the psychology of motivation, we have tried to point out where his views have been accepted, rejected, or modified by other writers, but many of these other writers have gone on to make positive contributions of their own which they regard as substitutes for much of the Freudian framework. It is difficult to do justice to the great variety of clinical contributions to the theory of motivation, but we can make a very brief survey of some of the major viewpoints. Nearly all theorists who have worked with clinical data have accepted the first four characteristics of the Freudian scheme. That is, they have agreed that motivation is one of the fundamental variables of human personality, that motives are persistent, that they are often unconscious, and that they are tensional in character. By and large, these same people have also vigorously rejected the sixth characteristic of Freud's scheme, namely, the insistence upon the basic somatic, instinctual nature of motivation. They can be discussed therefore in terms of what attitude they have taken toward point five, that is, in terms of whether or not they have accepted a "monistic" view of motivation

for this reason that psychoanalytic therapy emphasizes the working out of adult conflicts in terms of the readjustment of the primary biological aims of which later motives are simply reflections. The practical significance of this viewpoint is that it leads naturally to the reinterpretation of all adult motivational goals in terms of those of childhood. We have already seen, for instance, how Alexander found it useful to explain a need for security and support in terms of the primary oral drives of infancy.

Later strivings are, if possible, referred to sublimations, deflections, fixations, or regressions of the primary biological instinct which unfolds according to a regular and inevitable pattern of growth and development. Nowhere is this clearer than in the tendency to explain adult male motivation in terms of the Oedipus complex. Freud argued that one of the first and most important object choices of the libido, after various parts of the body, would be the mother. Furthermore, the attachment of the libido to the mother is so strong that the male child especially wants to eliminate all competitors for the mother's love, particularly the father. The hostility toward the father in turn arouses on the one hand fear of retaliation, and on the other hand guilt for hating an object (the father) to which the libido is also attached. In this situation a number of motives appear to be present: a primary desire for the mother, a desire for aggression against the father, a need for the father's love and approval, fear of punishment, and a need for the reduction of the anxiety resulting from the conflict of motives which in turn causes a forgetting or repression of the whole complex. A thorough analysis of how each of these motives arises would be difficult to make, if indeed it has ever been made in any rigorous fashion by psychoanalysis. But whatever their origin, these motives become the primary ones in the explanation of behavior which may occur many years after the original Oedipus situation. It is in this way that all contemporary motivation tends to be referred to, and explained in terms of, much earlier development of a biological instinct and its various object choices.

In a general way this viewpoint of Freud's has been very influential. Many clinical psychologists, anthropologists, and personality psychologists have come to believe that the early years of childhood are of great importance in developing the basic motivational structure of an individual. On the other hand, this belief has been subject to violent attack by men like Lewin, and Allport, or more recently Orlansky (1949), and even by psychoanalysts who began within the Freudian framework. Horney, who may be considered typical of so-called neo-Freudians, has objected particularly to what she calls Freud's "instinctivistic and genetic psychology" (1939, p. 8). She and others in her group have emphasized the importance of cultural, environmental, or sociological factors in motivational development. In other words, she believes that motives are genuine learned products of experience and do not simply reflect always the aim-inhibited striving of a primary biological instinct. In her words, "A prevailingly sociological orientation then takes the place of a prevailingly anatomical-physiological one," and the "one-sided emphasis on genesis" is relinquished (1939, p. 9). Her view comes close to the position taken in Chapter 10 that there are special reasons why early childhood experiences are of greater importance in motivational development than later ones, but that they do not therefore continue to mold, almost single-handed, all adult motivational strivings. From this standpoint motives are the product of *all* learning experiences to which the initial childhood ones contribute heavily, but certainly not exclusively.

Other Views of Motivation

In discussing Freud's contribution to the psychology of motivation, we have tried to point out where his views have been accepted, rejected, or modified by other writers, but many of these other writers have gone on to make positive contributions of their own which they regard as substitutes for much of the Freudian framework. It is difficult to do justice to the great variety of clinical contributions to the theory of motivation, but we can make a very brief survey of some of the major viewpoints. Nearly all theorists who have worked with clinical data have accepted the first four characteristics of the Freudian scheme. That is, they have agreed that motivation is one of the fundamental variables of human personality, that motives are persistent, that they are often unconscious, and that they are tensional in character. By and large, these same people have also vigorously rejected the sixth characteristic of Freud's scheme, namely, the insistence upon the basic somatic, instinctual nature of motivation. They can be discussed therefore in terms of what attitude they have taken toward point five, that is, in terms of whether or not they have accepted a "monistic" view of motivation and if so, in terms of what primary motive they have put in the place of the libido. The monistic theorists may be most easily summarized. Like Freud they have tended to trace all motivation, all strivings, to a single basic motive, but they have disagreed as to what it is.

One of the earliest alternative theories was presented by Adler (1917), who argued that the libido or sexual motivation was really secondary to the drive for power or mastery. He started with the fact that all children begin life necessarily as being smaller and more helpless than the adults in their environment. The child as a result repeatedly observes that he is less able to get what he wants than are the adults in his circle. This arouses in him a strong need to compensate for his observed inferiority and all striving is directly or indirectly aimed at overcoming the initial, biologically-given helplessness. This is an ingenious notion, but Adler, like Freud, was apparently so concerned with universalizing his finding that, in the view of outside observers, he tended to warp all observations on the psychology of motivation to fit his particular scheme. This has been the pitfall of all monistic theories of motivation. The tendency has been to discover one motive and to be so impressed with its importance that the whole of experience is interpreted in the light of that one motive.

Horney (1939), who acknowledges a debt to H. S. Sullivan, has done likewise. As we have seen, she rejects the libido concept, but puts in its place another primary motive, namely, the need for security and safety in a potentially dangerous world. Like Adler she starts with the fact that a child is small and relatively powerless. From this fact, however, and from her clinical observations, she infers that the child wants not mastery, as Adler inferred, but security against threat. She emphasizes "all those adverse influences which make a child feel helpless and defenseless and which make him conceive the world as potentially menacing. Because of his dread of potential danger the child must develop certain 'neurotic trends' permitting him to cope with the world with some measure of safety." (1939, p. 10.) To her, basic anxiety in all its manifestations is sufficient, along with some primary satisfactions (1939, p. 73), to account for all man's complicated motivational tendencies. Her position can incorporate the latest cultural and sociological findings because the dangers which a child perceives may be thought of as culturally defined at least in part. Her view may also be considered consistent with the one adopted by the experimental psychologists who have thought of motivation as primarily a matter of anxiety or tension reduction (cf. Miller and Dollard, 1941).

As a final example of a monistic theory we may turn to men like Goldstein (1940), Rogers (1948), and Lecky (1945), who argue that man's primary motive is the drive for self-consistency, or integration. Rogers, on the basis of his nondirective interviewing data, has repeatedly noted what he first called a "positive growth influence" which seems to lead the person to make positive efforts at self-correction even in the midst of some very negative experiences. This "growth influence" has later been identified with the drive for self-consistency (1948) or the desire for maintaining a picture of the self which is coherent and integrated. It is this drive which therefore will prevent the incorporation into the self-concept of certain ideas which are alien to the total picture. Put in this way it is obvious that the drive has much in common with the Gestalt conception of forces working for *closure* in the perceptual field. The theory is not sufficiently developed to be considered a complete motivational scheme as yet, but the present indications are that Rogers and his co-workers are thinking in terms of parallels with Gestalt, perceptual forces. Another interpretation of the meaning of the self-consistency motive is given below in Chapter 14.

These are merely selections from a number of theories that have taken an essentially monistic view of motivation. There are other theorists, equally influential, who have rejected the monistic approach altogether. Among these we may mention only three—Allport, Lewin, and Murray. Allport reacted strongly against the whole Freudian interpretation of motivation. His scheme, therefore, differs at almost every point from Freud's, but his most serious objection was to the tying of adult motivations to infantile biological ones. He therefore developed the concept of *functional autonomy* which was a kind of "Declaration of Independence" for motives (1937). He believes that biological drives, or as he calls them, "deficit stimuli," might serve to account for the behavior of infants, and might even serve as the original basis for the development of psychogenic motives, but once formed, the psychogenic motives no longer have any connection whatsoever with their historical antecedents. They continue to function autonomously, under their own "steam," without any further dependence on biological states or conditions. In his theory he does not go much beyond providing evidence for the fact that motives do appear to function autonomously. That is, he does not suggest *what* motives should be used to conceptualize the human adult personality. His position seems to be rather that one should use whatever motives are appropriate to the individual case rather than rely on a few which are "common to all men." This is because he does not really conceive of the motivational aspect of personality as separable from the trait aspect. As we have seen in an earlier chapter, his traits "drive" as well as "direct." Consequently he has what might be described as a particularistic conception of motivation. Accurate as such a position may be, it does not promote a science of personality because one of the purposes of science is to economize in the description of a given personality in its entire richness and variety. This shortcoming of his scheme is perhaps illustrated by the failure of any one to use it in describing an individual case, unless one regards as an example of its use the case descriptions made by clinical psychologists who utilize whatever motives may come to mind for summarizing an individual life history. While such a procedure is convenient, it scarcely leads to the development of any general motivational concepts which are consistent enough to form a scheme which can be used for the scientific purpose of economical personality description.

The same criticism may be made of Lewin (1935). He, like Allport, was structurally rather than historically oriented in his theory. As an experimentalist he has perhaps contributed more to our empirical knowledge of the psychology of motivation than almost any other person, but as a theorist his contribution has consisted largely of "situational" or field analyses of motivated behavior. Thus in the example quoted in the beginning of the chapter where Dembo is describing the behavior of a person trying to solve an impossible problem, she as a student of Lewin represents the situation conceptually by a visual plot of "field forces" and "valences" (1931). The visual plot may also be symbolized in terms of topological geometry. The approach is to take an event consisting of a person interacting with his environment and then to try and conceptualize the behavior that results from this interaction in terms of the fewest number of abstract concepts which will account adequately for the behavior. Thus, in a situation like Dembo's, if the person moves toward an object and picks it up, the person is represented as being pushed by a "force" toward the object and the object is represented as having positive valence for the person. The situation may be diagrammed thus:

Such a description can then be complicated by the addition of other field forces until the visual plots become quite complicated and even three-dimensional.

Once more it would be impracticable to go into Lewin's whole conceptual system in any detail. We have presented this much in order to show why it is that his system does not lend itself to the conceptualization of the individual life. It does lend itself to accurate cross-sectional depictions of *unique* person-environment interactions. But no one yet has seriously attempted to write a life history of a particular person in Lewinian terms. It certainly could be done (cf. Lewin, 1946), but the question remains as to whether it could be economically done and also as to whether the results would be of any general value in writing up the life history of another person. This is not a criticism of Lewin's approach for the type of situational analysis for which it was originally intended. It is simply a restatement of the limitations of any particularistic motivational scheme as far as conceptualizing the life history of a single person is concerned.

Murray's need system (1938) may be described as pluralistic rather than particularistic. It can best be summarized in terms of the way in which it was constructed. Murray brought together a large number of different psychologists with different theoretical orientations and had them work together for a period of two or three years on the problem of constructing a conceptual scheme for personality which would succeed in handling case study materials collected on a group of individuals who were studied intensively over this period. In other words, Murray was the first person historically to make a major effort to conceptualize adequately the concrete normal individual life in all its richness and variety (cf. also Polansky, 1941). The psychoanalysts who had made somewhat similar attempts had always been guided by the desire to find out what was wrong with the person so that they could cure him. Consequently the personality pictures which they drew were warped to some extent by their purpose. Psychoanalytic case studies tend to be one-sided and to emphasize the maladjustments of the individual rather than the areas of normal functioning because it is the problem areas of personality with which psychiatrists are chiefly concerned. Murray at least faced the problem as we have defined it here—namely, the problem of trying to give an adequate conceptual picture of the total personality. In order to do this he drew on the contributions of as many different schools as he could. What he was trying to do and how he went about doing it are both important in understanding the results which he obtained.

On the motivational side he ended up with a rather extensive list of concrete needs drawn in part from the different backgrounds of the psychologists cooperating with him. These needs have the advantage over the particularistic ones of Allport or Lewin of being generally applicable to more than one life or one situation. They are concrete, extensively defined, and taken together do provide a complete motivational system for summarizing the dynamic aspect of personality. But they have the disadvantage of being so heterogeneous that it is difficult to fit them into a system. They suffer from the defects of any particularistic scheme in appearing to be a collection of need *names* which are not related to one another in any way and which seem so extensive as to be scarcely more economical than the original behavior they are supposed to represent.

Murray recognizes this problem in part and attempts to relate his needs to each other first by a general definition and then by stating the general aims which groups of them are supposed to serve. His general definition is as follows: "A need is a construct (convenient fiction or hypothetical concept) which stands for a force (the physico-chemical nature of which is unknown) in the brain region, a force which organizes perception, apperception, intellection, conation, and action in such a way as to transform in a certain direction an existing, unsatisfying situation." (1938, p. 124.) He then goes on to state that the existence of a need can be inferred from the direction in which the unsatisfying situation is transformed, from the "typical behavioral trend" or "typical mode" of responding, or from the "manifestation of satisfaction with the achievement of a certain effect." But this raises some difficulties that he never fully resolves. Are needs to be thought of primarily in terms of the characteristic *mode of response* used to gratify them or in terms of the inferred goal of behavior of any sort? Murray states later that "an operational definition of a need in terms of actones is out of the question" (1938, p. 244), but in practice his need definitions often lean heavily on such characteristic actones.

As Murray would be the first to point out, a person may show abasive, affiliative, or achievant behavioral trends, all in an attempt to satisfy his n Achievement, conceived as the need for certain goal satisfactions (however vague). That is, an outside observer looking at his behavior could infer that he has abased himself, or allied himself with some superior person with the goal of getting ahead in the world. Although he has shown abasive rather than achievant attitudes and behavioral trends, it would be a mistake to infer that he therefore shows n Abasement. It would simplify matters if Murray's needs were conceived always in terms of the inferred *goals* of behavior rather than in terms of the behavioral trends usually characterizing the means of attaining them. In this way they would fulfill the purpose of the motive concept in psychological theory more closely which, as we defined it at the beginning of the chapter, is to group together a variety of different behavioral trends around a common cause or a comon goal. To put the matter in terms of our approach to theory, Murray's need concept should be "purified" of its trait (consistent behavior) connotations just as Allport's trait concept should be cleared of its dynamic connotations.

Murray has imposed on his individual needs an overarching goal system which serves in part to meet the objections that his needs are not sufficiently related and not sufficiently goal-oriented. Table 11.1 classifies some of his twenty or more different manifest needs under the four general status aims he says they may serve (1938, p. 150). Curiously enough the breakdown he makes here is very similar to the one made in Table 10.2, in which we considered the *kinds of problems* the infant is confronted with in socialization. Thus "to defend status" defines problems of *protection*; "to raise status" involves problems of *mastery*; "to ally with others" suggests problems of *affection*; and "to reject or attack hostile objects" is at least tangentially related to problems of *control* or learning about reactions to frustration. Such an analogy suggests the basic aims, or strategies of the organism can be reduced to a limited number with considerable agreement on all sides. Unfortunately the more important problem of relating these aims in a systematic way to operations for measuring them still remains.

TABLE 11.1

Classification of Murray's Needs in Terms of Approximate Status Aims

Status aims	*Related needs*
1. To raise status	n Achievement n Dominance n Exhibition
2. To defend status	n Autonomy n Counteraction n Harmavoidance n Defendance
3. To ally with others for mutual protection	n Abasement n Affiliation n Nurturance
4. To reject or attack hostile objects	n Aggression n Rejection

Murray attacked this problem with characteristic vigor by relating each of the general aims to a series of sub-needs as listed on the right-hand side of Table 11.1 and by specifying a great variety of ways of measuring each sub-need. Two difficulties emerged in the process. First, the general classification of status aims was lost sight of in the analysis of the need structure of an individual case, and remained therefore a theoretical order added to a basic heterogeneity without producing any real integration. Here, as elsewhere in Murray's book, the solution to the different viewpoints held by his contributors seems to have been compromise and addition rather than simplification and integration. The second difficulty lay in the sheer multiplicity of the operations listed for measuring a given need. Future research workers in the field of personality will doubtless find the richness of detail with which he worked at this problem extremely useful. Clinicians have certainly been provided by it with the only motivational vocabulary which competes at all with the psychoanalytic one. But as a practical method of measurement Murray's system falls of its own weight. The only way to take into account all the manifestations of a need for a given individual is to weigh and synthesize them in an essentially intuitive fashion to arrive at a final judgment expressed as a rating. Table 11.2 suggests the difficulty and subtlety of this process by listing *part* of the defining operations for a single need in his system. A person who has familiarized himself with these need expressions (and those

TABLE 11.2

n Dominance (n Dom) As Described in Murray's
Explorations in Personality

Desires and Effects: To control one's human environment. To influence or direct the behavior of Os by suggestion, seduction, persuasion, or command. To dissuade, restrain, or prohibit. To induce an O to act in a way which accords with one's sentiments and needs. To get Os to cooperate. To convince an O of the 'rightness' of one's opinion.

Feelings and Emotions: Confidence.

Trait-names and Attitudes: Dominative, forceful, masterful, assertive, decisive, authoritative, executive, disciplinary.

Press: infraDom: Inferior Os; p Deference: Compliance; p Abasement. supraDom: Superior Os; p Dominance; p Rival.

Gratuities: Children, servants, disciples, followers.

Actions: General: To influence, sway, lead, prevail upon, persuade, direct, regulate, organize, guide, govern, supervise. To master, control, rule, override, dictate terms. To judge, make laws, set standards, lay down principles of conduct, give a decision, settle an argument. To prohibit, restrain, oppose, dissuade, punish, confine, imprison. To magnetize, gain a hearing, be listened to, be imitated, be followed, set the fashion. To be an exemplar.

Motones: To beckon, point, push, pull, carry, confine.

Verbones: Commands: 'Come here'—'Stop that'—'Hurry up'—'Get out,' etc.

Mesmeric influence: To hypnotize.

ideo Dominance: To establish political, aesthetic, scientific, moral, or religious principles. To have one's ideas prevail. To influence the 'climate of opinion.' To argue for one cause against another.

socio Dominance: To govern a social institution.

Fusions: The commonest fusion is with n Agg (Autocratic power).

Coercion: To force an O (by threats) to do something, etc.

Statements in Questionnaire

1. I enjoy organizing or directing the activities of a group—team, club, or committee.
2. I argue with zest for my point of view against others.
3. I find it rather easy to lead a group of boys and maintain discipline.
4. I usually influence others more than they influence me, etc.

(Reproduced by permission from H. A. Murray, *Explorations in Personality.* Copyright, 1938, Oxford University Press.)

of the twenty to thirty other needs in the system) can doubtless produce a rating of the strength of various needs and a picture of their various fusions and interrelations which will correlate fairly highly with the judgments of another person similarly trained (cf. Murray, 1938), but the fact remains that the whole procedure involves a refinement of essentially clinical methods of analysis rather than a contribution to personality theory. As we pointed out in our discussion of ratings (Chapter 6), theory is not likely to advance so long as measurements are made in terms of judgments based on partially unknown (or unreportable) behaviors in a variety of unknown circumstances on the basis of an unknown process of weighing and synthesizing. The next step theoretically is to translate Murray's highly suggestive descriptions into a variety of measures of motivation which can be systematically studied in controlled situations and related to each other in clearly understood ways.

The Hierarchy of Motives. Maslow (1943a, 1948) has integrated most of the approaches to motivation so far discussed into an overall scheme which is organized according to a hierarchical principle of relative prepotency. He argues that the physiological tensions, for instance, are prepotent until they are satisfied, at which point other motives take over:

> It is quite true that man lives by bread alone—when there is no bread. But what happens to man's desires when there *is* plenty of bread, and when his belly is chronically filled? *At once other (and 'higher') needs emerge* and these, rather than physiological hungers, dominate the organism. And when these in turn are satisfied new (and still 'higher') needs emerge and so on. (1943a, p. 375.)

His list of needs in order of basic importance to the organism is as follows:

1. Physiological needs
2. Safety needs
3. Love and belonging needs
4. Esteem needs (needs for achievement and recognition)
5. Self-actualization need
6. The desires to know and understand

Most of these needs have previously been emphasized by one writer or another—the physiological tensions by biologists; safety by Horney, Sullivan, *et al.*; love and belonging by the psychoanalysts (although love is not synonymous with sex either for them or for Maslow); esteem by Adler; and self-actualization by Goldstein, Rogers, *et al.* Maslow is uncertain as to where his cognitive needs fit into the structure, but he feels certain that they exist perhaps as a function of intelligence and of gratification fairly high up the scale of lower-order needs. What he has done is to place the various emphases of other theorists in an order of importance such that lower needs must be gratified before higher ones can function adequately. He illustrates the point by a fable:

> Let us say that A has lived several weeks in a dangerous jungle, in which he has managed to stay alive by finding occasional food and water. B not only stays alive but also has a rifle and a hidden cave with a closable entrance. C has all these and has two more men with him as well. D has the food, the gun, the allies, the cave, and, in addition, has with him his best loved friend. Finally, E, in the same jungle, has all of these, and in addition is a well-respected leader of his band. For the sake of brevity we may call these men respectively the merely surviving, the safe, the belonging, the loved, and the respected. (1948, p. 409.)

He then goes on to state: "But this is not only a series of increasing need-gratifications; it is as well a *series of increasing degrees of psychological health.*" In short, his hierarchy is a means of defining psychological adjustment and the conditions necessary for creativity and happiness. As such it is a somewhat unique departure from psychopathological theories of motivation which have stressed the tensional, *need* characteristics of motivation. Whatever its shortcomings, his scheme certainly has the virtue of stressing the importance of studies of the consequences of *need-gratification* to supplement our studies of *need-frustration.* Like so many other of the motivational schemes we have discussed, its worth will also finally depend on the evidence which is brought in by such experimental studies.

Clinical Measures of Motivation. How does the clinician arrive at his inferences about motivation? We have seen in a general way how Freud proceeded to analyze a memory lapse by asking for free associations from the subject. In the last chapter we illustrated how Karl's imaginative productions could be used to make inferences about certain basic affective associations laid down in childhood. We have also made some guesses as to the meaning of his presolution responses to the stimulus word "success" in a tachistoscopic recognition test. Is there any method in all this madness? How does the clinician arrive at his hypotheses, his dynamic interpretations, his "wild guesses" or whatever you want to call them?

Furthermore, how does he go about finding out whether his guesses are right?

To begin with, most clinicians have found that fantastic material is the best hunting ground for motivational analyses. Freud got his start in analyzing free associations and dreams; he then went on to apply similar methods of interpretation to other such unrealistic or odd behavior as slips of the tongue, memory losses, parapraxes, etc. Murray, who has been perhaps the most influential exponent of motivational analysis in America, has had his greatest success in analyzing controlled daydreams or imaginative productions produced for his Thematic Apperception Test. The reason for the apparently unique value of imaginative material for dynamic analysis probably lies in the fact that fantasy is by definition less influenced by the autochthonous, culture-pattern variables that produce schemata and less influenced also by the past learned responses (traits) of the subjects. We will return to this problem in Chapter 15. For the moment we will have to accept it as a historical fact, at any rate, that fantastic material lends itself most readily to analysis in motivational terms.

Not all fantasy material is fantastic (in the sense of "unreal"). Even within a myth or imaginative story or dream there are real and unreal elements. Let us take the following myth, which is a condensation of a Navaho tale, as an example.

Abstract by Katherine Spencer of "The Stricken Twins" (W. Matthews, *The Night Chant,* 1902, pp. 212-65).

A poor family, consisting of a woman, her mother, her husband and their son and daughter, live in Canyon de Chelly. They do not have corn nor sheep but live on wood rats, seeds and wild fruits. The adolescent daughter hears a strange voice while gathering yucca alone; her family pays no attention to her tale. The hearing of voices is repeated four times, and on the fourth day Hastse Yalti appears and asks her in marriage. The girl is shy in his presence and does not answer his questions until the fourth repetition. She fears to ask permission of her family because he is "too fine a man." When he proposes marriage in secret, she is afraid of not being able to keep the secret. After the fourth repetition of his request, she agrees. They meet on each of four successive days and not again. She is remorseful and fears to face her parents lest they learn her secret and kill her. When four months later she feels motions within her, she still does not talk to her family; twin boys are born at the end of nine months. Her family asks whether this happened when she heard voices. She protests that she doesn't know who the father is, that it must have happened in her sleep. Her brother takes her side saying that she knows no more than she tells, that perhaps the holy ones are responsible and that in any case it is good to have their number increased.

As the twins grow to boyhood, they wander often from home and their family has difficulty keeping track of them. When about nine years old, they leave home and their tracks end mysteriously. The possibility of their kinship to the holy ones is remembered and their mother thinks they may have gone in search of their father. After five days, the twins reappear; the elder is blind and carries the younger who is lame. They tell their story—how they wandered a short way and rested in a rock shelter; how its roof closed over and trapped them; how they were finally let out by the Squeaking God only to find themselves thus maimed.

The first part of the story dealing with the family and its living arrangements is "realistic" and may be taken to reflect the way in which the Navaho live in family units and usually raise corn or sheep for a living. But then we are told of a daughter who has intercourse with a God or spirit in secret in a way which suggests the "Virgin Birth" story. What are we to make of this? Why should she fear telling her family if he is "too fine a man"? Why should they kill her if they learn her secret? Why does she give birth to twins? Why are the twins injured in this particular, totally unreal way of a cave closing over them? All these and many other questions arise in the course of reading this story. They arise chiefly over portions of the material which do not make "sense," which are not logical, rational, or consistent with what one would expect on the basis of the normal, culturally-patterned representation of the world and what happens in it.

As a first step in motivational analysis then, the clinician usually isolates or discovers certain "unusual," unreal, or fantastic behavioral elements. Having isolated them he has several choices of how to go about discovering what they mean.

1. Free association. In psychoanalysis, particularly in its early years, the method of choice was to ask the patient to free associate around the inexplicable occurrence until an explanation popped up, just as in the case of the man who had forgotten the word *aliquis*. There are two objections to this method, one theoretical, the other practical. On theoretical grounds, it is hard to know whether or not the solution "found" by the patient is suggested by the analyst. Who is to say when the patient should stop free associating? Should he stop only when he finds an interpretation that suits the analyst or himself? What criteria of suitability are there? On practical grounds free association is time-consuming and

often not practicable for studying normal people or their imaginative products, especially when they are not around (as in the myth above). While free association will continue to have suggestive value in clinical situations, it has come to be supplemented frequently by other methods.

2. Empathy and recipathy. Murray has perhaps been more directly concerned with the problem of diagnosis of motivation than any other person. He begins by rejecting two obvious approaches—namely, trying to infer what a person is trying to do from the trend of his behavior or simply asking him, "What are you trying to do?" (1938, p. 245.) Instead he recommends what he calls an essentially "intuitive process." By this he does not mean "uncontrolled, free-floating intuition," but "critical empathy" and "recipathy." By empathy he means essentially "feeling with" the person whose behavior is to be interpreted, "putting oneself in the place of another" (1938, p. 247). As the myth unfolds (for example) "we feel something and we imagine that the other person [telling the myth or story] feels the same." Recipathy is the complement of empathy. "The E sets himself opposite to, rather than flowing with, the subject's movements and words, and becoming as open and sensitive as possible, feels how the subject is affecting him (the E). . . . if he feels that he is being swayed to do something, he imagines Dominance; if he feels anxious or irritated, he infers Aggression, and so forth." (1938, p. 248.)

How would these processes be a help with our Navaho myth? Suppose we identify for a moment with the god Hastse Yalti in the story. Does it make us feel that he has played a trick on the girl? She is shy and impressed by him and he wins her over in secret despite her initial fears. He has tricked her family and as further proof of his potency produces twins. From the girl's viewpoint we might feel by recipathy that here was a powerful being and she is so much in his power that she submits even though she fears that her family will kill her if they find out. From all of this we might form the hypothesis on the basis of empathy and recipathy that the male Navahos who tell this story are fulfilling in this portion of it a simple desire to appear powerful over women and that they have doubts about this potency ordinarily or they would not need to express it in so disguised and elaborate a manner. Such an interpretation gains added support from knowledge that in real life parents would be highly unlikely to kill or even disapprove a girl for wanting to marry "too fine a man." At the manifest level the girl's desire to keep the affair a secret doesn't make sense; if we assume that the purpose of the secrecy is to gratify the storyteller's wish to appear powerful, then it does make motivational sense.

3. Symbolism. Psychoanalysts, though they also use empathy in a less explicit way than Murray suggests, are more apt to make motivational inferences in terms of symbols or "body language," as we have already seen. Thus in the next portion of our Navaho myth the twin boys are caught in a cave (claustral symbol) which closes down on them and maims them in a way which obviously would suggest to the psychoanalyst castration by the female. In fact, the injuries of the boys are in the classical tradition: one has a mutilated leg (penis), the other is blinded (symbolizing injury to the scrotum). In these terms the dynamic content of the story is that man (Hastse Yalti represented by his sons) is punished by woman for his sexual conquest over her. The limitations of this type of symbolic interpretation have already been discussed: the point here is simply to illustrate how the clinician goes about his job of forming hypotheses about the motivational content of fantasy material from translating events into body language.

4. Logical inference. Tomkins (1947) has not been satisfied with these more intuitive approaches and has attempted instead to use more traditional methods of drawing logical inferences from imaginative material. Specifically he applies John Stuart Mill's canons of logic to his data. The best way to illustrate how this approach works is to quote one of his own examples:

B. Method of difference.

Consider now the relationship between these stories.

1. This is someone who has just lost a person very dear to him. He is in the depths of despair. Life has lost all its meaning for him and he doesn't want to go on living. But then he meets a woman who understands the way he feels and gradually he forgets his sorrow and he finds again that there is meaning in life.
2. This is the picture of a man who is mourning someone who was very close to him. Nothing seems to matter very much to him since her death. He sees no more point in living. Death comes as a welcome relief from his misery.

The relationship between these stories illustrates Mill's method of difference. "If an instance in which the phenomenon under investigation occurs, and an instance in which it does not occur, have every circumstance in common, save one, that one occurring only in the former, the circumstance in which alone the two instances differ is the effect or cause or an indispensable part of the cause of the phenomenon." Thus in 1 and 2, there is the loss of a love object, and a consequent depression. But in 1 there is the intervention of a new love object who understands him; and the outcome is regeneration. In 2, there is no new love object, and the outcome is a continuation of the depression to its end in death. Thus we may say that recovery from depression is the effect of the intervention of another love object.

(Reproduced by permission from S. S. Tomkins, *The Thematic Apperception Test.* Copyright 1947, Grune and Stratton.)

In motivational terms, we could infer from this analysis that the subject has a need for a woman's love. Tomkins illustrates Mill's other canons (methods of agreement, concomitant variation, agreement and difference, etc.) in similar fashion. His approach is undoubtedly used by many clinicians. Thus in interpreting Karl's TAT stories we will find that so long as women go on loving men no matter how the men transgress, they will come out all right in the end. But in the one story in which a woman (a sister) turns against a man, she is sorry the rest of her life. Here we would be tempted to infer that Karl has so strong a need for nurturance, love, and support from women that any thought of their turning against a man must be punished. But there are difficulties with this approach too. It is difficult, for one thing, to find instances which "have every circumstance in common, save one" or meet other such requirements of Mill's canons. For another, the average "depth" psychologist would feel that this approach is too formal and superficial by itself and would not get as readily at concealed motivation as the other techniques already discussed.

There are many psychologists who regard any of the approaches outlined as leading essentially to nonsense or at the most to an elaborate mythology that psychoanalysts and others have built up until they have become victims of it. Such a view is partly correct. Certainly there has been far too much uninhibited enthusiasm for the kind of speculative motivational analysis just illustrated. But a sharp distinction must be made between forming or *entertaining* a motivational hypothesis and *accepting* it as proven. The methods described deal with how motivational hypotheses are generated, not with how they are proved or disproved. This is an important difference which is far too often overlooked. Many clinicians are so impressed with their ability to make *any* kind of sense out of fantastic events that they tend to believe whatever sense they find, without further attempts to check it. Experimentalists on the other hand are so oriented around checking hypotheses that they often seem incapable of generating any good ones. Both approaches are needed.

But how can motivational hypotheses of the sort we have been describing be checked? Personality psychologists have tended to be most impressed by confirmation of a hypothesis by another interpreter working independently either with the same or a different set of facts (cf. Allport, 1942; Hall, 1947). While agreement of two judges working independently on the same data has some checking value, we are apt to be more impressed when confirmation of a hypothesis comes from a totally new and previously unknown source of information. Thus, for instance, we may feel more secure in our interpretation of the Navaho myth when we find that Navaho men are disadvantaged with respect to Navaho women according to the way the social structure is organized and that they lose more decisions to their wives when disagreements arise (Strodtbeck, 1950). These (and other data too detailed to discuss here) support our interpretation of the Navaho myth that men feel a need for increased power over women and that they fear the consequences of such impulses toward self-assertion.

While agreement among different interpretations does add to the probability that a hypothesis is correct, it is by no means foolproof. After all, a great many wise people agreed for a long time that the earth was flat. The fact of the matter is that hypotheses about motivation such as we have been discussing can and should be checked in exactly the same way as any other hypothesis is checked in science. The requirements are that the hypothesis and the events to which it is supposed to apply be stated as explicitly and clearly as possible and that it then be checked by an appeal to all the relevant facts. These two simple criteria are seldom met in dynamic analyses. Often the interpretation is so tortuous that it is impossible to discover to what events it is supposed to apply; thus any possibly negative finding may be dismissed on the grounds that the fact in question was not really relevant to the motive previously inferred. Or not all the facts are examined: it is easy to find facts that will illustrate a hypothesis. What about the ones that are overlooked? For example, we have not as yet explained in our Navaho myth why the brother took his sister's side when her truancy was discovered. To avoid selective use of facts, it is often desirable *first* to list the facts to be explained, so that none may be disregarded in the effort after an interpretation. Or an interpretation may be worked out on part of the facts and used to predict (or postdict) what would happen in other cases. A useful illustration of the importance of considering all the facts is provided by R. K. White's value analysis of Richard Wright's autobiography, *Black Boy* (1947). White first read the document carefully as a clinician would and made an intuitive motivational analysis of its contents. Then he developed a careful scoring system for classifying dynamic content which he applied to the whole book. When he compared the results of the quantitative approach to the intuitive one, he found that they agreed in most respects, but that intuitively he had greatly underestimated the importance of Physical Safety as a value to Richard Wright. In short, a careful examination of *all* the facts led him to modify his analysis of Wright's motivational structure.

Karl's Motives. In practice the clinical psychologist is thoroughly "dynamic." No matter what his theoretical or methodological orientation may be, in terms of any of the approaches just described, the average clinician constantly interprets test data and patients' actions in motivational terms. Much of the interpretation appears to the average theoretically minded psychologist as highly speculative, but we would fail to touch on an important, if unsystematic, body of empirical data if we were to leave the clinical approach without at least attempting to give the flavor of a dynamic interpretation of a particular person. In doing so we will not be able to apply the careful methodological checks just suggested, but we will be able to show more fully how motivational hypotheses are generated and may be elaborated into an over-all picture of a person's motivational structure. Without further apology then let us take our case, Karl, and attempt to analyze his motives, more or less as a clinician would.

To begin with, let us turn to the kind of data which has most often and most easily been interpreted in dynamic terms—to his fantasy productions. Murray's Thematic Apperception Test, to the extent that it has tended to elicit fantasy or daydreams in a series of standardized situations, has moved a step beyond Freud's dream analysis methodologically, but its interpretation follows the same principles that Freud first applied with such success. We have already seen in the previous chapter how Karl's TAT strongly suggested the presence of the following thema (from Table 10.8):

Rejection (Desertion)	→	n Aggression n Affiliation	→	Conflict Anxiety	→	frequent projected aggression
A		B		C		D

For simplicity's sake let us refer to this as the "Desertion-Aggression" thema. It appears in story 3, in which an orphaned girl is taken advantage of by a predatory male; in story 10, in which a young man who is deserted by his wife commits suicide; but most vividly of all in story 13, which is reproduced in full below:

13MF. A young man with his head buried on his arm, a woman lying on a bed behind him.

(Here's a good one.) That is a good one. This man has always been a strong character. (pause) The girl in the picture is his daughter. She has just died. Despite the fact that this man is a strong character, he has been sensually attracted to his daughter. Nevertheless, he does love her dearly inasmuch as she is the image of her mother, who had deserted him years before. They have lived alone together for years. His loneliness, perhaps, and his love for his wife, led him to have intercourse with his daughter. She not being aware of the incestuous spirit involved, was nevertheless willing and so it continued for a time with the man suffering from periods of remorse, but nevertheless, attempting to justify his action, and now his daughter had fallen sick and she had died. He is crushed and broken, that she is gone, because he had loved her dearly. However, because of his burning passionate desire, he has drawn down the covers from her naked body . . . (pause) This has upset him considerably. He realizes the shame of his deed, his past performances. His life will never be a happy one because he will be haunted by these ghosts of the past, of his wife's desertion and of his betrayal of his daughter's purity.

All the elements of the thema are here: (A) The man is deserted by his wife and in his loneliness (B) he seduces and betrays his daughter (fusion of aggression with desire for love); (C) he is overcome by remorse (guilt and anxiety); and (D) she dies because of illness (aggression projected into an impersonal agent). The fusion of sex and aggression is particularly vivid in the man's "burning passionate desire" for a dead body.

In fact, it is so vivid that it suggests we look further for this particular type of action by men in Karl's stories. It occurs in fact fairly frequently. Both stories 3 and 4 deal with predatory males who seduce and then toss aside innocent, loving women. This gives us more information about Karl's desertion-aggression thema by

[illegible]

[illegible]

goal objects involve [illegible]
about women, both [illegible]
having them (because [illegible]

In addition to the [illegible] there is another theme [illegible] successful achievement." [illegible] mendous achievement built [illegible] at the peak of his fame, leaves [illegible] son; his mother hopes he will [illegible] what happens! He has little talent [illegible] gives it up for something else. [illegible] lies the same theme. In story 7 a [illegible] up the great career expected of him as a [illegible] "in the footsteps" of his [illegible] his relatives' death by conquering [illegible] boy goes off to Africa and attempts to "follow [illegible] steps" by becoming a big-game hunter. [illegible] his purpose and "will probably perish [illegible] being exposed to an icy blast." This story [illegible] low because of its possible [illegible]

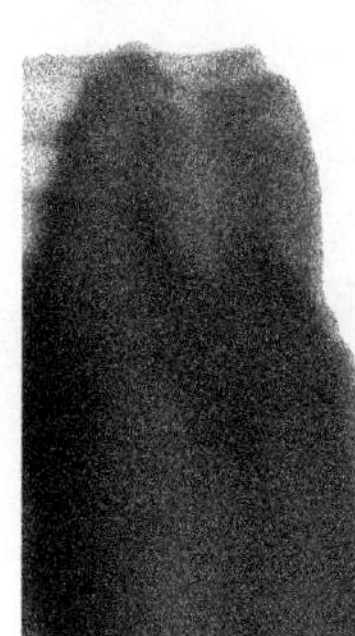

8 BM. An adolescent boy with a dim [illegible] background.

The young man is a city boy [illegible] the [illegible] school. His hobby is hunting and the gun [illegible] His father was a big game hunter, explorer [illegible] expeditions in the wilds of Africa he was [illegible] others [illegible] colleagues. He was [illegible] operation was necessary to save his life. [illegible] his friends performed the crude operation. [illegible] died, but he left sufficient fortune to [illegible] is still living, but hopes her son will not [illegible] boy dreams of following in his father's footsteps [illegible] an expedition as soon as he is able. His mother [illegible] but to no avail. He will be a successful [illegible]

suggesting that the source of desertion is a woman (see story 13) and that the need for love *and* aggression are consequently aimed at her. Since these two aims are somewhat contradictory, they are fused here in a kind of sadistic sexuality which permits partial gratification of both needs and, curiously enough, has no ill effects for the woman, though it does for the man (in story 4). The reaction of the women to the bad, predatory men in these stories (3, 4, 5, and 6) is interesting and illuminating. In stories 3 and 4 they go on loving, in simple innocence, and manage to come out of their experiences wiser and braver for them. In story 5, however, when the woman, here a sister, turns against her brother for wrongdoing, he dies and she is forever after tortured by remorse. The moral seems to be that women *must go on loving,* no matter what men do. If they do, they will be rewarded; if they do not, they will be punished. Finally in this series comes story 6, which contains two women: a mother who is trying to hold her lawyer-son to his high ideals and a wife who is urging him to let her "bad" brother off. If we assume, as is often the case with stories of this sort, that the male character has split here into its "bad" (id) and "good" (super-ego) aspects, then the story makes good sense in terms of what has gone before. The "bad" side of man will be let off from his "crimes" by the intervention of a loving woman (here his sister, cf. story 5), but the "good" side which is his conscience, inherited from and supported by his mother, will continue to suffer guilt long afterward. Here it is apparent that the female image has split into a loving, forgiving nurturant aspect represented by a lover (see also stories 14 and 18), and a demanding aspect represented by the mother. Through all of this run three basic ideas: (1) Men betray women's love and trust through acts of deceit, sexuality, aggression, wrongdoing, etc.; (2) women, especially lovers, must forgive and nurture men; (3) men must suffer guilt for their wrongdoing, especially if they are forgiven (or get away with it).

What can be concluded from all this about Karl's motives? First of all, it is clear that he has a strong *fear of rejection* coupled with an intense *need for affiliation* and *nurturance.* For reasons which will become clearer in the next chapter we will adopt the practice of speaking of fears (avoidance motives) and needs (approach motives) separately. In the present case the two are largely complementary but this is not always the case. Also, either the fear or the wish may be very much stronger than the other, even when they are complementary. Secondly, probably as a result of the rejection-affiliation conflict and subsequent insecurity, Karl has a strong *n Aggression* coupled with an equally strong fear of expressing his own Aggression (*f Aggression*), which results in (a) projection of aggression into impersonal agents, (b) fusion of aggression with sexuality (sadism), or (c) intrapunitiveness (guilt or aggression turned against the self). Furthermore, it is clear that these two motive conflicts are intimately tied up with women as the main goal objects involved, and that he will be extremely ambivalent about women, both loving and needing them on the one hand, and hating them (because they demand or desert) on the other.

In addition to the desertion-aggression thema just discussed, there is another thema in Karl's TAT which centers around "unsuccessful achievement." In story 1, for instance, there is a tremendous achievement build-up for the young boy: His father dies at the peak of his fame, leaves his old and valuable violin to his son: his mother hopes he will play it: all depends on him. And what happens? He has little talent; he cannot play very well and gives it up for something else. Stories 7 and 8 continue more or less the same theme. In story 7 a brilliant young biologist gives up the great career expected of him as a scientist who is to follow "in the footsteps" of his professor, in order to go off and "avenge his relatives' death by conquering disease." In story 8 the young boy goes off to Africa and attempts to "follow in his father's footsteps" by becoming a big-game hunter, but he too doesn't fulfill his purpose and "will probably perish . . . like a hothouse plant being exposed to an icy blast." This story is reproduced in full below because of its possible interpretation as a typical Oedipus thema:

8 BM. An adolescent boy with a dim surgical operation scene in the background.

The young man is a city boy . . . the lad is . . . who is away at Prep school. His hobby is hunting and the gun he sees belonged to his father. His father was a big game hunter, explorer, traveler, but on one of his expeditions in the wilds of Africa he was accidentally shot by one of his cohorts . . . colleagues. He was far from civilization . . . an immediate operation was necessary to save his life. Only a First Aid kit being available his friends performed the crude operation. It was unsuccessful. The man died, but he left sufficient fortune to take care of his son. The boy's mother is still living, but hopes her son will not be a big game hunter. But the boy dreams of following in his father's footsteps and is planning to go on an expedition as soon as he is able. His mother will try to dissuade him, but to no avail. He will be a successful hunter, but probably will perish in the jungle from some dread disease, much like a hot house plant being exposed to an icy blast.

In traditional psychoanalytic terms this story would be interpreted as reflecting an Oedipus conflict, since it has all the elements of the classical situation. The aggression against the father is represented by his father's being killed in a hunting expedition. His desire to take his father's place is shown by his attempt to take over his father's gun (penis symbol) and follow in his footsteps in a hunting expedition (intercourse symbol). The guilt arising from these two motives and from his own love for his father is illustrated by his own punishment and death for what he has done. Particularly significant is the statement that he will die "like a hot house plant being exposed to an icy blast" because this apparently refers to a form of sexual inhibition which he practiced as a boy. The following remarks in his autobiography are relevant: "My period of masturbation was from about 12, eighth grade, well into high school. . . . I was afraid of getting caught. I was told it would lead to insanity. [Also older fellows told him when he thought about it to put a cold pack on his head; or stick it in cold water; also to think of the cold arctic.]"

To follow through on the Oedipal interpretation of these stories we could reinterpret the father-daughter incest story, reproduced above, as a projection of his own desires for his mother and their dreadful consequences. While such an interpretation may seem appealing in its simplicity, there are certain difficulties in the way of its too ready acceptance. (1) Why should Karl love his mother? What evidence we have suggests that she did not treat him particularly well, certainly not in a manner which would readily set up such a strong affectional tie as this explanation requires. This question may seem foolish to a psychoanalyst who thinks in terms of a libido with rather fixed object choices which are not influenced by circumstances, but it is not foolish to a learning psychologist who regards affective choice as a function of principles which govern the formation and strengthening of any associational bonds. (2) Why is Karl so energetic and so ambitious? On the surface at least, as we have seen in previous chapters, he wants very much to get ahead in the world. It is possible to explain this ambitiousness as aim-inhibited striving. That is, since he is frustrated in his desire for his mother by guilt and anxiety, the motivational energy which would normally flow in this direction becomes diverted to getting ahead in the world. But even this objectively does not seem to cover the facts very well because his autobiographical account of his sexual experiences does not indicate undue anxiety or inhibition over sexual matters. On the contrary, in all of his TAT stories and in all that he says about sex, there seems to be little evidence of repression or anxiety. Technically at least, we would not expect him to work so hard for a substitute goal (achievement) unless the original aim had been seriously inhibited by anxiety. (3) Why does his motivational pattern differ from that of any other son in the family? Karl has two brothers and, although we have no data on their adjustment to life, his description of them in his autobiography indicates that their motivational pattern is different from his own. This raises the problem of whether the Oedipus complex, as it is usually summarized, is sufficiently specific to give the unique variations in motivational patterning that occur from one son to another. The scheme has the disadvantage of being so general and so universal that it loses some value for the explanation of individual differences in motivational development. (4) Why does Karl show such an extreme need for support and security? The analysis in terms of the Oedipus complex has little to say on this point, yet it is sufficiently clear from all that we know of Karl that one of the major driving forces in his life is his lack of self-confidence and his desire, not so much for sexual experience with women, but for the support and nurturance that they can give him. Any adequate motivational analysis must cover this point.

But perhaps the most important reason for not accepting the Oedipus hypothesis, at least in its simplified form, is that there are other more complete ways of accounting for these same story elements. To carry the "unsuccessful achievement" thema one step further, for instance, we find that Karl himself gives reasons for his heroes' inadequacies which fit closely with other things we know about him. In story 8 he stresses the importance of *belonging* by speaking of the "migrant workers" as "shiftless fellows" who have "no future, no purpose, no destination. They are merely nonentities in the scheme of social progress." The theme is taken up again in story 14, which tells of a boy with wild achievement dreams who is trying to throw off the "shackles of mental oppression," and in story 18, which points out that the "key to the lock is the girl he loves." In short, these stories seem to be pointing the moral that love is necessary for achievement. The reason why the boys in the earlier stories did not succeed is that they did not *belong*; they were orphans, or went against their parents' wishes, or did not have the strong nurturant love that will "make the future a bright one indeed." There is throughout this thema a strong sense of the importance of achievement combined with a deep feeling of personal inadequacy. From the viewpoint of the Oedipus thema the inadequacy must be attributed to competition with the loved father for the mother, a competition which should produce strong guilt feelings. From the broader viewpoint, which is supported by Karl's own statements, the inadequacy is due to the feeling of desertion and rejection, and can be remedied only by strong nurturant love. The Oedipus complex is flexible enough to handle this, of course, by arguing that the desertion feeling is itself a result of guilt from incestuous desires for the mother, but in a way this is the trouble with the Oedipus thema: it is flexible enough to account for anything, and for that reason it may be better to attempt to analyze the motivational forces involved without reference to it. If the second explanation is adopted, the overt and disguised sexual content of these stories may be seen as a working-through of the "unsuccessful achievement" or "inadequacy-security" thema. In these terms the possible sexual connotations of the death of a boy in Africa for following in his "father's footsteps" means simply that sexual material has been used to express his basic inadequacy. Similarly the father-daughter incest story may be taken more at its face value as indicating the peculiar fusion of sex and aggression that desertion leads to. In short, the incest thema becomes *manifest* content expressing the fusion of two latent needs for aggression and for affiliation. There seems no reason to assume that the sexual material is always primary and everything else derivative.

What has our consideration of the "achievement-inadequacy" thema added to our conception of Karl's motives? Two things: (1) an awareness that achievement is a very strong motive for him and (2) that he regards achievement as impossible without love and security. The first point establishes the importance of another motive in addition to the Aggressive and Affiliative needs already discovered, and the second point begins to establish the hierarchy of motives or their interconnections.

There is one final thema in Karl's stories which deserves mention. It is illustrated first in story 6, where the young lawyer finally disregards his mother's advice, lets his brother-in-law off easy, and suffers the "tortures" of conscience ever after. It crops up again in story 8, where the son goes to Africa against his mother's wishes and dies once he gets there. The same idea is expressed in story 10, where the son marries "against his mother and father's wishes" and is subsequently punished in the form of desertion by his wife, and finally by death at his own hand. In all these stories the consequence of disobedience is suffering. We can therefore infer that Karl shows signs of a *need for Abasement,* or conformity or obedience. While the evidence for this need is not as strong in the TAT as for the needs previously discussed, there is plenty of evidence from his autobiography and behavior in high school that he was a "well-behaved, well-mannered" boy who, by and large, conformed to adult standards of good behavior. We know that great stress was placed on obedience in his authoritarian family and it is therefore no surprise to find that in fantasy the consequences of disobedience are serious, even though consciously he may no longer regard rebelliousness as much of a vice (cf. Chapter 8). This suggests that we may be dealing here with an avoidance motive, with a *fear of disobedience* or disapproval, rather than with a positive need for Abasement. The only difficulty is that such a need fuses readily with Karl's dominant need for Affiliation and becomes a strong need complex supporting an external trait of conformity, at least so long as this trait will satisfy such a fusion of needs. It then becomes hard to distinguish n Abasement from f Disapproval.

Can we summarize our clinical analysis of Karl's motivational structure in any simple manner? The problem is a difficult one, just as it was when we attempted to schematize his ideational structure in Chapter 8, largely because we have no systematic methods for solving it, but Table 11.3 makes an attempt.

TABLE 11.3

Main Sources and Interrelations of Karl's Motivational Structure

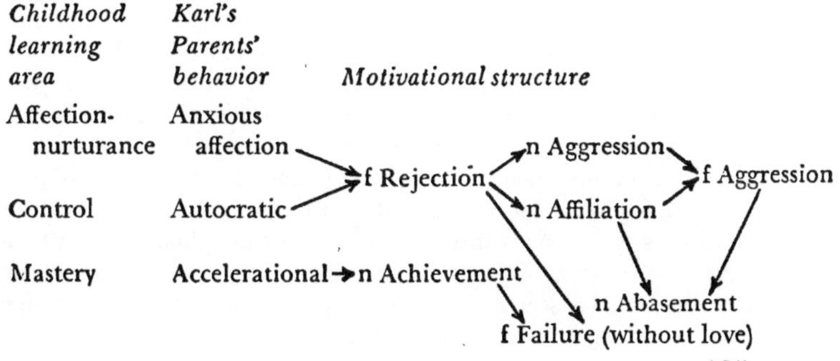

The table is arranged so as to suggest how motives derive largely (but not entirely) from certain key socialization experiences as discussed in the last chapter. Since the full argument for this relationship will not be made until the following chapter, it will have to be temporarily accepted on faith here until a firmer basis for it can be established later. At any rate, whatever its origin, the core of Karl's motivational structure seems to be fear—fear of rejection in particular. This motive is somehow connected with his achievement strivings, perhaps in accordance with the demands of the conditional love formula: "If I do well (or succeed), I will be loved." Certainly the obverse of this formula is clearly present in Karl's thinking: "If I am not loved, I can't succeed." In either case Karl is deeply concerned about achievement either through the direct stress placed on it by his parents or because he perceives it as connected with the love he needs so intensely.

The other major consequence of his basic insecurity (f Rejection) is the simultaneous arousal of n Affiliation and n Aggression, which in turn initiate a central motivational conflict over expressing Aggression (f Aggression). The reason for this conflict is the fear that expressing aggression will only serve to increase rejection, a fear which reinforces n Aggression by adding to f Rejection and thus sets up a vicious circle. As the Rorschach analyst puts it, "A vicious cycle is demonstrated in that hostility gives rise to anxiety, which further reinforces and intensifies hostile reactions. . . ." The consequences of this Aggression-Affiliation conflict are: 1) strong motivational support for the kind of abasement and conformity which suppresses the dangerous aggression by reaction formation; and 2) a general increase in over-all anxiety level or in the sum of his avoidance motives which require "defensive" as opposed to "constructive" behavior (cf. Chapters 12 and 13). The psychiatrist, Dr. Benjamin Simon who interviewed Karl describes his motivational structure as follows:

> Ego ideal development in this man is extremely diffuse, and uncrystallized and has been shifting a good deal. The need for achievement at a direct expression is low. There is no definite planning or organization of his future life but beneath this there is an extremely powerful driving force which forces achievement at the present time. There is a lack of goal which is adequately sublimatory rather than a lack of drive. . . . Need for love and security is extremely intense and is seen throughout in uncrystallized form. The super ego at the normal expressive level appears to be minimally active but is seen to be strongly present in the phobias which are protecting him against his hostile trends.

In short, the psychiatrist confirms our analysis at many points and in particular the conclusion that his motivational system is fear-ridden and held together by avoidance forces more than by positive goals. For this reason it will probably show evidences of considerable internal strain and stress and will not function smoothly in an integrated fashion. We need therefore not be surprised to find the Rorschach analyst stating that "emotionally he is very labile" and that "although there is an attempt to express mature, warm emotions in interpersonal relationships, he is unable to sustain this."

Lest the interconnections traced in Table 11.3 seem too completely dynamic and independent of external press, it should be remembered that at many points there are reality factors which support the motivational structure. An adequate discussion of the relation of motives to the rest of personality (the ideological system, for instance) will have to be postponed to Chapter 15, but perhaps an illustration which also confirms our analysis will serve to remind us of the interrelations. We have argued that Karl feared to express aggression because of his strong n Affiliation, the aim of which is opposed to n Aggression. But there is also a strong reality factor supporting his f Aggression: he has a tremendously powerful physique and has reason to fear the consequences (for Affiliation) of becoming aggressive. A study by Stone (1950) has shown that football players in general show the same kind of projection in their fantasied aggression as Karl does: they tend to picture impersonal agents as killing people. Stone's explanation is that they fear the rejection and disapproval that might come from expressing their potentially dangerous hostility so much that they project hostile impulses away from themselves into impersonal forces. In short, it is not *just* because Karl has a strong n Affiliation that he fears and projects his aggression: he projects it also because he has learned that for anyone so powerful as he to express aggression means in reality an increased likelihood of rejection.

Our summary interpretation of Karl's motivational structure is doubtless incomplete and certainly difficult to support on the basis of logical inferences from experimentally established facts, but its purpose has been to show how clinical data are customarily utilized to arrive at a picture of a person's motivational structure. There is obviously much room for improvement in this type of analysis, but we must first understand the kind of data and hypotheses it makes use of before turning to an experimental approach to motivation in the next two chapters.

NOTES AND QUERIES

1. It is possible to generalize Freud's tendency to dichotomize human motivation by classifying all needs as centering around security or around self-esteem (cf. Maslow and Mittelmann, 1941). This particular breakdown has attracted a good many theorists. Thus Fromm (1941a) has spoken vividly of the wish "to swallow up" which suggests the active, sadistic, masterful, self-esteem drives and the wish "to be swallowed up" which suggests the passive, masochistic, affiliative, dependent, security drives. What advantages has such a scheme? Is there any biological basis in primitive pleasure and pain for such a breakdown? Would hunger, for instance, lead into the development of active or passive drives? How about contact gratifications (from sucking, cuddling, etc.)?

2. Do you feel that Karl had been brought up on the conditional love formula so that he was interested in achievement in order to gain love or do you think he developed a "conditional achievement" schema to the effect that he had to be loved in order to achieve? Is there any real difference between these two formulations? How could you set up a crucial test to determine which is the correct interpretation or do you think such a test already exists in the data presented?

3. Turn back to the Rorschach interpretation of Karl given in Chapter 5 and select all the statements in it that have to do with his motivation (its origins, elements, or interrelations). Compare the result with the analysis of his motivation made in this chapter largely on the basis of the TAT. Do they disagree at any point? Do you have any particular difficulties in answering this question? How could they be met in the future?

4. C. S. Hall (1947), in discussing the interpretation of dreams, reports the following example (told by a female college student):

> I dreamed last night I was in a train station with my sister. We were supposed to make a certain train, but for some reason neither of us could find the right track. It was most confusing and all that I can remember is the two of us racing about trying to find that train in a large depot that had many tracks and entrances.

What feeling do you get if you empathize with the dreamer? What motives are suggested by your analysis? Check your interpretation with the one given by Hall, which is supported by other dreams in the series. Can the content of this dream be translated into "body language"? Does such a translation add anything to the meaning of the dream?

5. Kardiner (1945, p. 175) gives an example of how he as a psychoanalyst would interpret a series of associations in dynamic terms. They were given by Mangma, an Alorese male informant, to the ethnographer Cora DuBois in the opening interview about his life history and ran as follows:

> (1) hunger; (2) stealing; (3) mother gave me bad food, unripe cassava, and refused me good food—resentment; an earthquake occurred; (4) I shoot a dog; the owner breaks my bows and arrows and beats me; (5) mother wants me to cut the fields, I refuse, she ties my hands up; (6) I run away from home; (7) I begin gardening on my own; (8) I won't let mother get my harvest; (9) he boasts of his gardening exploits; (10) fights with his friends; (11) fantasy about raising bride price; (12) planting a garden and the father and mother eat it; (13) is falsely accused of sleeping with a girl by people who want to get his money; and this starts a financial war with the family; (14) I'm cheated again, etc. . . .

Try to interpret this series of associations in dynamic terms, assuming that the choice of episodes (and particularly their sequence) is determined by motivational factors. What would you infer his major motives to be on the basis of this material? Compare your analysis with Kardiner's (1945, pp. 175-177).

6. Some psychoanalysts have been sensitive to the criticisms advanced primarily by anthropologists against the universality of certain dynamically important conflicts and complexes. Alexander, for instance, states,

> Children who exercise early sexual freedom probably have less anxiety in connection with their genital pleasure sensations than do children of our Western civilization. On the other hand Stärcke and I succeeded in demonstrating the early biological precursors of the castration fear. We showed that it is based on the repeated experience of the emotional sequence: pleasure followed by pain and frustration. The castration threat, customary in the sexually repressed Victorian era, only reinforces the universal emotional attitude: to expect pain and evil after pleasure and gratification. (From Kluckhohn and Murray, 1948, p. 332.)

What do you think of this way of maintaining the universality of the castration complex? Do you think there is a "universal tendency to expect pain and evil after pleasure and gratification"? Would it be possible to disprove such an assertion? How does Alexander's definition handle the two instances of "castration" fear dis-

cussed in this chapter—one in the Navaho myth of "womb" injury and one in Karl's story of the boy who got "cut down like a hot house plant being exposed to an icy blast"? Does the use of the term "castration" add to the understanding of the motivational conflicts involved?

12

Motivation: Experimental Approach

> If the Balinese is kept busy and happy by a nameless, shapeless fear, not located in space or time, we might be kept on our toes by a nameless, shapeless, unlocated hope of enormous achievement.
>
> —Gregory Bateson, quoted in Kluckhohn (1949, p. 227)

Since experimentalists have been interested in working up from simple biological motives, they have usually worked with animals. The extent to which this is true is illustrated by Miller's recent summary of the literature on "Learnable drives and rewards" for the revised edition of the *Handbook of Experimental Psychology* (1950). In this very complete and up-to-date survey of the experimental literature on learned motives, there is scarcely a reference to a study in which human beings were used as subjects. Albino rats were nearly always preferred. The reason for this lies in two basic assumptions: first, that all motivation, whether of rats or humans, begins in the form of simple biological tensions like hunger or thirst; and second, that all the more complex motives are learned on the basis of their connection with these primary biological drives. Since rats have the same tensions as do human beings and since they apparently learn in the same way, it becomes economical and much simpler to study the acquisition of drives in rats or other animals. The large number of studies that have been aimed at trying to discover how secondary, nonphysiological drives are acquired is indicative both of the importance of the problem and of the lack of progress that has been made to date. Most elementary texts are eloquent on the subject of how a tension like hunger serves to motivate an organism, but, as students often complain, they become vague and discursive when attempting to discuss the complex motives which are obviously of much more central importance in determining the behavior of human adults. The gap in our knowledge would be most strikingly revealed if any clinical psychologist attempted to deal with his case material in terms of the simple biological tensions which fill the chapters on motivation in experimentally-oriented psychology texts today.

Having frankly faced the limitations of our knowledge in this field we can turn to a consideration of the several serious attempts which have been made to solve the problem of how secondary drives are acquired. First of all, let us look at some typical results on teaching animals secondary drives. At the very simplest level there is an experiment like the one performed by Bugelski (1938), who taught rats to press a bar in a Skinner box to get food. When the bar was pressed by the rat, it made a click in dropping a food pellet into the tray in front of him. After the bar-pressing habit had been firmly established by a number of rewards (or reinforcements), the food delivery mechanism was adjusted so that when the bar was pressed no food was delivered, but the click continued to sound. Rats in whom the habit was extinguished under these conditions kept pressing the bar longer than rats for whom both the click and food delivery were stopped at the same time. This result has been interpreted by Bugelski and Hull (1943) to mean that the click had acquired "secondary reinforcing power." That is, by association with the food reward, it had acquired the power to reward the bar-pressing response by itself and thus delay extinction of that response as compared with a group which was not given such sub-goal reinforcement.

Miller (1950) has argued that the real test of the power of an acquired reinforcing agent is whether or not it can be used to produce new learning. So other experimenters have attempted to get rats to *learn a new habit* in order to receive the stimulation from a formerly neutral object which has acquired secondary reward value from prior association with a primary reward like food. A typical experiment of this sort is reported by Saltzmann (1949). In one condition he had white rats run down an alley to get food in a very distinctive goal box. After a number of reinforcement trials which were to give the distinctive goal box reward-value by association with primary food reward, he placed the box at the end of a simple U-type maze to see whether the rats would learn to make the correct choice to get into the familiar goal box even though it did not contain food in the maze situation. He found that the goal box showed a "rapid loss of reinforcing properties" after continuous reinforcement in the runway training unless he interpolated reinforcing trials on the runway during the maze learning. In both his experiment and in Bugelski's, the acquired rewarding power of the cues associated with primary reward was slight and transitory, and far from the strength which acquired rewards obviously have in human beings.

One explanation for the characteristically rapid loss of reinforcing power of secondary rewards has been that rats are not as capable of symbolic functioning as are human beings. This suggests a study of acquired rewards in higher animals. Wolfe (1936) and Cowles (1937) have both reported extensive experiments in which chimpanzees were taught to associate discs with food rewards (oranges or bananas). Cowles found that "chimpanzees readily performed work to obtain discs which were immediately exchangeable for food" (1937, p. 93), that "with certain training, they consistently worked for groups of ten to thirty tokens before exchange" and that "under these conditions the tokens were adequate incentives for the acquisition and retention by these animals of numerous habits comprising the following types: simple left- or right-position habits, complex five-choice position habits, visual size- and color-pattern discriminations, and delayed response. Entire habits requiring up to twenty trials, as certain position habits, may be completely learned in one session with food-tokens as the sole differential reinforcing agent, prior to any reception of food reward." (1937, p. 94.) In other words, it does seem to be true that chimpanzees, who are capable of greater symbolic functioning than rats, can learn to respond to acquired rewards in much the same way as human beings respond to an acquired reward like money. Nevertheless, there is still a considerable difference between the value of the food-token to the chimpanzees, and the value of many secondary rewards such as money, social approval, affection, and the like to human beings. Cowles concludes, "Comparisons of their strengths as incentives for the acquisition and retention of responses showed that the food-token was slightly less efficacious than the directly received food and much more efficacious than the tokens which yielded no food upon exchange." (1937, p. 94.) He found other evidence that the secondary rewards were less powerful than the primary and in all cases quickly lost their reward value if they could no longer be exchanged for food. Even in these experiments then, there is not much evidence for the acquisition of a motive which has anything like the persistence and strength of human psychogenic needs, many of which may become so powerful that they lead to the frustration of primary biological needs as in asceticism, martyrdom, training for athletic contests, etc.

How can the persistence and power of acquired motives as they appear in clinical case studies be reconciled with the relative weakness of such motives as produced in the laboratory? Allport simply asserts (1937) that psychogenic motives cut themselves loose from their biological antecedents and continue to function autonomously "under their own steam." Sherif has postulated the existence of "ego motives" (1948) to solve the problem. But such "solutions" merely restate the problem; they do not explain how such "ego motives" arise or become functionally autonomous. Another solution, this time of more testable nature, has been suggested by Mowrer, who has emphasized the great importance of anxiety reduction in secondary drives (1939). Fear and anxiety are readily produced in a rat by shocking him. Miller, for instance, has shown that the compartment in which a rat is shocked acquires secondary drive value of sufficient strength to motivate a rat to learn a new habit to escape the compartment even when shock is no longer given in it (1948). Thirteen of his twenty-five animals learned to turn a little wheel which dropped a door and enabled them to escape from the compartment in which they had been shocked. Furthermore, when turning the wheel was ineffective, the rats were able to learn a new habit of pressing a bar to escape. Even though nearly half of his rats failed to acquire the secondary drive in sufficient strength to induce learning, Miller's study suggests that anxiety reduction is more potent as a secondary reinforcing agent than the so-called "positive" secondary reinforcing agents such as the click or the goal box associated with food in Bugelski's or Saltzmann's experiments.

The potency of anxiety reduction is shown even more clearly in a study by Farber (1948). He trained rats to go consistently right or left in a T-maze to get food. When the habit had been fairly well fixated, he introduced shock after the rat had made his turn at the choice point and just before he entered the goal box which contained food. In this way the goal box should have come to represent both food reward and safety (escape from fear or anxiety). After a considerable amount of training of this sort, Farber attempted to extinguish the habit by removing food from the preferred side, putting it in the other goal box, and omitting shock altogether. Most of his rats shifted their preference eventually from the formerly rewarded turn to the new one. But the rats who had been shocked took much longer to reverse their choice. Most significant of all, two rats continued to make the wrong choice for ten trials a day for twenty-five days, and finally could be extinguished only by massing the extinction trials. In other words they had so strongly fixated a response of turning in a certain way that removing the food reward and omitting the shock did not cause them to give up the "maladaptive" response over a very long period of time. The explanation for this persistence apparently is that the goal box continued to reduce the anxiety which had been associated with shock received in that arm of the choice of the T-maze. This experiment, together with some similar ones by Maier and his associates (1949), is practically unique in having demonstrated the acquisition of a motive which approaches the persistence and strength of acquired motives in adult human beings.

Such findings and some theoretical considerations have persuaded some authors that all learned motives have a fear or anxiety reduction element in them. Such a view recommends itself not only because it tends to explain the persistence of acquired drives. It is also consistent (as we have seen) with the general Freudian position on the importance of anxiety. Thus, as Mowrer has pointed out (1939), a great many frustrating, anxiety-producing situations arise in the course of human socialization and it is not too farfetched to suppose that most behavior is directed at reducing these anxieties. Support for this general position has been drawn from the psychoanalytic view of socialization as essentially annoying, frustrating, or tension-producing. Finally, the whole viewpoint is consistent with the conception of *primary* drives as annoying, persistent tensions which, like hunger pangs, keep activating the organism until they are removed or reduced by gratification of some sort

The Tension Reduction View of Motivation. Miller and Dollard (1941) fitted many of these ideas into a systematic theory of motivation which has the advantage of being simple, economical, and explicit; and it can therefore be rather quickly summarized. To them "a drive is a strong stimulus which impels action. Any stimulus can become a drive if it is made strong enough. The stronger the stimulus the more drive function it possesses." (1941, p. 18.) They explain secondary drives very simply as follows: "Drive value is acquired by attaching to weak cues responses producing strong stimuli." (1941, p. 66.) In other words, a weak or indifferent cue is connected with responses producing a strong stimulus and thereby acquires the power to arouse a drive. As an example they cite the ability of the cues from being on shipboard to arouse nausea (strong response-produced stimulation) after an experience of seasickness. The cues, by acquiring a connection with nausea, have the capacity to initiate action (leaving the ship, taking a pill, etc.), which will continue until the nausea is somehow reduced.

To Miller and Dollard, rewards are events which produce a reduction in the drive stimulus. "Rewards are thought of as events producing a reduction in the drive, that is, in strength of stimulus. . . ." (1941, p. 28.) As to secondary rewards, "just as it is possible for previously neutral stimulus situations to acquire drive value, so also is it possible for previously neutral stimulus situations to acquire reward value. Relief from anxiety is an acquired reward. Receiving money, social approval, and higher status are other events with acquired reward value." (1941, p. 30.) Presumably they have all been associated with reduction in primary drives. "Any cue that acquires the capacity to inhibit or relax a response which produces strong stimulation becomes able to serve as an acquired reward." (1941, p. 64.) The click which delayed extinction in Bugelski's experiment cited above has acquired reward value because it has been associated with a reduction in hunger stimulation.

This theory, because of its simplicity and wide influence, demands careful consideration. In the first place there is an obvious objection to the theory which the authors have foreseen and met in a somewhat unusual way. How do they account for instances of strong sensory stimulation which do not act as drives but as rewards? Sexual stimulation, the thrills of a roller-coaster ride, or a bright light in a dark wood at night may all serve as rewards although on the surface at least they represent an increase rather than a decrease in sensory stimulation. Miller and Dollard reply to this by stating that they are referring to a reduction in "total" stimulation. When we look more closely into what they mean by this, it appears that they mean *central* stimulation rather than *sensory* stimulation defined in the conventional way as "energy change activating receptors" (1941, p. 59). "For example, a frightened person lost in the dark may suddenly see a bright light, which has become to him a cue to the relaxed behavior characteristic of food and safety. The light may produce a moderate increase in the amount of stimulation reaching him through his eyes, but a marked decrease in the amount of stimulation from anxiety responses." (1941, p. 65.) In short, it appears that what the authors mean by a reduction in stimulation is a reduction in cortical activity. Thus while they continue to define a drive as strong response-produced stimulation, they mean by a response "any activity within the individual which can become functionally connected with an antecedent event through learning" (1941, p. 59). Thus nearly any neural event in the central nervous system, so long as it occurs after the first synapse, may be thought of as a response in their sense of the word. Thus their scheme has a somewhat deceptive behavioral reference because they use the terms stimulus and response, although they do not mean by these terms what other psychologists have conventionally meant. Because of this confusion in terminology, it might be better to restate the theory in other terms. Thus one might say that a drive is represented by a state of heightened cortical activity, and reward by a reduction in cortical activity. Even when restated in these terms the theory has some serious drawbacks which have been pointed out by various writers.

Self-Contradiction in the Explanation of Learning. One of the most fundamental difficulties with the theory is that tension reduction is supposed to be rewarding and consequently is responsible for the fixation of a learned response. Yet at the same time tension reduction cannot strengthen the connection between the cue and the response-produced tension itself. If it did, we would have the paradox of the reduction in anxiety reinforcing or strengthening the anxiety response. Miller has recognized this objection (1950) and has phrased it this way, "If a reduction in the strength of fear can reinforce the response of bar-pressing, one might ask why doesn't the eventual reduction in the strength of the fear stimulus reinforce the fear response enough to prevent it from being subject to experimental extinction?" In short, why doesn't the reduction in anxiety reinforce the anxiety response? The situation may be diagrammed very simply as in Table 12.1.

TABLE 12.1

Diagram of the Way in Which Reduction of a Fear Response (Rf) Reinforces Bar-Pressing

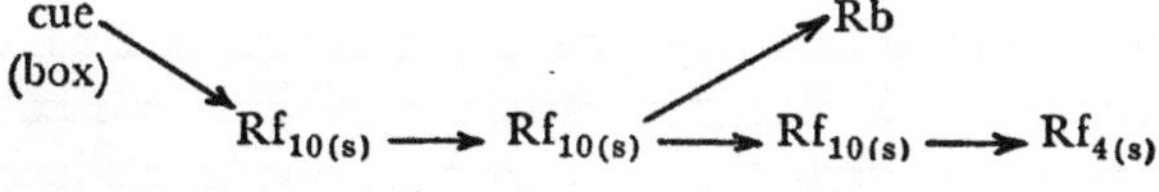

Response-produced stimulation

Cue → Rf_{10}	Acquired fear response based on prior shock in the box resulting in strong response-produced stimulation, $Rf_{10(s)}$.
$Rf_{10(s)}$ → Rb	Acquired bar-pressing response connected with fear-produced stimulation (as cue) and *reinforced* by reduction in fear stimulation $Rf_{4(s)}$ through escape (or avoidance).
Cue → Rf_{10}	*Not reinforced by reduction in fear stimulation* $Rf_{4(s)}$

[illegible]

[illegible]

[illegible]

[illegible]

The reduction in fear stimulation, $Rf_{4(s)}$, serves at one and the same time *to strengthen* the bar-pressing response and *not to strengthen* the fear response. This contradiction has been resolved by Mowrer (1947) by assuming that there are two kinds of learning, one involving association by simple contiguity which is responsible for the original connection of the situation with fear, and the other based on reduction in tension which is responsible for reinforcing the instrumental bar-pressing response. Miller (1950) does not feel it necessary to make such an *ad hoc* division in the learning process. He argues instead that, since fear stimulation dies out gradually, the visceral responses most closely associated with reduction in fear involve less intense fear stimulation and will therefore be most strongly reinforced by the reduction in fear. Consequently, progressively weaker fear responses will be strengthened by their own reduction. This explanation is ingenious but it endows a simple event with some rather remarkable properties. Reduction in fear now simultaneously strengthens another response (bar pressing) and weakens itself. To be consistent, it would appear that one might also argue that the bar-pressing response has also tended to die out (as a stimulus trace) before it is reinforced and it too might therefore be extinguished (not reinforced) by the anxiety reduction. In short, so many apparent contradictions and complications arise from the drive reduction hypothesis as an explanation of learning that many feel it cannot be an accurate description of motivation and that it would be better to revise it thoroughly than to shore it up with *ad hoc* assumptions.

Activity Level. If all drives are strong stimuli and all reductions in stimulation rewarding, why would it not follow that inactivity would be so rewarding that the organism would ultimately be reduced to a state of quiescence? Unless lying on a bed in a dark room has universally been connected with strong stimulation, it should be the state to which we all tend to return according to the tension-reduction hypothesis. Yet the facts of the matter seem to be that the organism, at times at least, seeks stimulation. As Murray points out (1938) in the passage quoted earlier, children in particular seem to have an "activity drive" or at the very least seem to seek the stimulation resulting from muscular activity. Any theory which appears to put quiescence as the final goal of existence flies in the face of many observational facts. Of course, it is possible to get around these stubborn facts by making various assumptions about "tension" and neural activity. Thus Miller and Dollard would doubtless argue that the activity of children is reducing central stimulation despite the obvious increase in peripheral stimulation. Although this may be neurologically possible, it does not seem likely. Murray, who in a later publication has adopted a form of the tension-reduction hypothesis (Kluckhohn and Murray, 1948), has assumed that it is the *process* of reducing tension that is rewarding, rather than the end result. Thus children are active because the *dying out* of activity is pleasurable. People put themselves in "thrilling" situations because the escape from mild fear or anxiety is pleasurable. The mechanism involved here seems to be like that of hitting yourself because it feels so good when you stop. Once again attempts to shore up the tension-reduction hypothesis seem more complicated than revising it to begin with.

Phenomenological Facts. The tension-reduction hypothesis not only runs into problems in trying to account for the high level of activity which human beings show but also has difficulty accounting for the phenomenological side of motivation. Subjectively, reward sometimes involves anxiety reduction but by no means always. More often it seems to involve anticipation of pleasurable stimulation. A man who is striving to get ahead in the world is driven phenomenally as much by the promise of success as he is by the fear of failure. The anticipation of being a "big shot," a captain of industry, a college professor, etc., may induce strong central stimulation but it is markedly different from the strong visceral (or central) stimulation attending anxiety (the fear of being a dismal failure). Phenomenologically at least there is clear difference between the state of mind which attends hope of success and that which attends fear of failure or deprivation. The tension-reduction hypothesis attempts to subsume both of these states under a single principle, but in so doing appears to do violence to the positive side of striving experiences. Of course, it is not essential for a psychological theory to follow the facts of phenomenology closely. On the contrary, it has become fashionable to ignore such data as too unreliable to serve as a basis for scientific hypotheses. Nevertheless, recent experiments by McClelland, Atkinson, Clark, and Roby (1949) on the projective expression of needs are providing a kind of reliable phenomenological data which will have to be accounted for by any over-all theory of motivation. These experiments, as we shall see later, clearly show that motivation increases imaginative anticipations *both* of success (reward) and failure (punishment). Any theory which is phrased wholly in terms of anticipations of punishment (anxiety) is taking account of only part of the phenomenological facts.

Appetite. The tension-reduction hypothesis has also run into considerable difficulty in dealing with some of the facts concerning simple biological drives like hunger from which it was originally derived. Young (1949) in particular has performed a long series of experiments on hunger in rats which have led him to conclude that "rats develop drives to run to foods which they *like* (find enjoyable) rather than to foods which they *need* (require nutritionally)." (1949, p. 119.) It would be impossible to summarize all the experiments he performed which led him to this conclusion, but perhaps his most significant finding is that rats will run or learn a new response to get a palatable food like sugar, even when they are completely satiated nutritionally with no known biological tension. In general this might be explained as an instance of secondary reinforcement in which the sugar continued to serve as a reward even in the absence of the biological tension with which it had been associated. But the difficulty with this hypothesis is that Young and others have repeatedly found that there is no simple one-to-one relationship between the reward value of an object and its capacity to reduce biological tension, although such a correlation might be expected on the basis of the secondary reinforcement principle. Thus, for instance, saccharin has no nutritional value, yet rats clearly prefer it to casein, which *does* meet their primary food needs. How could saccharin have acquired its greater reinforcing power if never associated with reduction in hunger tension? It could be expected to have some reinforcing power by generalization since it is similar to other sweet tastes which are need-reducing, but why so much as compared with foods which are always need-reducing? And what is perhaps more significant, why doesn't its reinforcing power extinguish since it is not associated with need-reduction? (Cf. Sheffield and Roby, 1950.) In short, Young comes to the conclusion that there are two processes involved in motivation which he describes as follows: "When the head recepters, especially those of taste and touch and smell, come in contact with the food there is an affective arousal which we have designated as enjoyment. Different intensities or degrees of enjoyment are revealed directly by the feeding behavior of rats and by tests of preference. Distress produced by deprivation and the relief of distress through food ingestion are also affective processes which are importantly related to acceptance." (1949, p. 119.) In short, his conclusions are in agreement with the phenomenological facts cited above, all of which point to the importance of *both* pleasure and relief from tension as characteristics of motivation.

The Problem of Motive Strength. Our survey of the experimental basis of motivation theory has revealed two major shortcomings. The first lies in its inability to account for the obvious persistence and strength of so-called secondary or psychogenic motives, at least as they appear in the life histories of concrete human beings. The second lies in the inability of the tension-reduction hypothesis specifically to account for much of the "pleasure-seeking" activities of the organism. Having defined our major difficulties clearly, we are in a better position to make suggestions as to how a more adequate theory of motivation may be formulated.

Let us begin where most theories of motivation have begun in recent years: with two simple assumptions—namely, that the important psychogenic motives are learned (not instinctual), and that they are somehow acquired by association with primary biological pleasure and pain. For the moment let us put aside the pleasure-pain problem and ask what it is that makes this particular kind of learning so persistent and powerful. Psychologists have studied the learning process in the laboratory in great detail. They have set up nonsense syllable pairs for human beings to associate, distinctive goal boxes for rats to associate with food pellets, and token rewards for chimpanzees to associate with oranges or bananas. In all of these learning situations, what the organism acquires is rather rapidly forgotten. Certainly it shows none of the persistence which we must assume characterizes human motivation. Yet the stubborn fact remains that psychologists believe motives are learned in the same way as other responses are learned. What is the solution to this apparent paradox?

So far, the only clue we have mentioned is that avoidance learning is harder to extinguish than other kinds of learning—a clue which, as we have just seen, has led to the elaboration of a theory of secondary motivation which is based on the notion of anxiety reduction and which we have found inadequate on other grounds. But suppose we take a closer look at avoidance learning. Why is it relatively harder for the rat to unlearn an avoidance response? Naïvely we could say that he keeps running to avoid a nonexistent shock simply because he doesn't know it has been turned off. His learned response *prevents* him from finding out that conditions have changed. But can't this situation be generalized? Are there not many situations in which the rat or the human being would have difficulty in discovering that conditions are now changed from what they were before—conditions that do not necessarily involve avoidance learning? In general we might predict that the more disorderly and confused the original conditions of acquisition were, the harder it would be to set up conditions which were sufficiently different from them for the organism to perceive the difference and unlearn a response no longer appropriate.

Let us follow this clue a little further: very few laboratory experiments are sufficiently "messy" and disorderly to make the discrimination between learning and extinction difficult for the animal. In their zeal for experimental control, psychologists may have overreached themselves. They have usually provided *one* cue that is always relevant, *one* response which is always appropriate to the reward, and *one* particular set of time relations between the events in the cue-response-reward sequence. The reasons for such careful control are excellent. If psychologists are to be able to determine the relations among their analytic units (cue-response-reward) they must control some while they systematically vary others. But it is just this control which may be creating the difficulties for explaining the persistence of certain types of "real life" learning. For the fact of the matter is that in life there is seldom any such regularity in the conditions of learning as we introduce normally into laboratory experiments. Stimulus, response, and reward do not occur in any regular sequence. Sometimes a response is rewarded, sometimes not; sometimes it is punished. Sometimes a reward is so delayed that it is difficult or impossible for the organism to determine what response was instrumental in producing it. In fact, learning in natural life situations often takes place under such irregular, changing, and inconsistent conditions that an experimenter who is absorbed in his consistent cue-reward sequences might wonder how anything is *ever* learned under such conditions. But things *are* learned under such conditions and when they are, they should be very hard to unlearn because the learning is so general in the first place, so compounded of different cues, responses, rewards, and punishments, that it will be hard for the person ever to discover that conditions have changed, that some general expectation he has formed is no longer being confirmed.

Fortunately the mature organism has developed its symbolic and anticipatory capacities to the point where such irregularities in external conditions are usually not so important. Language is a great help to human beings. Thus Johnny has no difficulty in learning that he is being punished for having filched some cookies three hours earlier rather than for riding his tricycle, which is what he is doing when his father discovers his theft. A rat might have trouble figuring out what the punishment was for. But Johnny's father simply tells Johnny that he is punished because he stole the cookies, and, if Johnny understands language, the act of stealing cookies will be symbolically redintegrated and directly associated with the punishment that follows. So it is with many situations. Our symbolic capacities free us from too great a dependence on external regularities and enable us to produce the same kind of regularities internally as the experimenter produces by control of external conditions.

But not always. Sometimes associative connections must be formed under such irregular conditions that they should be very difficult to regularize symbolically. This should be particularly true of early childhood before symbolic control has developed to any very great extent. Following our clue has now led us back to the position taken in Chapters 10 and 11 that early childhood ought to be the time when the opportunity to form strong, generalized, and persistent associations is greatest. As we discovered in Chapter 10, there are many reasons based on learning theory why early childhood experiences should have the great importance assigned to them by the psychoanalysts discussed in Chapter 11. Many of these same reasons would lead us to expect that these experiences may form the basis we have been seeking for the formation of the strong secondary motives that obviously persist for long periods in a person's life. In the first place, if we accept the principle of mass action or the greater over-all responsiveness of the infant to stimulation, it would be logical to assume that many more of the infant's associations would have an affective component. Since pleasure and pain (or affective arousal) are easier to produce in an organism which has not yet developed its discriminatory or symbolic capacities, it should follow that many more situations in infancy would get associated with affective states than would be true later on.

In the second place, the connection for the infant between a situation or response and the state of affective arousal must be very

vague and general at best, before symbolic control has been achieved. Whatever else can be said about the behavior of parents, it must be much more irregular than the behavior of an animal experimenter trying to get a rat to acquire a strong secondary drive. There are inevitably delays, inconsistencies, and indeterminacies in the association of situations and responses to primary pleasure and pain. For example, if Johnny gets praised occasionally for doing a variety of things like building blocks, throwing a ball, saying a new word, etc., a general connection is set up between "doing something" and pleasure. Johnny is probably not quite sure what the "something" is that leads to pleasure because the reward occurs in a hit-or-miss fashion and because he can't tell the difference very well between one response and the next, but a very general connection is made. Because it is so general, the connection will also be hard to extinguish. Perhaps he isn't rewarded for throwing the ball on several different occasions. But in the first place, he may not perceive this (the lack of reward may be associated with some other act out of the many he is performing) and in the second, even if he did perceive it, that would be no reason to give up, since he was also not rewarded during the acquisition of the association. Furthermore, there are many other acts in the hierarchy associated with this type of reward which have not been extinguished.

For an older child, on the other hand, the specific connection between a particular response and reward would be much more easily formed and also more easily extinguished since a new (nonrewarded) situation could be more easily distinguished from the old, particularly after the use of language had developed to the point where the parents could explain the situation was different. In short, early childhood would seem to be the ideal time to form strong, affective associations which are so general that they will be hard to extinguish. So we now have a hypothesis as to how persistent secondary motives are acquired and why childhood is so important in their formation. Our next problem is to attempt to state more precisely what conditions lead to the development of (a) strong and (b) general associations of an affective nature. Actually there will be some overlap in our treatment of these two attributes of motivational associations for the simple reason that resistance to extinction is commonly used to measure *both* strength of an association and its generality. Nevertheless, each attribute has also some different measuring operations: strength may also be measured by amplitude, frequency of occurrence in competition with other responses, and latency; generality may be inferred from the irregularity of the conditions of learning. Hence the two attributes will be treated separately in the following discussion, although they are inseparable in some cases.

Conditions Influencing Primarily the Strength of Affective Associations. (1) Primacy. In Chapter 10 we discussed briefly why early associations should have some advantage over later ones just because they occurred first and would not therefore be assimilated into a pre-existing apperceptive mass. But we did not specifically discuss the problem of strength. As a matter of fact, there are a number of animal experiments which show that early associations are stronger. Hunt's initial study of feeding frustration in young rats (1941) is a case in point. He found that if rats were irregularly deprived of food in infancy they tended to hoard more as adults, when deprived of food again, than did rats whose initial feeding frustration occurred after the organism had matured. Why should this be so? An explanation apparently requires the notions that deprivation cues get associated with anxiety or affective arousal, that hoarding is an instrumental response which reduces this anxiety, and that *the affective arousal is more intense in infancy than later.* Consequently, when the cues are reinstated in adulthood they arouse a greater anxiety in the rats deprived in infancy, which in turn motivates more instrumental hoarding behavior. Similar results have been obtained by Wolf (1943), who has reported the relatively greater permanent effect of early over late sensory deprivation in rats. Animals whose eyes or ears had been temporarily sealed off during the nursing period consistently performed less well in a competitive situation in adulthood which required the use of these sense modalities, despite the fact that tests of the sensitivity of sight or hearing under noncompetitive situations showed no impairment. Rats which had been deprived later in life did not show the same inadequacy in the face of adult frustration. While the results of this experiment cannot be interpreted with any great certainty, they can be understood in terms of a hypothesis which states that the early-deprived rats had formed a strong association between frustration and dependence responses involved in nursing which was reinstated when frustration occurred in later life. Again the evidence is that the early association has a stronger or more permanent effect.

Unfortunately it is difficult to perform comparable experiments on human infants and to observe their effect in later life. Most reports at the human level have dealt with motor and intellectual rather than motivational phenomena. Thus Dennis has reported (1938) that marked deprivation of social stimulation in young human infants had little effect on their motor development. In a very well-known study McGraw compared the development of a pair of identical twins, Johnny and Jimmy, after treating Johnny to very unusual, accelerative training techniques. She found that the untaught twin caught up very quickly with his brother and the two showed no marked differences later in motor coordination and intellectual capacity. Nevertheless, she did find (1935, 1939) that the special training had had rather marked effects on such personality variables as self-confidence and initiative. Jimmy remained much more cautious than his accelerated brother. This suggests that generalized learning in infancy involves primarily affective pleasure-pain associations which will influence the motivational or emotional aspects of personality in later life more than the purely intellectual or motor aspects.

(2) Involvement of the Autonomic Nervous System. We have been arguing that affective arousal (pleasure and pain) is somehow at the root of motivational associations. Affective arousal is normally accompanied by some kind of discharge over the autonomic nervous system which is characteristically conceived as both *intense* and *diffuse*. From this we may infer that one of the reasons why affective learning is stronger or harder to extinguish is that it is more intense, more diffuse, perhaps more "primitive" than associations involving more highly differentiated cortical control. Mowrer (1947) has been so impressed by the differences between learning which involves the autonomic as compared with the central nervous system that he has been led to the conclusion that different kinds of learning are mediated by the two systems. He argues that learning proceeds according to the contiguity principle in the autonomic system and according to the law of effect in the central nervous system. The evidence which he accumulates for two kinds of learning is considerable but it does not lead necessarily to his conclusion that the distinction between the two depends on whether the autonomic or the central nervous system is involved. On anatomical grounds one simply cannot make as sharp a distinction between the two nervous systems as Mowrer's theory requires. Nevertheless, autonomic discharge *can* be taken as a sign of the fact that a central state of considerable intensity and diffuseness has been aroused and one can reason from this that associations involving the autonomic effector system will be stronger and harder to extinguish than those which do not lead to such a discharge. The exact reason why this is so is not known but a suggestion can be made: perhaps affective states are less under cortical control and are therefore less easily aroused symbolically in their full intensity. If this were so, one could argue that they will be harder to extinguish, just as it is hard to extinguish any response which cannot readily be evoked symbolically. One of the benefits of psychotherapy may be that affective states are sufficiently reinstated to become associated with symbolic cues, which can then be attached to new responses which will take the place of the old, maladaptive, affective ones.

Whatever the reason for the apparently greater intensity of affective states associated with autonomic discharge, it again seems likely that they are more apt to be aroused in early childhood (cf. Jersild, 1942). Prior to the development of cortical control, nearly any stimulus will involve some autonomic discharge. As the child matures, the affective component apparently gets less and less and more and more specifically attached to certain cues or responses. This suggests that motives may become progressively harder to form with age although clearly a traumatic incident at any age should be sufficient to form the kind of strong affective association that is required. The only difficulty is that even here the association is apt to be much more specific (e.g., a phobia) than the generalized hedonic associations required for "true" motivation. Aside from their greater susceptibility to autonomic involvement, children are also more apt to be subjected to the kinds of experiences which lead directly to affective arousal. They are less able to protect themselves against relatively intense pains such as being stuck by a pin, severe colic, falling out of bed, etc. They are subjected to a great deal more direct reward and punishment by parents, etc. It is in these terms that we can best understand McGraw's finding that generalized associations involving affective arousal from early reward and punishment for roller-skating, climbing boxes, etc., had more permanent effects than the rather specific instrumental associations involved in acquiring such particular motor skills.

(3) Time Discrimination and Intensity. The psychoanalysts have not been slow to recognize the greater affective intensity of early childhood experiences, but as might be expected they tend to attribute them to other, more subjective factors. Chief among these has been the suggestion that the intensity of pleasure and pain is greater because the infant has not as yet learned to discriminate time, to anticipate in particular that certain experiences will come to an end. Affective states for the infant should have in consequence a certain "timeless" quality which is difficult for adults to comprehend and which psychoanalysts have tried to get them to comprehend by stepping up the vividness of the language they use to describe the infant's phenomenal world. Perhaps Flugel (1945) presents the most common-sense description of the infant's inferred states of mind, based on much stronger statements made by child analysts like Susan Isaacs and Melanie Klein. "The very young child, with no more than a minimal appreciation of time, is unable to bear tension; he does not possess the knowledge, so consoling to older human beings, that loss, frustration, pain, and discomfort are usually but temporary and will be followed by relief. Consequently a very small change in a situation (e.g., a less comfortable posture or pressure of his clothes, a less easy grasp of a nipple or a less ready flow of milk) will convert a pleasant satisfying stimulus into an unpleasant dissatisfying one." (1945, p. 109.) "In moments of satisfaction everything is well, and the breast—and later the mother—is an entirely good object, the prototype perhaps of the fairy godmother or genie who fulfills all wishes completely and instantaneously. At moments of dissatisfaction the child feels that all is lost, that he is overwhelmed by distress, and that the object or parent is entirely bad, hostile, and frustrating." (1945, p. 117.) While many experimentalists (cf. Orlansky, 1949) would doubtless object to the anthropocentric language used by Flugel and the psychoanalysts in an attempt to explain the child's world of experience, yet they could certainly agree that the absence of time discrimination would give an "all-or-nothing" characteristic to pleasure or pain experiences which would probably serve to make them more intense than for older organisms that can anticipate the cessation of either pleasure or pain. This lack of discrimination alone would go a long way toward explaining why it is that associations formed between events and pleasure and pain in early childhood should have a persistence and affective intensity that would be hard to equal in the laboratory.

(4) **The Paradoxical Effects of Frequency of Reward.** Nearly all learning theorists assume that the frequency of occurrence of an

association has something to do with increasing its [illegible]th, even though they may disagree as to whether frequency cau[illegible] or merely carries the influences which produce an increase in strength. They also commonly assume that persistence or resistance to extinction is a measure of the strength of an association. Yet there have always been some facts that do not fit both of these assumptions. Sometimes, the more frequently a response has been reinforced the *easier* it is to extinguish. How can an operation both strengthen and weaken a response at the same time? Pavlov (1927) found that conditioned salivary responses which had been greatly overlearned could sometimes be extinguished on a single trial. Under these circumstances, how could trials to extinguish be a measure of the strength of a connection? Obviously, one or the other of the original assumptions must be in error. The question has come up again and again in learning theory in the controversy over whether a partially learned discrimination can be reversed without loss of learning time (cf. Hilgard and Marquis, 1940). The so-called "continuity" theorists have accepted both of the two assumptions just stated and argued that the more frequently one response to a discrimination situation has been reinforced, the longer it will take to extinguish that response and shift to the opposite one. The noncontinuity theorists have argued that this does not seem to be necessarily so.

Without going into the intricacies of this particular argument, we can note that frequency of reward has two effects which should influence the extinction process differently. In the first place, frequency probably permits the association to be strengthened as the continuity theorists argue. However, in the second place, the more frequent the reward has been, the easier it is for the organism to perceive that there has been a change in conditions when the reward is withdrawn in the extinction condition. The stronger the original association, the more distinctive and specific it is and the greater the contrast with the new situation in which the animal no longer receives reward under the same conditions. Consequently the animal should find it easier to discriminate the new (extinction) situation from the old (acquisition) situation. Really the animal is faced with a *problem in successive discrimination* which will be easier in direct relation to the distinctiveness of the difference between conditions of learning and extinction. The greater the frequency of reward during acquisition, the more distinctively different a series of non-rewarded trials and the easier extinction should be. If original learning is pushed far enough, as in the case of Pavlov's overlearning experiments, a single nonreinforced trial may be sufficient to distinguish the new situation from the old and to produce the appropriate response of not responding. To summarize, the more frequently an association is reinforced, the stronger it will become, but also the more specific and in consequence the more easily extinguished. Evidence for these two conflicting effects of the frequency of reward has been discovered by Gwinn (1950) working with the fear response in rats. He found that when he increased the frequency of strong shocks which mature rats received in a compartment, the rats ran out of the compartment faster on the first few extinction trials, which is consistent with the first assumption that frequency of an association increases its strength. But he also found, paradoxically, that the same rats *extinguished more quickly,* which is consistent with the second assumption that these rats were able to distinguish the non-shock situation in extinction from the shock situation in training more easily than the rats who had only been shocked a few times during training.

The bearing of this point on the formation of motives in human beings is interesting, although somewhat conjectural at this stage. Learning psychologists who have attempted to apply their principles to child rearing have up to now usually argued that the way to strengthen a desirable habit or attitude is to reward it consistently. Thus it might be suggested that if Johnny's father wants Johnny to strive for achievement, he ought to reward Johnny for any little efforts toward achievement that he makes. In the light of our present analysis this might strengthen the specific response of achieving for daddy's approval, but if Johnny ever found himself in a situation where approval was not forthcoming, we might expect that the response would also extinguish rather rapidly. It is on just such a basis that we could distinguish between a *habit* of achieving in response to specific situations to get a specific reward and an achievement *motive* which is based on a generalized association between *various* responses and *possible* achievement rewards.

Again, age at which stress is placed on achievement (or other forms of adjustment) seems important. A parent may be extremely consistent in stressing achievement (from his viewpoint) but may begin his consistent disciplining at too early an age for the child to discover and symbolize the consistency. If so, he will tend to develop what we have just called an achievement motive rather than an achievement habit. Thus Friedman (1950), in studying the extent to which children in various cultures were required to do things for themselves, found that early stress on independence training was significantly related to the amount of achievement motivation expressed in the mythology of the cultures concerned. Later stress, however, was not as closely related to mythological n Achievement, which suggests that children in such cultures did not develop the strong *generalized* affective associations needed for high imaginative n Achievement but developed instead achievement "habits" which, as in the hypothetical case of Johnny, would be more specifically tied by language to particular situations and rewards.

Conditions Affecting Primarily the Generality of Affective Associations. Frequency of reward is a good transition from conditions increasing strength to those increasing generality of associations since, as we have seen, it serves simultaneously to increase strength and decrease generality, particularly if continued long enough. What are some of the other conditions influencing generality of associations, particularly as they may be present in childhood, when motives are presumably learned? Linton has considered the problem in a general way as follows:

"The more specific a response the easier it is to extinguish it. The reason for this is fairly obvious. Laboratory experiments have shown that habits are extinguished either when they fail to achieve the desired ends or when they expose the individual to too much punishment. Owing to environmental or other changes, a response which is linked with a single situation or with a very small number of situations, can easily become subject to the conditions which will lead to extinction. More generalized responses on the other hand, are likely to be rewarded in connection with some situations even when they are unrewarded or punished in connection with others. It is a common experience that while specific patterns of overt behavior are fairly easy to extinguish, value-attitude systems are extremely hard to extinguish. Such systems tend to survive even when their overt expressions have been inhibited in many situations and to reassert themselves with almost undiminished vigor when new situations involving the particular value factor arise." (1945, p. 115.) If the word *motive* is substituted for the phrase "value-attitude system" in this quotation, it summarizes in a general way one of the main reasons why motives are so persistent.

Furthermore, Linton goes on to link the formation of generalized value-attitudes to early childhood. They "seem to be easy to establish in childhood but exceedingly difficult to establish in adult life" possibly because of "some inability on the part of the small child to differentiate between related situations" (1945, p. 116). In short, he has stated our general thesis that affective associations laid down in childhood are often so exceedingly general because of the child's undeveloped powers of discrimination that they persist because it is difficult to produce the conditions that would make it possible to extinguish them. This argument assumes that associations do not decay simply through disuse, which seems a safe assumption in view of the fairly overwhelming evidence that it is what happens *in time* rather than time itself that causes forgetting (cf. McGeoch, 1942). What more specifically are some of the conditions that promote generality of initial learning?

1. Lack of Symbolic Control. We have already discussed above the great advantages that human beings have in being able to free themselves from environmental sequences by symbolic manipulation. The use of symbols, especially language, favors specificity of learning largely because it enables the child to make the discrimination much more easily between when it is appropriate to make a response and when it is not. He can group together what would otherwise be a large number of complex experiences, often separated by varying time intervals, under a single heading and say, for instance, "Oh, mummy loves me if I try hard." The younger child does not have this advantage: all he can learn is that there is a vague class of activities which is followed by something pleasant (e.g., "mummy's love"). Since he cannot define the boundaries of the class very well or decide whether a given act belongs to it or not, he may, if pressure for achievement is put on him at this age, learn to "be kept on his toes by a nameless, shapeless, unlocated hope of enormous achievement," as Bateson so nicely phrases it. Language also makes it easier to decide when effort is *not* called for. If the child has named the class of activities which require effort (e.g., schoolwork), he can the more readily distinguish activities that do not require effort (e.g., household chores). But if the independence training is itself so general that no such specific learning is possible, or if it occurs so early in life that adequate symbolization is impossible, then we have the conditions for the formation of an extremely general achievement association which will be very hard to extinguish.

2. Generalized Threats and Promises. We have also already mentioned the fact that avoidance learning may be hard to extinguish because it leads to a response which does not permit the person to discover that the situation is changed. Technically this is somewhat different from general learning, but it delays extinction in the same way. Furthermore, it suggests a type of learning situation which may prevent unlearning because the responses are instrumental to goals which are so high, vague, or indeterminate that *it is impossible for the person to evaluate how well he is doing.* At one extreme, a child may be punished regularly for stealing candy. He knows he will be spanked if he takes it and may learn to inhibit this response. Later on he may try taking it again and if he goes unspanked will soon extinguish the inhibitory response. At the other extreme, a child may be told if he steals candy that "something bad" will happen to him, his conscience will hurt him, God will disapprove, etc. This too will in time inhibit his response but now if he breaks through this inhibition at any time he has no way of knowing accurately whether he is being punished or not. "Something bad" may not happen immediately, but it may later; sins may be stored up in heaven, etc. In short, prohibitions established on the basis of vague threats are much harder to unlearn than those established by direct punishment, just as Mackinnon discovered (cf. Murray, 1938). The same argument holds for vague promises of reward. The vaguer and more general they are, the harder it will be for the child to discover whether the achievement behavior (for instance) he is showing does or does not lead to the promised gratifications.

3. Irregularity of Original Learning Conditions. For a number of years learning theorists have known that random reinforcement during learning will delay extinction over what it is for 100 per cent reinforcement (cf. Humphreys, 1939). Many studies summarized by Jenkins and Stanley (1950) have shown that this phenomenon is very general and occurs whether reinforcement is periodic (e.g., every second minute), aperiodic (e.g., randomly distributed around two minutes), or in fixed ratio (e.g., for every third response). An explanation of the delay in extinction can readily be made in terms of our analysis of the influence of frequency of reinforcement on the distinctiveness of acquisition as compared to extinction conditions. Whenever reinforcement occurs with less than 100 per cent regularity, acquisition conditions become more similar to extinction conditions and it gets harder for the animal to discriminate between the two and learn to stop responding. Stated in its most general form, our proposition is that *any method of increasing the similarity between acquisition and extinction will delay extinction.*

But randomizing reinforcement is only one way of making the discrimination between learning and extinction difficult. Many other kinds of irregularities may be introduced. Even in these experiments the correct *response* is never varied (as it often would be in life situations), nor are the revelant *cues.* In other words, in a typical experiment bar-pressing remains the response which produces the food, although it may not bring food on a particular occasion. McClelland and McGown (1950) performed an experiment in which the reinforcement factor was held constant at 100 per cent but the relevant cues and responses to receiving food were varied. They trained two groups of white rats to associate a goal box with food, one in the standard specific way and the other in an irregular, "general" way. The goal box consisted of a circular alley. In the specifically-trained group a barrier was inserted in the alley and food reward on the training days was *always* placed just in front of this barrier. Consequently the rats in this group learned to enter the circular alley, turn left, and run a certain fixed distance to find a food pellet. They learned to associate a particular left-turning response, a particular location in the alley, and a particular time delay with food reward.

The group of rats which received generalized reinforcement training were treated quite differently. They too were always fed in the circular alley but there was no barrier in it and the reinforcement was given in such a way as to prevent the animal from associating any particular response, or portion of the alley, or time delay with food reward. This was done by leaving the food rewards in different sections of the circular alley and by sometimes feeding the animal only when he *stopped* in a certain section of the alley. In other words, the occurrence of the food reward in the goal alley was so irregular with respect to time and place and so inconsistent with respect to the response reinforced that the rats must have formed only a very general association between the circular alley and food reward. After both groups of rats had received 100 per cent reinforcement in the goal alley on three successive days in this fashion, the crucial test was made of determining which group would continue to run into the alley longer when the food reward was withdrawn. Both groups showed evidence of the fact that the goal alley, by being associated with food, had attained some secondary reinforcing power. That is, both groups ran into the goal alley more often and faster on the test day than did control groups which had not received reinforcement in it. The group which had been rewarded for a specific response during training extinguished rather rapidly as in all other experiments of this sort. But the general group behaved quite differently. In the first place, the rats in this group ran into the goal alley significantly faster than the specific animals did, showing that the generalized training had developed a more powerful secondary reward. In the second place, they showed little evidence of extinction in the twenty-five extinction trials given them. On the contrary, they showed slight evidence of a tendency to run faster at the time when the "specific" animals had definitely begun to extinguish

So far then as this experiment goes, it confirms the hypothesis that generalized learning is stronger (speed-of-running measure) and will persist longer than specific learning. It tests the hypothesis however, only in an over-all fashion. Actually three factors associated with reward were controlled in the specific group and varied in the general group—namely, the response, the time delay, and the place where the food was. Each of these should be studied separately to discover whether it is the variation in the responses rewarded or the place rewarded or the delay of reward which accounts for the persistence of the secondary reinforcing power of the goal alley. Needless to say, all these factors are varied under the normal conditions in which the child is learning something. Prior to the development of language there must be a good many associations which can best be described as "something good" following "something" else at some time or other.

A peculiarly important form of irregularity in learning not so far mentioned is that in which both reward and punishment (or pleasure and pain) get mixed up in the same association. Suppose the rats in McClelland and McGown's experiment had also been shocked occasionally just as they were eating the food. What would have happened then? Would this have delayed extinction still more? As a matter of fact there is some evidence on this point: Drew (1938) found that electrifying the food a rat was eating greatly increased the rate of consumption. What is being built up here is an association which involves elements both of pleasure and pain—an association which appears to be "stronger" and should be harder to extinguish by non-reward if Farber's previously reported similar experiment (1948) may be taken as indicative of what would happen.

Such associations have very great importance in psychoanalytic theory and in understanding the problems of neurosis. In these areas the term *ambivalence* is commonly applied to them. How such mixed, ambivalent associations are supposed to be acquired in early childhood is again clearly described by Flugel (1945). After pointing out that a very small change in the situation may "convert a pleasant satisfying stimulus into an unpleasant dissatisfying one," he states: "Thus the child can both love and hate the same objects in rapid succession or alternation and his love and hate alike tend to work on the all-or-nothing principle—there are not the qualifications and quantitative variations that are found in later life." (1945, p. 109.) The breast which does not supply the milk may be regarded as "bad" or frustrating one moment and as "good" the next, when milk flows and satisfies hunger. Thus many objects must in the beginning be associated *with both pleasure and pain* in ways that the infant is incapable of separating. As both Lewin (1935) and Miller (1944) have pointed out, ambivalence or an approach-avoidance conflict is one of the most serious and insoluble types of conflict. As such it may create a secondary disturbance or tension which becomes an important and persistent new motive with tension reduction as its goal. But note in particular that associations which contain pain and punishment to begin with should be exceedingly difficult to extinguish by additional punishment or non-reward later on. Theorists have wondered why a child's love for his mother may persist despite all sorts of discouragements, punishment, evidence of dislike and rejection, etc. One of the reasons may well be that the child acquired his original regard for his mother under conditions which contained a good deal of punishment to begin with. So the "new" punishing situations are not sufficiently different from the "old" learning conditions to make the unlearning of the old response likely or even possible. Ambivalent associations should be harder to unlearn than nonambivalent ones, if this reasoning is correct.

4. **Unreproducibility of the Conditions of Learning.** A related but somewhat different reason why early learning may be so general that it is hard to extinguish arises from the fact that many of the discriminations a child subsequently makes have not been made at the time the learning in question took place. Chief among these is the distinction between self and not-self, between inner and outer sensations. In Flugel's words, "There is no adequate distinction between sensations and their accompanying feelings and impulses, nor —more important still—between these feelings and impulses and

the associated outer objects." (1945, p. 110.) In short, things happen in the child's life—pleasurable things and painful things—and the child has no clear notion as to whether the pain comes from within (proprioceptive sensations) or without (sensations from the eye or other distance receptors). Thus the pleasure from sucking may become associated *both* with internal hunger sensations and with external visual ones (the breast). We could expect then a kind of generalized association between eating pleasure and a set of cues not yet discriminated into inner and outer sources which we might label *proto-perceptive*. Later on, however, the child discriminates quite clearly between what happens inside him and what happens in the outside world. Now suppose we had the job of extinguishing an association involving proto-perceptive cues after the inner and outer discrimination had been clearly established. Would it not be difficult? How could we go about reestablishing the cue situation which was present when the association was learned? What we would be most likely to do is to reproduce the external part of the cue compound (e.g., the mother) and expect that new associations learned to this aspect of the compound would replace the old ones. But such a procedure would probably not be very efficient, although some retroactive inhibition through partial similarity in the cue situations should occur. In short, it may be hard to unlearn some early affective associations because they were learned *under cue conditions which cannot be reinstated and attached to new responses.* This point need not only apply to inability to distinguish inner from outer stimuli, of course; it should hold for any peculiar cue conditions of infancy that are hard to reinstate. In fact, the same argument was presented in a more general way in Chapter 10, in which we pointed out that as children grow larger it becomes difficult to reinstate exactly what they perceived when they were small and looking at the underneath surfaces of the world. And if cue patterns cannot be reproduced with a fair degree of accuracy, it will be difficult to unlearn the associations involving them.

For all these reasons and for others which are closely related, affective associations formed in early childhood are apt to be strong and very resistant to unlearning or forgetting. From the theoretical viewpoint there is no reason why such associations could not be formed *at any time in life* but more of the conditions we have laid down are apt to occur in childhood, particularly at the preverbal level. Thus we have made a beginning at least toward solving one of the two major difficulties associated with contemporary theories of motivation—namely, the difficulty of explaining their extraordinary persistence and strength in the light of our knowledge of the transitoriness of most laboratory learning. Now let us turn to the second major difficulty.

Pleasure and Relief: A Two-Factor Theory of Motivation. In discussing the tension-reduction hypothesis as a theory of all motivation, we were led to criticize it on the grounds that it does not do justice to important pleasure-seeking drives by reducing them all, superficially at least, to pain-avoiding ones. Must we have a monistic theory of motivation? Or can we legitimately speak, as Bateson does in the quotation placed at the beginning of this chapter, of the Balinese being "kept busy by a nameless, shapeless fear, not located in space or time" while we Americans are "kept on our toes by a nameless, shapeless, unlocated hope of enormous achievement"? Certainly there is ample subjective evidence for a difference between "hope" and "fear" motives, and there is also good evidence that primary pleasure is *not* derived only in the course of reducing biological needs. But is the distinction between pleasure and pain drives that seems indicated a useful one? What evidence is there that these two kinds of motives influence behavior differently? Unless we can show that they have differential effects on behavior, we can be accused of arguing for a "difference that doesn't make a difference." What are the facts on this point?

1. **Frustration-Produced Instigation.** The authors of *Frustration and Aggression* (Dollard *et al.*, 1939) were impressed by the difference between ordinary goal seeking (the primary instigation-action sequence) and the aggression which appeared whenever this process was interfered with. They state, for instance, "The dependent definition of aggression is, *that response which follows frustration, reduces only the secondary, frustration-produced instigation, and leaves the strength of the original instigation unaffected.*" (1939, p. 11.) It is important to note that aggression is not conceived here as a response which will satisfy the original instigation. This strongly suggests that the second, frustration-induced behavior sequence involves a different kind of motive from the original instigation-action sequence, since the goal response of the two sequences is conceived as different. In being aggressive, a person may satisfy his secondary instigation but may ruin his chances to obtain the gratification sought in the original action sequence. Aggressive behavior may be adaptive in the sense that it satisfies the frustration instigation and

nonadaptive in the sense that it may not satisfy the original instigation.

Maier (1949) has been so impressed by differences of this sort that he has been led to the conclusion that not all behavior is motivated. Some of it, he believes, is instigated by frustration but has no goal, and hence is not motivated. His own research has involved producing abnormal fixations in rats that were trained to jump from a platform to one of two windows to get food. By making exceedingly difficult and frustrating the discrimination of which window was correct, Maier eventually succeeded in making his rats behave "abnormally." Many of them developed jumping responses which were extraordinarily stereotyped, resistant to change, and nonadaptive in the sense of being no longer instrumental in obtaining food for the animal. In fact, sometimes the responses became so strongly fixated that even when Maier removed the cards on the windows so that the rats should have been able to see the food, they continued to jump abortively to one side. From many such experiments he concludes that frustration produces behavior which differs in many important respects from motivated behavior. Specifically he reports some of his contrasts as follows:

1. A problem situation produces stereotyped behavior in the frustrated individual, whereas it produces variable behavior in the motivated individual.

2. Responses produced under frustration, in so far as they show fixation, are rigid and stereotyped to a degree that exceeds responses produced by rewarded learning. Thus the motivated individual is characterized by plasticity and the frustrated individual by rigidity.

6. The method of guidance is highly effective for altering frustration-produced responses but it has no great value for replacing reward-learned responses.

9. Frustration-instigated responses are either nonconstructive or destructive in nature whereas motivated responses are constructive.

10. The response expressed during frustration is influenced to a great extent by its availability to the organism, whereas the response expressed in the state of motivation is influenced more by anticipated consequences than by availability. (Maier, 1949, pp. 159-60.)

In all of these points as well as his others Maier seems to be describing important differences between behavior motivated by pleasure-seeking and by pain-avoiding. Yet he regards frustration-produced behavior as not motivated at all, stating, for instance, that "the frustration process produces behavior that is purely an end in itself and not a means to an end." (1949, p. 161.) One can accept his descriptive differences between the two types of behavior without being forced to this interpretation. It would seem simpler to assume that his frustrated rats developed an avoidance motive in the course of trying to satisfy an approach motive (desire for food). When the problem of discriminating which card was correct grew too difficult for them, they might have made the adaptive response of not jumping at all, except that Maier did not permit this response. The rats were forced to jump either by an air blast or an electric shock. It is therefore not so surprising that in time they would become oriented around escaping or avoiding the jumping stand rather than approaching the food compartments. In one sense at least this could be regarded as an "adaptive" response in that it brought momentary relief from pain and tension. So it is possible to rephrase Maier's findings in terms of a contrast between avoidance and approach behavior or behavior motivated by pleasure or pain. In these terms Maier's results can be very simply restated as showing that *avoidance motives produce behavior which, generally speaking, is more rigid or less variable than behavior produced by approach motives,* a fact which has been well attested by other research as well (cf. Sears, 1942; Patrick, 1934). Some of his other conclusions, such as the greater "destructiveness" of anxiety-produced behavior, are congruent with the approach of the Yale group to frustration and aggression (1939) and still others, such as the importance of guidance for changing frustration-produced responses, need reinterpretation in terms of other experiments on avoidance learning (cf. Hilgard and Marquis, 1940). But however his results are interpreted, they strongly support the view that behavior motivated by pain or anxiety is different in many important respects from behavior motivated by pleasure or hope.

2. The Effect of Punishment. If punishment is used to inhibit an avoidance response, it may have a very different effect from what it would have on an approach response. Maier found that punishment may actually *increase* the strength of abnormal fixations in an experiment which showed that "punishment on 100 per cent of the trials causes fewer animals to abandon a response than does punishment on 50 per cent of the trials." (1949, p. 37.) The same result has been reported by Gwinn (1949) in an entirely different situation. He trained rats to run in a circular alley to avoid a shock until they reached a place where they could jump out. If, after he had established this avoidance response, he attempted to inhibit it by placing a new shock at a spot just before the escape compartment, he found that the rats tended to run out longer and faster than if no such punishment were given. The situation might be compared to a boy running down a dark street at night because he is afraid of ghosts. If someone shouts at him to stop, he may actually run faster because the supposed inhibitor may actually add to the general anxiety which he is attempting to avoid by running. Punishment for an approach response, on the other hand, sets up a conflict between approach and avoidance motives which should cause a steady decrease in the approach response as the avoidance drive grows stronger. In short, punishment may increase the strength of an avoidance response while it should only decrease the strength of an approach response.

3. **Different Performance Gradients.** One of the most persuasive arguments for a two-factor theory of motivation is provided by the studies of conflict behavior summarized ably by Miller (1944). Miller postulates that the gradient of avoidance behavior is considerably steeper than the gradient of approach behavior. Perhaps the simplest illustration of this phenomenon is provided in an experiment by Brown (1948) in which rats were placed in a single alley with food or shock at either end. The rats were fitted with a small harness to which was attached a recording device which would measure the strength with which they pulled in either direction. If they were placed near the shock, they pulled away from it for a short distance and then stopped. If, however, they were placed at the other end of the alley from the food, they began pulling toward the food nearly as strongly as they did when near to it. The results are summarized simply in Figure 12.1 which is reproduced from Miller's article.

Miller is able to deduce from the difference in the steepness of avoidance and approach gradients a number of the known facts about conflict. Once again it appears to be extremely useful to treat avoidance and approach drives as functioning differently, although in the previous Miller and Dollard book (1941) both hunger and escape from shock are treated as essentially similar instances of tension reduction.

Indirect support for the differential effect of the two kinds of motives on behavior can be found in an experiment reported by Clark and McClelland (1950), who studied the relationship between

FIGURE 12.1

Gradients of Approach and Avoidance

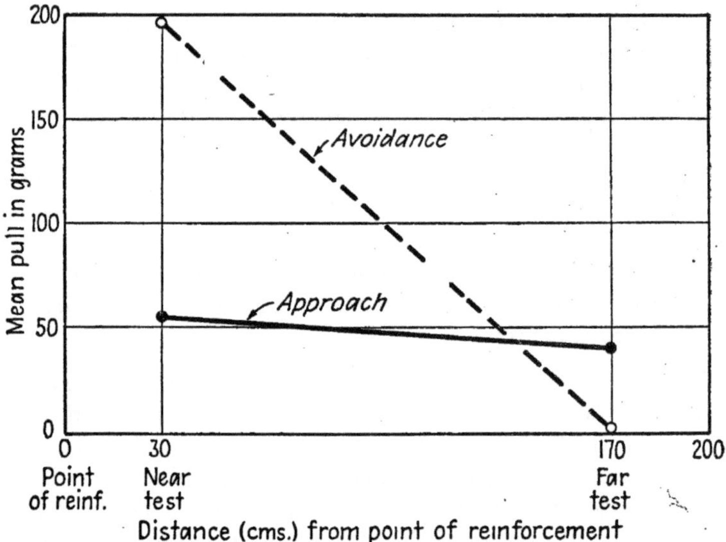

The approach gradient represents the force with which rats under a 48-hour hunger drive pulled against a restraining harness at different distances from the point at which they had been fed. The avoidance gradient shows the force with which rats pulled away from the point at which they had received a strong shock on the previous trial. (Reproduced with permission from Miller, 1944, p. 434. Copyright by The Ronald Press.)

high imaginative achievement motivation and performance output on successive minutes of an anagrams test. They discovered at least two achievement-related motivational factors in a factor analysis of their results. One was characterized by high imaginative concern with achievement and high performance in the middle section of the anagrams test. The other factor was characterized by high output in the last minutes of the test and by a high rating for achievement drive by a psychiatrist and clinical psychologist who had studied the subjects involved intensively. On the basis of these findings Clark and McClelland argue that the subjects who do well on the central portion of the anagrams test are motivated more by the positive hope of success, a hope which, like the anticipation of food in Brown's experiment, leads them to work harder or show evidence of learning at a considerable distance from the point of reinforcement. The other group of subjects, on the other hand, appear to be motivated by the fear of failure and consequently work hard at the last moment to avoid failure. Again the fear gradient is steeper and motivates avoidance behavior only as the point of punishment grows very near. Some slight further support for this two-factor theory was found by studying the anticipations of failure attributed to characters in the stories that the subjects wrote for a Thematic Apperception Test. It was found that the subjects who worked hard in the last few minutes of the anagrams test introduced such anticipations of failure into their stories significantly more often than the subjects who did not do well on the last few minutes of the test. In other words, it was true that the subjects who did well at the last moment were generally more preoccupied with fear of failure.

4. **Double Gratification.** There is considerable evidence that situations which involve both pleasure and relief from tension are more rewarding than either alone. A number of writers (cf. Wright, 1937) have pointed out how the pleasure of certain activities like riding in a roller coaster or eating seems to be artificially increased by dangers and difficulties. Stagner (1937) argues, for instance, that tabus and restrictions have greatly increased the reward value of sexual activity in Western society. As an example of a need which is not heightened by scarcity he mentions the physiological need for oxygen. Presumably, if oxygen were difficult to get, its reward value would likewise be increased. The logical explanation for this increase in reward value through scarcity appears to be that two motives are satisfied when the reward is obtained—one involving pleasure, the other relief from anxiety or tension. Festinger has even noted the phenomenon in rats by demonstrating that they can be induced to choose a nonpreferred food by introducing difficulties in the way of attaining it (1943). Price (1949) has studied the phenomenon cross-culturally and has noted a number of instances in which cultures appear to impose blocks in the way of gratification in order to enhance that gratification. It is easiest to explain these facts in terms of both pleasure and relief contributing to over-all gratification.

5. **The Effect of Approach and Avoidance Motives on Different Kinds of Human Behavior.** So far we have been dealing largely with experimental data from studies of rat behavior. When we come to the human level there is also ample evidence that approach and avoidance motives have quite different effects. Clinically, as we saw

in the last chapter, it is convenient and perhaps absolutely necessary to speak of some people as being motivated primarily by fear, others by hope or promise of success. In fact, the whole idea of defense mechanisms is based primarily on the notion that anxiety produces a kind of rigid, defensive, avoidance behavior which can be clearly distinguished from more flexible and constructive approach behavior (cf. Horney, 1937), a notion which is supported by Maier's findings on abnormal fixations in rats. But aside from this general theoretical argument there is also considerable experimental evidence for the differential effects of the two kinds of motives on different types of behavior. Let us sample it a little to get an idea of its extent. Take *imagination* first. McClelland, Birney, and Roby (1950) found that experimentally-induced anxiety produced an increase in the frequency of from six to ten imaginative story characteristics nearly all of which were *negative* in nature, such as aggression, death of a friend or relative, grief, and the like. In contrast, experimentally-induced ego-involvement increased about an equal number of positive and negative story characteristics (McClelland, Clark, Roby, and Atkinson, 1949). In other words, subjects who were made temporarily insecure (anxious) had more thoughts dealing with unhappiness, anticipated disaster, etc., than did subjects whose n Achievement had been temporarily aroused. The most reasonable interpretation of the insecure subjects' state of mind is that they wanted relief from anxiety, while the achievement-oriented subjects were thinking in terms both of possible success and of possible failure.

Similar results have been obtained in studies of the *level of aspiration* which is commonly assumed to be a joint product of hope of success, fear of failure, and the desire to be accurate (cf. Lewin, Dembo, Festinger, and Sears, 1944). Many research workers who have interviewed subjects after the level of aspiration have been able to tease out which ones were motivated primarily by hope or fear. Thus P. Sears (1940, 1941), for instance, found one group of children (characterized by high D or difference scores) who set their levels of aspiration high either as a goad to achievement or as a way of gaining social approval. She found another group (characterized by low D scores) who seemed to be using the level of aspiration as a defense mechanism, since by placing their level of aspiration low they could avoid the pain of failure. Once again the behavioral effects of these two motives are sufficiently different to warrant treating them as distinct.

Some data obtained at Cambridge University in England on the *performance* of airplane pilots in the Cambridge cockpit (Davis, 1948) can be explained on a similar basis. In these studies two kinds of individuals could be distinguished, one of which tended to break down under pressure rather suddenly and the other of which did not. The performance of the individuals who tended to break down was characterized by very small tolerance for error—in trying to keep a dial pointer at a certain position, for instance. Excellent and exact maintenance of the pointer on the target for a considerable length of time was often followed in these people by a sharp break in performance followed by disorganized behavior. The other group of subjects showed a much wider tolerance for error but also less tendency to break down. A reasonable interpretation of these facts is that the first group is motivated primarily by the desire to keep the pointer exactly on the target whereas the second group is motivated more by the desire to avoid too great a deviation from the target. In this particular instance the second type of motivation is more adaptive in the long run, though less precise. Other evidence of the differential effects of the two kinds of motives on work output has been referred to above in the study by Clark and McClelland (1950), which showed greater output near the end of the task for those presumably motivated primarily by fear of failure.

Finally, differential effects have likewise been found in *recognition* and *memory*. McClelland and Liberman (1949) have reported that subjects with lower achievement motivation tend to avoid recognizing words connoting failure whereas subjects with higher n Achievement see words connoting success significantly more quickly. Atkinson (1950b) has obtained a similar result in memory for completed and incompleted tasks. The subjects with low n Achievement tend to recall significantly more completed tasks while those with high n Achievement tend to recall more incompleted tasks. In both cases the subjects with low achievement motivation seem to be "chiefly concerned with avoiding failure, or with achieving a minimal level of aspiration, whereas the group of subjects with high n Achievement is concerned more directly with achieving success or attaining a maximum level of aspiration." (McClelland and Liberman, 1949, p. 251.) In the particular case of n Achievement, avoiding failure seems to characterize low motivation and attaining success to characterize high motivation, but there is no theoretical reason why this should be so for all motives. It may be true only for achievement motivation or it may be an artifact of the way in which level of achievement motivation is determined in these studies by summing achievement characteristics in imaginative stories written under standard conditions. The important point is that data from such widely different classes of behavior as imagination, level of aspiration, performance, recognition, and memory all point to the existence of two kinds of motives which influence behavior differently.

Notes for a Revised Theory of Motivation. Now that we have surveyed both the clinical and experimental evidence on the nature of motivation, can we bring together our findings in brief summary form? To attempt to do so will help to show how far we have come and will perhaps indicate the way in which further thinking about motivation might proceed. Suppose, to begin with, we try to define motivation. In terms of our previous discussion a motive becomes *a strong affective association, characterized by an anticipatory goal reaction and based on past association of certain cues with pleasure or pain.* Such a definition has a number of important implications which should be explored a little.

1. All motives are learned. That is, they are based on affective arousal, but they are not the occurrence of affective arousal itself. Apparently what happens is that certain cues (either in the affective state or in the external conditions producing it) get associated with the affective state so that they can partially redintegrate it on a later occasion. It is this *anticipation of change in affective state* which is here defined as a motive. What, then, is the state of affective arousal itself, when it occurs? Subjectively we would call it an *emotion.* Thus according to this view emotions are not motives but are the basis for motives. To make the point clearer, suppose we consider happiness or pleasure for a moment. When the person is experiencing it we call it an emotion, but if it or the conditions producing it give rise simultaneously to anticipations of a change in affective state (either an increase or decrease in pleasure, or increase or decrease in pain), then a motive may be said to be involved. In short, it is the anticipatory goal response or redintegrated change in affective state which is the motive and which gives the motive its *directing* power as compared with an emotion which is an affective arousal *now* with no associated reference to another affective state.

Consider the other side of the picture for a moment. What happens when pain fibers are stimulated? At least theoretically when the stimulation first enters the brain, a motive has not been aroused as yet, although the pain may produce a central excitatory state which in turn results in diffuse bodily changes and perhaps also in some overt reflex behavior. It is not until the pain cues off through past association anticipated changes in affective level (either pain reduction or pain increase) that a motive can properly be said to have been aroused according to our definition. Landis and Hunt's work (1939) on the startle pattern illustrates the two phases in this sequence. First, a sudden strong stimulus like a pistol shot will evoke a pattern of reflex crouching responses of very short latency which they named the startle pattern. Second, some time after this, avoidance responses like prolonged blinking of the eyes or withdrawal will appear. These latter we would consider to be the product of an avoidance *motive* cued off by the loud stimulus—a motive which takes longer to produce its effects on behavior than the strong stimulus because association fibers are involved. The reflex startle responses, on the other hand, are not, strictly speaking, motivated but are produced reflexly by the central state of affective arousal resulting from the impact of the strong stimulus. Thus we cannot speak of a strong stimulus as a motive, although for all practical purposes strong stimuli like pain become associated so frequently and early in life with decreases (or even increases) in pain that they come to cue off motivational associations with great dependability. To summarize once more: every motive is learned, *it must involve two points on an affective continuum*: a present state (either positive, negative, or neutral) which redintegrates through past learning a second state involving an increase or decrease in pleasure or pain over the present state. It is this redintegrated change which we are referring to when we speak in the general motive definition of an "anticipatory goal reaction."

2. What are the conditions which give rise innately to the states of affective arousal, anticipation of which is assumed to be motivating? There are several possibilities. A simple, but apparently inadequate, notion is the one adopted by Troland (1928) to the effect that there is *beneception* (sensory processes indicating a condition favorable to survival of the individual or species) and *nociception* (sensory processes indicating a condition detrimental to survival). These correspond roughly to receptor activities giving rise to pleasure and pain and, in a sense, attempt to define pleasure and pain objectively in terms of the relation of sensations to survival. (Cf. Young, 1936.) Another possibility is Miller and Dollard's assumption (1941) that any stimulation, if it is strong enough, will produce the affective

arousal which is necessary for a motivational association. We have objected to this idea not because it is wrong but because it seems incomplete and does not do justice to the pleasure-seeking activities of the organism, which suggests still a third possibility—namely, that a moderate increase in stimulus intensity in any sense modality may lead to pleasure and a further increase to pain. Figure 12.2, reproduced from Woodworth (1938, p. 498), illustrates the idea, using some data from Engel on the effect of stimulus intensity on judgments of pleasantness-unpleasantness for various tastes. Although at present such an inference would be highly speculative, we might adopt the hypothesis that these results could be generalized to *any* sense modality. If so, it would mean, for instance, that stimulation of the eyes or the ears would be pleasurable and sought by the organism up to a point, until at very high intensities pain would appear and avoidance motives aroused. The actual curves would presumably differ for various sense modalities just as they do for the different tastes in Figure 12.2. Pain would presumably look something like the "bitter" curve showing a very narrow range of pleasurable intensities ("tickle").

While such a notion is intriguing and would explain readily certain apparently paradoxical phenomena like the drive for activity (to get stimulation from proprioceptors), our case for approach and avoidance drives need not depend on its ultimate validity. For all we know now there may be other conditions such as hormonal effects on the central nervous system or certain *patterns* of neural activity (cf. Hebb, 1949) which give rise to pleasure and pain. Essentially, the problem is the old one of trying to discover what the conditions are for producing emotion. Whatever explanation finally turns out to be correct, it should include the notion that reward, approval, etc. (perhaps initially derived from contact gratifications) leads to one type of motivational association and punishment to another. That is, both positive (approach) and negative (avoidance) motives should be distinguished because they have different effects on behavior.

The argument for this position has already been given. It need only be added here that in practice we may distinguish these two kinds of motives by the symbols *n* for need and *f* for fear. Thus we speak of n Achievement when the person's primary goal is to enjoy the glories of success, and of f Failure when a person's primary goal is to avoid the misery and disgrace of failure. Note that we do not speak of n Failure-relief, although such terminology would be consistent with our general view of motivation. The reason for this is

FIGURE 12.2

The Pleasantness-Unpleasantness of Taste Sensations as a Function of Stimulus Intensity

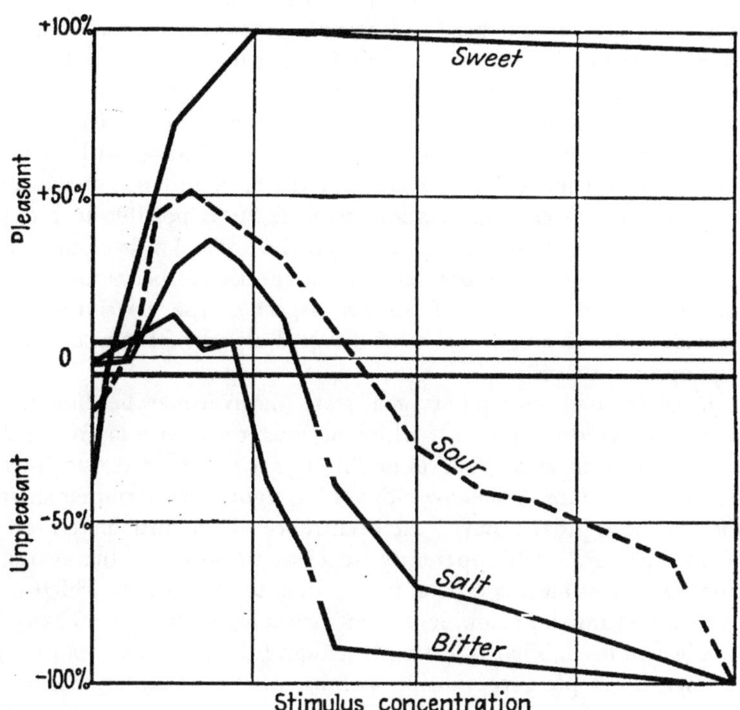

Preponderance of "pleasant" or "unpleasant" judgments in relation to the concentration of a sapid solution. The ordinate gives percent "pleasant" minus percent "unpleasant." The abscissa is proportional to the concentration, the full length of the baseline standing for 40% cane sugar, for 1.12% tartaric acid, for 10% salt, and for .004% quinine sulphate (all by weight). The two parallel lines just above and below the zero level signal the fact that there is typically a neutral zone between pleasant and unpleasant.

Bitter, as shown by its curve, gave at best only a slight preponderance of "pleasant" over "unpleasant" judgments. Sweet always gave a preponderance of "pleasant" except at a very low concentration. Sour and salt are intermediate. The curve for sour has been slightly smoothed.

(Reproduced by permission from R. S. Woodworth, *Experimental Psychology* [data of R. Engel]. Copyright 1938 The Macmillan Co.)

that while approach motives are named most easily in terms of the goal which terminates a behavior sequence, avoidance motives are named most easily in terms of the "origins" of a behavior sequence. Relief from tension may be obtained in such a variety of ways that it is easier to name the need in terms of the source of tension rather than in terms of the mode of relief adopted. It is probable that theorists like Miller and Dollard (1941) and Mowrer (1939) have been led to stress the drive stimulus aspect of motivation rather than its goal aspect largely because they have been dealing with avoidance motives where it is easier to define the drive in terms of the cue aspect of the affective association involved. It is possible to recognize the important differences between these two kinds of motives and yet to see how they both arise from affective associations which may be named in terms of the cue aspect of the association for avoidance drives and in terms of the goal aspect of the association for approach drives.

3. An aroused anticipatory goal state (motive) may be disrupted by the occurrence (a) of cues which no longer give rise to an anticipated change in affective level or (b) of cues that give rise to interfering associations. Somehow motives have got to be terminated. In the case of approach drives, the occurrence of the anticipated state of affective arousal is apparently sufficient to break up the association. One possible reason for this is that the sensations which accompany eating (for example) are not associated with further changes in affective level. That is, eating is seldom followed after a point by an increase in pleasure, possibly because of some adaptation effects in the sense modalities producing pleasure. It may even be associated with pain from overeating, if with anything, so that in time it will set off an interfering anticipation of pain which will produce other (avoidance) behavior. This illustrates again why a state of affective arousal is not itself a motive (though it may cue off one). A satiated animal may be in a state of affective arousal (pleasurable internal sensations) but not be motivated because anticipated goal states are not being tripped off. But how about the other side of the picture? Why doesn't the occurrence of anticipated pain lead to disruption of the fear motive? To some extent it does: a person may actually experience some relief (reduction in motivation) when a feared event occurs. But the difficulty is that the feared event, if it is itself painful, will continue to cue off anticipations of relief from pain by transfer from past similar situations in which pain has been repeatedly followed by reduction in pain. Thus *new* motivating

associations are aroused when the pain actually occurs in a way which does not happen when pleasure actually occurs.

From all this we might infer that there are certain anticipated goal states which are so vague and generalized that it would be impossible for them to occur in such a way as to provide cues that would no longer arouse anticipations of further changes in affective level. It is for this reason that motives like n Achievement may be so insatiable. A sub-goal success may actually cue off new associations of further success and pleasure, particularly if the cues which give rise to anticipated success were not very specific to begin with (see below). On the other hand, of course, n Achievement may be disrupted not by actual achievement, but by other "distractors," e.g., by other motivational associations or perhaps by frustration. Frustration is a mechanism which seems to act as a kind of safety valve to prevent a need from dominating central processes too long. That is, if an anticipatory goal state is aroused for a sufficient length of time without at least partial fulfillment (or disruption), the effect is painful and the pain itself will in time disrupt the motive state, primarily by introducing a new motivational association, namely, the need for tension reduction or avoidance of pain (cf. Chapter 13). This may also explain why very intense motives may be self-defeating and insatiable. If they are intense they should build up to the frustration-disruption threshold sooner and the organism becomes mobilized around avoiding pain rather than attaining the original goal. Thus a vicious circle may be set up in which a person has very little opportunity to display the instrumental responses which might have fulfilled the original motive directly.

4. What has become of the traditional notion that all psychogenic motives are built on primary biological drives? Strictly speaking we should no longer think in this fashion. States of biological need have no unique function in producing motives; they are merely *one* of the conditions which dependably (in all individuals) give rise to motivational associations. The crucial factor in all motives is the association of certain cues with affective arousal of various sorts. Thus sight of food becomes a means of arousing the hunger *motive* through frequent association with the pleasurable sensations and the relief from tension that accompany eating. Consequently we can see how the cues that arise from deprivation and from the biological needs it produces are not qualitatively different from any cues (like sight of food) which may get associated with the goal response of eating. That is, the class of cues resulting from states of

tissue need is not essential for the formation of motives in any special way. But it may lead with greater dependability to the formation of a motivational association because deprivation cues are *always* followed by eating (unless the animal dies) whereas with a cue like sight of food there may not be 100 per cent reinforcement, since the animal may have his eyes closed when he eats, etc. Deprivation or biological need cues are also more persistent than other cues and may in fact continue to bombard the organism until the biological need is removed. This does not operate to increase drive strength *directly,* as has often been assumed, but it has the same effect indirectly since the affective eating associations evoked by these cues will be aroused over and over again until the condition which produces the cues is terminated by eating or by death. That is, the function of the biological cues is to arouse eating associations with increasing frequency as deprivation increases until these associations engage the entire attention of the organism and competing associations are driven out (cf. the discussion in Chapter 13 of the way in which a hypothetically increasing thirst condition may gain control of the associational processes). It is theoretically just as possible, although considerably less likely, that cues in the external environment should serve to arouse a motivational association to the exclusion of all others (as when a man is completely absorbed in winning the 100-yard dash). If we put the cues arising from food needs in the same class as other cues that may get associated with eating, the "paradox" of the "salted nut phenomenon" disappears. Hebb puts it this way: "Consider the salted nut phenomenon. Ordinarily, one can take salted nuts or let them alone—until one has eaten a mouthful, when it becomes much harder to let them alone. Hunger has increased: but how? A lack of food cannot be increased by eating something, and stomach contractions are stopped by chewing and swallowing. If, however, we consider hunger to be neither a particular condition of the body, nor a set of sensations from the stomach, but an organized neural activity that can be aroused (like any other conceptual process) in several ways, the puzzle disappears." (Hebb, 1949, pp. 199-200.) In short, sensations from the stomach or from heat loss in a state of food need have no special motivating properties: they get associated like any other set of cues, though more dependably, with the pleasure and relief accompanying eating and thus are capable of arousing the hunger motive like any other set of cues. The advantage of this interpretation is that it makes complex motives like n Achievement in no way dependent on continued satisfaction of biological needs like hunger. The hunger *motive* and the achievement motive have exactly the same status theoretically: they are both learned and both based on the formation of associations between certain cues and changes in states of affective arousal.

5. The persistence of a motive throughout the life history of an individual is a function of a number of variables, among which are the following: (a) the absolute frequency of occurrence of the cue-pleasure (pain) association: hunger is a reliable motive because the association between certain sensations (stomach contractions, sight of food) and eating occurs several times a day throughout the lifetime; (b) the generality of the association and ease with which it may be extinguished; (c) the stress (intensity of pleasure-pain) involved in the association at the time it is formed; (d) the age at which the affective association is formed—the earlier it is formed the likelier conditions (b) and (c) are to obtain. Hence the most persistent motives are more likely to be laid down early in childhood, especially at the preverbal level, although there is no reason why they could not be formed at any time in life. These points are all drawn from the previous discussion of the generality of affective associations and the difficulty of extinguishing them if laid down early in life.

6. The presence of a motive may be inferred either (a) indirectly based on knowledge of past cue-affective arousal associations or (b) directly based on imaginal goal states. Our inferences under condition (a) may be based on our direct knowledge of the particular individual we are studying (as when we infer that the rat has acquired a hunger motive based on the association during habituation of being handled by the experimenter and being fed) or by extrapolation from the experience of other individuals (as when we infer that this individual has an n Achievement because we have observed that he has been exposed to the same conditions which have led to the development of n Achievement in other members of his group). Working with antecedent conditions from which inferences about motive states are drawn is difficult, especially with human beings, and we do better to work directly with their anticipated goal states as measured in imagination (cf. McClelland, Atkinson, Clark, and Lowell, 1950). That is, the simplest measure we can obtain of the strength of the achievement motive in a human individual is to observe the frequency with which he thinks about achievement as measured through imaginative productions. These measures are "purer" than others like a consciously stated level of aspiration

which is usually a joint product of a number of motives. Thus, for instance, when a person explicitly sets or chooses an achievement goal in a level of aspiration situation, it is not clear whether he is motivated primarily by n Achievement, f Failure, or a desire to be accurate in his judgments in forecasting. For this reason, we will delay discussing the level-of-aspiration technique until Chapter 14, when we can put it in the context of the self-picture. Other techniques of measuring motivation, such as increased sensitivity to perceptually related words, explicit conscious estimates of motivational strength, answers to questions, etc., all seem relatively less pure than imaginal goal states largely because they are relatively more influenced by other factors in addition to the motive to be measured.

7. Motives are individually acquired but certain situations will produce pleasure or pain with such regularity either through biological or cultural arrangements that the probability of certain *common* motives developing in all people is very high. As we have seen, Allport objects (1937) to thinking in terms of "a few motives common to all men." Since all motives are learned, is it not likely that each person will learn a different set? While in general this is true, the degrees of freedom are in fact considerably reduced by certain invariants in the process of adjustment. The first invariant is obviously the biological arrangement for making certain sensations innately pleasurable and painful. For instance, if we argue that certain sweet tastes are pleasurable, and certain aches and pains are unpleasurable, the likelihood of strong affective associations getting formed around eating is very high indeed. In short, the probability of certain internal cues arousing anticipated pleasure or relief from tension in eating is, practically speaking, 1.00. We can therefore speak of a motive common to all men. But what about motives where the arrangements are cultural rather than biological? The situation is not essentially different. Socialization occurs in all cultures for all individuals and it involves certain common problems in all cultures. Thus the likelihood of certain cues getting associated with reward or punishment is fairly high for all men. Take the matter of achievement, for instance. All individuals in all cultures must learn to some extent to do things for themselves—e.g., learn to walk, talk, eat by themselves, fish, hunt, read, or whatever. In the course of mastering these various problems, it is highly likely that certain mastery cues (effort, difficulty, incompletion, etc.) will get associated with affective arousal and will produce in time centrally motivating anticipations of success or failure. These associations may be rela-

tively weak in cultures which do not stress independence training early, or relatively strong in other cultures where great stress is placed on early achievement. They may be predominantly hopes of enormous achievement, as in middle-class America, or fears of failure and inadequacy, as in Bali or Alor. But whatever the variations in the strength or kind of n Achievement associations, the fact remains that *some associations* of this sort are laid down in all individuals in all cultures, at all times, simply because with very few exceptions everybody is faced at one time or another with achievement problems. Exactly the same argument can be used for the three other general classes of learning problems listed in Table 10.2. That is, we could expect generalized affective associations to develop in connection with protection and support problems (n Nurturance-Succorance), in connection with problems of affection (n Affiliation, or f Rejection), and in connection with avoidance of frustration and disapproval by self-control (n Approval, n Recognition, n Abasement, etc.) as well as in connection with problems of mastery. The argument of course does not require that the particular breakdown of learning problems we made in Table 10.2 be the basis for deciding what common motives will necessarily be formed. All it states is that the basis for assuming that there are common motives is the fact that there are common learning problems which every individual must face in the process of socialization. This does not of course exclude the possibility that there are also idiosyncratic learning problems for each individual which will produce motives which may be different from those of any other person either in intensity or in their pattern of interrelationships. Nevertheless even here it may turn out to be more convenient, at least for a general science of personality, to treat these idosyncratic motives as instances of special affective associations within the general class of affective associations commonly developed by all men facing similar problems.

NOTES AND QUERIES

1. According to the proposals for a theory of motivation briefly outlined at the end of the chapter, is it necessary to distinguish as sharply as Miller and Dollard have between secondary drive and secondary reward? What would be the difference between these two concepts in terms of these proposals?

2. Is all behavior motivated as motivation is defined in this chapter?

3. What exactly is meant by a primary drive and what is the difference between it and a motive? Can a primary drive stimulus be defined in terms of the probability of its getting associated with a state of affective arousal?

4. Can reward and pleasure be independently measured? How about punishment and pain?

5. Can frustration be considered a motive? If so, what is its anticipatory goal state? Can aggression be considered a goal state which reduces frustration?

6. Make a list of the "dependable motives"—the ones you think would be likely to develop in the course of meeting common problems of socialization all over the world. Compare the motives we utilized to describe Karl's motivational structure in Chapter 11 with the ones on this list. Comment on any discrepancies between the two lists.

7. In Wolf's experiment on the effects of sensory deprivation in infancy on the responses of adult rats to competitive situations, what measure of the strength of the early association is being used? Does the measure permit you to conclude whether the early association is stronger or more general? Can you think of any way of measuring what response was actually acquired in infancy to test the hypothesis advanced in the text? (Cf. p. 445.)

8. Design a training situation which should endow poker chips for chimpanzees with a relatively inextinguishable reward value, according to the principles laid down in the text.

9. According to the propositions advanced to explain the acquisition of motives, explain two ways in which a man of forty-five might acquire an intense interest in politics.

10. When is a condition of affective arousal sufficient to form a motivating association? Suppose a man is embarrassed on a particular occasion in front of a girl. In what sense does or does not the association formed (girl-affective arousal) become a motive?

11. According to the principles discussed of what makes extinction easy, why should Maier have found that guidance for his abnormally fixated rats was a more effective way of changing their behavior than punishment?

12. Explain how intense sensations could be cues which arouse motivational associations formed on the basis of past experience by all men in all cultures. Could you design an experiment which might show that such associations were acquired gradually and that there-

fore intense sensations could not be considered drives before the associations were formed?

13. Why should animal experimenters be having difficulty finding evidence for a gradient of primary reinforcement? Is there reason to expect that there should be no such thing? (Cf. Spence, 1947.)

14. A number of authors (Webb, 1948; Leeper, 1948) have pointed to the connection between motivation and emotion, arguing that under certain conditions emotions can operate as drives. Is this view consistent with the proposals for a theory of motivation advanced in this chapter? Are there conditions in which emotions will not serve as motives?

15. Why doesn't the sight of food arouse the hunger motive in a satiated person?

16. The generally accepted intimate connection of motivation with early socialization raises the question of the theoretical relationship between motives and the kind of schema laid down in early childhood that we discussed in the last chapter. Are these early, largely preverbal schemata the same thing as motives?

13

The Effects of Motivation on Behavior

The experimental studies of motivation we have just reviewed have provided us with a theoretical framework which should be general enough to include eventually the higher-level clinical interpretations of motivation discussed earlier. But neither of these approaches to motivation has provided us with much information about how motives influence human behavior. Does a motivated organism behave in distinguishably different ways from an unmotivated one? Fortunately, there is a considerable body of information on this point which comes neither from the clinic nor from the study of rats but from experimental studies of human motivation. It is this body of data which must claim our attention now as we set aside the more theoretical issues with which we have been concerned and attempt to get some idea of how motives influence behavior.

It is fortunate that such a body of data exists, that psychologists like Lewin outside the clinic or the rat laboratory have been interested in human motivation. The study of rats has given us a good deal of information, particularly about the acquisition of motives, but it has told us very little about how they function in human beings. Clinical psychologists, on the other hand, have given us too much information about how motives function in human personality but often with too little critical evaluation of their interpretations. The reason for this is a simple, practical one. As we concluded earlier, clinical psychologists turned readily to the motivational concept because they needed a concept which would be useful in tying together or accounting for a variety of very different responses —just as they needed the trait concept to account for consistent, similar responses. Therefore, in characterizing a motive they were driven to make inferences about its nature *from its many particular effects.* They reasoned from consequents to antecedents, from specific and varied responses to an underlying motive. Such a procedure has run into a number of serious difficulties as compared with the experimental approach of having the motive under control and observing its effects on behavior. In the first place, it has led to a serious confusion between motivation and causation. Clinicians often make statements which sound as if discovering the motive for an act is all that is needed to account for the act. For instance, a man may be said to have become a surgeon because cutting people up satisfies a basic (preferably unconscious) motive, e.g., a sadistic urge. Such a motive may in fact be involved, but obviously much more is needed to account for such a decision. In our terms a man decides to become a surgeon not only because of some underlying need, but also because of his conceptions of what a surgeon's life is like, of what is required of him in the way of service to others (schemata), and because of his past adjustments to similar situations (traits of emotional control, etc.). We need both the trait and schema variables as well as the motive variable to explain any particular choice like this. In short, causation is larger than motivation but the method clinicians use of studying motivation by attempting to find a single explanation for a variety of responses tends to overstress the importance of the motivational variable as the causative factor.

A second difficulty arises from the fact that so long as there is no independent measure of motivational strength, it is possible to attribute opposite effects to the same motive or the same effects to opposite motives. For example, psychoanalysts have been criticized for arguing that different effects, e.g., walking into a bar or across the street around a bar, have the same cause (desire for a drink), or for stating that when a person walks across the street he may do it (1) because he really wants to or (2) because he really wants to do just the opposite and is displaying reaction formation against his desire to enter the bar. It is possible of course to resolve these apparent contradictions by making assumptions about motives having different effects at different intensities, about conflicts of motives, etc., but so long as the method of approach does not involve experimental control of the variables in question, it will be difficult to prove or disprove such assertions.

Finally, clinicians must reason from such a variety of complex behaviors that it is a wonder they are ever able to make any rigorous inferences about underlying motives. Consider, for example, the entire range of symptoms in the neuroses and psychoses, or even the somewhat narrower range of defense mechanisms—reaction formation, projection, repression, undoing, etc. All these are customarily explained as being the result of motives of different strengths and varieties interacting sometimes in extraordinarily complex ways. How is it possible to get any coherent idea of how motives function from analyses based on such variety and complexity? The fact is that it has not been possible and that clinical methods of interpretation have to be supplemented by superior experimental methods which will permit a more rigorous study of the effects of motivation through the isolation and control of motivational variables.

It is easy enough to speak of the advantages of experimental studies of motivation but it is difficult to design ones that do not meet equally serious, though different, objections. Thus the motives that can be experimentally controlled have been traditionally limited to such things as hunger, which is hardly of much interest to the student of personality. Or the effects of motives which are studied include such behavior as speed of learning nonsense syllables, which again is a far cry from the complex defense mechanisms that the clinician wants to understand in motivational terms. For these reasons some recent studies on the projective expression of needs, by McClelland and associates (1949, 1950), seem especially useful in combining some degree of experimental control with an analysis of some of the variety of complex reactions studied in the clinic. These experiments have attempted to arouse experimentally not only simple physiological tensions like hunger but also some more complex psychogenic motives such as n Achievement and n Security. The value of experimental arousal lies particularly in the fact that it is easier to isolate the effect of the motivational variable *per se* on behavior as distinguished from the other variables that influence behavior. But it has another advantage as well which derives from the fact that if a motive can be induced, it may be induced at different levels of intensity and its presumably different effects observed. This may provide a way of resolving some of the apparently paradoxical effects clinicians have attributed to the same motive. Thus an increase in motivation at one level may *increase* efficiency and at another *decrease* it.

These experiments also have the advantage of measuring the effects of motivation on imagination or symbolic processes. Typically, subjects are asked to write brief imaginative stories in response to various pictures under the influence of hunger, n Achievement, or some other motivational state. Content analyses of the stories show which characteristics change as a result of the induced motivation. While it may be difficult to match in overt behavior in the laboratory some of the defense mechanisms or symptoms clinicians are interested in, it is not so difficult at the symbolic level. For instance, one of the story characteristics scored by McClelland *et al.*

is Ga+, which is defined as the anticipation of pleasure accompanying the successful outcome of a goal sequence. Induced achievement motivation increases the frequency with which statements appear in subjects' stories which can be classified as Ga+. The advantage of using such a behavioral measure lies in part in the fact that it falls in complexity somewhere between a simple overt motor response and a complex defense mechanism such as a delusion of grandeur which might be of interest to the clinician. We cannot produce delusions of grandeur in the laboratory very easily but we may be able to study the functioning of their symbolic prototype, the Ga+ response.

Other advantages from dealing with symbolic processes derive from the great variety of behavior they represent and the economy with which they represent it. It was probably for these reasons that Freud felt that his study of symbolic processes in dreams provided such an important avenue to the understanding of complex behavioral symptoms of mental disease. He states: "Experience has shown that the unconscious mechanisms which we discovered from our study of dream-work and which gave us an explanation of the formation of dreams also help us to understand the puzzling symptoms which attract our interest to neuroses and psychoses. A coincidence of such a kind cannot fail to excite high hopes in us." (1940, p. 57.) The reason for such a coincidence does not seem mysterious or hard to find. A single dream or imaginative story may pack into a relatively short space of time an amount of behavior which it would take hours to display overtly and a variety of responses which in some of their more bizarre forms could never be displayed overtly by a person under normal conditions. Symbolic processes provide a kind of behavioral shorthand, a shorthand which is both economical and efficient in representing a lot of a person's behavior. For the same reasons it can provide a useful index of the strength of motivation on the general assumption that the greater a person's imaginative or symbolic concern with a particular goal (Food, Achievement), the stronger his motivation in that area. Thus McClelland *et al.* (1949) have computed an over-all n Achievement score which is the sum of the achievement characteristics shifting under induced achievement motivation which appear in a given person's record under normal conditions. With such a score it is possible to divide people into groups with high and low motivation and to observe in what ways they react differently (cf. McClelland and Liberman, 1949). For all these reasons the studies of the projective expression of needs are particularly strategic in the analysis of the effects of motivation on behavior and we shall draw heavily, though by no means exclusively, on them in what follows.

Increased Instrumental Activity. One effect that nearly all theorists agree motivation has is that of energizing the organism or making it more active. At the biological level this is readily demonstrated. A large number of observations attest the fact that motives like sex or hunger lead to an increase in restlessness, in the total number of responses emitted by the organism (cf. Morgan, 1943). Problem-solving experiments show the same result: the motivated organism is more active, produces more vicarious trial and error, more energetic responses, etc. The same effect is found at the symbolic level. Subjects motivated either by hunger (Atkinson and McClelland, 1948) or by n Achievement (McClelland, Clark, Roby, and Atkinson, 1949) tend to attribute instrumental activity to characters in their stories more often than unmotivated subjects. That is, the people in the stories actually do something (make a decision, try a new mode of attack, etc.) in order to reach their food or achievement goals. Nor is this result confined to situationally-induced needs. Lowell (1950) and Clark and McClelland (1950) have shown that people who score high on n Achievement in their imaginative stories under normal conditions solve more arithmetic problems per unit time, learn to rearrange scrambled words faster, and show greater relative output in the middle of an anagrams test than do subjects with low imaginative n Achievement.

Increased motivation leads to increased output under an extremely wide range of conditions. In industry, for example, many studies have shown that added incentives will produce a spurt in output (cf. Moore, 1939) or that interest in one's work as brought about perhaps by the knowledge that one is being studied will increase output (the so-called "Hawthorne effect," cf. Roethlisberger and Dickson, 1939). McGeoch (1942) lists a large number of experiments which have demonstrated that learning increases in speed and efficiency under increased motivation or added incentives such as praise or reproof, rivalry, intent to learn, etc. Melton (1942) has concluded from all this that one of the major functions of motivation is to mobilize the resources of the organism for more efficient action or to release energy which may be used to produce faster output, more efficient learning, etc. The energizing effect of motivation is displayed either through an increase in the *number* of responses produced per unit time, in the *variety* of responses produced, or in the number of *relevant* responses.

But sometimes such an increase in response output does not lead to greater learning or performance *efficiency*, particularly if it is pushed far enough. Some work by Patrick (1934) patterned after earlier studies on animals by Hamilton (1916), illustrates the point. He placed human subjects in a compartment with four exit doors and gave them the problem of trying to discover and escape by the one unlocked door. Since the escape door on successive trials varied in a random fashion, the subjects could not solve the problem, but they could vary in the amount of rationality they showed in systematically trying out the doors, and in the speed, therefore, with which they got out. Patrick found that most human subjects were highly rational (avoiding repeated tries at the same door or the door unlocked on the previous trial, etc.) under normal motivating conditions. But when he stepped up their motivation by spraying them with needle showers or shocking them through their bare feet, the subjects showed more stereotyped, irrational, and inefficient behavior. Their behavioral output may have risen as motivation increased, but it was less efficient or adaptable. The same effect has been obtained by a number of animal experimenters who have shown that as the difficulty of a discrimination increases the strength of stimulus (e.g. punishment) which will produce optimum problem solving efficiency gets less and less (the so-called Yerkes-Dodson Law, cf. Young, 1936, pp. 280 ff.). In short, there would appear to be a curvilinear relationship between motivational intensity and the *efficiency* of performance, even though the sheer output of responses may continue to rise. The decrease in efficiency is probably due to the decrease in variability of the responses emitted, which in turn may be due to a decrease in the number of succeeding responses which will be influenced by any given response (cf. Miller and Frick, 1949). That is, the subjects' "memory span" is cut down and they tend to repeat unsuccessful responses more readily under very intense motivations.

The curvilinear relation between motivation and efficiency is illustrated nicely by a series of experiments on the effects of induced muscular tension on learning and work output. Muscular tension may not be exactly the same as motivation but it seems to accompany changes in motivation with such regularity that it may be thought of as one of the bodily mechanisms by which motivation achieves its energizing effects on performance. We may therefore study the effects of different intensities of induced tension with the same interest

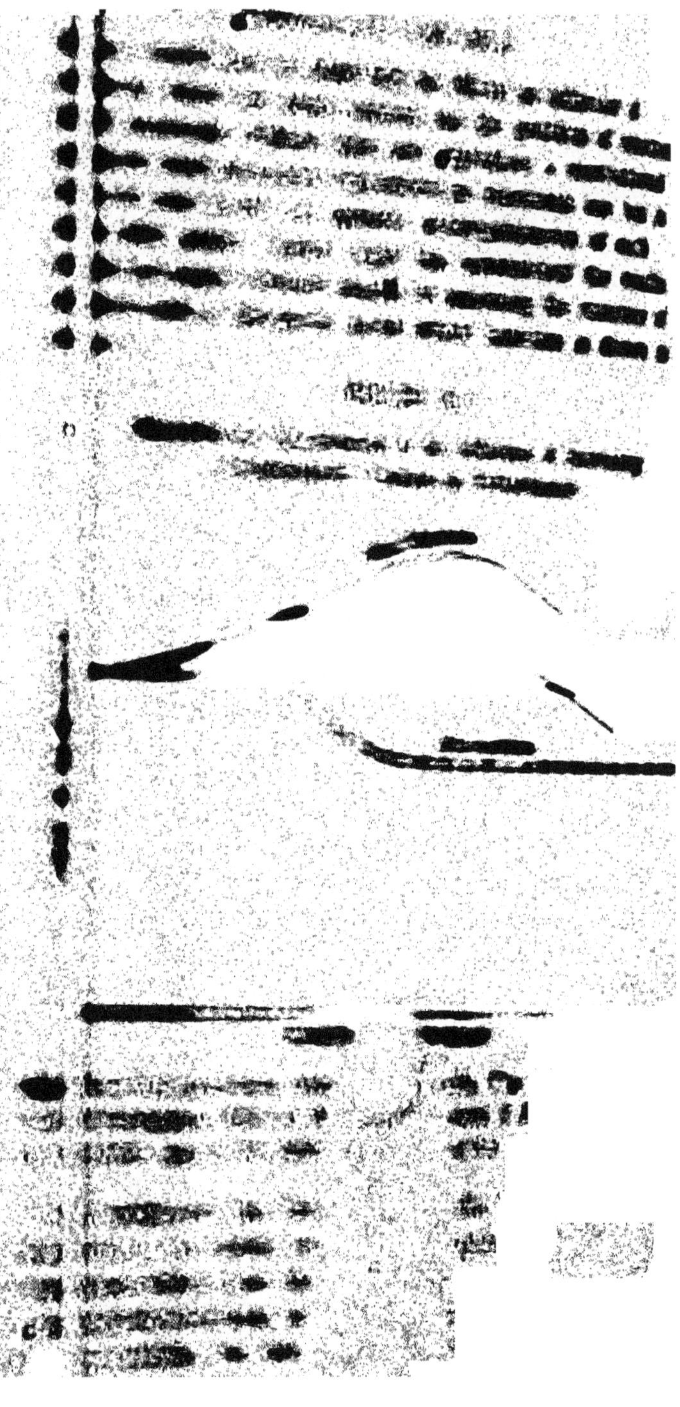

onses, suggesting again that it
f response which produces the

hift in the effect of motivatio
creases can be found in othe
then disrupt performance as
:lelland (1950) report that subj
ure actually perform better in
t, while Sears (1937) has clea
anticipations of failure will
a lowering of over-all score. C
s emphasized the incapacitati
surprising in view of the fact t
ıre suffering from the effects o
their writings one might b
s disruptive and leads the org
· have seen in an earlier cha
al position that motives are
luced if possible to a minim
this is as one-sided a view as
lways biologically useful in e
ms more efficiently. The fac
motive increases in intensity
ficiency of instrumental acti
ould appear that as far as adj
tain optimum level of mo
anxiety," which leads to m
little motivation leads to
isruption and [illegible] nse against
unsolved [illegible] discovery
is and why [illegible] ntensities

most striking [illegible] moti

that we would have in observing the effects on behav
adrenalin when our main concern was the problem o
duced muscular tension does not reproduce a mot
any more than adrenalin reproduces an emotional st
cases we may study the somatic accompaniments o
states with profit. Courts (1942) has summarized th
number of muscle-tension studies by assuming the ex
cilitative and a disruptive factor which function as
ure 15.1.

FIGURE 15.1

Hypothetical Explanation of the Influence of Inc
Dynamometer Tension on Performance

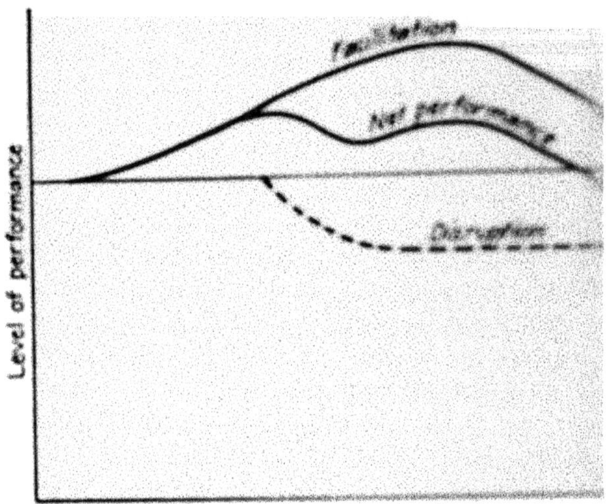

(Reproduced by permission from F. A. Courts, The Inf
on the Dynamogenic Effect of Muscular Tension. J. Exp
511. Copyright 1942 by the American Psychological Asso

As he points out, his "explanation of the data
two factors] is, of course,
performance curve is one
of experiments involving such diverse responses as
nonsense syllables, the knee jerk response, and p
pursuit rotor task. There seems to be clear evid
reason or another performance tends to fall off af
duced tension. The intensity level necessary to pro
off has also been found to be less with more comp

requ[illegible] [illegible]ore variable responses, suggesting again that it is the r[illegible] duction [illegible] the variability of response which produces the decreas[illegible] in performance.

Further support for this shift in the effect of motivation on pe[illegible] form[illegible] as its intensity increases can be found in other place[illegible] Fear m[illegible] first facilitate and then disrupt performance as it grow[illegible] more [illegible]nse. Clark and McClelland (1950) report that subjects wit[illegible] presumably mild fear of failure actually perform better in the la[illegible] minut[illegible] [illegible]f an anagrams test, while Sears (1937) has clearly dem[illegible] onst[illegible] that more severe anticipations of failure will interfer[illegible] with [illegible]rmance and cause a lowering of over-all score. Clinician[illegible] have [illegible] course, nearly always emphasized the incapacitating effec[illegible] of str[illegible] motives. This is not surprising in view of the fact that mo[illegible] pe[illegible] [illegible]hom they deal with are suffering from the effects of intens[illegible] dri[illegible] [illegible]ut to read some of their writings one might be led t[illegible] [illegible] that *all* motivation is disruptive and leads the organism t[illegible] [illegible] [illegible]ous defenses. As we have seen in an earlier chapter, th[illegible] [illegible] [illegible] supports the general position that motives are states [illegible] tensi[illegible] [illegible]hich ought to be reduced if possible to a minimum. Ou[illegible] pre[illegible] [illegible]nalysis suggests that this is as one-sided a view as the op[illegible] p[illegible] [illegible] that motives are always biologically useful in enablin[illegible] the [illegible]ism to solve problems more efficiently. The fact of th[illegible] matt[illegible] [illegible]ems to be that *as a motive increases in intensity it fir[illegible] leads [illegible]n increase in the efficiency of instrumental activity an[illegible] [illegible] [illegible]ecrease.* Thus it would appear that as far as adjustme[illegible] [illegible] [illegible]d there is a certain optimum level of motive i[illegible] te[illegible] [illegible] level of "creative anxiety," which leads to maximu[illegible] pro[illegible] [illegible]lving efficiency. Too little motivation leads to sluggis[illegible] ness a[illegible] [illegible]ertia, too much to disruption and defense against anxiet[illegible] The theoretical problems still unsolved are the discovery of wh[illegible] this [illegible] [illegible] optimum intensity is and why higher intensities lead [illegible]

Interrelatedness. One of the most striking effects of motivation [illegible] the way [illegible] which it brings together or relates diverse aspects of t[illegible] organism[illegible] activities. It organizes responses, introduces trends in[illegible] behavior [illegible], as McGeoch puts it, provides "orientation and dire[illegible] tion" for behavior (1942). From the outside observer's viewpoin[illegible] as we have seen, it is this capacity of the motive concept to ma[illegible] sense ou[illegible] [illegible] varied responses which distinguishes it from our oth[illegible] that we would have in observing the effects on behavior of injecting adrenalin when our main concern was the problem of emotion. Induced muscular tension does not reproduce a motivational state any more than adrenalin reproduces an emotional one, but in both cases we may study the somatic accompaniments of such central states with profit. Courts (1942) has summarized the results of a number of muscle-tension studies by assuming the existence of a facilitative and a disruptive factor which function as shown in Figure 13.1.

FIGURE 13.1

Hypothetical Explanation of the Influence of Increasing Dynamometer Tension on Performance

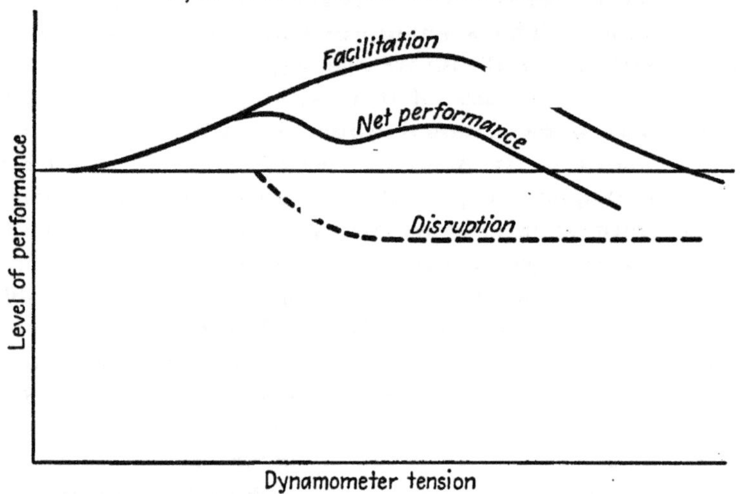

(Reproduced by permission from F. A. Courts, The Influence of Practice on the Dynamogenic Effect of Muscular Tension. *J. Exp. Psychol.*, 30, 504-511. Copyright 1942 by the American Psychological Association.)

As he points out, his "explanation of the data [in terms of the two factors] is, of course, hypothetical" (1942, p. 509). But the net performance curve is one that has been obtained for a large number of experiments involving such diverse responses as memorization of nonsense syllables, the knee-jerk response, and performance on a pursuit rotor task. There seems to be clear evidence that for one reason or another performance tends to fall off at high levels of induced tension. The intensity level necessary to produce the falling off has also been found to be less with more complex tasks which require more variable responses, suggesting again that it is the reduction in the variability of response which produces the decrease in performance.

Further support for this shift in the effect of motivation on performance as its intensity increases can be found in other places. Fear may first facilitate and then disrupt performance as it grows more intense. Clark and McClelland (1950) report that subjects with presumably mild fear of failure actually perform better in the last minutes of an anagrams test, while Sears (1937) has clearly demonstrated that more severe anticipations of failure will interfere with performance and cause a lowering of over-all score. Clinicians have, of course, nearly always emphasized the incapacitating effects of strong motives. This is not surprising in view of the fact that most people whom they deal with are suffering from the effects of intense drives. But to read some of their writings one might be led to conclude that *all* motivation is disruptive and leads the organism to adopt various defenses. As we have seen in an earlier chapter, this conclusion supports the general position that motives are states of tension which ought to be reduced if possible to a minimum. Our present analysis suggests that this is as one-sided a view as the opposing one that motives are always biologically useful in enabling the organism to solve problems more efficiently. The fact of the matter seems to be that *as a motive increases in intensity it first leads to an increase in the efficiency of instrumental activity and then to a decrease.* Thus it would appear that as far as adjustment is concerned there is a certain optimum level of motive intensity, a level of "creative anxiety," which leads to maximum problem-solving efficiency. Too little motivation leads to sluggishness and inertia, too much to disruption and defense against anxiety. The theoretical problems still unsolved are the discovery of what this area of optimum intensity is and why higher intensities lead to inefficiency.

Interrelatedness. One of the most striking effects of motivation is the way in which it brings together or relates diverse aspects of the organism's activities. It organizes responses, introduces trends into behavior, or, as McGeoch puts it, provides "orientation and direction" for behavior (1942). From the outside observer's viewpoint, as we have seen, it is this capacity of the motive concept to make sense out of varied responses which distinguishes it from our other concepts and makes it so useful. From the internal frame of reference, as reflected in Thematic Apperception stories written under the influence of motivation, this characteristic of motives is also very evident. In the first place the motive operates to produce more need-related imagery. If a subject is hungry and is asked to identify a series of ambiguous stimuli, he will see more of them as food-related than if he is not hungry (McClelland and Atkinson, 1948). Similarly, if his n Achievement is aroused, pictures presented to him will more often suggest stories dealing with achievement (McClelland, Clark, Roby, and Atkinson, 1949). In short, the need operates to draw more and more of the subject's associations into its orbit. Thus we might suppose that as motive intensity increases, more and more of the organism's perception and behavior will be related to it until under the extreme pressure of a need, as when a person is dying of thirst in the desert, nothing is left which is *not* related to the need.

One of the striking results of the experiments on the projective expression of needs is the increase in future references in the stories written by motivated subjects. For example, in the experiment on n Achievement, two of the story characteristics which increased most markedly were: *general imagery* and *anticipatory goal responses.* The general imagery category was defined as involving stories which dealt with long-term achievement concerns, such as graduating from school, attaining a life goal, inventing something of use to the world, choosing a vocation, etc. The category dealing with anticipation of goal responses was scored whenever characters in the stories were anticipating success and its gratifications or failure and its unpleasant consequences. In both cases it is as if the need has served to relate present achievement experiences to future ones, to promote understanding of the present in terms of a wider context. In contrast, a group of subjects who were not motivated for achievement told stories which dealt with specific achievement tasks that had no general or long-term implications. Motives seem to be serving to tie the present to the future, the specific to the general and the long-run.

There is still another way in which motivation appeared to increase interrelatedness in these experiments. The stories written under achievement motivation contained more individuals who were either helping or actively hindering the person in the story who was attempting to carry out an achievement-related behavioral sequence. The specific categories involved were named *nurturant* and *hostile press*. In other words, if a picture contained two people, one might typically be perceived as having an achievement concern and the other as actively hindering or helping him. Extra people in the pictures lost their neutral status and were seen as actively involved in the achievement situation. It is as if the motive in question served to sensitize the subjects to the nurturant or hostile possibilities of other people. The situation seems to be comparable to the one in which a chimpanzee perceives a stick as the means to the end of pulling in an orange which is just beyond his reach, or to the one in which a boy who is in love with a girl sees someone else who dates her as a rival almost immediately. This phenomenon in exaggerated form appears in delusions of reference and persecution. A motive may become so intense that objectively disinterested people are perceived as threatening or concerned in some way with the frustration or fulfillment of the motive in question.

What evidence is there that this capacity of a motive to interrelate aspects of the person's symbolic processes in these experiments is a general characteristic of motives? We should remember in the first place that according to the theoretical assumptions proposed in the last chapter motives are based on strong generalized affective associations. It follows from this that one could expect motives when aroused to involve a variety of responses, since they are general to begin with. It is differentiation of sub-goals and specifically relevant responses that appears to be progressively learned. Generality or interrelatedness of responses associated with pleasure or pain exists from the beginning. In the second place, it has been common practice in learning theory to assume that reinforcement or reward serves to set up a goal gradient—in a maze situation, for instance. It is a fact that errors near the end of a maze are eliminated more quickly than those farther from the end. To explain this fact Hull (1943) and others have spoken of a delay of reinforcement gradient which is responsible for the stronger and more rapid fixation of correct responses near the reward. Regardless of the exact theoretical interpretation, the fact remains that all theorists assume that somehow reward or motivation serves to relate events which occur earlier in a maze to events or responses which occur later in the maze. The goal gradient is simply an attempt to express this relationship more precisely. The assumption that motivation somehow increases the interrelatedness of successive responses is essential to any learning theory which accounts for the progressive elimination of errors in a complex behavioral chain, especially since the errors may be distant in space and time from the point of reinforcement.

There is other evidence for interrelatedness from other types of experiments. Zatzkis (1949) has discovered that people with high imaginative n Achievement use different grammatical categories in an achievement-related task such as writing a theme. Specifically they use more future tenses, more generalized or abstract nouns, and more clauses indicating retroactive or proactive relationships. In short, the motive appears to influence not only the ideas which a person has but also the linguistic forms which he chooses to express those ideas. The changes in language, like the changes in ideas, strongly suggest that the presence of a motive tends to increase relationships in time and between the particular and the general. An experiment by Klein and Schoenfeld (1941) on the effects of ego-involvement is relevant here. Subjects were asked to perform a variety of tasks and also to rate how confident they were that they had done well after completing each task. An intercorrelation of the confidence ratings under normal working conditions showed a low and insignificant relationship. However, if the subjects were ego-involved, which is to say, if their n Achievement was aroused, the intercorrelation of the confidence ratings rose to the level of significance. In other words, the introduction of the achievement motive served to relate responses which had formerly been unrelated. All the tasks were now perceived as relevant to an achievement goal.

As final support for the hypothesis that motivation increases interrelatedness we need only refer back to the kind of situation which originally gave rise to the motivational concept in clinical situations. In the *aliquis* episode discussed in Chapter 11, Freud successfully related the forgetting of a word to an event (sexual intercourse) which had occurred earlier in the person's life history. To tie together these two events, which were separated in time and different in form, he suggested the existence of an underlying motive, namely, guilt or, as some would currently phrase it, the need for tension reduction. Now if we turn this situation around and, instead of reasoning from effects to causes, ask what effects the motive produces, we come to the conclusion that the motive has different but related effects (forgetting a word, disguised free associations, etc.). This may sound as if we have reasoned in a circle, but what we have added above is the experimental finding that when we induce motivation we do in fact get an increase in the interrelationships that the motive concept was originally devised to explain.

Sensitization. Organisms which are in a state of motivation seem more sensitive to some kinds of environmental cues than to others.

As Morgan (1943) has put it, a drive or instinct seems to operate in part at least by reinforcing "some sensory stimulations and not others" (Hebb, 1949, p. 191). There seems to be a lowering of perceptual if not sensory thresholds to specific kinds of stimulation and furthermore, when the drive-related stimulation is suprathreshold, it appears more vivid than when the organism is not motivated (reinforcing effect). This may be the mechanism which accounts for the increased interrelationships mentioned in the previous section, but the experimental literature on the sensitizing effects of motivation is sufficiently large to warrant separate treatment. In the experiments by McClelland *et al.* on the projective expression of needs, this effect was most noticeable in the changed character of goal statements in the motivated subjects. Increased motivation did not increase the number of successful outcomes of achievement-related stories, but it did increase the number of times that a successful outcome was associated with a positive affective statement. Specifically this meant that there was no increase in the number of statements such as "He will achieve his goal" but there was in the number of statements which ran, "He will achieve his goal and be happy ever after." In other words, goal situations had become more vivid or more affectively toned, for the motivated group. The increased vividness of the achievement goal was also reflected by such conative statements as "He wants to get ahead" or "He is striving to complete the task in time," etc. Such explicit statements of need for achievement were much more frequent in the motivated groups.

Perceptual sensitization produced by motivation has been measured in two main ways: in terms of changes in the characteristics of a need-related object or in terms of the speed of recognition of the object. As an illustration of the first approach, an experiment by Bruner and Goodman (1947) is typical. They asked poor and rich children to adjust a diaphragm with a circular opening to the same size as coins of different value held in their hands. They found that the poorer children tended to overestimate the size of the coins to a greater extent than did the rich children. Yet the same difference was not obtained when cardboard discs instead of coins were used. In other words, the need-related objects (coins) were overestimated more than the unrelated objects (cardboard discs). McClelland and Atkinson (1948) have reported similar effects for hunger. They found that when they presented subjects with ambiguous stimuli supposedly representing food-related and unrelated objects and asked them which was larger, the hungry subjects said the food-related object was larger much more often than did the satiated subjects. In a further experiment McClelland, Atkinson, and Clark (1949) report that achievement-motivated subjects gave larger estimates of the amount of money supposedly represented by an ambiguous stimulus significantly more often than a control group of subjects. Sensitization seems to be a very general effect which increases the vividness of goal objects in all dimensions—clarity, brightness, size, hedonic tone, etc. In extreme cases it may be the basis for hallucinations. A thirsty man in the desert not only sees everything in relation to his thirst drive, *what* he sees is more vivid—i.e., a water "mirage" appears larger, brighter, clearer, more affectively toned, etc., the greater his desire for water.

The second measure of sensitization has been recognition time. As Postman, Bruner, and McGinnies point out, "That a generalized set lowers the recognition threshold for specific stimuli within its compass, has, of course, been known since the early work of the Wurzburg School." (1948, p. 153.) These authors report confirmation of this relationship in an experiment which tested the speed of word recognition for subjects whose scores on the Allport-Vernon Study of Values Test were known. They found that most of the subjects recognized words which were related to their high values faster than words related to their low values when the words were rapidly exposed in a tachistoscope. Furthermore, in considering the guesses which the subjects made before correctly recognizing the word being exposed, they found significantly more value-related hypotheses for the high-value words than for the low-value words. In short, the particular needs or values in question seem to make ready the recognition or production of need-related words. This readying, sensitizing, or "priming" process seems to be one of the major effects of motivation. Further evidence for it has been obtained by McClelland and Liberman (1949) in an experiment which shows that subjects with high imaginative n Achievement recognize success-related words faster than do subjects with low imaginative n Achievement. This is not surprising when it is remembered that the n Achievement score is itself derived from the readier production of achievement-related imagery in a storytelling situation. In other words, one can think in terms of a central motive state (Morgan, 1943) which leads to both the readier production of achievement-related responses and the readier recognition of achievement-related stimuli.

The sensitization effect we are discussing here is very similar to what has sometimes been called *wish fulfillment*. There seems to be a tendency for motivation to mobilize memory, perception, and imagery in a way which is related to gratification of the need in question. For example, Knapp reports an experiment (1948) in which students were asked to recall statements they had read previously concerning the spread of Communism in Western Europe. The material was so arranged that there were an equal number of statements indicating that Communism was either gaining or losing ground. Those students who recorded themselves as moderately opposed to the spread of Communism in Europe tended to recall the anti-Communist statements better. They remembered, in accordance with their wishes, that Communism was losing ground. Many similar experiments could be cited. In fact some authors, notably Sherif, have been so impressed with the pervasiveness of this phenomenon that they argue it is the chief effect of motivation. Sherif (1948) cites as evidence the great preoccupation with food observed among conscientious objectors who took part in a starvation experiment at the Laboratory of Physiological Hygiene at the University of Minnesota. In fact, the subject's intense preoccupation with food seems to show a very widespread sensitization effect, as the following excerpt from the report on the experiment shows:

> The intensive preoccupation with food made it difficult for the men to concentrate upon the tasks they had intellectually decided they would work on. If a man tried to study, he soon found himself daydreaming about food. He would think about foods he had eaten in the past; he would muse about opportunities he had missed to eat a certain food when he was at this or that place. Often he would daydream by the hour about the next meal, which was not very far away: "Today we'll have menu No. 1. Gee, that's the smallest menu, it seems. How shall I fix the potatoes? If I use my spoon to eat them I'll be able to add more water. Should I make different varieties of beverages tonight? Haven't had my toast yet today. Maybe I should save some for a midnight snack with my buddy. What kind of a sandwich could I make? Maybe I'd better write these ideas down, so I don't forget them. If I eat a little faster the food would stay warm longer —and I like it warm. But then it's gone so quickly. . . . (Sherif, 1948, pp. 80-81.)

A similar sensitization tendency has been more or less assumed to operate to shift goal estimates upward in level-of-aspiration experiments. Most writers have agreed with Frank (1938) that the choice of a particular level of aspiration is determined by three factors: the desire to do well, the desire to make an accurate judgment, and the desire to avoid failure. The first of these motives is supposed to push the estimate upward; the others to hold it down. Unfortunately there is no direct experimental evidence that an increase in motivation produces an increase in the size or amount of the goal which is desired (level of aspiration), although such an effect would be expected on the basis of much of the evidence already cited. The obvious test of observing the effects on level of aspiration of induced motivation has apparently not been made. A somewhat relevant experiment has been performed by Taylor, however (1948). He studied the effects on level of aspiration of the ingestion of dexedrine, a drug which produces a central excitatory state which is apparently something like the motivational one. He found that dexedrine did produce an increase in the final goal estimates for performance and also in the average discrepancy scores, giving support to the general proposition that motivation-like states increase goal expectations. Similar trends can be found in Gould's (1939) and P. Sears' (1941) case studies of individuals with high levels of aspiration. Often, but by no means always, such people were judged by the experimenter as having stronger motivation than people with low average discrepancy scores.

Anxiety. The sensitization effect is by no means universal. In fact, there seems to be just as much evidence for a contradictory trend, a tendency for an increase in motivation to mobilize imagery concerned with deprivation and loss of the goal in question. In McClelland and Atkinson's experiment (1948) there was an increase in food-related imagery which accompanied the increase in hunger, but the increase was not in terms of goal objects or things which could be eaten. In their second experiment (1948) on the effect of hunger on written stories they also found a marked increase in the number of stories dealing with food *deprivation* (e.g., black-market activities). Similar results were obtained in a study of the effect of induced n Achievement on perception. The same subjects who under the influence of achievement motivation "saw" more money in response to one item, "saw" lower grades in response to another item which called for four grades on a report card. Other subjects who were similarly motivated wrote many more stories with themas that dealt with *loss of achievement.* Furthermore, both in the hunger and achievement experiments one of the most significant shifts which occurred in story characteristics was in the frequency with which characters in the story expressed a *need* for food or achievement.

It is possible that this marked increase in concern with deprivation or lack of the goal in question might be a result in these experiments of having induced the needs by deprivation or failure. Gebhard (1949) reports that experiences of success or failure are very important in determining the favorableness with which a particular task is regarded. Thus one might argue that prior experiences of failure, for instance, carry over to the new task of writing stories and are projected into those stories as a result of this particular experience rather than as a result of the increase in motivation. Further evidence from an experiment in which n Achievement was aroused without as much induced failure (McClelland, *et al.,* 1949) supports this conclusion in part in that the number of deprivation themas decreases although they do not drop to the level obtained in a low n Achievement group. The difficulty is that frustration is one of the surest ways to provide cues for arousing a strong motivating state. Lambert (1950), for instance, has argued from rat data that frustration adds to the intensity of an over-all drive state for the organism. Consequently, to avoid using it as a means of arousing a motive may "purify" the effects of the motive but at the same time prevent observation of the motive's effects at the most intense levels.

Fortunately there is considerable evidence from other sources that an increase in motivation produces an increased concern with deprivation and failure. In Knapp's experiment (1948) referred to above, the subjects who rated themselves as extremely opposed to the spread of Communism in Europe tended to recall better the *pro-Communist* statements in direct contradiction to their intense wishes in the matter. Here it is as if the increase in motivation had produced the direct opposite of wish fulfillment. The highly motivated subjects remembered facts which would justify their worst fears. A similar effect was obtained by Murray (1933) when he had some little girls rate pictures for maliciousness before and after a frightening game of "Murder." The induced fear produced an increase in the estimates of maliciousness of the faces in the pictures presented for rating. One might have expected that in line with the sensitization effect discussed above, the increase in the need for relief from tension would have operated to make faces more friendly. Yet the opposite was true. Anxiety, not wish fulfillment, accompanied the increase in need. Similar effects have long been noted in clinical data. The existence of a strong motive is often inferred from the presence of anxiety in a dream, for instance. A boy who is mildly in love may spend some of his time daydreaming in wish-fulfilling fantasies of future happiness, but as his love grows more intense, elements of anxiety and anticipations of the possible loss of his loved one begin to creep in. The experiments by McClelland *et al.* (1949) on the projective expression of needs show that increased motivation leads to the projection of anticipations both of success *and failure.* Postman and Solomon (1950) report that nearly as many subjects recognized *incompleted* tasks significantly faster as recognized completed tasks faster in accordance with the expectations of the wish-fulfillment or sensitization hypothesis. Whitfield (1949b) states in contradiction to the findings on experimental starvation that in a collection of five hundred dreams in Germany after World War II, when most of the people were starving, only two or three dealt with food. How can these apparently contradictory trends be reconciled with the sensitization effects reported above?

The Effects of Motivation at Different Intensity Levels. One way to clear up some of this confusion is to assume that motives of different intensities arouse different expectations through past association and reinforcement and that some regular stages can be distinguished in the person's imaginative or thought processes as a motive increases in strength. Figure 13.2 represents an attempt to put together in a preliminary, schematic way some of the different findings we have just discussed on sensitization, anxiety, etc., as they may appear in response to motives of different strengths.

In this schematic figure* the frequency of goal imagery and deprivation imagery have been separately plotted to show the presumably different effects of motivation at different intensity levels. In the first or wish-fulfilling stage, motivation is weak enough to be "satisfied," as it were, with goal images. In fact, evidence from Atkinson and McClelland's experiment on hunger (1948) shows that just after eating there appears to be a somewhat greater number of references to completed food goal sequences than later on. It is in this stage that the sensitization effect, at least as far as the *production* of goal imagery is concerned, is most obvious. Under certain conditions this concern with pleasant goal fantasies may give the impression that the subject is repressing unpleasant thoughts, but actually it is a kind of "pseudo repression," not motivated by fear as with very high levels of motivation but by simple wish-fulfilling desires. An increase in motivation can bring a person in this stage out of his daydream back into "reality." In the second stage of motive intensity,

* I am especially indebted to Dr. R. H. Knapp for his guidance in thinking through this problem.

FIGURE 13.2

The Hypothetical Effect of Increased Motive Intensity on Thought Processes

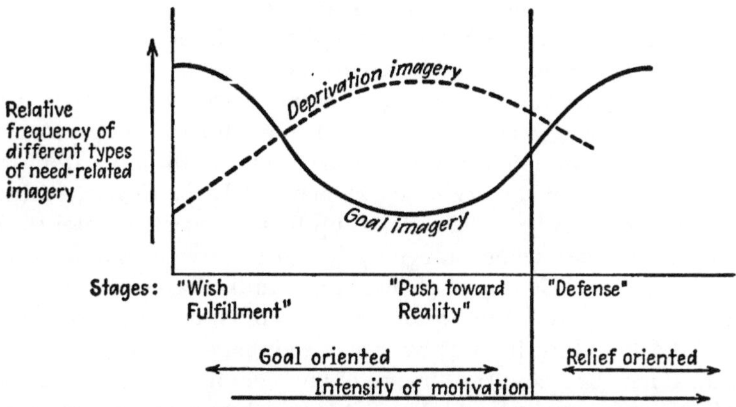

there is a "push toward reality," an increasing awareness of the need, of the obstacles to the satisfaction of the need, and of instrumental ways of overcoming the obstacles. Deprivation imagery tends to replace goal imagery in the spontaneous productions of the subject. This is the conscious anxiety stage. However, the sensitization effect probably persists over into this stage as far as *recognition* is concerned. To put the matter very briefly, a subject in this stage who is hungry will spontaneously concern himself more with means of getting food and with the absence of food, but if a food-related stimulus should be presented to him, he will perceive it more vividly (as larger, brighter, with faster recognition, etc.) than at an earlier stage of motivation. "A hungry person may prefer not to think of a beefsteak at all, but if he sees one it may appear larger and juicier than normal." (Sanford, 1937.) This "push toward reality" has obvious adaptive significance. It prepares the organism to satisfy the need by focusing attention on obstacles, by increasing readiness to respond to goal-related stimuli *if presented,* by energizing activity (see above), etc.

But if motivation is pushed still higher, a change occurs. The concern with need and with deprivation grows apparently so intense that it becomes painful and the organism is now oriented in a new direction—namely, toward a relief from anxiety rather than toward attainment of the original goal. The appearance of this new motive reverses some of the trends which have so far appeared. Need and anxiety imagery tend to drop out of awareness because their presence is too painful. In their place arrives a kind of defensive goal imagery which is very different in its function from the goal imagery obtained with weak motivation. It is this stage which may be represented by the defensive recall of completed tasks in some of the task interruption experiments (cf. Rosenzweig, 1943).

We may picture the sequence of events described abstractly here with a concrete imaginary episode. Let us suppose that a man is driving through a desert when his car breaks down miles from the nearest water. In the beginning he may not be particularly thirsty and he imagines he will be picked up by some passing motorist. As the hours under the hot sun go by, his thirst increases and he begins to imagine delicious cool drinks, thick milk shakes, or ice cubes tinkling in a glass. As more hours pass, his thirst becomes more acute and the unrealistic images give way to an intense preoccupation with how thirsty he is and the absence of any sign of water in the desert. He may now begin to think up various schemes for getting water out of his car or to search in the surrounding territory for a spring, but he no longer spends much time in idle dreams of cooling drinks. Instead, he is active, anxious, and very conscious of his thirst. If we assume that many hours pass by, his thirst increasing in intensity all the time, his anxiety may become so acute and so painful that the bounds of reality begin to break down and he may begin to have hallucinations or see mirages of water in the distance or think that he actually hears the tinkle of ice cubes in a glass. Eventually he may, as it were, lose consciousness of his thirst altogether and become delirious, existing in a fantasy world in which his needs are being gratified. Such a reconstructed picture is consistent with clinical reports of instances of intense motivation, with experiments like Dembo's on prolonged frustration (1931) and with the facts we have just been reviewing. It is as if increasing awareness were at first useful in preparing the organism to satisfy the need in question, and then beyond a certain point of intensity it becomes so painful that there is a need for defense and repression.

Such a conclusion is, of course, entirely in line with the clinical findings of psychoanalysis. In fact, in the cases with which clinicians normally deal, the motives involved are often in the upper, relief-oriented phase of motive intensity as pictured in Figure 13.2. The substitute, unreal gratifications of dreams, the repression of motives, and the various neurotic symptoms which clinicians find, all seem characteristic of this end of the motivation continuum as we have analyzed it. Since experimental and clinical psychologists have normally been dealing with different ends of the motivation continuum, it is not so surprising that their conclusions at times have seemed to be contradictory. What the experimentalists need to do is to push their motive intensities, if possible, to the level obtained in neuroses to see whether the effects observed by clinical psychologists can be obtained. This will naturally be difficult to do, but the results to date strongly suggest that the findings of the two approaches will be found to be consistent, if motivational intensity level is taken into account.

Variations in the Effects of Motive Intensity. Our schematic diagram of the different stages in the effects of motivation on behavior is of course much too simple. Our knowledge at present is too sketchy to fill it out in much detail, but two modifications must be made even now—one dealing with different kinds of motives and one with the interaction of the concrete situation with motivational intensity. We have been persuaded by a number of facts reviewed in the preceding chapter that there are at least two kinds of motives which should be distinguished for practical purposes, namely, approach motives and avoidance motives. Does an avoidance motive go through the same stages in its mobilization of imagery as an approach motive? Apparently not. Figure 13.2 was designed primarily with approach motives in mind; avoidance motives apparently shift more quickly into the "defense" stage of orientation. Figure 13.3, reproduced with modifications from Atkinson (1950), illustrates the differential effect of ego orientation on the two kinds of motives as far as recall of interrupted tasks is concerned. What this figure shows is that as the experimenter made it clearer and clearer to the subjects that the tasks which were interrupted were related to personal success and failure, the subjects who were presumably motivated primarily by hope of success recalled significantly more interrupted or incompleted tasks, while the subjects who were motivated by fear of failure recalled fewer of these tasks. If it is assumed that the two motives are of equal strength, obviously the subjects with the "fear" motive are in the "defensive" stage during ego orientation while the subjects with the "hope" motive are in the "reality" stage. they are remembering incompleted tasks so that they can complete them and achieve more success. Actually Atkinson's separation of the two motivational groups was based on the fact that the subjects presumably motivated by fear had *lower* TAT n Achievement scores while those presumably motivated by hope had higher n Achieve-

FIGURE 13.3

The Effect of Different Instructional Orientations on Recall of Interrupted Tasks for Two Kinds of Achievement Motives

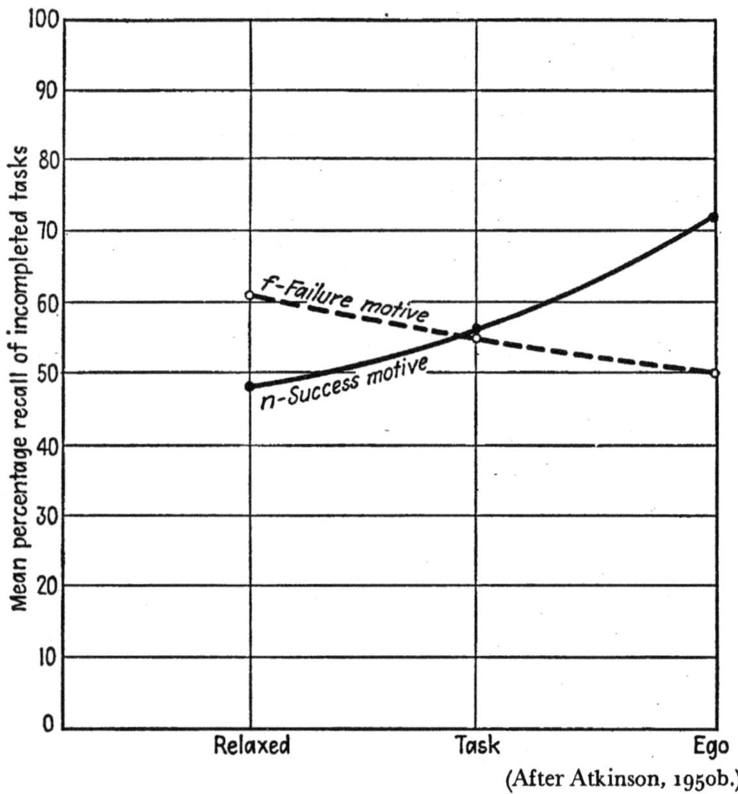

(After Atkinson, 1950b.)

ment scores. Apparently, as far as achievement motivation is concerned, there is considerable evidence that low motivation is associated with avoiding obvious failure (cf. also McClelland and Liberman, 1949). If this is so, it is clear that our picture of the stages of orientation accompanying an increase in motivational strength in Figure 13.2 is too simple. Lower motivation (represented in this case by f Failure) produces *more* "reality-oriented" activity (recall of incompleted tasks) under relaxed conditions and *less* reality-oriented activity under ego-involved conditions than does high motivation. It looks as if a weak motive, if it is a fear motive and if the situation is ego-involved, can produce a defensive reaction while a stronger approach motive is producing a realistic instrumental response. In this case the "defensive stage" would be associated with *lower* motivation rather than higher as schematized in Figure 13.2. What all this adds up to is that whether a person is in the "wish-fulfilling," "reality," or "defense" stages depends not only on level of motivation but also on the nature of the motive and the nature of the situation.

Nor should this be surprising. After all, the different kinds of imagery supposedly associated with different motivational levels are aroused presumably because of past experience with what has happened or with what has led to reward after such motive intensities have been experienced. One could expect that in a general way concern with instrumental activities, for instance, has been a response which would have led to satisfaction for a number of people with motives of moderate strength. Hence we might expect to find a *general* tendency in a large number of people for a large number of motives for this type of imagery to appear in connection with motives of moderate strength. But by the same argument one might also assume that a large number of people had discovered that the way to handle a fear motive is to avoid thinking about the situation that gives rise to the fear. Thus one might expect somewhat different stages in the development of associations to avoidance and approach motives of increasing strength. The same reasoning applies to the nature of the situation. The associations aroused will be determined in part by past experience (particularly so when imagination is involved) but also in part by the nature of the present situation. Thus in Atkinson's experiment the subjects with high n Achievement did not *recall* so many interrupted tasks under a relaxed orientation, nor did they *complete* as many tasks initially. Although their TAT records showed that they had high achievement motivation, they were disinterested in this situation since it was explained to them that what they did had no relevance to their personal success. When the instructions were ego-oriented, however, the situation changed. Now these same subjects produced a large amount of instrumental activity (recall of incompleted tasks), but it required a combination of high achievement motivation plus a situation which could lead to reward to produce this response. Intense motivation alone was not enough.

A further illustration of this same kind of relationship between the nature of the situation and level of motivation can be found in a study of n Aggression among football players by Stone (1950). He obtained TAT records of aggression among football players both during and after the season and compared them with the TAT records of a matched control group of subjects obtained at the same times. He found that the football players and control subjects produced an almost exactly equivalent amount of imaginative aggression during the season, but that afterward the football players showed significantly less aggression and what aggression appeared was more projected than for the controls, i.e., it was as violent but the source of the aggression was predominantly impersonal rather than personal. To explain this somewhat complicated finding, he was forced to assume that during the season the players had to mobilize their aggression to handle the problems of playing football successfully, but that under normal conditions they did not have to since they were bigger than other people and had very little fear of being unable to defend themselves against attack. So after the season, when there was no further need to mobilize their aggressive responses, their over-all aggression count decreased significantly. But it was projected further from the self and attributed to impersonal agents because these same football players had reason to be anxious over showing aggression both because they now had to inhibit a response frequently rewarded in the immediate past and because they had doubtless learned through past experience that their superior strength, unless carefully controlled, might lead to rejection by others. The point of introducing this analysis here is that it illustrates in a number of ways how the nature of the situation (the football players' experiences with aggression) will be influential in determining the kind of aggression imagery a person displays. Thus the football players are in the "defensive" stage after the season with respect to their aggression motivation (e.g., they project it into impersonal agents), presumably not because their level of motivation is high (in fact, it seems to be lower than for the controls) but because the experiences that they have recently been through and that they have had previously in their life histories have led them to be anxious over their own aggressiveness.

One might wonder in view of all this variety whether it is proper to speak of stages of orientation associated with increasing motivation at all. Perhaps not. Our knowledge is too limited at the present time to be sure. But it seems to simplify matters a little to assume that there are such stages which are the result of certain common experiences for large numbers of people and that they may be modified by uncommon experiences or by a shift from an approach to an avoidance motive.

Conflicts and the Need for Anxiety Reduction

So far we have been talking about the effects on behavior of a single motive operating alone, but normally several motives are active at the same time and often in opposition to each other. Can we say anything about the effects on behavior of such conflicts? The problem has been dealt with very extensively in the clinic because abnormalities of behavior are often caused by just such conflicts. It has also been dealt with in the laboratory under the heading of reactions to conflict or frustration. Lewin (1935), Miller (1944), and others have made extensive analyses of various types of conflicts and the modes of solution to which they lead. At the simpler levels these solutions may best be described as goal-oriented. For instance, when a motive is blocked—e.g., when Johnny wants some ice cream and doesn't have a nickel, he may beg his mother for one, look in his other pants pockets, etc. If such further instrumental activity fails, Johnny may be persuaded to accept some substitute goal such as a promise that he will get ice cream tomorrow or a story after supper that night. In short, in this simple type of blocking situation, the reaction to frustration is either *to vary the instrumental activity* or *to accept a substitute goal* (cf. Sears, 1941; McClelland and Apicella, 1945).

When conflict is more intense, as for instance when two motives are involved, behavior is apt to be characterized by oscillation and possibly compromise. The person may be forced to give up or delay one goal response in order to obtain another or he may try to adopt a course of action which partially satisfies both goals (cf. Hovland and Sears, 1938). Many complex actions are frequently interpreted by clinicians in terms of the joint operation of conflicting motives. For example, a Bryn Mawr college student on the suburban train to Philadelphia handed her ticket to the conductor upside down. Why? Certainly we cannot explain the behavior in terms of a consistent trait of behaving in this way in the past. We cannot conclude that this is her conception (schema) of the way a passenger should behave toward a conductor on a train. Nor does it seem reasonable to assume that this was instrumental activity representing a single motive such as the desire to behave aggressively toward the conductor by causing him inconvenience. Instead, we learn on analysis that this peculiar response was the result of a conflict of motives. She wanted to ride all the way to Philadelphia on a ticket which was good only part way. We might explain her action as a simple method of attaining this wish by concealing the destination written on her ticket, except for the fact that it was the most obvious way of calling the conductor's attention to her particular ticket. The technique most likely to have been successful would have been for her simply to hand him her ticket and hope that he would forget her destination in the confusion of the many other tickets that he had to take. Consequently, to explain her action fully a clinician would be apt to assume another motive was also active—a desire to conceal her dishonesty. Her action could then be interpreted as a compromise which partially satisfied her desire to be dishonest and her desire to be honest, but which in the process satisfied neither motive completely. Many individual actions can be explained as the joint products of several motives, as Freud so ably demonstrated in his early analyses in *The Psychopathology of Everyday Life.*

Sources of Anxiety. Very little of general significance can be said about such compromises as we have been describing. Each is more or less unique in the individual case and its effect is likewise unique or at most classifiable under such general headings as oscillation, compromise, varied instrumental activity, and substitution. However, as the conflicts become more acute, a new element enters the situation—namely, anxiety. As we have suggested above, anxiety produces some markedly different effects on the organism which are best described as *defensive* rather than *goal-oriented.* In other words, as conflict grows more intense, a new motive arises—the need for relief from the tension produced by the conflict. The person's behavior becomes more and more oriented around the reduction of anxiety rather than the attainment of the original goals. Actually this new motive for anxiety reduction may develop not only (1) from conflicts of motives but also (2) from an increase in the intensity of a single motive, and (3) from a motive which has been primarily a fear or avoidance motive from the beginning. The last two sources have already been discussed to some extent in previous sections. So a brief review here is all that is necessary.

Motive intensity as a source of the need for anxiety reduction. Figure 13.2 shows how it is conceived that any motive, if it becomes intense enough, may orient the organism around defense and anxiety reduction if it continues to be unsatisfied. And apparently the stronger a motive becomes, the more difficult it is to satisfy it and the more painful frustration of it becomes. As usual, the psychoanalysts have characterized this source of anxiety in vivid terms. They are apt to speak of "fear of the Id" or fear of the strength of instinctual tendencies. To get a colorful word-picture of what they mean, let us turn to a quotation from Flugel: "A vivid impression of the way in which the infant can come to feel threatened and overmastered by its own aggressiveness is conveyed for instance by Riviere: 'The child is overwhelmed by choking and suffocating; its eyes are blinded with tears, its ears deafened, its throat sore; its bowels gripe, its evacuations burn it.' Thus the child's autogenous aggression, the biological purpose of which, as manifested for instance in crying, is no doubt to get others to relieve its needs, may threaten to destroy its owner, and it is the impotence of the child in face of the mounting tension which makes uncontrolled and unrelieved aggression appear as a situation of acute danger." (Flugel, 1945, pp. 110-111.) While this description may appear unnecessarily imaginative, it does illustrate how an intense enough motive may actually disrupt itself (cf. Chapter 12) and create a new need for anxiety reduction.

Indirect support for this hypothesis comes from the analysis of the relation between frustration and aggression made by Dollard, *et al.* (1939). It can be argued (see below) that some kinds of aggression at least are not instrumental to attaining a blocked goal, but help discharge or express a person's anxiety. Consequently if we find a case in which this type of aggression is frequent, we can argue that anxiety level is also high. Doob and Sears (1939) report on the basis of a questionnaire study that aggressive responses were reported increasingly often as the subjects rated their frustrated motives as more intense. Rephrased in our terms this would suggest that as motive intensity increased, anxiety level increased, which in turn increased the likelihood that an aggressive response would appear. The only difficulty with this and other similar evidence reported by Dollard *et al.* (1939) on the relation between intensity of frustration and increased frequency of aggression is that they do not always distinguish between *instrumental* aggression (an increased effort to get at the blocked goal) and *goal response* aggression (a defensive attempt to reduce anxiety level). Thus their findings do not unambiguously support the hypothesis that motive intensity, if pushed high enough, will produce a new need for anxiety reduction, which is reflected in an increase in *goal response aggression.*

Fear as a source of the need for anxiety reduction. Motives which involve pain-avoidance from the beginning probably develop into needs for anxiety reduction rather readily. In fact, one might wonder whether they are not actually the same thing. The only reason for keeping them separate is the rather traditional notion that fear and anxiety are different, that simple pain-avoidance is different from anxiety reduction. The distinction appears to be based in part on the fact that learning will increase in efficiency with a mild pain-avoidance drive (e.g., electric shock), and then decrease with higher intensities of shock. Thus Dodson (1915) has shown that kittens will learn an easy light-dark discrimination faster and faster as shock intensity is increased, but if the discrimination is difficult, they will learn more slowly if the shock is pushed beyond a certain optimal point. The assumption has been that with high intensities of shock the animal becomes so oriented around escaping pain (defensive behavior) that he shows less efficient problem-solving behavior. Another reason for making the distinction between simple avoidance and anxiety reduction motives is provided by some experiments at a much more complex personality level on *rigidity* of behavior under the influence of anxiety. Here considerable research indicates that anxious persons abandon a previously successful mode of response less easily than people who are not anxious (cf. Adorno, *et al.*, 1950; Christie, 1949; Harris, 1951). An anxious person is less flexible in his approach to new problems, more rigid in his perception of ethnic differences, etc. This again suggests defensive concern with reduction in anxiety rather than instrumental problem-solving behavior such as may be obtained with simple pain-avoidance drives. The contrast is perhaps highlighted most sharply by perception experiments, some of which show better recognition for shock- or pain-associated material (McCleary and Lazarus, 1949) and some of which show poorer recognition for anxiety-associated material (Postman and Bruner, 1948).

So far we have suggested that this difference is due to a simple increase in the intensity of the fear motive, which would make this a special case of the principle discussed in the previous section. Actually it may not be intensity which is responsible for the shift from instrumental to defensive behavior, but some other characteristic of the fear-producing situation. For example, if a person is standing in the street and sees a truck bearing down on him, he will normally fear injury and adapt to the situation by simply stepping to one side. This we might call instrumental avoidance behavior which can occur when the source of danger and the means of avoiding it are both fairly well defined. Faster recognition of shock-associated words could be explained on this basis. However, if the nature of the danger is unknown or unspecifiable so that no problem-solving response is really possible, then the person may have to resort to defensive measures to reduce his anxiety (attempts at withdrawal, aggression, etc.—see below). Poorer recognition after generalized induced failure could be explained on this basis. Or take a further example. To tell a subject he is maladjusted is to threaten him in a non-specific way: he thinks of this as "something bad" but he doesn't know exactly what is wrong and therefore cannot attack the danger in a problem-solving way. Under these conditions his thoughts turn significantly more often to such "defensive" measures as aggressing against others or introducing others in an affiliative relationship (McClelland, Birney, and Roby, 1950). Thus the shift from instrumental to defensive behavior in response to a fear-producing motive may be a function of the *non-specificity of the danger* (rather than its intensity), and/or the unavailability of methods of coping with it.

Conflicts of motives as a source of the need for anxiety reduction. The third source of anxiety—namely, from the conflict of motives—is more directly relevant to this section. As we suggested earlier, two incompatible motives may operate in such a way that a person finds it impossible to satisfy both, even partially. The conflict is much more acute than when a motive is simply blocked by a barrier. The person may be torn between two opposing wishes, between wish and fear for the same event (e.g., marriage), or between two opposing fears as in Maier's experiments (1949) in which the rat is punished if he doesn't jump and punished if he does. In all such cases the conflict of motives may produce so much oscillation, so much anxiety, that the major goal response becomes simply the relief from tension. A simple illustration at the experimental level of how conflict may increase over-all tension has been worked out by Sears (1950) and others (Hollenberg and Sperry, 1950) using doll-play in children. They started with the assumption that children who were frustrated at home, as measured by data collected from parent interviews, would express more aggression in doll-play. In other words, they started with the assumption of Dollard *et al.* (1939) that frustration raises the over-all instigation to aggression or, as we have been calling it, n Aggression. They found that while there was a tendency for this to be so, punishment for aggression in the home was even more likely to raise the frequency of aggression in doll-play. They explained this in terms of a conflict theory as follows: the frustrated children developed a stronger n Aggression; if they were punished for expressing aggression, they developed a conflicting f Aggression (fear of expressing aggression);

the conflict between these two opposed motives (or more specifically over the mode of expressing aggression) was itself a further source of frustration which would increase the over-all n Aggression. Hence the frustrated and *punished* group of children would have a higher n Aggression than any other group. But this could not be discovered directly in the home situation since their overt aggression was inhibited there. It could be discovered in the doll-play situation, however, presumably because the doll house with its parent and sibling figures was on a generalization gradient with the real home. That is, the similarity of the doll situation to the home situation would tend to evoke both n Aggression and f Aggression, but since the generalization gradient for an avoidance motive is steeper than for an approach motive (cf. Chapter 12), it would not evoke both exactly as in the home situation, but would evoke more of the impulse to aggression than its inhibition. Thus the tendency of the frustrated and punished children to display more aggression in the doll-play situation is explained by reference to two hypotheses—one that conflict over expressing aggression increases over-all n Aggression, which is of particular interest to us here; and the other that gradients of generalization for approach and avoidance motives are different, as previously assumed. The role of such conflicts in increasing the need for tension reduction has been treated theoretically by Whiting (1950) and is supported by Maslow's distinction between deprivation and threat (1943b) and by Gwinn's work (1949) on the facilitative effects of punishment on a running response in rats (cf. Chapter 12).

The clinical evidence for the importance of such conflicts of motives in raising over-all anxiety level is also very widespread. Nearly all the findings on guilt and shame are relevant here since both of these states result from conflicts over what a person wants to do (or has done) and what he feels he should do. Psychoanalysts are apt to describe the conflict in terms of the contradictory demands of the impulse life (the Id) and the demands of society (the super-ego). As Flugel puts it: "Undoubtedly one of the most important results of the formation of the super-ego is the development of that peculiar mental condition which we often describe as guilt or the sense of sin—a condition that is perhaps peculiar to the human race. . . ." (1945, p. 143.) Of special importance is the kind of conflict in which the self is perceived as the source of the difficulty which is usually the case when we speak of guilt or a sense of sin. In such cases the self may appear to be the object against which instrumental activity (or perhaps aggression) should be directed, which in turn increases fear and anxiety. There seems no reason to believe that these conflicts at a higher level will obey any different principles from the ones discussed in connection with the doll-play experiments. They have been mentioned here to suggest that they might be handled in exactly the same terms.

Modes of Reducing Anxiety. The effects of anxiety on behavior can best be thought of in terms of the clinical literature on defense mechanisms or the ways in which people attempt to reduce anxiety. The literature is so extensive that it is beginning to be possible to arrive at certain generalizations. To review all the factual evidence on which such generalizations are based would be manifestly impossible, however, since it would involve reviewing the whole range of symptoms in mental disease. Even naming and describing the various defense mechanisms that have been isolated by different workers in the field would be difficult. All that we can hope to do is classify these defense mechanisms according to their several different modes, hoping thereby to indicate the different directions in which anxiety may be reduced.

McClelland and Apicella (1945) have reviewed the previous literature on reactions to frustration extensively in their attempt to devise a classification scheme which would cover all the reactions they obtained in an experimental frustration situation. The scheme which they developed as a result of this investigation is reproduced in Table 13.1 to give a fuller idea of the kind of reactions they obtained and how they defined various categories of classification. They distinguished between *goal-oriented* reactions (attack and substitution) and *defense-oriented* ones (withdrawal and limitation). This is necessary since in any concrete frustration situation reactions occur which are aimed both at obtaining the blocked satisfactions and at reduction of anxiety. The person may shift from one mode of adjustment to another. As they put it, "no mode of adjustment to frustration is completely satisfactory, so a variety of responses are usually attempted, each of which has its goal, but all of which do not fit into a coordinated functional behavior sequence." (1945, p. 385.) Recognizing this constant shifting about in the concrete frustration situation we shall nevertheless pay attention here only to the defensive reactions because we are interested for the moment in frustration not as a single barrier but as a source of conflict-produced tension or motivation, the general goal of which is tension reduction. McClelland and Apicella (1945) were able to distinguish two goals of defensive behavior aimed at decreasing failure, one a kind of denial of the motivation involved (withdrawal) and the other a kind of denial of the reality of the frustration (limitation). In addition they recognized that anger and aggression appeared to have an anxiety-reducing function which did not fit very well into their scheme anywhere. We shall follow their scheme in general and add anger and aggression as a separate method of tension release.

1. Withdrawal. The simplest reaction to a pain-producing situation appears to be to escape from it altogether. The mechanisms of escape have been variously named: e.g., *inhibition, going out of the field, repression.* The primary aim of escape seems to be to reduce the *instigation* to act, as shown in Table 13.1. At one level the subject may in effect say, "I give up" or "I quit," indicating that he refuses to struggle, which is often a way of reducing tension because it eliminates the feedback to drive intensity level from continued conflict (cf. Whiting 1950). At another he may consciously try to forget or inhibit the anxiety-producing situation; he may try to escape it altogether by doing something else, particularly when he is caught between two fears; or he may attempt to reduce anxiety by repressing from consciousness the conflict which gives rise to it. The last mechanism has received most attention from the time that Freud first called attention to it, because it occurs in cases of more severe anxiety which apparently continues to affect the person's behavior even though out of consciousness (cf. Haggard, 1943).

In the process of trying to withdraw from the conflict-producing situation, an individual may adopt some rather unusual measures. *Reaction formation* is one. Here the person is so anxious to prevent the occurrence of the painful situation that he does the direct opposite of the thing he wishes to avoid. A reformed alcoholic approaching a tavern may go so far as to cross the street to avoid a conflict-producing situation. Mowrer (1940) has observed similar behavior in rats that have been taught to press a pedal to avoid a shock. When he added a shock to the pedal, he observed that some of the rats when put into the situation tended to get as far away from the pedal as possible, as if they were actively rejecting their impulse to press it to avoid the shock that was coming. *Phobias* are similar means of making certain that the person will avoid the conflict-producing situation. Thus we find that the psychiatrist says about Karl that his phobias are "protecting him against his hostile trends." In his case the anxiety over expressing aggression is apparently so great that he must protect himself against symbolic representations of it (as in his fear of fire).

It is interesting to speculate on the theoretical possibility that some secondary motives produce so much anxiety that the motive is given up or abandoned altogether. Since we have taken the position that motives are learned, it is at least logically possible that the affective associations on which they are based could be unlearned or markedly altered because of the anxiety they produce. If this happened, one would have a person whose life would be governed largely by primary pleasure and pain and perhaps by the need for relief from anxiety as the only remaining acquired motive. The behavior we would expect from such a person corresponds to the behavior sometimes obtained in schizophrenia, particularly of the simplex and hebephrenic types. In these mental diseases it does appear as if the hierarchy of learned motives has collapsed due to the pressure of anxiety. It is, of course, impossible to say at this stage of the game what causes the collapse, but it is at least logically possible that the cause may lie either in a defect in the formation of the original strong affective associations on which secondary motives depend or in the unusual pressures to which they are subjected in later life.

2. **Conversion and Limitation.** Just as a person may escape anxiety by withdrawal or giving up, he may also attempt to get relief by altering the situation which produces the anxiety. This does not refer to restriving or renewed attempts at solving the conflict, but to attempts at reducing anxiety by changing the *interpretation* of the frustration which produces the conflict. What is involved is perhaps best illustrated by Anna Freud's discussion (1937) of the way children may deny reality when they are under conflict. They may simply say that it is "not so" that they have been bad. They may reverse the real facts, "lie," or pretend that the world is different and more in line with their wishes. She argues that children are better able than are adults to reduce their tensions by altering reality. But adults use the same approach: when they do, it is called *rationalization.* People reduce the anxiety connected with a conflict situation by reinterpreting the situation so that it is no longer as painful. McClelland and Apicella (1945) found, for instance, that students who failed at a particular card-sorting task frequently explained the failure by stating that they had been up late the night before, or that the cards were too sticky to sort, or that it was too hot in the experimental room to work efficiently, etc. (See Table 13.1.)

TABLE 13.1

Classification of Verbal Reactions (R's) to Experimentally Induced Failure

			Related Clinical Mechanisms
. WITHDRAWAL			
Instigation aimed at decreasing failure	Any R directed at changing or avoiding instigation to act		
A. Ego extrication	R avoids by detaching ego from need to continue	"That's about the best I can do." "I can't get it."	Performance without conscious ego-involvement, automatisms
B. Rejection	R avoids by trying not to continue	"Have I got to stay here 'til I get 45?" "You couldn't take me away from this for awhile."	Repression Negativism Encysting Aus dem Felde gehen
. ATTACK			
Instrumental Act aimed at increasing success	Any R aimed at overcoming obstacle to get achievement		
A. Intensified R including aggression	R is an attempt to break through what are perceived as obstacles to success	(Slamming cards)	Fixation Persistent non-adjustive affective R
1. at self		"C——, I'm good."	Suicide
2. at experimenter		"I know I failed you s——."	Displaced aggression
3. at cards		"Come here you b——."	Displaced aggression
4. at psychology		"Thank G——, I don't take this stuff."	Displaced aggression
B. Varied R	R is an attempt to solve problem by circumventing obstacle	(Shifting deck or sorting method) "Keep your eyes on me or I'll cheat."	Instrumental act regression Instrumental act phantasy Asking for help
. LIMITATION			

	Definition	Sample Remarks	Related Mechanisms
. LIMITATION—*Continued*			
A. Rationalization	R limits by explaining inapplicability of super ego standards for performance	"I could do better if I couldn't see you." "I didn't get enough sleep last night." "It's too hot."	Rationalization Projection Delusions
B. Isolation	R limits by referring failure to unimportant super ego standards	"All right, so I am a far-below-average card-sorter." "You won't tell anyone, will you?"	Isolation Conversion symptoms
C. Humor	R limits by referring failure to inappropriate super ego standards	"I'm a homicidal maniac." "I'm ignorant . . . a freak." "I hope you brought your supper."	Silliness Cynicism
. SUBSTITUTION			
Goal Response aimed at increasing success	Any R aimed at getting some secondary satisfaction out of the situation		
A. Anger, excitement	R is a seeking for satisfaction by "release of tension" or by "drowning anxiety"	(Swearing) "Ah, s——!" "G—— d——."	Catharsis, masochism Hysterical crying
B. Socially approved R's	R is a seeking for satisfaction by making socially approved R's to failure	"I'm sorry." "I'll do my damnedest." "This is miserable."	Confession Apology Nonchalance
C. Subgoal satisfaction	R is a seeking for satisfaction through subgoal achievement in task	"I'll set a poor level." "That's some better." (Predicting failure accurately)	Changes in level of aspiration
D. Sympathism	R is a seeking for satisfaction by asking for comfort from E	"Honest, you make me feel just terrible."	
			Goal response regression Identification Indirect compensation

Other clinically defined defense mechanisms which belong under this heading include: *isolation,* or the attempt to repress not the whole conflict but its painful affect; *undoing,* or the attempt to take back an act as if it had never occurred; *projection,* or the attempt to defend oneself by attributing an undesirable characteristic to someone else; and *conversion symptoms,* or the attempt to reduce psychic tensions by converting them into somatic disorders. In all these mechanisms the person is trying to reduce anxiety by substituting a less severe type of tension, by altering the situation in some way or by changing the interpretation of the facts which would normally be given. We might oversimplify the aim of this type of defense by calling it *conversion of fact,* just as we might call the preceding aim *conversion of drive.*

Here, too, we could predict that the overdevelopment of this mode of defense might lead to particular mental disorders. Conversion hysteria has already been mentioned. Others would include paranoia and probably paranoid and catatonic schizophrenia. In all these disorders the person seems to be frantically engaged in attempting to restructure his conception of reality in order to make it less anxiety-producing. If he succeeds in restructuring it in a way which is fairly close to reality, he may develop into a case of true paranoia. If he succeeds only partially and inconsistently, his behavior is characterized by the silly and absurd delusions of the paranoid schizophrenic. If he does not succeed at all but simply keeps working at the problem, he may withdraw into a catatonic stupor in which he continues nevertheless to work at his problem frantically, if we are to believe the reports of individuals who have come out of such stupors (cf. Boisen, 1936). If all these attempts at reinterpretation fail, one might expect a regression to the simple *withdrawal* method of dealing with anxiety. It may be for this reason that catatonic and paranoid schizophrenics tend to slip back into the simple and hebephrenic forms of the same disease.

3. Aggression and Punishment. One of the most mysterious ways of relieving tension is by expressing aggression or by receiving punishment. The theoretical nature of these phenomena is not at all well understood, although they have been the subject of extensive study both by clinical and experimental psychologists. The authors of *Frustration and Aggression* simply state *"the occurrence of any act of aggression is assumed to reduce the instigation to aggression."* (1939, p. 50.) Since they have previously defined the instigation to aggression as being produced by frustration, it follows that they regard aggression as tension reducing. As they point out, this is entirely in line with the psychoanalytic doctrine of *catharsis* which is based on the observation that expression of the emotions reduces intensity, at least temporarily. Thus a psychoanalytically oriented writer like Flugel can write: "Now the infliction of punishment, inasmuch as it implies the natural reaction of aggression, tends to relieve the outraged feelings of those who have been hurt; after its infliction their anger abates, and they tend to regard the incident as closed." (1945, p. 145.)

Yet it is still not clear why aggression should be tension-reducing. The authors of *Frustration and Aggression* attempt to tie up the aggressive response with a strong goal-oriented, attack response on the obstacle to the original instigation. Thus they say *"the strongest instigation, aroused by frustration, is to acts of aggression directed against the agent perceived to be the source of the frustration."* (1939, p. 39.) And they can define aggression independently as *"an act whose goal response is injury to an organism (or organism-surrogate)."* (1939, p. 11.) One difficulty with such a formulation is, as McClelland and Apicella point out, that many explosive, violent acts do not seem aggressive in this limited sense of being directed against some object. Anger seems to *precede* aggression and to have, like the expression of other intense emotions, some tension-reducing capacity of its own *prior* to the discovery of some object against which it may be directed. It is for this reason that these authors put anger and aggression in the category of substitute satisfaction (see Table 13.1). Other theorists do not attempt to derive the tension-reducing capacity of the expression of the emotions, but simply accept it as instinctive. Horney, for instance, has made the suggestion in discussing masochism (1935) that violent expressions of emotion may relieve anxiety by "overwhelming" or "drowning" it. This is consistent with the idea, discussed below in Chapter 14, that the integrity of the self-schema is intimately tied up with the perception of potency which may be violently asserted in such outbursts of emotion. That is, primitive anger may be an attempt at reducing anxiety by an act of self-assertion which serves to maintain the self-image in face of threats from the outside. In this sense anxiety as a threat from without may be "drowned" by a violent outburst of self-will. Whatever the final explanation is, the fact remains that the expression of anger and aggression often does appear to reduce anxiety, at least temporarily, in a way which is not clearly tied up with the instrumental character of the aggressive response in attaining the goal which the person has been prevented from reaching.

Further evidence for this view lies in the fact that aggression does not always strike the source of frustration. It may be *displaced,* if anxiety is associated with expressing it toward the real source of frustration. Thus a child may have a relatively strong instigation to express aggression toward a parent due to the frustrations of socialization but, because of fear of punishment or loss of love, he may not express this aggression directly but displace it toward substitutes, as in the doll-play situation. In such cases it is hard to see how the satisfaction in striking substitutes, etc., derives from the instrumental character of the aggressive response in attaining the original goal. Aggression appears rather to relieve anxiety in some as yet unclearly understood fashion.

The most startling direction which aggression may take is against the self. It is startling because it seems hard to understand, on the surface at least, why self-inflicted pain should reduce anxiety. Yet the phenomenon of self-aggression, *masochism,* or *nemesism,* as it has sometimes been called, is well known and has been extensively treated in the literature. Flugel describes a simple example thus: "The other day I was watching a mother feed her little girl of two. The child resisted the soup that was being offered her in a spoon and endeavored to push away the mother's hand with considerable show of force and displeasure. After a while, however, the mother still persisting, the child suddenly altered her behavior, seized the spoon herself and, without changing in any other way her combative expression, pushed it into her own mouth with quite unnecessary violence and poured the contents down her throat. There occurred indeed a quite unmistakable reversal in the direction of the child's aggression; from being directed against the mother, it was turned against the child's own self, in a way that fulfilled the mother's wishes, but with a kind of savage energy which was quite foreign to the mother's attitude." (1945, pp. 78-79.) Flugel finds the phenomenon so ubiquitous that he adopts the term *need for punishment* to explain it and derives the need for punishment in part from the child's discovery that punishment frequently terminates anxiety-producing occasions. Thus he supposes that the child learns through experience that when he has been bad he will be punished and the punishment serves to express *and end at the same time* the parents' disapproval. In time he may learn to try to bring tension-producing situations to an end by punishing himself in some way. In these terms one can see how the child succeeded, by forcing the food down his own throat, in terminating the anxiety which arose out of the conflict over eating, even if he frustrated his original wish still more in doing so. This seems to be a case in which there is a shift from behavior which is instrumental to the wish not to eat to behavior which is defensive in that it is aimed at reducing the anxiety arising in the course of frustration of the original motive. In the same vein Flugel goes on to explain such paradoxical phenomena as the fact that children sometimes are happier after punishment (cf. Levy and Munroe, 1938), the fact that some people are happier under the external pressure of disaster or harsh treatment and worry more when things go well, and the fact that some people commit suicide. People in a depressive psychotic state even go so far as to introject the faults of others and then blame themselves for these faults. In short, many people often show a considerable amount of hostility toward themselves and appear to need punishment which, when it occurs, relieves their anxiety. The trouble is, as Flugel himself recognizes, that punishment and frustration under other circumstances increase rather than allay anxiety. Self-aggression doesn't *always* produce relief; sometimes it increases anxiety. Why? The fact is that we do not as yet clearly understand the function of self-aggression nor exactly in what sense or under what conditions it produces relief from anxiety. We simply know it occurs with considerable frequency.

The authors of *Frustration and Aggression* have gone a little further and attempted at least to state conditions under which self-punishment is more likely to occur. In the first place, they state that "*instigation to self-aggression should be relatively stronger when the source of frustration is perceived to be the self than when it is perceived to be some external agent.*" (1939, p. 48.) This would appear to be true on the surface. Thus a person who has two strong conflicting motives or who feels that he is constantly failing to live up to his ego-ideal standards ought to perceive himself as the source of the anxiety which is so painful to him. Since it has been assumed by these authors that aggression toward the source of frustration is instinctively relieving, it follows that the person in such a conflict would be more apt to become aggressive toward himself. There are two difficulties with this position. One is the problem of why aggression, particularly if directed against the self, should relieve tension, especially when it apparently does not do so all the time. The second arises from the fact that the person's perception of the source of frustration is often not very accurate. Thus a person may wrongly introject the fault of another and blame himself for it, or he may project onto another the blame which in reality is his own. Yet, in the present state of our knowledge, we cannot say why he introjects or projects. Consequently it does not help too much to say that self-aggression occurs when the self is perceived as the source of frustration.

The second reason for self-aggression is inhibition of aggression by the self rather than by an external agent. "Restraint by an external agent of an act of aggression, consequently, should instigate aggression against that agent; and self-restraint of an act of aggression should instigate aggression against the self." (Dollard *et al.*, 1939, p. 48.) There seems to be evidence for this statement in Mackinnon's finding (Murray, 1938) that intropunitive subjects (those who tend to blame themselves) were more often subjected to "psychological" discipline in their childhood than were extrapunitive subjects who tend to blame others when things go wrong. In other words, the intropunitives had been restrained from aggression and other unsocial acts as children, not by external force, but by the development of internal standards of conscience. Consequently these internal restraints would more often be perceived as frustrators by them and aggression should consequently be more often directed against the self for imposing them—which was, in fact, the case.

Finally, aggression tends to be directed against the self when other avenues of aggression are inhibited. This suggests "an inverse relationship between the occurrence of different forms of aggression" (1939, p. 51), in support of which the authors of *Frustration and Aggression* cite the following instance. "In the sleep-deprivation experiment, the subject who made the gory drawing was rated as expressing the most overt aggression. In a self-administered algesimeter test he pricked (injured) himself with the least pressure of any subject. By contrast, another subject, who seemed to be slightly nauseated by the experiment, was rated as expressing the least overt aggression and, in the algesimeter test, he inflicted more injurious pressure upon himself than did any of the other subjects." (1939, p. 52.) The idea that one channel of aggression can substitute for another is derived originally from Freudian theory and has received very wide acceptance, but actually there is very little direct evidence to support it. In fact, Stone's study (1950) of the effects of rewarded overt aggression among football players indicates if anything that there is a *positive* rather than an inverse relation among the various forms of aggression. Those players who showed high aggression on the field tended to show high covert aggression too. For every case of a player who, as in the above quotation, was low in overt aggression and rated as high in self-aggression, there was an opposite case of a man who was either high on overt aggression and high on self-aggression or low on overt aggression and extrapunitive, etc. Furthermore, the football team as a whole showed no evidence of a decrease in imaginative aggression after an afternoon of expressing overt aggression in football practice. All of these facts tend to throw some doubt on the idea that there is a kind of reservoir of aggression which may be lowered by expression through various channels which may substitute for each other if one happens to be blocked. There is at least as much evidence for the alternative hypothesis that expression of aggression in any form *increases* the probability of expression in other ways by generalization and transfer.

So while the clues suggested by Dollard *et al.* (1939) as to when self-aggression occurs represent an important step forward, they leave many problems still to be solved. In addition to the difficulties mentioned already, one could argue, as some theorists have, that instead of self-punishment being derived from displacement inward of aggression toward others, it is really primary (in the sense of overriding anxiety by violent masochistic emotion) and aggression outward a secondary learned development (the discovery of an object against which the violence can be directed). For another thing, the explanation of the need for punishment in terms of aggression displaced inward does not appear to account very well for all the facts discussed by Flugel. For instance, he notes that *reparation* and *confession* often serve as substitutes for self-punishment. Confession in particular, which has been recognized for centuries as a means of allaying anxiety, does not seem to have as its aim the injury of the self—an aim which it should have if it is an example of aggression displaced inward. The whole question needs further study.

The overdevelopment of the aggressive and self-punishing methods of reducing anxiety ought to lead to violent emotional displays or to severe self-accusations. Both characterize the manic-depressive psychosis which has been traced by Flugel (1945), Freud, and other psychoanalysts to the tendency to adopt aggression and self-punishment as defenses against anxiety. So the particular classification we have made of the three major modes of defense against anxiety has at least the advantage of running parallel to the traditional psychiatric classification of the major psychoses. Thus we have related schizophrenia (especially the simplex and hebephrenic types) to withdrawal as the dominant mode of defense, paranoia and paranoid schizophrenia to conversion of facts, and manic-depression to aggression and self-punishment. This is, however, no more than an interesting coincidence: we clearly do not know enough about defense mechanisms or about these psychoses to make any rigorous connection between them. The value of the classification lies solely in suggesting that the breakdown proposed here has been found of use elsewhere. For the point of all this discussion is that *some* classification, *some* simplification among the thousand and one defense mechanisms identified in the clinical literature, has got to take place before we can proceed to the next step of trying to find the conditions which lead to one defense rather than another. We are in the position of a biologist who must identify and classify his species of animal before he can study the conditions under which it thrives, disappears, etc. To the extent that a mechanism like aggression in all its forms can be identified, the conditions of which it is a function can be systematically investigated. By the same token we need to define other major types of defense so that they can be studied in the same way.

Lest this discussion seem too general, consider the problem of *regression* for a moment. Here is a defense mechanism which was derived originally from psychoanalytic theory about stages in the development of the libido, and as such has received extensive treatment in the clinical literature. Lewin has also been interested in it and has demonstrated that regression in the sense of primitivization or dedifferentiation of behavior occurs as one result of frustration (Barker, Dembo, and Lewin, 1940). There have also been extensive animal studies on the subject (cf. Sears, 1943). But on closer analysis it appears that there are many different kinds of regression and that progress in the field is not likely to be made until they are distinguished from each other. Sears, for instance, points out that there is *instrumental act* regression—e.g., a return to an earlier mode of attaining a goal, as when a rat frustrated in one habit returns to an earlier one—and there is also *goal-response* regression—e.g., the return to an earlier form of gratification when a later and presumably more mature one is frustrated, as when a person frustrated in heterosexual activity returns to autoeroticism. But we can push the distinctions still further: If our previous analysis is correct, we would have to argue that neither instrumental or goal-response regression is *necessarily* a defense mechanism. Technically it is possible for either to be part of the adjustment to the original instigation (varied instrumental activity or substitute goal) rather than defenses against anxiety which has arisen out of conflict and frustration. Regression *as a defense* will doubtless be found to obey different laws from regression which is a means to attaining in some form the originally frustrated goal response. Furthermore, after such a breakdown as this it may seem preferable to define regression in such a way that it fits under such general modes of defense as withdrawal or conversion so that the process of discovering general principles will be simplified. In short, it is only as we make our taxonomy of the defense mechanisms simpler and more systematic that we will be able to learn more about the conditions under which they occur in much the same way as we have begun to explore the nature of aggression.

Conditions Influencing the Choice of Defense Mechanism. Is there anything at all that can be said about the factors which determine the appearance of one mode of reducing anxiety rather than another? Anna Freud says quite frankly that "the considerations which determine the ego's choice of mechanism remain uncertain." (1937, p. 54.) She is undoubtedly correct and part of the reason lies in the way in which the defense mechanisms are defined: since they overlap, have no agreed-upon operational definitions, and are not related in any systematic way, it has been difficult to do any systematic research on them. Still, some very general and obvious conditions are known to influence the choice of reaction. For instance, past experience is known to have an effect: people apparently tend to use one type of reaction with a fair degree of consistency. The many positive and significant correlations obtained by Murray and his co-workers (1938) among reactions of the same group of subjects to different test situations would lend support to this hypothesis. As a specific example of this sort Sarason and Rosenzweig (1942) report a significant correlation of .54 between inability to recall failures in the interruption-of-tasks experiment and tendency to give predominantly "glossing over" (impunitive) reactions to frustration in the Picture-Frustration Study. Rephrased in our terms, this finding means that subjects behaved consistently in at least two situations in the extent to which they used withdrawal as a means of handling potential anxiety.

As further evidence of the effect of learning Keister (1938) has shown that children can be taught to adopt new methods of handling frustration. Actually her concern was to get the children to show less defensive behavior and more problem-solving behavior. She found that by encouragement, gradual increase in difficulty of tasks, etc., she could get children to postpone the "giving up" or withdrawal response and to work longer and harder at the task of trying to lift a heavy box off a toy. This demonstrates that learning does have an effect on the type of reaction a person gives to frustration, although it does not specifically treat the problem of which mode of defense is likely to be chosen, granted that some particular one is necessary.

Anticipation of punishment should at least theoretically influence the choice of reaction, and Dollard *et al.* (1939) assume that it does. Specifically, they state that the fear of punishment tends to inhibit aggression and therefore to shift emphasis to other types of adjustment (e.g., withdrawal or conversion). As an illustrative example, Doob and Sears (1939) have shown in a questionnaire study on types of reaction to frustration that in general the greater the fear of punishment, the more the subjects' reactions shifted from aggression to some substitute response. The only difficulty with this finding is that it does not deal specifically with the problem of whether the person is oriented around anxiety reduction or around attaining the original goal in some form. That is, we know from previous discussion of Maier's (1949) and Gwinn's (1949) studies of rats and from the doll-play studies that punishment for a response may add to the total instigation to make the response, provided the response is aimed at reducing tension in the first place. In short, it is not at all clear that punishment of an anxiety-reducing response will necessarily inhibit it though it is clearer that punishment of a response which is simply instrumental to attaining a particular goal *will* tend to inhibit it.

Is there a natural hierarchy of reactions within the defense category? This possibility has not been fully explored. One could argue, for instance, that the first defense is anger-aggression, the second rationalization or reality conversion, and the third withdrawal, and that one could expect such a sequence of responses among people who were subjected to increasingly intense anxieties. Such a possibility does not seem very likely. McClelland and Apicella (1945) found no evidence for a regular sequence of responses on the first, second, and third reactions to frustration as anxiety was presumably getting more intense due to the cumulative effects of previous frustration. What seems more likely is that there is a hierarchy of defensive reactions for a given individual which can be discovered through prolonged frustration (cf. Dembo, 1931), but which is different for different individuals. The question still remains open, as Anna Freud says, as to what the factors are which determine the position in the hierarchy.

A Conceptual Problem. Can modes of reducing anxiety be considered in any sense to be needs or motives? If a person adopts a consistent mode of handling anxiety by withdrawal, could he not be said to have a high n Autonomy? In similar fashion a person who used rationalization, etc., as a defense might be considered to have a high n Defendance, one who used aggression as having high n Aggression, one who used self-aggression as having a high n Abasement, and the like. What exactly is the difference, if any, between a consistent mode of defense and a need? To answer such a question we will have to go back a little in our conceptual scheme and recall that we have previously argued that avoidance drives are based on strong affective associations involving pain or fear of pain. On this basis we were led to speak of fear drives such as f Rejection as distinct from drives such as n Affiliation. With this in mind we can diagram the situation rather simply as follows:

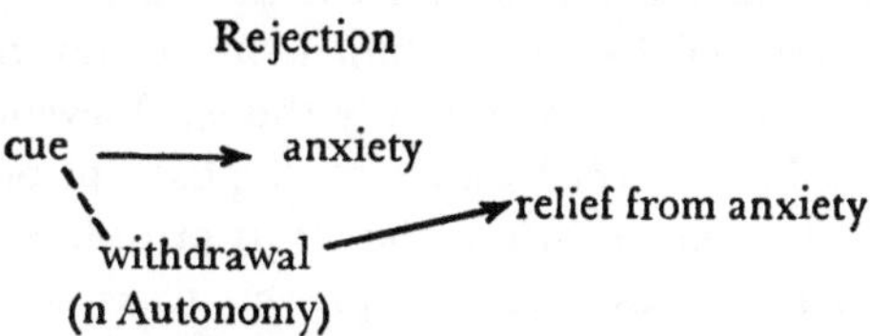

This diagram shows how a cue (a woman, for instance) might come to arouse by past association a fear of rejection and how a particular means of reducing this anxiety might be developed, such as withdrawal, which we can name n Autonomy with some reservation. The reason for the reservation is that n Autonomy may also be based on strong *positive* affective associations, as, for instance, when a person develops a love for the woods because of strong sensuous and activity pleasures gained there, etc. In the diagrammed situation it is still the strong negative affective association which is really primary and one might suppose that the particular mode of reducing the anxiety involved in it (n Autonomy) might vary more since it is presumably secondary and based on somewhat later, more highly discriminated learning than is the affective association on which it is based. Thus it seems slightly preferable in this case to talk about f Rejection and modes of handling it rather than about n Autonomy, even though we may recognize that defensive modes function in many respects like motives since they get strongly associated with the positive affect associated with relief from tension. Actually at the present stage of our knowledge this is largely a conceptual problem which can best be resolved when we know more about how such needs function as compared with needs based on positive affective associations.

Karl's Motive Structure As Derived From Its Effects. Throughout this chapter we have emphasized the importance of studying the effects of experimentally induced motivation on behavior. The results of such studies can also be used to gain insight into the individual case. If, for instance, we know that motives of high intensity have such and such effects on imagination, we would seem justified in concluding that a person who shows those imaginal characteristics under normal conditions would be a person with high motivation in that area. At least this is the assumption in terms of which McClelland, Atkinson, Clark, and Lowell have operated (1950) with some success. More explicitly a man's score for a particular motive like n Achievement can be obtained by having him write stories under standard conditions and then counting up only those achievement characteristics appearing in his record which, on the basis of previous experimentation, are known to shift as the result of induced achievement motivation. In Karl's case, for example, his n Achievement score is +12, which is the highest in the initial sample in which the range was from —4 to +12 with a mean of 3.13 and standard deviation of 4.25. Thus we have direct confirmation for the hypothesis based on a clinical analysis of his TAT in Chapter 11 that Karl has a very high n Achievement. The justification for totaling up the achievement characteristics in this way is partly practical: it produces a score which relates in a meaningful way to a number of other behavioral characteristics; and partly theoretical: it seems likely that a person with high n Achievement will spend more of his time thinking about achievement problems and working out new and different angles on them so that when he is asked to write stories, he will be more likely to produce a larger number of different achievement-related responses.

What is perhaps more interesting is a study of the particular kinds of imagery Karl used in writing his stories under standard conditions to the four slides used to get a measure of his achievement motivation. All four of his achievement stories contained *general* achievement imagery (long-term concern with success or failure) and three of them had a plot centering around achievement. Furthermore, three contained an explicitly stated wish for achievement, some kind of instrumental activity, and some anticipation of future success or failure. In short, there is every indication that Karl's record contains the future references, interrelatedness, and sensitization so characteristic of high motivation in any field. But what about the deprivation characteristics? Here his record is interesting. None of his plots deals with what is technically called a "deprivation thema" —a plot in which a person is in a serious achievement difficulty which he has to overcome. On the other hand, two of the three instrumental acts are unsuccessful, as are three of the four outcomes. And affect is negative in two out of three cases. In short, this begins to look like the "inadequacy thema" all over again that we found in the full TAT and analyzed in Chapter 11. Karl has intense concern with and hopes of future and long-run success, but there is no indication of realistically successful next steps. In fact, in two cases when the hero of the stories is blocked in his achievement efforts, he turns to some substitute goal or activity, which is a rather rare characteristic of such stories (McClelland, Clark, Roby, and Atkinson, 1949). If our argument about the three stages in thinking associated with increasing drive is correct, then Karl would have to be described as between the "reality-oriented" and "defensive" stages. There is some reality orientation (instrumental activity) but it is unsuccessful and there is not the usual concern with obstacles to be overcome (deprivation thema, blocks) which is usually associated with this stage. The defensive orientation is indicated by the emphasis on goal affects and anticipations of long-run success. His head is in the clouds as he stumbles over his next steps. His motto might be: *ad astra per aspera,* with emphasis on the stars rather than the difficulties which are not clearly perceived.

Although such an analysis as this is interesting and suggestive, it should be taken as no more than that, since there is as yet no evidence as to how representative the sample of his achievement ideas is which is obtained in response to these four pictures. Atkinson (1950a) has found that even the over-all achievement score obtained by summing characteristics has a reliability of only .60 to .70 at most, which is not adequate for interpretation of individual scores.

The stability of sub-characteristics such as we have been dealing with here is not known. Thus the only value of such an analysis is that it illustrates how some of the trends discussed earlier may be found in the individual case and how, ultimately, more precise quantitative indexes can be found for some of the qualitative methods of TAT analysis discussed in Chapter 11.

Finally, we should like to know something about Karl's reactions to frustration, his modes of handling anxiety. There is considerable information on this point in his case materials, some of which has already been mentioned in other connections. More specific treatment of the problem will be avoided here because we will want to ask for predictions as to how he handles frustration in the prediction questionnaire in Chapter 15.

NOTES AND QUERIES

1. What is the difference between a trait and defense mechanism? Is one easier to alter or extinguish than the other? What criteria would you set up for determining whether a given pattern of responses was one or the other?

2. Can you set up criteria which will distinguish behaviorally between instrumental and goal-response aggression? Stone (1950) in his study of football players, for instance, felt that he must be able to distinguish between aggression which was just pushing another player out of the way (instrumental aggression) and which was hitting someone unnecessarily. He managed to get several criteria of difference that he could use in movies of a game. Can you think of some? Is the distinction an important one? Should the two kinds of aggression obey different laws?

3. Is instrumental aggression the same thing as "Obstacle Dominance" in the Rosenzweig Picture-Frustration Study? (cf. Rosenzweig, Fleming, and Clarke, 1947). Try to fit the other categories used to score this test into the general classification of defense mechanisms adopted in this chapter.

4. Can you think of ways of distinguishing between the "pseudo repression" caused by simple autistic fantasies at low levels of motivation and "real" repression caused by anxiety at high levels of motivation? Should repeated attempts to remember on different occasions have different effects on the two kinds of repression? Should an increase in motivation or a threat of punishment for not remembering have different effects?

5. It has sometimes been argued (cf. Langer, 1943) that fantasy is primarily wish-fulfilling, which is a somewhat inaccurate translation of Freud's contention that all dreams are motivated. Evaluate this argument in terms of the evidence for the effects of motivation on imagination. Are there reasons why covert trial and error should obey different laws from overt trial and error?

6. Introspection as practiced in the early days of psychology has largely fallen into disuse. Why? In what sense has it been taken out, dusted off, and used again in experiments reported in this chapter?

7. Is there a difference between reactions to frustration and modes of reducing anxiety? Does it depend on how you define "frustration"? Point out the difference, for instance, between "reactions to barrier" and "reactions to threat" (cf. Maslow, 1943b).

8. There has been no discussion in this chapter of the extensive literature on whether motivation facilitates learning or only performance (cf. Postman, 1947, for a discussion). In terms of our theoretical analysis, make a case for its influencing either. Under what circumstances, for instance, will one association (such as the affective one involved in a motive) facilitate the acquisition of another association? Or why should increased output of responses result from the arousal of an affective association as compared with other types of associations? How might increased output of responses actually facilitate learning?

9. What do you think is the explanation for the fact that experimentally starved subjects in Minnesota were constantly obsessed by thoughts of food while starving people in Germany apparently were not? Is it a difference in intensity level of motivation or in the situation? If the latter, what is the critical difference in the two situations and how would you go about testing any hypothesis you arrive at?

Part Five

SUMMARY AND INTEGRATION

14

Conceptions of the Self

Every book on personality should have a chapter on the self. Traditionally, as Allport points out (1943), the concept of the ego or self has been central in the study of personality, but it has been neglected in recent years largely because psychologists have not been able to figure out operations for performing experiments on the self. Our problem then is a difficult one. On the one hand, we may accept the conviction that the self is important; on the other, we must treat it without the benefit of any considerable body of experimental data. Since much that has been written about the self is in the nature of speculations which cannot easily be proved or disproved, we shall try to limit ourselves to speculations which either have or could have operational definitions.

In terms of our over-all scheme for analyzing personality, the self clearly belongs in the category of schemata. Included among the ideas a person has about the world is one about the nature of himself. It is one of the most important ideas that he has and has many characteristics, only a few of which we will be able to discuss in detail. In many ways, the schema a person has of himself is like a conception that another person might have of him. For example, we have developed a rather extensive, somewhat coherent picture of Karl. Although Karl has not been guided by any such systematic purpose as ours, he too has built up a self-conception out of years of experience with himself, which is doubtless like ours in many respects. In fact, he has many more data to build on than we do: all of his experiences of himself are "firsthand," whereas ours are secondhand at best. He has the whole population of episodes to draw on; we have only a sample. His advantage may be compensated for to some extent by the fact that we are presumably more disinterested than he and should therefore be in a better position to interpret much of what has happened to him. However, anyone working in personality should have a healthy respect for an individual's own picture of himself—if for no other reason than that he is speaking out of very much more experience than anyone else could ever have. Occasionally psychotherapists forget this; so it has been a healthy corrective to have Rogers (1942) emphasizing in his writings on nondirective therapy the great importance which should be attached to the person's self-picture and self-knowledge.

Starting with this therapeutic orientation, Rogers and his students have collected some of the best empirical data on ideas about the self. A typical recorded interview contains remarks like the following:

S166. Solved self-centeredism and selfishness. Solved my worry problems a great deal. In fact, I'm not worrying about appearance so much any more. People are gonna like me whatever I wear. If they don't like me as I am, they won't like me at all. And why put on an act? I used to put on acts all the time. They were to cover up, though. They were to cover up for myself. I didn't want people to know. I was terribly shy. I still am, but—I acted beyond them. That is, put on an acting air of superiority to cover up because I felt so inferior to them. I tried to make them feel inferior to me. That's why I never had any friends. Oh, I had a few. It wasn't till I—I really didn't start living until January of this year. Then I started everything. That's when I stopped bucking the teachers. That's when I stopped trying to antagonize people. That's when I tried to get friends. That's when I began to get friends. (Snyder, 1947, p. 79.)

So much of the content of these interviews is oriented around the self that it has become customary to summarize them with self-characterizing statements like the following:

I don't worry about my appearance any more—and not so much about self-consciousness.

I'm depressed about having to go home in three weeks.

Girls are puzzling and annoying; how to behave with them worries me.

I hate my appearance; I've always tried to compensate for it.

I like to pity myself. (Snyder, 1947, p. 86.)

If we look closely at statements like these, we note that they are not unlike those which a psychologist might make about a student after studying him. That is, the boy describes himself as having certain traits (socially inhibited, fussy about his appearance), certain role perceptions ("Girls are puzzling and annoying."), etc. In other words, he has observed his behavior just as a psychologist might have, and out of his experience with himself he develops rather unsystematically a self-picture which is similar in many respects to the one that the scientist might develop using the same data. The important point is, however, that the person may make mistakes in conceptualizing himself (just as the outside observer may!). He may wrongly evaluate something that happened to him or something that he did and the resulting picture which he draws may be distorted in some very important way, at least in terms of the judgment of others working from the same data. It is this discrepancy between the self-concept and the "real" self as the therapist sees it which forms the basis for much maladjustment, according to Rogers (1942, 1947).

Karl's Conception of Himself. To get an idea of the nature and extent of some of these discrepancies in the conception of the self let us take a look at Karl's self-picture. He gives us a fairly complete description of himself as an adolescent as follows:

> I was always cooperative and obedient, a good student, but influenced by others which sometimes led me into trouble. I was always sensitive and my feelings were and still are easily hurt.
>
> I went to school, grammar school, at five, graduated at thirteen years of age. Very good marks, head of the class of eighteen. I always liked geography and history. Got the best marks in these courses. Liked math least of all although I received good marks in it. I had many friendships (got along alright with the teachers) and was regarded favorably by other boys and girls. I was always bashful around girls and was kidded a lot about it. I was very gregarious. In the younger days, third and fourth grade, I was occasionally picked on, but after a couple of fist fights which I was goaded into I was left alone.
>
> In high school my marks were excellent. I was at the head of the class, in many activities, president of the class for four years, on the football team, all-state guard, editor of the school paper. I worked well with all groups. My high school days were very happy and gratifying ones. I was very ambitious, wished to become a chemical engineer. I always did my work conscientiously and thoroughly and never wasted a minute. I always went to Sunday school, kept myself pure and led a fairly model life. I graduated when seventeen years of age. I was confident working in groups when I knew the people, received cooperation and was usually chairman or a "wheel." I was very anxious to get ahead in the world and was very zealous toward going to college.
>
> For amusement I played sports, went to the movie shows, etc., but not as much as the average. I was sometimes more content to sit home and read. I did a great deal of reading during my youth. I had no particular heroes. I always liked the cowboy heroes of the Westerns, Tarzan, and others in the Saturday serials. I looked up to my football coach to an extent but not too greatly.

In this brief space he makes it clear what his traits were (e.g., bashful, gregarious, sensitive), what his conceptions were of what happened to him of importance (president of the class, on the football team, editor of the school paper), what his motives were ("I . . . wished to become a chemical engineer"), and also how he evaluated himself ("I was very confident working in groups . . . led a fairly model life"). These aspects of personality are touched on in typical self-descriptions just as they are in descriptions by psychologists trying to give an adequate theoretical formulation.

Karl's autobiography was written, however, some six to eight years after the period which this section describes. Would it not then be particularly subject to errors of memory or systematic biases? What evidence have we that Karl really had a similar picture of himself at the time these things were taking place? Fortunately we have some such evidence. A day or two after he arrived at college, when he was seventeen, he took the Strong Vocational Interest Test, which contains a long section entitled "Rating of Present Abilities and Characteristics." His answers to this section of the test will provide us with information on two points: (a) the extent to which his recollected self-picture agrees with the one he had at the time and (b) the extent to which an "over-all" picture agrees with one based on answers to a number of very specific questions. His answers to this section of the Strong Test are reproduced in full in Table 14.1.

TABLE 14.1

Karl's Answers to Part VIII of the Strong Vocational Interest Blank When He Was Seventeen

Part VIII. Rating of Present Abilities and Characteristics. Indicate below what kind of a person you are right now and what you have done. Check in the *first* column ("Yes") if the item really describes you, in the *third* column ("No") if the item does not describe you, and in the *second* column (?) if you are not sure. (Be frank in pointing out your weak points, for selection of a vocation must be made in terms of them as well as your strong points.)

		YES	*?*	*NO*
361	Usually start activities of my group	X		
362	Usually drive myself steadily (do not work by fits and starts)		X	
363	Win friends easily	X		
364	Usually get other people to do what I want done		X	
365	Usually liven up the group on a dull day	X		
366	Am quite sure of myself		X	
367	Accept just criticism without getting sore	X		
368	Have mechanical ingenuity (inventiveness)			X
369	Have more than my share of novel ideas			X

370	Can carry out plans assigned by other people	X	
371	Can discriminate between more or less important matters	X	
372	Am inclined to keep silent (reticent) in confidential and semi-confidential affairs		X
373	Am always on time with my work		X
374	Remember faces, names, and incidents better than the average person		X
375	Can correct others without giving offense	X	
376	Able to meet emergencies quickly and effectively	X	
377	Get "rattled" easily		X
378	Can write a concise, well-organized report	X	
379	Have good judgment in appraising values		X
380	Plan my work in detail	X	
381	Follow up subordinates effectively		X
382	Put drive into the organization	X	
383	Stimulate the ambition of my associates	X	
384	Show firmness without being easy	X	
385	Win confidence and loyalty	X	
386	Smooth out tangles and disagreements between people	X	
387	Am approachable	X	
388	Discuss my ideals with others	X	

Check in the first, second, or third column at the right according as the first, second, or third statement in each item below applies to you.

	(1)	(2)	(3)	(1st)	(2nd)	(3rd)
389	Feelings easily hurt	Feelings hurt sometimes	Feelings rarely hurt	(X)	( )	( )
390	Usually ignore the feelings of others	Consider them sometimes	Carefully consider them	( )	( )	(X)
391	Loan money to acquaintances	Loan only to certain people	Rarely loan money	(X)	( )	( )
392	Rebel inwardly at orders from another, obey when necessary	Carry out instructions with little or no feeling	Enter into situation and enthusiastically carry out program	(X)	( )	( )
393	When caught in a mistake usually make excuses	Seldom make excuses	Practically never make excuses	(X)	( )	( )

TABLE 14.1 (*Continued*)

	(1)	(2)	(3)	(1st)	(2nd)	(3rd)
394	Best-liked friends are superior to me in ability	Equal in ability	Inferior in ability	( )	(X)	( )
395	Handle complaints without getting irritated	Become annoyed at times	Lose my temper at times	( )	(X)	( )
396	Borrow frequently (for personal use)	Borrow occasionally	Practically never borrow	( )	(X)	( )
397	Tell jokes well	Seldom tell jokes	Practically never tell jokes	( )	(X)	( )
398	My advice sought by many	Sought by few	Practically never asked	(X)	( )	( )
399	Frequently make wagers	Occasionally make wagers	Never make wagers	(X)	( )	( )
400	Worry considerably about mistakes	Worry very little	Do not worry	( )	(X)	( )

(Reprinted from Vocational Interest Blank for Men [Revised] by Edward K. Strong, Jr. with permission of the author and of the publishers, Stanford University Press.)

What kind of a self-picture emerges from such a multiplicity of specific remarks about himself? The Strong Test scoring schemes are of no assistance to us because they are not designed for content analyses of this sort. Yet there is a great deal of information contained in his self-ratings that we should be able to use somehow. In fact, methodologically such ratings seem superior to the kind of over-all picture of himself that Karl gives some years later in his autobiography, since an over-all picture can be more easily slanted than a large number of specific judgments. Our approach to this material can be along the lines we adopted in making an inductive analysis of his answers to the questionnaire on religious attitudes: We can list in one column the characteristics he says he has, those which he denies, and those which he is doubtful about. If this is done, his statements about himself can be rather easily summarized under four main headings:

1. I am a self-starter, have lots of drive and initiative and energy. I don't hang back. (Items 361, 363, 365, 372, 376, 382, 383, 384, 385. 386, 398, 399)

2. My relation to others is very important to me. I need friendship and am sensitive in social relations. (Items 363, 367, 375, 389, 391, 393, 398)

3. I am not too sure of myself or self-confident, especially in telling others what to do. (Items 362, 364, 366, 379, 381, 389, 395, 397)

4. I am efficient in doing a job but don't possess unusual abilities. (Items 368, 369, 373, 374, 378, 380)

For the most part this picture is supplementary to the one which he gives in his autobiography, and agrees with it in most essentials. However, it serves to organize somewhat differently the perception of the self. Thus in the Strong Test he makes it much clearer that his leadership, as reflected in the various positions he held in high school, was of the stimulating sort but that he was so sensitive to the opinions of others that he found it difficult to be an authoritarian leader. This is stated somewhat indirectly in his autobiographical sketch as follows: "I was very confident working in groups when I knew the people, received cooperation and was usually chairman or a 'wheel.' " Here he does imply that his leadership is dependent upon the confidence of others and that this is very important to him. But the answers to repeated individual items make it clearer just how sensitive he was and how dependent his leadership was on the cooperation of others. Furthermore, the Strong answers emphasize more than the autobiography how energetic he conceived himself to be, possibly because in writing an autobiography he did not want to overpraise himself. But the two pictures are essentially congruent and serve to support one another and reinforce interpretations which might be drawn from either one.

Karl's Conception Compared with Ours. Now how does all this agree with the picture we have formed of Karl? We may not have as much data as he did, but we have better techniques for analyzing aspects of his behavior which he doubtless did not focus on, and we may feel that we are freer from systematic biases than he was. Table 14.2 presents a summary list of the traits we concluded he had in Chapter 7 and tests the extent to which he mentions the same or similar traits either in his autobiographical statement or in his answers to the Strong Test.

TABLE 14.2

Comparison of the Extent to Which Karl Perceives His Traits As We Have Conceptualized Them

Karl's traits (Chapter 7)	*Relevant autobiographical comments*	*Relevant answers to items on the Strong Test*
1. Energetic	"in many activities" "on the football team," etc.	361, 376, 377, 382
2. Expansive		
3. Non-analytic		374 (378)
4. Fluent	"I did a great deal of reading"	(369), 382, 383, 365
5. Outer orientation		388, 399
6. Variable in performance		362, 373
7. Emotionally labile	"my feelings were and still are easily hurt"	366, 389, 395
8. Emotionally expressive		372, 388
9. Gregarious	"many friendships" "very gregarious"	363, 375, 383, 385, 386, 387, 390, 391
10. Submissive, adaptable	"cooperative, obedient" "influenced by others"	364, 370, 381 (382), (392)
11. Conscientious	"I always did my work conscientiously and thoroughly"	371,396

In this table the item numbers in parentheses in Column 3 indicate responses which do not seem consistent with columns 1 and 2. On the whole there is considerable agreement between our perception of Karl's traits and his own, although it is difficult to make any precise estimate as to the amount of agreement. More striking than any disagreements are the number of instances in which there is no information on a particular trait. Neither in the autobiography nor the self-ratings is there any statement which can be readily related to a trait of "expansiveness," for instance. The reason for this is probably that such a trait did not appear important either to Karl or to Strong in making up his Vocational Interest Self-Rating Scale, whereas "gregariousness" seemed of central importance to both. Thus it is apparent that the amount of congruence between a self-picture and a systematic trait conceptualization will be a function of the conceptual common ground of each.

Congruence will also be in part a function of the "negative" tone of the trait in question. Karl says little or nothing in his autobiography about his "variability" in performance. In fact, from such statements as "I always did my work conscientiously and thoroughly and never wasted a minute," we would be led to infer that he was a regular, methodical worker who always handed his papers in on time, etc. Yet in the more specific self-ratings he confesses that he is irregular much as we had concluded from his performance on an anagrams test as reported in Chapter 6. He sees that he has difficulty "driving himself steadily" (Item 362) and is "not always on time with his work" (Item 373). This discrepancy is important theoretically because it illustrates how a fact about the self may be recognized but not organized into a higher-order self-picture. The reason for such an omission need not be some complex repression mechanism but may simply be an inability to fit such a fact into an over-all consistent picture. Karl knows that he was conscientious and thorough—and he was not deceived in this as both his high-school and college teachers would testify—but irregularity, unpunctuality, etc. do not seem to fit in particularly well with this dominant trait. So he omits them from the over-all self-picture. A similar discrepancy is apparent in his description of his drive and energy which appears on certain issues to be inconsistent with his description of his submissiveness, suggestibility, etc. Thus on the one hand he states that he can "put drive into an organization," "win confidence and loyalty," etc., and on the other that he can*not* "follow up subordinates effectively," "get others to do what he wants done," etc. As we have already pointed out, he is more aware of this inconsistency and has attempted to resolve it in terms of leading when he has the cooperation of those working with him.

Agreement on Other Personality Variables. So far we have demonstrated that except for omissions and some negative traits Karl's self-picture is pretty much in agreement with ours, at least so far as traits are concerned. What about our other personality variables—schemata and motives? As far as his ideas and role conceptions are concerned we relied very heavily on his own statements in determining our analysis of what they were. So there would be little point to checking our picture with his statements again. If we did, we would find that he overlooked certain things (future orientation, for instance) largely because he was not looking for them and did not see their importance from our particular frame of reference. With motives the situation is a little more complicated. He knows that he is very ambitious but he probably does not judge his n Achievement to be as unreal as we do and as dependent on a much more basic n Security. Again we have evidence that whereas he is aware of isolated experiences (e.g., bashfulness with girls) that we would regard as related to n Security, he is not able to integrate them into anything like an adequate estimate of the strength of his own security needs or of their sources in his past history. He knows that he is sensitive and easily upset emotionally, but he doesn't know why. He recognizes the great importance that friendships have to him, but again doesn't know why. In fact the self-picture in the field of motivation seems much less adequate than in the other two areas. It is probably for this reason that dynamic psychologists have been able to impress the general public so much: they have been able, more or less, to tell people things about themselves that they didn't already know. While this is important in spreading confidence in psychotherapy it should not lead systematic personality theorists to overstress the importance of dynamic formulations. From the theoretical viewpoint, whether the person knows about one of the characteristics we assign him or not does not determine the importance of that characteristic in understanding and predicting his behavior. What the self-picture leaves out may be of particular use in explaining irrational, or neurotic, behaviors, but that doesn't make what is included in the self-picture any more or less important in an over-all theoretical scheme. On the other hand, what *is* included, since it forms another of the more or less stereotyped schemata in terms of which the person functions, is of great importance in understanding many aspects of a person's behavior.

SELF-POTENCY

With this empirical introduction into the general nature of self-schemata, we can now proceed to treat them more systematically as "emergents" with certain general characteristics. One of the most important of these is a sort of "areal" characteristic or dimension which defines what is included as part of the self. That is, there seem to be degrees of nearness to the self, differences between "me" and "mine": The "essential me" seems perceptually different from "my books, my clothes, my friends"; the self-schema seems to contract and expand. Allport has referred to this "areal" characteristic as the *extension of the self* and described it thus:

"And still the process goes on. Possessions, friends, one's own children, other children, cultural interests, abstract ideas, politics, hobbies, recreation, and most conspicuously of all, one's *work,* all lead to the incorporation of interests once remote from the self into selfhood proper." (1937, p. 217.) But Allport does not make it clear on what basis such things are incorporated into the self. A suggestive hypothesis is that there is a dimension of *self-potency,* to use Bruner's term (1950) on which objects, events, experiences, and the like are ordered as being near or far from the self. Several people have suggested that the perception of *power* or *control* determines whether or not something is perceived as part of the self. Thus Rogers states that perhaps the basis for incorporating an event into the self is the awareness "of a feeling of control over some aspect of his world of experience" (1948, p. 17). Thus we say our foot "goes to sleep" and "it becomes an object to us rather than a part of self" (1948, p. 17). As Hamlet puts it:

> Was't Hamlet wronged Laertes? never Hamlet.
> If Hamlet from himself be ta'en away,
> And when he's not himself does wrong Laertes,
> Then Hamlet does it not, Hamlet denies it.

The reason why lack of control is associated with the "not-self" probably lies in childhood experiences. As Piaget points out (1930), it is the resistance to the child's intentions which forces him originally to discriminate between himself and others, between "wish" and "reality."

In short, the associations run as follows:

Freedom, wish = self
Restraint = other (not-self)

If this formula is correct, it is easy to see how anything associated with a subjective feeling of intent, with an act of will, tends to be incorporated into the self, whereas anything which happens in a way which appears to be beyond self-control is considered ego-alien. Thus we may even speak of "my conscience" as if it were an ego-alien force making us do something. As such it is out along the dimension of self-potency and not part of the "real self." There seem to be stages of control by the self defining a true perceptual dimension of distance from the self which might be summarized as follows:

Me	My body	My	My	Strangers,
"Free will"	My conscience	belongings	friends	Physical universe etc.

→ Perceptual dimension of self-potency

This analysis suggests why it is that "free will" is such a central notion in thinking about the self; it is the very core of self-consciousness: destroy it and you destroy the basis for distinguishing between the self and the not-self. This analysis also suggests that objects, people, etc. get related to the self to the extent that they are perceived as controlled by the self or *are subject to ego's motives* in the broadest sense. Thus, even a God can become *my* God if I believe that in some way he is influenced by what I am thinking, feeling, or doing. My body, since it is usually subject to my control, is very intimately tied up with "me"; the same is true of my possessions and my friends though to a lesser extent. The issue of how far this ego-control extends has become especially acute in American society because, as we have seen in Chapter 8, our culture stresses the importance of individual self-determination. Recognizing that such an emphasis does lead to attempts to overexpand the boundaries of ego-control, Americans make free use of the terms "selfish" and "egocentric" as sanctions against a lawless extension of individual potency.

The attribute of self-potency also contributes to the emergent character of the self-schema. Apparently there is a certain minimum of ego-control necessary to maintain the integrity of the self-schema. A person who loses the perception of control completely and becomes a "pawn of circumstances" or a "creature of his impulses" is usually described as schizophrenic. In normal people this minimum level of self-potency, which probably differs for different individuals, can be maintained by substituting one form of potency for another whenever the self is perceived as checked or frustrated. Allport has summarized this process neatly as follows: "Note especially Anderson's statement that 'success in one area may more than compensate for failure in many areas.' Only in terms of ego-psychology can we account for such fluid compensation. Mental health and happiness, it seems, does not depend upon the satisfaction of *this* drive or *that* drive, it depends rather upon the *person's* finding *some* area of success *somewhere*. The *ego* must be satisfied, not the hunger drive, nor the sex drive, nor the maternal drive, however insistent these segmental tensions may be." (1943, p. 466.)

Translated into our terms, what Allport appears to be saying is that a certain minimum level of self-potency is necessary to maintain the integrity of the self-schema and that it is only in terms of such a self-schema that such matters as ego-involvement, threat, frustration-tolerance and certain kinds of substitution make much sense. To take a simple example, let us suppose, as the authors of *Frustration and Aggression* do (1939), that Jimmy wants an ice cream cone, but his mother won't let him have it. This is a simple blocking or deprivation of a segmental drive. However, let us suppose that Jimmy has been subjected to many previous frustrations (that, for instance, he feels basically unloved and rejected, his security drives blocked); now the added frustration of being unable to have an ice cream cone may mean something different. It may appear as a *threat,* to use Maslow's term (1943b). The reason it appears as a threat, according to our argument, is that the minimum level of self-potency has been approached. A person can stand a certain amount of frustration and restraint without destroying the self-potency percept which is so basic to the self-schema, but not an indefinite amount. This may be, in effect, an explanation of what is meant by *frustration-tolerance* (cf. Rosenzweig, 1944). The closer the over-all frustration level gets to destroying the percept of self-potency, the more the individual feels threatened and the less his tolerance for new frustration. In some cases, of course, the self-schema may become disorganized from the loss of the sense of self-potency and the person may become either an amnesia case or a psychotic. In short, there appears to be an over-all sense of self-potency which may be raised or lowered by actions or frustrations in different areas of life.

Does the fact that we have spoken of a certain minimum necessary sense of self-potency suggest that there is some over-all emergent motive, perhaps a *self-actualization* drive, as Goldstein calls it (1940)? Perhaps, but actually the adjectives "minimum necessary" tend to conceal the fact that there are all degrees of organization and disorganization of the self-picture. It is difficult to pick an arbitrary level of organization of a self-schema and speak of the person as striving to maintain or enhance that level. Nevertheless, the point is well worth stressing for those who prefer, as we have, to speak of several separate motives that the over-all fulfillment or frustration of these motives contributes to the sense of self-potency which is probably the key attribute of the self-schema, a schema which in turn is absolutely central to the person's total adjustment to life. Though we may want to make distinctions among motives for the sake of analytic convenience, we must recognize that what happens to each of them contributes to the over-all self-picture and that Allport is essentially correct in saying that events such as successes and failures have an impact on the person as well as on segmental drives.

As a corollary of this analysis we can see how it is that psychotherapy makes some of its gains. Rogers (1947) has pointed out that the chief characteristics of a maladjusted person are a sense of bewilderment and of lack of control, as illustrated in the following two statements: "She is perplexed and almost unacquainted with what is going on in herself." "She feels unable and unwilling to function in any responsible or social way." (1947, p. 360.) One of the things that the therapist does is to give the patient a perception of control over his feelings, ideas, impulses, etc. by discussing, interpreting, or integrating them into some kind of a "rational" symbol system. To symbolize is to increase the possibilities of control (cf. Chapter 10). Thus this particular value in therapy is not especially dependent on the *kind* of explanation evolved to account for the puzzling ego-alien aspects of behavior. *Any explanation that the patient accepts as making sense will increase his perception of control and self-potency which are so essential to his self-schema and ultimate adjustment.* Such an analysis suggests why it is that nearly any kind of therapeutic system has some beneficial results—whether it be Christian Science, Freudian or Jungian psychoanalysis, or Rogers' technique of helping the person to work out his own interpretation.

SELF-CONSISTENCY

Another general characteristic of the self-schema is its internal organization—in particular its consistencies and inconsistencies. It can be thought of as having a certain structure with parts which vary in the consistency of their over-all integration or relation to one another. Like any other schema it consists essentially of a cluster of memories centered around a common element. In Chapter 9 we treated in some detail mother and father images: the self-image is similar, although more important because the self is a common element in many more experiences than is any other object. Its structure or consistency is of course a product of a long period of acquisition. Unfortunately, not much is known about developmental stages in the self-picture. Various child psychologists have concerned themselves with *when* the child becomes self-conscious (as suggested by the increasing use of first-person pronouns, for instance). Schilder (1935) has speculated on the contents of the self-image, particularly as reflected in the "body image," and has argued that portions of the body become central to the self-image, not according to the perception of potency as we have argued, but in order of their contribution to over-all sensory gratification (first the mouth, then the anus, the genitals, etc., in familiar psychoanalytic fashion). But on the whole not much is known about how the self-schema is formed and the only conclusions about its structure that can be drawn are very general: (1) The self-schema at any particular moment in a life history is likely to be inadequate and inconsistent with respect to the total range of experiences to which the person has been subjected. To get all the events that have happened over many years to a single person into one "system" is difficult and not likely to have been accomplished smoothly. Psychoanalysts in particular have pointed out that inconsistencies may arise (a) through different experiences at different stages in the life history and (b) through the incorporation into the self-schema of feelings, actions, etc. which do not really "belong" to it. For instance, as Flugel points out, at a very early age the infant

> has not learnt the distinction—later of such far-reaching import—between the self and the not-self. He does not clearly recognize the difference between a disagreeable outer stimulus and an unpleasant tension in himself. . . . There is no adequate distinction between sensations and their accompanying feelings and impulses, nor more important still—between these feelings and impulses and the associated outer objects. . . . Thus the sensations of hunger are not separated from the distress and anger aroused by these sensations, nor is anger, with its accompanying tendency to suck and bite aggressively, separated from the mother's breast which is failing to satisfy hunger. . . . (1945, 109-110.)

Much psychoanalytic writing of this sort has been highly imaginative, and so far rests for validation largely on fantasies of children and adults, yet the kernel of truth in it all seems to be that strong inappropriate elements persist in the self-schema, elements which are inappropriate in the sense that they incorporate impulses into the self that belong to the outer world or project into the outer world impulses that belong to the self. The process of forming the self-schema is by no means orderly, neat, and sensible. (2) The self-schema attains a certain minimum degree of stability and consistency as an organized hierarchy of response tendencies of different strengths. Certain attributes are more frequently associated with the self than others, just as certain characteristics are ascribed more frequently to one's mother, to Germans, or to schoolteachers (cf. Chapters 8 and 9). The strongest associations, those at the top of the hierarchy, are usually the ones which define identity: e.g., one's name, residence, age, origin, relations, and the like. Occasionally, even such central elements in the schema may be unavailable to conscious recall, apparently as a defense against anxiety. If so, we say the person is a victim of amnesia or is in a "fugue state." In such cases the self-schema does not appear to be totally lost: responses lower on the hierarchy continue to function. Syz reports the case (1937) of a man who could not remember who he was but who could react appropriately to certain things belonging to himself, etc. The methods for determining the hierarchy of responses in the self-schema appear to be the same as we outlined in Chapter 9 for getting at role perceptions or parent "images." (3) Like any other schema, the self-picture maintains a certain consistency and stability by its very "shorthand," stereotyped character. In Chapter 8 we saw how one of Bartlett's subjects boiled down a long story into a few sentences. Similarly a person tends to develop an over-all conception of himself which is greatly simplified and necessarily leaves out many elements, particularly inconsistent ones. We have seen, for instance, how Karl was able to describe himself fairly briefly. A person may go even further and think of himself very economically as "a successful businessman," "a skillful lover," "stupid but happy," "not living up to potentialities," etc. The economy of such self-symbolizations is obvious but it also has its disadvantages: as in all stereotyping, it is often difficult to break down the symbols into the elements for which they stand and a certain rigidity or resistance to change or to inconsistent information develops. The very economy of organizing one's self-schema under the heading of "stupid but happy" makes any reorganization of experiences more difficult because a new symbolization would require a breakdown of the old one, a period of uncertainty and confusion, trial and error for a new schema, etc. It seems likely that the ability to break down a self-stereotype is tied up with the basic security needs of the person. The "persona," as Jung calls it, is less readily discarded for a new one the more insecure the person is.

Unsymbolized Portions of the Self-Schema. Implicit in our analysis so far has been the assumption that the conscious or symbolized self-schema is only a portion of the total self-schema. The push toward simplification of any symbolizing process tends to leave out many experiences which are directly relevant to the self—particularly, as we have seen, the inconsistent ones or perhaps the ones that have been formed early in life and are later replaced by others. It is time we took a more systematic look at these unconscious portions of the self-schema and especially at how the observer infers they exist. In the process we can learn more about the organization of the self-schema—its consistencies and inconsistencies.

To return for a moment to Karl, we found that he does not consciously recognize the importance of his basic need for security, at least to the extent that we would stress it. In short, his conception of his motives does not agree entirely with ours. He does state that he is sensitive in his relation to others, particularly when questioned in detail on a self-rating scale, but nowhere is this information organized into a conscious recognition of what we would call his driving need for security. Instead he emphasizes his desire to get ahead in the world. We argue on the basis of some of the same information as he has that actually ambition is secondary to the need for security or fear of rejection. The interesting point is this: To what extent does Karl function as if security is all-important to him? One could argue that the experiences he has had, both of his own behavior and the behavior of others toward him, would lead to the development of a security schema not unlike the one which an outsider would judge he had from noting the same facts. This schema would continue to influence his behavior even though it is not consciously symbolized by him at all accurately. As Rogers puts it, "the concept of self is made of selected perceptions, and does not include all perception" (1948, p. 20.) Some perceptions, in fact, are "denied by the conscious self because they are inconsistent with the concept of self." (1948, p. 21.) We may argue in the present case that Karl *would continue to react* in terms of an unconscious organization of experiences which we would call f Rejection or n Affiliation, although these motives are not fully or accurately represented in consciousness as part of his self-picture.

There are two slightly different conclusions which can be drawn from this argument. (1) Karl has a strong unrecognized f Rejection which is in no way a part of the self-schema, either conscious or unconscious; (2) Karl has a strong f Rejection which is not consciously included in the self-picture but which under certain conditions can be shown to be recognized as belonging to the self. The latter view takes the position that the subject's over-all conception of himself is pretty much what an outside observer's would be but is distorted in the process of conscious verbalization, either because of an inadequate conceptual scheme or because of motivational pressures to make the self-picture socially acceptable.

No clear-cut decision between these two viewpoints is possible at the present time, but there is considerable evidence to show that characteristics may be unconsciously assigned to the self which are quite different from the ones that are consciously assigned to the self. Such discrepancies may be measured either (1) through unconscious self-judgments or (2) projection experiments in which it is assumed that the self is really identifying with some character in the projection and assigning him traits that belong to the self.

Conscious and Unconscious Self-Judgments. A promising technique for determining the difference between conscious and unconscious self-schemata is that of the "unrecognized self-judgment" as devised by Wolff (1933, 1943) and standardized by Huntley (1940). Wolff found that when a person's own forms of expression were given him for judgment, he often failed to recognize them but reacted to them nevertheless in a way which was quite different from the way in which he reacted to the expressions of others. He also found that these unconscious self-judgments were quite different from conscious self-judgments. Huntley used Wolff's techniques under more controlled conditions. First he obtained, without the subject's knowledge, various records of his "expressive forms." The forms included such things as pictures of clasped hands, handwriting, part-profiles, retold stories which had been phonographically recorded, etc. Six months later a number of forms, including his own, were presented to the subject for characterization. As in Wolff's experiments about two-thirds of the subjects failed to recognize their own forms—e.g., clasped hands, handwriting (if reversed in a mirror), etc. Huntley could therefore compare the characterization of recognized and unrecognized self-expressions with characterizations of the expressions of others. In one experiment he made up samples of five characterizations by a particular person, including one about himself, and handed the samples to outside judges to be ranked in order of favorableness. The distribution of ranks for the unconscious self-characterizations (S-judgments) was very peculiar. It is reproduced in Figure 14.1.

FIGURE 14.1

Relative Favorableness of Self-Judgments Made Without Recognition (Men Alone) and With Recognition (Men and Women)

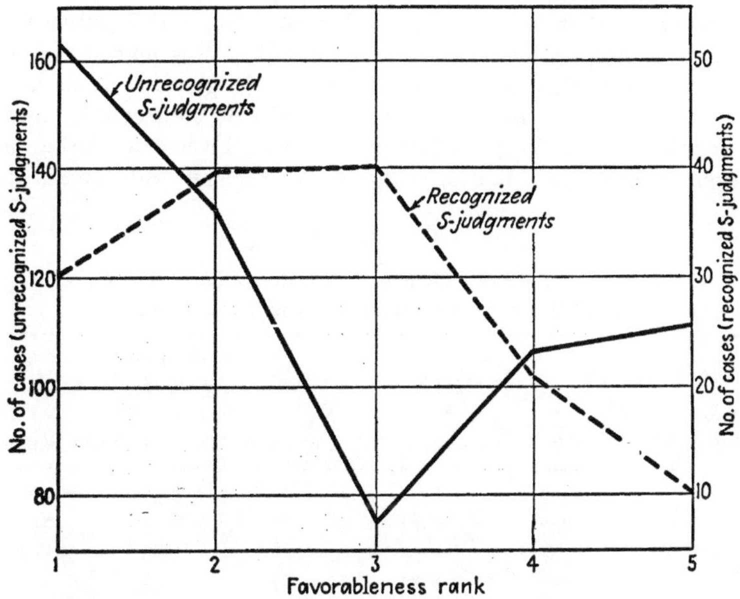

The findings are grouped for all forms, since the data reveal no characteristic differences. The numbers on the abscissa indicate the position in which the S-judgment was ranked, so that all instances in which it was ranked as most favorable are grouped at 1, etc.

(Reproduced with permission from C. W. Huntley, Judgments of Self Based Upon Records of Expressive Behavior. *J. Abnorm. Soc. Psychol.*, 35, 398-427. Copyright 1940 by the American Psychological Association.)

The unrecognized self-judgments (solid line) were significantly more often ranked by outside observers as first in favorableness. Interestingly enough, there seems to be a bi-modal tendency with significantly fewer unrecognized self-judgments being ranked in the middle position. The dotted line shows the way the *recognized* self-judgments were distributed in favorableness by the judges. They were ranked significantly more often than would be expected by chance in the middle position, with significantly fewer in the fourth and fifth positions and also in the first position. In short, most people tend to write conscious self-characterizations that are moderate in favorableness, whereas they write unconscious self-characterizations that are usually very favorable, occasionally very unfavorable, but not so often moderate.

In another experiment Huntley used graphic ratings of expressive forms rather than free characterizations of them. This permitted a somewhat simpler quantitative treatment than was possible when the characterizations were ranked by outside judges. By this method he was able to compare the average ratings by the subject of his own recognized and unrecognized expressions with his average rating *of others'* expressions. Table 14.3 shows some of the results he obtained.

TABLE 14.3

Comparison of the Self-Judgments With the Judgments of Others
(Sum of the results for all characteristics and all forms)

Stage of Recognition	*No.*	*Mean (S-O judgments)*	*Sigma of the mean*	*C.R. of the difference between the Mean and Zero*	*Sigma*
I	1520	+.46	.063	7.32	2.51
II	232	+.81	.134	6.05	2.04
III	132	+.95	.138	6.89	1.58
IV	192	+.25	.167	1.49	2.32
V	228	+.33	.134	2.47	2.02

(Reproduced with permission from C. W. Huntley, Judgments of Self Based Upon Records of Expressive Behavior. *J. Abnorm. Soc. Psychol.*, 35, 398-427. Copyright 1940 by the American Psychological Association.)

In column 3 of the table the average of the self-judgments (S) is subtracted from the average judgment of others (O). Since "for all the stages of recognition the means are positive . . . the *S-judgments are on the average more favorable than the judgments of others.*" (1940, p. 415.) Huntley discriminated five stages in recognition starting with non-recognition (Stage I) and ending with complete self-recognition (Stage V). As the table shows, the S-judgments increased in favorableness as the suspicion of recognition grew (Stage I to Stage III) but as it increased to complete self-recognition they tended to decrease in favorableness again. Some of the explanation for this may perhaps be found in the last column of the table labeled "Sigma." This column gives the standard deviations of the distributions of self-judgments. It is significantly larger for Stage I (non-recognition) than for Stage V (recognition). As a consequence Huntley concludes: *"There is a reliable tendency for the S-judgments to be more extreme in the instances of non-recognition than they are when recognition has taken place."* (1940, p. 416.) As the standard deviation decreases from Stage I to Stage III and the favorableness increases at the same time, it looks as if some of the unfavorable judgments noticed in the figure reproduced above (Fig. 14.1) tend to drop out as recognition increases. It is as if the unfavorable ratings, representing the most negative aspects of the self-schema, are more unconscious and give way as recognition increases to ego-enhancing characterizations which in turn give way to more conventionally favorable self-judgments. He found very similar relationships when he compared the self-judgments to judgments *by* others. Here too the self-judgments were *more favorable* and *more extreme* than the judgments by others of the same expressive forms.

These findings confirm the fact that unconscious self-characterizations are *different* from conscious characterizations. They also tend to confirm the hypothesis that unconscious judgments tend to be more extreme, i.e., less reality-bound. But this experiment is only a beginning. It provides us with a technique which could be used to sample extensively a person's unconscious self-schemata. The data so far reported from Huntley deal only with such over-all characteristics as *favorableness* and *extremeness*. Actually he had the subjects rate the various self-expressions on many such traits as "Originality –v– Unoriginality." We could therefore easily extend his approach to include all of the traits in our standard list (Chapter 7), and perhaps even all the motives and ideas we have attributed to Karl. That is, we could proceed to determine how Karl conceives of himself in terms of all these variables when he does not know he is characterizing himself as compared with how he conceives of himself when he does know he is characterizing himself. The discrepancies between the two self-pictures might tell us much about how his values shape his conscious self-picture (see below) and more about why he behaves in certain ways that are puzzling to himself.

Projection of Self-Attributes. A most fruitful notion clinically has been Murray's assumption (1938) that a person will describe himself more fully, honestly, and adequately, particularly in his more unpleasant aspects, when he is telling a story about someone else with whom he identifies. The original Freudian notion was specifically that a person would tend to project his *rejected* impulses into another person. Murray generalized this idea in the Thematic Apperception Test and he and others have demonstrated that often a person in telling an imaginative story will attribute to the hero characteristics which seem to belong to himself. If this is true, we have another method of getting at unconscious self-schemata.

The chief difficulty lies in trying to determine which parts of the hero's character are really a reflected image of the self, and which parts are borrowed from a story just read, a friend's behavior, etc. All our knowledge of imaginal processes (cf. the discussion of mother and father images in Chapter 9) makes us aware of their extreme fluidity. Murray himself is very cautious on this point. Although his primary assumption for the Thematic Apperception Test is that "the attributes of the heroes (needs, emotional states and sentiments) represent tendencies in the subject's personality," (1943, p. 14), he states later that "the conclusions that are reached by an analysis of TAT stories must be regarded as good 'leads' or working hypotheses to be verified by other methods, rather than as proved facts." (1943, p. 14.) He cautions in particular against leaning too heavily on the assumption that what is strong in imagination is also strong in the subject's manifest personality. "What is revealed by the TAT is often the very opposite of what the subject consciously and voluntarily does and says in his daily life." (1943, p. 16.)

How then are we to proceed? In general, three methods have been used to determine whether or not a projected image refers in any sense to the self: (1) Inferences based on known part-similarities, (2) confirmation by other data, and (3) systematic comparison of self- and other-judgments.

1. Reasoning on the basis of partial similarities runs as follows: certain people in the stories are more like the subject with respect to such variables as age, sex, situation in life, etc. If these individuals (usually the heroes) consistently have certain characteristics which are not attributed to other individuals in the stories and which are not simply stereotyped characteristics of any person with that age-sex status, then these characteristics may be said to be related to the self-schema of the person telling the story. The *nature* of the relationship, of course, is still to be determined. Karl describes many of his young, male characters (whom he would be most likely on the basis of partial similarity to identify with) as weak, vicious, and aggressive, always betraying women. Since we know that in normal life he is mild, cooperative, gregarious, and sensitive (by his own self-description), we are left with the question of just what this nega-

tive, projected "self"-picture means. This involves problems of TAT interpretation which are too complex to go into here, except to mention that their solution will depend on an analysis of the motives which might produce such a discrepancy in conscious and unconscious self-pictures. For the moment we will have to be content with the hypothesis that unconsciously (if we accept the part-to-whole argument) he has a very negative opinion of himself.

2. Confirmation with other data of hypotheses suggested by the TAT is the method preferred by most clinicians. As a typical example we may turn to one of Karl's stories which runs as follows:

> These fingers look like the fingers of fate which have this innocent young man in their clutches. This fellow has led a normal life, and good upbringing. As he was going out into the world, he has been obsessed by a fear of the unknown. These fingers of fate seem to have him in their clutches. He feels he is bound to the grim wheel of necessity from which he cannot escape. He is constantly haunted by those things which he cannot grasp. Those factors in life which weigh on his mind and which oppress his daily life. This fellow is caught in a more or less hopeless tangle. He doesn't quite know where he's going or what he is doing. He tries to break away. He tries to break away from what he considers fate, but is unable to. His resolution and courage to lead an emancipated life seem to fail. He feels like a trapped animal, as if every path he took were a blind alley. This leads to an obsession in the form of a sense of failure. He feels he cannot help himself, yet that he can. He feels alone in the world. He is at a loss at times to describe his feelings. Nobody seems to understand. The one thing that will snap him out of this, where he will seek to free himself from a shackled existence . . . where he will assert himself and conquer his doubts and fears, the thing that will do the most toward putting him on the right road will be for him to marry the girl he loves. Otherwise this chap's life is in vain. He will not be accomplishing anything worthwhile. He will lead a blighted existence, but were he, as I said before, to love the right girl and marry her, the future would be a bright one indeed. This chap has the qualities inherent in him of a good sound citizen and member of society. But the key to the lock is the girl he loves. That's all. (Does he marry or not?) Yes, he does, this man will break the bounds. It may take time, but he will be at peace and his spirit emancipated, and his life will be a happy one.

Is Karl talking about himself in this story? A strong hint that he is lies in the fact that the young man in the story is pictured as overcoming his difficulties only if he loves and marries the right girl. "The key to the lock is the girl he loves." We know from Karl's autobiography that he too views romantic love as the great solution to his problems. In fact he describes his life situation in much the same terms as he uses in talking about the hero of his story. With one of the main elements in the plot identified in this way as belonging to Karl, the interpreter feels safer in assuming that *other* attitudes, feelings, impulses, etc. attributed to the hero in this story also relate to Karl. This need not be true, of course, but the probability that they are so related seems increased. Often the inference need not be extended much beyond identifying an idea as belonging to the subject's conscious self-schema, since the way in which it is expressed imaginatively may give a fuller and more honest picture of it than the way he describes it consciously. Sometimes the imaginative picture does no more than give a fuller notion of the *intensity* of the affect associated with an idea which the person consciously expresses—a fact which is clearly in line with Huntley's finding that partially recognized self-descriptions tend to be more extreme. In the present instance this seems to be the case: Karl's imaginative description of the importance of love to his hero comes somewhat closer to our conception of the intensity of his f Rejection and n Affiliation than does his conscious self-picture (see above). Unfortunately this method of determining whether the person is talking about himself in a TAT is also hazardous. We cannot be certain that even when the person says "that looks like me," he will proceed to talk about himself in a freer fashion. He *may* promptly tell a story about someone else: the only guard against this is to multiply evidence from several different sources.

3. Somewhat more precise estimates of unconscious self-conceptions can be drawn from systematic comparisons of self-judgments with characteristics attributed to others. In an ingenious experiment somewhat like Huntley's, Sears (1936) had a group of fraternity brothers rate each other and themselves on such traits as *obstinacy, stinginess,* and *bashfulness*. He found that men who were considered stingy by others but who did not judge themselves to be stingy attributed more stinginess to others. A plausible explanation appears to be that they conceived themselves as stingy but rejected the idea (hence the lack of conscious insight), which led them to distort the scale of judgment so they could be pushed toward the generous end by making everyone else stingier than they were. The technique is one other way of getting at an unconscious self-schema since it is hard to imagine how the subjects could have distorted the scale of projected attributes in this particular way without some implicit recognition of their own stinginess.

Nevertheless the approach is by no means foolproof. It would certainly not be safe to infer that a person who attributes more than an average amount of stinginess to others is himself stingy. For one thing, the relationship Sears found was not perfect. For another, it holds only for those without insight. And for a third, it does not hold for other traits like bashfulness. In fact the people who attributed most bashfulness to others were those who were judged to be least bashful and knew it (as reflected in self-ratings). In short, under certain conditions the trait a person attributes to himself will be attributed to others and under certain other conditions its opposite will be. And it may be difficult to determine which set of conditions is operating in a particular case (e.g., whether the person has insight or not). Nevertheless the technique does suggest a way of drawing systematic inferences about unconscious self-schemata from conscious judgments of self and from characteristics projected into others.

A more recent development along these lines is the sentence completion test which may be designed to evoke characterizations of the self and of others. An example will show best how it may be used for this purpose. Karl was administered a form of this test devised by Dr. Jules D. Holzberg which contained fifty items dealing with conceptions of self and of others on matters relating to achievement and security. The test was administered twice so that all items which referred to the self in the first form could be rephrased so as to refer to another person in the second form and vice versa. Using the answers which Karl gave to this test, we can arrive at a more exact test of our hypothesis that he has a conscious conception of himself as being very ambitious and an unconscious conception as being greatly in need of security (fearing rejection, etc.).

In Table 14.4 we have selected out twenty-seven pairs of statements from his sentence completions, at least one of which relates to achievement. The statements on top are from Form A of the test, which he took first, and the ones on the bottom are from Form B, which he took second. For example, he gave the top answers in items 23, 24, 25, 26 consecutively on one occasion and the bottom answers to the same items consecutively on another occasion. The answers have been rearranged to make direct comparison easier. He was under instructions to answer the items as quickly as possible so that he doubtless was only half-conscious at the most that he was answering the same rephrased items on the two occasions. His answers have been scored in terms of whether or not he attributes more achievement competence or concern to himself than to others.

TABLE 14.4

Karl's Sentence Completion Test Results for Achievement-Related Statements

+ self has greater achievement competence or concern
— other has greater achievement competence or concern
O neither has greater achievement competence or concern

Karl's completions are in italics

1. Mike's fondest ambition is *to travel around the world.*
+ My fondest ambition is *to earn a comfortable fortune.*

3. Joe was uneasy because *he saw others succeeding.*
— I was uneasy because *there were too many people around me.*

4. When he saw that the others were doing better than he was, Joe *dug in and tried hard.*
O When I saw that the others were doing better than I was, I *became angry and tried to do better.*

6. When he failed at something, he *sat down and thought it over.*
+ When I failed at something, I *tried again.*

8. Bob feels proud when he *has his sweetheart with him.*
+ I feel proud when *I'm on top.*

9. + I wish for *all good luck and happiness.*
Bob wishes for *happiness.*

12. When luck turned against him, Joe *decided to turn over a new leaf.*
+ When luck turned against me, I *dug in to fight harder.*

15. He thinks of himself as *a great man.*
O I think of myself as a *superior person.*

16. O I would rather *be rich than president.*
Harry would rather *drink beer than study.*

21. Discouragement made him *try harder.*
— Discouragement made me *a little sad.*

23. + I try hard *sometimes.*
Frank tries hard *but just can't win.*

24. The thing which bothered Harry's conscience was *only doing a half-way job.*
O The thing which bothered my conscience was *I could do better than I do.*

25. + I always wanted to be *a man of power.*
Bob always wanted to be *a better man than I am.*

26. When people disapproved of John's ideas, *he didn't give a damn.*
+ When people disapproved of my ideas, *I gave them some more advice.*

27. In coming to a decision, he *got excited about it.*
+ In coming to a decision, I *decide in a hurry.*

28. Tom's ability to succeed *depended on his enthusiasm.*
O My ability to succeed is *potential and latent.*

29. O When I compete against others, I *try to do my best.*
When Bill competes against others, he *tries hard.*

32. Bud worries over *nothing at all.*
+ I worry over *the things I don't do.*

33. + I brag about *myself and achievements.*
Fred brags about *women and drinking.*

34. + I am afraid when *others know more than I do.*
He is afraid when *others threaten his position.*

35. — I am driven to great efforts to *make money.*
Bud is driven to great efforts to *reach his life's goal.*

36. When he attempts to reach difficult goals, he *doesn't try too hard.*
+ When I attempt to reach difficult goals, I *sometimes try and sometimes do not.*

39. + My greatest worry is *not to live a life worth living.*
Tom's greatest worry is *his wife.*

41. If Fred could only *do his best.*
— If I could only *settle down.*

45. + My greatest ambition is *to be powerful in influence.*
His greatest ambition is *to do good in the world.*

46. Bob's defeat made him *get on the ball.*
O My defeat made me *knuckle down and get to work.*

50. He often thinks of himself as *being greater than he is.*
+ I often think of myself as *a man of destiny.*

Of the twenty-seven statements dealing with achievement, the self shows more competence or concern in sixteen instances, the other person in four, and neither in seven. Chi-square for the twenty items showing a preference is 7.2, $P<.01$.

This significantly greater frequency of achievement-related sentence completions as well as an inspection of the answers themselves definitely confirms the hypothesis that he attributes more achievement concern or competence to himself than to others. The difference comes out most clearly in items like number 39 in which he states that his greatest worry is not to live a life worth living while Tom's greatest worry is his wife. Exactly the same contrast is made in items 8 and 33. In all these cases Karl is presenting himself as being more concerned with achievement while Bob or Joe or Fred is more concerned with love or security. "I brag about myself and my achievements." "Fred brags about women and drinking," etc.

This suggests that a test should be made to check whether or not Karl sees himself as having greater security concern than he sees others as having. Table 14.5 gives the necessary data.

TABLE 14.5

Karl's Sentence Completion Test Results for Security-Related Statements

+ self has greater security attainment or concern
— other has greater security attainment or concern
O neither has greater security attainment or concern

Karl's completions are in italics

2. + My greatest fear is *to be left alone.*
His greatest fear is *of fire.*
3. Joe was uneasy because *he saw others succeeding.*
+ I was uneasy because *there were too many people around me.*
7. — I feel sorry when *I see people as they are.*
Jack feels sorry *when he has no money.*
8. Bob feels proud when *he has his sweetheart with him.*
— I feel proud when *I'm on top.*
9. O I wish for *all good luck and happiness.*
Bob wishes for *happiness.*
13. He is most troubled *by imaginary evils.*
O I am most troubled *by the unknown.*
16. — I would rather *be rich than president.*
Harry would rather *drink beer than study.*
17. — I suffer most from *others' criticisms.*
He suffers most from *being alone.*
20. — I feel hurt when *some inferior person tells me what to do.*
He feels hurt when *the others refuse to recognize him.*
31. — My hero is *the individual.*
His hero is *God.*
33. — I brag about *myself and achievements.*
Fred brags about *women and drinking.*
34. —I am afraid when *others know more than I do.*
He is afraid when *others threaten his position.*
37. Bill is afraid of *too many little things.*
— I am afraid of *neither God, man, nor beast.*
39. — My greatest worry is *not to live a life worth living.*
Tom's greatest worry is *his wife.*
40. — I dream a great deal about *impossible situations.*
He dreams a great deal about *wine, women, and song.*
42. O The main thing in my life is *to have fun and be happy.*
The main thing in John's life is *to be happy.*
44. When the other men avoided him, Bob *felt hurt but kept his spirits up.*
+ When the other men avoided me, I *felt hurt.*
47. — I usually feel shocked when *someone crosses me up.*
He usually feels shocked when *he meets women.*

Of the eighteen paired statements dealing with security (affiliative relations), the self shows more attainment or concern in three instances, the other person in twelve, and neither in three. Chi-square for the sixteen items showing a preference is 5.4, $P < .05$.

Once again the evidence is good that Karl conceives of other people as being more concerned with happiness, affiliative relationships, loneliness, etc., than he is. To put it in another way, he conceives of Bob or Fred or Joe as being more dependent on others than he is. Perhaps the difference is brought out as clearly in item 31 as anywhere. He states that "My hero is the individual" while "His hero is God." This puts the contrast in almost classical terms. It is as if Karl is saying that he values the individual because the individual is enough—he can stand alone, on his own feet. But he apparently thinks of others as being more dependent and therefore as valuing God. Throughout history there has been a repeated shift in man's emphasis on the importance of the individual or the importance of God depending on whether or not man felt, like the Greeks, confidence in himself and his achievements or, like the Hebrews, a constant sense of failure and need for the support of an all-powerful God. Karl certainly *consciously* puts himself on the side of faith in the individual, but his repeated insistence that Tom or Joe is interested in security relationships (from beer and women all the way to God) makes us doubt whether or not his conscious picture is entirely accurate.

Once again the logical hypothesis which these data appear to support is that Karl is actually operating in terms of a security schema which is of far greater importance to him than he realizes. But can we assume that the security needs which he attributes to others really represent his own unconscious self-schemata? Maybe he just thinks that other people are more interested in security than he is. That *might* be all these results mean. The argument on this point would run somewhat as follows. We could start with a null hypothesis that security is a matter of no particular concern to him. If this were so it would appear reasonable to expect an equal number of security statements in his description of himself and of others. Since there are not an equal number of statements in these categories, we are forced to conclude that either he personally is interested in security and projects this interest into others or that the people he has met have been more interested in security than would be normal. We can at least tentatively reject the second alternative on the ground that there is no reason to assume that the people he has met have somehow been preselected to have a greater security concern than most people. This leaves us with considerable logical support for the hypothesis that it is *he* who is so interested in security but who for some reason disowns this interest and attributes it to others. In short, the results of the Sentence Completion Test support fully the hypothesis arrived at from the TAT stories and autobiographical statements that Karl is operating consciously in terms of a concept of himself as being independent and ambitious and unconsciously in terms of a conception which heavily emphasizes the need for security.

Ego Strength. Many psychologists have been very much interested in describing the consequences of the kind of discrepancy in the self-schema that we have been discussing. In general they have taken the view that, the less a person is able to adjust to reality, the greater the inconsistency between his conscious and unconscious self-schemata. Rogers describes the matter as follows:

> Psychological maladjustment exists when there is a significant number of perceptions experienced by the organism which are denied symbolization, and consequently are not organized into a consistent system related to the self-concept. When this situation exists, psychological tension results. (1948, p. 28.)

This describes exactly what has happened in Karl's case: there are a number of security-related experiences which he has not integrated or symbolized into his conscious self-picture although he projects them in a way which suggests that he recognizes their self-relevance. Whenever such discrepancies exist, the person is less integrated and we may refer to him as lacking in *ego strength*. The term *ego strength* has been used quite widely to refer to the extent to which a person can deal with reality effectively, particularly in the face of difficulties. What we are suggesting is that an important basis for ego strength is an accurate self-picture, e.g., one which includes all the significant self-related perceptions even though they may be inconsistent or unfavorable.

Several kinds of discrepancies in the self-schema have been discussed by clinical psychologists. First of all there is the rather simple case like Karl in which the discrepancy is not great but involves largely a question of emphasis: what Karl needs is a fuller realization of the importance of security to him. Then there is the case of the paranoid self-picture in which the discrepancy is also not great but is very carefully worked out with such tremendous motivational support that it is hard to reorganize it. Such a person's self-schema may be "strong" in the sense of rigid but it is not strong in the sense of dealing effectively with reality as it is judged by others. Finally, White (1943) has described the case of a college student he named Joseph Kidd, whose self-picture was scarcely built on experience related to himself at all but almost wholly on what he thought others expected of him. His ego strength was judged to be low because his self-picture constantly changed in accordance with the demands of the situation and apparently had no roots in actual self-perception. In such instances, as Rogers puts it, "The concept of self in other words is based almost entirely upon the perception of others' values and contains a minimum of perception of one's own experiences. Since the values held by others have no necessary relationship to one's actual organic experiencings, the discrepancy gradually comes to be experienced as a feeling of tension and distress." (1948, p. 30.)

Does this mean that incorporating inconsistent or even damaging personal experiences into the conscious self-schema will contribute to ego strength? Apparently it does. Certainly psychoanalysis and nearly all other psychotherapies proceed on this assumption. Furthermore, whenever psychiatrists happen to study a group of normal people, they are usually surprised to discover many of the same conflicts which they usually hold responsible for mental disease. Their first reaction may be: How can people appear so normal when they carry around such a terrific load of conflict, guilt, and the like? One possible explanation is that with "normal" people, more of such experiences are accurately symbolized in the self-picture which prevents the kind of ineffectual adjustment that must result whenever a person is trying to respond in terms of one kind of a conscious self-schema and another kind of unconscious one. Herein lies one of the other advantages of psychotherapy: It fills out the self-picture and makes it more nearly accurate, so that the person can respond in terms of a total picture which, even though full of conflict, is presumed to be better than an incomplete or incorrect one.

Self-Evaluation

The self-schema can be described not only in terms of the dimensions of potency and consistency, but also in terms of evaluation. At least in our culture it is nearly impossible for a person to describe himself without adding a value judgment of some sort. Huntley

—definitely not the *bored sophisticate* type—although enthusiasm for such things as skiing is definitely wearing off.

Start talking about a subject I'm familiar with and *you're likely to be snowed under.* In other words, I like to talk—not because, as is the case with my kid brother, I'm fascinated by the sound of my own voice, but because I can't seem to resist the urge to let other people know interesting things. I can't keep a secret, however. I have more than an average sense of *pride*—call it stubbornness if you will.

Particularly interesting in this sketch is the shift in the last line from the use of the word *pride* to the word *stubbornness.* Obviously the shift is made not because the term *stubbornness* is more descriptive, but because it has a somewhat different (less favorable) value connotation. From such self-descriptions as these and from those given in the recorded interviews of Rogers and his associates (1942, 1947) it is readily apparent that personal behavior is nearly always viewed in terms of values. The person sees his behavior as being guided by certain values and usually makes a judgment as to whether or not he has successfully behaved in a way which measures up to

Characteristics of Self-Evaluation. A judgment requires at least two points of reference: something must be compared to something else. When the person judges himself he holds the self or some aspect of it up against some standard and finds the result satisfying or unsatisfying. Now there are two aspects of this process of comparison which are particularly striking: (1) the extent to which the self is judged as a whole and (2) the extent to which both the part of the self being judged and the value in terms of which it is being judged may be unknown to the judge. Why should the self be judged as a whole? We have already dwelt on the "emergent," stereotyped character of the self-schema. It is simply part of the economy of the schematizing process which tends to reduce the self-schema to a formula which can therefore be more easily evaluated as a whole, as "good" or "bad," "progressive," "conservative," "sinful" or what not. This does not mean, of course, that parts of the self-schema are not differently evaluated. The student whose sketch was quoted above was clearly able to distinguish between his "bad" temper and his "good" insight into himself. It does mean, however, that judgments in one area may *transfer* to others and that there is an over-all "sentiment of self-regard," as McDougall called it, which may be raised or lowered at least minimally by every success or failure the

found, for instance, that the most striking distortion in self-judgments occurred in what he called the "favorableness" dimension. Karl in his Sentence Completion Test seems to be taking a rather dim view of that security-concerned portion of himself which we argued he projected into others: "Harry would rather drink beer than study" . . . "Fred brags about women and drinking" . . . "Tom's greatest worry is his wife" . . . "He dreams a great deal about wine, women and song," etc. It is as if he is disowning *and criticizing* this aspect of himself. In his autobiography he uses value standards in describing his performance in high school: "I was cooperative and obedient . . . a good student." When members of a psychology class were asked to write ten-minute personality sketches of themselves in class, a very large percentage held themselves up to standards for judging. The following is a somewhat extreme example:

When I speak or think of my personality, I think of it in terms of character traits. Perhaps the best way to discuss the question is to look at what I consider to be "my bad traits" and "my good traits."

Bad

A. I have a very bad temper which is revealed, however, only at certain times.

B. I am prone to become sulky on certain occasions, which is brought about mainly because of my temper.

C. I am *too* critical of certain individuals and situations.

Good

A. I am able to understand my faults and as a result have made a conscious effort to correct them (particularly the bad temper).

B. I am very meticulous on almost all counts; in conjunction with this I am conscientious about any work which I undertake.

C. I find it easy to adjust myself to situations including those unfamiliar to me.

D. I am easy to get along with, except when my temper gets the upper hand.

Here is another one, in a somewhat lighter vein, although the tendency toward evaluation is definitely present even here. The phrases suggesting self-judgment have been italicized for emphasis.

—My personality

It's sort of a quiet one—when I'm sober. *Not too outstanding* in any form. I can keep up a *pretty good banter* with most any girl for the first two or three dates, but then I run out of amusing anecdotes and really have to think hard for something amusing to say. I'm enthusiastic by nature

—definitely not the *bored sophisticate* type—although enthusiasm for such things as shaving is definitely wearing off.

Start talking about a subject I'm familiar with and *you're likely to be snowed under.* In other words, I like to talk—not because, as is the case with my kid brother, I'm fascinated by the sound of my own voice, but because I can't seem to resist the urge to let other people know interesting things. I can keep a secret, however. I have more than an average sense of *pride*—call it *stubbornness* if you will.

Particularly interesting in this sketch is the shift in the last line from the use of the word *pride* to the word *stubbornness.* Obviously the shift is made not because the term *stubbornness* is more descriptive, but because it has a somewhat different (less favorable) value connotation. From such self-descriptions as these and from those given in the recorded interviews of Rogers and his associates (1942, 1947) it is readily apparent that personal behavior is nearly always viewed in terms of values. The person sees his behavior as being guided by certain values and usually makes a judgment as to whether or not he has successfully behaved in a way which measures up to those values.

Characteristics of Self-Evaluation. A judgment requires at least two points of reference: something must be compared to something else. When the person judges himself he holds the self or some aspect of it up against some standard and finds the result satisfying or unsatisfying. Now there are two aspects of this process of comparison which are particularly striking: (1) the extent to which the self is judged as a whole and (2) the extent to which both the part of the self being judged and the value in terms of which it is being judged may be unknown to the judge. Why should the self be judged as a whole? We have already dwelt on the "emergent," stereotyped character of the self-schema. It is simply part of the economy of the schematizing process which tends to reduce the self-schema to a formula which can therefore be more easily evaluated as a whole, as "good" or "bad," "progressive," "conservative," "sinful" or what not. This does not mean, of course, that parts of the self-schema are not differently evaluated. The student whose sketch was quoted above was clearly able to distinguish between his "bad" temper and his "good" insight into himself. It does mean, however, that judgments in one area may *transfer* to others and that there is an over-all "sentiment of self-regard," as McDougall called it, which may be raised or lowered at least minimally by every success or failure the

found, for instance, that the most striking distortion in self-judgments occurred in what he called the "favorableness" dimension. Karl in his Sentence Completion Test seems to be taking a rather dim view of that security-concerned portion of himself which we argued he projected into others: "Harry would rather drink beer than study" . . . "Fred brags about women and drinking" . . . "Tom's greatest worry is his wife" . . . "He dreams a great deal about wine, women and song," etc. It is as if he is disowning *and criticizing* this aspect of himself. In his autobiography he uses value standards in describing his performance in high school: "I was cooperative and obedient . . . a good student." When members of a psychology class were asked to write ten-minute personality sketches of themselves in class, a very large percentage held themselves up to standards for judging. The following is a somewhat extreme example:

When I speak or think of my personality, I think of it in terms of character traits. Perhaps the best way to discuss the question is to look at what I consider to be "my bad traits" and "my good traits."

Bad

A. I have a very bad temper which is revealed, however, only at certain times.
B. I am prone to become sulky on certain occasions, which is brought about mainly because of my temper.
C. I am *too* critical of certain individuals and situations.

Good

A. I am able to understand my faults and as a result have made a conscious effort to correct them (particularly the bad temper).
B. I am very meticulous on almost all counts; in conjunction with this I am conscientious about any work which I undertake.
C. I find it easy to adjust myself to situations including those unfamiliar to me.
D. I am easy to get along with, except when my temper gets the upper hand.

Here is another one, in a somewhat lighter vein, although the tendency toward evaluation is definitely present even here. The phrases suggesting self-judgment have been italicized for emphasis.

–My personality

It's sort of a quiet one—when I'm sober. *Not too outstanding* in any form. I can keep up a *pretty good banter* with most any girl for the first two or three dates, but then I run out of amusing anecdotes and really have to think hard for something amusing to say. I'm enthusiastic by nature

—definitely not the *bored sophisticate* type—although enthusiasm for such things as shaving is definitely wearing off.

Start talking about a subject I'm familiar with and *you're likely to be snowed under*. In other words, I like to talk—not because, as is the case with my kid brother, I'm fascinated by the sound of my own voice, but because I can't seem to resist the urge to let other people know interesting things. I can keep a secret, however. I have more than an average sense of *pride*—call it *stubbornness* if you will.

Particularly interesting in this sketch is the shift in the last line from the use of the word *pride* to the word *stubbornness*. Obviously the shift is made not because the term *stubbornness* is more descriptive, but because it has a somewhat different (less favorable) value connotation. From such self-descriptions as these and from those given in the recorded interviews of Rogers and his associates (1942, 1947) it is readily apparent that personal behavior is nearly always viewed in terms of values. The person sees his behavior as being guided by certain values and usually makes a judgment as to whether or not he has successfully behaved in a way which measures up to those values.

Characteristics of Self-Evaluation. A judgment requires at least two points of reference: something must be compared to something else. When the person judges himself he holds the self or some aspect of it up against some standard and finds the result satisfying or unsatisfying. Now there are two aspects of this process of comparison which are particularly striking: (1) the extent to which the self is judged as a whole and (2) the extent to which both the part of the self being judged and the value in terms of which it is being judged may be unknown to the judge. Why should the self be judged as a whole? We have already dwelt on the "emergent," stereotyped character of the self-schema. It is simply part of the economy of the schematizing process which tends to reduce the self-schema to a formula which can therefore be more easily evaluated as a whole, as "good" or "bad," "progressive," "conservative," "sinful" or what not. This does not mean, of course, that parts of the self-schema are not differently evaluated. The student whose sketch was quoted above was clearly able to distinguish between his "bad" temper and his "good" insight into himself. It does mean, however, that judgments in one area may *transfer* to others and that there is an over-all "sentiment of self-regard," as McDougall called it, which may be raised or lowered at least minimally by every success or failure the

person experiences. Much more experimentation on this point is needed, however.

Another even simpler reason for judging the self as a whole is the fact that the self tends to be judged as a whole by other people, particularly the parents. "Johnny, you're a good boy, and I love you" may be the refrain that one son hears over and over again. Or he may hear what Freud is said to have heard from his father: "You'll never amount to much." (Sachs, 1944.) When the young Sigmund set out to prove his father wrong, to prove that he *would* amount to something, he was accepting the tendency of his parents to judge himself *as a whole.* Such seems often to be the case. Since we are treated and judged as separate individual wholes by others we tend to regard ourselves in the same light.

The fact that both of the points of reference in the judging process may be unconscious has been especially emphasized by psychoanalysis. It is easy enough to understand the judging process when the student says, "I have a temper . . . that is bad." Three things are involved: (a) the perception that he is aggressive at times, (b) a value of aggression control, and (c) a comparison of (a) with (b) which leads to the judgment "my temper is bad." But sometimes we only have (c) or the *affect* associated with (c). The person may simply feel guilty, may punish himself for days and be completely unable to verbalize his offense. He can neither perceive what act or thought was wrong nor what value he is judging himself in terms of. All that he or we as observers have to go on is the end result of the judging process: misery, suffering or euphoria, or perhaps some strange or "symptomatic" act.

Drawing inferences about the nature of a person's values either from explicit statements or from such end-products of self-judgment has been a favorite exercise of psychoanalysis. It has led on the one hand to a tremendous literature on the structure of value systems (super-ego, ego-ideal) and on the other, to an increasing concern for improving the methods by which such inferences are made. On the whole it looks as if speculation about the nature of value structures in the self-schema like the super-ego has outrun its methodological base. We will therefore spend some time in the pedestrian task of attempting to show how inferences about personal values may be more solidly based on fact and then pass on to a brief summary of some of the better-attested characteristics of the super-ego and ego-ideal as contained largely in psychoanalytic writings.

Methods of Measuring Self-Relevant Values. 1. One of the most popular methods of getting at an individual's value schemata has been to use *statements of preference.* The Allport-Vernon Study of Values Test uses this approach. A typical item on this schedule runs as follows:

> The main object of scientific research should be the discovery of pure truth rather than its practical applications. a. Yes b. No

If the subject rates *yes* in preference to *no,* he is scored as being more interested in theoretical values than in economic ones. Actually such an approach does not seem to differentiate sufficiently between general interests which are important to the subject and what we have been calling here *self-relevant* values, e.g., values which are part of the frame of reference in terms of which the person perceives himself. A preference seems to be analogous to what Hull (1943) means by *habit strength*: it refers to the frequency with which a certain choice or type of response will occur as compared with certain others. As in the case of habit strength there are a good many factors which will influence the strength of a choice, e.g., motivational strength, past reinforcement, etc. *One* of these factors may be some kind of a self-relevant value but since all factors determine the choice, it is hard to determine what the choice signifies with respect to such a value. Although this does not mean that this method of approach to defining a person's values is of no use, it does mean that interpretation of the results will be complicated, that preference scales give a more unambiguous measure of what we have called *ideas that have weight for the person* or *interests* (cf. Chapter 8), and that therefore some of the other methods of measuring values are simpler to use in practice.

2. *Statements of aspiration* represent a somewhat more direct attempt to get at a person's values. They may range all the way from answers to a simple question like "What do you want to be when you grow up?" to involved level of aspiration procedures. The difficulty with simple straightforward questioning about personal values has been that it has seemed to be more successful at getting social norms than at getting the actual values the person lives by and judges himself in terms of. Thus, for instance, Riecken (1950) found that answers to such questions as "What are the three most worthy ambitions an individual may have?" and "What are the three things you would most like to teach your children?" were very stereotyped—e.g., most people seemed to be choosing from a restricted

range of socially agreed-upon virtues. He found further that the answers tended to resist change in a manner which suggested that they were not very closely related to direct personal experiences, but represented social stereotypes.

Some of the standard level-of-aspiration techniques seem more adaptable to the purpose we have in mind here, although care must be taken to structure the experimental situation so as to get unambiguous information. The general approach involves simply asking the subject to make some kind of a judgment of how well he is going to do on a particular task. His judgment ordinarily involves his perception of his own past performance as well as the value which he places on doing well in this particular situation. The typical sequence of events in a judgment of this sort is diagrammed below after Lewin, Dembo, Festinger, and Sears (1944).

FIGURE 14.2

Typical Sequence of Events in a Level of Aspiration Experiment

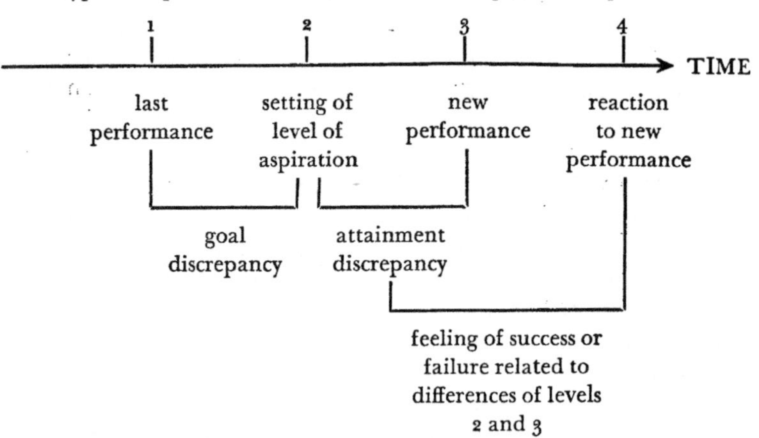

Four main points are distinguished in a typical sequence of events in a level of aspiration situation: last performance, setting level of aspiration for the next performance, new performance, and the psychological reaction to the new performance. The difference between the level of the last performance and the level of the new goal is called goal discrepancy; the difference between the goal level and that of the new performance is called attainment discrepancy. This difference is one of the bases of the reaction at the point 4.

(Reproduced with permission from Hunt, J. McV. (Editor), *Personality and the Behavior Disorders,* p. 334. Copyright 1944 by the Ronald Press Company.)

The level of aspiration technique has been very widely used because it is readily adaptable to any type of performance situation and because the subject's estimates can often be quantified. Most of the work in the field has centered around the experimental variables which will influence the stated level of aspiration or the discrepancy between the level of aspiration and the last performance (D-score). From the viewpoint of personality theory the interest in the level-of-aspiration technique is somewhat different. It centers in the question: How can we use such a method to get an idea of the inner goal structure of the person or of his conscious and unconscious self-relevant values? If the technique is to be used for this purpose there are several lines along which research can proceed.

a. *Simplification of the Meaning of the Goal Estimate.* Further attempts must be made to clarify the meaning of the stated level of aspiration to the subject. As Gould (1939) has pointed out on the basis of extensive interview material, the answer to the simple question "What will you do next time?" has a variety of different meanings to different subjects. To one subject the score which he gives may be an "incentive" which he has chosen in order to improve his performance; to another subject the score may represent what he realistically expects to do; to still another it may be a low value he chooses to protect himself against failure because he confidently expects to surpass it. As Lewin *et al.* (1944) state, the actual level of aspiration represents the "action goal" which is determined by a multitude of factors, whereas what we are interested in corresponds more nearly to the "ideal goal" or the value which the subject attaches to doing well in this particular task.

How the ideal self-goal is to be measured is a difficult problem which has not as yet been satisfactorily solved. Investigators like Festinger (1942) have, it is true, asked the subjects what they would *like* to get next time. The resulting goal choices are much less influenced by the past performance of the subject or by comparisons with other groups. They are "unrealistic" as compared with the judgments made by a group of subjects who are asked to state what they *expect* to do next time. To this extent they might seem to come closer to stating the subject's ideal goal at least with respect to achievement on this particular task. As one subject put it, "the estimate was what I thought I ought to get and I was trying hard to reach the estimate I set for myself." (Festinger, 1942, p. 195.) The only difficulty with this solution to the problem is that such estimates sometimes become so unreal, fanciful, or playful that they are not really self-related at all. Thus if you were to ask somebody, "How much money would you like to make?" the chances are he might answer something like, "Oh, a million dollars." On the basis of such an answer it would probably be incorrect to conclude that making a million dollars was part of the person's ego ideal in any very serious sense. The trick seems to be to get the subject to make a realistic aspiration statement in a performance context without allowing it to be too much influenced by actual performance in that context. If it is too much influenced, then the level of aspiration becomes not a goal statement but something of an expectation statement or perhaps an ego defense against failure. At the moment it looks as if Festinger's question is the best solution to this problem, although there are others. For example, asking for levels of aspiration in a task situation in which the subject does not know how well he is performing might give a better picture of his true "goal level." Or a public statement of aspiration level with private knowledge of performance scores might also give an indication of how much the subject valued achievement, at least in a social context. If the problem is properly seen as one of determining the subject's valuation of achievement (or some other goal), various ways of accomplishing this by modifications in the standard level of aspiration technique will suggest themselves. As it is, the theoretical meaning of many goal estimates is not clear.

b. *Study of Other Than Achievement Goals.* The level of aspiration technique could be used for values other than that of achievement. Nearly all the research to date has dealt with achievement goal estimates. There is no reason, however, why the technique should be limited to this type of situation. A person may be asked to state a goal with respect to any kind of performance. For instance, a child might be asked to record, either privately or publicly, how obedient he would like (or expect) to be in a series of situational tests involving obedience or following commands. Wright's experiment on altruism in children (1942) is illustrative of an approach which might be adopted. She used the following task situation: "A child, confronted with a desirable and less desirable toy, was asked to give one away and keep the other for himself. In one case the other person was his best friend; in another case a stranger." (1942, p. 220.) This situation is comparable to determining the achievement level of aspiration by noting which of a series of tasks of differing difficulty a subject chooses. By varying the difference in the desirability of the toys, Wright could have obtained a measure of the child's level of aspiration with respect to generosity or altruism. That is, she might have found the place at which the child shifted from generosity to selfishness as she increased the difference in desirability between the two toys. This would yield an estimate of the child's "aspiration" with respect to generosity or altruism. It is unfortunate that the term *level of aspiration* has tended to be restricted to achievement situations. It could certainly be extended to a number of other value situations such as this. And if it were, much more information on an individual's value structure could be obtained by using it.

c. *Comparison of Goal Choices With Other Measures of Goal Importance.* Responses in level of aspiration situations can be studied to get at differences in explicit and implicit values. There has been much discussion among workers in the field over the relation between the stated level of aspiration and the "real" or "true" level of aspiration. For instance, Gould reports (1939) the case of a student who set a conscious level of aspiration which she concluded on the basis of an interview was considerably below his real level of aspiration. He stated that he was satisfied with a B average in school although practically no mark of his was ever below a B and his average was A—. In his own words, "I feel if I set myself too high a mark I'll be disappointed when I don't get it and if you set too low a mark I felt I might be discouraged." (1939, p. 52.) He apparently set a low conscious level of aspiration in order to protect himself against possible failure. Gould concludes, "The fact that he only experienced success when his performance was quite a bit *above* the estimate, seems conclusive proof his conscious level of strivings and expectations is restricted to 'minimum' expectations, and that he is actually motivated by a higher repressed level of striving." (1939, p. 53.) Gardner (1940) has argued against making any elaborate inferences about the "true" level of aspiration on the ground that they involve a lot of qualitative interview data which do not justify the use of the term *level* of aspiration implying a quantifiable figure. In spite of this, it has proved possible to utilize in particular the subject's *feelings* of success and failure as a measure of the implicit level of aspiration. Jucknat rated the reaction of her subjects to their performance all the way from "very good success" through a six-point scale to "very strong failure" (cf. Lewin, *et al.*, 1944, p. 338).

As Gould suggests, these feelings of the subject may be a better index of the implicit value placed on achievement than the stated aspiration level which is a product of so many other forces. Furthermore, knowledge of implicit as well as explicit goals will put us in a much better position to study the value structure of the individual, just as when we compare conscious and unconscious self-judgments by the Wolff-Huntley technique.

3. *Statements of self-judgment* may under certain conditions be the easiest of all to interpret. We have already given a number of illustrations of such self-judgments in discussing the Wolff-Huntley technique and in demonstrating how self-evaluation characterizes the self-schema. The values implicit in such judgments may be studied more systematically in one of two ways. The first involves a simple frequency count of the values implicit in a self-description. If we apply this approach to Karl's description of himself in his adolescence quoted earlier in the chapter we arrive at the results given in Table 14.6.

TABLE 14.6

Karl's Self-Description Scored for Implicit Values

A. Scored sample

I was always cooperative (Affiliation) and obedient (Standards), a good student (Achievement) but influenced by others (Affiliation) which sometimes led me into trouble. I was always sensitive and my feelings were and still are easily hurt (Personal Adjustment).

B. Value frequency count for entire section

Non-aggression	1	Peace, Passivity	0
Affiliation	8	Nurturance	0
Achievement	13	Respect, Tolerance	0
Autonomy	1	Sentience	
Moral Standards	5		
Personal Adjustment	2		

This table shows the method by which many statements can be referred to values implied by the use of self-descriptive adjectives (cf. Allport and Odbert, 1936). The set of value categories used in this particular analysis are drawn in part from Murray's list of needs (1938) and is not of course in any sense definitive. One might argue that a free description of this sort is certain to leave out certain important value areas because of instructions the subject gives himself as to what the psychologist would be interested in. While this is a disadvantage, it has its positive side. One could argue that it is precisely those values in terms of which a person *chooses* to describe himself that are of importance to him. Thus we know from Karl's Social Distance scale and from the "Vices" test (Chapter 8) that he values tolerance and has great respect for others, if he is specifically asked about these things. The fact that he does not choose any episode or characteristic which reflects this value in describing himself may suggest that these are not self-relevant values. This does not mean that they are not important values to him at the symbolic level but it does mean that they are not intimately tied up with his self-schema. Achievement, Affiliation (which may account for his high Tolerance), and concern about Moral Standards, on the other hand, are values of great importance to him personally, at least as judged by this particular method of scoring his values.

The other method of getting at values through self-judgments involves using the Wolff-Huntley technique of asking for ratings on unrecognized forms of self-expression. By themselves, whether positive or negative, such judgments presumably reflect the importance of the characteristic being judged in proportion to the extent to which they deviate from a middle judgment or from the mean of similar judgments made of other people's forms of expression. Thus, for instance, a subject might be handed a rating slip containing the following scale to be filled out in response to his own mirrored (and unrecognized) handwriting:

Does this suggest a person who is | ✓ |

Uncooperative — Cooperative

If he checked it as indicated and if he checked other people near the middle of the scale, we might be justified in concluding that Affiliation was an important self-related value. If we had ratings on the same scale of *recognized* self-expressions we would have even more to go on. If, for instance, his conscious self-judgment of cooperativeness is near the middle of the scale, we might infer that he values modesty and does not want to appear too self-centered. Other discrepancies between conscious and unconscious judgments would lead to other kinds of inferences. For example, if he rated himself very high consciously on cooperativeness, but only in the middle of similar self-judgments unconsciously, we might want to infer that his Affiliation orientation was simply for the sake of appearances (Standards) and that this value implicitly was not particularly self-relevant.

4. This kind of analysis comes close to making inferences about value structure from the *kinds of defenses* the person adopts, which is the fourth method of finding out about self-relevant values. As we suggested earlier, clinicians use this method predominantly in drawing inferences about the nature of a person's value system. Suppose, for instance, a person shows a symptomatic act—e.g., in Erickson's well-known hypnotized subject (1939), suppose he says "shut the bore" instead of "shut the door" when he attempts to act in accordance with his desire to shut off the bore who is talking to him. The fact that he does not openly tell the bore to shut up is attributed to some "inhibiting force," to some value schema which prevents such an openly hostile act. Freud gives dozens of similar examples in his *Psychopathology of Everyday Life*. The compromises or symptomatic acts are used in each case to infer (a) what the person wanted to do or say and (b) what the value schema (super-ego) was which distorted the intention. An exactly similar approach is used in analyzing symptoms or milder defense mechanisms. As Alexander points out (1942), a tiger does not need to rationalize his aggression but a man does. Why? Because the man has a set of values which causes him to feel ashamed or guilty for his aggressive impulses and he consequently must defend himself against this anxiety by producing good reasons for his aggressive acts. Similarly, any of the other defense mechanisms—reaction formation, denial, undoing, projection, etc. (cf. A. Freud, 1937)—are seen as compromises worked out by the ego in response to conflicts between essentially antisocial drives and social value schemata belonging to the self-schema and called the *super-ego*.

At the moment we are not so much interested in the results of this approach as we are in considering it as a *method* of drawing inferences about self-relevant values. Obviously as it has been used it involves a great deal of specialized reasoning applicable only to each particular defense as it occurs in a particular person. Can we generalize the method into something which might be used more systematically? One way of doing this has already been suggested in our analysis of level aspiration techniques—e.g., we can compare affect (feelings of success and failure) with consciously set goals and draw inferences from the resulting discrepancies about implicit values. For instance, if a person sets a very high level of aspiration, consistently fails to reach it, and records no particular failure feelings, we may infer that he values conformity greatly but is less concerned either with accuracy (predicting what he will do) or with achievement. Or if he sets his goal low, consistently surpasses it, and shows little feeling of success, we may want to infer that he has strong prohibitions against failure, that his actual achievement goal is higher than set, etc. Brachmachari (as reported in Flugel, 1945) has demonstrated how this sort of approach may be systematically applied in a questionnaire type of study. He asked a number of questions about conventional moral issues on which respondents were asked to record their attitude, their conduct, and the conflict they felt over the issue. For instance, one of the questions was, "Ought we to do our utmost to adhere to the conventional code of sexual morals which condemns all forms of direct sexual satisfaction except marriage (e.g., extra-marital intercourse, homosexuality, masturbation)?" (Flugel, 1945, p. 65.) The subjects rated their attitude and conduct on a scale which ranged from —5 (disagreement) to +5 (complete agreement) and any conflict they felt over the discrepancy between attitude and conduct on a scale from 0 to 5. The results on the "Conventional Sex Morals" item and two others are given in Table 14.7.

TABLE 14.7

Attitude, Conduct, and Conflict with Respect to Various Issues of the Moral Code

		Attitude	*Conduct*	*Discrepancy*	*Conflict*
1. Conventional sex morals	men	+1.12	+1.51	+0.39	1.32
	women	– .02	– .02	– .36	.92
2. Physical courage	men	+1.51	+1.23	– .28	1.39
	women	+ .10	+0.79	+ .69	.91
3. Avoid borrowing	all	+3.26	+ .54	–2.72	1.10

(Reproduced with permission after Brachmachari from J. C. Flugel, *Man, Morals and Society*. Copyright 1945, International Universities Press.)

The discrepancies in various ratings are particularly important for getting at latent values. For instance, why should the men say they behave better on the average with regard to sex morals than they think they should? More than this, why should they feel so much conflict over the issue as compared with women when their conduct is in fact *better* than they consciously require, while women fall slightly short of their aspirations and feel less conflict? Flugel argues that these inconsistencies may be easily explained in terms of a much severer implicit prohibition against unconventional sexuality than the men are willing to admit publicly. Why shouldn't they admit it? To explain this (which Flugel does not attempt) we may have to assume some other value, placed perhaps on being "reasonable" and not "old-fashioned." The other two items also show some interesting discrepancies. Notice how a relatively great discrepancy between attitude and conduct on borrowing is associated with less conflict than is produced by a very small discrepancy over "Physical courage." One is tempted to argue, as Flugel does, that to avoid borrowing is a "nominal ideal without any deep moral feeling behind it" (1945, p. 67). The other two ideals (sex and courage) on the other hand, may be so important to the person that only small discrepancies between attitude and conduct can be tolerated without acute anxiety. Hence the conscious level of aspiration may be actually lowered *below* what it is for "Borrowing" as a means of reducing the discrepancy. Whatever conclusions are finally reached from such arguments as these, the *method* of analyzing discrepancies systematically like this seems a much better way of drawing some of the same kind of inferences about unconscious value schemata that have customarily been drawn by clinicians from the analysis of defenses and symptomatic acts.

Characteristics of Value Schemata. Even though the methodology for studying self-relevant values has been poorly developed to date, a great deal has been written about this aspect of the self, largely by psychoanalysts. Much of it must be regarded by experimentalists as highly speculative in nature, but certain points stand out as so important that they warrant our attention, even if we regard them only as hypotheses to be checked by some of the improved methods just suggested. To begin with it has become common practice to distinguish between the *ego-ideal* and the *super-ego,* both of which are from our viewpoint clusters of values within the self-schema. Although the exact nature of the difference between these two structures is not agreed upon, a distinction suggested by Alexander and Flugel seems most convenient. They both feel that it is best "to use the 'super-ego' for the more unconscious and irrational elements, and the 'ego-ideal' for more conscious and adaptable ones." (Flugel, 1945, p. 77.) The advantage of this distinction is that it is in line with our previous discussion about conscious and unconscious portions of the self-schema and how each develops in the socializing process (cf. Chapter 10).

If we follow this suggestion, we may conveniently describe the characteristics of each by contrasting them one with the other as in the following list:

	Ego-ideal	*Super-ego*
1.	Conscious (symbolized)	Unconscious (unsymbolized)
2.	Self-potent	Ego alien
3.	Source in explicit cultural values	Source in implicit cultural values
4.	Realistic	Irreal, rigid
5.	Dominant mode of reaction is instrumental	Dominant mode of reaction is defensive

As they stand, these characteristics look somewhat more mysterious, speculative, and dichotomous than they really are, for each one refers to an aspect of our previous discussion. Thus by "conscious" and "unconscious" is meant the *degree* to which the person can verbalize the value standards which guide his behavior. Both in our discussion of conscious and unconscious portions of the self-schema and in our discussion of methodology, we have given illustrations of how it can be shown that implicit standards are different from explicit ones. Our second distinction between the ego ideal and super-ego follows from the first. Self-potency is normally associated with the ego ideal since potency is the distinguishing characteristic of the conscious self-picture. A person normally thinks of his ideals as if they were under his control. He may disown his conscience almost, at times, as if it were a foreign body. He speaks of his conscience as *making* him do something, as if it were really ego-alien. Socrates listened to his "daimon," to the voice of his conscience, which told him what to do. In speaking of it he treated it as essentially outside his direct control. His experience seems fairly characteristic. Flugel reports an introspective study by Frenkel and Weisskopf on the differences between wishes and duties, which supports the view that duties are conceived as *external* forces acting on a person who may question their power to move him, while wishes (and corresponding ideals) seem much closer to the self and "impel more vigorously to action." (Flugel, 1945, p. 18.)

The reason for making such a distinction between the ego-ideal and super-ego can perhaps be made clearer by tracing the development of each. The ego-ideal, as we are using the term here, is derived largely from the conscious verbalized, systematic teachings of adults in the environment of the growing child. Its sources are largely ideals that are held up before the child by various members of his culture whether in the home, in school, in Sunday school, Boy Scout organizations, or through the examples set by movie stars, heroes of the comic strips, and other juvenile literature, etc. The values in the ego-ideal are the explicit values of the culture in which the person lives and since he learns them explicitly, he can reproduce them explicitly; that is, he knows what they are and can formulate them verbally if asked.

The super-ego, on the other hand, derives from the implicit values of the culture which the child often learns about from the behavior toward him of members of the culture. Here *early* child training is particularly important because much of it occurs before the child's linguistic discriminations have developed very highly (cf. Chapter 10). Normally the parent does not explain why he punishes Johnny so severely for soiling his pants, partly because at this age Johnny would not understand what he was talking about and partly because the parent would probably find it difficult to verbalize the value which led him to spank Johnny. Almost from birth the child begins to learn what is right and what is wrong from the way in which he is rewarded and punished, but the early value schemata which he develops from such treatment are necessarily *unverbalized.* This does not mean that his behavior is not guided by such schemata. Curiously enough, some behaviorists have argued against the importance of early childhood discipline on the grounds that the child was too young to formulate verbally the somewhat complicated super-ego standards he is supposed to learn according to the psychoanalysts. The fact is that it is just because he is too young to formulate these standards verbally that they may later assume such overwhelming importance in determining his behavior. If he could formulate them and verbalize them, they would be conscious and subject to the control which symbolization brings. It is therefore not surprising to find that much of the content of the super-ego consists of prohibitions or rules of conduct which derive from early parental disciplines.

For the same reason the super-ego tends to be harsher and more rigid than the ego-ideal which is represented symbolically in consciousness. The super-ego's notions of "right" and "wrong" are more primitive, archaic, infantile, and far less adaptable to subtle differences in the external situation. Thus a man may realize on the basis of more mature learning that under certain circumstances it is wiser not to tell the whole truth in order to save another person from suffering, yet in so doing he may suffer severe "qualms of conscience" for violating the rigid implicit standard of truthfulness that admits of no shades of gray. One of the clearest ways of distinguishing between explicit ego-ideal standards and implicit super-ego ones is to observe what happens when the person fails to live up to one or the other. Falling short of a conscious ideal may lead to feelings of disappointment, to revision downward of the level of aspiration, or to renewed efforts to reach it. In short, blocking leads to goal-oriented striving (cf. Chapter 13). But with the super-ego, failure is a different matter. Since the standard is stricter and less adequately understood, falling short results in vague uneasiness or unfocalized anxiety and the person becomes organized around defending himself against this anxiety rather than toward instrumental means of solving the original conflict. In other words, the person is most apt to become defense-oriented rather than goal-oriented according to the distinction made in the last chapter. To summarize once more: a large part of the human being's success in dealing with his environment is dependent upon his ability to symbolize portions of it and to manipulate and control it through these symbols (words, numbers, images etc.). Since the super-ego standards are less adequately symbolized, failure to live up to them can be less effectively dealt with: it tends to result in generalized anxiety which the person copes with by defending himself as best he can against it. It is not hard to see from this argument why we have learned most about how the super-ego functions from the defense mechanisms and symptoms characteristic of neurosis.

Relation of Motives to Self-Relevant Values. All of this discussion has drawn on many of the same kinds of arguments we used to define the nature of motives. Just exactly what is the difference between a motive and an explicit or implicit self-relevant value? One way of looking at the problem is to regard the motive as what makes a value self-relevant. We have argued above that not all values in the sense of ideas which are important to a person (e.g., future orientation) are used in evaluating the self. Could it be that a person's motives determine which important ideas will be used in self-judgments? Suppose we take Karl who, if our analysis is correct, has very strong security and achievement drives. We would argue then that any value which was perceived as fulfilling either or both of these drives would become self-relevant for Karl. And in fact this seems to be the case: in describing his characteristics, he implies achievement and affiliative standards most often, in rating vices he places courage as the most important virtue (personal achievement of security), etc. Other values, such as tolerance, which he accepts as important in his society, seem less clearly self-relevant. They do not fulfill either of his main motives.

Another conclusion follows from this analysis: the most rigid self-relevant values will tend to be the implicit super-ego ones since they will tend to be tied up with motives which are also based on unsymbolized general affective associations (cf. Chapter 12). In this case we can picture the learning of the motive and of the goal which will satisfy it as going on at the same time. The implicit value is the state which is generally associated with disrupting the motive in much the same way that food is the goal or terminal state of the hunger motive. They are in no sense independent of each other and two terms are hardly necessary to distinguish one from the other.

With explicit or ego-ideal values, however, the situation is different. As we have pointed out, they tend to develop *after* motives have been acquired; they are more realistic, more easily influenced by changes in the situation, etc. They are therefore to some extent independent of motives and in time may even take over many of the functions of motives in determining choices. One of the striking things about Frenkel and Weisskopf's study (cf. Flugel, 1945) was that as people got older the distinction between wishes and duties (implicit values) became less marked. What people thought they should do and what they wanted to do became the same thing. One explanation of this finding is that as motivation becomes more differentiated in terms of conscious goals and values, the power of the implicit motives and values laid down in childhood begins to lessen and the person no longer perceives himself as divided into two parts with essentially different aims warring against each other. He responds more in terms of the situation and less in terms of the strong affective associations laid down in childhood, which means that the function of his motives has been taken over to some extent by his cognitively arrived-at values.

NOTES AND QUERIES

1. In spite of our resolution at the beginning of this chapter, many of the concepts introduced to explain the different characteristics of the self-schema do not as yet have operational definitions. Consider self-potency, for example. How could you set up an experiment which would determine whether there were any general stages in the perception of objects, people, etc., as near or far from the self? Granted you found some general trends for groups of peo-

ple, how would you determine the stages on this dimension for a single individual? How would you test the hypothesis that the dimension involved is organized around the perception of potency? What are some alternative ways in which it might be organized? How about similarity, for instance? For methods of measuring schemata refer back to Chapter 9. Would the sequence of recall of elements presented in varying orders be helpful? How about the sequence of free associations starting with various self-related words or stages in the recognition of self-related words? Can you think of developmental studies which might show how the self-schema is organized as it is acquired? Design at least one good experiment in this field.

2. How could you measure whether or not the "integrity" of the self-schema was being "maintained"? What constitutes "integrity" and what constitutes "maintenance"? We have spoken of a certain "minimum level" of self-potency as being "necessary." How could you determine what the minimum level was for a given person? What is it "necessary" for? Could the shift from "instrumental" to "defensive" reactions to frustration be determined with any accuracy? How? If so, how would the result bear on problems of "integrity" of the self-schema? Can you think of any way of inducing changes experimentally in the perception of self-potency?

3. Design an experiment which would test Jung's hypothesis that the *persona* (hierarchy of self-related responses) is less readily shifted in insecure people. This involves finding a measure of self-perception, a method of inducing a change in it, and a way of measuring security-insecurity. Consult Frenkel-Brunswik (1949) and Bruner and Postman (1949) for methods of measuring perceptual resistance to incoming, inconsistent information. Then figure out a way to provide a person with information that he is different from what he thinks he is, etc.

4. The hypothesis is advanced in the text that Karl has not had experience with people who are unusually concerned with security and that therefore his attribution of security concern to others is a reflection of his own security problems. Is there evidence that would throw doubt on the first part of this argument? Make a careful study of his security-related sentence completions so as to be able to evaluate how serious the objection is that this evidence raises.

5. Make a study of the sentence completions (or other test items) which involve reactions to the real or assumed superiority of other

persons. Comment on any differences you find between Karl's statements of his own and of others' reactions to such situations.

6. The text argues that ego strength is largely a function of the *completeness* of the self-picture in incorporating information about the self. Could it be a function of other aspects of the self-picture as well? What ones? How about self-potency or self-consistency? How would you test any hypotheses you advance? Is improvement in adjustment to life a good measure of ego strength? Refer back to the different pictures of Hawk and Helmler in Chapter 3. Is it possible to have a "strong" ego under one set of conditions (e.g., peacetime) which is "weak" under others (e.g., wartime)?

7. Various suggestions have been made in this chapter and others as to why psychotherapy is effective. Bring them together and evaluate them. Design experiments for testing at least one. Refer to the methods of content analysis practiced by Rogers and his students if necessary (cf. Curran, 1945, for a review of them).

8. What is the difference between an idea (Chapter 8) and an idea in terms of which the self is judged (Chapter 14)? Which would you call a "value" and why? Is the difference the same as between a self-relevant and a non-self-relevant value? Give examples of each.

9. What is a simple statement of choice, such as "I like peanuts," a measure of? How does it differ from a measure of choice made by observing the frequency with which the person buys peanuts over a period of time? Does one measure necessitate the concept of the self-schema? Can a rat have a concept of the self? How would you know?

10. The statement is made in this chapter that the super-ego is more "primitive," "archaic," and "infantile" than the ego-ideal. Try to provide operational definitions for each of these three adjectives. Do you have better luck with adjectives like "rigid" or "extreme"? Design an experiment or cite evidence from the chapter which shows that implicit values are more rigid or extreme than explicit ones.

11. Collect evidence or design experiments which would test the hypothesis that self-relevant values with high cognitive support (e.g., belief in the value of science or Christianity) can function like motives or replace them in later life. How would self-relevant values be particularly likely to lead to the acquisition even late in life of the strong affective associations which we have argued are the basis of motives?

15

Interrelation Among the Basic Personality Variables: Predicting the Concrete Act

The job of analysis is done. We have picked our way slowly but systematically through the mass of facts about personality, and concluded that we need at least three basic constructs and one derived one to handle personality in its entirety. We have dissected Karl and studied separately the aspects of his behavior which we have classified under each of these constructs. Now the problem is one of synthesis. What are the relations among the basic constructs we have used to describe personality? Can we give an integrated picture of Karl's personality or are we like "all the king's horses and all the king's men" unable to put Humpty-Dumpty together again? The problem of synthesis is certainly no easy one, and it is the one on which personality theorists have most often failed. It is relatively easy to give a fairly complete description of one aspect of personality at a time and to pretend it is the whole story—which is what the psychoanalysts have often done in dealing only with the motivational or dynamic aspect of personality. But our job is more difficult because our level of aspiration is higher. We now want a *complete* picture even though we may have to sacrifice some of its details to get it.

To begin with a fresh and somewhat less analytic viewpoint, let us consider the organism as a whole, functioning in its environment. As Lewin (1935) has so aptly phrased it, behavior (B) is a joint function of the personality (P) and the environment (E), or: $B = f(P, E)$. Now for the sake of convenience let us consider only the P term in this formula. In a way, that is exactly what we have been doing throughout this book. Our aim has been to consider the person apart from any particular environmental situation and to try to discover what conceptual scheme best fits all of his behavior in all such situations. That is, considering the nature of the environment and of the person's known reactions to it, we have attempted to build up a brief hypothetical scheme of him which will enable us to predict his [illegible] behavior in specific situations. The theoretical constructs used in our hypothetical scheme have not been many. There [illegible] three basic variables—trait, schema, and need—and one derived variable—the self-schema. They are listed in Table 15.1 along [illegible] their chief determinants (antecedent conditions) and measures.

The Chief Determinants and [illegible] Constructs

Determinants	[illegible]	Measures
1. Reinforcement in [illegible] ilar situations	[illegible]	of a response [illegible] similar situ[illegible]
2. Changes in stimulation [illegible] particularly as [illegible] terned by cultu[illegible]	[illegible]	Perceptual responses when external determi[illegible] nants are maximized ("cognition")
3. Undifferentiated [illegible] placed on [illegible] goal responses, [illegible] ticularly early [illegible]	[illegible]	Imaginative goal re[illegible] sponses when external determinants are min[illegible] imized
4. Specific acts and [illegible] D as perceived [illegible] the self	[illegible]	Comments about or judgments of the self

Since constructs [illegible] in proportion to the ease with which they can be measured and made to vary as the function of antecedent conditions, a special effort has been made to tie each construct down at both ends in terms of these two prerequisites. Such tying-down [illegible] to some of the determinants, but incompleteness of [illegible] seems preferable to leaving the matter vague. For example, the general argument is not changed by assuming that it is contiguity rather than reinforcement which accounts for trait formation. Two other general points should be noted about the table before [illegible] into it in detail. First, the terms H and D for Habit and Drive respectively are used because of the close analogy of two of [illegible] constructs to these constructs as used by Hull in his *Principles of Behavior Theory* (1943). The parallel is not exact, particularly in the *antecedent conditions needed to produce a drive,* but it has seemed worth making in this symbolic fashion since ultimately we may hope that all such theoretical super[illegible] tures will grow together, and be consistent one with the other. The S construct is not fully developed Hull, but other behavior theorists, notably Tolman (1948a), I emphasized the importance of this primarily perceptual variab econd, the table represents a spelling out of the P variable in win's equation cited above, which may therefore be rewritten as ows:

$$B = f(H, S, I\ )(E)$$

Such an equation is purely programm c, of course. It says nothing about the nature or form of the re nship among the variables. These can be worked out only in ter f the measures of each one.

Trait Measures. Let us turn the e to these measures. Generally speaking, we will get a pu measure of any particular variable if we eliminate or control nfluence of other variables when we are measuring it. Thus, f mple, when we are interested in a particular trait such as a hievement trait (t Achievement) like working hard, we measu e consistency of a certain class of "working hard" responses, w he person's perception and motivation in various tasks are held tant (cf. Chapter 7). If the person's perception of a particular t hanges, if for instance he becomes ego-involved, the condition getting a "pure" measure of t Achievement have been violate d what we actually get is contaminated by the introduced v on in the perceptual (or motivational) factors which determ ehavior. The fact is that most traits have been measured with other two factors more or less well controlled, which is doubt hy we have been able to develop the trait concept in the fir ce, but nevertheless more explicit attempts to control the oth riables would purify our measures of the trait variable. Ideally, re testing for the presence or absence of a given trait in a partic ew situation, we ought to have a measure of how a person perce he situation, and what his motives are at the moment. Since t s impracticable in many instances, we often have to assume th at he will perceive the situation in a culturally normal fashion (termined by consensus of other cultural members) and bring to ulturally normal motives (e.g., desire to cooperate with the rimenter, etc.). We may summarize this discussion by attemp to give a more or less formal definition of a particular trait as t Achievement.

t Achievement is the inference that erson will respond or less consistently by working hard in a standardized

us to predict his unknown behavior in specific situations. The theoretical constructs used in our hypothetical scheme have not been many. There are three basic variables—trait, schema, and need—and one derived variable—the self-schema. They are listed in Table 15.1 along with their chief determinants (antecedent conditions) and measures.

TABLE 15.1

The Chief Determinants and Measures of the Basic Hypothetical Constructs Used in Our Conceptualization of Personality

Determinants	*Construct*	*Symbol*	*Measures*
1. Reinforcement in similar situations	Trait	(t or H)	Consistency of a response in past or similar situations
2. Changes in stimulation particularly as patterned by culture	Schema	(s or S)	Perceptual responses when external determinants are maximized ("cognition")
3. Undifferentiated stress placed on certain goal responses, particularly early in life	Need or Motive	(n or D)	Imaginative goal responses when external determinants are minimized
4. Specific acts and S, H, D as perceived by the self	Self-Schema	(sS)	Comments about or judgments of the self

Since constructs such as these are useful in proportion to the ease with which they can be measured and made to vary as the function of antecedent conditions, a special effort has been made to tie each construct down at both ends in terms of these two prerequisites. Such tying-down may do violence to some of the determinants, but incompleteness of this sort seems preferable to leaving the matter vague. For example, the general argument is not changed by assuming that it is *contiguity* rather than *reinforcement* which accounts for trait formation. Two other general points should be noted about the table before we go into it in detail. First, the terms H and D for Habit and Drive respectively are used because of the close analogy of two of our constructs to these constructs as used by Hull in his *Principles of Behavior Theory* (1943). The parallel is not exact, *particularly in the antecedent conditions needed to produce a drive,* but it has seemed worth making in this symbolic fashion, since ultimately we may hope that all such theoretical superstructures will grow together, and be consistent one with the other. The S construct is not fully developed in Hull, but other behavior theorists, notably Tolman (1948a), have emphasized the importance of this primarily perceptual variable. Second, the table represents a spelling out of the P variable in Lewin's equation cited above, which may therefore be rewritten as follows:

$$B = f\,(H, S, D, sS)\,(E)$$

Such an equation is purely programmatic, of course. It says nothing about the nature or form of the relationship among the variables. These can be worked out only in terms of the measures of each one.

Trait Measures. Let us turn therefore to these measures. Generally speaking, we will get a purer measure of any particular variable if we eliminate or control the influence of other variables when we are measuring it. Thus, for example, when we are interested in a particular trait such as an achievement trait (t Achievement) like working hard, we measure the consistency of a certain class of "working hard" responses, when the person's perception and motivation in various tasks are held constant (cf. Chapter 7). If the person's perception of a particular task changes, if for instance he becomes ego-involved, the conditions for getting a "pure" measure of t Achievement have been violated and what we actually get is contaminated by the introduced variation in the perceptual (or motivational) factors which determine behavior. The fact is that most traits have been measured with the other two factors more or less well controlled, which is doubtless why we have been able to develop the trait concept in the first place, but nevertheless more explicit attempts to control the other variables would purify our measures of the trait variable. Ideally, before testing for the presence or absence of a given trait in a particular new situation, we ought to have a measure of how a person perceives the situation, and what his motives are at the moment. Since this is impracticable in many instances, we often have to assume that he will perceive the situation in a culturally normal fashion (as determined by consensus of other cultural members) and bring to it culturally normal motives (e.g., desire to cooperate with the experimenter, etc.). We may summarize this discussion by attempting to give a more or less formal definition of a particular trait such as t Achievement.

t Achievement is the inference that a person will respond more or less consistently by working hard (a) in a standardized class of

us to predict his unknown behavior in specific situations. The theoretical constructs used in our hypothetical scheme have not been many. There are three basic variables—trait, schema, and need—and one derived variable—the self-schema. They are listed in Table 15.1 along with their chief determinants (antecedent conditions) and measures.

TABLE 15.1

The Chief Determinants and Measures of the Basic Hypothetical Constructs Used in Our Conceptualization of Personality

Determinants	*Construct*	*Symbol*	*Measures*
1. Reinforcement in similar situations	Trait	(t or H)	Consistency of a response in past or similar situations
2. Changes in stimulation particularly as patterned by culture	Schema	(s or S)	Perceptual responses when external determinants are maximized ("cognition")
3. Undifferentiated stress placed on certain goal responses, particularly early in life	Need or Motive	(n or D)	Imaginative goal responses when external determinants are minimized
4. Specific acts and S, H, D as perceived by the self	Self-Schema	(sS)	Comments about or judgments of the self

Since constructs such as these are useful in proportion to the ease with which they can be measured and made to vary as the function of antecedent conditions, a special effort has been made to tie each construct down at both ends in terms of these two prerequisites. Such tying-down may do violence to some of the determinants, but incompleteness of this sort seems preferable to leaving the matter vague. For example, the general argument is not changed by assuming that it is *contiguity* rather than *reinforcement* which accounts for trait formation. Two other general points should be noted about the table before we go into it in detail. First, the terms H and D for Habit and Drive respectively are used because of the close analogy of two of our constructs to these constructs as used by Hull in his *Principles of Behavior Theory* (1943). The parallel is not exact, *particularly in the antecedent conditions needed to produce a drive,* but it has seemed worth making in this symbolic fashion, since ultimately we may hope that all such theoretical superstructures will grow together, and be consistent one with the other. The S construct is not fully developed in Hull, but other behavior theorists, notably Tolman (1948a), have emphasized the importance of this primarily perceptual variable. Second, the table represents a spelling out of the P variable in Lewin's equation cited above, which may therefore be rewritten as follows:

$$B = f(H, S, D, sS)(E)$$

Such an equation is purely programmatic, of course. It says nothing about the nature or form of the relationship among the variables. These can be worked out only in terms of the measures of each one.

Trait Measures. Let us turn therefore to these measures. Generally speaking, we will get a purer measure of any particular variable if we eliminate or control the influence of other variables when we are measuring it. Thus, for example, when we are interested in a particular trait such as an achievement trait (t Achievement) like working hard, we measure the consistency of a certain class of "working hard" responses, when the person's perception and motivation in various tasks are held constant (cf. Chapter 7). If the person's perception of a particular task changes, if for instance he becomes ego-involved, the conditions for getting a "pure" measure of t Achievement have been violated and what we actually get is contaminated by the introduced variation in the perceptual (or motivational) factors which determine behavior. The fact is that most traits have been measured with the other two factors more or less well controlled, which is doubtless why we have been able to develop the trait concept in the first place, but nevertheless more explicit attempts to control the other variables would purify our measures of the trait variable. Ideally, before testing for the presence or absence of a given trait in a particular new situation, we ought to have a measure of how a person perceives the situation, and what his motives are at the moment. Since this is impracticable in many instances, we often have to assume that he will perceive the situation in a culturally normal fashion (as determined by consensus of other cultural members) and bring to it culturally normal motives (e.g., desire to cooperate with the experimenter, etc.). We may summarize this discussion by attempting to give a more or less formal definition of a particular trait such as t Achievement.

t Achievement is the inference that a person will respond more or less consistently by working hard (a) in a standardized class of performance situations, (b) under the influence of a class of motives limited in range and intensity. Within the limits set by (a) and (b), t Achievement will vary in strength and consistency as a direct function of the amount of reinforcement received for such behavior in previous similar situations.

What this definition says in brief is that other things being equal (e.g., needs and schemata), t Achievement will vary as a function of reinforcement (reward or punishment) for the class of responses defined as belonging under t Achievement in previous situations. This means that we could build any amount of t Achievement into an individual if we had control over his life history. Since we do not have such control, we must be content with building in habits or traits in rats and discovering the principles of their formation or with discovering the strength or consistency of t Achievement in a particular person by measuring the consistency of this response pattern in a variety of situations in which schemata (perceptions) and needs are approximately the same. Unfortunately, to require that the schemata and needs be the same or *standardized* in test situations is not to say very much. We still have to determine under *what* motivational-perceptual conditions we want to test for t Achievement. Should we limit our measures of t Achievement to those situations in which the motive is to cooperate with the experimenter and the tasks are laboratory games? Or should we attempt to control these variables at a somewhat higher level, say in a study situation in which the motivation involved may be n Achievement and the task perceived as something on which people in our culture are supposed to do well? What are the relationships between t Achievement, measured when S and D are at one determination, and t Achievement when they are at another? These are all questions which cannot be answered at the present time, although there is no reason why they could not be answered by empirical observations within the theoretical framework presented here.

Schema Measures. When we turn to the *schema* construct, the situation is similar. Again we want to measure the person's "perception of the situation" providing past experience and motivation are standardized. Such standardization is assumed in normal experiments on the attributes of sensation. That is, we bring in a normal subject off the street and ask him to judge whether a tone he has just heard is higher or lower than the tone he heard earlier. Implicit in the procedure are the assumptions, first, that the subject has had a normal experience with sounds of different pitches and has learned to make judgments of higher and lower, and second, that his motivation is to do what the experimenter asks him to do rather than, for example, to show aggression toward him. Provided both these assumptions are valid, we may then proceed to measure perceptual responses as a function of changes in stimulation. If either of our two assumptions is not valid, that is, if either motivation or past experience does not fall within a normal range, then our response measure is an "impure" indicator of perception and normally we discard the results. Once again we may attempt to summarize this discussion with a formal statement, using achievement as our example:

> s Achievement is the inference as to what class of situations a person will define as achievement-related (a) under the influence of a class of motives limited in range and intensity and (b) within certain limits as to the specific kinds of past experiences (reinforcements) he has had in this area. Within the limits set by (a) and (b), s Achievement for any person will vary as a direct function of the cultural definition of achievement-related situations (i.e., what others in his group say is achievement-related).

Note that in this statement we have shifted from the reporting of a simple sensation ("that is blue") to the reporting of a complex cultural idea ("that is achievement-related"). But the two cases are on the same continuum, although the latter is less well defined than the former. That is, it is the culture which defines a certain class of stimuli as being a "sound" and another class of situations as being "achievement-related," although we normally do not speak of a culture pattern as often in the first instance as we do in the second. The important difference between the two cases is that there is more room for variation in the latter in the way people perceive (report) the stimulus pattern. But in both cases, if we are interested in how a particular person perceives it, we control his needs and idiosyncratic past experiences and measure his response to the stimulus pattern as compared with the consensus among responses given by other people to it. This is so easily done for simple sensory and perceptual patterns that whole schools of psychology have developed which ignore or attempt to dispose altogether with the past experience and motivational determinants of behavior. This has been particularly true of Gestalt theory, which in its more extreme forms (cf. Krech and Crutchfield, 1948) has sometimes attempted to absorb the other variables used here in a somewhat "totalitarian" manner.

One of the major "peculiarities" or difficulties with drawing inferences about the schema construct (or any perception, for that matter) is that we are often not as interested in the *intensity* or *strength* dimension as we are in the case of traits or motives. As we discovered in Chapter 8, we want to know *what* a person's ideas are, what *pattern* of elements they consist of, more than how *strong* they are. This requires the development of some kind of mathematics (e.g., matrix algebra) which is different from the one we are accustomed to use in handling simple variations in strength or intensity.

Need Measures. Our measure of motivation is on shakier ground than our measures of schemata or traits. It consists of counting and classifying goal imagery of various sorts in a test situation for which there is no specifically relevant learned response and in which the present external stimulus determinants are minimized. In short, we use the ordinary test of free association or imagination in which the stimulus "constraints" are reduced and in which the person ordinarily would not have acquired directly appropriate responses on the basis of his past experience. This suggests why it is that products of imagination, whether in the form of dreams, free associations, or Thematic Apperception Test productions, have given rise to the concept of motivation, since it is in imagination that the other two major determinants of behavior (past experience, stimulus conditions) are greatly reduced in importance. It also suggests why other measures of motivation such as self-ratings or goal choices have not proven as fruitful. In both these cases schemata and habits enter more fully into the determination of the response, which consequently becomes an "impure" measure of motivation. In short, to get a good measure of motivation the influence of the other variables must be controlled and preferably minimized. While this view would not be generally held among experimental psychologists, we have seen in the chapters on motivation how those who have worked extensively in the field of human motivation—from Freud and Murray to the experimental work of McClelland and associates—have by and large worked with imaginative products. With this as background we may attempt to make a formal statement of the nature of the motive construct, again using achievement as an example:

> n Achievement is an inference as to the extent to which the person's behavior is guided by anticipated or past achievement satisfactions or dissatisfactions (a) in a standardized class of situations (b) within certain limits as to the specific kinds of past experiences (reinforcements) the person has had in those situations. Within the limits set by (a) and (b), n Achievement is a direct function of the amount of undifferentiated stress placed on achievement, differentiation being a positive growth function of the age at which stress is applied.

This definition draws heavily on the arguments in Chapter 12 and Chapter 10 in stating that, other things being equal, a need is directly determined by the undifferentiated stress placed on certain cue-response sequences primarily in early childhood. It differs from the traditional experimental approach which has conceived of deprivation as the chief antecedent condition for motivation.

Our argument has been that while deprivation may be a condition for the arousal of a motive which has already been established, we are more concerned here with how the motive got established in the first place. And the best guess at the present time seems to be that early socialization procedures are very important in establishing more or less permanent affective associations which lie at the root of motivational trends, at least as measured in adulthood in imagination. While this guess also has the support of years of psychoanalytic experience and theorizing, nevertheless it should be regarded as much less firmly established than the antecedent conditions associated with our other two basic personality variables.

Once again we must note in passing that those who have been primarily interested in needs or motives have tended also to be somewhat "imperialistic" and to disregard in consequence the other variables influencing behavior (cf. Fenichel, 1945). Thus, to read some psychoanalysts one would think that perception was *wholly* determined by motivation and that stimulus determinants were of little or no importance. As we have noted in Chapter 13, it is all too easy to find such statements as that a surgeon cuts people up because of a strong unconscious, sadistic drive. Nor is it enough to amend this statement as Alexander has (1942) to the effect that the surgeon may cut off someone's leg partly for altruistic motives, although these motives may also be involved. A complete and more correct statement would be that the concrete act (cutting off someone's leg) is a joint function of certain motives, aggressive or altruistic, certain schemata (ideas about his job) and traits (skills or habits reinforced in similar past situations). In this as in all other similar cases, we must beware of imperialistic tendencies on the part of those theorists who work exclusively with the data on which only one of our three constructs is based.

Little has been said about the fourth construct (Table 15.1)—namely, the self-schema—largely because it has been treated more fully in the preceding chapter and because it is a derivative concept rather than a "basic" one. That is, as we have tried to make clear, the self-schema is derived from the observation of one's own behavior and involves an implicit conceptualization of the self which is not theoretically unlike the conceptualization an outside observer might construct, although it may be inaccurate in many places. The reason why this particular schema is included in Table 15.1 is that it seems to have an *emergent* quality which differentiates it from other schema. When the self-schema is aroused (as in ego-involvement) it seems to enter independently along with traits, schemata, and motives into determining concrete acts.

Relations Among the Personality Variables. So far we have treated these basic personality variables as if they were completely independent. Such is not the case. It would be premature to attempt to state what the relationships are (particularly since they may vary from individual to individual), in the absence of any experimentation directed at precisely this point. However, it may be worth listing some sample relationships which are either indicated by previous experimentation or which are suggested by the nature of the constructs themselves.

1. As n Achievement increases in intensity in an individual, the number of situations defined by the individual as achievement-related (s Achievement) will also increase. This follows from the evidence in Chapter 13 that motivation increases the perception of the relatedness of events.

2. As n Achievement increases in intensity, t Achievement, when defined as efficiency, will first increase and then decrease (cf. Chapter 13).

3. As s Achievement increases in importance (clarity, cognitive support) for the individual, the more t Achievement becomes tied to external stimulus patterns—to promptings from without. In other

words, the more important the culturally defined patterns of achievement become for the individual, the more his persistence and achievement activities will be tied to situations which are defined by the culture as achievement-related and the less "consistent" his t Achievement will become *in all situations.*

4. As t Achievement increases in consistency and importance, the more n Achievement gets attached to means rather than ends. There are probably some individuals whose goal satisfactions come from working hard rather than from accomplishing something with that hard work (cf. Allport, 1937).

Such statements merely illustrate the kinds of interrelationships which may exist among the basic variables we have been discussing. Many more could be listed, but there would be no point in doing so since none of them has been explicitly subjected to experimental attack. The point in listing them at all is to show how the particular hypothetical constructs we have used in developing our theoretical system of personality do suggest hypotheses as to interrelationships in the personality structure that can be tested. And, as we argued in Chapter 4, one of the tests of the usefulness of a hypothetical construct is the ease with which it generates such hypotheses. Finally, it should be noted, that we have worked out our illustrations solely in terms of achievement-related schemata, traits, and motives, not because there is any peculiar virtue about this particular area of personality, but because more is known about interrelationships here than elsewhere. The same approach should be applicable to other areas of personality as well.

Final Conceptualization of Karl's Personality. With this theoretical introduction we may now turn our attention to the concrete problem of trying to summarize all the inferences we have made throughout the book about Karl's traits, schemata, and motives. This is no easy task. In the first place it is very complex. We have already summarized in several places different aspects of his personality and now we must try to summarize and relate these summaries. Even more troublesome are the interpretive problems which arise from not having collected data on him properly in the first place. Now that we have developed a conceptual scheme which suggests what the operations are for measuring various traits, schemata, and motives, we should be in a much better position to go back to our subject and explore his personality structure systematically. However, the data came first and gave rise to the conceptual scheme and were not specifically collected in terms of it. The dilemma may be made clearer by an analogy. It is as if we had gone out to discover the basic attributes of sound by collecting naïve reports from a number of subjects on auditory stimulation. After analyzing and correlating these reports, we might arrive at the attributes of pitch, loudness, etc., at which point we would ordinarily return to experimentation and study each of them separately with the others more or less under control. We would not attempt to use the miscellaneous observations we started with to derive statements of the relation between pitch and loudness, etc. Yet this is almost exactly what we will now attempt to do for Karl. The process, therefore, must necessarily be intuitive and inexact. If our over-all scheme is any good at all, it should suggest ways of collecting data more systematically on a person so as to arrive at a more coherent, consistent, and adequate theoretical picture of him. Ultimately, we should be able to develop critical tests which, like the tests in qualitative analysis in chemistry, will enable us to determine the bonds and linkages among various traits, schemata, and motives.

Yet we must do the best we can with Karl because a summary personality picture of him is necessary to complete our theoretical analysis. First of all we may begin with listing the major traits, schemata, and motives which we have discovered in our analysis of him. Table 15.2 summarizes these data.

The traits selected are the ones which Karl shows most consistently according to our analysis in Chapter 7. There are doubtless many others which he shows to a moderate degree, but they do not interest us as much as these, partly because we must simplify the picture, and partly because only a fair degree of consistency may mean that the trait dimension is irrelevant to this particular personality. The schemata in the table have been grouped under three headings, representing first, the general cultural orientations discussed in Chapter 8; second, the role model themas discussed in Chapter 9; and finally, the general themas derived primarily from fantasy reflections of socialization procedures discussed in Chapter 10. The needs or motives listed are stated both positively and negatively in line with our general theoretical position taken in Chapters 11 and 12 that approach and avoidance motives may usefully be distinguished. Not all the motives are of the same strength, but there is not much we can do about representing this fact in the absence of adequate measures of motive strength. In general, *the smaller the serial number, the stronger the motive is estimated to be.* In some cases motives

TABLE 15.2

List of Karl's Important Traits, Schemata, and Motives According to Prior Analyses

Traits (Chapter 7)

T 1. Energetic
T 2. Expansive
T 3. Global, nonanalytic thinking
T 4. Fluent
T 5. Outer orientation
T 6. Variable in performance
T 7. Emotionally labile
T 8. Emotionally expressive
T 9. Gregarious
T 10. Submissive, adaptable
T 11. Conscientious

Schemata (Chapter 8)

S 1. Happiness: every person should be happy
S 2. Loneliness: a man stands alone without strong solidary support
S 3. Individual achievement: every man must be a success by his own efforts
S 4. Optimism-progress: man is increasing his knowledge and control of nature
S 5. Fear of others: the world is full of potentially dangerous competitors, authoritarian figures, etc.

Role themas (Chapter 9)

Thema 1. Men are strict, hardworking, but insecure and unhappy.
Thema 2. Women are demanding and insecure but ideally nurturant.
Thema 3. An adolescent boy should conform to adult norms of good behavior to be a success.

General themas

Thema 4. The way to resolve the conflicts in the cultural ideology (S1-S5) is through romantic love, the love of God, and a service occupation (Chapter 8).
Thema 5. People expect more of me than I can accomplish (Chapter 10).
Thema 6. Desertion (rejection) leads to a conflict of aggressive and affiliative desires which is resolved by repressing and projecting aggression and accentuating affiliation (Chapter 10).

Needs

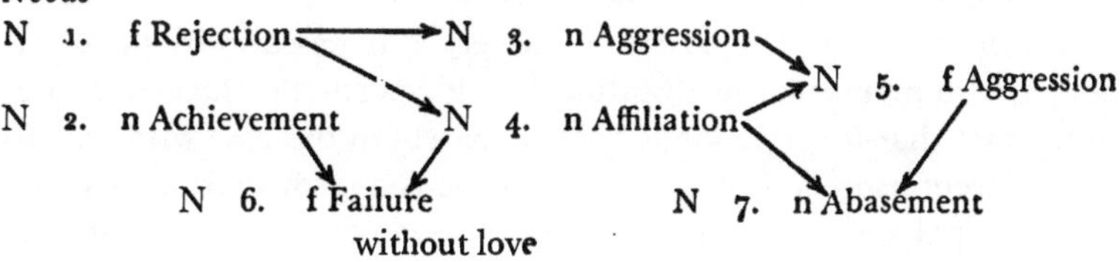

are opposed to each other and in some cases not. n Aggression and f Aggression produce conflict since under ordinary circumstances Karl cannot satisfy both needs by the same act. Generally speaking, as we have seen, f Aggression wins out and he is cooperative and friendly to all. On the other hand, fear of being rejected can reinforce n Affiliation, as seems to be the case, and a particular act, notably dreaming about a warm, all-embracing love, may satisfy both needs simultaneously. However, some conflict is still involved since any close love-relationship he enters into should, for a time at least, arouse fear of rejection and desertion more intensely. Finally, n Achievement and f Failure may also partly reinforce each other and partly interfere with one another. In Karl's case it would appear that they are nearly evenly balanced at a fairly high level of intensity which would suggest some irregularity in actual performance, particularly since this motive complex seems so intimately tied up with the security motives and dependent on their satisfaction.

Granted that Table 15.2 represents an adequate sample of the traits, schemata, and motives in Karl's personality, how are we to bring them into relationship to each other? How are we to put Humpty-Dumpty together again? This is the same problem that we met in part in Chapter 8. Matrix analysis can be helpful here as it was there. That is, each individual item in Table 15.2 can be compared with every other item and a judgment made first as to whether the two items are related and secondly as to whether the relationship is mutual or in one "direction" or another. Such an approach is a way of making sure that all relationships are systematically explored. Yet in the end the final picture will unfortunately still depend a good deal on the synthesizing and integrating capacities of the human mind until some better techniques are developed. Table 15.3 represents an attempt at a synthesis of the data in Table 15.2.

In this diagram we have chosen to place the motives at the center in line with notions about "depth" psychology, traits on the outside as more peripheral aspects of personality, and schemata in between. What these "layers" represent is largely convenience in pictorial design, although some justification for this particular hierarchy lies in the fact that it corresponds approximately to the ease with which the different aspects of personality can be changed. Presumably the motivational structure, having been laid down earlier in life, is

TABLE 15.3

Attempted Synthesis of Karl's Personality Structure

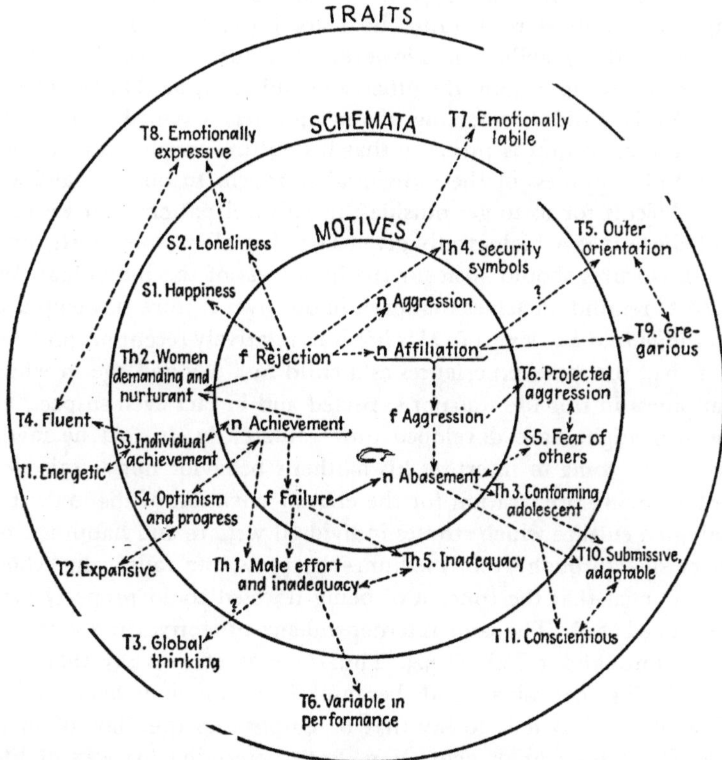

not easily modified, whereas traits, being products of later learning, could be altered provided conditions change sufficiently (either within the person or within the environment). This method of portraying the relations among our variables is defective at many points, as all diagrams must be, but it does suggest several of the most important features of the over-all personality structure.

In the first place the arrows indicate that many of the relationships between motives and schemata are mutual rather than one-sided. To take a concrete instance, we have represented the strong f Rejection which activates Karl as interacting with rather than determining his idea that individuals should be happy. Psychoanalysts often talk as if a motive operates solely as a selective device which searches among the ideas present in a culture and picks those which are most suited to its purpose. If this were so, we could simply say that Karl believes the happiness of an individual to be supremely important because he fears rejection and has such a strong need for affiliation. However, it is just as feasible to turn this relationship around the other way and to argue that the reason why Karl's childhood feeling of rejection has assumed such major importance to him is precisely that his culture emphasizes the welfare and happiness of the individual so much. In our day and age it is difficult for us to get outside this cultural pattern and we tend to believe it is a biologically given fact that all people at all times in all cultures should wish for the happiness of the individual. We need to remind ourselves that even in our own culture this emphasis on *individual happiness in this life* is of relatively recent origin. Had Karl had the same experiences as a child in a day and age in which happiness in this life was not expected and in fact even suspect, his motives might have developed quite differently. In fact he might even have come to interpret his mother's behavior not as rejection but as loving preparation for the eternal salvation of his soul. It is only in a culture which stresses individual welfare and happiness on every side through every medium—the press, the radio, the school system, etc.—that the concept of being rejected could properly have developed at all. The same interdependence of motives and schemata exists throughout Table 15.3. Thus it is as true to say that Karl inhibits his aggressive trends because of his conscious belief in the "law of love" as it is to say that he emphasizes the "law of love" because of his fear of aggression. Both determine his way of life. Likewise the cultural emphasis on lack of solidary relationships ("loneliness") increases his fear of rejection and his fear of rejection stresses the isolation of the individual in the culture and so on. Some relations between motives and schemata seem to be primarily in one direction, as, for example, the relation between his conflicts over achievement and the "inadequacy" thema. But most of the relations are reciprocal.

It should also be noted that the table, in stressing relationships between motives and schemata, does not adequately picture the relations among the schemata themselves. This is compensated for to some extent by Figure 8.1 which does show some of these relationships. Finally, the traits are pictured as being products of motive-schemata complexes for the most part, although they are dependent on recurrent environmental situations in a way which is not clearly indicated in the diagram. This accounts for the traits which are not dynamically connected with any particular motivational complex. That is, some traits are more dependent upon recurrent situational determinants than on recurrent dynamic ones. Thus in the case of imaginative fluency, for example, we could argue that this trait was developed in part out of an interaction of a strong need for achievement and a fear of rejection (forcing introversion) and in part out of the cultural emphasis on adventure, optimism, and progress, but there must also have been a contribution made by Karl's hereditary intellectual equipment. The same would appear to be true for his energy. This could be modified by his needs and schemata, but the biological determinant of this trait makes a rather large contribution to it. In short, as we have seen in the trait theory chapter, certain traits seem largely determined by and get their names from the physical aspect of the person-environment interaction (e.g., bicycle-riding, physical motility, etc.). These traits fit less well in the table than those which are determined and named primarily in terms of the individual's reaction to the environment (e.g., gregariousness, submissiveness, etc.).

The many different relationships schematically represented in Table 15.3 need not be described here in full, since one of the purposes of such a table is to condense what might take many pages to describe. The reader can work out these relationships for himself and should do so in preparation for predicting how Karl will behave in a variety of concrete situations in a college environment. But before turning to this test of the adequacy of our conceptual scheme, we must pursue our theoretical analysis of the interaction between the person and his environment a little further.

The Problem of Prediction. If we return for a moment to our formula $B = f(P, E)$, we note that so far we have achieved a better understanding of the P term in the equation. In a certain sense this is a satisfaction in itself because one of the purposes of our scientific inquiry is the understanding of personality structure. If the job of Table 15.3 has been well done, we should feel that we have a better understanding of Karl's personality structure. Nevertheless we want to know more. We want to be able to predict what Karl will do on a certain occasion or in certain situations. This desire for prediction does not simply reflect our American concern for social engineering—for predicting the behavior of human beings so that we can control it. Rather, prediction will test the adequacy of our formulation of the P term in the equation, provided we have a knowledge of the E term. That is, if we know the nature of the concrete environmental situation, then our knowledge of the personality structure, if it is correct, should enable us to predict the specific behavior which will occur. If we attempt to predict the behavior on the basis of knowledge of the personality structure *alone* without knowledge of the environmental situation, our predictions will not be an adequate test of the conceptualization of the personality system. On the other hand, the more accurate our knowledge of the environmental situation, the better should be our test of the adequacy of the personality conceptualization when we predict what the person should think or do in response to that situation. But doesn't this make testing our conceptualizations difficult, if not impossible? How can we know ahead of time exactly what situation a person will meet? As we have seen in Chapter 4 there will always be some uncertainty about predicting what a person will be doing tomorrow, just as there will always be some uncertainty about predicting what a certain chemical will be doing at 5 P.M. on the afternoon of March 24th. Prediction in science does not necessarily refer to future events. Thus we may build up a conceptual scheme for a person like Karl on the basis of some behavioral facts and then attempt to predict how he will react in other situations, the nature of which is known because they have in fact already occurred to him. It is for this reason that we have withheld part of our knowledge about Karl, particularly the part dealing with his behavior in a college environment. If we can describe accurately the general character of his environment in college or the specific character of test situations in college, we can test the adequacy of our conceptualization of his personality by predicting on the basis of his personality *and the situation* what his behavior in a variety of concrete instances should be and then checking this behavior against what he actually did. If we can predict better than chance, if we can predict better than we could after knowing the nature of the environment alone, if we can predict better than on the basis of knowing the environment plus the intuitive knowledge gained by reading a portion of his autobiography earlier, then and only then can we feel justified in concluding that our systematic attempt at conceptualizing his personality has added anything to our understanding of him.

Perhaps the situation is made clearer by Table 15.4, which diagrams the interrelationships among personality variables, environmental variables, and predicted behavior.

TABLE 15.4

Interaction of Personality and Environment on a Particular Occasion Showing How Behavior May Be Predicted

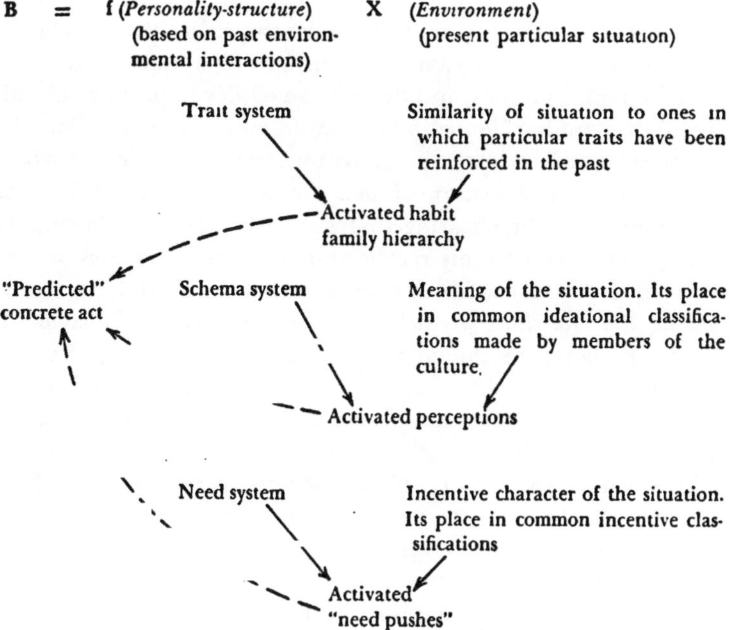

This table has been designed to show aspects of the environment which are relevant to the arousal of trait systems, schema systems, or drive systems respectively. Not shown in the table is the way in which the environment may determine a concrete act directly, independently of what systems it arouses in the personality. In other words, a particular environmental situation *permits* only a limited number of responses. The organism cannot do anything at all. If we are trying to predict, for example, what Karl will do on a Strong Vocational Interest Test we must limit our predictions to a Like, Indifferent, or Dislike response. No other response, except refusing to answer, is possible in this situation or at least counted if it occurs. Knowledge of the environmental situation then narrows the range of possible responses within which we are to predict what the person will do. This limitation is more apparent for overt responses than it is for covert ones. Murray (1938) has emphasized that we must not only predict what a person will do but what he thinks and feels. That is, it would be just as important for us to predict that Karl feels intensely hostile toward the college which forces him to take the Strong Vocational Interest Test (if he thought this to be so) as it would be to predict that he chooses a particular "Like" alternative in answer to a certain question. These feelings, emotions, and the like are harder to predict not only because they are less limited by the nature of the situation, but also because they cannot immediately be observed. The scientist has to rely on some indirect measure of them such as one of the physiological signs of emotion, the swearing that Karl does under his breath, or, what is most common, his recollection and report of how he felt afterward. Nevertheless Murray seems to be theoretically correct in insisting that we must predict both overt and covert behavior. If we attempt both, we should realize that it is more important to specify the nature of the situation for overt behavior since it places greater constraints on what a person can do than it does for covert behavior.

To return to Table 15.4, just how are the various aspects of the environment related to the various personality systems in the left-hand column? The relationships can probably be explained most easily in terms of an example. Let us try to predict Karl's behavior on a particular occasion. Suppose he is on his way upstairs to his room to study one evening at college. On his way he passes by another room and sees a boy sitting at his desk. What will he do? Will he stop and chat? Or will he continue on his way to his room? In trying to predict we can first of all eliminate, according to the suggestion made above, certain responses as being impossible or improbable because of the nature of the situation. We can rule out the possibility of his calling his mother on the telephone to ask her what he should do, since there is no telephone in the college dormitory. We can rule out his suddenly sitting on the floor in a Buddha-like posture, not because it is physically impossible, but because it is highly unlikely in such a situation in our culture. On similar grounds we can rule out the possibility of his suddenly jumping over the stair railing or out the window and dashing himself to bits on the ground below. And so on.

Instead we may limit ourselves to the most likely probabilities, namely, his going on to his room or his stopping to talk with the other boy. To help predict which response he will choose, we will turn first of all to the aspect of the situation which is related to any relevant trait system. The question we ask here is simply this: Is this situation similar to other situations in which Karl has shown similar behavior? If it is similar we can argue that it will activate a habit family hierarchy, in which one of the responses which has high positive "excitatory potential" will be entering the room and talking with the other boy. In this particular instance we know that this situation is similar to other situations in which Karl has displayed a trait which we have called "gregariousness." We know that on many previous similar occasions, Karl has stopped and talked with others or shown related behavior. It should definitely help our prediction to know that the situation is similar to other situations in which he has displayed a consistent response of gregariousness and will therefore tend to activate this class of responses on this occasion.

Coming on down Table 15.4 we arrive at the aspect of the environment which is labeled "meaning of the situation." This is none other than our old friend, the cultural pattern defining the nature of the situation. How does the college culture "define" the nature of this situation? If we know that in the culture such a chance meeting in the evening is defined by other members of the group as an occasion for sitting around and "bulling," it will help us predict what Karl will do, because it will help us predict how he will *perceive the situation.* On the other hand, if we know more, if we know that the boy is studying for a written examination he is to take the next morning, we may be able to state that Karl perceives the situation differently since it is a pattern in this culture not to interrupt somebody who is cramming for an exam. In short, knowing the place of a particular situation in the cultural ideological framework will help us predict what schemata will be aroused in Karl—

what perceptions and ideas he will have about the situation. These in turn should help us predict what he will do.

Finally we want to know what motives the situation is likely to arouse in Karl. Here again we should know what the incentive characteristics are of stopping and talking with another person. This is like asking what drive food is related to. In short, we are asking what potentialities the situation has for gratification of various drives. We cannot ask this in the abstract, but must decide it in cultural (or sometimes individual) terms, in terms of whether members of the culture (or Karl) commonly perceive the situation as offering opportunities for the gratification of a particular drive. In the present instance we can say with some certainty that stopping and talking with a friendly fellow student should be a sufficient incentive to arouse Karl's strong n Affiliation. We have referred to such an activated drive as a "need-push" borrowing a term from Tolman (1948b), who uses it in much the same sense. A *need-push* is the strength of a particular need on a particular occasion resulting from the interaction of the environment and the person's need system. It is seldom enough to know that any *one* need has been aroused by a situation. In this situation we can argue that motives other than n Affiliation will also be aroused in Karl. What about his n Achievement, for example, when he sees the other boy studying? Or perhaps the boy is not very friendly, in which case we might assume that his f Rejection is high enough to motivate him to go on up to his room. Making a prediction under such circumstances would seem extremely hazardous. It is particularly so in the present instance because our example is hypothetical. We have no particular occasion and no particular fellow student in mind.

Nevertheless, on the basis of a consideration of all these factors we would seem justified in predicting that on *many* such occasions Karl would stop in and talk. Our prediction for a number of such occasions is certain to be better than it is for any particular one of them. We can even make some quantitative predictions such as that, out of a hundred such opportunities, Karl will enter the room in 80 or 90 per cent of the cases. The instances in which he does not enter would be attributed to special factors such as those we have mentioned: e.g., a boy studying for a written examination, an unfriendly boy, or an especially strong arousal of Karl's own n Achievement. What we are saying is that Karl's trait of gregariousness, his perception of the situation as one calling for social interaction, and his strong n Affiliation are sufficient to override such factors and lead him to enter the room *on most occasions.* Our prediction is firmly based on a knowledge of Karl and on a knowledge of this type of situation with the limitation it places on possible responses and with the interpretation normally given it by members of the college culture. We must know both the person and the environment to make successful predictions.

There are occasions in which we are eager to predict or explain a particular response at a particular point in time rather than a number of responses to a class of situations as in the example just given. This usually occurs when something striking has happened to the individual or when he has behaved in some unusual manner. That is, ordinarily we do not care whether he entered Joe's room on the night of January 20th at 9 P.M. His behavior on that occasion is *uninteresting* according to our usual standards and gains importance only as it is lumped in with a lot of similar responses on similar occasions. This does not mean that we could not explain what he did on that particular evening if we wanted to. The fact is that we are usually not interested in taking that much trouble. However, suppose that he entered Joe's room on that particular evening and threw Joe out of the window. This would make that particular event "interesting" and we as psychologists would feel ourselves called upon to explain it in detail. Yet there is no difference between this behavior and any other behavior he might have shown so far as accounting for it theoretically is concerned. The problem of explanation and the method of finding an explanation are the same in both cases. It just happens that socially we are more often likely to want an explanation of striking or abnormal behavior. In the past it has been possible to distinguish those theorists who are interested primarily in abnormal personality from those who are interested in normal personality largely on the ground of whether they are interested in explaining a striking bit of behavior (a symptomatic act) or a general trend of behavior. The clinical psychologist or psychoanalyst has been forced by the nature of his profession to consider chiefly unusual episodes, whereas the psychologist dealing with normal personality has been most often concerned with general trends. This split in interest has led to some unfortunate theoretical differences which might not have arisen had these people worked with the same data and seen the theoretical connections between the two types of prediction and explanation.

SUMMARY AND INTEGRATION

Karl's College Environment. With this theoretical introduction to the nature of prediction based on a knowledge of personality structure and environmental structure, we can return to our concrete illustration and take the next step toward predicting how Karl would behave in college. This involves analyzing as a sociologist or cultural anthropologist would the nature of the environment into which Karl was plunged on his entrance into college. After we have given as adequate a "clinical" description of his college culture as we can in a short space, we will then be ready to test the adequacy of our formulation of his personality structure by making many specific predictions as to how he behaved in that college environment.

The college which Karl entered was a small, private, New England institution for men which we will call Bowhurst. He entered before World War II when enrollment was around seven hundred and the threat of war was still distant, although it was to begin to disrupt the normal college way of life by the end of his sophomore year. Like most such colleges, Bowhurst is isolated from the New England town in which it is situated, although there are many more opportunities for spending an evening in town at the movies or in the local taverns than in a rural college community as described by Newcomb (1943). The students at Bowhurst are predominantly from fairly well-to-do, middle-class families in business and the professions. Although some students are from a private-school, lower-upper-class background, there are fewer of this type than at other New England colleges with more social prestige. In fact, Bowhurst usually gets the prize students of the public high schools like Karl, some very good students from private schools of lesser prestige, and poorer students from the private schools that prepare primarily for Harvard, Yale, Princeton, and Dartmouth. The predominance of upwardly mobile public-school boys gives the college a serious atmosphere on the whole as compared with more upper-class New England colleges, but there is a sufficient admixture of upper-class private-school customs to have a profound effect on the social life of the college.

Any boy entering Bowhurst is faced with two major adjustment problems: one to his studies, and the other to his social life. On the formal educational side, Bowhurst is a liberal-arts college which is supposedly nonvocational, although a certain amount of preprofessional training for medicine and other such fields is offered.

The student usually starts out in large classes fulfilling generalization requirements and then goes on to concentrate in a particular field of study where the classes will be smaller and he will get more attention from the instructor. On the whole, Karl will have little contact with the faculty outside the classroom. The typical student regards his performance in his courses as the most important part of his life, particularly in his freshman year. There is a falling-off of his interest usually in his sophomore year, which is reflected in lower grades and is known in administrative circles as the "Sophomore Slump." This usually corresponds with the period in which the student is making major readjustments in his social life from the norms he carried over from secondary school. As far as the educational environment is concerned, Karl will find college different from his particular high school in the following respects: (1) he will be more on his own with regard to how he performs his work in courses; (2) there will be no girls in the classes or readily available for social life during the week; (3) the general intellectual level of his fellow students will be higher and there will therefore be increased competition for good marks; (4) his classes will generally be larger since he came from a very small high school in a small town; and finally, (5) there will be many more upper-class boys who will have the habit and ability to spend money on liquor, women, cars, and other signs of conspicuous consumption.

Socially the most important aspect of life at Bowhurst is the fraternity system. Three-fourths or more of the student body belong to one of the dozen or so fraternities. A great many of the freshmen are pledged within the first week at college. Those who are not are unacceptable to the "Brethren" either because they belong to minority groups (Negroes, Jews), or because they are personally unattractive ("meat balls"). Some students disbelieve so strongly in the fraternity system, particularly in its race prejudice, that they refuse to join when asked. The fraternities are ordered in a rough kind of prestige hierarchy in which contributing factors are tradition, scholastic average of the house, the importance of its members in campus life, and the wealth and family background of some of its members. The fraternity house is the center of social life on the campus. The great majority of students start eating at the house where they are pledged the second week they are on the campus, and from then on it becomes more and more the center for recreation, study, and friendships. Dating is infrequent during the week and is relatively rare even on week ends since the nearest girls' college is some miles away. Approximately three times a year an attempt is made to make up for this deficiency all at once by inviting girls for week-end parties centered around the fraternity houses. These "house parties" are the occasions for conspicuous "sowing of wild oats" and for gaining a certain amount of prestige by so doing.

The houses on the whole are relatively independent of control by the college so long as the members do not get into serious trouble. After freshman year most fraternity members go to live at the houses and from then on they regulate their own social life almost entirely through the fraternity organization. This is consistent with the college policy of attempting to get the students to assume adult responsibilities, a policy which is perhaps most conspicuously represented outside the fraternity by the honor system, the self-administered code of honor which governs student behavior in preparation for classes and during examinations. One of the explicit justifications for the fraternity system is that it gives the students training in self-government and helps them in the transition from irresponsible adolescence to responsible adulthood. It does play this role to some extent. House officers, at least, have responsible functions to perform and the fraternity must often make responsible decisions as to disciplining members, planning social functions, getting the pledges to study, etc. But the difficulty is that the fraternity also provides the occasion for the forming of age-mate "gangs" or cliques which may simultaneously institutionalize irresponsible behavior. Most of the faculty disapprove of the fraternity system, especially because of the race prejudice which many of the fraternities show, but also because they regard prejudice as merely symptomatic of the irresponsible behavior which results from putting students too much on their own.

The fraternity has several functions other than accelerating or retarding a transition to adult responsibility. Explicitly at least it is supposed to promote brotherhood, loyalty, and tolerance, at least for fellow members of the same fraternity. Since the method of selecting new members for the fraternity involves hasty decisions on both sides, most houses consist of a group of men of rather heterogeneous background who, according to the explicit fraternity code, must learn to like or at least tolerate each other. Furthermore, the fraternity does exercise some responsibility for trying to get its members to study harder, particularly freshmen and those who seem in danger of flunking out. On the ideological side, most fraternities tend to be conservative since they are often dominated by the private secondary-school boys who are most experienced and interested in fraternity social life. There are exceptions to this rule, of course, but unlike Bennington as described by Newcomb (1943) there is almost certainly not at Bowhurst, at least within the fraternities, an atmosphere of declining conservatism from freshman to senior year.

Outside the fraternities there is little of great social importance except for athletics. The fraternities do urge their members to go out for extracurricular activities in order to increase the prestige of the fraternity, and some importance is attached to student government, though it is generally considered to be a "tool" of the more important, autonomous fraternity units. As for athletics Bowhurst is no exception to the usual college rule. One can achieve considerable prestige through participation on college athletic teams, but with the exception of football and possibly basketball, the importance of even this is not too great. Excellence in scholarship also brings prestige, as does participation in the college paper, dramatics, and other extracurricular clubs, although to a decreasing extent. On the whole the student body at Bowhurst seems rather apathetic about extracurricular activities, at least as compared with the popular ideal of a college, and as compared with the ideal it holds up for itself occasionally. This is probably because the autonomous fraternity unit is the main center of social life.

Prediction Questionnaire For Karl. Our general theoretical orientation is complete. Now it remains to put it to the practical test. With some knowledge both of Karl's personality structure and of the college environment which he entered, we can turn to an attempt to predict what he will do in a number of different situations in that college environment. Table 15.5 reproduces again Part I of the prediction questionnaire which was to have been filled out on an intuitive basis at the end of Chapter 4. Part II of the questionnaire, which is contained in the instructor's manual, should also be filled out by the student to observe the way in which our systematic analyses can be used in predicting concrete acts. After this, Part II of Karl's autobiography, also in the instructor's manual, should be read and the questionnaires scored before continuing to the next section, which presupposes a knowledge of Karl's subsequent history in college.

TABLE 15.5

Prediction Questionnaire (Part I) for Karl

When he entered college, Karl took the Strong Vocational Interest Test so that we have his reactions to a good many specific questions. Circle Like (L), Indifferent (I), or Dislike (D) as you think he did. A second part of the questionnaire asks you to predict certain general aspects of his behavior and performance in college. Your answers will be compared with his actual behavior.

A. Excerpts from the Strong Vocational Interest Blank (Strong item numbers are given in the second column from the left, beginning 191, etc.)

1.	191	Handling horses	L	I	D
2.	192	Giving "first aid" assistance	L	I	D
3.	193	Raising flowers and vegetables	L	I	D
4.	194	Decorating a room with flowers	L	I	D
5.	195	Arguments	L	I	D
6.	196	Interviewing men for a job	L	I	D
7.	197	Interviewing prospects in selling	L	I	D
8.	198	Interviewing clients	L	I	D
9.	199	Making a speech	L	I	D
10.	200	Organizing a play	L	I	D
11.	211	Pursuing bandits in sheriff's posse	L	I	D
12.	212	Doing research work	L	I	D
13.	213	Acting as yell leader	L	I	D
14.	214	Writing personal letters	L	I	D
15.	215	Writing reports	L	I	D
16.	216	Entertaining others	L	I	D
17.	217	Bargaining ("swapping")	L	I	D
18.	218	Looking at shop windows	L	I	D
19.	219	Buying merchandise for a store	L	I	D
20.	220	Displaying merchandise for a store	L	I	D
21.	221	Expressing judgments publicly regardless of criticism	L	I	D
22.	222	Being pitted against another as in a political or athletic race	L	I	D
23.	223	Methodical work	L	I	D
24.	224	Regular hours of work	L	I	D
25.	225	Continually changing activities	L	I	D
26.	226	Developing business systems	L	I	D
27.	227	Saving money	L	I	D
28.	228	Contributing to charities	L	I	D
29.	229	Raising money for a charity	L	I	D
30.	230	Living in the city	L	I	D
31.	231	Climbing along edge of a precipice	L	I	D

TABLE 15.5 (*Continued*)

32.	232	Looking at a collection of rare laces	L	I	D
33.	233	Looking at a collection of antique furniture	L	I	D

Comparison of interest between two items. Indicate his choice of the following pairs by checking (√) in the first space if he preferred the item to the left, in the second space if he liked both equally well, and in the third space if he preferred the item to the right. Assume other things are equal except the two items to be compared.

34.	321	Street-car motorman	.. .. ..	Street-car conductor
35.	322	Policemen	.. .. ..	Fireman (fights fire)
36.	323	Chauffeur	.. .. ..	Chef
37.	324	Head waiter	.. .. ..	Lighthouse tender
38.	325	House to house canvassing	.. .. ..	Retail selling
39.	326	House to house canvassing	.. .. ..	Gardening
40.	327	Repair auto	.. .. ..	Drive auto
41.	328	Develop plans	.. .. ..	Execute plans
42.	329	Do a job yourself	.. .. ..	Delegate job to other
43.	330	Persuade others	.. .. ..	Order others
44.	331	Deal with things	.. .. ..	Deal with people
45.	332	Plan for immediate future	.. .. ..	Plan for five years ahead
46.	333	Activity which produces tangible returns	.. .. ..	Activity which is enjoyed for its sake
47.	334	Taking a chance	.. .. ..	Playing safe
48.	335	Definite salary	.. .. ..	Commission on what is done

(Reprinted from the Vocational Interest Blank for Men (Revised) by Edward K. Strong, Jr. with the permission of the author and publishers, Stanford University Press.)

B. Predictions about college adjustment

Karl took Ethics, German, Mathematics, English, and Chemistry during Freshman year.

49. Karl's average grade for the year was:
(check Honors, Average, Below average)

A− B+ C	B− C+ C	C− D+
..Honors	..Average	..Below average

T F 50. He got an A in his Freshman year
T F 51. He got an E in his Freshman year (flunked a course)
T F 52. He did his best work in Mathematics
T F 53. He was elected an officer of the Freshman class
T F 54. He played football in his Freshman year

Roughly 75% of the students receive a bid for a fraternity at the men's college which Karl attended

TABLE 15.5 (*Continued*)

T F 55. Karl joined a fraternity

T F 56. Karl joined one of the "high prestige" fraternities

T F 57. He tried out for the editorial staff of the college paper during his freshman year

58. Check how many friends you think he made
    ..Few
    ..Average number
    ..Many

59. Check how deep and lasting these friendships were
    ..Deep and lasting
    ..Average depth and duration
    ..Superficial and short-lived

The following items refer to his Sophomore year.
He elected German, Mathematics, Physics, Spanish, and Chemistry.

60. Karl's average grade for his Sophomore year was:

A− B+ B	B− C+ C	C− D+
..Honors	..Average	..Below average

T F 61. He got an A in his Sophomore year

T F 62. He got an E in his Sophomore year (flunked a course)

T F 63. He was elected an officer in the Sophomore class

64. Check the amount of drinking you think he indulged in
    ..Very little or none
    ..Average amount
    ..A lot

65. Check the amount of student roughhousing or fighting he was involved in
    ..Very little or none
    ..Average amount
    ..A lot

66. Check the amount of heterosexual activity he was involved in
    ..Very little or none
    ..Average amount
    ..A lot

67. Check the amount of time you think he spent in "bull sessions" sitting around and talking with other students
    ..Less than average
    ..Average
    ..More than average

T F 68. He changed his vocational ambition during this period

T F 69. He gave up playing football to study harder

T F 70. He took on a lot of outside work

Accounting For Karl's Later Development. Anyone who has attempted to fill out the prediction questionnaires, checked his answers against the answer key, and read the second portion of Karl's autobiography is likely to feel that the whole procedure is not really justified. How is it possible to know whether Karl would check at a given moment that he liked "looking at shop windows"? Perhaps he himself would not choose the same response if he took the test over again. While it is true that the balance of factors contributing to any particular response may be so equal that prediction must be indeterminate, still one should, with a knowledge of Karl's personality structure, be able to predict correctly more often than chance. The advantage of a number of small items is precisely that they do not make the predictor's knowledge stand or fall on the prediction of any one particular response, nor do they permit the judge to predict in such general terms that almost any response would serve to confirm his guesses. Furthermore, some of the particular items actually tap trends of considerable importance in Karl's personality. While we might feel that "looking at shop windows" does not, we should certainly fail to have understood him well if we could not predict that he would like "entertaining others," or "continually changing activities."

A more serious objection than this lies in the inability to state precisely in some of the items what the nature of the environmental situation was. It is true we have described in a general way what the college environment was like. In some instances we have even been able to specify quite accurately the nature of the stimulus conditions as, for instance, when we asked for an estimate of Karl's recognition thresholds to various words. In still other places we required only a prediction of Karl's subjective reactions (e.g., to his course failures) which, as we have seen, are not limited in the same way by the nature of the environmental situation. But in many cases the environment is bound to determine the nature of his response to some extent. For instance, when we want to know how he reacted to his first sexual intimacy with a girl, does it not depend to some extent on how *she* reacted? Or when we are asked to predict what kind of a job he took after graduating from college, does it not depend on what jobs he was offered? Presumably he did not have complete freedom of choice; he may have wanted to go on to graduate school, for instance, but not have been able to because of lack of money. In such cases the predictor must take such environmental press into account as best he can, recognizing that because of such "unknowns" his predictions will not be perfect but should still be better than chance because of his knowledge of the person in the (P,E) interaction.

Still another objection to the prediction procedure arises from quite a different source. Have we not weighted the dice in *favor* of correct prediction by basing our knowledge of Karl's personality structure on a number of measures which were taken *after* the responses to be "predicted" were made? Are we "predicting" at all in such cases? For instance, we know from Karl's religion questionnaire and Allport-Vernon test scores discussed in Chapter 8 that he was very much interested in religion. From this knowledge we would be more likely to guess correctly that he studied evangelical religion at night school during the war. But the tests referred to were taken by Karl several years *after* he underwent a strong religious conversion, went to night school, and returned to college prepared to "preach the Gospel, come what may." In one sense we would not be predicting his turn to religion after dropping out of college unless we had measures *prior* to that time which showed that he had a strong religious interest. Certainly it would have been better if we had had them. But in another sense, a theoretical personality picture need not be so time-bound. What we try to do in constructing such a picture is to make inferences from one set of measures (taken at one point in time) to some general constructs and principles which will enable us to estimate what the person will do at another point in time, which may be *either earlier or later.* As Allport points out (1942), we may "predict" or "postdict." In either case we may be able to confirm our hypotheses about consistent trends within the personality. The advantage that prediction has arises from engineering considerations: if we can predict, we can control. But this is not a decisive value as far as theory is concerned. Prediction is always more indeterminate than postdiction anyway, since we cannot specify the nature of the environmental press nearly as well before it occurs.

But we cannot dispose of this difficulty quite so easily. A careful consideration of the timing of our measures may require a change in some of our interpretations. Let us take a look at our TAT analyses in Chapters 10 and 11 in particular. Two of the most important themas in Karl's TAT deal with "desertion" and "inadequacy" respectively. Now Karl's experiences in the four years prior to his taking the test appear peculiarly likely to have been responsible for these themas. In the first place, the girl with whom he was deeply in love deserted him and married another. In the second, he had in effect flunked out of college and failed to live up to the very high hopes both he and his parents had held for him when he entered. What would be more natural than for these two experiences to color his imaginative productions? What right had we then to draw inferences from such material about his motivational structure and even to connect it with his early childhood experiences? While we must acknowledge the force of this objection, there are a number of reasons why it does not undermine the kind of conclusions we drew from his TAT. In the first place, we must recognize that the traumatic experiences in question are already four years old. Since he was deserted by his first love (a desertion which incidentally he tends to minimize in his autobiography), Karl has had a religious conversion, has nearly married her sister, and has spent a year overseas. As far as flunking out is concerned, he has in the meantime returned to college and obtained an 88 or B+ average in his first semester. None of this disproves the importance of the earlier traumatic incidents, but it does suggest strongly that if they are important, it is because they have become woven into his "basic personality structure" and not because they are simply recent episodes that color his imagination in a way which is *unrepresentative* of his over-all adjustment to life. There has been plenty of time for them to get assimilated into and to alter the nature of Karl's previous apperceptive mass. Furthermore, if, in fact, they had been incidents which were markedly inconsistent with Karl's expectations about security and achievement as laid down early in life, we could reasonably expect them to have been reworked in a quite different fashion by this time. In short, the case for interpreting the TAT as we did rests largely on the assumption that such specific episodes as these have tended by this time to get integrated into the personality structure to such an extent that their direct influence on imagination is *typical* of his basic personality trends.

The case does not rest wholly on this point, however. We can even abandon the position that earlier motivational learning influenced the subsequent schematizing of these episodes and argue that they were the determining factors in Karl's *contemporaneous* motivational structure. For, in the end, it is his motivational structure *now* that we are interested in. We may speculate as to how it arose, but such speculations may be considered of secondary importance. Such an extreme stand is neither necessary nor entirely justified, however. The fact of the matter is that the analysis of motivation and schema structure based on the TAT and the "desertion" and "inadequacy" themas in it is supported at many points independently by autobiographical episodes from an earlier period (e.g., his timidity and insecurity as a child, his bashfulness before girls, etc.). And, what is perhaps most convincing of all, we can use the analysis of motivation made *after the War* to explain (or postdict) the behavior which led up to the crucial failure in his sophomore year *before the War*. In short, we can accept the "inadequacy" and "desertion" themas as reflecting two prior incidents and still use the way they are woven into the stories to explain why both incidents occurred in the first place.

Despite all the objections to the prediction procedure (many of which could disappear if the data had been collected with the final conceptual scheme in mind), it has one great advantage. It forces the person who may think he understands the case material to test that knowledge in a very precise and often exasperating fashion. Anyone who tries it is almost certain to come out convinced that he did not understand Karl nearly so well as he thought he did—which is a good thing. Too often we read through a case study, written by a psychoanalyst perhaps, in which we are absolutely astonished at the ingenuity and skill with which he makes everything hang together. Yet for the scientist the nagging question must remain: Are any of these wonderful character sketches stated in terms of hypotheses that can be critically tested? It is easy enough in writing a case study to find *illustrations* that will confirm a hypothesis. But suppose we ask the question, how could any of this interpretation be *disproved*? That is a far more difficult question—and one that cannot be answered as far as most clinical personality sketches are concerned. Most of them are written in such a way that they are capable of illustration but not of proof or disproof. Our study of Karl is unfortunately no real exception. But by submitting it to the test of actual prediction of unknown behavior we have at least drawn attention to its shortcomings and demonstrated the need for this kind of testing of personality sketches which might otherwise seem too pat and persuasive. Anyone who has tested his knowledge of Karl in this fashion is not very likely to accept uncritically the interpretation of some of the later episodes in his life to which we must now turn our attention.

Behavior To Be Accounted For. It would be impracticable to attempt to deal efficiently with every one of the 120 items in the prediction questionnaire in terms of our theoretical picture of Karl.

We must therefore limit ourselves to some key behavioral items. Generally speaking they will be ones that are particularly striking or persistent such as,

> Why did he fail so badly in his second year at college after such a good beginning?
> Why did he get into fraternity fights?
> Why did he drink so much as compared with other students?
> What explained his conversion to evangelical religion?
> Why was he such a good hypnotic subject?
> Why did he volunteer for overseas ambulance duty?
> Why did he return to college and make such a good record after the war, only to return to his earlier habits in his senior year?

In tackling such major adjustments as these, we may be led to emphasize the importance of one determinant over the others. Thus the very way in which these questions are asked suggests that we should search primarily for motivational explanations. Yet our theoretical position is that traits, schemata, and motives enter into the determination of any act. To avoid undue emphasis on any one of these we can select four representative types of adjustment for intensive study, one in which all three determinants enter about equally, and three in which either a trait, a schema, or a motive respectively seems to be the crucial factor.

Joint Determination of an Act. Karl engaged in a considerable amount of student roughhousing and fighting and on one occasion was picked up by the police as a ringleader in a big row. How are we to account for this behavior? On the *motivational* side we have argued that he has a strong n Aggression, which, however, is normally kept so in check by his f Aggression that he appears extremely mild and cooperative. On the *schema* side, we can observe that a certain amount of fraternity fighting is culturally normal and that Karl in time would learn about this culture pattern. On the *trait* side, we know that he has received a good deal of rewarded training in being aggressive on the football field. It is therefore not so surprising that when the opportunity (E factor) presents itself, Karl will be found in the midst of the fray. Contributing factors are undoubtedly his strong n Affiliation and his strong trait of Gregariousness. He *wants* to be "one of the boys" and habitually practices being one of them, so that when they get in a fight, the total "excitatory potential" attached to the response of joining in should be very high indeed. The only inhibiting factor—f Aggression-expression—

would also tend to be weakened because, as we have seen, it is supported largely by his fear of Rejection—a fear which should be lessened in a social situation in which everyone is being aggressive. In this case it would be difficult to point to any one factor as being absolutely decisive in determining his participation in fighting. No factor alone would probably have been enough. Had he not had a strong n Aggression, his training in aggression on the football field would probably not have been enough. Had he not had experience in being aggressive, his n Aggression would probably not have led him so often (or so effectively!) into fights. Had student fighting not been a culture pattern, he almost certainly would not have started anything, as his normal mildness indicates. So, in this case, we seem to need all three of our hypothetical variables to account for what he did.

Traits As Decisive Determinants. Karl gives as one of the reasons why he fell down in his sophomore year the fact that he was into too many different things. To us this is a familiar trait. In high school he was active in everything—athletics, clubs, course work, etc. In fact, we have noted that energy and variability are two of his outstanding traits. In college he tended to react as he had before; he transferred his previously successful patterns of responses to the new situation. He was active in everything his freshman year and was elected President of the Freshman Class. The success story of his high school days seemed about to repeat itself. But in the end the trait proved maladaptive: his attempt to do everything in the more complex atmosphere of college proved impossible and ultimately contributed to his failure in his sophomore year. If we are interested in accounting for his wide participation in all sorts of activities in his freshman year or perhaps in his election as President of the Freshman Class, then the most useful single factor to consider seems to be the trait variable. The college situation (schema variable) and his complex of motives were sufficiently similar at first to what they had been in high school for his past adjustment in high school to be the decisive factor in determining how he responded on entering college. It is exactly to account for such consistencies in behavior in similar situations under similar motivation that we need the trait variable. To be sure, even here, the other variables entered into determining the *form* of the concrete act; he had to perceive what clubs and activities were available in college, and he had to have n Affiliation and n Achievement as he had had before in order for him to react as he did. But the *decisive* factor in this case seems to be his traits or consistent modes of adjustment to similar situations.

Schemata As Decisive Determinants. Among other things Karl joined a fraternity when he entered college. Why? The simplest answer would be that it was the "thing to do." It was, in short, a modal response for freshmen at Bowhurst, a culture pattern. Here motivation and traits do not seem to be the decisive factors. Given a student with motives within a certain range (who is not, for instance, too autonomous) and with traits within a certain range (not so deviant as to be unacceptable), the "meaning of the situation" as it is defined by the other people in the situation should lead him to join a fraternity. It is "expected" behavior. Again Karl's motives doubtless contributed: he had a strong n Affiliation which would be more easily gratified in a fraternity situation. So did his traits: anyone as gregarious as he is would almost certainly have chosen to join. But none of these things by themselves would have led to this particular response, although they may have made a certain range of responses more likely. The decisive factor appears to be the cultural or social norm which Karl had every opportunity to perceive both before he came to college and after he got there. Had it not been the "thing to do" for students to join a fraternity, it is likely that his motives and traits would have found other outlets—perhaps in clubs and class activities.

Motives As Decisive Determinants. When we turn to motivation, we are plunged in the midst of what is considered the "normal" way of explaining behavior. Actually, as we have seen earlier, it is the normal way of explaining abnormal or unusual behavior, and is not of such decisive importance in accounting for such everyday occurrences as why Karl got involved in so many activities, or played football, or went to class every day, or joined a fraternity. Nevertheless, it does play a decisive role in many kinds of behavior. Take Karl's drinking, for instance. Drinking parties are part of the cultural pattern at Bowhurst. As Karl makes clear, it was this social norm which started him on the "habit of drinking acquired at college." Furthermore, his strong trait of gregariousness and his strong n Affiliation would predispose him to conviviality. But there is something unusual about his drinking behavior. In time it became "abnormal" for his culture. It interfered with his work, led him into fights, and tended to transform him from an extremely conscientious student into an undependable and erratic one. Why did drinking attract him

so? Here it appears useless to search among his traits, based on past modes of adjustment in "similar" situations, or to look to the culture pattern which in fact frowns on the excesses to which Karl went. In the words of a fraternity brother:

When he returned in the fall of 194–, he surprised everyone by his restraint from drinking. As the year progressed, however, he took up drinking again and as a result has become more frequently intoxicated. This has led to disturbances in the House, partly his own fault and partly the result of his friends urging him on. Among the remaining friends, this has created some ill-feeling toward him. His friends claim he would be a good man, if he did not drink. They also fear his aggressive tendencies when intoxicated.

Karl apparently concurs in this judgment when he states at the end of his autobiography, "Also I drink too much beer which I shouldn't." To explain this we will have to look to his motivational structure. We do not have to look far. It would not take much imagination to arrive at the hypothesis that social drinking might be a rather specific medicine for the peculiar motivational conflicts which beset Karl. We have stressed again and again the importance of the following motivational complex in his life:

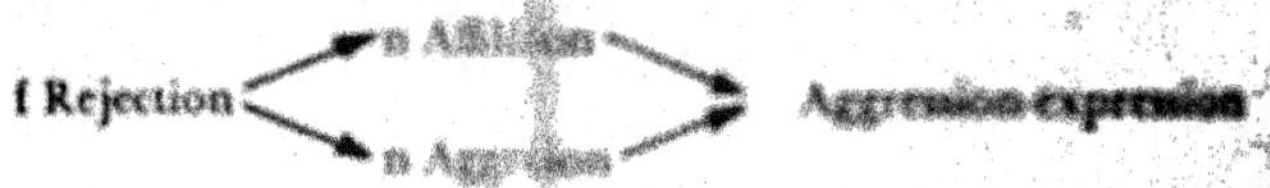

Although there is unfortunately as yet little experimental evidence on the subject, clinical and introspective reports seem unanimous in agreeing that one of the effects of alcohol is to decrease anticipations of failure, to reduce anxiety, to remove inhibitions, or to "drown the super-ego." Whatever terminology is used, the effect of this process in Karl's case would be to decrease the avoidance motives at each end of this pattern (f Rejection and f Aggression) and to allow the fuller expression of n Affiliation and n Aggression. This permits not only the direct gratification of two of Karl's central needs which are normally frustrated but produces considerable "secondary gain" by reducing the conflict between the needs and fears. This is particularly true of aggression. If our analysis is correct, Karl's strong n Aggression is ordinarily inhibited by an even stronger f Aggression-expression; his calmness and placidity must be won at considerable cost. The conflict between two such strong response tendencies must be very high and in itself produce a strong need for anxiety reduction (see section on conflict of motives in Chapter 13). Drinking, if it serves to weaken f Aggression (by weakening anticipations of rejection resulting from [illegible] pressing aggression), should not only permit expression of n A[illegible] sion, but should also reduce the conflict between the two motive[illegible] d the anxiety which the conflict produces.

Unfortunately, drinking is g[illegible] medicine only so long as it lasts. As his fellow student's comme[illegible] how, Karl's drunken aggressiveness realistically increases the a[illegible] nt of rejection from his fellows, which on the "day after" shou[illegible] ly serve to reactivate even more strongly his f Rejection, his gu[illegible] having been aggressive, and his general over-all anxiety level. [illegible] in turn makes it more imperative that he seek a release by dr[illegible] ng. So a vicious circle tends to be set up. While such an interpr[illegible] n may seem completely *ad hoc,* there are several facts that su[illegible] it. First of all, Karl's insecurity pattern is commonly found in [illegible] studies of alcoholics. Secondly, he tends to drink in this wa[illegible] hen he is in the fraternity group. While he was away durin[illegible] he gave up drinking almost entirely. While there may h[illegible] other reasons for this, it still suggests strongly that the R[illegible] -Affiliation-Aggression complex, strongly aroused by an int[illegible] p, was responsible for his drinking. He was n[illegible] a [illegible] ker. Above all, he had to have affiliation even if it was [illegible] of good-natured kidding which he said he enjoyed. He [illegible] stibly drawn into contact with others and required [illegible] ance from them that they liked him or were n[illegible] e puts it, he "tried to keep away from groups" but [illegible]

Dynamic Explanations of Re[illegible] ons to Frustration. Sometimes reactions to frustr[illegible] easily accounted for in terms of traits. A person m[illegible] sistent mode of responding to a particular kind of [illegible] ncreased effort or striving to increased difficulty su[illegible] d into children by Keister (1938). Sometimes frustration res[illegible] ay be most easily accounted for by an analysis of cultur[illegible] s, as in the case of "ritualized" swearing in our own cult[illegible] most often, as the psychoanalysts have made clear, fr[illegible] des an almost unexcelled opportunity to study a per[illegible] nal structure. We have previously noted how Dembo's stu[illegible] tration (1931) strongly indicated the need for a dynamic [illegible] ion of behavior, and how Freud's motivational schemes origi[illegible] veloped out of analyzing people who were frustrated, anxi[illegible] lefending themselves against anxiety. It is no accident that an [illegible] ment for diagnosing motivational

so? Here it appears useless to search among his traits, based on past modes of adjustment in "similar" situations, or to look to the culture pattern which in fact frowns on the excesses to which Karl went. In the words of a fraternity brother:

> When he returned in the fall of 194–, he surprised everyone by his restraint from drinking. As the year progressed, however, he took up drinking again and as a result has become more frequently intoxicated. This has led to disturbances in the House, partly his own fault and partly the result of his friends urging him on. Among the remaining friends, this has created some ill-feeling toward him. His friends claim he would be a good man, if he did not drink. They also fear his aggressive tendencies when intoxicated.

Karl apparently concurs in this judgment when he states at the end of his autobiography, "Also I drink too much beer which I shouldn't." To explain this we will have to look to his motivational structure. We do not have to look far. It would not take much imagination to arrive at the hypothesis that social drinking might be a rather specific medicine for the peculiar motivational conflicts which beset Karl. We have stressed again and again the importance of the following motivational complex in his life:

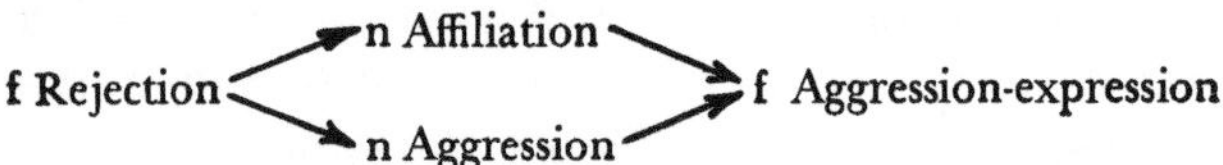

Although there is unfortunately as yet little experimental evidence on the subject, clinical and introspective reports seem unanimous in agreeing that one of the effects of alcohol is to decrease anticipations of failure, to reduce anxiety, to remove inhibitions, or to "drown the super-ego." Whatever terminology is used, the effect of this process in Karl's case would be to decrease the avoidance motives at each end of this pattern (f Rejection and f Aggression) and to allow the fuller expression of n Affiliation and n Aggression. This permits not only the direct gratification of two of Karl's central needs which are normally frustrated but produces considerable "secondary gain" by reducing the conflict between the needs and fears. This is particularly true of aggression. If our analysis is correct, Karl's strong n Aggression is ordinarily inhibited by an even stronger f Aggression-expression but his calmness and placidity must be won at considerable cost. The conflict between two such strong response tendencies must be very high and in itself produce a strong need for anxiety reduction (see section on conflict of motives in Chapter 13). Drinking, if it serves to weaken f Aggression (by weakening anticipations of rejection resulting from expressing aggression), should not only permit expression of n Aggression, but should also reduce the conflict between the two motives and the anxiety which the conflict produces.

Unfortunately, drinking is good medicine only so long as it lasts. As his fellow student's comments show, Karl's drunken aggressiveness realistically increases the amount of rejection from his fellows, which on the "day after" should only serve to reactivate even more strongly his f Rejection, his guilt for having been aggressive, and his general over-all anxiety level. This in turn makes it more imperative that he seek a release by drinking. So a vicious circle tends to be set up. While such an interpretation may seem completely *ad hoc,* there are several facts that support it. First of all, Karl's insecurity pattern is commonly found in case studies of alcoholics. Secondly, he tends to drink in this way only when he is in the fraternity group. While he was away during the war, he gave up drinking almost entirely. While there may have been other reasons for this, it still suggests strongly that the Rejection-Affiliation-Aggression complex, strongly aroused by an intimate group, was responsible for his drinking. He was not a "solitary" drinker. Above all, he had to have affiliation even if it was in the form of good-natured kidding which he said he enjoyed. He was irresistibly drawn into contact with others and required constant assurance from them that they liked him or were not rejecting him. As he puts it, he "tried to keep away from groups" but he could not.

Dynamic Explanations of Reactions to Frustration. Sometimes reactions to frustration may be most easily accounted for in terms of traits. A person may develop a consistent mode of responding to a particular kind of blocking, e.g., increased effort or striving to increased difficulty such as was trained into children by Keister (1938). Sometimes frustration responses may be most easily accounted for by an analysis of culture patterns, as in the case of "ritualized" swearing in our own culture. But most often, as the psychoanalysts have made clear, frustration provides an almost unexcelled opportunity to study a person's motivational structure. We have previously noted how Dembo's study of frustration (1931) strongly indicated the need for a dynamic interpretation of behavior, and how Freud's motivational schemes originally developed out of analyzing people who were frustrated, anxious, and defending themselves against anxiety. It is no accident that an instrument for diagnosing motivational

so? Here it appears useless to search among his traits, based on past modes of adjustment in "similar" situations, or to look to the culture pattern which in fact frowns on the excesses to which Karl went. In the words of a fraternity brother:

> When he returned in the fall of 194–, he surprised everyone by his restraint from drinking. As the year progressed, however, he took up drinking again and as a result has become more frequently intoxicated. This has led to disturbances in the House, partly his own fault and partly the result of his friends urging him on. Among the remaining friends, this has created some ill-feeling toward him. His friends claim he would be a good man, if he did not drink. They also fear his aggressive tendencies when intoxicated.

Karl apparently concurs in this judgment when he states at the end of his autobiography, "Also I drink too much beer which I shouldn't." To explain this we will have to look to his motivational structure. We do not have to look far. It would not take much imagination to arrive at the hypothesis that social drinking might be a rather specific medicine for the peculiar motivational conflicts which beset Karl. We have stressed again and again the importance of the following motivational complex in his life:

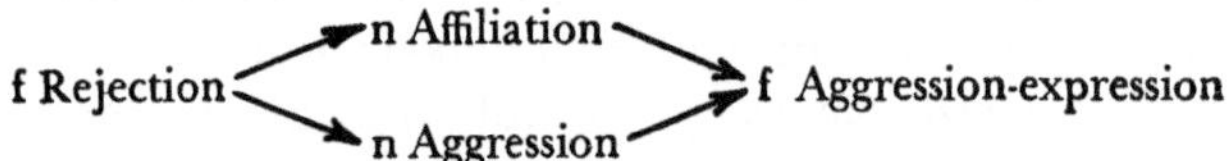

Although there is unfortunately as yet little experimental evidence on the subject, clinical and introspective reports seem unanimous in agreeing that one of the effects of alcohol is to decrease anticipations of failure, to reduce anxiety, to remove inhibitions, or to "drown the super-ego." Whatever terminology is used, the effect of this process in Karl's case would be to decrease the avoidance motives at each end of this pattern (f Rejection and f Aggression) and to allow the fuller expression of n Affiliation and n Aggression. This permits not only the direct gratification of two of Karl's central needs which are normally frustrated but produces considerable "secondary gain" by reducing the conflict between the needs and fears. This is particularly true of aggression. If our analysis is correct, Karl's strong n Aggression is ordinarily inhibited by an even stronger f Aggression-expression but his calmness and placidity must be won at considerable cost. The conflict between two such strong response tendencies must be very high and in itself produce a strong need for anxiety reduction (see section on conflict of motives in Chapter 13). Drinking, if it serves to weaken f Aggression (by weakening anticipations of rejection resulting from expressing aggression), should not only permit expression of n Aggression, but should also reduce the conflict between the two motives and the anxiety which the conflict produces.

Unfortunately, drinking is good medicine only so long as it lasts. As his fellow student's comments show, Karl's drunken aggressiveness realistically increases the amount of rejection from his fellows, which on the "day after" should only serve to reactivate even more strongly his f Rejection, his guilt for having been aggressive, and his general over-all anxiety level. This in turn makes it more imperative that he seek a release by drinking. So a vicious circle tends to be set up. While such an interpretation may seem completely *ad hoc,* there are several facts that support it. First of all, Karl's insecurity pattern is commonly found in case studies of alcoholics. Secondly, he tends to drink in this way only when he is in the fraternity group. While he was away during the war, he gave up drinking almost entirely. While there may have been other reasons for this, it still suggests strongly that the Rejection-Affiliation-Aggression complex, strongly aroused by an intimate group, was responsible for his drinking. He was not a "solitary" drinker. Above all, he had to have affiliation even if it was in the form of good-natured kidding which he said he enjoyed. He was irresistibly drawn into contact with others and required constant assurance from them that they liked him or were not rejecting him. As he puts it, he "tried to keep away from groups" but he could not.

Dynamic Explanations of Reactions to Frustration. Sometimes reactions to frustration may be most easily accounted for in terms of traits. A person may develop a consistent mode of responding to a particular kind of blocking, e.g., increased effort or striving to increased difficulty such as was trained into children by Keister (1938). Sometimes frustration responses may be most easily accounted for by an analysis of culture patterns, as in the case of "ritualized" swearing in our own culture. But most often, as the psychoanalysts have made clear, frustration provides an almost unexcelled opportunity to study a person's motivational structure. We have previously noted how Dembo's study of frustration (1931) strongly indicated the need for a dynamic interpretation of behavior, and how Freud's motivational schemes originally developed out of analyzing people who were frustrated, anxious, and defending themselves against anxiety. It is no accident that an instrument for diagnosing motivational states like Murray's TAT contains pictures which deal almost wholly with frustration, aggression, grief, misery, and despair. As many a person has asked on first seeing them, why shouldn't there be more cheerful scenes? Does not the TAT necessarily force people to give a gloomy one-sided view of themselves? Why not a *Sentience* Apperception Test which will evoke thoughts of what the person enjoys in life?

While there is some force to these objections, the rationale for the approach to motivation via frustration seems to run something like this: frustration acts like a prism to a ray of light. It breaks up the stream of behavior and the analyst can more easily observe what is contributing to it. The practical point apparently is that it is not as easy to discover what a person's motives are, or in what hierarchy they are arranged, so long as they are being gratified, so long as the organism is functioning smoothly and normally. Motives seem to influence behavior in more striking and easily detectable ways when they are not being gratified. In our terms, the reason for this would perhaps lie in the fact that so long as motives are not blocked, behavior gives a better picture of cultural patterns and traits than of motives. Thus the Sentience Apperception Test might tell us a good deal about how a person enjoys himself (traits) and what kinds of recreation he accepts out of the cultural patterns governing enjoyment (schemata), both of which are important things to know about him, but it would not give us much information about his motives. Recreational traits or schemata can be supported by such a variety of motives that only frustration will show which motives are operative in a particular case. At least this is the argument. Whether it will prove to be true when the present-day emphasis on defensive, tension-reducing motives is balanced by a study of pleasure-seeking motives is another question.

Let us take Karl's reactions to his scholastic failure in his sophomore year as an example of the way in which such reactions shed light on motivational structure. Above all he was terribly afraid of what his parents would think and was obsessed by a sense of inadequacy and failure. In other words, he showed both high shame and high guilt. The shame we can attribute to his strong f Rejection which we traced to his parents' authoritarianism (in part) in the first place: the guilt has a more complex history. To account for it we need to assume that he valued achievement highly (and there is every evidence that it was a central part of his self-picture supported both by a lower-middle-class culture pattern and by a strong n Achievement). Scholastic failure then constituted a serious interference with his ambitious plans and hopes for himself. Realistically it would have been difficult for him to blame anyone else but himself for failing. But dynamically it was also consistent for him to do so partly because we argued that he identified strongly enough with his parents to adopt their attitudes toward himself, and partly because his strong n Aggression, being inhibited in direct expression because of f Rejection, would be likely to be displaced to *some* object—an object which would probably turn out to be the self whenever there was any realistic likelihood that the self was the frustrating agent. In short, there are several important reasons why he should feel intropunitive or guilty in response to failure-frustration, and most of them lie in his motivational structure rather than in his trait or schema structures.

Karl's subsequent reactions to frustration are also revealing as far as his motives are concerned. When he left school after his failure, he fell deeply in love the following summer with a girl who turned out to be a *nurse* and who was also *religious*. If we regard his n Achievement as in part supported by a strong desire for love (the "conditional love" complex popularized by Margaret Mead, 1942), then this behavior makes sense. Frustrated at getting love and affection and security through academic success, he falls back on a more direct method of getting the strong nurturance and affiliation he needs. What is more, the girl is especially suited to give him what he wants so badly because she is older, a nurse by profession, and religious—the perfect picture of the strong, nurturant woman he needs. No wonder this love affair meant so much to him! But again he was frustrated; she left him and married someone else. It was at this point that he became deeply religious, started attending an evangelical, fundamentalist Bible school at night, and decided to "preach the Gospel come what may." Again we must turn to his motives to account for his behavior. There is nothing in his trait structure that would lead us to expect it. His exposure to the Bible through his mother's influence and his contact with Sunday school as a boy doubtless produced the schemata which made such an act possible, but it is only in terms of his strong and by now repeatedly frustrated needs for Affiliation, Nurturance, or Security that we can make good sense out of this conversion experience. We can furthermore account in these same terms for the ease with which his newfound religious convictions get transformed once he is back in college where his affiliation needs are more directly met by fraternity associations, by early scholastic success, and by renewed drinking bouts, and where these same needs would be apt to be frustrated, if he should continue to persevere in a kind of religious belief which would be the object of ridicule among many of his associates.

Such a motivational analysis of Karl's reactions to frustration could be carried further to explain many other erratic aspects of his behavior. It is dramatic, intriguing, and perhaps especially impressive to the everyday observer who is not aware how difficult it is to submit such dynamic interpretations to critical tests and who is accustomed to think in terms of culturally normal behavior. But we must not be overimpressed by the drama of motivational analysis. It has its place, especially in explaining unusual behavior. But after all, Karl is by and large a *normal* product of our culture. Perhaps 95 per cent or more of his responses, which cover the way he thinks, talks, and reacts in everyday life, can be best accounted for in terms of his internalization of culture patterns (schemata) and his consistent modes of adjustment to recurrent problems (traits). Motives get to be decisive only in a small number of cases, which tend to get blown up beyond their real importance because they are unusual and dramatic. They have "surprise" value and attention focuses on them for that reason, but this should not lead us away from our central theoretical task, from our responsibility to give a balanced account of the whole personality. To do this job adequately, we need to explore systematically the person's traits and schemata (including his self-schema), as well as his motives. If we approach the problem from at least three angles, we will be in a better position to fulfill our assignment as a scientist in the field of personality, which is to create the best possible theoretical model (personality structure) which will account in simplest terms for the most important portions of a single individual's behavior. It goes without saying that we are far from having reached any such goal as yet, nor are we likely to reach it any time soon. But if we know where we are going and have some knowledge of how to start, we will have taken the first steps toward reaching it.

NOTES AND QUERIES

1. Why should ego-involvement (cf. Klein and Schoenfeld, 1941) introduce a correlation among a number of responses which were formerly uncorrelated? Work out the solution in terms of the schematic formula, B = f (H, S, D, sS) (E). Generalize your solution.

How else would it be possible to introduce correlations among responses by manipulating variables in this equation?

2. Reconsider the question in the light of this chapter as to whether all behavior is *motivated.* Does this question have anything to do with what is the *decisive* determinant of a response?

3. Explain why Karl was a good hypnotic subject in terms of the conceptual scheme we have worked out for him. Read Murray (1938, pp. 453 ff.) for clues.

4. Select any of the interpretations in this chapter and try to design a test which would clearly confirm or disprove it. In a sense any response Karl makes is a test of *some* hypothesis, but what is the difficulty of using it to test any particular one? What is the advantage of stating the hypothesis before you know what the response is?

5. One of the difficulties with a multiple-variable, schematic equation is that since the relations among the variables are not prescribed, you are left free to manipulate them any way you like to account for a response. Can you see any method of meeting this difficulty? Is making the "settings" for the variables before you know the response any help? Can you think of any way in which more precise relations between various schemata, traits, and motives can be worked out?

6. Are you worried by the thought that in the far-distant future we might actually be able to build a theoretical picture of a person which would account for his behavior?

7. In working out the nature and relations among various traits, schemata, and motives, what are the great advantages of working with groups of people rather than a single person? What are the disadvantages?

8. Why did Karl volunteer for overseas ambulance duty? Would you say a trait, a schema, or a motive was chiefly responsible?

9. Could exactly the same response be produced by different combinations of the basic variables? Work out an example of a response which might be produced by different determinants and show how you would set about discovering what they were in each case. Take the reasons given for Karl's participation in fraternity fighting, for instance, and compare them with some different hypothetical reasons why another student might participate and show how the different "settings" of the personality variables in these two cases should lead to different behavior on certain other occasions.

10. Why did Karl enjoy being kidded? Attempt to deduce this

reaction in as rigorous a fashion as possible from the general theoretical picture of his personality. What makes rigor difficult?

11. Sheldon states (cf. Chapter 5) that mesomorphs are apt to be fond of alcohol just as Karl is. Attempt to show how this generalization might be derived from the kind of motivational complex which is likely in our culture to develop in men with powerful physiques (cf. discussion of Stone's study of aggression in football players in Chapters 11 and 13 as well as the discussion in this chapter). Set up an experiment to test your hypothesis.

12. In what sense is heredity contributing to the "habit of drinking" in the case discussed in question 11? Explain how heredity may increase the probability of the development of a certain trait, schema, or motive without actually determining it with a probability of 1.00. Give a concrete example. Can you think of a case in which heredity determines a response with a probability of 1.00 in human beings? In other animals?

References and Author Index

References are listed alphabetically by date of publication. The numbers in italics after each reference give the pages of the text on which the reference is cited.

ABERLE, D. F., COHEN, A. K., DAVIS, A. K., LEVY, M. J., and SUTTON, F. X. 1950. The functional prerequisites of a society. *Ethics,* 60, 100-111. — *378, 379*

ADLER, A. 1917. *Neurotic constitution.* New York: Moffat, Ward. — *402*

ADORNO, T. W., FRENKEL-BRUNSWIK, E., LEVINSON, D. J., and SANFORD, R. N. 1950. *The authoritarian personality.* New York: Harper. — *504*

ALEXANDER, F. 1942. *Our age of unreason.* Philadelphia: Lippincott. — *4, 10, 11, 89, 356, 570, 585*

ALLPORT, F. H. 1937. Teleonomic description in the study of personality. *Character and Pers.,* 5, 202-14. — *105*

ALLPORT, F. H., and FREDERIKSEN, N. 1941. Personality as a pattern of social trends. *J. soc. Psychol.,* 13, 141-82. — *102*

ALLPORT, G. W. 1937. *Personality, a psychological interpretation.* New York: Holt. — *4, 15, 37, 53, 56, 63, 66, 74, 75, 89, 98, 100, 101, 102, 117, 149, 186, 201, 202, 206, 207, 208, 214, 215, 217, 218, 220, 221, 229, 235, 363, 403, 433, 474, 539, 587*

ALLPORT, G. W. 1942. *The use of personal documents in psychological science.* New York: Social Science Research Council. — *30, 49, 50, 51, 70, 71, 89, 94, 105, 417, 608*

ALLPORT, G. W. 1943. The ego in contemporary psychology. *Psychol. Rev.,* 50, 451-78. — *42, 529, 540*

ALLPORT, G. W., GILLESPIE, J. M., and YOUNG, J. 1948. The religion of the post-war college student. *J. Psychol.,* 25, 3-33. — *284*

ALLPORT, G. W., and ODBERT, H. S. 1936. Trait-names: a psycho-lexical study. *Psychol. Monogr.,* 47, No. 211. — *233, 568*

ALLPORT, G. W., and POSTMAN, L. 1947. *The psychology of rumor.* New York: Holt. — *244, 246*

ALLPORT, G. W., and VERNON, P. E 1931. *A study of values.* Boston: Houghton Mifflin. — *257, 258, 259*

ALLPORT, G. W., and VERNON, P. E. 1933. *Studies in expressive movement.* New York: Macmillan. — *131, 132, 133, 134, 230, 231*

ANGELL, R., *see* Gottschalk and others (1945).

ANGYAL, A. 1941. *Foundations for a science of personality.* New York: Commonwealth Fund. — *102, 103*

APICELLA, F. S., *see* McClelland and Apicella (1945).

ARRINGTON, R. E., *see* Thomas and others (1933).

ASCH, S. E. 1946. Forming impressions of personality. *J. abnorm. soc. Psychol.,* 41, 258-90. — *54, 293, 294, 342*

ATKINSON, J. W. 1950a. Development of an equivalent form of the projective measure of achievement motivation and an exploratory study of picture differences. Unpublished Ph. D. thesis, Univ. Mich. — *523*

ATKINSON, J. W. 1950b. A projective measure of achievement motivation in the interruption of tasks experiment. Unpublished Ph.D. thesis, Univ. Mich. — *46, 228, 465, 497, 498*

ATKINSON, J. W., and MCCLELLAND, D. C. 1948. The projective expression of needs. II. The effect of different intensities of the hunger drive on thematic apperception. *J. exp. Psychol.,* 38, 643-58. — *482, 492, 494*

ATKINSON, J. W., *see also* McClelland and Atkinson (1948), McClelland, Atkinson, and Clark (1949), McClelland and others (1949, 1950).

BALDWIN, A. L. 1942. Personal structure analysis: A statistical method for investigating the single personality. *J. abnorm. soc. Psychol.,* 37, 163-83. — *34*

BALDWIN, A. L. 1946. The study of individual personality by means of the intraindividual correlation. *J. Personality,* 14, 151-68. — *208, 209, 210, 211, 212*

BALDWIN, A. L., KALHORN, J., and BREESE, F. H. 1945. Patterns of parent behavior. *Psychol. Monogr.,* 58, No. 3. — *41, 348, 349, 352, 353, 354, 363, 364*

BALDWIN, A. L., KALHORN, J., and BREESE, F. H. 1949. The appraisal of parent behavior. *Psychol. Monogr.,* 63, No. 4. — *349, 352*

BALES, F. 1950. *Interaction process analysis.* Cambridge, Mass.: Addison-Wesley Press. — *32, 307, 326*

BARKER, R., DEMBO, T., and LEWIN, K. 1940. Frustration and regression: an experiment with young children. *Univ. Ia. Stud. Child Welfare,* 18, No. 1. — *518*

BARTLETT, F. C. 1932. *Remembering: a study in experimental and social psychology.* Cambridge: Cambridge Univ. Press. — *59, 246, 247, 249, 342*

BATESON, G. 1942. Social planning and the concept of "deutero-learning." In T. M. Newcomb and E. L. Hartley (Eds.), *Readings in social psychology.* New York: Holt, 1947. — *254*

BATESON, G. 1944. Cultural determinants of personality. Chapter 23 in J. McV. Hunt (Ed.), *Personality and the behavior disorders.* New York: Ronald Press, 1944. — *334, 366*

BECK, S. J. 1944. *Rorschach's test.* New York: Grune and Stratton. — *52, 170*

BELL, John. 1948. *Projective techniques.* New York: Longmans, Green. — *34, 44, 132, 133, 134, 136, 139, 141, 146, 147, 159*

BENJAMIN, J. D., and EBAUGH, F. G. 1938. The diagnostic validity of the Rorschach test. *Amer. J. Psychiat.,* 94, 1163-78. — *147*

BERGMANN, G., and SPENCE, K. W. 1944. The logic of psychophysical measurement. *Psychol. Rev.,* 51, 1-24. — *77, 78, 80*

BIRNEY, R. C., *see* McClelland, Birney, and Roby (1950).

BODER, D. P. 1940. The adjective verb quotient: a contribution to the psychology of language. *Psychol. Rec.,* 22, 310-43. — *155*

BOGARDUS, E. S. 1928. The measurement of social distance. In T. M. Newcomb and E. L. Hartley (Eds.), *Readings in social psychology.* New York: Holt, 1947. — *270*

BOISEN, A. T. 1936. *The exploration of the inner world.* New York: Willett and Clark. — *512*

BOWERS, A. M., *see* Healy and others (1930).

BRALY, K. W., *see* Katz and Braly (1933).

BREESE, F. H., *see* Baldwin and others (1945, 1949).

BREUER, J., and FREUD, S. 1895. *Studies in hysteria* (trans. by A. A. Brill). New York: Nervous and Mental Disease Publishing Co., 1936. — *94*

BRONNER, A. F., *see* Healy and others (1930).

BROWN, J. F. 1936. *Psychology and the social order.* New York: McGraw-Hill. — *290*

BROWN, J. S. 1948. Gradients of approach and avoidance responses and their relation to level of motivation. *J. comp. physiol. Psychol.,* 41, 450-65. — *461*

BROWN, N. O. 1947. *Hermes the thief.* Madison, Wis.: Univ. Wis. Press. — *68*

BRUNER, J. S. 1950. Personality dynamics and the process of perceiving. Chapter 7 in the University of Texas symposium on perception and personality. — *253, 539*

BRUNER, J. S., and GOODMAN, C. C. 1947. Value and need as organizing factors in perception. *J. abnorm. soc. Psych.,* 42, 33-44. — *46, 261, 489*

BRUNER, J. S., and POSTMAN, L. 1949. On the perception of incongruity: a paradigm. *J. Personality,* 18, 206-23. — *325, 342, 577*

BRUNER, J. S., POSTMAN, L., and ROD-

RIGUES, J. 1950. Stimulus appropriateness and ambiguity as factors in judgment. Unpublished paper. — *250, 294, 325*

BRUNER, J. S., *see also* Postman and Bruner (1948), Postman and others (1948).

BUGELSKI, R. 1938. Extinction with and without sub-goal reinforcement. *J. comp. Psychol.*, 26, 121-34. — *432*

BUSEMANN, A. 1925. Die Sprache der Jugend als Ausdruck der Entwicklungsrhythmic. Jena: Fischer. — *155*

CANTRIL, H., *see* Sherif and Cantril (1947).

CARMICHAEL, L., HOGAN, H. P., and WALTER, A. A. 1932. An experimental study of the effect of language on the reproduction of visually perceived form. *J. exp. Psychol.*, 15, 73-86. — *250*

CARMICHAEL, L., KENNEDY, J. C., and MEAD, L. C. 1949. Some recent approaches to the experimental study of human fatigue. *Science*, 110, 445. — *45*

CATTELL, R. B. 1946a. *Description and measurement of personality*. Yonkers-on-Hudson, New York: World Book Co. — *54, 55, 72, 105, 164, 171, 177, 180, 183, 184, 199, 200, 201, 203, 208, 213*

CATTELL, R. B. 1946b. The riddle of perseveration. *J. Personality*, 14, 229-67. — *173, 177*

CENTERS, R. 1947. The American class structure. In T. M. Newcomb and E. L. Hartley (Eds.), *Readings in social psychology*. New York: Holt, 1947. — *313*

CHILD, I. L., POTTER, E. H., and LEVINE, E. M. 1946. Children's textbooks and personality development: an exploration in the social psychology of education. *Psychol. Monogr.*, 60, No. 279. — *252, 253, 314*

CHILD, I. L., *see also* Whiting and Child (1950).

CHOTLOS, J. W. 1944. A statistical and comparative analysis of individual written language samples. *Psychol. Monogr.*, 56, No. 2, 77-111. — *151, 153*

CHRISTIE, J. R. 1949. The effects of frustration on rigidity in problem solution. Unpublished Ph.D. thesis, Univ. Calif. (Berkeley). — *504*

CHRISTIE, J. R. 1950. The effect of some early experiences in the latent learning of rats. Unpublished dittoed paper. — *363*

CLARK, R. A. 1947. The problem of closure in mental organization. Unpublished Honors thesis. Middletown, Conn.: Wesleyan Univ. — *171*

CLARK, R. A., and MCCLELLAND, D. C. 1950. A factor analytic integration of imaginative, performance, and case study measures of the need for achievement. Unpublished paper. — *81, 86, 461, 465, 482, 485*

CLARK, R. A., *see also* McClelland, Atkinson, and Clark (1949), McClelland and others (1949, 1950).

CLARKE, H. J., *see* Rosenzweig and others (1947).

COHEN, A. K., *see* Aberle and others (1950).

COLE, L. E. 1939. *General psychology*. New York: McGraw-Hill. — *391*

CONANT, J. B. 1947. Presidential address before the American Association for the Advancement of Science. Excerpts in *Amer. Psychol.*, 3, 67. — *4*

COTTRELL, L. S. 1942. The adjustment of the individual to his age and sex roles. *Amer. sociol. Rev.*, 7, 617-20. — *316, 318*

COURTS, F. A. 1942. The influence of practice on the dynamogenic effect of muscular tension. *J. exp. Psychol.*, 30, 504-11. — *484*

COWLES, J. T. 1937. Food-tokens as incentives for learning by chimpanzees. *Comp. Psychol. Monogr.*, 14, No. 71. — *433*

CRESPI, L. P. 1945. Public opinion toward conscientious objectors: III. Intensity of social rejection in stereotype and attitude. *J. Psychol.*, 19, 251-76. — *315*

CRUTCHFIELD, R. S., *see* Krech and Crutchfield (1948).

CURRAN, C. A. 1945. *Personality factors in counseling*. New York: Grune and Stratton. — *36, 578*

DAVIS, A., and DOLLARD, J. 1940. *Children of bondage.* Washington: American Council on Education. — *312, 347*

DAVIS, A., and HAVIGHURST, R. J. 1946. Social class and color differences in child-rearing. *Amer. sociol. Rev.,* 11, 698-710. — *351*

DAVIS, A., and HAVIGHURST, R. J. 1947. *Father of the man; how your child gets his personality.* Boston: Houghton Mifflin. — *313, 347*

DAVIS, A., and HAVIGHURST, R. J. 1948. The measurement of mental systems. *Sci. Mon., N. Y.,* 66, 301-16. — *199*

DAVIS, A. K., *see* Aberle and others (1950).

DAVIS, D. F. 1948. *Pilot error.* Air Ministry 3139 A. London: His Majesty's Stationery Office. — *465*

DEMBO, T. 1931. Der Ärger als dynamisches Problem. *Psychol. Forsch.,* 15, 1-144. — *42, 383, 384, 404, 496, 521, 615*

DEMBO, T., *see also* Barker and others (1940), Lewin and others (1944).

DENNIS, W. 1938. Infant development under conditions of restricted practice and of minimum social stimulation: a preliminary report. *J. genet. Psychol.,* 53, 149-58. — *446*

DESCARTES, René. 1637. *Discourse on method* (Veitch's trans.). LaSalle, Ill.: Open Court Publishing Co., 1946. — *100*

DICKSON, W. J., *see* Roethlisberger and Dickson (1939).

DILTHEY, W. 1894. Ideen über eine beschreibende und zergliedernde Psychologie. *Gesammelte Schriften,* Vol. 5. Leipzig and Berlin: Teubner, 1924. — *66*

DILTHEY, W. 1910. *Das Erlebnis und die Dichtung, Lessing, Goethe, Novalis, Hölderlin.* Leipzig: Teubner. — *66*

DODSON, J. D. 1915. The relation of strength of stimulus to rapidity of habit-formation. *J. Anim. Behav.,* 5, 330-36. — *504*

DOLLARD, J. 1937. *Caste and class in a southern town.* New Haven: Yale Univ. Press. — *29*

DOLLARD, J., DOOB, L. W., MILLER, N. E., MOWRER, O. H., and SEARS, R. R. 1939. *Frustration and aggression.* New Haven: Yale Univ. Press. — *92, 371, 391, 458, 460, 503, 505, 512, 513, 515, 516, 517, 520, 540*

DOLLARD, J., and MOWRER, O. H. 1947. A method of measuring tension in written documents. *J. abnorm. soc. Psychol.,* 42, 3-32. — *30, 31*

DOLLARD, J., *see also* Davis and Dollard (1940), Miller and Dollard (1941).

DOOB, L. W., and SEARS, R. R. 1939. Factors determining substitute behavior and the overt expression of aggression. *J. abnorm. soc. Psychol.,* 34, 293-313. — *503, 520*

DOOB, L. W., *see also* Dollard and others (1939).

DREW, G. C. 1938. The function of punishment in learning. *J. genet. Psychol.,* 52, 257-67. — *455*

DUBOIS, C. 1944. *The people of Alor.* Minneapolis: Univ. Minn. Press. — *147, 334, 337, 351, 360*

DUDYCHA, G. J. 1936. An objective study of punctuality in relation to personality and achievement. *Arch. of Psychol.,* 29, No. 204. — *204*

EBAUGH, F. G., *see* Benjamin and Ebaugh (1938).

EISENBERG, P. 1940. The motivation of expressive movement. *J. gen. Psychol.,* 23, 89-101. — *134*

ELKIN, F. 1943. Harold Holzer. *J. abnorm. soc. Psychol.,* 38, 48-86. — *xiv*

ENKE, W. 1930. Die Psychomotorik der Konstitutionstypen. *Z. angew. Psychol.,* 36, 237-87. — *131*

ERICKSON, M. H. 1939. Experimental demonstrations of the psychopathology of everyday life. In S. S. Tomkins (Ed.), *Contemporary psychopathology.* Cambridge, Mass.: Harvard Univ. Press, 1943. — *570*

ERICSON, M. C. 1947. Social status and child-rearing practices. In T. M. Newcomb and E. L. Hartley (Eds.), *Readings in social psychology.* New York: Holt, 1947. — *313*

EYSENCK, H. J. 1947. *Dimensions of personality.* London: Routledge and Kegan Paul. — *104, 117, 118, 179*

FARBER, I. E. 1948. Response fixation under anxiety and non-anxiety conditions. *J. exp. Psychol.*, 38, 111-31. — *434, 455*

FENICHEL, O. 1945. *The psychoanalytic theory of neurosis.* New York: Norton. — *585*

FERNBERGER, S. W. 1948. Persistence of stereotypes concerning sex differences. *J. abnorm. soc. Psychol.*, 43, 97-101. — *324*

FESTINGER, L. 1942. Wish, expectation, and group standards as factors influencing level of aspiration. *J. abnorm. soc. Psychol.*, 37, 184-200. — *565*

FESTINGER, L. 1943. Development of differential appetite in the rat. *J. exp. Psychol.*, 32, 226-34. — *463*

FESTINGER, L., *see also* Lewin and others (1944).

FISKE, D. W. 1949. Consistency of the factorial strictures of personality ratings from different sources. *J. abnorm. soc. Psychol.*, 44, 329-44. — *187, 191, 192, 193, 194, 196*

FLEISCHMAN, D. L. 1949. Notes of a retiring feminist. *American Mercury*, 68, 161-68. — *295*

FLEMING, E. E., *see* Rosenzweig and others (1947), Rosenzweig and Fleming (1949).

FLUGEL, J. C. 1945. *Man, Morals and Society.* New York: International Universities Press. — *302, 448, 456, 457, 503, 506, 513, 514, 517, 543, 571, 572, 573, 576*

FOSBERG, I. A. 1941. An experimental study of the reliability of the Rorschach psychodiagnostic technique. *Rorschach Res. Exch.*, 5, 72-84. — *146*

FRANK, J. D. 1938. Level of aspiration test. In Murray, H. A., *Explorations in personality*, 461-71. New York Oxford Univ. Press. — *491*

FREDERIKSEN, N., *see* Allport and Frederiksen (1941).

FRENKEL-BRUNSWIK, E. 1949. Intolerance of ambiguity as an emotional and perceptual personality variable. *J. Personality*, 18, 108-43. — *183, 577*

FRENKEL-BRUNSWIK, E., *see also* Adorno and others (1950).

FREUD, A. 1937. *The ego and the mechanisms of defense.* London: Hogarth Press. — *397, 509, 519, 570*

FREUD, S. 1904. The psychopathology of everyday life. In *The basic writings of Sigmund Freud.* (Trans. and ed. by A. A. Brill.) New York: Modern Library, 1938. — *385, 391*

FRFUD, S. 1909. Analysis of a phobia in a five-year-old boy. *Collected Papers.* Vol. III. London: Hogarth Press, 1925. — *94*

FREUD, S. 1910. History of the psychoanalytic movement. In *The basic writings of Sigmund Freud.* (Trans. and ed. by A. A. Brill.) New York: Modern Library, 1938. — *386, 387*

FREUD, S. 1918. Totem and Taboo. In *The basic writings of Sigmund Freud.* (Trans. and ed. by A. A. Brill.) New York: Modern Library, 1938. — *17, 96, 333*

FREUD, S. 1927. *The ego and the id.* London: Hogarth Press. — *11*

FREUD, S. 1930. *Civilization and its discontents.* New York: Norton. — *392*

FREUD, S. 1940. *An outline of psychoanalysis.* New York: Norton, 1949. — *378, 481*

FREUD, S., *see also* Breuer and Freud (1895).

FRICK, F. C., *see* Miller and Frick (1949).

FRIEDMAN, G. A. 1950. A cross-cultural study of the relationship between independence training and n Achievement as revealed by mythology. Unpublished Honors thesis, Harvard Univ. — *357, 367, 450*

FROMM, E. 1941a. *Escape from freedom.* New York: Farrar and Rinehart. — *428*

FROMM, E. 1941b. Hitler and the Nazi authoritarian character structure. In T. M. Newcomb and E. L. Hartley (Eds.), *Readings in social psychology.* New York: Holt, 1947. — *305*

GARDNER, J. W. 1940. The use of the term "level of aspiration." *Psychol. Rev.*, 47, 59-68. — *567*

GEBHARD, M. 1949. Permanence of experimentally induced changes in the attractiveness of activities. *J. exp. Psychol.*, 39, 708-13. — *493*

GESELL, A., and others. 1940. *The first five years of life.* New York: Harper. – 36, 350

GESELL, A., and ILG, F. L. 1943. *Infant and child in the culture of today.* New York: Harper. – 350, 378

GETZELS, J. 1950. The elicitation of specific information using projective techniques. *Bull. of the Laboratory of Social Relations, Harvard Univ.,* 2, No. 4. – 44

GILLESPIE, J. M., *see* Allport and others (1948).

GLUECK, S., and GLUECK, E. 1950. *Unraveling juvenile delinquency.* Boston: Commonwealth Fund. – 147

GOLDSTEIN, K. 1940. *Human nature in the light of psychopathology.* Cambridge: Harvard Univ. Press. – 403, 541

GOLDSTEIN, K., *see also* Hanfmann and others (1944).

GOODMAN, C. C., *see* Bruner and Goodman (1947).

GOODRICH, H. B., and KNAPP, R. H. 1950. Unpublished report for the Committee on Education of Scientists. Middletown, Conn.: Wesleyan Univ. – 179

GORER, G. 1948. *The American people.* New York: Norton. – 264, 270, 305, 306

GOTTSCHALK, L., KLUCKHOHN, C., and ANGELL, R. 1945. *The use of personal documents in history, anthropology and sociology.* New York: Social Science Research Council. – 46, 4[illegible]

GOULD, R. 1939. An experimenta[illegible] ysis of "level of aspiration." [illegible] *Psychol. Monogr.,* 21, 1-[illegible] 565, [illegible]

GREEN[illegible] 1941 *Mea*[illegible] *hu*[illegible] *vior.* [illegible]ew [illegible] P[illegible]

G[illegible] P. 1940. [illegible]ties. *Rev.,* 47. [illegible]

[illegible] F. R. [illegible]lty [illegible] associ[illegible] Ch[illegible] J. M[illegible] *Pe*[illegible] *and* [illegible]dis[illegible] York:[illegible] G. [illegible]ect[illegible] nent [illegible]ate[illegible]

J. [illegible] *Psychol.,* 59, [illegible] – 460, 506 [illegible]

G[illegible] G. [illegible] 1950. Resistance to ex[illegible]tinc[illegible] of learned fear drives and avo[illegible] behavior. Unpublished p[illegible] – 440

HAGG[illegible], F. A. 1943. Some conditions det[illegible] adjustment during and rea[illegible] following experimen[illegible]tall[illegible] stress. Chapter 40 in S. [illegible] Tomk[illegible] (Ed.). *Contemporary psy[illegible]path[illegible].* Cambridge, Mass.: Har[illegible] Univ. Press. – 508

HALL [illegible] S. 1947. Diagnosing personality [illegible] analysis of dreams. *J. abnorm.* [illegible], 42, 68-79. – 417, 438

HAM[illegible] C. V. 1916. A study of per[illegible] [illegible] reactions in primates and [illegible] *Behav. Monogr.,* 3, No. 13. [illegible]

HANA[illegible]LY, N. G. 1937. Memory trace for[illegible] in recall and recognition. *Ar[illegible] Psychol., N. Y.,* 31, No. 216. – [illegible]42

HAN[illegible], E., and KASANIN, J. 1937. A [illegible] hod for studying concept form[illegible]. *J. Psychol.,* 3, 521-40. – 183, 263

HAN[illegible], E., RICKERS-OVSIANKINA, M., and GOLDSTEIN, K. 1944. Case La[illegible] *Psychol. Monogr.,* 57, No. 4. – [illegible] 168

HARL[illegible], H. F. 1949. The formation of [illegible] sets. *Psychol. Rev.,* 56, 51-65. [illegible]

HARR[illegible] 51. The effects of stress on [illegible] mental set in problem sol[illegible] [illegible]blished Ph.D. thesis. H[illegible] – [illegible]

H[illegible] and MAY, M. A. 1928. [illegible] the nature of character. [illegible] *dies in deceit.* New York: [illegible] – 60, 20[illegible] 06, 207

[illegible] R. J., [illegible] nd Hav[illegible] (1946. [illegible] 1926. [illegible] *kindred* [illegible] *ers of* [illegible] Vols.) New [illegible] Mac[illegible] W., [illegible] E., and Bow[illegible] *structure and* [illegible] *analysis.* New [illegible] For[illegible] 340

HEBB, D. O. 1[illegible] T[illegible] [illegible]anization of *behavior*. New Y[illegible] [illegible]iley. — *460, 473, 480*

HELSON, H. [illegible] [illegible]ion-level as a basis for a [illegible] [illegible]e theory of frames of referen[illegible] [illegible]chol. Rev., 55, 297-313. — [illegible]

HERTZ, M. R. [illegible] [illegible]eliability of the Rorschac[illegible] [illegible]est. *J. appl. Psych*[illegible]. 1[illegible], 4[illegible] [illegible]6

HILGARD, E. R., a[illegible] [illegible]quis, D. G. 1940. *C*[illegible] [illegible]*l learning*. New York: A[illegible] [illegible]tury. — *343, 449, 46*[illegible]

HOGAN, H. P. [illegible] [illegible]ichael and others 19[illegible]

HOLLENBER[illegible], E., a[illegible] S[illegible], M. 1950. Some a[illegible] [illegible]gression in doll play. P[illegible] [illegible]n press). — *505*

HOLLINGSHEAD, A. B. [illegible] *Elmtown's youth*. New Y[illegible] — *312, 313, 314*

HOLLINGWORTH, H. [illegible] [illegible] The inaccuracy [illegible] [illegible]*ch. Psychol*., N. Y[illegible] [illegible]*44*

HOLZBERG, J. D. R[illegible] test interpretati[illegible] [illegible]*46*

HOLZBERG, J. D. [illegible] [illegible]ompletion Test. — [illegible]

HORNEY, K. 19[illegible] [illegible]em of feminine mas[illegible] [illegible]*nal. Rev*., [illegible], 241-[illegible]

HORNEY, K. 1[illegible] *T*[illegible] [illegible]*tic personality of* [illegible] [illegible]k: Norton. — *464*

HORNEY, K. 1[illegible] [illegible]*in psychoanalysis*. New [illegible] [illegible]ton. — *303, 334, 33*[illegible]

HOVLAND, C. I., [illegible] R. 1938. Exper[illegible] [illegible]onflict: I. Types [illegible] [illegible] modes of resoluti[illegible]. *J. ex*[illegible] [illegible], 23, 177-93. — *317, 50*[illegible]

HULL, C. L. 192[illegible] [illegible]*le testing*. Yonkers-on-Hudson: [illegible]ld Book Co. — *25*

HULL, C. L. 1943. *Pri*[illegible]*les of behavior*. New York: Appleton-Century. — *216, 316, 391,* [illegible]*, 487, 563, 580*

HULL, C. L., and MONTGOMERY, R. P. 1919. Experimental investigation of certain alleged relat[illegible] between character and handwriting. *Psychol. Rev*., 26, 63-74. — *131, 134*

HUMPHREYS, L. G. 1939. The effect of random alternation of reinforcement on the acquisition and extinction of conditioned eyelid reactions. *J. exp. Psychol*., 25, 141-58. — *453*

HUNT, J. McV. 1941. The effects of infant feeding-frustration upon adult hoarding in the albino rat. *J. abnorm. soc. Psychol*., 36, 338-60. — *358, 303, 445*

HUNT, J. McV. (Ed.). 1944. *Personality and the behavior disorders*. New York: Ronald Press. *See* Bateson (1944), Guthrie (1944), Lewin and others (1944), Maller (1944), Miller (1944), Mowrer and Kluckhohn (1944), Rosenzweig (1944), Sheldon (1944), White (1944).

HUNT, W. A., *see* Landis and Hunt (1939).

HUNTLEY, C. W. 1940. Judgments of self based upon records of expressive behavior. *J. abnorm. soc. Psychol*., 35, 398-427. — *546, 547, 548, 549*

ISRAELI, N. 1932. The social psychology of time. *J. abnorm. soc. Psychol*., 27, 209-13. — *262*

JENKINS, W. O., and STANLEY, J. C. 1950. Partial reinforcement: a review and critique. *Psychol. Bull*., 47, 193-234. — *345, 361, 453*

JERSILD, A. T. 1942. *Child psychology* (Rev. Ed.). New York: Prentice-Hall. — *447*

JONES, E. 1944. The psychology of religion. In S. Lorand (Ed.), *Psychoanalysis today*. New York: International Univ. Press. — *305*

JUCKNAT, M. 1937. Leistung, Anspruchsniveau, und Selbstbewusstsein. (Untersuchungen zur Handlungs- und Affektpsychologie: XX. Ed. by Kurt Lewin.) *Psychol. Forsch*. 22, 89-[illegible] — *42*

KALHORN, J., *see* Baldwin and [illegible] (1945, 1949).

KARDINER, A., and [illegible] [illegible]945. *psychological fro*[illegible] New York: Colu[illegible] [illegible]Pre[illegible]

GESELL, A., and others. 1940. *The first five years of life*. New York: Harper. — *36; 350*

GESELL, A., and ILG, F. L. 1943. *Infant and child in the culture of today.* New York: Harper. — *350, 378*

GETZELS, J. 1950. The elicitation of specific information using projective techniques. *Bull. of the Laboratory of Social Relations, Harvard Univ.,* 2, No. 4. — *44*

GILLESPIE, J. M., *see* Allport and others (1948).

GLUECK, S., and GLUECK, E. 1950. *Unraveling juvenile delinquency*. Boston: Commonwealth Fund. — *147*

GOLDSTEIN, K. 1940. *Human nature in the light of psychopathology*. Cambridge: Harvard Univ. Press. — *403, 541*

GOLDSTEIN, K., *see also* Hanfmann and others (1944).

GOODMAN, C. C., *see* Bruner and Goodman (1947).

GOODRICH, H. B., and KNAPP, R. H. 1950. Unpublished report for the Committee on Education of Scientists. Middletown, Conn.: Wesleyan Univ. — *179*

GORER, G. 1948. *The American people.* New York: Norton. — *264, 270, 305, 306*

GOTTSCHALK, L., KLUCKHOHN, C., and ANGELL, R. 1945. *The use of personal documents in history, anthropology and sociology*. New York: Social Science Research Council. — *46, 47, 50*

GOULD, R. 1939. An experimental analysis of "level of aspiration." *Genet. Psychol. Monogr.,* 21, 1-116. — *492, 565, 567*

GREENE, E. B. 1941. *Measurements of human behavior.* New York: Odyssey Press. — *180*

GUILFORD, J. P. 1940. Human abilities. *Psychol. Rev.,* 47, 367-94. — *172*

GUTHRIE, E. R. 1944. Personality in terms of associative learning. Chapter 2 in J. McV. Hunt (Ed.), *Personality and the behavior disorders.* New York: Ronald Press. — *70*

GWINN, G. T. 1949. The effects of punishment on acts motivated by fear. *J. exp. Psychol.,* 39, 260-69. — *460, 506, 520*

GWINN, G. T. 1950. Resistance to extinction of learned fear-drives and avoidance behavior. Unpublished paper. — *450*

HAGGARD, E. A. 1943. Some conditions determining adjustment during and readjustment following experimentally induced stress. Chapter 40 in S. S. Tomkins (Ed.), *Contemporary psychopathology*. Cambridge, Mass.: Harvard Univ. Press. — *508*

HALL, C. S. 1947. Diagnosing personality by analysis of dreams. *J. abnorm. soc. Psychol.,* 42, 68-79. — *417, 428*

HAMILTON, G. V. 1916. A study of perseverance reactions in primates and rodents. *Behav. Monogr.,* 3, No. 13. — *483*

HANAWALT, N. G. 1937. Memory trace for figures in recall and recognition. *Arch. Psychol., N. Y.,* 31, No. 216. — *342*

HANFMANN, E., and KASANIN, J. 1937. A method for studying concept formation. *J. Psychol.,* 3, 521-40. — *183, 262*

HANFMANN, E., RICKERS-OVSIANKINA, M., and GOLDSTEIN, K. 1944. Case Lanuti. *Psychol. Monogr.,* 57, No. 4. — *167, 168*

HARLOW, H. F. 1949. The formation of learning sets. *Psychol. Rev.,* 56, 51-65. — *254*

HARRIS, R. A. 1951. The effects of stress on rigidity of mental set in problem solution. Unpublished Ph.D. thesis, Harvard Univ. — *504*

HARTSHORNE, H., and MAY, M. A. 1928. Studies in the nature of character. (2 Vols.) *Studies in deceit.* New York: Macmillan. — *60, 204, 205, 206, 207, 315*

HAVIGHURST, R. J., *see* Davis and Havighurst (1946, 1947, 1948).

HEAD, H. 1926. *Aphasia and kindred disorders of speech.* (2 Vols.) New York: Macmillan. — *244*

HEALY, W., BRONNER, A. F., and BOWERS, A. M. 1930. *The structure and meaning of psychoanalysis.* New York: Knopf. — *337, 340*

HEBB, D. O. 1949. *The organization of behavior*. New York: Wiley. — *469, 473, 489*

HELSON, H. 1948. Adaptation-level as a basis for a quantitative theory of frames of reference. *Psychol. Rev.*, 55, 297-313. — *245, 254*

HERTZ, M. R. 1934. The reliability of the Rorschach ink-blot test. *J. appl. Psychol.*, 18, 461-77. — *146*

HILGARD, E. R., and MARQUIS, D. G. 1940. *Conditioning and learning*. New York: Appleton-Century. — *343, 449, 460*

HOGAN, H. P., *see* Carmichael and others (1932).

HOLLENBERG, E., and SPERRY, M. 1950. Some antecedents of aggression in doll play. *Personality* (in press). — *505*

HOLLINGSHEAD, A. B. 1949. *Elmtown's youth*. New York: Wiley. — *312, 313, 314*

HOLLINGWORTH, H. L. 1909. The inaccuracy of movement. *Arch. Psychol., N. Y.*, 2, No. 13. — *244*

HOLZBERG, J. D. Rorschach test interpretation for Karl. — *142-146*

HOLZBERG, J. D. Sentence Completion Test. — *553-56*

HORNEY, K. 1935. The problem of feminine masochism. *Psychoanal. Rev.*, 22, 241-57. — *513*

HORNEY, K. 1937. *The neurotic personality of our time*. New York: Norton. — *464*

HORNEY, K. 1939. *New ways in psychoanalysis*. New York: Norton. — *393, 394, 395, 398, 399, 401, 402*

HOVLAND, C. I., and SEARS, R. R. 1938. Experiments on motor conflict: I. Types of conflict and their modes of resolution. *J. exp. Psychol.*, 23, 477-93. — *317, 501*

HULL, C. L. 1928. *Aptitude testing*. Yonkers-on-Hudson: World Book Co. — *25*

HULL, C. L. 1943. *Principles of behavior*. New York: Appleton-Century. — *216, 316, 391, 432, 487, 563, 580*

HULL, C. L., and MONTGOMERY, R. P. 1919. Experimental investigation of certain alleged relations between character and handwriting. *Psychol. Rev.*, 26, 63-74. — *131, 134*

HUMPHREYS, L. G. 1939. The effect of random alternation of reinforcement on the acquisition and extinction of conditioned eyelid reactions. *J. exp. Psychol.*, 25, 141-58. — *453*

HUNT, J. McV. 1941. The effects of infant feeding-frustration upon adult hoarding in the albino rat. *J. abnorm. soc. Psychol.*, 36, 338-60. — *358, 363, 445*

HUNT, J. McV. (Ed.). 1944. *Personality and the behavior disorders*. New York: Ronald Press. *See* Bateson (1944), Guthrie (1944), Lewin and others (1944), Maller (1944), Miller (1944), Mowrer and Kluckhohn (1944), Rosenzweig (1944), Sheldon (1944), White (1944).

HUNT, W. A., *see* Landis and Hunt (1939).

HUNTLEY, C. W. 1940. Judgments of self based upon records of expressive behavior. *J. abnorm. soc. Psychol.*, 35, 398-427. — *546, 547, 548, 549*

ISRAELI, N. 1932. The social psychology of time. *J. abnorm. soc. Psychol.*, 27, 209-13. — *262*

JENKINS, W. O., and STANLEY, J. C. 1950. Partial reinforcement: a review and critique. *Psychol. Bull.*, 47, 193-234. — *345, 361, 453*

JERSILD, A. T. 1942. *Child psychology* (Rev. Ed.). New York: Prentice-Hall. — *447*

JONES, E. 1944. The psychology of religion. In S. Lorand (Ed.), *Psychoanalysis today*. New York: International Univ. Press. — *305*

JUCKNAT, M. 1937. Leistung, Anspruchsniveau, und Selbstbewusstsein. (Untersuchungen zur Handlungs- und Affektpsychologie: XX. Ed. by Kurt Lewin.) *Psychol. Forsch.* 22, 89-179. — *42*

KALHORN, J., *see* Baldwin and others (1945, 1949).

KARDINER, A., and others. 1945. *The psychological frontiers of society*. New York: Columbia Univ. Press. —

KARDINER, A. (*Contd.*) *305, 334, 335, 336, 344, 347, 356, 366, 368, 429*

KASANIN, J., *see* Hanfmann and Kasanin (1937).

KATZ, D., and BRALY, K. W. 1933. Verbal stereotypes and racial prejudice. In T. M. Newcomb and E. L. Hartley (Eds.), *Readings in social psychology*. New York: Holt, 1947. — *294, 295*

KATZ, L. 1947. On the matric analysis of sociometric data. *Sociometry*, 10, 233-41. — *280*

KAUFFMAN, P. E., and RAIMY, V. C. 1949. Two methods of assessing therapeutic progress. *J. abnorm. soc. Psychol.*, 44, 379-85. — *31*

KEISTER, M. 1938. Behavior of young children in failure. In R. Updegraff, and others, *Studies in pre-school education*. Univ. Ia. Stud. Child Welfare, 14, 29-82. — *519, 520, 615*

KELLEY, D. M. 1947. *22 cells in Nuremberg; a psychiatrist examines the Nazi criminals*. New York: Greenberg. — *18*

KELLEY, H. H. 1949. The effects of expectations upon first impressions of persons. *Amer. Psychol.*, 4, 252. — *293, 294, 325*

KELLEY, P. M., *see* Klopfer and Kelley (1942).

KENDALL, M. G. 1948. *Rank correlation methods*. London: Griffin. — *24*

KENNEDY, J. C., *see* Carmichael and others (1949).

KLEIN, G. S., and SCHOENFELD, N. 1941. The influence of ego-involvement on confidence. *J. abnorm. soc. Psychol.*, 36, 249-58. — *227, 488, 618*

KLOPFER, B., and KELLEY, P. M. 1942. *The Rorschach technique*. Yonkers-on-Hudson, New York: World Book Co. — *53*

KLUCKHOHN, C. 1946. Personality formation among the Navaho Indians. *Sociometry*, 9, 128-32. — *349*

KLUCKHOHN, C. 1947. Some aspects of Navaho infancy and early childhood. In G. Roheim (Ed.), *Psychoanalysis and the social sciences*. New York: International Universities Press. I, 37-86. — *366*

KLUCKHOHN, C. 1949. *Mirror for man*. New York: McGraw-Hill. — *431*

KLUCKHOHN, C., and KLUCKHOHN, F. R. 1947. American culture: generalized orientations and class patterns. Chapter 9 in *Conflicts of power in modern culture*. Symposium of Conference in Science, Philosophy, and Religion. — *260, 261, 268, 281, 302, 340*

KLUCKHOHN, C., and LEIGHTON, D. 1947. *The Navaho*. Cambridge, Mass.: Harvard Univ. Press. — *251, 281, 304, 305, 337, 338, 359*

KLUCKHOHN, C., and MOWRER, O. H. 1944. Personality and culture: a conceptual scheme. *Amer. Anthrop.*, 46, 1-29. — *240*

KLUCKHOHN, C., and MURRAY, H. A. 1948. *Personality in nature, society, and culture*. New York: Knopf. — *264, 358, 379, 429, 439*

KLUCKHOHN, C., *see also* Gottschalk and others (1945), Leighton and Kluckhohn (1947), Mowrer and Kluckhohn (1944).

KLUCKHOHN, F. R. 1950. Dominant and substitute profiles of cultural orientations: Their significance for the analysis of social stratification. *Social Forces*, 28, 376-93. — *255, 256, 262, 263, 264, 269, 303*

KLUCKHOHN, F. R., *see also* Kluckhohn, C., and Kluckhohn, F. R. (1947).

KNAPP, R. H. 1948. Experiments in serial reproduction and related aspects of the psychology of rumor. Unpublished Ph.D. thesis, Harvard Univ. — *491, 493*

KNAPP, R. H., *see also* Goodrich and Knapp (1950).

KOFFKA, K. 1935. *Principles of Gestalt psychology*. New York: Harcourt, Brace. — *224, 244*

KOMAROVSKY, M., and SARGENT, S. S. 1949. Research into subcultural influences upon personality. In S. S. Sargent and M. W. Smith (Eds.), *Culture and personality*. New York: Viking Fund. — *292*

KORZYBSKI, Alfred. 1941. *Science and sanity*. Lancaster, Pa.: Science Press. — *152*

KRECH, D., and CRUTCHFIELD, R. S. 1948. *Theory and problems of social psychology*. New York: McGraw-Hill. — *22, 239, 584*

LAMBERT, W. W. 1950. The acquisition and extinction of instrumental response sequences in the behavior of children and rats. Unpublished Ph.D. thesis, Harvard Univ. — *493*

LANDIS, C., and HUNT, W. A. 1939. *The startle pattern*. New York: Farrar & Rinehart. — *467*

LANGER, W. C. 1943. *Psychology and human living*. New York: Appleton-Century. — *525*

LASKER, G. W. 1947. The effects of partial starvation on somatotype. *Amer. J. phys. Anthrop.*, 5 (New Series), 323-33. — *121*

LECKY, Prescott. 1945. *Self-consistency, a theory of personality*. New York: Island Press. — *403*

LEE, D. D. 1940. A linguistic approach to a system of values. In T. M. Newcomb and E. L. Hartley (Eds.), *Readings in social psychology*. New York: Holt, 1947. — *252*

LEEPER, R. W. 1948. A motivational theory of emotion to replace "emotion as disorganized response." *Psychol. Rev.*, 55, 5-21. — *477*

LEIGHTON, D., and KLUCKHOHN, C. 1947. *Children of the People*. Cambridge, Mass.: Harvard Univ. Press. — *338, 339, 347*

LEIGHTON, D., *see also* Kluckhohn and Leighton (1947).

LEVINE, E. M., *see* Child and others (1946).

LEVINSON, D. J., *see* Adorno and others (1950).

LEVY, D. M. 1937. Primary affect hunger. *Amer. J. Psychiat.*, 94, 643-52. — *350, 356*

LEVY, D. M. 1943. *Maternal overprotection*. New York: Columbia Univ. Press. — *356*

LEVY, J., and MUNROE, R. 1938. *The happy family*. New York: Knopf. — *515*

LEVY, M. J., *see* Aberle and others (1950).

LEWIN, K. 1935. *A dynamic theory of personality*. New York: McGraw-Hill. — *456, 478, 501, 579*

LEWIN, K. 1946. Behavior and development as a function of the total situation. Chapter 16 in L. Carmichael (Ed.), *Manual of child psychology*. New York: Wiley. — *405*

LEWIN, K., DEMBO, T., FESTINGER, L., and SEARS, P. S. 1944. Level of aspiration. Chapter 10 in J. McV. Hunt (Ed.), *Personality and the behavior disorders*. New York: Ronald Press. — *223, 464, 564, 565, 567*

LEWIN, K., *see also* Barker and others (1940).

LEWIS, O. 1949. Husbands and wives in a Mexican village: a study of role conflict. *Amer. Anthrop.*, 51, 602-10. — *322*

LIBERMAN, A. M., *see* McClelland and Liberman (1949).

LIEBMAN, J. L. 1946. *Peace of mind*. New York: Simon and Schuster. — *4*

LINDSAY, A. D. 1935. *Introduction to Plato's Republic*. New York: Everyman's Library, Dutton, 1942. — *5*

LINTON, R. 1945. *The cultural background of personality*. New York: Appleton-Century. — *75, 295, 296, 297, 298, 451, 452*

LINTON, R. 1949. Problems of status personality. In S. S. Sargent and M. W. Smith (Eds.), *Culture and personality*. New York: Viking Fund. — *290, 303, 317*

LOOMIS, A. M., *see* Thomas and others (1933).

LORGE, I. 1949. *The semantic count of the 570 commonest English words*. New York: Bureau of Publications, Teachers College, Columbia Univ. — *251*

LOVELL, C. 1944. The effects of special construction of test items on their factor composition. *Psychol. Monogr.*, 56, No. 6. — *177*

LOWELL, E. L. 1950. A methodological study of projectively measured achievement motivation. Unpublished M.A. thesis. Middletown, Conn.: Wesleyan Univ. — *482*

LOWELL, E. L., *see also* McClelland and others (1950).

LUNDBERG, G. A. 1926. Case work and the statistical method. *Social Forces,* 5, 61-65. — *105*

MCALLESTER, D. P. 1941. Water as a disciplinary agent among the Crow and Blackfoot. *Amer. Anthrop.,* 42, 593-604. — *41, 333*

MCCLEARY, R. A., and LAZARUS, R. S. 1949. Autonomic discrimination without awareness: an interim report. *J. Personality,* 18, 171-79. — *504*

MCCLELLAND, D. C. 1942. Functional autonomy of motives as an extinction phenomenon. *Psychol. Rev.,* 49, 272-83. — *218*

MCCLELLAND, D. C., and APICELLA, F. S. 1945. A functional classification of verbal reactions to experimentally induced failure. *J. abnorm. soc. Psychol.,* 40, 376-90. — *42, 501, 507, 509, 520*

MCCLELLAND, D. C., and ATKINSON, J. W. 1948. The projective expression of needs. I. The effect of different intensities of the hunger drive on perception. *J. Psychol.,* 25, 205-32. — *78, 227, 486, 489, 492*

MCCLELLAND, D. C., ATKINSON, J. W., and CLARK, R. A. 1949. The projective expression of needs: III. The effect of ego-involvement success and failure on perception. *J. Psychol.,* 27, 311-30. — *490*

MCCLELLAND, D. C., ATKINSON, J. W., CLARK, R. A., and LOWELL, E. L. 1950. *The achievement motive.* Unpublished monograph. — *473, 480, 522*

MCCLELLAND, D. C., BIRNEY, R. C., and ROBY, T. B. 1950. The effect of anxiety on imagination. Unpublished paper read at the Eastern Psychological Association Meetings. — *371, 464, 480, 505*

MCCLELLAND, D. C., CLARK, R. A., ROBY, T. B., and ATKINSON, J. W. 1949. The projective expression of needs. IV. The effect of the need for achievement on thematic apperception. *J. exp. Psychol.,* 39, 242-55. — *23, 30, 33, 42, 81, 82, 85, 439, 464, 480, 482, 486, 493, 494, 523*

MCCLELLAND, D. C., and LIBERMAN, A. M. 1949. The effect of need for achievement on recognition of need-related words. *J. Personality,* 18, 236-51. — *85, 465, 481, 490, 498*

MCCLELLAND, D. C., and MCGOWN, D. R. 1950. The effect of non-specific food reinforcement on the strength of a secondary reward. Unpublished paper. — *345, 454, 455*

MCCLELLAND, D. C., *see also* Atkinson and McClelland (1948), Clark and McClelland (1950), Riecken and McClelland (1950).

MACCORQUODALE, K., and MEEHL, P. E. 1948. On a distinction between hypothetical constructs and intervening variables. *Psychol. Rev.,* 55, 95-107. — *83, 84*

MCGEOCH, J. A. 1942. *The psychology of human learning.* New York: Longmans, Green. — *216, 218, 332, 341, 342, 344, 482, 485*

MCGOWN, D. R., *see* McClelland and McGown (1950).

MCGRAW, M. B. 1935. *Growth: a study of Johnny and Jimmy.* New York: Appleton-Century. — *365, 446*

MCGRAW, M. B. 1939. Later development of children specially trained in infancy. *Child Developm.,* 10, 1-19. — *446*

MACLEOD, R. B. 1947. The phenomenological approach to social psychology. *Psychol. Rev.,* 54, 193-210. — *86, 88*

MAIER, N. R. F. 1949. *Frustration. The study of behavior without a goal.* New York: McGraw-Hill. — *435, 459, 460, 505, 520*

MALLER, J. B. 1944. Personality tests. Chapter 5 in J. McV. Hunt (Ed.), *Personality and the behavior disorders.* New York: Ronald Press. — *186*

MANN, T. 1948. *Doctor Faustus.* New York: Knopf. — *17*

MARQUIS, D. G., *see* Hilgard and Marquis (1940).

MARQUIS, D. P. 1941. Learning in the neonate: the modification of behavior under three feeding schedules. *J. exp. Psychol.,* 29, 263-82. — *343*

MASLOW, A. H. 1943a. A theory of human motivation. *Psychol. Rev.,* 50, 370-96. — *410*

MASLOW, A. H. 1943b. Conflict, frustration and the theory of threat. Chapter 45 in S. S. Tomkins (Ed.), *Contemporary Psychopathology*. Cambridge, Mass.: Harvard Univ. Press, 1943. — *506, 525, 541*

MASLOW, A. H. 1948. Some theoretical consequences of basic need gratification. *J. Personality*, 16, 402-16. — *42, 410, 411*

MASLOW, A. H., and MITTELMANN, B. 1941. *Principles of abnormal psychology*. New York: Harper. — *428*

MATTHEWS, W. 1902. *The night chant, a Navaho ceremony*. New York: Memoirs of the American Museum of Natural History, Vol. 6. — *412*

MAY, M. A., *see* Hartshorne and May (1928).

MEAD, L. C., *see* Carmichael and others (1949).

MEAD, M. 1942. *And keep your powder dry*. New York: Morrow. — *302, 359, 617*

MEEHL, P. E., *see* MacCorquodale and Meehl (1948).

MELTON, A. W. 1942. Learning. In W. S. Monroe (Ed.), *Encyclopedia of Educational Research*. New York: Macmillan, 667-86. — *482*

MELTON, W. A., and VON LACKUM, W. J. 1941. Retroactive and proactive inhibition in retention: evidence for a two-factor theory of retroactive intuition. *Amer. J. Psychol.*, 54, 157-73. — *345*

MERRILL, B. 1946. A measurement of mother-child interaction. *J. abnorm. soc. Psychol.*, 41, 37-49. — *27, 28, 30, 35, 41, 51, 52*

MERTON, T. 1948. *The seven storey mountain*. New York: Harcourt, Brace. — *xiv*

MILL, J. S. 1873. *Autobiography*. New York: Holt. — *9, 10*

MILLER, G. A., and FRICK, F. C. 1949. Statistical behavioristics and sequences of responses. *Psychol. Rev.*, 56, 311-24. — *483*

MILLER, J. G. 1942. *Unconsciousness*. New York: Wiley. — *99*

MILLER, N. E. 1944. Experimental studies of conflict. Chapter 14 in J. McV. Hunt (Ed.), *Personality and the behavior disorders*. New York: Ronald Press. — *456, 461, 462, 501*

MILLER, N. E. 1948. Studies of fear as an acquirable drive: I. Fear as motivation and fear reduction as reinforcement in the learning of new responses. *J. exp. Psychol.*, 38, 89-101. — *434*

MILLER, N. E. 1950. Learnable drives and rewards. Mimeographed chapter for S. S. Stevens (Ed.), *Handbook of Experimental Psychology*. New York: Wiley. — *431, 432, 437, 438*

MILLER, N. E., and DOLLARD, J. 1941. *Social learning and imitation*. New Haven: Yale Univ. Press. — *346, 403, 435, 436, 461, 467, 470*

MILLER, N. E., *see also* Dollard and others (1939).

MILLS, T. 1950. Interaction process analysis applied to TAT stories. Unpublished paper. — *32, 307*

MITTELMANN, B., *see* Maslow and Mittelmann (1941).

MONTGOMERY, R. P., *see* Hull and Montgomery (1919).

MOORE, H. 1939. *Psychology for business and industry*. New York: McGraw-Hill. — *482*

MORENO, J. L. 1946. *Psychodrama*. Vol. I. New York: Beacon House. — *326*

MORGAN, C. D., *see* Murray and Morgan (1945).

MORGAN, C. T. 1943. *Physiological psychology*. New York: McGraw-Hill. — *85, 482, 489, 490*

MOWRER, O. H. 1939. A stimulus-response analysis of anxiety and its role as a reinforcing agent. *Psychol. Rev.*, 46, 553-65. — *434, 470*

MOWRER, O. H. 1940. An experimental analogue of "regression" with incidental observations on "reaction-formation." *J. abnorm. soc. Psychol.*, 35, 56-87. — *342, 508*

MOWRER, O. H. 1947. On the dual nature of learning—a reinterpretation of "conditioning" and "problem-solving." *Harvard Educ. Rev.*, 17, 102-48. — *438, 446*

MOWRER, O. H., and KLUCKHOHN, C. 1944. Dynamic theory of personality. Chapter 3 in J. McV. Hunt (Ed.), *Personality and the behavior disor-*

ders. New York: Ronald Press. — *56, 57, 75, 360, 362*

MOWRER, O. H., *see also* Dollard and others (1939), Dollard and Mowrer (1947), Kluckhohn and Mowrer (1944), Whiting and Mowrer (1943).

MUNROE, R. L. 1945. Three diagnostic methods applied to Sally. *J. abnorm. soc. Psychol.*, 40, 215-27. — *150*

MUNROE, R. L., *see also* Levy and Munroe (1938).

MURRAY, H. A. 1933. The effect of fear upon estimates of maliciousness of other personalities. *J. Psychol.*, 4, 310-39. — *493*

MURRAY, H. A. 1938. *Explorations in Personality*. New York: Oxford Univ. Press. — *33, 34, 45, 48, 82, 135, 193, 214, 252, 256, 257, 300, 358, 360, 379, 384, 393, 405, 406, 407, 408, 409, 410, 414, 438, 453, 516, 519, 549, 568, 596, 619*

MURRAY, H. A. 1943. *Thematic Apperception Test manual.* Cambridge, Mass.: Harvard Univ. Press. — *550*

MURRAY, H. A. 1949. Thematic Apperception Test. Stories given by 6 subjects. Cambridge, Mass.: Harvard Psychological Clinic. — *307*

MURRAY, H. A., and MORGAN, C. D. 1945. A clinical study of sentiments. *Genet. Psychol. Monogr.*, 32, 3-311. — *64, 65, 163, 280*

MURRAY, H. A., *see also* Kluckhohn and Murray (1948).

NAEGELE, K. D. 1949. From De Tocqueville to Myrdal: A research memorandum on selected studies of American values. Comparative study of values working papers, No. 1. Laboratory of Social Relations, Harvard Univ. — *260*

NEWCOMB, T. M. 1943. *Personality and social change.* New York: Dryden Press. — *600, 603*

NEWCOMB, T. M., and HARTLEY, E. L. (Eds.). 1947. *Readings in social psychology*. New York: Holt. — *251, 252, 254, 270, 294. See also* Bateson (1942), Bogardus (1928), Centers (1947), Ericson (1947), Fromm (1941b), Katz and Braly (1933), Lee (1940), and Whorf (1940).

OLDFIELD, R. D., and ZANGWILL, O. L. 1942. Head's concept of the schema and its application in contemporary British psychology. Part II. Critical analysis of Head's theory. Part III: Bartlett's theory of memory. *Brit. J. Psychol.*, 33, 58-64; 113-29. — *244*

OLSON, W. C. 1929. *The measurement of nervous habits in normal children.* Minneapolis: Univ. Minn. Press. — *26*

ORLANSKY, H. 1949. Infant care and personality. *Psychol. Bull.*, 46, 1-48. — *362, 377, 401, 448*

ORNE, M. T. 1949. An experimental study of hypnotic age regression. Unpublished Honors thesis, Harvard Univ. — *324*

O.S.S. ASSESSMENT STAFF. 1948. *Assessment of Men.* New York: Rinehart. — *58, 71, 72-74, 195-98, 326*

OVERSTREET, H. A. 1949. *The mature mind.* New York: Norton. — *4*

PARSONS, T. 1949. *Essays in sociological theory.* Glencoe, Ill.: The Free Press. — *13, 297, 311, 312*

PARSONS, T. 1950. Toward a sociology of culture. Unpublished manuscript. — *259, 266, 269, 270, 272, 274*

PASCAL, G. R. 1943a. Handwriting pressure: its measurement and significance. *Character & Pers.*, 11, 235-54. — *132*

PASCAL, G. R. 1943b. The analysis of handwriting: a test of significance. *Character & Pers.*, 12, 123-44. — *135, 136*

PATERSON, D. G. 1930. *Physique and intellect.* New York: Appleton-Century. — *117, 131*

PATRICK, J. R. 1934. Studies in rational behavior and emotional excitement: II. The effect of emotional excitement on rational behavior of human subjects. *J. comp. Psychol.*, 18, 153-95. — *483*

PAVLOV, I. P. 1927. Conditioned reflexes (trans. by G. V. Anrep). London Oxford Univ. Press. — *449*

PETERS, H. N. 1946. The mirror-tracing test as a measure of social maladaptation. *J. abnorm. soc. Psychol.*, 41, 437-48. — *172*

PIAGET, J. 1926. *The language and thought of the child* (trans. by Warden). London: Kegan Paul. — *252*

PIAGET, J. 1930. *The child's conception of physical causality* (trans. by Gabain). New York: Harcourt, Brace. — *252, 539*

POLANSKY, N. A. 1941. How shall a life-history be written? *Character & Pers.*, 9, 188-207. — *98, 405*

POSTMAN, L. 1947. The history and present status of the law of effect. *Psychol. Bull.*, 44, 489-563. — *525*

POSTMAN, L., and BRUNER, J. S. 1948. Perception under stress. *Psychol. Rev.*, 55, 314-23. — *504*

POSTMAN, L., BRUNER, J. S., and MCGINNIES, E. 1948. Personal values as selective factors in perception. *J. abnorm. soc. Psychol.*, 83, 148-53. — *46, 490*

POSTMAN, L., and SOLOMON, R. 1950. Perceptual sensitivity to completed and incompleted tasks. *J. Personality*, 18, 347-57. — *494*

POSTMAN, L., *see also* Bruner and Postman (1949), Bruner and others (1950).

POTTER, E. H., *see* Child and others (1946).

PRESSEY, S. L. 1921. A group scale for investigating the emotions. *J. abnorm. soc. Psychol.*, 16, 55-64. — *94*

PRICE, T. 1949. A cultural device for the heightening of experience. Unpublished Honors thesis. Middletown, Conn.: Wesleyan Univ. — *463*

RADKE, M. J., and TRAGER, H. G. 1950. Children's perceptions of the social roles of Negroes and Whites. *J. Psychol.*, 29, 3-33. — *325*

RAIMY, V. C., *see* Kauffman and Raimy (1949).

RAY, W. S. 1947. An instructional film for use in the fidelity of report experiment. *J. Psychol.*, 24, 293-312. — *26*

RHODES, W. E. 1948. Psychoanalytic theory and transcendent religious involvement in thirty young men. Unpublished Honors thesis. Middletown, Conn.: Wesleyan Univ. — *284, 309*

RICHARDS, T. W. 1946. *Modern clinical psychology*. New York: McGraw-Hill. — *106*

RICKERS-OVSIANKINA, M., *see* Hanfmann and others (1944).

RIECKEN, H. W. 1950. Changes in attitudes and personality among participants in a work service program. Unpublished Ph.D. thesis, Harvard Univ. — *563*

RIECKEN, H. W., and MCCLELLAND, D. C. 1950. Value categorization of written material. Unpublished paper. — *33, 568*

ROBERTS, J. W. 1950. A survey of the control of his own culture possessed by each of four individuals in four different cultures. Unpublished paper. — *260*

ROBY, T. B., *see* McClelland, Birney, and Roby (1950), Sheffield and Roby (1950).

RODRIGUES, J., *see* Bruner and others (1950).

ROE, A. 1949. Psychological examinations of eminent biologists. *J. consult. psychol.*, 13, 225-46. — *13, 147*

ROETHLISBERGER, F. J., and DICKSON, W. J. 1939. *Management and the worker*. Cambridge, Mass.: Harvard Univ. Press. — *482*

ROGERS, C. R. 1942. *Counseling and psychotherapy*. New York: Houghton Mifflin. — *529, 531, 561*

ROGERS, C. R. 1947. Some observations on the organization of personality. *Amer. Psychologist*, 2, 358-68. — *380, 531, 542, 561*

ROGERS, C. R. 1948. A comprehensive theory of personality and behavior. Unpublished tentative draft. — *403, 539, 545, 558, 559*

ROSENBLITH, J., and WHITE, B. 1949. The influence of meaning on size judgments in young children. Unpublished paper. — *325*

ROSENZWEIG, S. 1943. An experimental study of "repression" with special reference to need-persistive and ego-defensive reactions to frustration. *J. exp. Psychol.*, 32, 64-74. — *228*

ROSENZWEIG, S. 1944. An outline of frustration theory. Chapter 11 in J. McV. Hunt (Ed.), *Personality and*

ROSENZWEIG (*Contd.*) *the behavior disorders.* New York: Ronald Press. — *541*

ROSENZWEIG, S., and FLEMING, E. E. 1949. Apperception norms for the Thematic Apperception Test. II. An empirical investigation. *J. Personality,* 17, 483-503. — *370*

ROSENZWEIG, S., FLEMING, E. E., and CLARKE, H. J. 1947. Revised scoring manual for the Rosenzweig Picture-Frustration Study. *J. Psychol.,* 24, 165-208. — *524*

ROSENZWEIG, S., *see also* Sarason and Rosenzweig (1942).

ROURA PARELLA, J. 1948. El mundo historico social. Mexico, D. F.: Instituto de investigaciones sociales, Universidad Nacional. — *67*

RUST, R. M. 1948. Some correlates of the movement response. *J. Personality,* 16, 369-401. — *39, 84, 187*

SACHS, H. 1944. *Freud, master and friend.* Cambridge, Mass.: Harvard Univ. Press. — *12, 562*

SACHS, H. 1948. *Masks of love and hate.* Cambridge, Mass.: Sci-Art Press. — *15*

SALTZMANN, I. J. 1949. Maze learning in the absence of primary reinforcement: a study of secondary reinforcement. *J. comp. physiol. Psychol.,* 42, 161-73. — *432*

SANFORD, F. H. 1942a. Speech and personality. *Psychol. Bull.,* 39, 811-45. — *32, 152, 153, 155*

SANFORD, F. H. 1942b. Speech and personality: a comparative case study. *Character & Pers.,* 10, 169-98. — *151, 152*

SANFORD, R. N. 1937. The effects of abstinence from food upon imaginal processes: a further experiment. *J. Psychol.,* 3, 145-59. — *495*

SANFORD, R. N., *see also* Adorno and others (1950).

SARASON, S. B., and ROSENZWEIG, S. 1942. An experimental study of the triadic hypothesis: reaction to frustration, ego-defense, and hypnotizability. II. Thematic Apperception Approach. *Character & Pers.,* 11, 150-65. — *519*

SARBIN, T. 1944. The logic of prediction in psychology. *Psychol. Rev.,* 51, 210-28. — *99, 105*

SARGENT, S. S., and SMITH, M. W. (Eds.). 1949. *Culture and personality: Proceedings of an interdisciplinary conference.* New York: Viking Fund. *See* Komarovsky and Sargent (1949), Linton (1949).

SCHILDER, P. 1935. *The image and appearance of the human body.* London: Paul, Trench, Trubner. — *542, 543*

SCHOENFELD, N., *see* Klein and Schoenfeld (1941).

SCHRÖDINGER, E. 1945. *What is life?* New York: Macmillan. — *394*

SEABROOK, W. B. 1940. *Witchcraft, its power in the world today.* New York: Harcourt, Brace. — *17*

SEARS, P. S. 1940. Level of aspiration in academically successful and unsuccessful children. *J. abnorm soc. Psychol.,* 35, 498-536. — *464*

SEARS, P. S. 1941. Level of aspiration in relation to some variables of personality: clinical studies. *J. Soc. Psychol.,* 14, 311-36. — *464, 492*

SEARS, P. S., *see also* Lewin and others (1944).

SEARS, R. R. 1936. Experimental studies of projection: I. Attribution of traits. *J. soc. Psychol.,* 7, 151-63. — *552*

SEARS, R. R. 1937. Initiation of the repression sequence by experienced failure. *J. exp. Psychol.,* 7, 151-63. — *42, 145, 485*

SEARS, R. R. 1941. Non-aggressive reactions to frustration. *Psychol. Rev.,* 48, 343-46. — *501*

SEARS, R. R. 1942. Success and failure: a study of motility. Chapter 13 in Q. McNemar and M. Merrill (Eds.), *Studies in personality.* New York: McGraw-Hill. — *16, 26, 35, 42*

SEARS, R. R. 1943. *Survey of objective studies of psychoanalytic concepts.* New York: Social Science Research Council. — *35, 95, 396, 518*

SEARS, R. R. 1950. Forms of fantasy aggression in young children. Unpublished paper delivered at Eastern Psychological Association Meetings. — *505*

SEARS, R. R., and WHITING, J. W. M. 1950. Projection and displacement in doll play. Unpublished paper. — *360*

SEARS, R. R., and WISE, G. W. 1950. Relation of cup feeding in infancy to thumbsucking and the oral drive. *Amer. J. Orthopsychiat.*, 20, 123-38. — *357, 396*

SEARS, R. R., *see also* Dollard and others (1939), Doob and Sears (1939), Hovland and Sears (1938).

SHEEN, F. J. 1949. *Peace of soul.* New York: Whittlesey House. — *4*

SHEFFIELD, F. D., and ROBY, T. B. 1950. Reward value of a non-nutritive sweet taste. *J. comp. physiol. Psychol.*, 43, 471-81. — *440*

SHELDON, W. H. 1944. Constitutional factors in personality. Chapter 17 in J. McV. Hunt (Ed.), *Personality and the behavior disorders.* New York: Ronald Press. — *117*

SHELDON, W. H., and STEVENS, S. S. 1942. *The varieties of temperament.* New York: Harper. — *118, 121, 122, 123, 124, 125, 126, 127, 128, 129, 158, 620*

SHELDON, W. H., STEVENS, S. S., and TUCKER, W. B. 1940. *The varieties of human physique.* New York: Harper. — *118, 119, 120, 159*

SHERIF, M. 1936. *The psychology of social norms.* New York: Harper. — *248*

SHERIF, M. 1948. *An outline of social psychology.* New York: Harper. — *434, 491*

SHERIF, M., and CANTRIL, H. 1947. *The psychology of ego-involvements.* New York: Wiley. — *15, 312, 346*

SIMMONS, L. (Ed.). 1942. *Sun Chief; the autobiography of a Hopi Indian.* New Haven: Yale Univ. Press. — *xiv, 248, 319, 320, 341*

SIMON, B. Case notes on Karl. — *119, 374, 426*

SIRJAMAKI, J. 1947. A footnote to the anthropological approach to the study of American culture. *Social Forces,* 25, 253-63. — *260*

SNYDER, W. U. (Ed.). 1947. *Casebook of non-directive counseling.* Boston: Houghton Mifflin. — *530*

SOLOMON, R., *see* Postman and Solomon (1950).

SPENCE, K. W. 1947. The role of secondary reinforcement in delayed reward learning. *Psychol. Rev.*, 54, 1-8. — *477*

SPENCE, K. W. 1948. The postulates and methods of behaviorism. *Psychol. Rev.*, 55, 67-78. — *81, 82*

SPENCE, K. W., *see also* Bergmann and Spence (1944).

SPERRY, M., *see* Hollenberg and Sperry (1950).

SPRANGER, E. 1928. *Types of men* (trans. by J. W. Pigors). Halle (Saale), Germany: Niemeyer. — *66, 67, 257*

STAGNER, R. 1937. *Psychology of personality.* New York: McGraw-Hill. — *74, 463*

STANLEY, J. C., *see* Jenkins and Stanley (1950).

STEVENS, S. S., *see* Sheldon and others (1940, 1942).

STODDARD, G. D. 1943. *The meaning of intelligence.* New York: Macmillan. — *163*

STONE, A. A. 1950. The effect of sanctioned overt aggression on total instigation to aggressive responses. Unpublished Honors thesis, Harvard Univ. — *36, 427, 499, 516, 524*

STOUFFER, S. A. 1949. An analysis of conflicting social norms. *Amer. sociol. Rev.*, 14, 707-17. — *322, 323*

STRODTBECK, F. 1950. A study of husband-wife interaction in three cultures. Unpublished Ph.D. thesis, Harvard Univ. — *326, 417*

STRONG, E. K., Jr. 1931. *Change of interests with age.* Stanford Univ., Calif.: Stanford Univ. Press. — *332*

STRONG, E. K., Jr. 1938. *Vocational interest blank for men.* Stanford Univ., Calif.: Stanford Univ. Press. — *112, 534, 605*

STRONG, E. K., Jr. 1943. *Vocational interests of men and women.* Stanford Univ., Calif.: Stanford Univ. Press. — *227, 316, 332*

SUTTON, F. X., *see* Aberle and others (1950).

SYMONDS, P. M. 1931. *Diagnosing personality and conduct.* New York: Appleton-Century. — *22, 23, 24, 25, 26*

SYZ, H. 1937. Recovery from loss of mnemic retention after head trauma. *J. gen. Psychol.*, 17, 355-87. — *544*

TAYLOR, J. H. 1948. The effect of ingestion of dexedrine on level of aspiration. Unpublished paper. Middletown, Conn.: Wesleyan Univ. — *492*

THOMAS, D. S., LOOMIS, A. M., and ARRINGTON, R. E. 1933. Observational studies of social behavior. Vol. I. *Social behavior patterns.* New Haven: Institute of Human Relations, Yale Univ. — *26*

THOULESS, R. H. 1931. Phenomenal regression to the real object. *Brit. J. Psychol.*, 21, 339-59. — *249*

THURSTONE, L. L. 1938. *Primary mental abilities.* Chicago: Univ. of Chicago Press. — *171, 172, 173, 174, 176, 199*

THURSTONE, L. L. 1944. *A factorial study of perception.* Chicago: Univ. of Chicago Press. — *176*

THURSTONE, L. L. 1947. *Multiple-factor analysis.* Chicago: Univ. of Chicago Press. — *178*

TOLMAN, E. C. 1948a. Cognitive maps in rats and men. *Psychol. Rev.*, 55, 189-208. — *242*

TOLMAN, E. C. 1948b. *The wants of men.* Berkeley, Calif.: Associated Students Store. (Mimeographed.) — *598*

TOMKINS, S. S. (Ed.). 1943. *Contemporary psychopathology.* Cambridge, Mass.: Harvard Univ. Press. — *397, 398. See also* Erickson (1939), Haggard (1943), Maslow (1943b), Wolf (1943).

TOMKINS, S. S. 1947. *The Thematic Apperception Test.* New York: Grune & Stratton. — *23, 415*

TRAGER, H. G., *see* Radke and Trager (1950).

TROLAND, L. T. 1928. *The principles of psychophysiology.* New York: Van Nostrand. — *467*

TUCKER, W. B., *see* Sheldon and others (1940).

VON LACKUM, W. J., *see* Melton and von Lackum (1941).

WALLER, W. 1932. *The sociology of teaching.* New York: Wiley. — *292*

WALTER, A. A., *see* Carmichael and others (1932).

WEBB, W. B. 1948. "A motivational theory of emotions . . . ." *Psychol. Rev.*, 55, 329-35. — *477*

WECHSLER, D. 1944. *The measurement of adult intelligence* (3rd Ed.). Baltimore: Williams and Wilkins. — *164, 165*

WERTHEIMER, M. 1945. *Productive thinking.* New York: Harper. — *244*

WHITE, B., *see* Rosenblith and White (1949).

WHITE, R. K. 1947. Black Boy: A value analysis. *J. abnorm. soc. Psychol.*, 42, 440-61. — *33, 418*

WHITE, R. W. 1943. The personality of Joseph Kidd. *Character & Pers.*, 11, 183-208; 318-60. — *559*

WHITE, R. W. 1944. Interpretation of imaginative productions. Chapter 6 in J. McV. Hunt (Ed.), *Personality and the behavior disorders.* New York: Ronald Press. — *43*

WHITE, R. W., TOMKINS, S. S., and ALPER, T. G. 1945. The realistic synthesis: a personality study. *J. abnorm. soc. Psychol.*, 40, 228-48. — *64, 65*

WHITEHEAD, A. N. 1925. *Science and the modern world.* New York: Macmillan. — *9, 96*

WHITFIELD, J. W. 1949a. Patterns of random behavior. Personal communication. — *44*

WHITFIELD, J. W. 1949b. Unpublished communication on medical research conducted in Germany after World War II for the British government. — *494*

WHITING, J. W. M. 1950. Effects of conflict on drive. Unpublished paper. — *506, 508*

WHITING, J. W. M., and CHILD, I. L. 1950. Child training practices and theories of disease: a cross-cultural study of personality development. Unpublished manuscript. — *41, 334, 356, 357, 361, 366, 367, 371*

WHITING, J. W. M., and MOWRER, O. H. 1943. Habit progression and regression—a laboratory study of some factors relevant to human socialization. *J. comp. Psychol.*, 36, 229-53. — *358*

WHITING, J. W. M., *see also* Sears and Whiting (1950).

WHORF, B. L. 1940. Science and linguistics. In Newcomb and Hartley (Eds.), *Readings in social psychology.* New York: Holt, 1947. — *250*

WISE, G. W., *see* Sears and Wise (1950).

WITKIN, H. A. 1949. The nature and importance of individual differences in perception. *J. Personality,* 18, 145-70. — *155, 182, 263*

WOLF, A. 1943. The dynamics of the selective inhibition of specific functions in neurosis. Chapter 31 in S. S. Tomkins (Ed.), *Contemporary psychopathology.* Cambridge, Mass.: Harvard Univ. Press. — *363, 445*

WOLFE, J. B. 1936. Effectiveness of token rewards for chimpanzees. *Comp. Psychol. Monogr.,* 12, No. 60. — *433*

WOLFF, W. 1933. The experimental study of forms of expression. *Character & Pers.,* 2, 168-76. — *546*

WOLFF, W. 1943. *The expression of personality.* New York: Harper. — *148, 543*

WOLFF, W. 1947. *The personality of the preschool child.* New York: Grune & Stratton. — *134, 136, 156, 157*

WOODWORTH, R. S. 1918. *Dynamic psychology.* New York: Columbia Univ. Press. — *217*

WOODWORTH, R. S. 1938. *Experimental psychology.* New York: Holt. — *253, 468, 469*

WRIGHT, B. A. 1942. Altruism in children and the perceived conduct of others. *J. abnorm. soc. Psychol.,* 37, 218-33. — *566*

WRIGHT, H. F. 1937. The influence of barriers upon strength of motivation. *Duke Univ. Series, Contr. to Psychol. Theory.,* 1, No. 3. — *463*

WRIGHT, R. 1946. *Black boy.* New York: Harper. — *xiv*

YOUNG, J., *see* G. W. Allport, and others (1948).

YOUNG, P. T. *Motivation of behavior.* New York: Wiley. — *467, 483*

YOUNG, P. T. 1949. Food-seeking drive, affective process, and learning. *Psychol. Rev.,* 56, 98-121. — *440, 441*

ZANGWILL, O., *see* Oldfield and Zangwill (1942).

ZATZKIS, J. 1949. The effect of the need for achievement on linguistic behavior. Unpublished M.A. thesis. Middletown, Conn.: Wesleyan Univ. — *33, 154, 488*

ZEIGARNIK, B. 1927. Über das Behalten von erledigten und unerledigten Handlungen, *Psychol. Forsch.,* 9, 1-85. — *97*

ZILBOORG, G. 1941. *A history of medical psychology.* New York: Norton. — *17*

Subject Index

CPSIA information can be obtained
at www.ICGtesting.com
Printed in the USA
BVHW01*2146210218
508809BV00004B/5/P

9 781528 073783